MW01628653

Engines You Can Build – Book 2

Engines You Can Build – Book 2

Engines You Can Build – Book 2

First Printing July 1994

Village Press
2779 Aero Park Drive
Traverse City, Michigan 49684

International Standard Book Number
0-941653-18-8
Library of Congress Catalog Card
Number 94-060489

Copy editing by Clover McKinley
Design and Layout by Luana Dueweke
and Jolyn Gildursky

Typeset and printed at Village Press,
Traverse City, Michigan, USA

INTRODUCTION

I'm very pleased to present to you *Steam and Stirling Engines You Can Build, Book 2,* a compilation of the best steam-and hot-air-powered engine projects to be published in *Live Steam,* 1982 through 1993. The primary purpose of this book, just like its predecessor, the first *Steam and Stirling Engines You Can Build,* is to provide the hobby machinist at any level of skill with some projects, designs, techniques, and guidance.

The projects are written by 22 different authors. The level of difficulty ranges from the very simple engines of John Aho, Andy Sprague, and Ray Colin, whose projects can be completed with little more than a drill press and hand tools, to the very sophisticated designs of Philip Duclos, Richard Mitchell, and Jeff Maier. Some are designs based upon prototype engines, and others are original. Also included are some suggested means of heating things up; there's a plan for an automatic electric model boiler, one for a very simple alcohol burner, and another excellent article on using propane gas to fire your engine. Chris Leggo, the author of the propane article, has updated it based upon new findings. You'll also find some fine techniques for creating more satisfactory lubrication, making a wood flywheel, or roll forming copper boiler heads.

Having bought this book, it appears that you are sincerely intent upon building one or more of these projects. Don't let the more sophisticated projects intimidate you. If you wish to have your skills improve and grow, just start with the first engine you believe you can build, and take it from there. In the process, you'll find your collection of operating engines expand as your stress level declines.

Bill Fitt edited the first *Steam and Stirling Engines You Can Build,* and I'm simply following his lead by introducing this second one. Bill once said, "The two main requirements necessary to get you into the Live Steam hobby are 1) decide and 2) begin!" And so say I! I hope you find it to be a rich resource.

Joe Rice

CONTENTS

CONTENTS

STEAM ENGINES

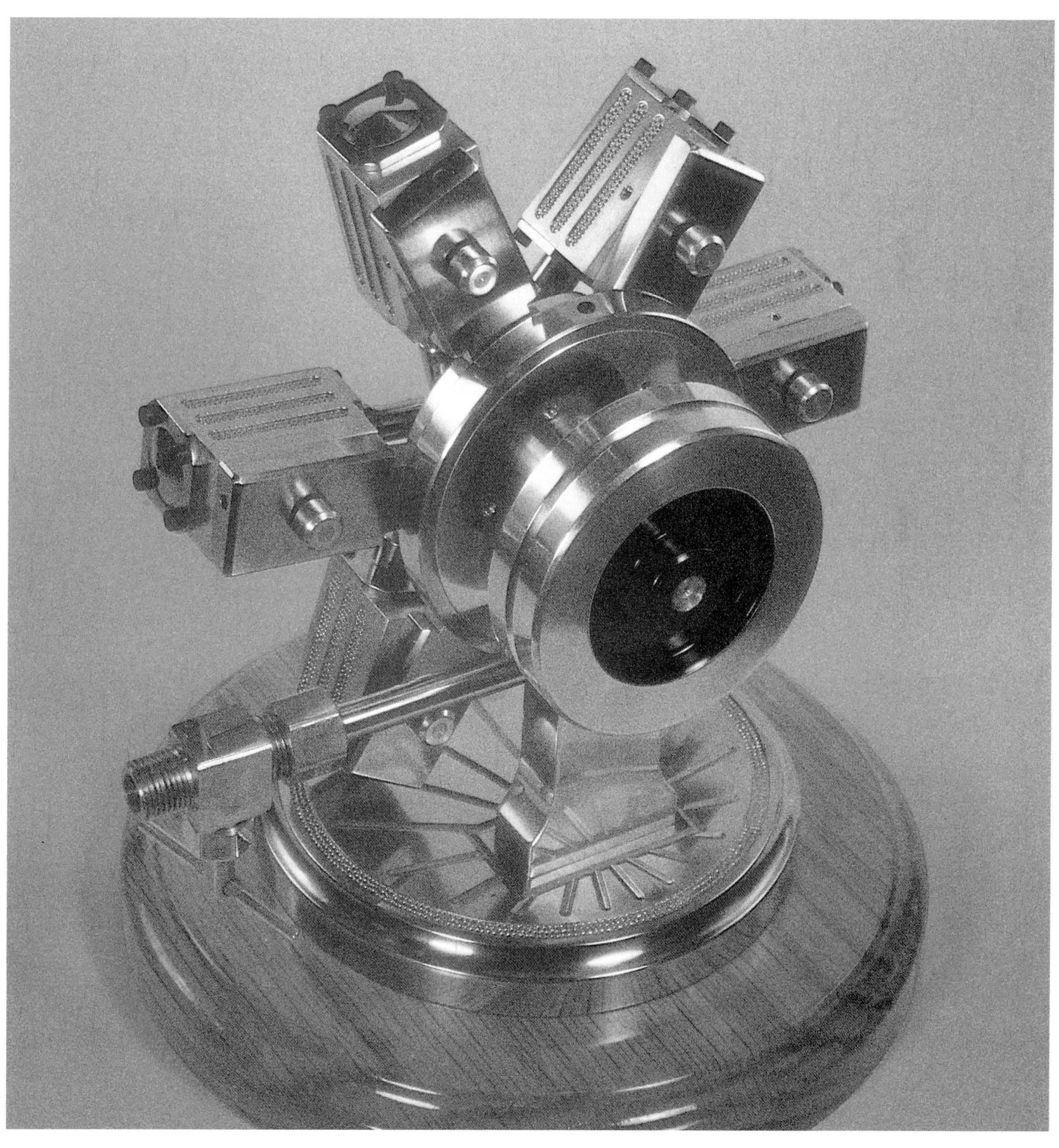

A Steam Engine for the Novice

By David Croft

Photos and drawings by the Author

An interest in live steam power affects us in a variety of ways. Some of us are keen on traction engines, some on steamboats, some on stationary engines and some on locomotives. For some of us our interests are in full size and for some they are in miniature. In my case, the interest is primarily in miniature locomotives, although to a lesser extent I have an interest in all the other fields. I often remember how difficult it was for me to get started in my hobby, and I wonder if others, particularly young people, experience the same difficulties I had, and whether they would appreciate some instruction to help them get started.

For a number of reasons I thought of scheming out a group of small beginners engines that would serve as exercises, give practice in working in a small machine shop, and instruction in some techniques not so well understood, ending up with a little piece of machinery that looks right, works well, and gives the builder some satisfaction. I thought of including a little theory, making use of a pocket calculator, and stressing a few methods I have found by experience to yield very accurate results and from which I get a lot of pleasure. I took into account what I considered to be extremely high costs, and tried to show how to build everything from scrap or surplus materials to save that precious commodity, money, for better tools.

As I write, I imagine I'm talking to a student, and this student is about 15 years old and keen. If you are not just this age, please bear with me. These instructions must serve prospective builders from a variety of backgrounds.

The first engine I ever built was from an article in *Popular Mechanics*, or *Popular Science*. I don't remember now, but it must have been about 1945 or even earlier. It was a single-cylinder vertical engine with a rotary valve, and its exhaust came out through a hole in the center of the crank-disk. To me, it was just the thing to power some imaginary model steamboat. But it would be necessary to machine the parts and that would require a lathe – one I did not have, nor had I ever used one. However, I had a friend at school whose father, I learned, was a tool and die maker, and he had a lathe in his basement workshop. Eventually, I was allowed to use this miraculous machine, a 10" Logan, and on it I turned a crankshaft, a flywheel, a main bearing/valve, a cylinder, and a piston. The rest I made with files, a hacksaw,

1 *An engine with a rotary valve now nearly 50 years old.*

2 *Front view, lubricator side.*

3 *Rear view, steam inlet side.*

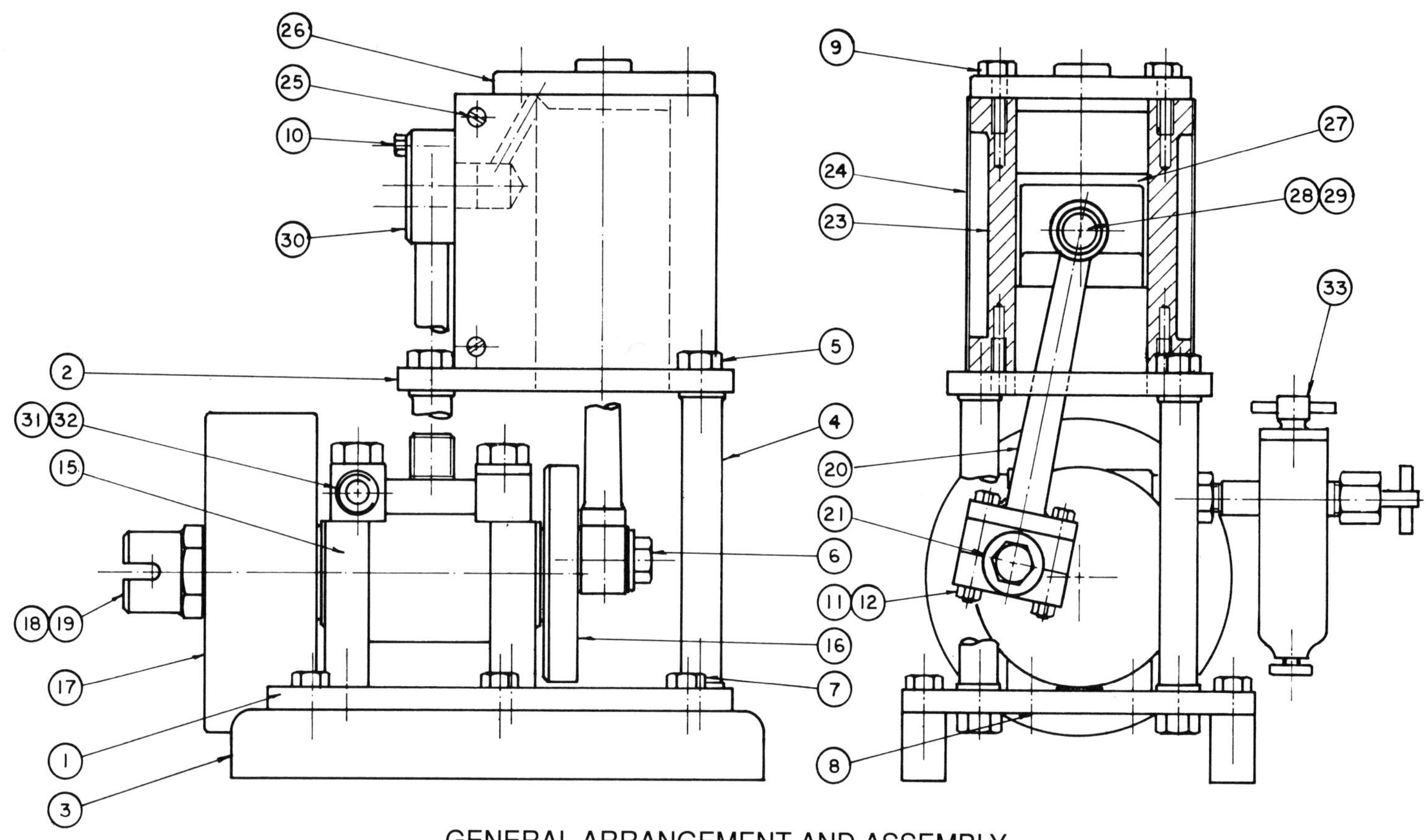

GENERAL ARRANGEMENT AND ASSEMBLY

a bench vise, and a soldering iron. The result worked, more by good luck, I think, rather than by good management! I still have it, and it will still operate. It reminds me how far we have come in nearly half a century (**Photo 1**).

Back in April 1981 *Live Steam*, a little novelty described by Elmer Verburg used the same type of valve. I thought we might use it once more in the first engine I propose to describe.

This engine is a single-cylinder vertical, and it would do very well as a power plant for a small boat. It is single acting, which means steam pressure pushes the piston down, but that energy stored in the flywheel during the "down" stroke is used to push the piston back up again, thereby pushing out the exhaust steam. There is one major disadvantage in a boat, however; it cannot be reversed.

I have tried to make this little engine look like a proper marine engine (**Photos 2, 3,** and **4**). All parts are made from appropriate materials, the cylinder being iron, but fabricated and so not requiring a casting. It is all held together with correctly proportioned hex head screws which you will make yourself. You will require a small lathe and either a vertical milling machine or a vertical slide attachment for the lathe. You will also need an assortment of drills, taps, dies, milling cutters and reamers. However, not wanting to overwhelm the prospective builder with high costs, I have tried to keep these to a minimum, and a list of small tools is included. Now let's get on with the individual pieces, and I will save further comments for each part in turn.

Frame

The logical place to begin is with the base or frame, and to work up from there. However, this engine is designed with the upper works supported on a plate or table, and this stands on four steel columns. Therefore, the baseplate and the table plate will be built together using the same setups to save time and to ensure accuracy.

Two scraps of 1/8" steel plate are required, one just over 2×2-5/8" and the other 1-1/2×2". They are plates for our purposes, but to the steel mill, this material is "sheet." If you can't find 1/8" material, then use 10, or 11, or even 12 gauge. You can compensate for the thickness later on. This steel should be cold finished or cold rolled. Don't use the kind with the black oxide scale on it as this requires so much more work to clean up. You will find what you need in just about any metal fabricating shop, and if you make friends with the shop foreman, he will give you all you need, as offcuts pile up underneath the big shear, and he has to clean it all up and put it out for the scrap dealer.

I'm going to spend quite a lot of time describing how I make parts such as these, but once I've done it, I won't have to do it again, as you can apply the same procedure to any other parts you like. I don't know a more accurate way to make small pieces, and the satisfaction of just putting parts together at assembly time, without the need to "fit," is the greatest satisfaction of all.

Set up the vertical milling machine vise carefully, making sure the jaws are parallel to the table. Then find the corner of the fixed jaw with a center finder. I simply hold a dowel pin in a collet in place of a cutter, and move the vise jaw beside it until it just pinches a feeler gauge. When you have done that satisfactorily, and raised the dowel pin clear of the jaw, moving the table over by the feeler gauge thickness plus half the dowel pin diameter puts the center of the spindle exactly in line with the edge of the vise jaw. Now repeat the operation using the end of the jaw, and the other axis. When complete, the center of the spindle is directly above one corner of the fixed jaw of the vise. I always use the upper right-hand corner (northeast corner, if you prefer). That way, as I turn the handles clockwise, the cutter moves in over the work. Finally, set the graduated collars to read "zero."

Now let's make some chips. Clamp the larger of the two plates in the vise, and mill a skim off of one long edge. Deburr it and turn it over for a skim on the opposite long edge. Remove from the machine and measure the width, which must be slightly more than 2.000". Replace in the vise, advance the cutter, and remove the excess. Measure again, and you should have exactly the width specified.

Now hold the plate flat by pinching the two newly machined edges and running one of the short edges past the side of the cutter. Reverse, repeat on the opposite end, measure, remove the excess, and there is an accurately formed blank. While you're at it, do the same thing on the smaller plate.

Next, put the larger plate back in the vise, again holding it flat by the long edges, and lining up one short edge with the "zero" end of the vise jaw. Now change the cutter over to a drill chuck with a small center drill, move to the first set of coordinates, and spot the hole with the drill. It is your choice here to either move on to each of the coordinates and do all the center holes first, or to change to the appropriate drill and finish each hole completely. I usually do the former method; I think it is generally quicker.

There is a cutout in this plate for clearance for the connecting rod big end, and another at the end for the flywheel. Drill 1/8" holes as shown at the four corners and larger holes in the middle just to remove material. Go back to a cutter, chew out most of the openings, and finally finish with a 1/8" end mill, going from one drilled hole to the next. You will find if you keep a pad of paper handy, you can record the readings on the dials so you can go back to them again without getting confused.

The baseplate is now complete and it is time for you to congratulate yourself because you have just made your first part by modern techniques. Isn't that better than marking it all out with marking blue and scribed lines, center punching, drilling, sawing, and filing? And whether you need it or not, it is so much more accurate. Some people have told me they get lost turning the dials, but I think it is just a matter of practice. Sometimes I draw in some guide lines lightly in pencil. Then, if I count one turn too many or too few, I see immediately that I'm out and can recheck. I no longer even keep marking blue.

This might be a good place to make a comment about dimensioning. If you see a dimension in fractions, you will know that the intention is to measure it with a scale, and if marking is required, a pencil is likely satisfactory. However, if the dimension is in decimals, you would expect to use a micrometer, or vernier caliper, or maybe one of those gorgeous digital readout instruments we have today. It seems foolish to me to specify diameters on lathe turned parts in fractions when the machine is fitted with dials that already read in decimals. Likewise the parts made on the miller. Raw material will be in fractions; benchwork, most sheet metal work, and references to accurate tools like reamers will all be in fractions. But parts made on machines will be dimensioned to suit the

4 Rear view, with coupling, flywheel and lubricator.

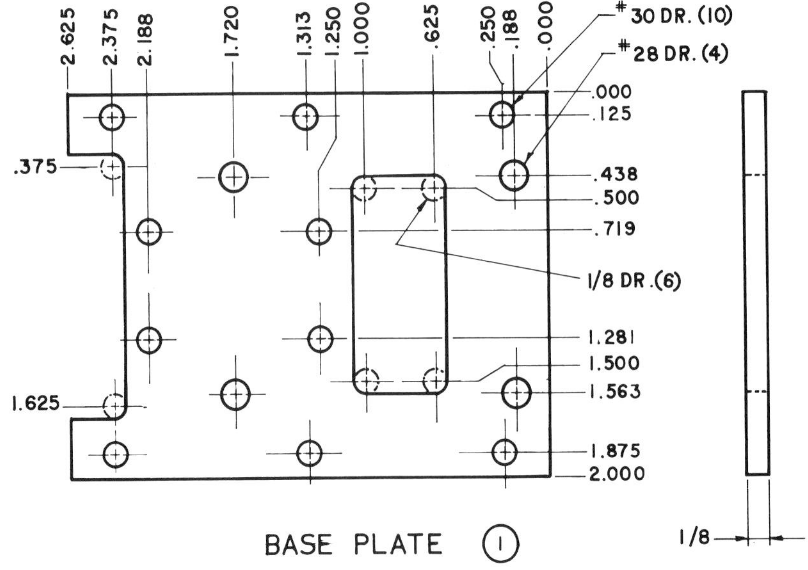

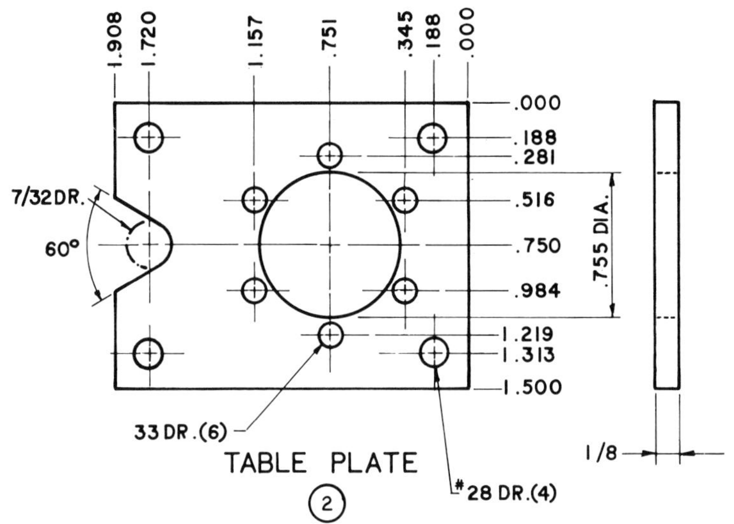

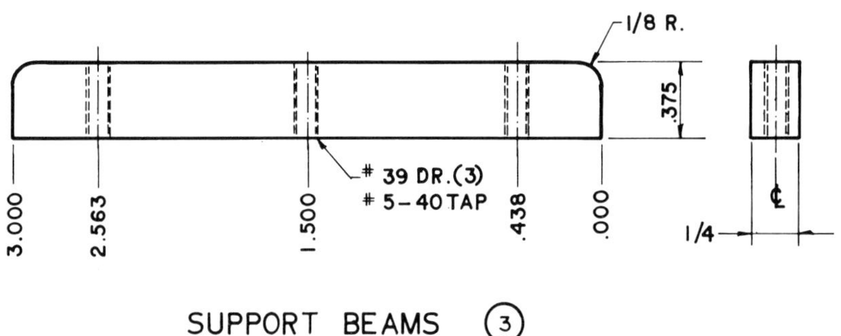

particular machine. I'm going to try to avoid talking about tolerances. That should come later.

The table plate is done in exactly the same way so I don't have to repeat. You will now see why my drawings are dimensioned the way they are. The decimal dimensions are not supposed to indicate anything special. Just follow them exactly, dialing the machine to whatever the drawing says. All I have to be responsible for is the accuracy of the original work, and hope it gets reproduced correctly.

Support Beams

The next parts you need are a pair of beams to stand the engine on. A model is spoiled for me if it is not made of appropriate materials. Beams would typically be timber shipping skids, and I think it would be quite in order to make them from a close grained wood. In real life, the engine would be lifted off these timbers and lowered into a hull, located on other timbers which are really part of the boat or ship. However, correctly or not, I have shown these beams made from strips of aluminum. They were cut from the edge of a piece of plate, 1/4" thick, clamped together, squared up in the mill and holes drilled and tapped exactly as described for the base. They were made complete in about half an hour. If you use wooden beams, you will have to change the method of fastening to either bolts and nuts, or wood screws. Miniature lag screws can be made from roundhead screws by reshaping the heads by milling or filing.

Columns

Four columns are required next. These are plain turning from 1/4" diameter steel rod. They could be left plain, but their appearance is much improved if a shoulder is formed at each end as shown on the drawings. Now is the time to compensate for the thickness variation of the material used for the table plate. If the plate is thicker than 1/8", shorten the columns by that difference; if it was thinner, lengthen them. I was asked recently by a beginner how to get accurate length on such parts. Well, it's simple. Face and finish one end. Cut off slightly too long, and face that end. Remove from the lathe, measure, rechuck, bring the facing tool up to just touch the work, lock the carriage and advance the tool by the difference between what you measured and what you need, finish the facing and complete the end. If you generally keep the top slide set parallel to the bed, you can conveniently use it to advance the tool.

Hexagon Screws and Nuts

By this time, you will have several parts made, and will be wanting to stand it up and begin the assembly. Therefore, you will need screws, so I might as well say what I want to say about screws, threads, hex heads and nuts.

As in the case of the use of the wrong materials, a model is spoiled for me when I see that commercial screws and nuts have been used to put it together. Threads are too coarse, and, except for specially made screws for models, hexagons are too large across flats, and too thin. This little engine has a bore of 3/4", and if it resembled a full sized machine with a 6" bore, the scale would be 1/8. So, using that scale for our example, look at the following chart of screw sizes.

Full Size ..... Pitch	⅛ Full Size ..... Pitch	Nearest Equivalent
1" ..... 8 tpi	⅛ ..... 64 tpi	5-44
¾" 10	3/32 80	3-56
½" 13	1/16 104	0-80
1¼" 7	5/32 56	8-36
1½" 6	3/16 48	10-32

There is no point in going further, for you will get the point. Even for the relatively large scale of 1/8, the National Fine Threads shown are way too coarse. Among the tools I would recommend that the beginning Live Steam model builder should buy are a full set of fine series taps and dies. I was very encouraged recently to discover a catalog of tools from a company called KBC Tools in which are listed

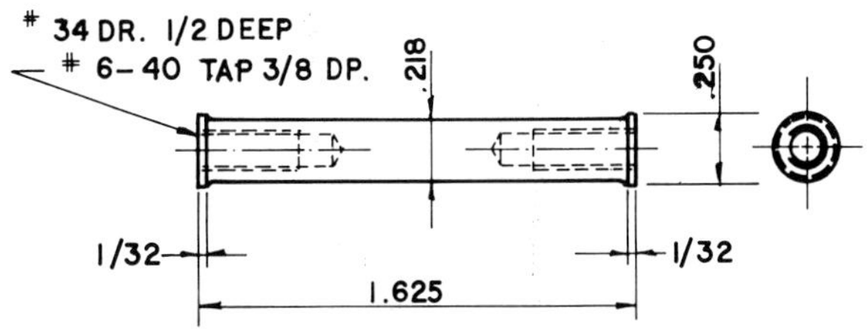

COLUMNS 4

HEXAGON HEAD SCREWS AND NUTS									
SCREW SIZE	DIA. D	PITCH		CORRECT HEX SIZE A/F	CORRECT HEAD B	CORRECT NUT C	FOR NEAREST HEX SIZE		
		NC	NF				A/F	B	C
0	.060	–	80	.090	.042	.054	3/32	.044	.056
1	.073	64	72	.110	.051	.066	3mm	.055	.071
2	.086	56	64	.129	.060	.077	1/8	.058	.075
3	.099	48	56	.149	.069	.089	5/32	.073	.094
4	.112	40	48	.168	.078	.101	5/32	.073	.094
5	.125	40	44	.188	.088	.113	3/16	.088	.113
6	.138	32	40	.207	.097	.124	7/32	.102	.131
8	.164	32	36	.246	.115	.148	1/4	.117	.150
10	.190	24	32	.285	.133	.171	5/16	.146	.188
12	.216	24	28	.324	.151	.194	5/16	.146	.188
1/4	.250	20	28	.375	.175	.225	3/8	.175	.225

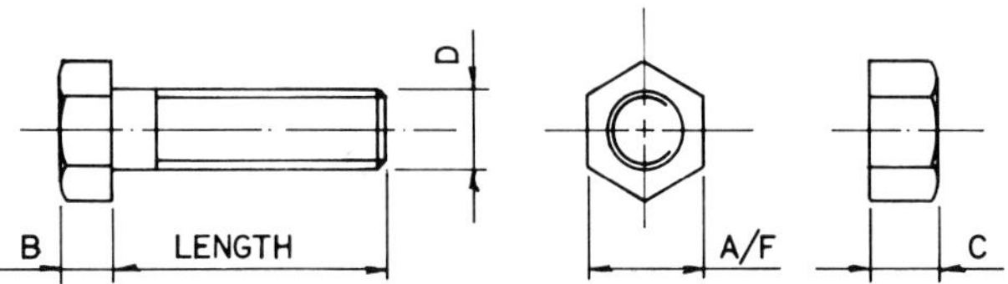

many pitches finer than National Fine. I see that for the above list, 5-60, 8-56, and 10-48 are all available. Let me make the usual disclaimer right now, I have no connection with this company, and only recently have they opened a branch here in Canada. They will be a convenient source of supply for U.S. builders, however, as they have branches in Detroit and San Francisco. Perhaps ***Live Steam*** could persuade them to advertise.

Returning to the model, as a general rule, all tapped holes in steel will be shown as National Fine (NF), while any in soft or brittle materials will be shown as National Coarse (NC). The reason for this is that fine threads in soft materials are much more likely to tear out, so the stronger coarse thread is used. In stronger steel, the tearing is less likely, and here the advantage of the fine thread is that the tap has a larger core diameter giving greater strength, and still has less material to remove. So, being less likely to break the tap, you win on two counts.

For the correct hexagon sizes, the

5 *Making hex screws. Locating the hex bar.*

6 Making hex screws. The diameter and length has been turned in one cut.

7 Making hex screws. The thread has been cut with a die in the tailstock die holder.

8 Making hex screws. Parting off with the rear tool post.

width measured across flats should be 1-1/2 times the diameter of the screw. This is generally true for both heads and nuts. Bolt heads are a little thinner than nuts, being just a little less than half the width across flats. That makes them about 0.7× bolt diameter. Nuts are about 0.9 × bolt diameter. You can look up the exact sizes in *Machinery's Handbook*. For model work, keep the hexagons a little on the chunky side if there is any doubt.

There have been a couple of articles in ***Live Steam*** recently on the manufacture of hex screws. I usually make them in batches, but find I can make only about 30 at a time before I go to pieces and start turning the wrong handles at the wrong time. Still for this engine, 30 screws is nearly enough, and besides they are different sizes, requiring different setups. The drawing shows the dimensions except for length of the screws you will need, and I suggest you make them all now. The length appears on the Bill of Material.

The method I use for making small hex screws is almost the same as that described by Gordon Carlson in his article in ***Live Steam*** July 1989. My lathe is one of the earliest Myford Super 7's, so I have the luxury of a rear tool post which I use for parting off. I also have a four-tool turret, so several tools can be mounted at the same time. I see many of the new machines have these same features, but if you are lacking either, follow Gordon's method. **Photos 5** through **8** show the process of making these small hex screws.

As an example, I will describe the making of the 6-40 screws specified for the attachment of the columns to the baseplate and table plate. Clamp the carriage to the lathe bed with the parting tool about 1/16" in front of the jaws of the three-jaw chuck. The top slide is set parallel to the bed. In one tool holder slot, mount a tool ground like a facing tool with a sharp or very tiny radiused end and plenty of clearance and top rake. This tool is going to reduce the 7/32" hex bar to finished diameter of 0.138" in one cut, so you might as well set it up to do just that right now. Set the cross slide index to read zero corresponding with this diameter. Now position the tool to the right of the parting tool by the length of the screw, the head thickness, and about 0.010" extra (0.375 + 0.102 + 0.010") and set the top slide index to read zero. Push the hex rod through the chuck until it touches the tip of the tool.

Face, turn down to finish diameter by advancing the top slide by 0.375", retract the tool with the cross slide to face under the head, and reset the top slide to zero. Some form of pencil line mark helps to locate which zero is the correct one! Now back off the cross slide enough to allow the tailstock die holder to be brought forward to cut the thread, and with that done, continue backing off the cross slide until the parting tool cuts off the screw.

Reset, and repeat as many times as necessary to make the batch of screws you are going to need. It makes sense to build up a stock while you have the setup. Don't forget to slightly round off or chamfer the end with a file before cutting the thread. It won't take a minute to do this much of each screw, more likely about 40 seconds.

The screws are not finished yet! As a second operation, make a threaded bushing in the three-jaw chuck, tighten each screw in turn into the bushing, set the facing tool to just touch the bushing and then back it off by 0.102". Again lock the carriage, and face off each screw in turn. Chamfer the corners lightly, either with a file or a form tool. This will take another 10 or 15 seconds. Now they're done!

One last comment about little hex screws. If you can't get a particular size of hex rod and decide to use the next bigger one, use the head thickness that goes with that hex size. For example, if you were using 1/4" hex in the above description, you would use 0.117" instead of 0.102".

To make nuts, face and center drill the end of the hexagon rod, and drill the tapping drill size. Add a chamfer with a file or cutter and part off before tapping. Each blank thus formed is then rechucked and tapped. The advantage is that the hole being tapped is a through hole instead of a blind hole, allowing the chips to clear better, and also, you don't end up tapping the length that will be destroyed when parting off.

Some people are unaware what the number sizes on machine screws indicate. For example, 5-40 – what does "5" indicate? Well, it is the diameter. To go from 5 to 6, the diameter increases by 0.013". As well, "0" has a base diameter of 0.060". Therefore, 1 has a diameter of 0.060" + (1 × 0.013") = 0.073", 2 has a diameter of 0.060" + (2 × 0.013") = 0.086" and so on. 5 is 0.060" + (50.013") = 0.125", which is convenient, since it is exactly 1/8". The tiny screws used by the HO railway people are 00, 000, and sometimes even 0000, being 0.047", 0.034", and 0.021" diameter respectively. Each diameter is 0.013" different from the next.

BILL OF MATERIALS

NO.	PART NAME	QTY.	MATERIAL	COMMENTS
1	Baseplate	1	steel	
2	Table plate	1	steel	
3	Support beam	2	aluminum	could be wood; see text
4	Column	4	steel	
5	Hex cap screw	8	steel	6-40 × 3/8" columns
6	Hex cap screw	1	steel	6-40 × 3/8" connecting rod
7	Hex cap screw	6	steel	5-40 × 3/8" support beams
8	Hex cap screw	4	steel	5-44 × 3/8" main bearing
9	Hex cap screw	12	steel	4-40 × 1/4" cylinder & cover
10	Hex cap screw	3	steel	2-56 × 1/2" header
11	Hex cap screw	2	steel	2-64 × 9/16" connecting rod
12	Hex Nut	2	steel	2-64 connecting rod
13				
14				
15	Main bearing	1	—	subassembly
	Body	1	steel	
	Bushing	1	bronze	
	Inlet pipe	1	brass	
	Exhaust pipe	1	brass	
	Transfer pipe	1	brass	
	Support plate	1	brass	
	Plug	2	brass	
16	Crankshaft	1	steel	
17	Flywheel	1	steel	
18	Collet	1	steel	
19	Coupling nut	1	steel	
20	Connecting rod	1	steel	subassembly
21	Washer	1	steel	No. 6 plain washer
22				
23	Cylinder	1	cast iron	brazed fabrication
24	Cylinder lagging	1	stove pipe	
25	Lagging screw	4	brass	0-80 × 1/8 roundhead
26	Cylinder head	1	cast iron	
27	Piston	1	aluminum	could also be cast iron
28	Wrist pin	1	drill rod	
29	Wrist pin pad	2	brass	
30	Header & pipe	1	brass	subassembly with copper tube
31	Ferrule	2	brass	
32	Union nut	3	brass	
33	Lubricator	1	—	subassembly
	Body	1	brass	
	Valve chamber	1	brass	
	Needle valve	1	steel	
	Gland nut	1	brass	
	Lock nut	1	brass	
	Cap	1	brass	
	Drain plug	1	steel	

List of Small Tools

As indicated in the text, the number of small cutting tools has been kept to a minimum. You may choose to buy a wider range of sizes than shown, but these will make a good start.

Drills

Set of number drills from 1 to 60. You won't need them all, but it is useful to be able to open up hole sizes gradually, and besides, they are usually sold in complete sets.

Set of fractional size drills from 1/16" to 1/2". The same comments apply.

Small center drills. Make sure you have numbers 1, 2, and 3, which are 1/8", 3/16", and 1/4" diameter respectively.

End Mills

Standard length end mills, 4-flute, in diameters of 1/8", 1/4", 5/16", 3/8", and 1/2". Two-flute end mills may also be used, and have the advantage of being center cutting, so the cutter may be plunged straight into the material.

Plain hand reamers 3/16", 1/4", 3/8", and 1/2" diameter.

Taps and Dies

Coarse series (NC) 2-56, 4-40, 5-40

Fine series (NF) 0-80, 2-64, 3-56, 5-44, 6-40

"Model Engineer" series 5/32-40, 3/16-40, 1/4-40, and 5/16-40

Taps are supplied in three styles, known as taper, plug and bottoming. "Taper" has little use in model building, and "plug" is the one to choose. For parts such as gland nuts, bottoming taps are necessary, but you can grind the point off a plug tap to make a suitable one. Therefore, I suggest you buy taps of each size, and stick to "plug" style.

Main Bearing and Valve

Getting back to the basic engine parts means the main bearing assembly should be next. This is one part I really can't say looks like full size since I don't suppose any full size engine was ever built with such a valve system. However, making it will be a good exercise, and it will give a chance to learn how to do another important function, silver brazing.

Silver brazing is the correct name for a process that has commonly been called silver soldering for many, many years. However, there is a higher strength version of common tin/lead solder that has a silver content, and to avoid confusion, the manufacturers have adopted this term as the correct one.

If you haven't tried the process before, you should practice on some odd bits before starting out on your carefully prepared engine parts. It is essential to have plenty of heat. However, it isn't necessary to have an oxy/acetylene outfit, although if you have one, use it. Air/acetylene makes a very good source of heat for the hobbyist. There are also several excellent propane torches available. Ask about these at a good welding supply company. It is important that the flame be slightly reducing; that is, it must not have any excess oxygen to combine with the metals being joined. That just causes them to burn. Silver brazing alloys and fluxes may be obtained from just about any welding supply.

... making it will be a good exercise, and it will give a chance to learn how to do another important function, silver brazing.

The manufacturer I am familiar with is Handy & Harman, and their general purpose alloy is called *Easy-Flo 45*, while the flux is known as *Handy Flux*. Again the usual disclaimer: there are other companies and equivalent products. I don't believe I can put instructions on how to silver braze in an understandable form, so I recommend you get some instruction from a teacher at the local technical school, a friendly welder, or get in touch with the local representative of the alloy manufacturer. The latter I have found to be very helpful. They even have films that are instructive.

Here are a few alternatives for the main bearing. If such a part were made in full size, the actual bearing would be bronze, and not brass. Follow suit in miniature; save your brass for pipe fittings! I originally planned the round center portion to be turned from a length of 3/4" diameter bronze rod, the bronze being obtained from that machine shop foreman friend you have by now made. It is usually known in the machine shop as "bearing bronze," and it is likely to be the common SAE 660 alloy. A 1-1/4" length of this is turned down to a shoulder 9/16" diameter by 9/32" long at each end, centered and drilled 23/64" through, all ready for reaming later on. This piece is supported

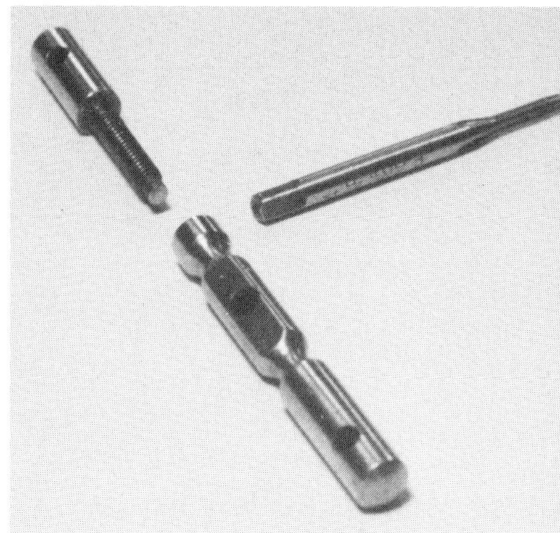

9 *Tiny taps deserve tiny tap wrenches. This one is homemade from 1/4" diameter drill rod.*

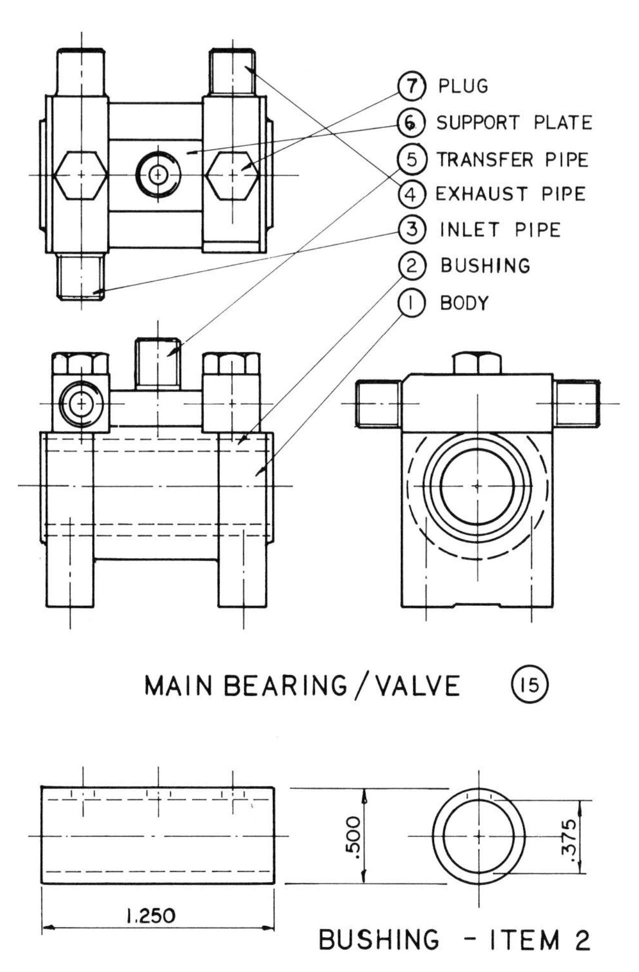

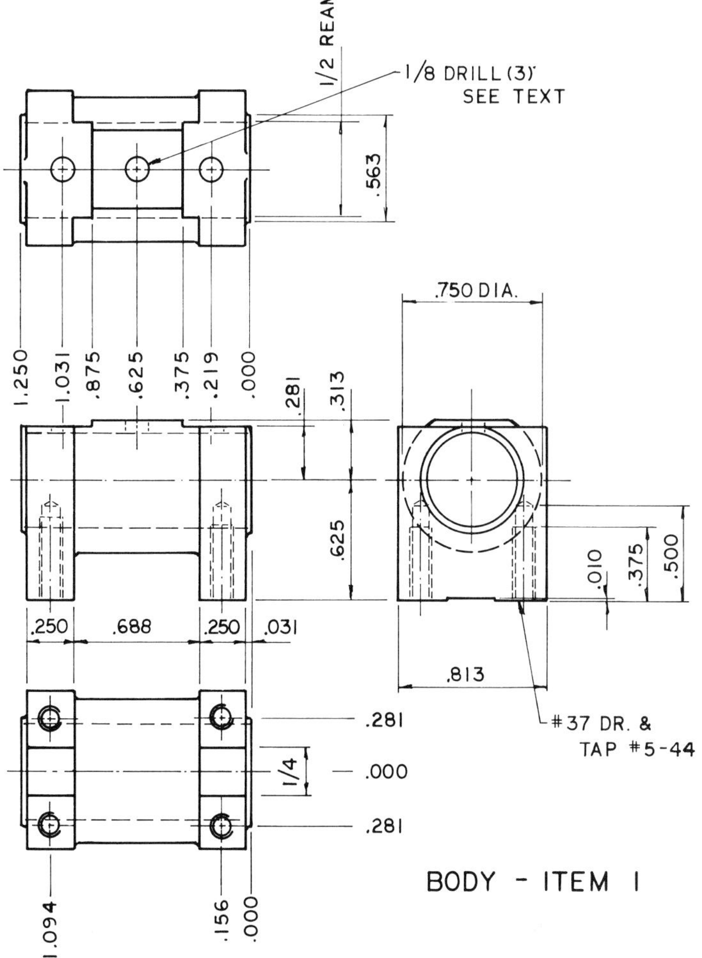

10 *Tapping in the milling machine. The tap is perfectly straight in the hole.*

in two legs cut from 1/4 × 1" steel flat with 9/16" holes drilled through them. The assembly is carefully milled on top for the brass parts, and the whole thing silver brazed at one heat.

I made mine exactly this way, except I turned the round portion of steel as well, drilled and reamed it 1/2" diameter, and later pressed in a commercial bush. But I found it a tedious method, and realized there was a much better way, as follows.

Start with a length of ordinary 1" square cold rolled or cold finished steel bar. Chuck this in the four-jaw, carefully setting it eccentrically, so you have slightly more than .625" (say .635") from center to one face, keeping it centered between the other two faces. Face the end, center, drill 31/64" × about 1-5/16" deep, and turn a shoulder 9/16" diameter × 1/32" long. Now turn down the portion in the middle to 3/4" diameter × 11/16" long leaving a 1/4" thick flange. Turn down some more to produce the second flange, and part off. You should be able to produce the whole piece in one setup this way, or you may prefer to re-chuck and face the rough end. You can use the same technique as on the columns to establish the length at 1.250". Now is the time to ream the hole 0.500" diameter (1/2" reamer). The advantage of this method is that the legs are automatically square and parallel, making the next step in the milling machine much more satisfactory.

Hold the part in the vise on the miller with the bottoms of the legs facing up. Push a piece of 1/2" round rod through the hole, and find the surface of this round with the cutter. Now lower the table 0.375" and this establishes the correct level to face off the feet. You can make a further cut along the center line about 1/4" wide × about .010" deep to produce four little pads – not necessary, but a nice little finishing touch. Change over to a drill chuck, find the center line, move over to the centers of the mounting holes which will be in the little pads, center, and drill No. 37 about 1/2" deep following with a 5-44 tap about 3/8" deep.

Now turn the whole thing over in the vise. Remember how you had the machine set up when you made the baseplate so you could dial in zero on the graduated collars, and you would be right over one corner of the fixed jaw? Using this feature, you can now go directly to the exact center of the shaft and be sure that when the holes are drilled, they truly will be right. And this is very important; an error here will affect the successful operation of the engine. Check your work, then go ahead and mill flats for the pipe connections, and drill the three holes for the ports. However, there is another use for these last three holes.

Several years ago, when Kozo Hiraoka described the construction of the three logging engines in ***Live Steam***, he showed many parts made by fabricating using silver brazing. He regularly screwed all the parts together with brass screws first, then silver brazed, and then filed off the screws. I adopted that method for my own work, and very highly recommend it as the ideal way to keep the pieces where they have to be while being heated.

Since the ports will be 1/8" diameter,

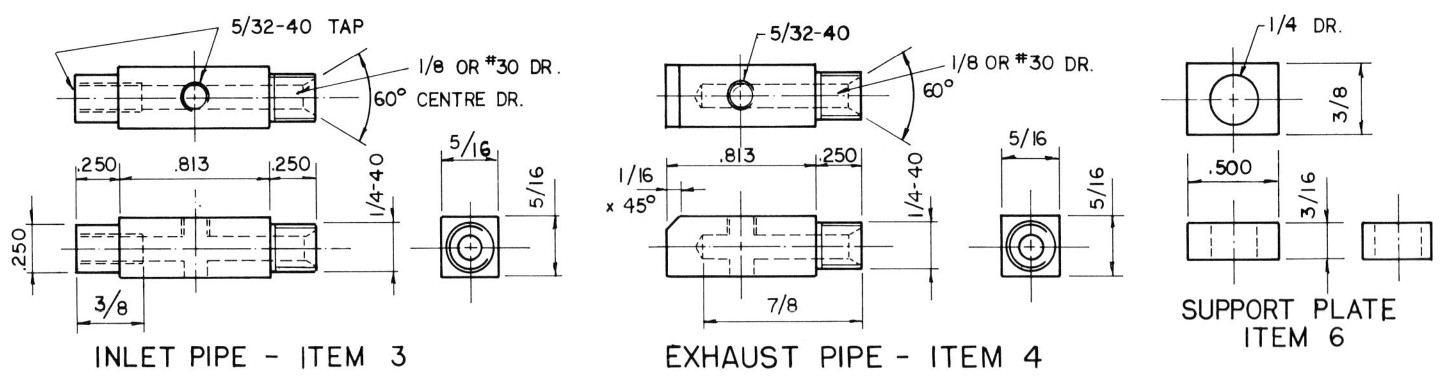

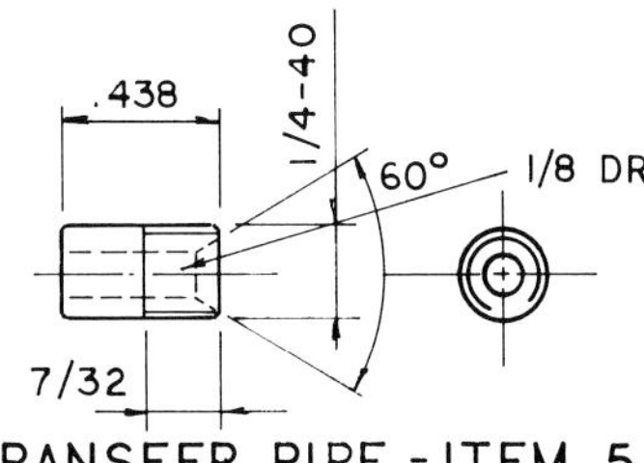

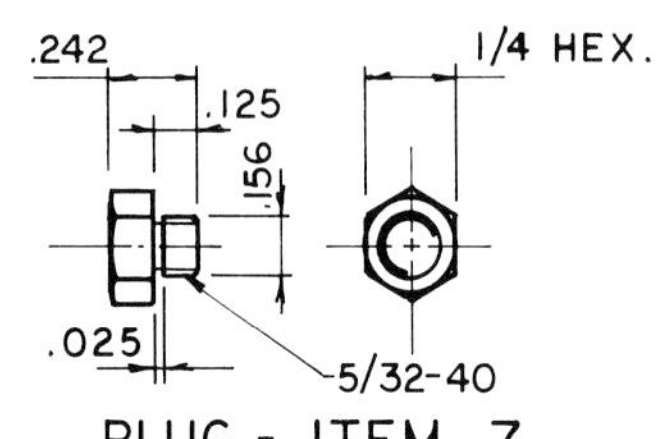

drill them smaller for now, suitable for tapping for Nos. 2, 3, or 4, coarse or fine as you prefer. Tap them and remove them from the machine.

At this point, the legs are still 1" wide, and must be narrowed down to 0.813". No great accuracy is required here but keep them symmetrical for the sake of appearance.

The four pieces on top for connecting the pipes are all made of brass, and they are pretty simple. I didn't have any 5/16 " square for the manifolds, but it took only a few minutes to saw up a bit of plate, and square up blanks in the miller. When they are done, put brass screws through the two manifolds and the connector in the middle, drop the little stiffening plate over the latter, tighten the screws, flux the whole thing, heat, and apply the alloy. Clean up carefully, and return to the milling machine.

This next operation will be a check on the last one in the miller. Remove the brass screws by using either a small end mill (center cutting), or a small center drill, and following with the body size drill for whatever size screws you used. Tap the holes for the brass plugs at the same time.

The bushing can be made from bronze rod or you can cheat a little and use a commercial one. If you use the commercial one, you will find it at another very useful source of supply, which, according to some letters in ***Live Steam***, is not so well known to model engineers and Live Steam enthusiasts. This is the local bearing supply and industrial hardware. Look under "Bearings" in the yellow pages. There are usually several in any town or city, and if the "minimum" order or "wholesale only" is a problem, you can try the competition.

These places sell all kinds of power transmission equipment, gears, pulleys, belts, motors, gearboxes, etc. Companies such as Boston Gear, Inc., and Browning are represented, and I am quoting a Boston part number for the bushing. It is an M68-10, and is 3/8" bore, 1/2" OD, and 1-1/4" long. If stock is a problem, try an M68-12, the same except 1-1/2" long, or try two shorter ones, M68-6, which are 3/4" long. These can be cut to length before assembly. They are made of the same bronze I mentioned earlier. You could use the sintered metal bushing (oilite), but it is not the correct material. You will want to pass the 1/2" reamer through the bore again, to remove burrs, but then you can push in the bushing. It should be the correct fit with no further work. Now, on the drill press, you can open the three ports to 1/8" or No. 30 drill. The bore will now need to be sized, so pass a 3/8" reamer through it. That completes the bearing assembly (**Photo 11**).

There is another product you can get from the local bearing supply, and that is bearing bronze, as mentioned earlier. Boston Gear supplies 13" lengths of cast bronze solid bars, as well as cored bars, in a whole range of sizes. This is a useful source for amateurs.

11 *The main bearing complete.*

Crankshaft

The crankshaft will be next – another nice little machining job. You will need a piece of steel shafting or plain cold rolled steel, 1-1/4" diameter. Cut off a piece about 2-5/8" long, face both ends and bring the length to 2.546". Put a small center hole in one end only. Now chuck this piece in the four-jaw chuck, eccentrically (the face without the center hole is the one you're going to work on). Use a dial indicator if you have one, and mount it in the tool post. The total reading on the dial will change 0.750", and you won't likely have an instrument with such a long stroke. No problem, just take a reading at one extreme, move the cross slide in or out by 0.750", rotate the work a half turn, and adjust until the reading on the instrument is the same as it was before.

It really is quite remarkable how quickly you can set up work accurately this way. If you don't have the dial indicator, just use the tip of a turning tool the same way, adjusting the jaws until the work clears the tool by the same thickness feeler gauge at the two extremes.

When all set, start turning away metal to form the crankpin. Work slowly, as even in a big chuck, it is badly out of balance and shakes at speed. Also, be careful not to exceed the 0.290" dimension, as you have already established the length of the shaft. Finish the pin diameter to 0.250", leaving a tiny radius where the pin joins the crank disk. Center drill the pin, and open out with a No. 33 drill (0.113") about 1/2" deep. Tap 6-40, just a few turns for now.

Change over to the three-jaw, or center carefully in the four-jaw, and put a small center hole in the middle of the crank disk. Be careful it isn't too big or you will find that a lathe center will foul the crankpin. Besides, a big hole looks terrible.

You can now set the shaft between centers, rotating it by means of a bar bolted to a faceplate and contacting the crankpin. It would be wise to put a soft bush around the pin to prevent it from being damaged. **Photo 12** should make this setup clear. Go ahead and turn down all the rest of the shaft to about 0.400" diameter. Remove from the lathe, and tap the rest of the 6-40 hole in the crankpin.

Now I'd like to break off for a little bit of theory. The next job is milling the ports, and it is tricky, so a little time getting the hang of what we are trying to do is time well spent. Refer to **Figures 1** through **6**.

These figures are views as if looking down the length of the crankshaft towards the flywheel. In Figure 1, the crankpin is at the bottom and is just about to begin to

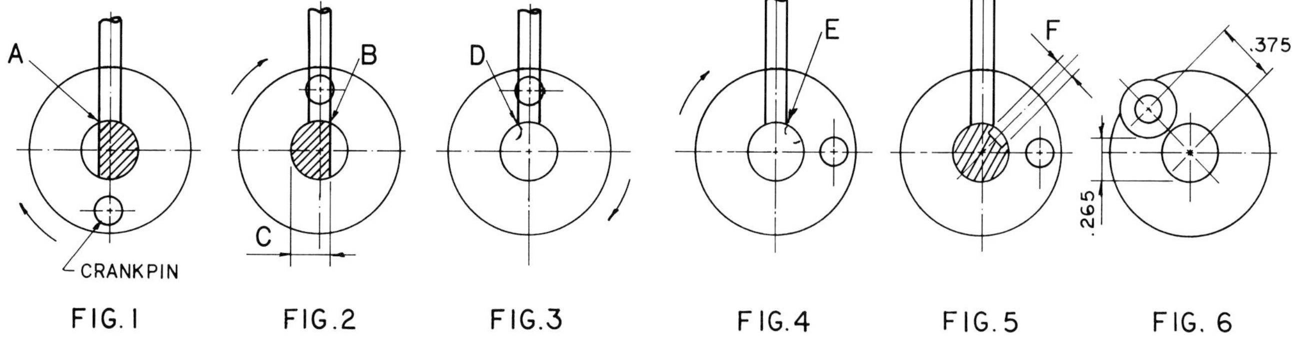

FIG. 1 FIG. 2 FIG. 3 FIG. 4 FIG. 5 FIG. 6

12 *Turning the crankshaft between centers.*

go back up. Therefore, the exhaust stroke is about to begin. The exhaust port is the unshaded area in the center, and the edge marked "A" is about to uncover the holes in the transfer pipe and, at the same time, the exhaust pipe. As rotation continues, the port remains open until the crankpin arrives at top dead center when the edge marked "B" closes it, as shown in Figure 2.

The port is clearly dimensioned by simply getting "C" correct, and it equals half the shaft diameter plus half the pipe diameter, but it is essential to keep it parallel to the axis of crankshaft and crankpin.

Now make the inlet port which joins the steam pipe to the transfer pipe. I have planned this engine with a fixed cutoff occurring at 90°. This is not exactly the same as 50% cutoff, but it's close. The port opens at "D" (Figure 3), and closes at "E" (Figure 4). The crank has rotated 90°, and you can see that the axis of the port is at 45°. 50% cutoff means that when the piston has moved half of the stroke, the steam supply is cut off, and the steam already in the cylinder expands, giving up its energy efficiently.

Theoretically, you could mill a flat for this port just the same as for the exhaust port, but it would be so shallow that the incoming steam would be severely restricted. Therefore, mill a shape with straight sides as shown in Figure 5. This can be done with a small slot drill or end mill, or a Woodruff key cutter. I happened to have one of the latter, so I used it (**Photo 13**). Dimension "F" takes a little figuring, which you may enjoy doing with a pocket calculator to check my work. This completes the theory.

I also happened to have a dividing head, and I used it to establish the angle. However, you don't need one of these expensive attachments. Try the following: Make a little bush exactly the same diameter as the crankshaft now is (I suggested about 0.400"). Ream the hole in it 1/4", and cut it off about 5/16" long. Slip this over the crankpin, and hold it with a washer and one of your 6-40 screws. Now lay this on the milling machine table with the disk in a slot and clamps pinching the shaft and pin down snugly. This establishes the correct orientation for the exhaust port, so you can do the milling.

To cut the inlet port means setting at

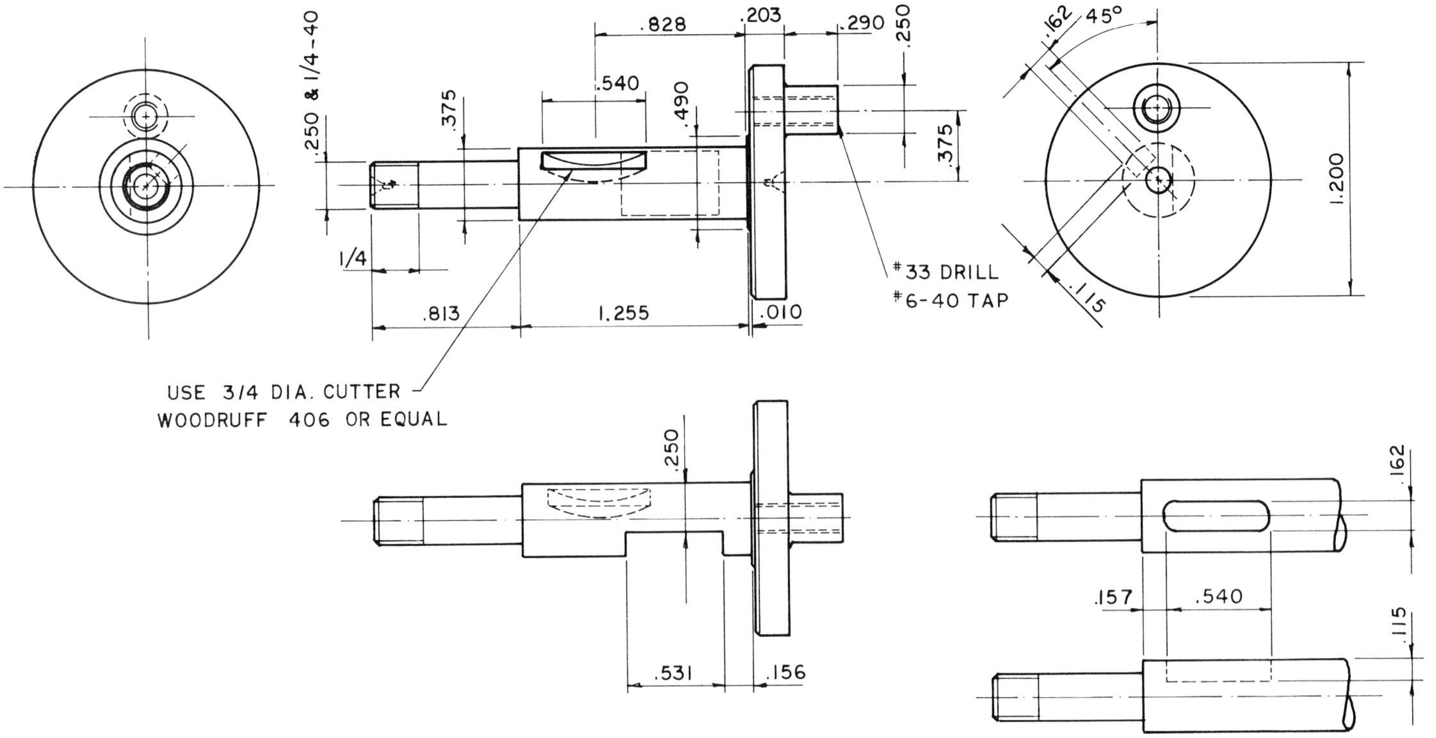

.250 & 1/4-40
.375
.540
.828
.490
.203
.290
.250
.375
1/4
.813
1.255
.010
#33 DRILL
#6-40 TAP
.162
45°
1.200
.115
USE 3/4 DIA. CUTTER
WOODRUFF 406 OR EQUAL
.250
.531
.156
.162
.157
.540
.115

CRANKSHAFT (16)

ALTERNATIVE INLET PORT
WHEN USING END MILL.

45°. Looking at Figure 6 and checking my trigonometry again, you will find the crankpin should be raised by 0.265". Use a piece of 1/4" material (a length of 1/4" keystock would be good) and a 0.015" feeler gauge as a shim, reset the clamps, and mill the port. I suggest you use a 1/8" cutter on center line first, and later move over 0.019" each way to get the correct width of 0.162". I made a bush just to set up to take the picture, and then wished I'd used it for the milling as it was obviously much quicker than setting up the dividing head. Be careful to allow for the larger diameter of crankshaft when cutting ports. The dimensions on the drawings are for the final diameter of .375".

When the ports are completed, go back to the lathe setup between centers again; turn the finish diameter to 0.375", and then the shoulder behind the crank disk. Establish the length of this journal at 1.255" using the top slide set parallel to the bed, and reduce the remainder to 0.250" diameter. Be careful to machine the best surface possible on the journal. Hold the 1/4" diameter part in the tailstock chuck, change back to the three-jaw, grip the disk in it, release the tailstock chuck, and cut about 5/16" of 1/4-40 thread at the end. Use a die in the tailstock die holder. Finally, between centers again, turn down the disk diameter to 1.200" and neatly chamfer its corners. So much for the crankshaft.

Flywheel and Its Mounting

Another of my pet aversions is the mounting of flywheels by means of setscrews. In fact, I dislike setscrews in any application and try to avoid them. By their very nature, flywheel hubs push sideways and will run out of true. To mount this flywheel, I have adopted a method I first remember seeing specified by Edgar T. Westbury, a prolific designer of little engines in England. Incidentally, for any of you who enjoy reading a good book, try reading Nevil Schute's novel, *Trustee From the Toolroom*. The hero of this story, one Keith Stewart, was supposed to be based on the real life Edgar Westbury.

The mounting is a split collet, and is made first. Chuck a piece of 1/2" steel shafting; set the top slide over to 5°, and turn a little cone slightly more than 5/8" long with the 1/2" diameter nearest the cutter and the small diameter nearest the chuck. Make sure the cutter is exactly on center or the cone won't be a cone. It will be a hyperbola instead. Center the end, drill 15/64", and finish with a 1/4" reamer. Part off at 5/8" or maybe 1/64" less. Don't disturb the top slide setting. Also, don't split the collet yet.

The flywheel (**Photo 14**) is made from 1-3/4" steel, or iron. I will have more to say about iron in connection with the cylinder. Don't use brass! While heavy enough, brass would have been far too expensive in real life and in a model makes the little machine look toy-like. Steel resembles iron in appearance, is cheap and readily obtained. Chuck a short piece, face, center drill, and take just a skim off the outside to clean up. Drill 3/8" diameter about 1" deep, and carefully bore a conical hole using the collet as a gauge. Be careful to keep the boring tool exactly on center!

The collet should stand proud of the wheel by not more than 1/32". If you accidentally go too far, face more off the flywheel blank. Now you can turn the grooves in the face. Be prepared to grind up some special tools for this as regular turning tools will be too big. Part off about 11/16" long, reverse in the chuck, face the opposite side to make the length just 0.625", and repeat the grooves. The collet must not stick out beyond this face. You may now split the collet with a thin saw blade, or a slitting saw in the miller if you have one. Be careful to remove all burrs from the saw cut.

The nut that holds the flywheel on also incorporates a coupling. Use a length of 7/16" hex steel, but put it in the milling machine first and cross-drill 3/32" diameter about 1/4" from one end, *exactly* across the diameter. Transfer to the lathe, do all the turning, drill, and tap. Before parting it off, however, go back to the milling machine to mill out the grooves. That way you have something to hold

13 *The inlet port has just been cut. Note how the 45° angle is obtained.*

it with. Then part off, and face the back. If you make a tiny register – say, 7/16" diameter by 0.005" deep – the corners of the hex won't scratch the wheel when tightened up. This completes all the rotating parts.

Cylinder

The cylinder comes next and this is the heart of the engine. Iron is the correct material to use. Normally the cylinder would be in the form of a casting but good iron castings are expensive these days, and besides, I'm trying to provide you with a design that doesn't require special supplies such as castings. Available, however, are sticks of cast iron from which you can machine up parts just as if you were using ordinary bar stock. I figured it might be possible to fabricate the shape we need for a cylinder by silver brazing, so this engine started life to prove if that was practical. And it was.

You may have to shop around a bit for the iron. Look up "Foundries" in the yellow pages. The ones that supply iron should have a selection of stock sizes. You need material that cleans up to 1-1/4" diameter. Alternatively, see if you can find an old sash weight or something like that. An old rusty lump in the back of Grandfather's barn might be just what you need. Be prepared for hard spots, though, in this kind of material. And you will get Grandfather's permission to take it first, won't you?

Start by chucking the bar, facing the end, and turning down a length of about 1-3/4" to 1.250" diameter. Then reduce the diameter about 3/4" from the end to 1.050" and extend this each way until you have formed a part that looks like a thread bobbin. Keep the flange about 7/32" thick for now, but make the distance between flanges as near 1-1/8" as you can manage. Center drill the face, and drill about 11/16" diameter, 1-5/8" deep. Change to a boring tool and open the bore to almost 0.750", say about 0.001" less. Part off, leaving the overall length just 1-9/16".

Mount the "bobbin" thus formed in the milling machine, establish the center line, and mill a flat 0.750" wide leaving the little corners at the flanges where the cutter comes through. Depth of cut is determined by just touching the cutter to the surface of the flange, which was turned to 1.250" diameter, and advancing 0.163". Don't try to do it all in one pass!

Next, square up a block of iron 0.750 × 0.382 × about 1-9/16". The 0.750" dimension should just locate in the little corners you left on the cylinder flanges.

The tricky part starts now. Nearly everyone told me I couldn't brave the iron. The problem is the graphite. The applications man at Handy & Harman gave me several suggestions, which I tried, but had varying results. The silver brazing alloy doesn't want to flow on, or wet the iron, and for this reason won't draw into the joint by capillary action. So I reasoned, why not put the alloy in the joint beforehand? The maximum strength joint should be about 0.002" thick. Over the area to be joined (3/4 × 1-1/2") meant a volume of alloy of 0.75 × 1.5 × 0.002 cubic inches. The wire size I had was 0.050" diameter. Dividing that volume by the X-section area of the wire gives

$$\frac{.75 \times 1.5 \times 0.002''}{0.050 \times 0.050'' \times (3.142/4)} = 1.146''$$

This much wire was snipped off, hammered flat, and cut into three pieces. Lay the block on a firebrick, smother in flux, put the three bits of alloy on top, place the cylinder in position, and slosh on lots more flux. Support a heavy bar between another brick and the cylinder to squish it down. Apply the heat carefully. I found that as the flux went clear and liquid, there, suddenly, was the little line of "gold" color all around the assembly, giving an excellent joint (**Photo 15**).

Slow cooling is important to avoid stresses and hard spots in the iron, so allow the cylinder to sit on the hot firebrick, and cover it up. A welder I used to know kept asbestos wool insulation for that purpose. Nowadays asbestos is a no-no, but try burying it in a pile of fiberglass torn from an insulation batt. When cool, wash in hot water, pickle in acid (6 parts water to 1 of hydrochloric acid, and add the acid to the water), and clean up in the usual way.

Chuck a length of aluminum bar in the lathe and turn down about 2" to 0.750" diameter so the cylinder is just a push fit on it. Now your little assembly can turn perfectly truly around its own axis and you can face both ends and establish its length at 1.500".

All the holes are drilled and tapped in the milling machine. Mount the cylinder in the vise, one end facing up, and using an indicator or an edge finder or the dowel pin-and-feeler-gauge technique, find the center of the bore. You will want to set the dials to zero, but note what they were so you can return them later. That way you don't lose the ability to find the corner of the vise jaw. Move to each of the six positions around the bore, center, drill, and tap 4-40 (**Photo 16**). Remember, coarse threads in brittle materials.

Reverse and do the same thing at the opposite end. You will now see why I specified 1.050" for the bobbin diameter, which is really larger than it should be, but it allows that the tapped holes you just made don't break through anywhere making the tapping difficult. If you feel more comfortable finishing the tapping by hand later, fine, but do start the tap in the machine to guarantee it is straight.

The 1/4" hole and the tapped holes for the steam pipe connection are done in exactly the same way. The connecting passage to the cylinder bore can be two No. 40 drilled holes. Hold the cylinder in a small machine vise which in turn is held in the bigger vise, and use a draftsman's 30-60 set square to set the angle at 30°. Offset from center line by 0.055", use a small center drill to get started on the sharp edge between bore and face, and drill through No. 40. Take it easy so the small drill doesn't snag and break when it meets the 1/4" hole. Move over 0.110" and repeat for the second hole. You should end up with two parallel holes and a neat thin wall in between. Trying to keep the wall thinner just invites the second hole to break into the first.

Last are the four tiny tapped holes in the corners of the flats of the steam chest to attach the lagging. Do add the lagging. So many models nowadays have it left off and the result looks "undressed." Look at the Stuart No. 10 cylinder on the front cover of ***Live Steam*** for January 1990. Com-

14 *The flywheel and its mounting collet. The collet is not yet split.*

pare that to the elegant wooden lagging on the big Tiny Power engine beside it.

I used 0-80 screws for mounting the lagging, as small a thread as I feel I can tap. My eyes no longer see the threads themselves. Beginners should be able to tap these little holes, and this makes a good practice job. Use the oiler as before. If you drill each hole 3/8" deep, the third and fourth should meet the first and second, which is good since you are no longer tapping blind holes. Don't attempt to drill straight through, as the drill won't likely stay straight. If you don't feel up to tapping 0-80, there is room for 1-72 or even 2-56, but by then the screw heads look too big. Tiny taps and small roundhead screws are available at hobby shops specializing in HO model railroad supplies. Roundhead screws are correct for this application.

The lagging itself is cut from a piece of blue stovepipe. It is cheap, the correct color and the correct material. I cut a strip with tin snips, a little oversize, wrapped it around the cylinder, tucking it into the corners with a length of 1/4" diameter rod, and persuaded it to be a close fit by tapping with a 4 oz. hammer. It can then be held with toolmaker's clamps while the corners are trimmed, hole positions marked, and center punched lightly putting little dimples into the tapped holes underneath. Remove it and drill No. 51 holes, replace, holding with the screws

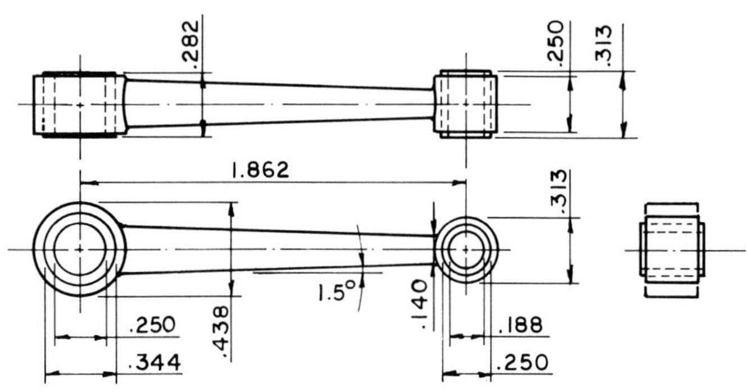

ALTERNATIVE SIMPLE CONNECTING ROD (20)

this time, trim the edges with a file, and polish with *Brasso.*

If you had a properly ground boring tool when you did the cylinder bore, the surface finish may be quite good enough as it is. However, treat yourself to a "honed" surface. In just about every town and city there are several automotive machine shops. These companies rebuild engines and transmissions and do related work. Almost all of them have a honing machine they usually use for sizing bushings. See if you can get the machinist to finish the bore of your cylinder for you, or better yet, get him to show you how to do it. Set the stream of cutting oil to flood your work while it's cutting – the object being to wash all the cuttings away, so there is nothing to gall or scratch. The resulting surface should delight you. A criss-cross pattern is what you want, and it will be dead true.

Connecting Rod

The next part is the connecting rod. Various styles of rod can be used, and by now I encourage you to not necessarily follow my instructions slavishly, but to adopt a shape you may have seen and which you find pleasing in appearance. On any engine with an overhung crank such as this one, it is possible to use a rod with a plain bushed journal at both ends.

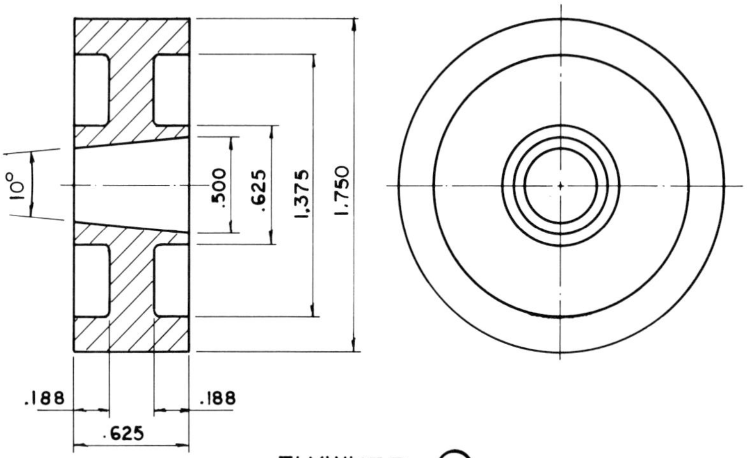

FLYWHEEL (17)

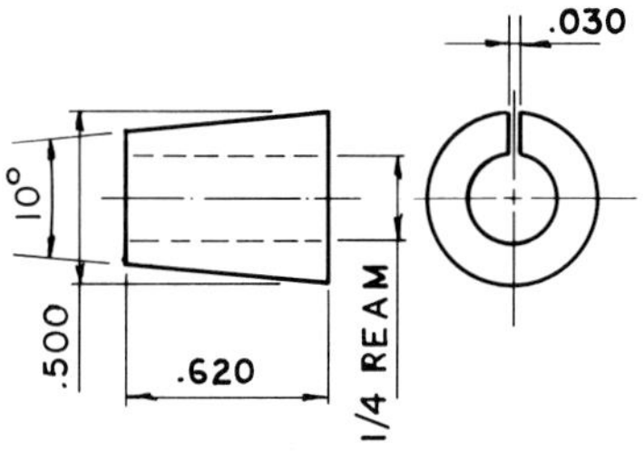

COLLET (18)

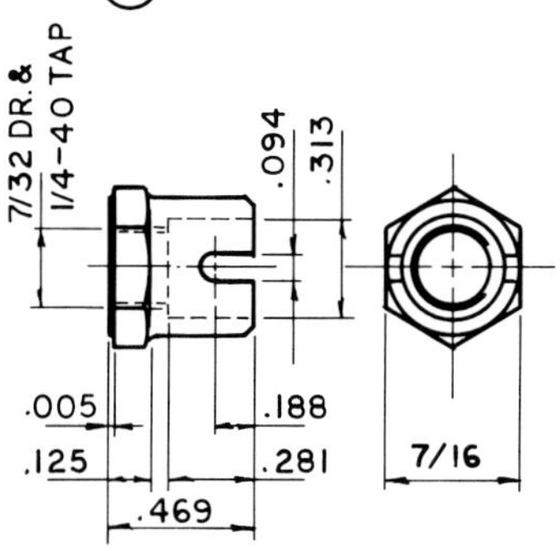

NUT (19)

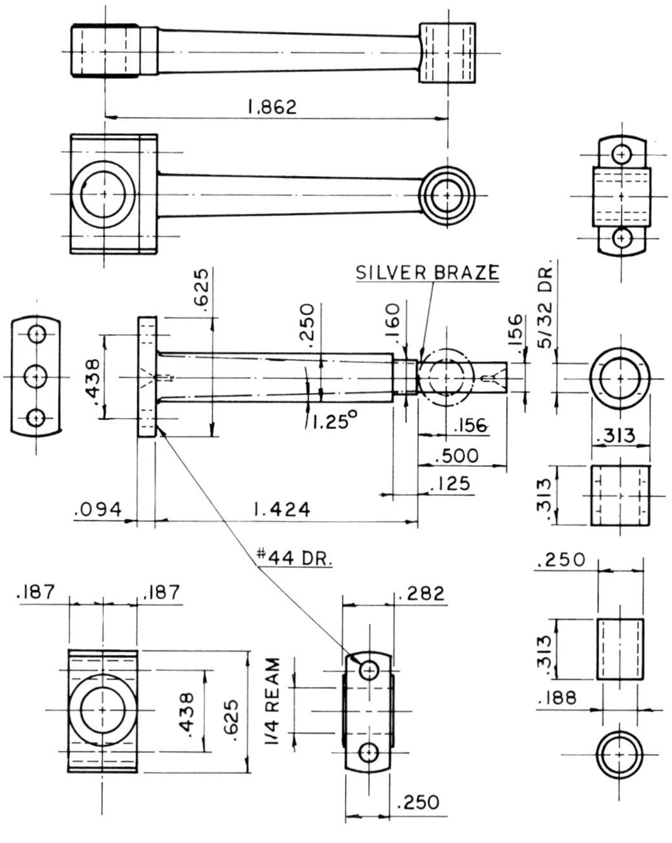

CONNECTING ROD (20)

15 *Note the brazing alloy at the joint on the cylinder.*

16 *The cylinder: lots of tapped holes!*

Then the "big end" looks like the Tiny Power M1 on the cover of ***Live Steam***, January 1990. The problem with this is that at assembly or disassembly, the rod has to be slipped over the end of the crankpin and it can't be without moving the whole crankshaft, or else disturbing the crosshead. In our engine the cylinder would be moved, and that requires disconnecting the transfer pipe. However, if this is not considered a problem, it allows for the simplest style to make and still follows correct "full size" practice. I'll describe both.

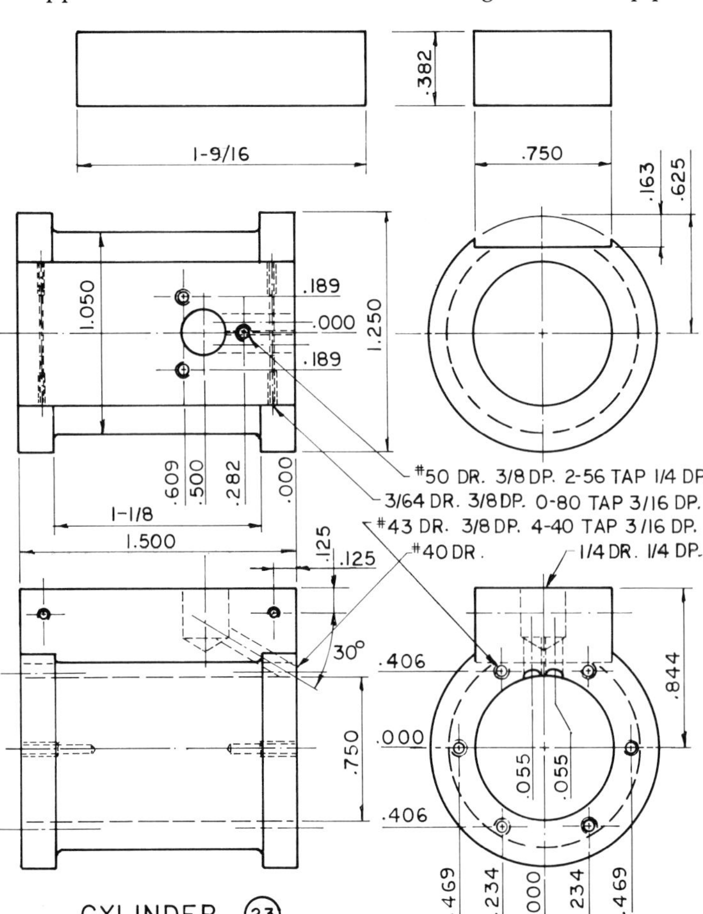

To make the simple connecting rod, start with a piece of 1/4 × 1/2" crs bar, chuck carefully in the four-jaw, and face and center drill one end. Allow enough material to form the boss for the "little end," and turn down the space between big end and little end to 1/4" diameter. Then turn the taper between them, supporting with the tailstock. Now, before parting off, transfer to the milling machine; carefully drill and ream through the center of each, maintaining exact center distance in preparation for pressing in bronze bushes. Saw off the part, go back to the lathe, face, and then by hand with a file, shape the two bosses. If you have the use of a rotary table, you can mill the radius at each end instead. Notice that this is the first handwork I have specified. I try to use files as little as possible, preferably only to remove burrs. Make up two bronze bushings and press them in. A touch of *Loctite* may help here.

A much more elegant connecting rod can be made by silver brazing a boss for the little end. For this style, start with a length of 1/4 x 5/8" (or more likely 1/4 × 3/4") steel, turn down a parallel portion at one end to 0.156" diameter, and center drill. Continue turning down the portion to the bolting flange to 1/4" diameter. Turn about another 1/8" to 5/8" diameter and also reduce the 1/4" diameter portion for about 1/8" to about 0.160" diameter. Do NOT turn the taper yet. I did, and what a problem I had then!

On a length of 5/16" diameter steel, cross drill a 5/32" hole about 3/16" from one end. Use the miller for accuracy. Transfer to the lathe and turn a boss just 0.312" long with the cross hole in the exact center. Drill through the length about 1/8" diameter.

This boss may now be pushed on to the end of the connecting rod. It won't go past the 0.160" part, so its lengthwise position is fixed and you can set it upright while the flat is at right angles. Pinch it to a firebrick with weights, flux it, and silver braze. Apply the alloy through the center hole in the boss, letting it flow outwards. It will make a beautiful joint. Clean up in the usual way.

Go back to the milling machine and clamp the flat in the vise. Now you can center, drill, and ream for the little end bush. Leave the tail in place for now because you still need the center hole. Saw off the excess material, upend in the vise, locate, center drill and drill for the two bolts. This is easy since you prepared the end when you turned the 1/8" at 5/8" diameter. With center holes at both ends, you can face the part and establish the length.

Next come the "big end brasses" which, of course, aren't brass at all. I cut two little bits from an old bronze bushing, and in the miller produced flats just 0.187" thick. I then tinned one face of each using ordinary plumber's soft solder, clamped them together with a pair of vise-grips, added a little flux, and heated. This process is called "sweating." When cool, I measured the thickness and found it to be just 0.375". So the solder only added 0.001". The little block thus formed was now squared up. As soon as I had proper reference points, it was easy to cross drill and ream for the crankpin and to drill for the two bolt holes. It was then bolted to the connecting rod. You may prefer to use commercial screws in order to avoid damaging the ones you carefully made for the job.

On a short piece of 1/4" diameter rod, center drill both ends so it will spin truly between centers. Poke it through the big end, mount between centers in the lathe, and carefully close the jaws of the four-jaw chuck around it. My error causes the bar between centers to deflect, and this is immediately seen when rotated. You may find it better to reverse one jaw of the chuck to support the little end, and you may also want to push something into the boss to prevent it being squeezed. Now remove the center bar, face, and turn a little register. This operation will also clean the face of the steel part. Reverse and repeat on the opposite side. Finally, hold in the three-jaw by the parallel portion and turn the bronze to 5/8" diameter to match the steel part.

17 *The transfer pipe and header.*

Dismantle, and working between centers, turn the taper. You will need to set the top slide over about 1-1/4 to 1-1/2°. Take light cuts, and change the angle as required to make it look right. Last, cut off the tailpiece and smooth the end. As for the simple connecting rod, you can make a bronze bush and press it into the little end.

Add a little reference mark on the bronze blocks and on the rod so you can reassemble the same way. Tiny center punch marks will do. Carefully heat the bronze blocks to melt the solder and let them come apart. Clean with a scrape on the file, reassemble with the correct bolts, and check that the bore is correct by passing the reamer through once more. And that should complete the connecting rod.

Piston and Wrist Pin

I have purposely left the piston until now in order to compensate for any collection of errors or buildup of tolerances. I found that the 1.862" dimension on the connecting rod was slightly too long, but I could vary the distance between wrist pin and piston top to make up for the error.

For material, iron would be ideal, and that is what would have been used in real life many years ago. However, considering the number of cars there are on the road, all with engines using aluminum pistons, I guess I don't have any objection if you use aluminum, too. Start with a piece of round slightly more than 3/4" diameter. Be careful to use an aluminum alloy that machines well. It is easy to pick up a surplus bit of bar that was meant for architectural purposes. It will weld fine, and it can be bent, but it machines terribly, the chips all piling up into a mess on the tip of the tool. What you need is a piece of 6061-T6, which is quite common in the machine shop, and gives a beautiful finish. Using the milling machine, drill across the bar exactly centered about 3/8" from the end and finish ream 3/16" for the wrist pin.

Transfer to the lathe, center, and drill 5/16" diameter by 1/2" deep. Push a piece of 3/16" rod through the wrist pin hole, bring the facing tool up to just touch it, clamp the carriage, and back off the top slide 0.218". This should establish the position of the bottom face. (If you are going to compensate for some minor error, the 0.218" will vary.) You can now open up the end of the piston to 0.688" diameter by about 0.188" deep.

Go back to the milling machine, holding the bar upright, and with the wrist pin hole parallel to the vise jaws, dig out the 5/16" hole to a slot, as shown on the drawing. Mill each side a little so the finished width is about 0.325". Return to the lathe once more, finish turn the outside diameter to as close a sliding fit in the cylinder as you can manage, part off, and face the top surface to give 0.625" total length. These little engines don't require piston rings or seals, relying on lubricating oil to keep them steam-tight. Small model airplane engines are a commercial example of this kind of fit.

The wrist pin can be a short piece of ordinary 3/16" drill rod. It doesn't need to be hardened, but you have the advantage of its ground surface and tough core to provide good wearing qualities. Drill through end to end 1/8" diameter and turn two little pads that locate in the end of the pin and prevent it from scratching the bore. Because these are meant to wear, they can quite correctly be made from brass.

Cylinder Head

This last part is made from the same material you used for the cylinder. Turn the outside diameter and the register diameter. You have an opportunity here to again compensate for any variation in the space between the piston top and the cylinder top when the piston is on top dead center. The register length should be made to give only a few "thou," say about 0.010", clearance. As you just did for the piston, move to the miller, locate the true center, and drill the six holes for attaching to the cylinder, exactly the way you did the corresponding tapped holes in the cylinder.

If your vise can be tilted, now would be a good time to mill a little 45° chamfer to deflect the incoming steam. An obvious alternative is to use a cutter such as a countersink with the point ground off.

Back to the lathe to part off, and then hold by the register to turn the top. The actual profile of the cylinder head can be varied to suit your preference as I suggested for the connecting rod. I think most full size engines had plain turned heads, and the bolt heads showed. However, on locomotives, a sheet metal cap shaped like the lid on a kitchen canister was regularly fitted over the head and became part of the lagging. I have shown such a shape on the drawings as an alternative.

Plumbing

The last few parts require practically no comments from me. "Pipe" is regularly made from copper tube, and the various ferrules and nuts are turned up from brass. The header on the transfer pipe should be drilled in the miller first and then finish turned. Soft solder a ferrule to a length of tube, add a nut, make a temporary assembly with the bearing, frame, columns, table, cylinder and header, and solder the tube into the header. That gives perfect length. Disassemble right away and clean everything, for the flux will cause the bright parts to corrode.

Displacement Lubricator

If this engine is never going to be used on steam, you may wish to stop here. Make another plug, the same as the two on the top of the bearing, and use it in the lubricator connection. Then run your creation on compressed air, and either oil manually or depend on a commercial air line lubricator to add the necessary oil.

The displacement lubricator does nothing on compressed air, but on steam, works as follows. Steam coming along the pipe to the engine also passes through a small orifice and into the space above the oil in the lubricator chamber. There, since it can't go anywhere, it cools and condenses, and the water thus formed, because it is heavier than the oil, sinks to the bottom. The oil level of course must rise, and eventually is squeezed back through the orifice and into the steam going into the cylinder.

Hold a piece of 1/4" brass hex in the lathe, and make a 5/32-40 locknut. At the same time, make a gland nut with a 3/16-40 thread. Doing these parts first allows you to use them as gauges for their mating pieces.

On the end of a length of 3/16" brass round, center, drill 1/16" diameter 7/32" deep, and continue with No. 60 drill for another 3/16". Turn the OD to 0.156" diameter for about 9/32", and thread 5/32-40. Part off, reverse, face, and establish length at 1.063" In the same way, drill, tap and thread the opposite end as shown.

Change over to 3/8" diameter brass rod and cross drill 3/16" diameter 5/16" from the end, using the milling machine. Cut off the rod about 1-1/4" long, finish the length, form the reverse curves at the bottom, drill and tap for the drain hole and the plug. The diagonal hole for the drain outlet requires special care, since if drilled too deep, it will cut into the valve seat and cause the drain to leak. Set up in the milling machine again to do this hole.

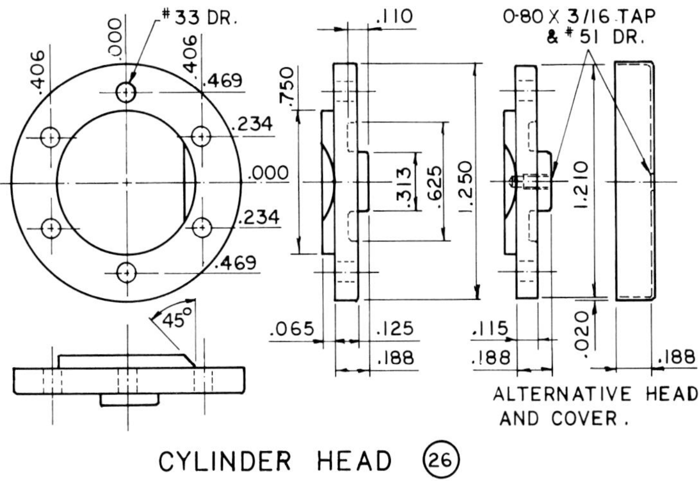

CYLINDER HEAD (26)

18 Piston, wrist pin, pad and connecting rod.

19 Reciprocating parts assembled.

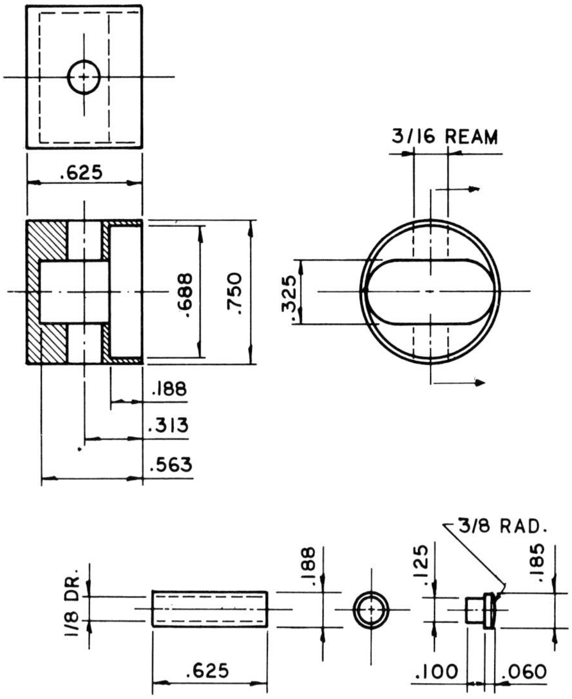

PISTON, WRIST PIN & PADS. (27) (28) (29)

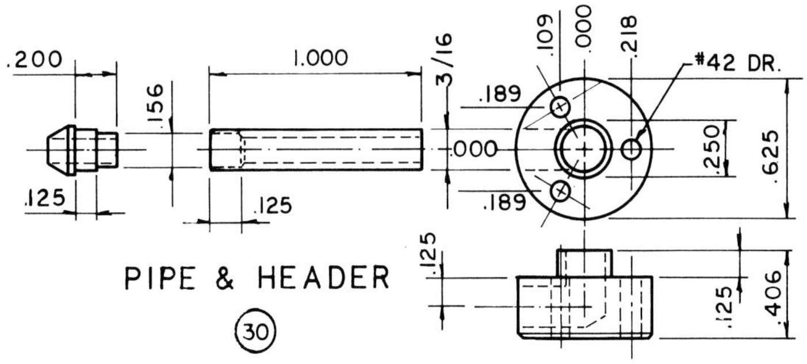

PIPE & HEADER (30)

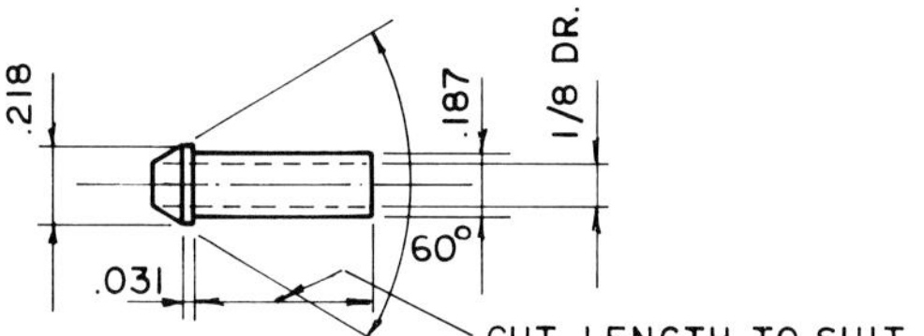

FERRULE (31)

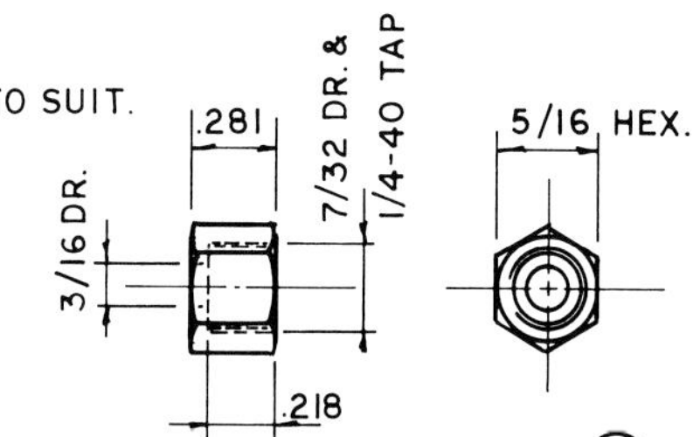

UNION NUT (32)

Assemble the 3/16" diameter part into the cross hole in the body and silver braze. If you center drill and open about 1/8" diameter down to meet the cross hole, you can add the brazing alloy through the hole, as described for the connecting rod.

When all cleaned up, drill out the body 9/32" diameter and tap 5/16-40 for the cap. A nice extra requires boring out the body below the cross hole to 5/16" diameter and squaring the bottom of the hole. That makes a nice job, and maximizes the amount of oil that can be held. Clear out the chips that have formed in the cross pipe.

The needle valve is next. Make it from a piece of coat hanger wire. I found that hanger wire is just about exactly 0.099" diameter, Perfect for threading 3-56. It is not the nicest stuff to machine, but it's not bad, and it certainly is cheap! Cross drilling for the handle takes some care but is not hard if you do it in the miller. Use a piece of wire for the handle and solder it in place.

The cap is made from the 3/8" brass

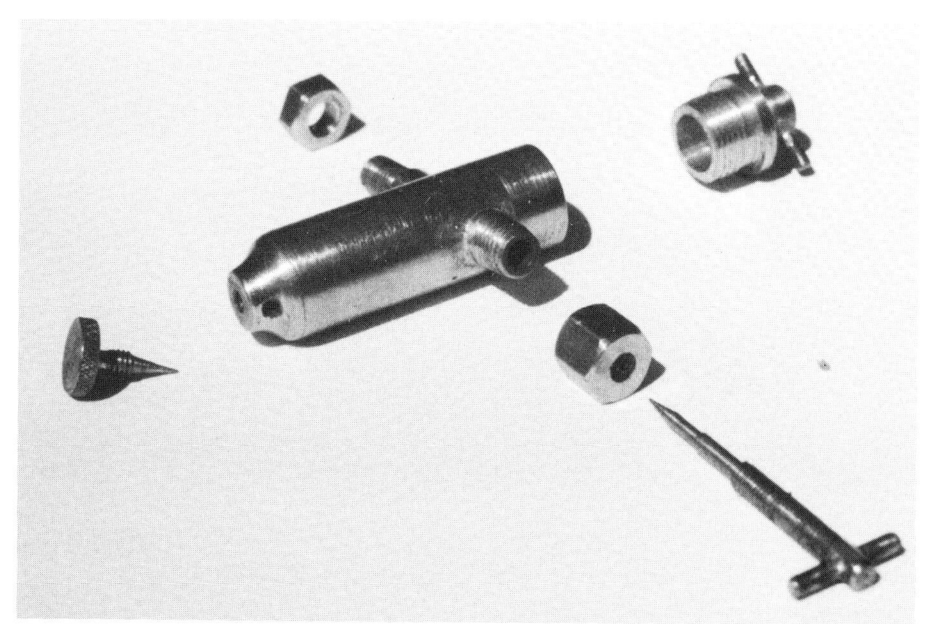

20 Component parts of the lubricator.

21 A complete displacement lubricator.

again. Cross drill for its handle first, 3/8" from the end. Then make the thread, hollow out, profile the top and part off. Solder in a wire handle as on the needle valve.

Last is the plug. This is plain turning from 1/4" diameter steel rod. Fine knurl if you have the tool.

Assemble as shown on the drawing. Use some strands of graphited yarn cut from "full size" valve packing to seal the needle valve gland.

Screw the finished unit into the port on the main bearing, and locate with the locknut. Fill with steam cylinder oil to the cross pipe. With steam on, open the needle valve just enough to establish traces of oil on the exhaust pipe. Note that it is possible to drain condensate and refill with oil while the engine is running. Opening the plug allows steam pressure to squirt out the condensate. Closing the needle valve and the plug allows the cap to be opened so more oil can be added.

Assembly Notes

You will surely have been putting the engine together as you have been going along, so by now you won't have anything left to assemble. I do have a couple of comments that belong under this heading, however.

22, a and b Two views of the 50-year-old rotary valve engine.

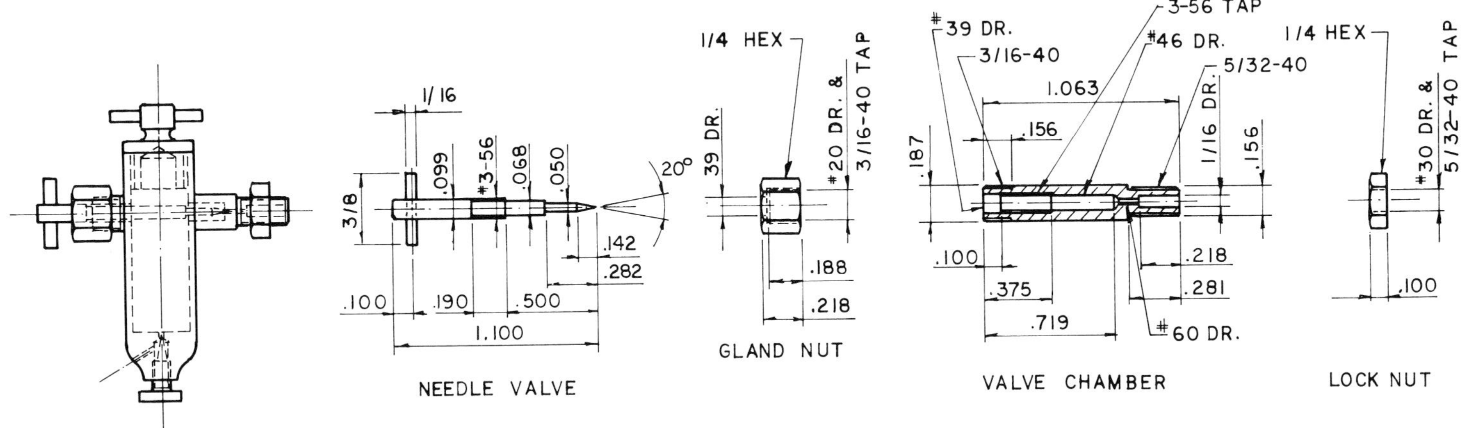

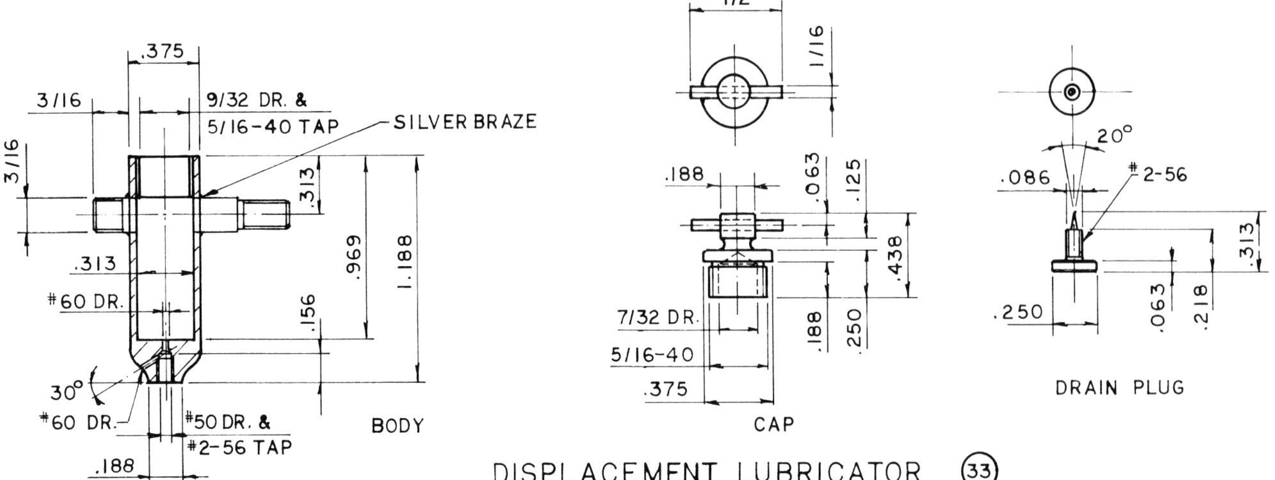

DISPLACEMENT LUBRICATOR (33)

23 *The engine set up on a base, coupled to a bicycle lighting generator as a load.*

24 *The engine running. Note the connecting rod and couplings are blurred.*

First, there is the matter of gaskets. I find that on little engines like this, the contact surfaces are so small that metal to metal joints are usually tight enough without the need for gasketing. However, sometimes there is a tell-tale weep of oil, and something has to be done about it. Paper gaskets used to be used, cut from the thinnest of commercial gasket paper, or from the glazed paper the butcher used for wrapping meat. Now there is a good alternative readily available and cheap, namely the sealant materials that come in a tube. One such is *Permatex,* which is a product of the Loctite Corp. This should be available in hardware stores or auto accessory stores. It makes an excellent seal, has practically zero thickness, and comes apart easily if it is necessary to dismantle.

Second, going back to the matter of putting the lagging on the cylinder, the purpose of the lagging is to hold insulation in place to reduce the flow of heat out from the cylinder. On the little engine, the effectiveness of this insulation is so slight due to its being so thin that you might as well leave it out. On the other hand, adding a little insulation makes your engine more realistic, and I recommend you do it anyway. Use a little slice cut from a fiberglass insulation batt.

I found that the end of the lagging strip tended to stick out a little from the surface of the steam chest, but a touch of five-minute epoxy, a material undreamed of in the days of steam, soon corrected that. The use of these space age materials, on a model of a steam engine that might have been built 100 years ago, doesn't bother me. I think it is because they are essentially invisible, and make the overall effect realistic.

This completes the description of the engine. If you have built it and if it has been your first, I hope you have enjoyed the project and are inspired to build many more. I can think of no more satisfying hobby.

25, a and b Two similar views of the engine running.

26 Plumbing parts. A pipe ferrule and a union nut.

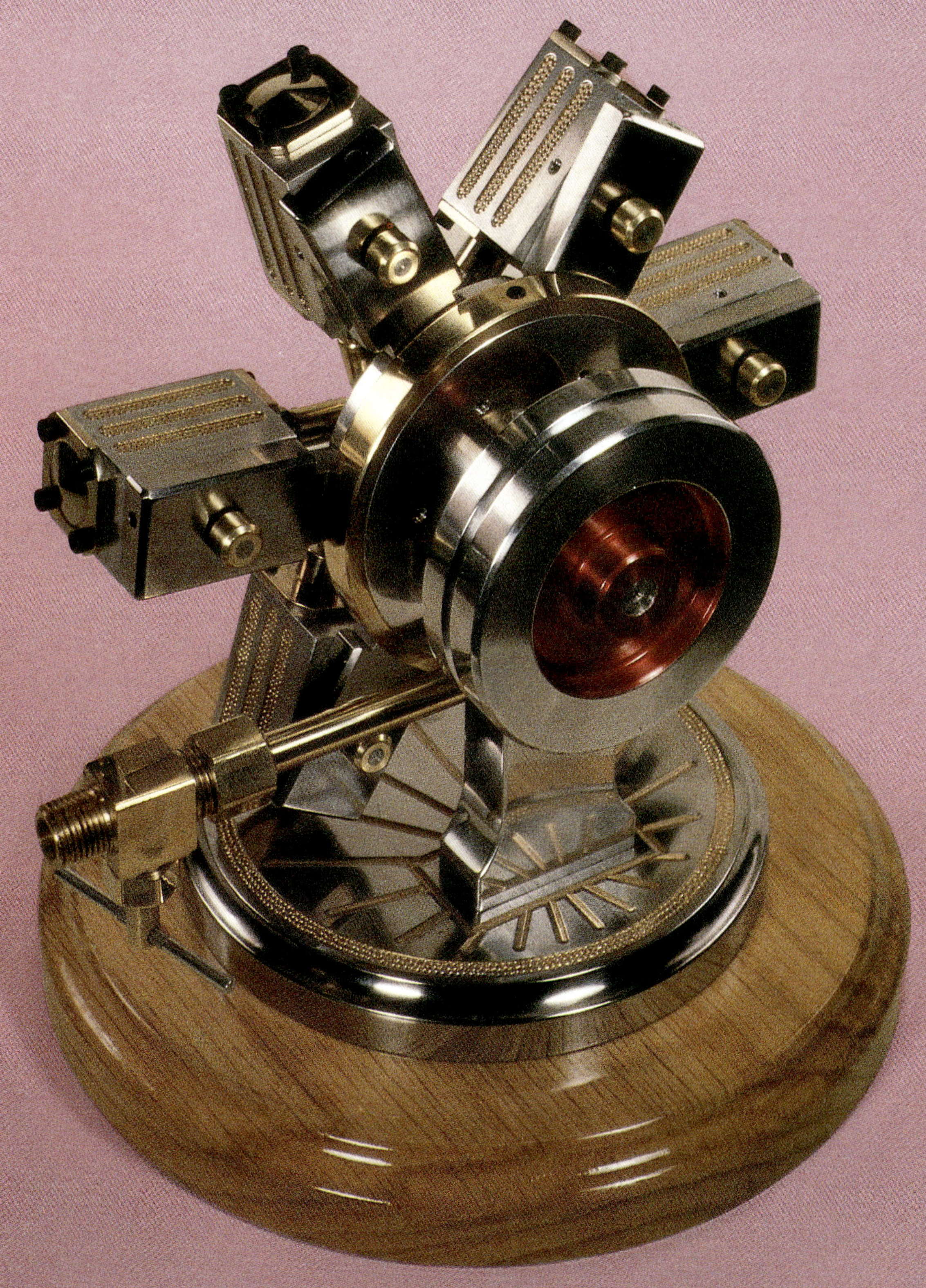

Philip Duclos' "HULA-HULA" ENGINE

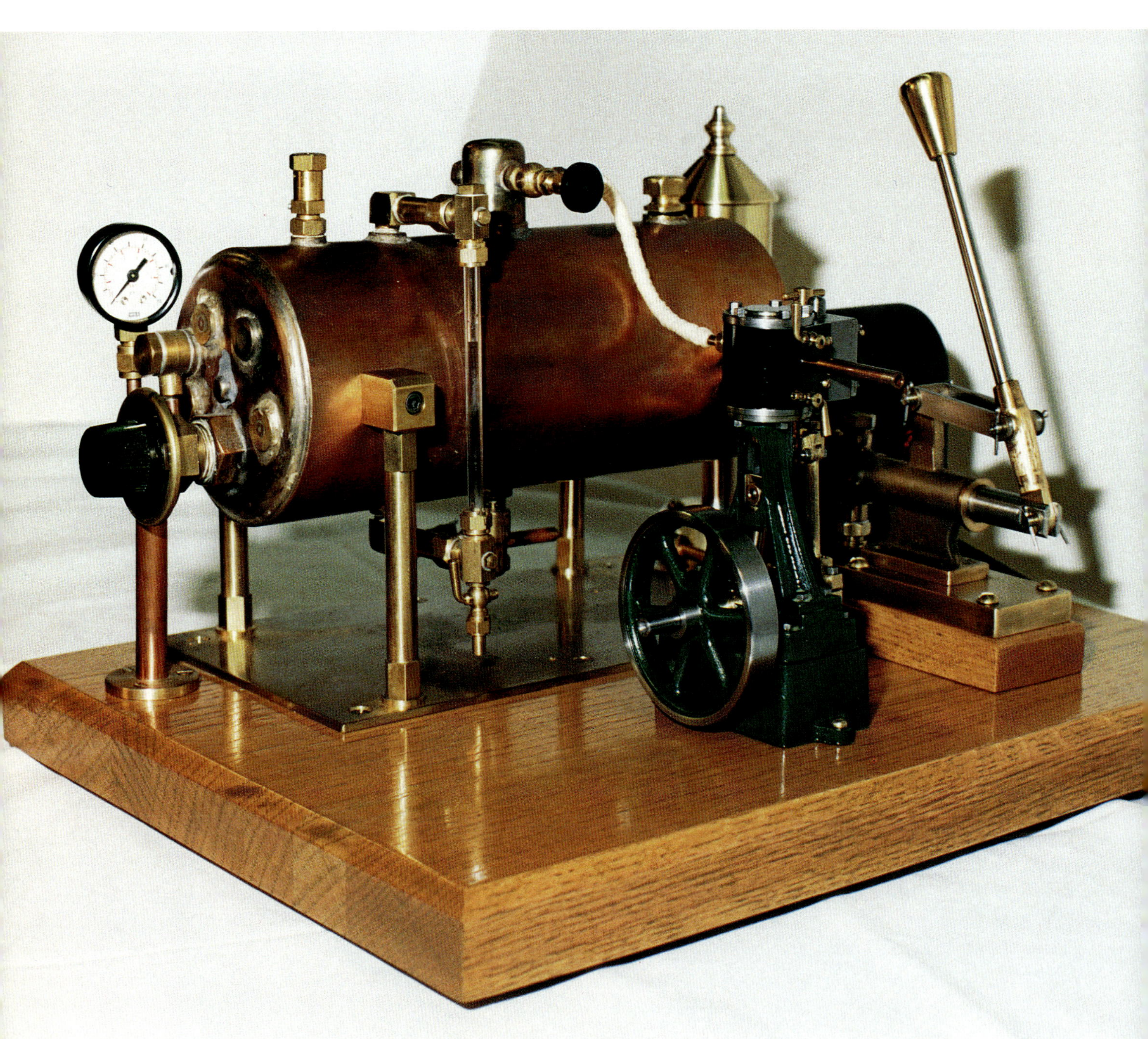

D.E. Johnson's ELECTRIC BOILER

Andy Sprague's SPEEDER

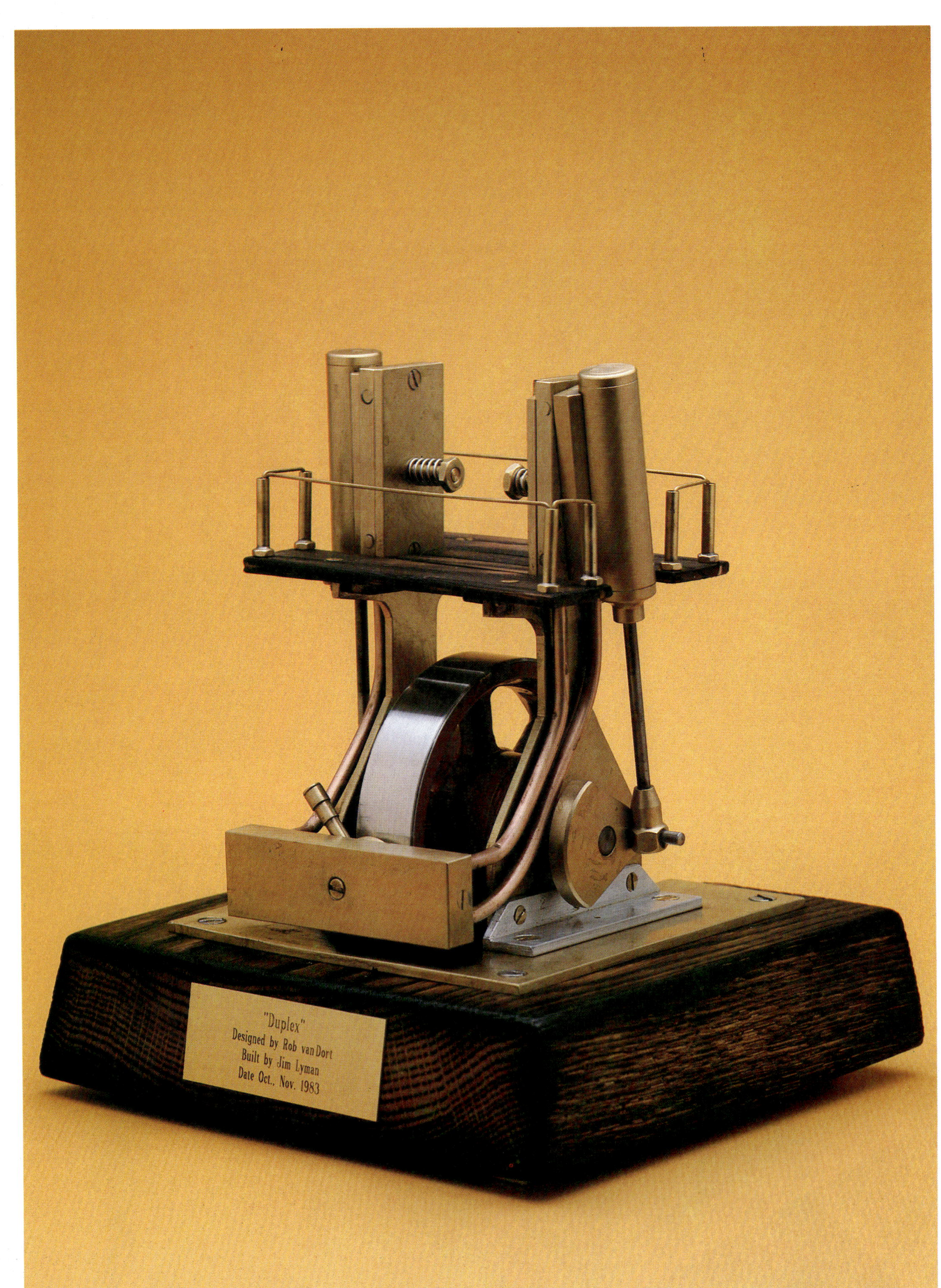

Jim Lyman's DUPLEX ENGINE

Andy Sprague's JUNKBOX STEAM ROLLER

Paul Jacobs' NDC-1

W. Marshall Black's "BRASSO" BEAM ENGINE

Andy Ross's STIRLING CYCLE ENGINE

Assembled engine, valve cover end

Assembled engine, output shaft end

An historical revival in miniature

Root's Engine

By R. S. Hedin

Photos by Author

The Scientific American of March 26, 1864, featured a description of a new steam engine designed by J. B. Root. I recently got a copy of this issue and made a model based on this description. No attempt was made to make an exact copy, as the original had many cored passages and other features that would be difficult to duplicate in a model.

The principle, as shown in the photos, is two rectangular pistons, one inside the other, working in a rectangular cylinder. The inside piston is driven by a crank and works vertically, while the outer piston moves horizontally. Steam is admitted at the end of each stroke so this is, in effect, a two-cylinder, double-acting engine with no dead center. The valve is in the cover housing and is an eccen-

Assembled engine, side view

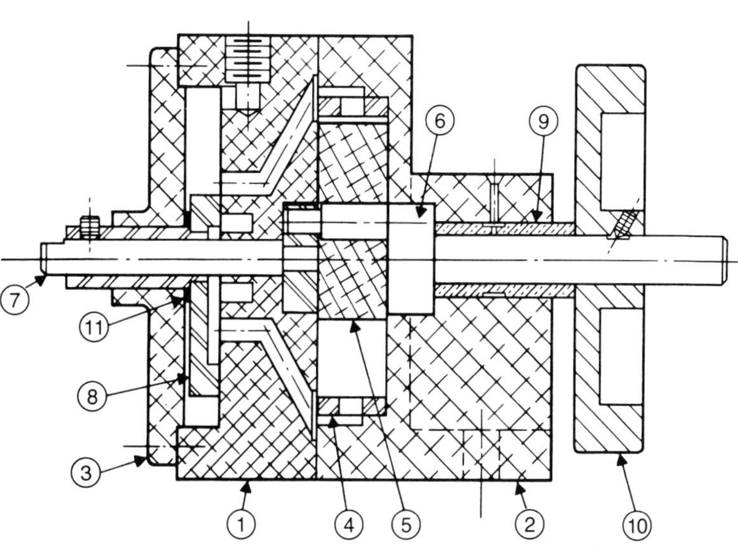

SECTION, ROOT'S ENGINE

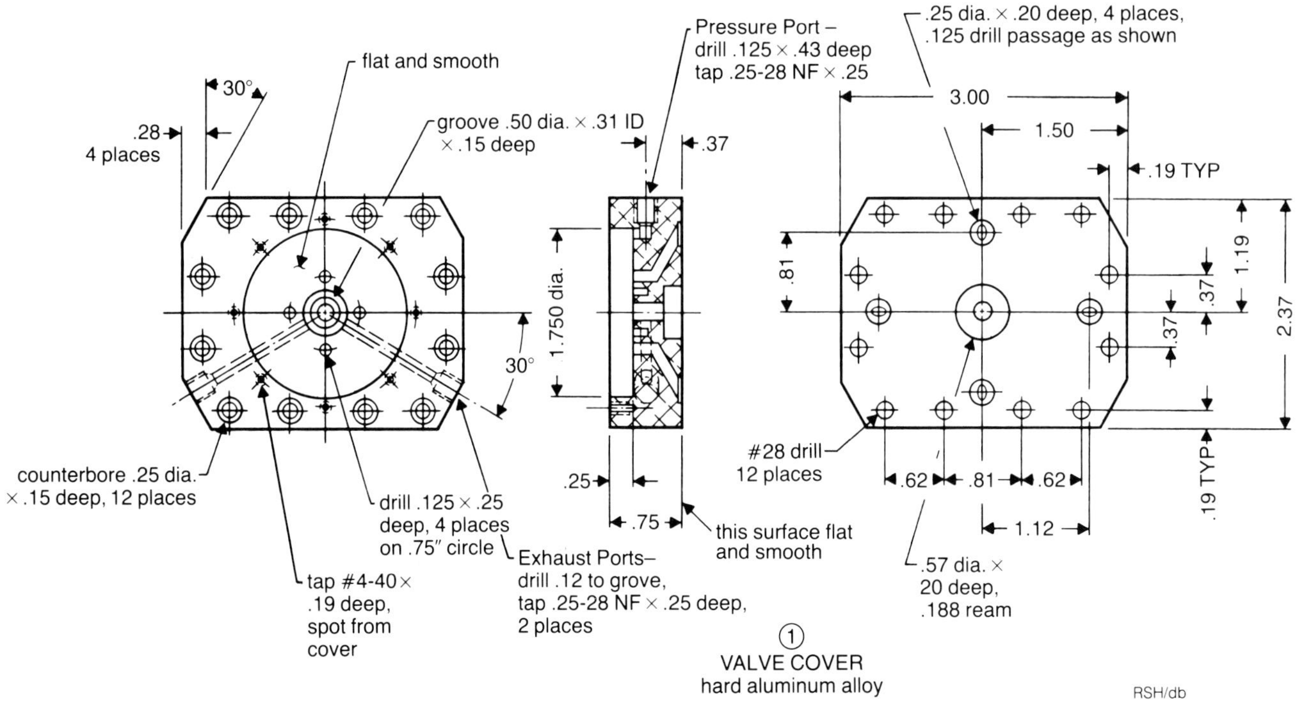

① VALVE COVER
hard aluminum alloy

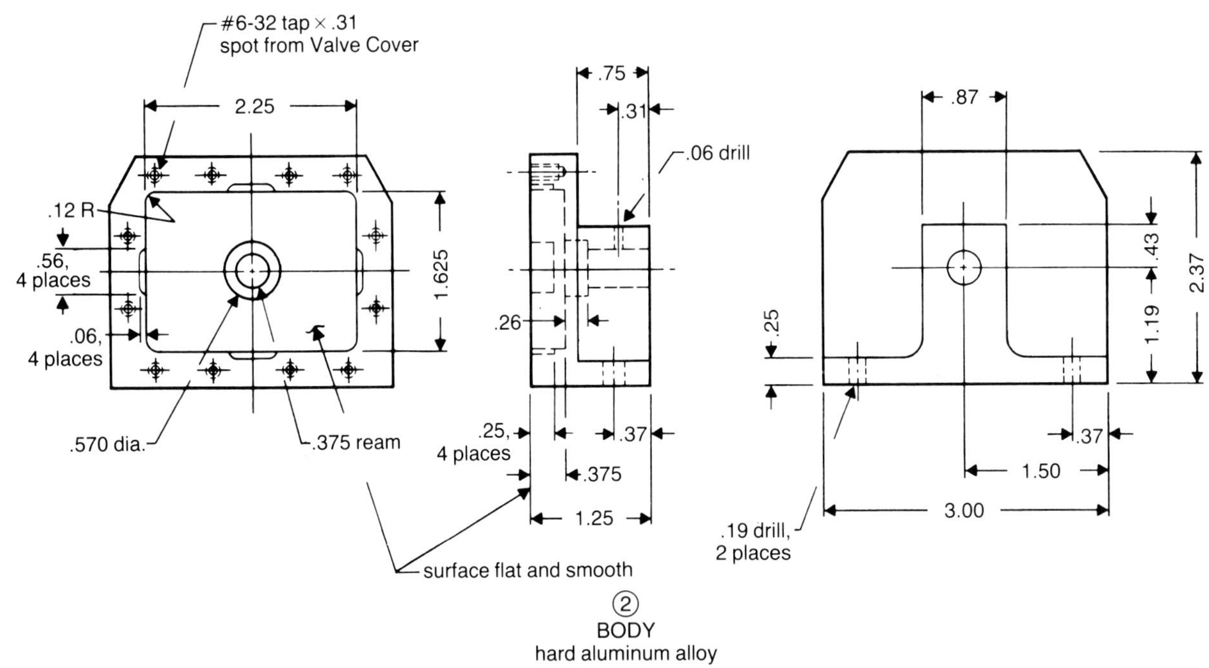

② BODY
hard aluminum alloy

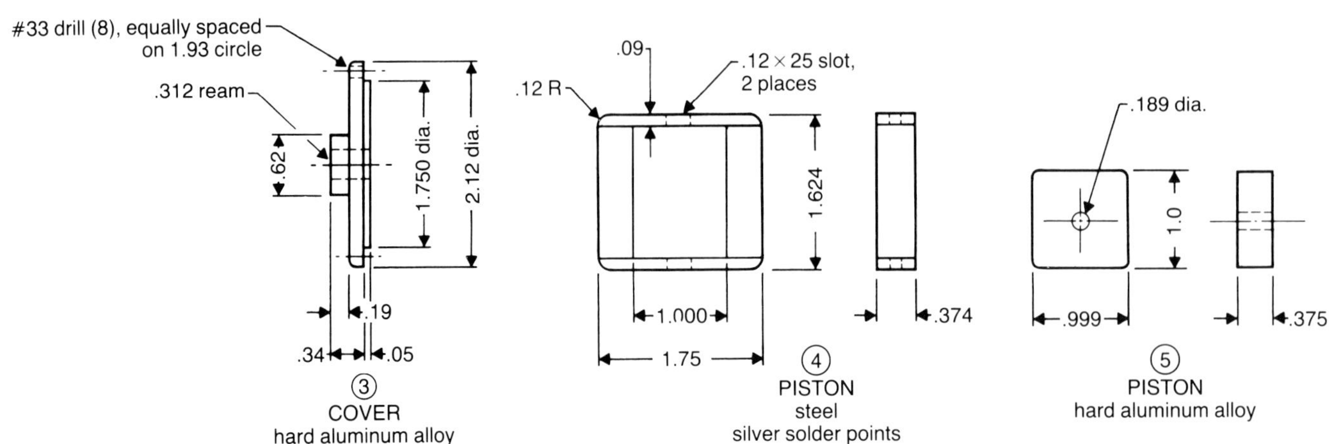

③ COVER
hard aluminum alloy

④ PISTON
steel
silver solder points

⑤ PISTON
hard aluminum alloy

Partial assembly of pistons and valve

tric round plate rotated by the crankshaft. It admits steam to each piston in turn through four ports and exhausts around the center. The valve is similar in action to a sliding D-valve. With the dimensions given, steam is admitted for nearly all of the piston stroke.

The bodies and the inner piston are made of hard alloy aluminum for easy machining and light weight. These were given a slight anodize treatment that accounts for the difference in color in the photos. The dimensions on the drawings are nominal and, depending on the stock used, may end up different. The three-place decimal dimensions indicate where close fits are required and the clearance between moving parts.

The steel piston is made of .375″ square stock and .375 x .093″ flat stock. The pieces are screwed together and silver soldered. (See previous issues of ***Live Steam,*** Kozo Hiraoka, for this technique.) Take a clean-up cut on all sliding surfaces to smooth and square them.

The crank can be made in a number of ways. If you're ambitious – one piece. The one in this model is made of three pieces fastened with bearing *Loctite.* Oil the parts as they are assembled. No gaskets are used between the valve cover and body, as this will affect the clearance of the pistons and cause leakage. If the mating surfaces are flat and smooth, there will be no problem with leaks. The valve is set 90° from the crank throw. The flat on the valve shaft and the set screw in the valve stem indicate this relationship after the engine is assembled. The engine is reversed by setting the valve 180° from its first position. Some nifty mechanism can be made for reversing without playing with a set screw. We leave this job for the reader.

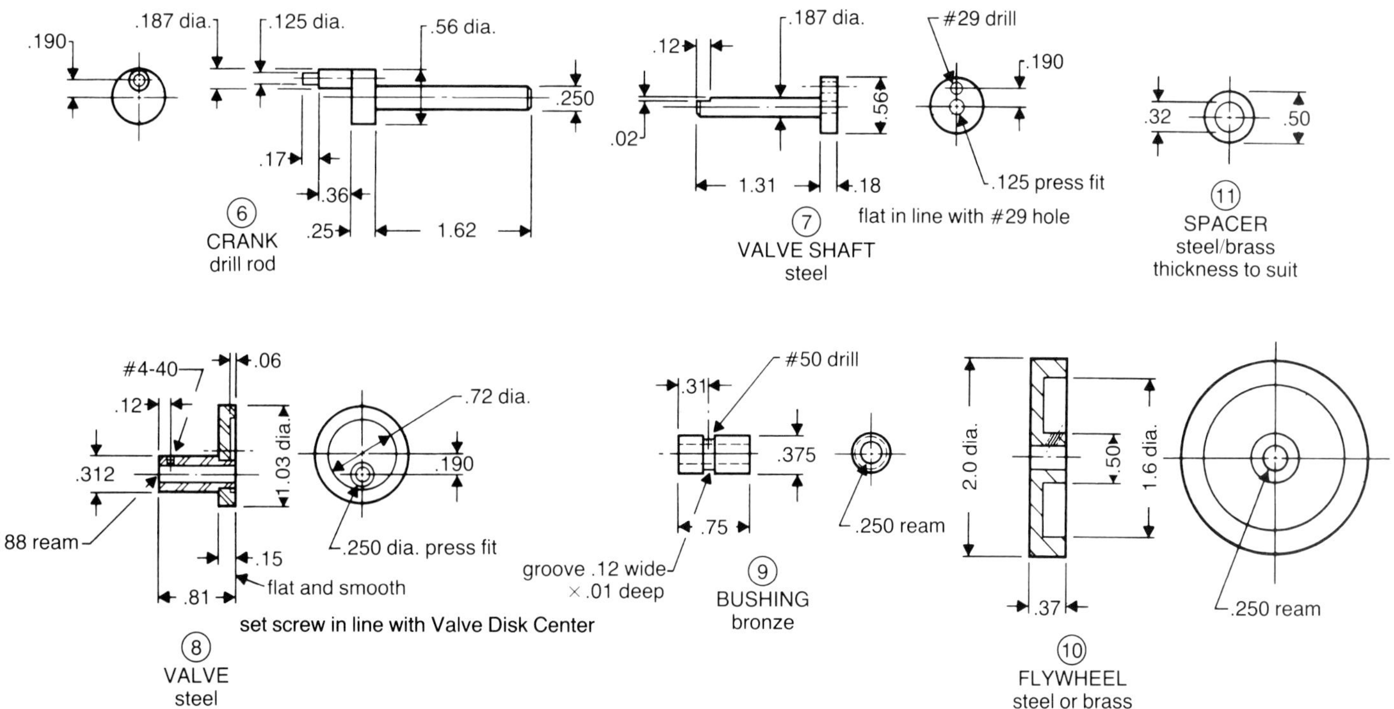

Finished parts

1

"Hula-hula" Engine

By Philip Duclos

Photos by Author

Approximately 75 years ago, model builders were constructing relatively lightweight single-action, six-cylinder radial steam engines, along with flash boilers. Okay! So what did they do with them? They were used as motive power for model airplanes! It must have been quite a sight to see one of them fly!

Our little motor certainly was not designed to power a model plane. Actually, it is more of a "showpiece" or "display" model. But its most unique quality comes from the fact that it is an *oscillating, dual-action* six-cylinder radial engine!

When this 1/2" bore motor is in action, the motion of the moving parts is very reminiscent of a fast wiggling hula-hula dancer – or better yet, six of them! (See the action in **Photo 1**.) The speed control is a common brass 1/8" pipe needle valve, and thus the engine can be adjusted from a slow "wiggle" of about 40 rpm to a blurry fast wiggle of perhaps 2,000 rpm.

In **Photo 2**, notice the flywheel on the rear side of the engine. Actually, it's for appearance only; the motor runs as well without a flywheel as with one!

Now, if you intend to operate the engine with compressed air as I did, almost

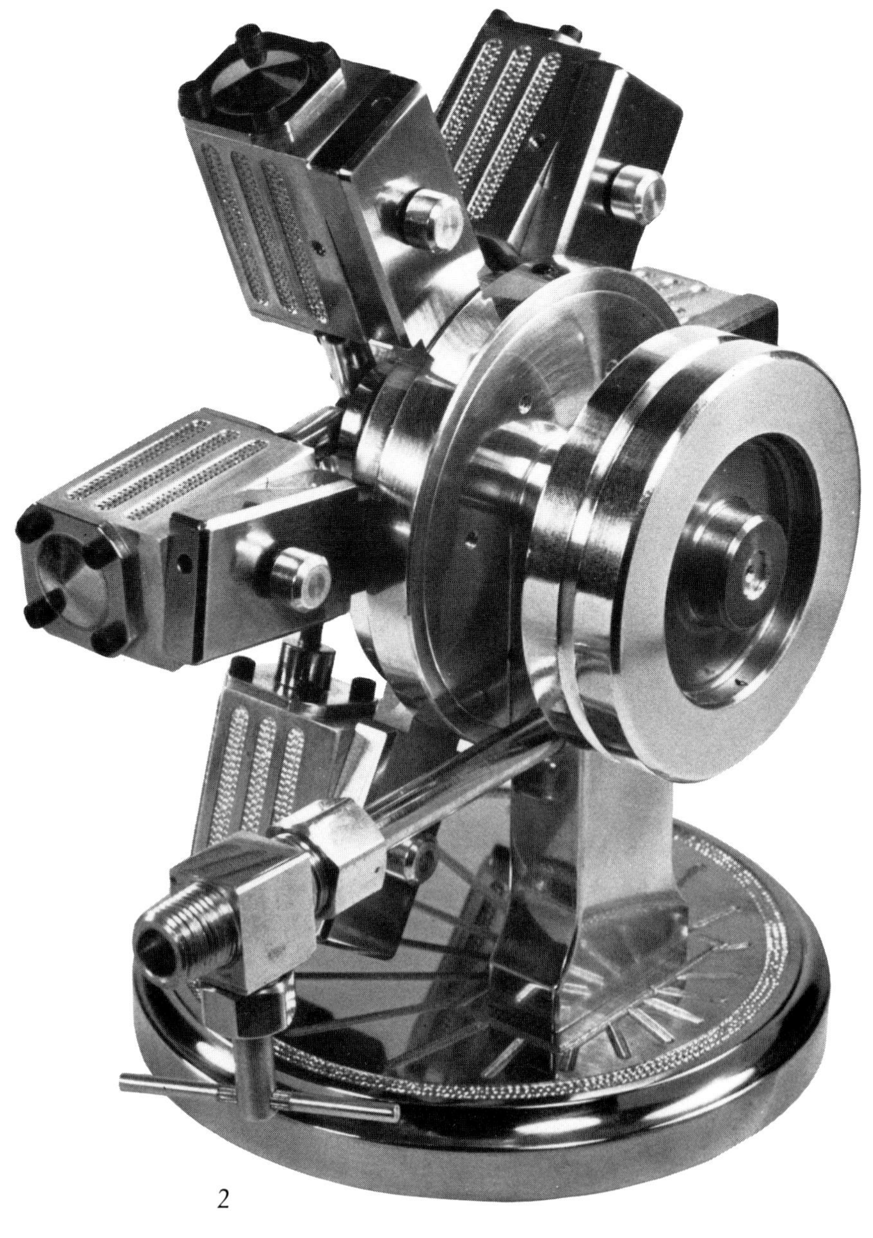

2

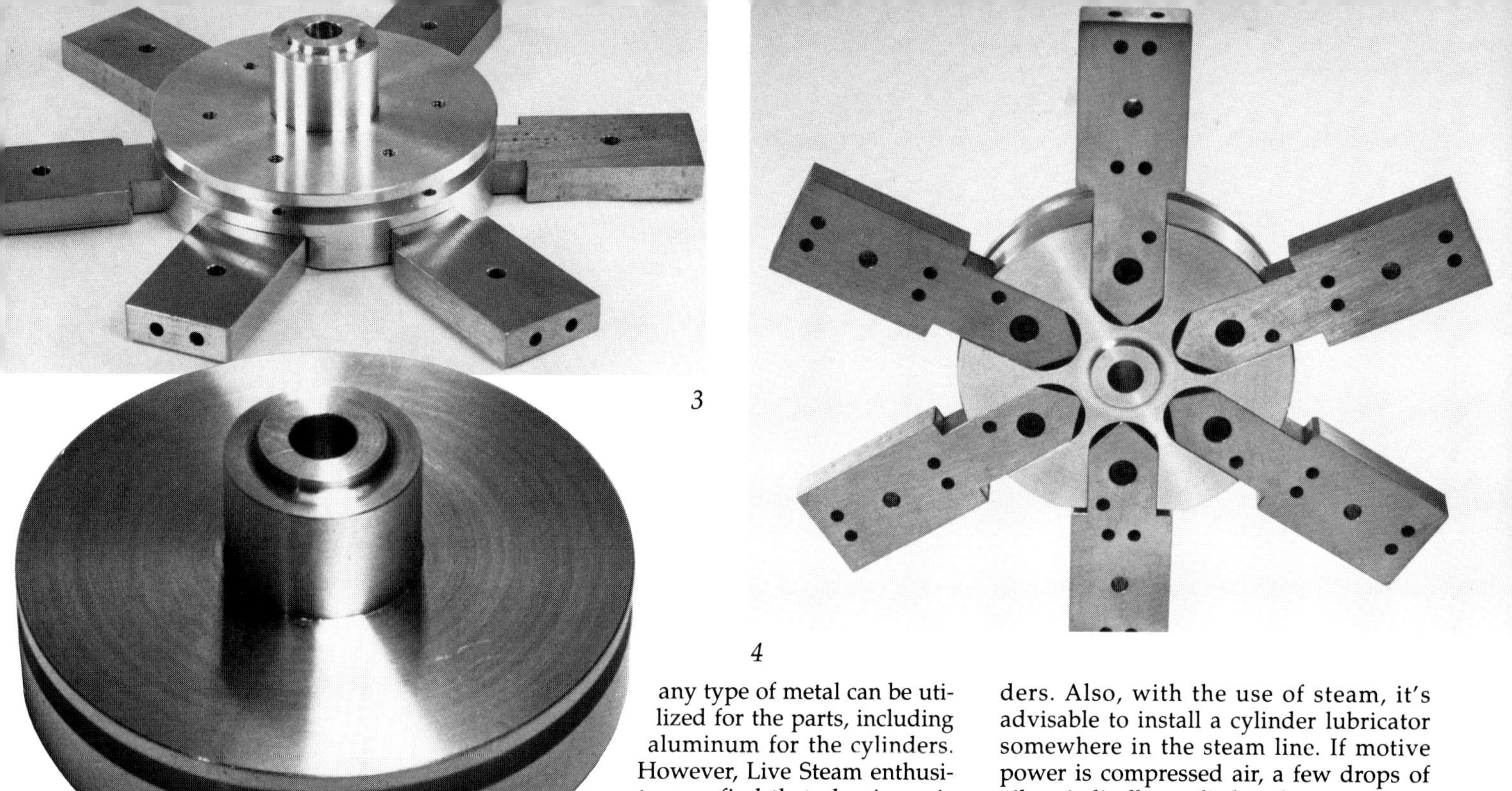

3

4

5

any type of metal can be utilized for the parts, including aluminum for the cylinders. However, Live Steam enthusiasts may find that aluminum is not the best choice for the cylinders. Also, with the use of steam, it's advisable to install a cylinder lubricator somewhere in the steam line. If motive power is compressed air, a few drops of oil periodically applied to the proper location will keep the motor running.

master cylinder slot
locate from cylinder backplate, 6 holes, 3/32"
locate from cylinder backplate, 6 holes; tap 4-40
30°
57½°
302½°
245°
.375" R
115°
½
2°
180°
.562
.250
⅛
3/32" oil hole; locate from body pillar
3/16
1/32
2.375
.030
5/32
1.125
master cylinder slot
148°
5/32" dia.
locate from body pillar; tap 6-32 2 holes, ⅜" deep
.250
11/16
ream .250"
½
.750
5/16
½

ENGINE BODY
aluminum, steel or brass
1 required

6

8

9

7

Before actural work is started on the engine, perhaps a brief explanation of some of the motor peculiarities would be appropriate. Visible in **Photos 3** and **4** are the six nearly completed steel backplates, bolted in place on the circular aluminum body. These are the cylinder supports; the one at the very bottom in Photo 4 is 1/4" shorter than the others and will hold the "master" cylinder; it is seen at its normal position at top left in Photo 1. The master piston rod is held rigidly to the master connecting rod unit. Another peculiarity is that the cylinder backplates are not positioned exactly 60° apart from each other, as you might imagine. The only two that are 180° apart are for the master cylinder and the one directly opposite. All of this maneuvering was necessary to standardize the location of all port holes in five of the cylinder backplates. The master backplate has only one port hole located differently.

Precise workmanship and plenty of polish will turn this project into an eye-catching showpiece – but even without the polish, it's still an "eye-catcher"!

Begin work by turning out the circular

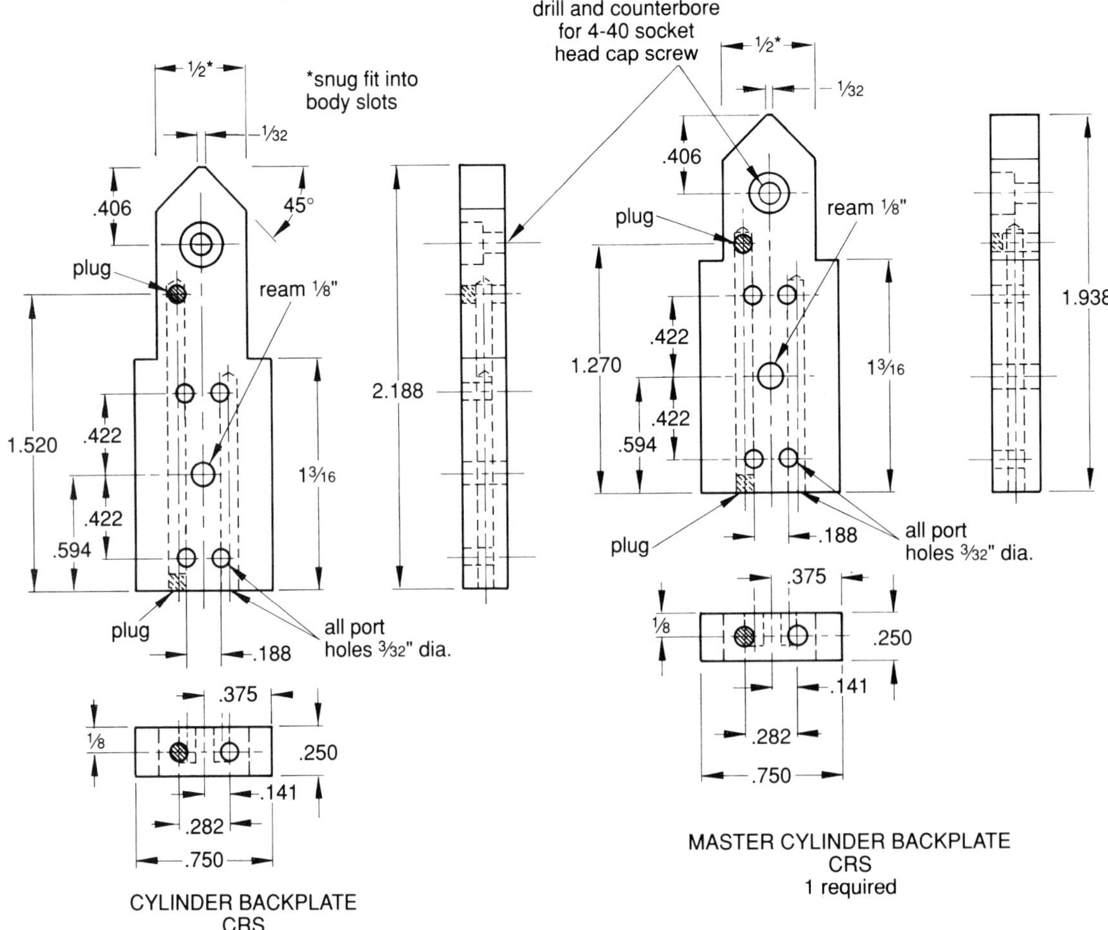

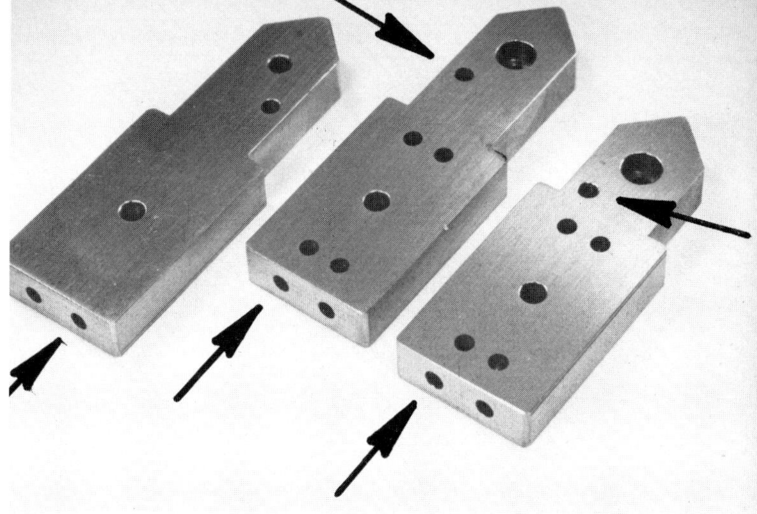

10 11

12 13

blank shown in **Photo 5.** The channel visible in the perimeter of the body will eventually be covered, thus becoming the manifold that transports steam or air pressure to the cylinders. The next operation on the body is performed by the milling machine. The body part must be held either by a small vise and V-block, or a chuck; these of course are secured to the rotary table. First, center the rotary table true to the mill spindle, then lock the cross slide. Crank the rotary around to its zero degree mark, for a movement later on, in a clockwise direction. Install an indicator in the mill spindle and place the work onto the rotary table.

With loosened clamps, shift the work by hand until it's centered true, then tighten the clamps. Use the longitudinal table travel for performing the next few operations. Now, move the work to the right enough to clear the spindle and install a sharp 1/2" end mill. Then position it to barely touch the surface of the work. Set the calibrated collar on the mill spindle to zero. Now move the cutter to the left to clear the work and lower it somewhat. The idea is to mill all six slots as close as possible to the same depth and length. Measure the actual diameter of the body. Subtract .750" from that and divide the result by 2. That amount will be the length of each slot. Now bring the end mill to barely touch the perimeter of the body. Set the calibrated collar on the longitudinal table travel to zero. It's advisable, when milling the slots, to gradually lower the cutter in steps of about .050" at a time. But before doing any cutting, check that the rotary table is set to its zero degree mark. The first slot to be cut will eventually be the one for the master cylinder. Proceed now to mill the first slot completely. Clear the end mill to the left from the work; crank the rotary clockwise 57-1/2°, and lock it. Mill the second slot. Crank the rotary around to 115° for the third slot, 180° for the next, then 245°, and finally 302-1/2°.

After milling the last slot, do not disturb the work or the height of the end mill, but move the cutter to the left to clear the body. Now proceed to crank the rotary around to its original zero setting; this will bring the master cylinder slot back to its previous position. Notice in **Photo 6** that it's necessary to mill two flats on the perimeter of the body to enable the shorter master cylinder backplate to seat properly against the inner curved surface of the slot. The overall length of this particular slot should be about 11/16". Then remove the body from the mill and set it aside.

Begin work on the cylinder backplates. 1/4 × 3/4" crs flat bar stock was employed for them. However, it may be advisable to lightly fly-cut or surface grind them, since it's important that these pieces are flat and parallel on both sides, and the edges square. Follow by machining them to the correct length; then prepare to form the step cuts on each that will make them a snug fit into the body slots. **Photo 7** indicates one method of doing this. First, measure the actual width of the slots in the body. Then measure the overall width of the backplates. From this, subtract the width of the slots and divide the result by 2. That amount will be the depth of the cut on each edge. After this, several backplates can be clamped together in an angle vise at 45°, and beveled as shown in **Photo 8**. Leave a narrow flat on the tip of the work, about 1/32" wide. Proceed by scribing center lines for the pivot shaft hole and port holes, and the two port holes on the outer end of the plate. All of these holes should be accurately drilled in the mill. Referring to **Photo 9**, the port holes on the end of the plate should be drilled prior to the four port holes on the face of the plate. These two port holes on the end are drilled rather deep, so spot drill them about 1/2" deep in the mill and finish drill with a drill press; it's much faster.

14

15

Please examine **Photo 10**. The four port holes on the face of the plate go only deep enough to intersect the two long port holes just drilled. The problem is that the long port holes are spaced farther apart than each pair of port holes on the face. This means if the four port holes were drilled down far enough to intersect the long holes, the drill would be forced to one side when it begins to penetrate the offset hole beneath. That reaction would probably elongate the hole being drilled. Avoid this disaster by first spot-drilling the hole with a No. 2 center drill. Drill as deeply with it as possible, but don't allow the 60° angle on the center drill to cut into the work. Proceed by installing a No. 46 drill and go just deep enough to intersect the long hole.

Finally, with a 3/32" end mill, deepen the hole until the tip of the cutter is approximately flush to the bottom curve of the horizontal hole. If a 3/32" end mill is unavailable, use a 3/32" drill; grind the cutting angle on it square across, similar to the tip on an end mill.

After completing the port holes, the plates should resemble the examples in **Photo 11**. The plate at the left has its back-side facing up. The center one is face up. The right one is the master backplate. The arrows indicate which holes will be sealed later on with short steel plugs. The

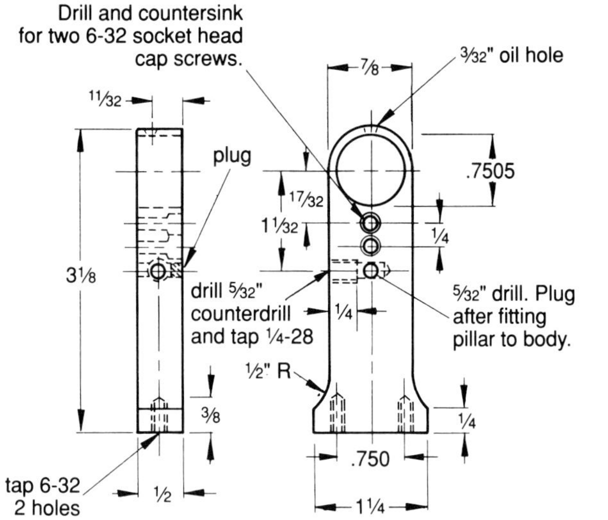

Drill and countersink for two 6-32 socket head cap screws.

3/32" oil hole

plug

drill 5/32" counterdrill and tap 1/4-28

5/32" drill. Plug after fitting pillar to body.

tap 6-32 2 holes

BODY PILLAR
aluminum or CRS
1 required

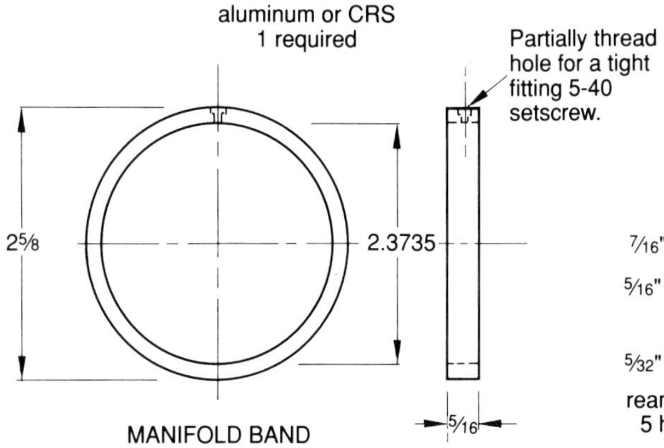

Secure the crankpin with *Loctite* 640, or solder, or press fit. 1 required.

"flat" for setscrew (optional)

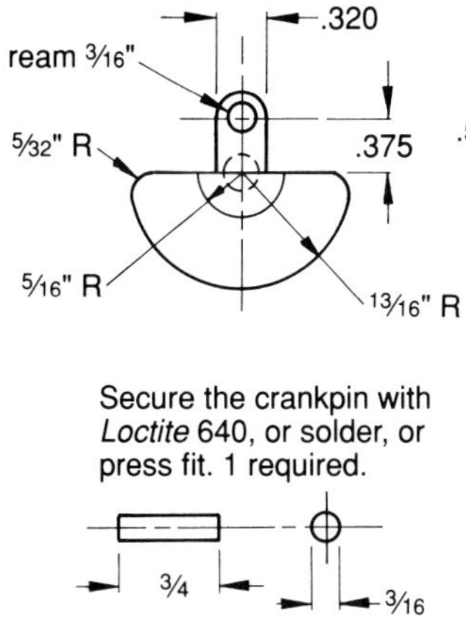

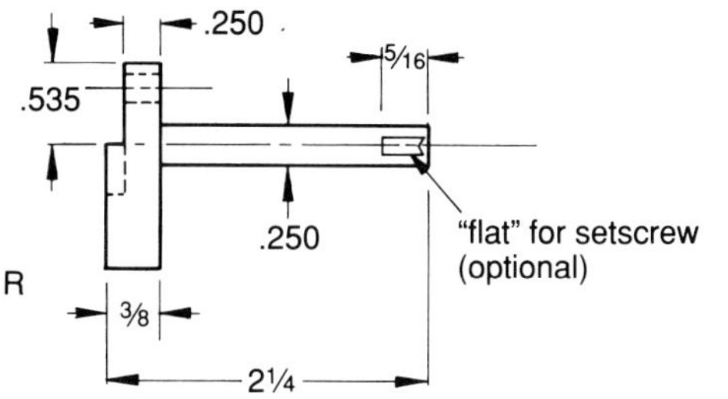

CRANKSHAFT
1 required CRS or HRS
crankpin: 1 required, drill rod or dowel pin

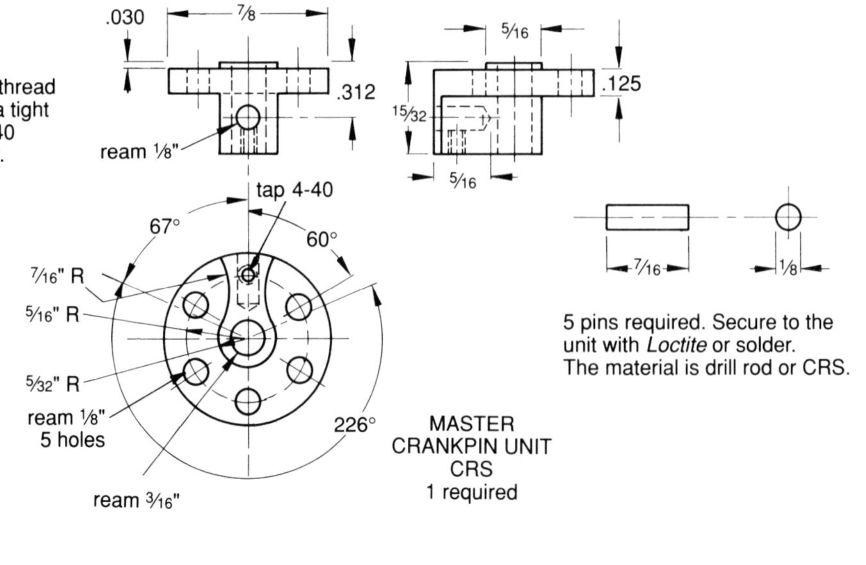

Partially thread hole for a tight fitting 5-40 setscrew.

MANIFOLD BAND
steel, aluminum or brass
1 required

5 pins required. Secure to the unit with *Loctite* or solder.
The material is drill rod or CRS.

MASTER
CRANKPIN UNIT
CRS
1 required

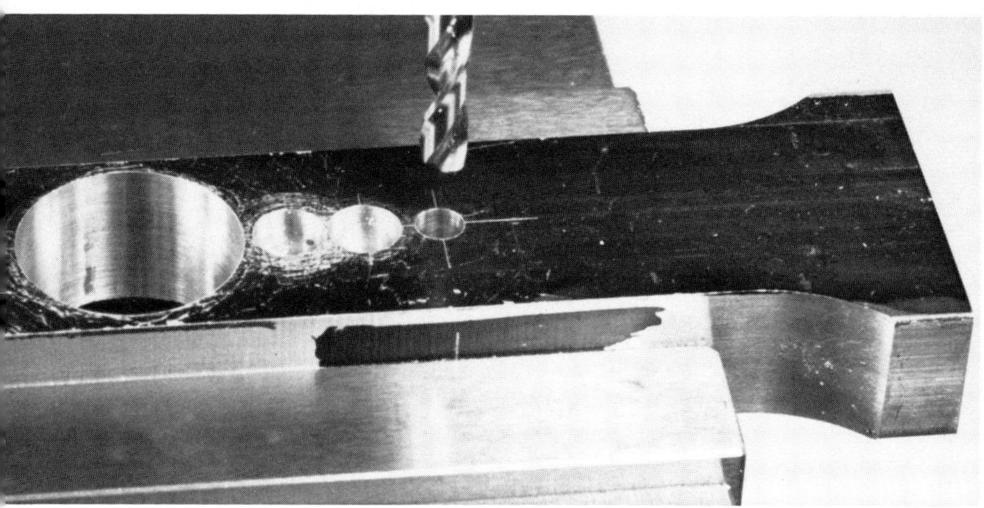

16

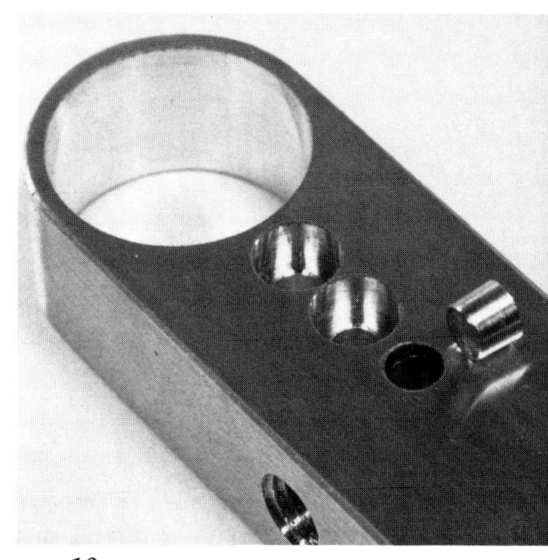

18

remaining port hole on the end of the piece will be the exhaust port hole; thus, the engine will revolve in a clockwise direction when viewed from the rear.

In preparing to bolt each backplate into place on the body, make certain the beveled tip on each one is seated against the curved edge in the body slots. As soon as all of the backplates are bolted in place, it's time to open up the port holes leading to the manifold channel in the body (**Photo 12**). Simply use the port hole indicated by the lower arrow to drill down far enough to reach the manifold channel. The upper arrow indicates the result.

The next step is to machine at least 12 port hole plugs. (It's a good idea to practice "hole plugging" on a scrap piece of metal first.) Machine the plugs with about a 4° inclusive taper on them. The small end of the plug should be close to the diameter of the port holes, and the plug length about 1/8".

17

21

19

20

22

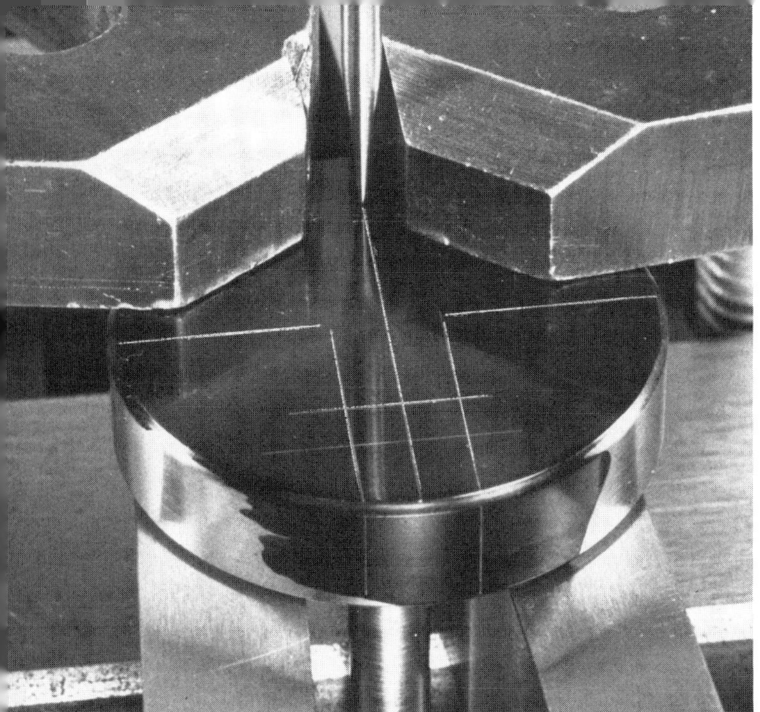

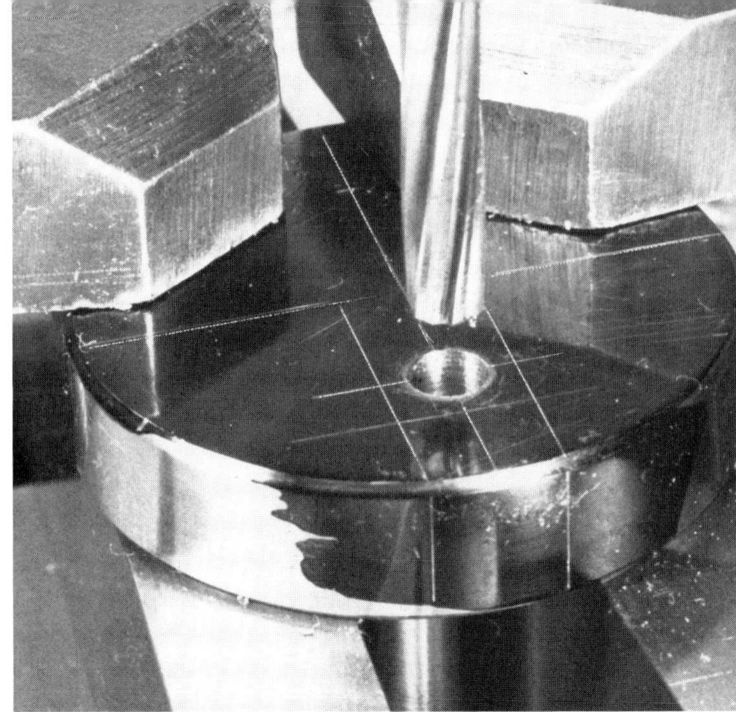

23 24

Approximately 1/32" of it should still extend above the surface after pounding (or pressing) it firmly in the hole. Then the surplus portion of the plug can be milled, filed, or ground off flush, leaving the plugged hole almost invisible (**Photo 13**). Notice, in this photo, the circular band that seals off the body manifold has been pressed into place (this will be done a little later on). Meanwhile, the arrow in the picture points to a socket setscrew plug that can be removed for periodically inserting a few drops of oil into the manifold to lubricate the cylinders. This is intended for those who utilize compressed air for motive power.

Concentrate now on producing the body pillar. The nearly completed pillar is

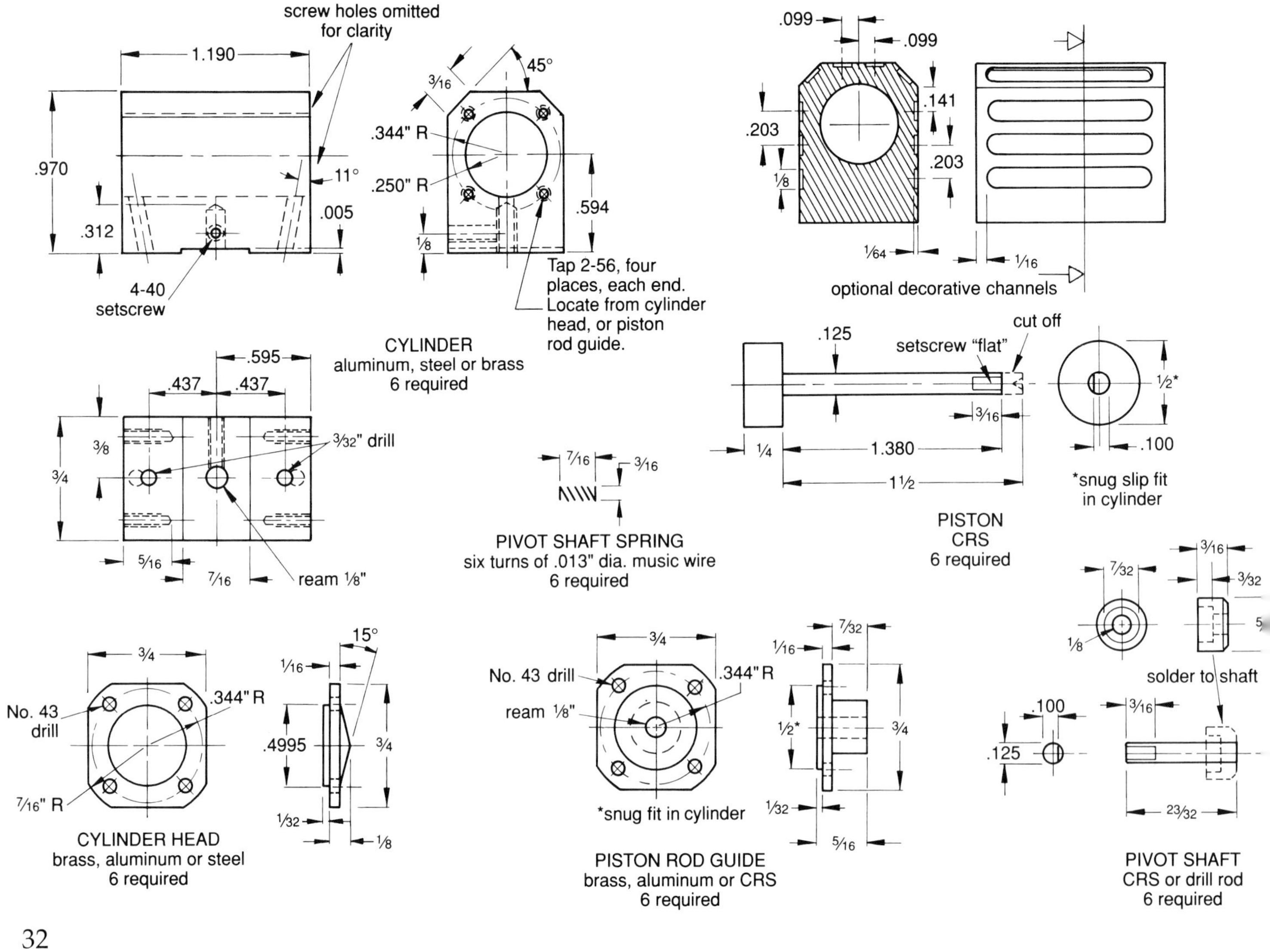

screw holes omitted for clarity
1.190
45°
3/16
.344" R
.250" R
.970
11°
.312
.005
.594
1/8
4-40 setscrew
Tap 2-56, four places, each end. Locate from cylinder head, or piston rod guide.
CYLINDER
aluminum, steel or brass
6 required
.595
.437
.437
3/8
3/32" drill
3/4
5/16
7/16
ream 1/8"
.099
.099
.141
.203
.203
1/8
1/64
1/16
optional decorative channels
.125
cut off
setscrew "flat"
1/2*
3/16
1/4
1.380
.100
1½
*snug slip fit in cylinder
PISTON
CRS
6 required
7/16
3/16
PIVOT SHAFT SPRING
six turns of .013" dia. music wire
6 required
3/16
7/32
3/32
1/8
solder to shaft
.100
3/16
.125
23/32
PIVOT SHAFT
CRS or drill rod
6 required
3/4
15°
1/16
No. 43 drill
.344" R
.4995
3/4
7/16" R
1/32
1/8
CYLINDER HEAD
brass, aluminum or steel
6 required
3/4
7/32
1/16
No. 43 drill
.344" R
ream 1/8"
1/2*
3/4
*snug fit in cylinder
1/32
5/16
PISTON ROD GUIDE
brass, aluminum or CRS
6 required

25 26

visible in **Photo 14.** Illustrated in **Photo 15** is an easy method of forming the contour on the pillar with the aid of a large end mill. The diameter of the end mill is not critical. Proceed by drilling, boring, or reaming the 3/4" hole in the pillar. Then the two counterbored bolt holes and the 5/32" port hole should be drilled completely through the pillar, as in **Photo 16.**

The arch at the upper end of the pillar is easily machined by mounting the work on a rotary table on the milling machine. After drilling or tapping all the required holes in the pillar, refer back to Photo 14. In order to bolt the pillar to the body in the proper position, scribe two center lines. The arrow points to a center line along the center of the master cylinder

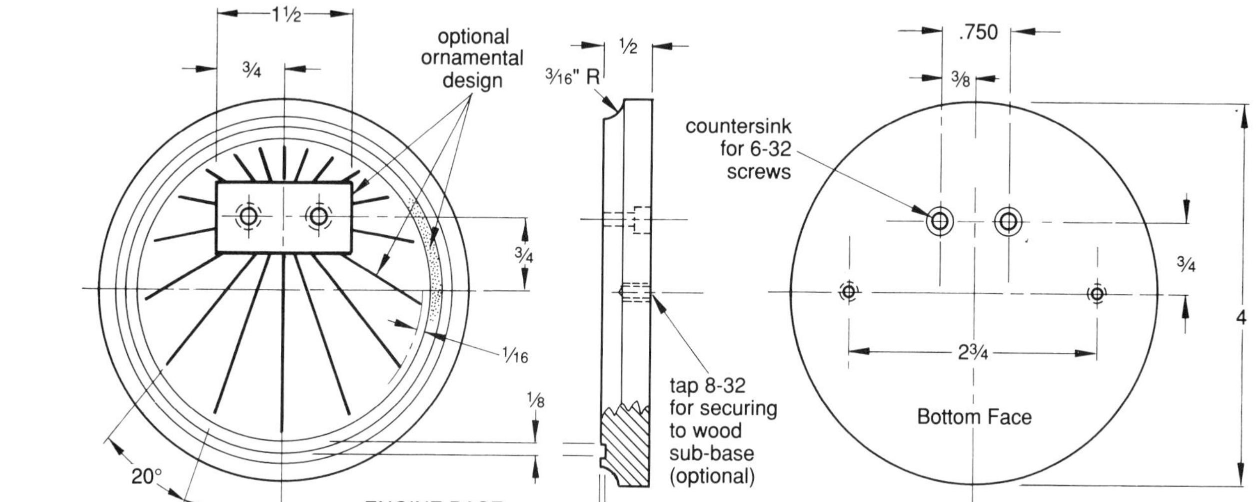

1½
¾
optional ornamental design
¾
1⁄16
⅛
20°
20°
½
3⁄16" R
tap 8-32 for securing to wood sub-base (optional)
1⁄64
ENGINE BASE
steel
1 required

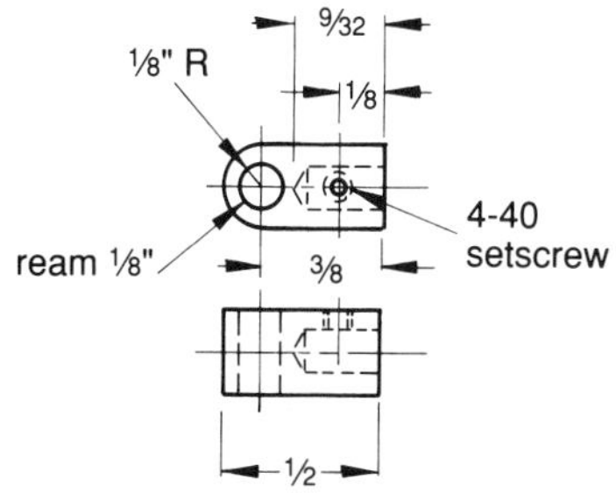

.750
⅜
countersink for 6-32 screws
¾
4
2¾
Bottom Face

9⁄32
⅛" R
⅛
ream ⅛"
⅜
4-40 setscrew
½
SLAVE CRANKPIN COUPLER
brass, CRS, or aluminum
6 required

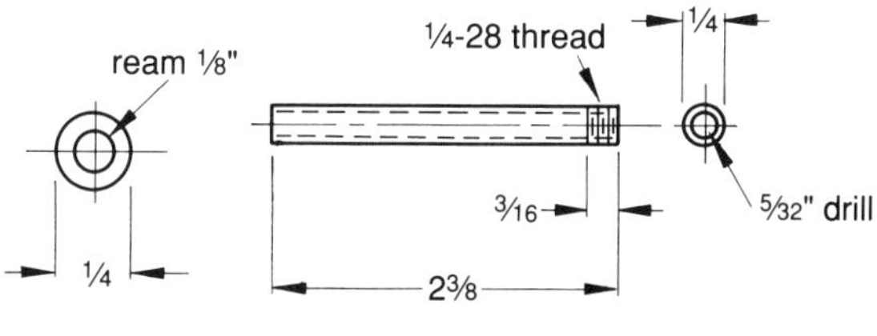

ream ⅛"
¼
¼-28 thread
¼
3⁄16
5⁄32" drill
2⅜
INLET EXTENSION PIPE
brass, aluminum or CRS
1 required

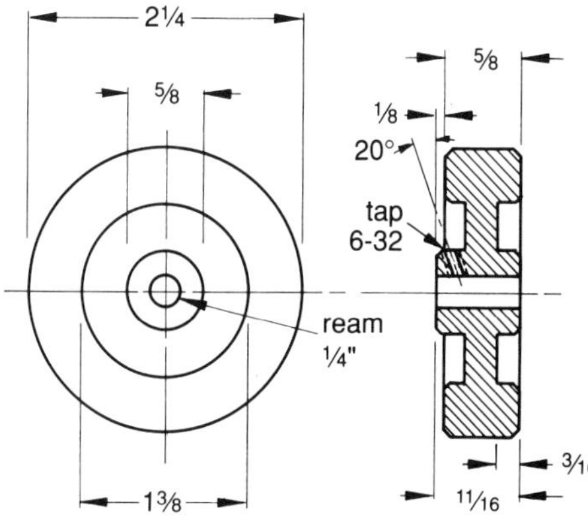

2¼
⅝
ream ¼"
1⅜
⅝
⅛
20°
tap 6-32
3⁄16
11⁄16
FLYWHEEL (optional)
aluminum

slot. Scribe the second line 148° from that. Now turn to **Photo 17**, and install the pillar on the body. Look down into the pillar bolt holes and center them to the scribed line on the body. Clamp the pillar to the body, and spot drill for the threaded holes. Also use the 5/32" port hole in the pillar to drill down into the manifold channel, only deep enough to open up the 5/32" hole into it. The outer end of the port hole is ready to be plugged in **Photo 18**. Fabrication of the band that seals the manifold is next; allow about .0015" for a press fit. **Photo 19** shows the band prior to pressing. Oh yes! don't forget to drill the oil hole for the crankshaft (**Photo 20**).

Speaking of crankshafts, its construction will follow (**Photo 21**). There are many ways of fabricating a crankshaft, but design often dictates how the crankshaft will be machined. The crankshaft, crank arm, and heavy counterbalance are all one piece. The master crankpin is a hardened steel dowel pin and is secured in place with *Loctite 640*. Machine the crankshaft as indicated in **Photo 22**. Part it from the stock piece, leaving enough material to face off the opposite end. Notice the setup in **Photo 23**.

Begin by scribing a center line across the disk, and then the outline for the crank arm, followed by the cross center line for the crankpin hole. It's important that the crankpin hole is drilled and reamed as squarely as possible, so mount the work on two parallels on the mill table. Position two loosened clamps to secure it; true up a wiggler in the spindle and bring it into position over the center line on the disk. Use the cross slide to advance the wiggler along the center line. By hand, slowly swivel the workpiece until the wiggler follows true all along the center line, then secure the hold-down clamps.

27

Set the calibrated collar on the longitudinal travel to zero, for use later on. Move the cross slide until the wiggler is centered over the cross lines for the crankpin hole. Drill and ream it (**Photo 24**). Without changing the setup, install a 5/8" end mill. Employ the longitudinal table travel to mill down a portion of the disk (**Photo 25**). As soon as the disk reaches .250" thick in the area being cut, lock the height adjustment on the mill to maintain the cutter position. Now move the longitudinal table travel back to its original zero setting, which should position the end mill over the center line of the disk. Then mill inwards 5/16" to form the arc in the counterbalance area. Continue by forming the crank arm (**Photo 26**).

The next item to tackle is the master crankpin unit, shown in **Photo 27**. This contrivance rides on the crankpin of the crankshaft. Notice the five "slave" crankpins that were soldered in place with low temperature silver solder (2% silver and 98% tin), often called jeweler's solder. This method was chosen because the holes for the slave pins are only 1/8" deep, so there was a question as to how effective *Loctite* would be. Choose whatever method you prefer; the pins could even be pressed in – providing they're pressed in straight.

Now refer to **Photo 28**. This setup is on the milling machine and the work is mounted in a chuck (or vise) on the rotary table. First, the blank for the master unit was machined in the lathe and the cutoff groove in it was placed 1/2" from the outer end to allow for facing the back end later on. The depth of the groove at this time is slightly more than 3/16". Center the blank true to the mill spindle and the rotary table; then set the calibrated collars on the longitudinal travel and the cross slide to zero, for returning to this position later on. Lock the cross slide. Install a 7/8" end mill (or one close to that size) and employ the longitudinal travel to bring the cutter to barely scratch the upper surface of the work.

Move the cutter to the right to clear the blank and lower it .312". Then crank the rotary table in a clockwise direction to its 67° mark. Gradually mill inwards and around the piece to the 293° mark on the rotary table. Stop milling when the hub diameter of the portion being formed

28

29

30

reaches 5/16", as in **Photo 29**. Now install a No. 2 center drill; move the longitudinal travel back to its zero setting, thus centering the spindle over the work. Crank the rotary table around to its zero° mark, then move the table to the left .313" and spot drill a "dimple" similar to the one in **Photo 30**.

Prepare to drill and ream the five 1/8" holes for the slave crankpins as illustrated in **Photo 31**. All of these holes are 60° apart, so begin by cranking the rotary around to its 60° mark for the first location, then 60° more for the second, etc. After this, move the work back to the lathe and part it from the stock piece. Mount it on a stub mandrel or a regular mandrel and face off the back side to the proper overall length; then form the little shoulder around the central hole on this face.

31

BILL OF MATERIALS

No. Req'd	Part	Material	Finished Size
1	Engine body	aluminum, steel or brass	2⅜" dia. × 1⅛"
5	Cylinder backplates	CRS	¼ × ¾ × 2³⁄₁₆"
1	Master cylinder backplate	CRS	¼ × ¾ × 1¹⁵⁄₁₆"
1	Body pillar	aluminum or CRS	½ × 1¼ × 3⅛"
1	Manifold band	steel, aluminum or brass	2⅝" OD × 2²³⁄₆₄" approx. ID × ⁵⁄₁₆"
1	Crankshaft	steel	1⅝" OD × 2¼"
1	Crankpin	steel dowel pin or drill rod	³⁄₁₆ × ¾"
1	Master crankpin unit	CRS	⅞" OD × ¹⁵⁄₃₂"
6	Cylinders	aluminum, steel or brass	¾ × .970 × 1.190"
6	Cylinder heads	brass, aluminum or steel	⅞" dia. × ⁵⁄₃₂"
6	Piston rod guides	brass, aluminum or steel	⅞" dia. × ⁵⁄₁₆"
6	Pistons	CRS	½" dia. × 1¾"
6	Pivot shafts	drill rod or CRS	⅛" dia. × ²³⁄₃₂"
6	Pivot shaft heads	brass or CRS	⁵⁄₁₆" dia. × ³⁄₁₆"
6	Slave crankpin coupler	brass, CRS or aluminum	¼" dia. × ½"
1	Engine base	CRS	4" dia. × ½"
1	Inlet extension pipe	brass, aluminum or CRS	¼" dia. × 2⅜"
6	Pivot shaft springs	music wire	.013" dia.
1	Flywheel (optional)	aluminum or steel	2¼" OD × ¹¹⁄₁₆"
6	Socket head cap screws		4-40 × ½"
48	Socket head cap screws		2-56 × ¼"
4	Socket head cap screws		6-32 × ½"
12	Socket setscrews		4-40 × ⅛"
1	Socket setscrew		5-40 × ⅛"
6	Socket head cap screws		4-40 × ⅜"

The slave crankpins can be made of drill rod, hardened dowel pins, or CRS. For gluing or soldering in place, the pins should have a fairly snug but free slip fit in the holes. Now scribe the cross center lines on the master crank unit for the 1/8" hole that will secure the master piston rod to the unit (**Photo 32**). Insert two 1/8" rods as shown, then drill and ream the hole to the proper depth. Proceed by drilling and tapping the 4-40 setscrew hole in the front surface. **Photo 33** shows the parts ready for assembly, either by silver soldering or by the use of *Loctite 640*. For silver soldering, the unit is placed on a flat heat-resistant surface, such as a piece of fire brick. Make certain the parts are free of oil, and apply liquid flux to the holes and pins before inserting them in place. After soldering with a torch (**Photo 34**), the work can be mounted again on a mandrel and the surplus solder lightly machined off.

Displayed in **Photo 35** are the essential parts for each cylinder. Notice that to the right of the pivot shaft spring is an O-ring. It could be substituted for the spring; either one is effective. All parts in the photo are identical for all cylinders.

When beginning work on the cylinder blanks, make certain the blocks are machined to size, with their sides square and parallel to each other. An example is illustrated in **Photo 36**. Naturally, the decorative channels on the blocks in **Photo 37** are optional. The block at the left in Photo 37 has only the channels on its surface. The other one has small round, slightly concave indentations applied with a punch and hammer – one at a time! An enlarged view of the punch marks being made on the engine base is shown in **Photo 38**. The diameter of the business end of the punch is about .050", and its tip is slightly convex.

First, it's best to practice "punch-marking" on a piece of scrap metal. When preparing to mill the ornamental channels in the blocks, attempt to standardize the procedure. Notice in **Photo 39** that the block is placed in line with the side edge of the vise jaws. Use the calibrated collars on the longitudinal and cross slide to control the spacing and length of the channels.

Complete the three channels on both sides first. Follow by forming the channel on each 45° bevel (**Photo 40**), and finally, the two channels on the upper surface of the work. Apply the ornamental indentations to all of the blocks before boring the cylinder holes. Use protective metal pads around the blocks when boring the cylinder hole (**Photo 41**). After boring, be certain to face off .002" or .003" from the outer end of the block to ensure that it's square to the cylinder hole – when the cylinder blocks are assembled on the engine, this end of the cylinder will be positioned facing towards the crankshaft. Put an identifying mark on this face of each cylinder.

After boring, scribe center lines on the base surface of the cylinder blocks for the pivot shaft hole and the two port holes. Drill and ream the pivot shaft hole first; it should be as square to this surface as possible, so use an accurate vise to hold the work. Continue by tilting the work 11° and drill the first port

36

32

33

34

35

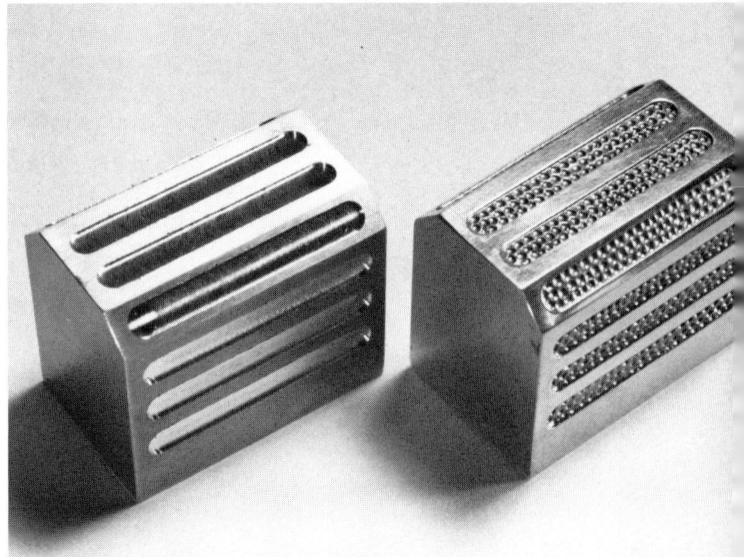
37

38 39

40

41

42

hole (**Photo 42**). Use a No. 2 center drill, then follow with a 3/32" drill. The block is now reversed in the vise and the remaining port hole drilled Proceed to **Photo 43**, and mill a very shallow clearance channel, perhaps .004" or .005" deep, and about 7/16" wide.

Turn out all of the blanks for the cylinder head and the piston rod guide. Two examples are visible in **Photo 44**. The left one is for the cylinder head; the 1/2" diameter by 5/16" long shank is mainly for easy gripping the blank while finishing it. The 1/2" diameter on this part should be a slip fit into the cylinder.

Turn to Photo 45. Mount the cylinder head blank in the mill, using a vertical indexer, or a chuck positioned on a rotary table. Center the work true to the mill spindle and the rotary. Now move the mill table the required distance to spot and drill the four equidistant bolt holes. While this setup is in place, also drill the bolt holes in the piston rod guide blanks. Then mill the "flats" on all of the blanks as indicated in **Photo 46**. Back at the lathe, the cylinder head blanks are gripped on about two-thirds of the length of the 1/2" diameter section.

Now let's take a look at **Photo 47**. At the left is the present blank. Above and to the right is what the next operation will produce by machining down the outer face to form a 1/2" diameter stub, and at the same time leaving the remaining flange 1/16" thick. A 15° angle cone is now cut out of the stub portion.

43

45

46

47

48

Finally, in **Photo 48**, position a cutoff tool *1/32" away* from the back face of the cylinder head and part it.

Finish the piston rod guides by gripping them on the 5/16" diameter section. Step-cut the exposed face as was done with the cylinder heads; however, the 1/2" diameter should be a very snug fit into the cylinder bore. Now face off the surplus portion of the 1/2" diameter section until it is 1/32" long. Conclude by carefully drilling and reaming the piston rod hole.

The piston and its rigid connecting rod shaft are machined integral. Make the piston rod about 1/8" longer than specified so it can be supported with a tailstock center during machining. Cut off the surplus end when completed. The diameter of the piston should be a very snug slip fit into the cylinder, and also the piston rod into the piston rod guide.

The five slave crankpin connectors are machined from a 1/4" round stock piece about 4" long. Use the lathe to accurately drill and ream the central hole in the end of the stock piece. Now transfer the entire rod to the end mill as shown in **Photo 49**. Employ a square to act as a stop to position the end of the rod about 1/2" from the side of the vise. Use an edge finder to center the spindle over the center line axis of the rod, then lock the appropriate table movement. Proceed to drill and tap the setscrew hole 1/8" in from the tip; then drill and ream for the crankpin hole (**Photo 50**). Take the work back to the lathe and cut off to proper length. Repeat the procedure for the remaining pieces.

Next, it will be necessary to round or bevel one end of each crankpin connector. An easily constructed fixture for doing this is visible in **Photo 51**. Simply tap a 5-40 hole close to the edge of a flat piece of scrap metal. Then center punch a dent on the side edge of the scrap metal, and in line with the threaded hole, to make the 5-40 screw turn with some resistance in the hole. Insert a 3" or 4" rod into the work to act as a handle. Grip this handle firmly while swinging the work around gradually to mill the radius. Use a 3/16" end mill.

After all of these parts are completed, including the pivot shafts, they should be assembled on the engine body to check for fit. The first cylinder to mount is the master cylinder, shown in **Photo 52**. Leave the cylinder head off, but install the piston as well as the piston rod guide. Insert the pivot shaft into the backplate and cylinder block and secure it with the setscrew on the side of the cylinder. Rotate the crankshaft until the master crankpin is closest to, and in line with, this cylinder. Have the head of the piston flush to the outer end of the cylinder. Also, the setscrew on the end of the piston rod should face upwards.

Now gently push inwards with the depth gauge to align the piston rod into the master crank unit. It may be necessary

49

50

51

52

53

54

55

56

57

58

to lift the parts up or down slightly to line up the piston rod to the hole. Push in the piston head to 3/32" from the outer end of the cylinder, then lock the setscrew on the master crankpin unit. The procedure for the remaining cylinders is almost identical, but always turn the crankshaft for each cylinder so the appropriate slave crankpin is in line with the center line of the cylinder before securing the piston rod to the crankpin connectors.

After preparing the circular blank for the engine base, scribe a center line across the face of the disk, and also the center lines for the two bolt holes (**Photo 53**). Then scribe lines for the ornamental rectangular design in the same area. Mount the work in a mill vise so the center line on the disk is at right angles to the vise jaw. Then proceed to drill the two bolt holes through the base.

A 1/8" solid carbide drill-pointed burr was utilized to engrave the designs in the base – if unavailable, use a sharp No. 3 center drill, and install it in the spindle. Position the point of the cutter in line with the scribed lines for the rectangular design – anywhere along the lines. Lower it to barely touch the surface, then set the spindle calibrated collar to zero. Now lower the cutter about .005" into the plate and carefully follow the scribed lines. Use caution when approaching the corners to avoid cutting beyond them.

The final width of the grooves is your choice, but a fair estimate would be about .080". Whatever width is chosen, take note of the total depth of the cut as indicated on the calibrated collar of the mill spindle. Now position the work in a small lathe chuck, center and clamp the chuck on the mill rotary table. Then form a 3/16" radius around the disk, as indicated in **Photo 54**.

Continue by forming the 1/8" wide by 1/64" deep channel illustrated in **Photo 55**. Following this, install a true running wiggler in the spindle and position it roughly over the center of the work. Crank the rotary table around to the zero degree mark, and lock it. Now loosen the chuck jaws holding the disk just enough to free it. The idea is to rotate the workpiece by hand, this way or that, and also move the mill table until the wiggler point is centered all along the center line (**Photo 56**). Now tighten the chuck jaws. Then center the spindle over the cross lines (**Photo 57**). Lock the longitudinal table travel. The rest of the "engraving" will be performed using the cross slide movement.

Notice in **Photo 58** how the completed lines will appear. The first line to engrave will be along the center line of the disk, so lower the cutter to barely touch the surface. Set the calibrated collar on the mill spindle to zero. All of the engraved lines are started by positioning the cutter over the grooves of the previously formed rectangular design, and then milling outward.

Now lower the cutter about one-half

of the previously determined total depth of the groove. Mill outwards to the circular scribed line near the perimeter. With the cutter still revolving, lower it to the required total depth and slowly mill back to the starting point. Now raise the cutter to pass over the rectangular design and then lower it to mill the short groove at the rear. Follow by raising the cutter again to clear the work. Crank the rotary table to 20° and continue with the next line in the same manner, then another 20°, and so on around. These decorative designs can be enhanced by coating them with gold paint, or any color to suit your fancy.

If a flywheel is not desired on the engine (**Photo 59**), then an end-play stop collar will have to be clamped to the crankshaft. Of course a pulley could serve the same purpose.

Be certain to clean and lubricate all of the moving parts of the engine for final assembly. If everything in the motor is proper, it will operate on fairly low pressure. Perhaps, if you have any "blowhard" friends, you could let them act as a source of energy – it will keep them breathless for a little while, anyway!

59

A Simple Steam Engine

By John A. Aho

Photos by Author

Here is an interesting project for a beginner or an advanced Live Steam buff. Recently rummaging through some old, olde, magazines, I came across *The Model Craftsman Home Mechanics Magazine*, dated January 1935 (price 25¢). In it was an interesting article on building this clever little steam engine, by Graham Anderson.

The action is very simple. The valve is lifted from its seat at the top of the stroke and seats itself when the piston moves down the cylinder. The exhaust is uniflow, through the port at the lower end of the stroke. There is a wide latitude in the permissible dimensions, as these may be varied to suit the available materials. In the construction of the engine, there are a few points that must be adhered to:

1) The exhaust port should be no less than one fourth of the stroke, measuring up from the top of the piston when in the lowest position (a ¾″ stroke calls for a 3⁄16″ exhaust port).

2) The lift of the valve need not be over 1⁄32″ and may be as little as 1⁄64″ if steam is dry.

3) The block on top of the ball should be a loose fit. This ball type of valve would not be practical in large sizes, since the weight increases as the cube of the diameter, but a 3⁄16″ or 7⁄32″ ball on a ⅛″ or 5⁄32″ opening is plenty large enough for a ½″ cylinder.

The valve is not mechanically closed, but takes a fixed time to do so. Therefore, the cutoff is later in the stroke as the speed increases, giving

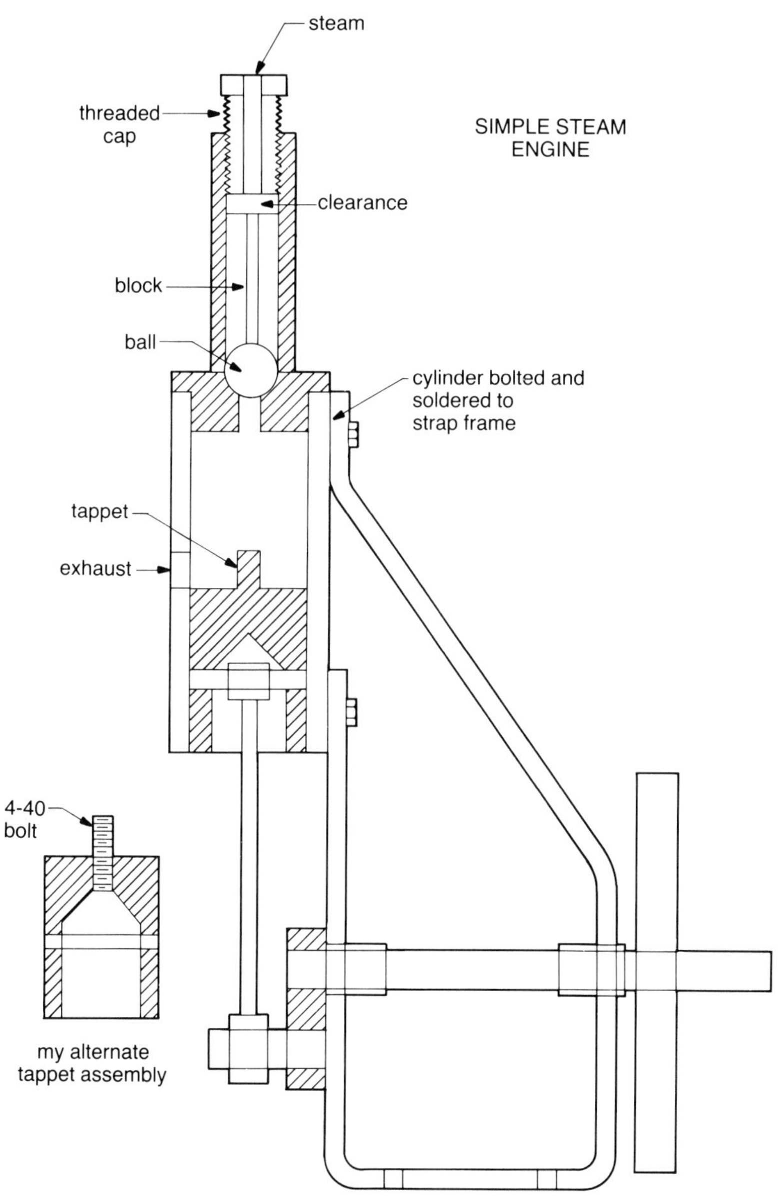

more power per stroke. Superheated steam is needed for high speed.

My engine has a 9/16″ diameter bore. The framework is from an Ericsson hot air engine which has a 1″ stroke. It had the crank assembly and a 3½″ flywheel. I used thick-walled brass tubing for the cylinder, which had enough material to drill and tap two 2-56 bolts to fasten the cylinder to the frame.

The piston is 1″ long with two oil grooves. Instead of machining a tappet to it, I drilled and tapped a 4-40 bolt to the center of the piston for the tappet. It made for easy adjustment for raising or lowering the tappet height for the ball lift. I also split the connecting rod so it was easier to take off and raise or lower the tappet for proper lift.

The engine took a little time to adjust properly, but once set, it operated beautifully. The block is a brass piece of rod and has two saw cuts lengthwise for steam passage. The clearance between the block and the threaded cap is very small, but there *must* be some clearance. The block on my engine is ¾″ long, but that dimension can vary. The cylinder diameters from ⅜″ to ½″ are ideal – the lighter, the better.

A small oscillating engine is shown in the photos – one of Elmer Verburg's designs – that can be operated from the same boiler by transferring the steam hose from one engine to the other.

Copied from original print in *Model Craftsman Magazine,* dated January, 1935, by Graham Anderson.

MR. deGROOT

H.R. LAMERS

Simplex & Duplex

By Rob van Dort

Photos by Author except where noted.
Original drawings by P.H. van Popta. Published through the courtesy of "Hed. Vereniging van Model-bouwers."

Usually the one- or two-cylinder oscillating steam engine is built in a rather squat form. We all know the compactly built marine engines often constructed as two-cylinder V-engines and, in my opinion, the ultimate, the four-cylinder engine as described lately by Jan Gunnarsson. Of course, these thoughts are not related to *scale* models of this type of engine, as used on paddle steamers, etc.

In designing *Simplex,* I have departed from this practice, as it was my aim to build an attractive stationary engine taking full advantage of the simplicity of the oscillating cylinder. I will describe the construction of the basic one-cylinder (*Simplex*) version, but it is just as easy to build the two-cylinder engine (*Duplex*), making it more powerful and self-starting if the two cranks are squared.

Duplex is capable of driving a small dynamo with 30 psi pressure. To make it run at moderate speed, a long stroke double-acting cylinder and a big flywheel are provided. Once the engine is ready, you can adorn it with steps, hand rails and paintwork to your own liking. The photographs of models shown here may give you some ideas (**Photos 1, 2** and **3**). While Mr. van Popta made the final construction plans from my sketches, the first *Duplex* prototype was built by Mr. de Groot **(1). Photo 2** shows the *Duplex* steamplant of Mr. Cramer and a "double-up" version – a real eye catcher **(3)** – by Mr. ter Steeg. Well, so much for the introduction.

Let's start with the construction of our *Simplex* steam engine. As we have to build the engine from the bottom up, we may as well start with the **Base Plate (107).** This can be made from brass, but any suitable piece of material will do as well. I used aluminum, 10 mm thick. Take care to choose the correct one for your engine, as they differ for the *Simplex* or *Duplex* version. Cut to size and scribe the two centerlines. Use these to mark out all holes and the rectangular opening for the Flywheel **(102, Photo 4).** The 3.5 mm diameter holes for the foundation bolts can be drilled right through. Those to be tapped M2 should be drilled 1.6 mm diameter. When brass is used, you can tap the necessary thread right away. In the case of steel, use some light cutting oil. Extra care should be taken when tapping these fine threads in aluminum, as it will most likely seize the tap. Use kerosene as a cutting aid and take the tap out frequently. The opening for the flywheel is a cinch if you have a milling machine. I do not, so I drilled some holes as big as my drill press would allow, and the finishing was muscle work with hacksaw and file.

MR. terSTEEG

When ready, finish this part with fine emery cloth.

Perhaps the best thing to do now is to make a wooden base block to mount the base plate on. Of course, in this block a "flywheel-pit" must be provided. Use long M3 screws with nuts and washers to fasten the base plate on the block showing the nut, as in real practice. Having a stable base plate now, we can start building up the engine, seeing it grow as we proceed.

The next parts will be the **Main Frame (101)** and **Bearing Assembly (118).** I used 50 x 2 mm brass bar stock, and 10 mm angle is readily available. It was a very straightforward job and a good exercise in marking out. Take care that the center heights of the axle bearing holes in the frame and bearing assembly are exactly the same, and measure the correct distance between the

Part No.	No. of Items	Description	Material
118	1	Bearing	for Simplex only
117	7	Bolt & nut M2	
116	1	Spring & nut M3	
115	1	Drilling jig	Steel
114	1	Piston & rod	Bronze and drill rod
113	1	Cylinder cover	Brass
112	1	Port block	Brass
111	1	Moving port block	Brass
110	1	Shaft	Silversteel (drill rod)
109	1	Cylinder	Brass
108	1	Cylinder cover	Brass
107	1	Base Plate	2mm brass
106	1	Angle	Brass
105	1	Crankshaft	Silversteel (drill rod)
104	1	Crank & pin	Steel
103	2	Bearing bush	Bronze
102	1	Flywheel	C. I. bronze
101	1	Frame	2mm brass

PISTON SUBASSEMBLY

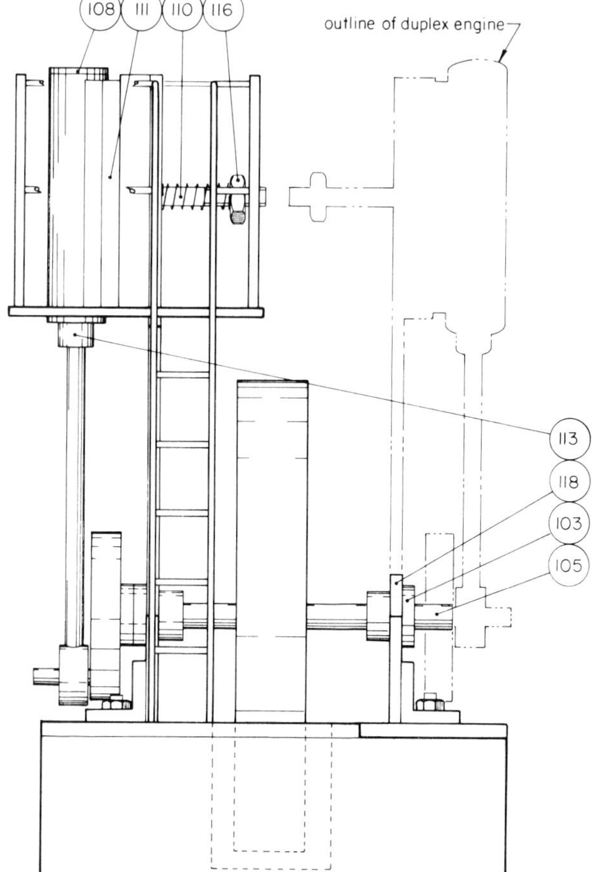

FRONT ELEVATION

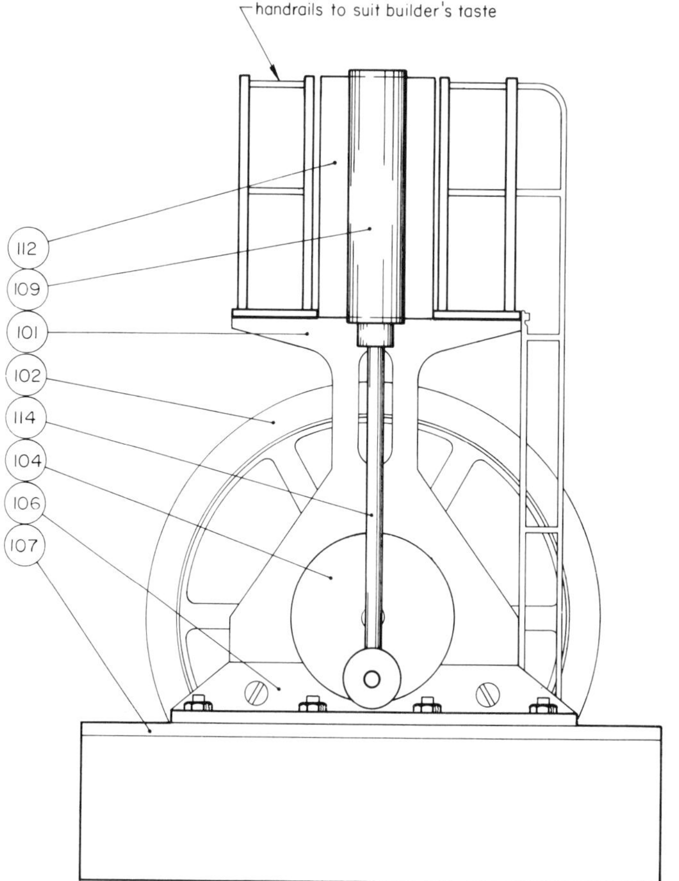

SIDE ELEVATION

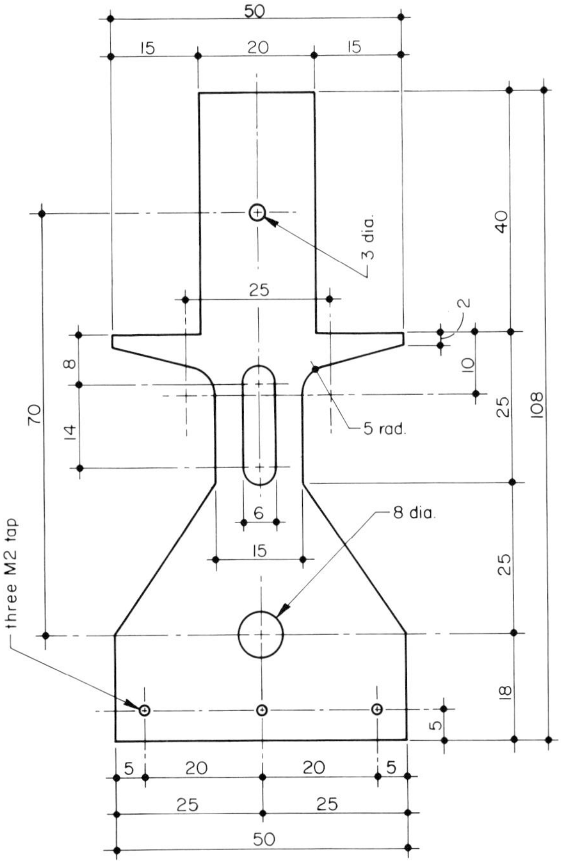

101 FRAME
2mm Brass, 1 required

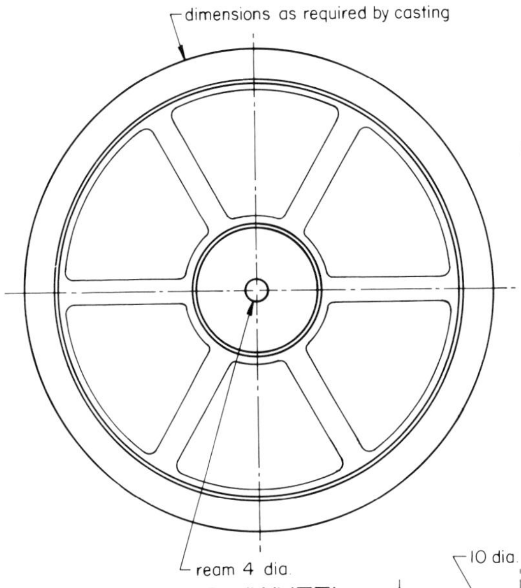

102 FLYWHEEL
Cast Iron, 1 required

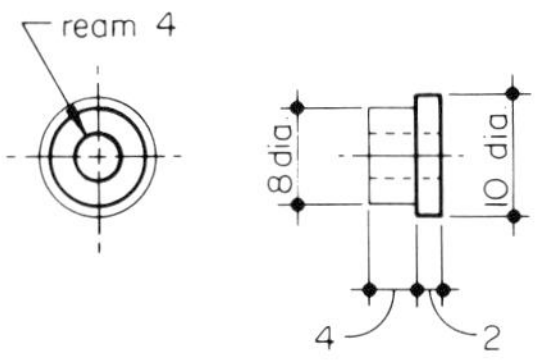

103 BEARING BUSH
Bronze, 2 required

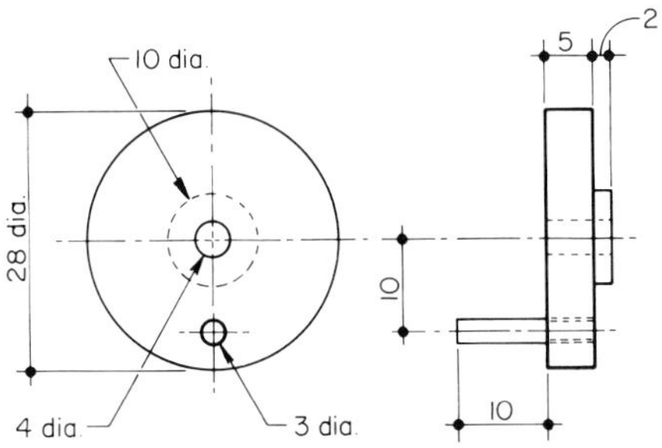

104 CRANK AND PIN
Steel, 1 required

crankshaft and cylinder pivot. Drill the holes for the bearing bushes 7.8 mm diameter and ream to 8 mm. The angle pieces are screwed to the frame and bearing but, of course, it is possible to use 2 mm rivets, securing the joint with soft solder afterwards. When using screws, hex-heads are better looking than round or cheese head stock. Next, turn the **Bearing Bushes (103)** from a bronze bar, drill 3.8 mm diameter and ream to 4 mm.

Press the bushes into the holes and soft solder to secure. Observe the correct position. The **Crankshaft (105)** is just a piece of 4 mm silver steel. To make the **Crank Disk (104)**, chuck a piece of 30 mm diameter bms in the three-jaw. Turn the outside to 28 mm diameter, face and turn the spigot. Center drill and drill a 3.8 diameter hole some 15 mm deep. Part off a disk of approximately 7 mm thickness, which can be done with a hacksaw. Ream the hole to 4 mm and press the disk on the shaft. Silver solder to secure. Now chuck the shaft and face off the disk to correct thickness. Do it most carefully. Scribe a 20 mm diameter circle to mark the place for the crank pin. Center pop, drill 2.4 mm and tap M3. The crank pin is just a piece of 3 mm diameter silver steel with M3 thread cut on one side. Be sure to hold the tap and die in the correct square position. Screw the crank pin home really tight and file off any protruding part on the backside. Polish the crankshaft assembly to a bright lustre. To finish all revolving parts, the **Flywheel (102)** may now be tackled. Let's assume that you have obtained a suitable casting (Stuart 7/73, 10/73). Remove the burrs, if any, from the rim and chuck in the three-jaw. Face off the rim and boss, center-drill and drill a 3.8 diameter hole. Ream to 4 mm. If necessary, just skim the inside of the rim. Turn the casting and do the same with the other side.

Now make the **Mandrel** as shown, and without taking it out of the chuck, cut the 4 mm thread. Put the wheel casting on it and finish the outside of the rim with *very light* cuts.

If you have to make your flywheel out of the solid, here is a method to mark the spokes. Once you have achieved the correct profile on both sides of the wheel, draw the desired form of the spokes on a piece of paper. Cut out the disk and make a hole of the same diameter as the flywheel boss. Paste the disk on one side of the flywheel, drill the necessary holes and cut out the unwanted material with a fretsaw (choosing brass makes this work a lot easier). Finish the spokes with the file. I have used this method because I like curved spokes. A set screw to secure the flywheel to the crankshaft will finish this part (**Photo 4**).

Erect the frame and side bearing and try to fit the crankshaft (**Photo 5**). Adjust the side bearing with some thin brass shims till the shaft runs light and true.

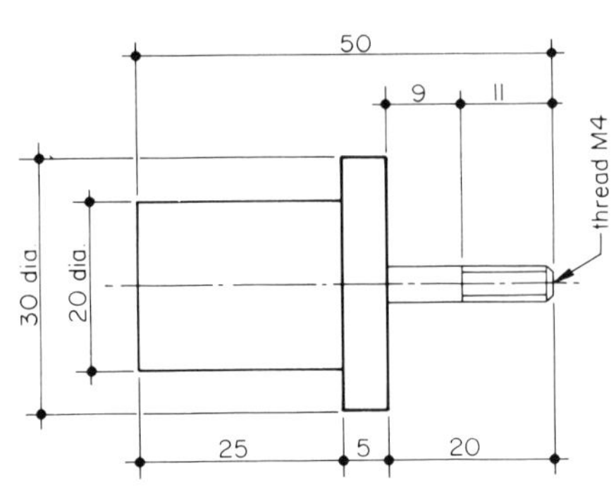

FLYWHEEL MANDREL

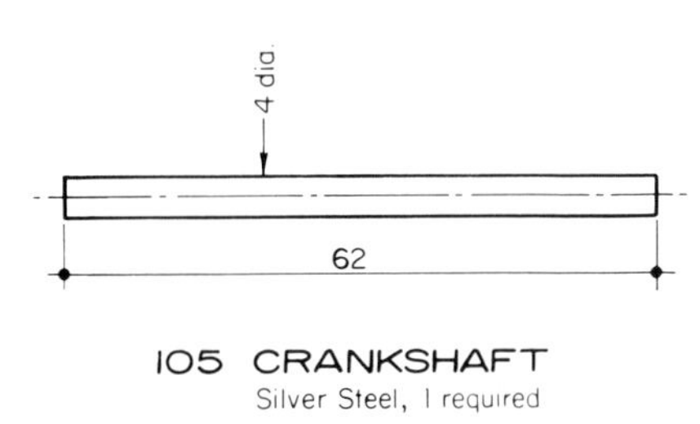

105 CRANKSHAFT
Silver Steel, 1 required

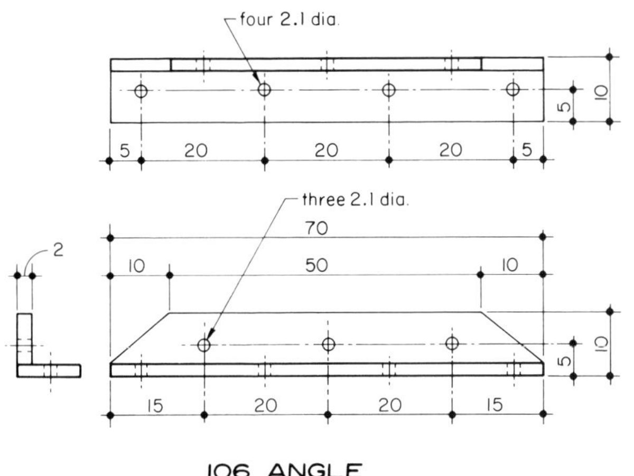

106 ANGLE
10 × 10 × 2 Brass, 1 required

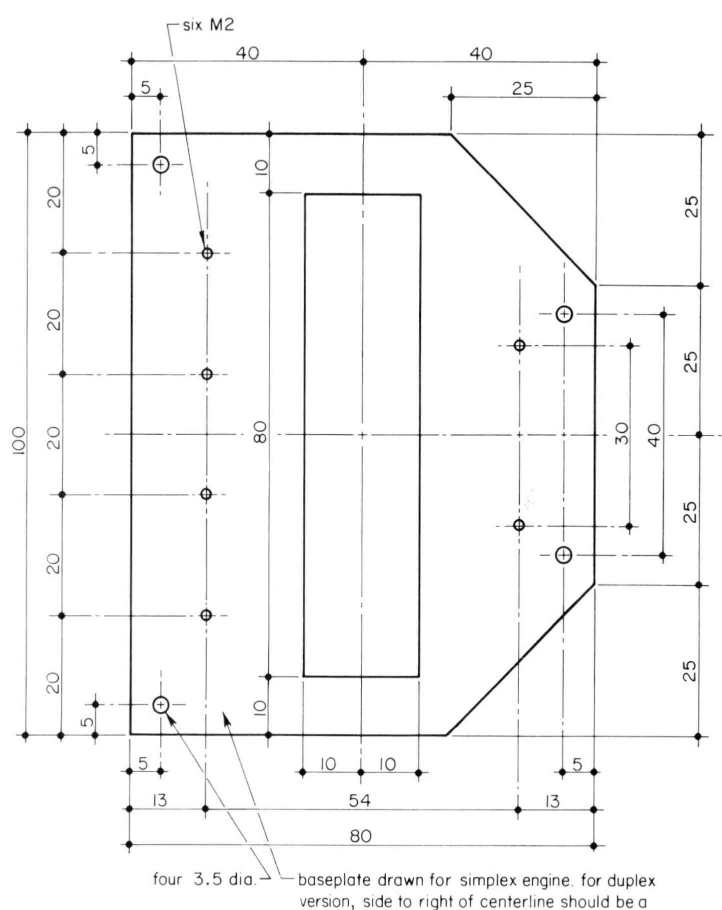

107 BASEPLATE
2mm Brass, 1 required

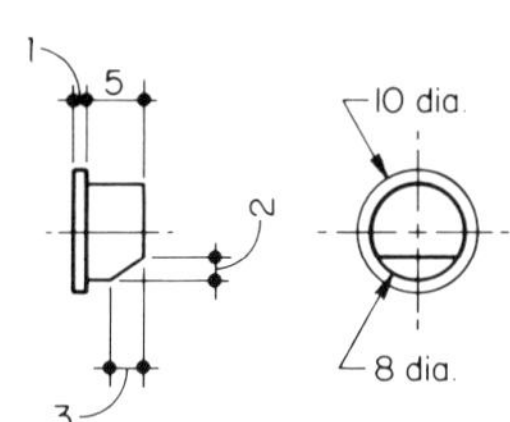

108 CYLINDER COVER
Brass, 1 required

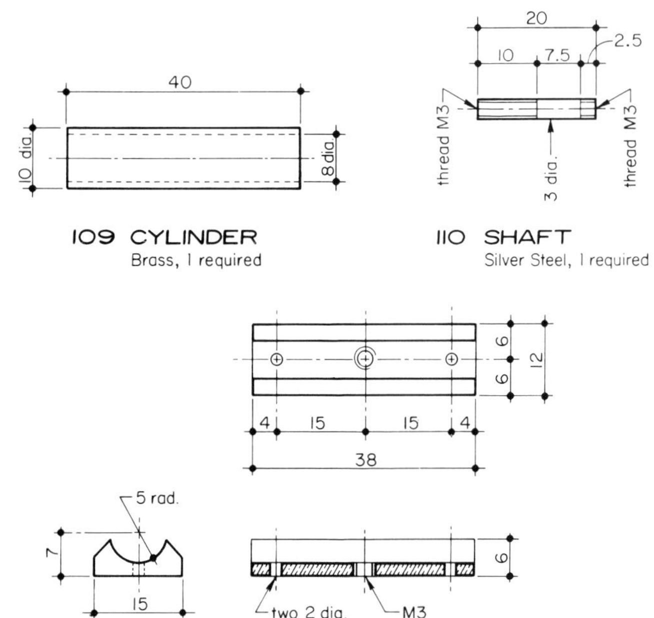

109 CYLINDER
Brass, 1 required

110 SHAFT
Silver Steel, 1 required

111 MOVING PORT BLOCK
Brass, 1 required

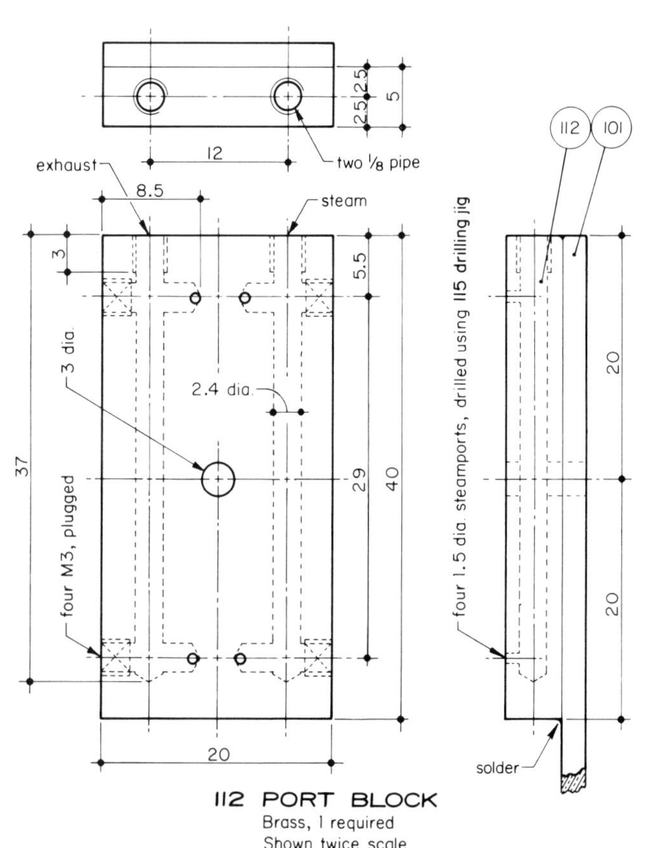

112 PORT BLOCK
Brass, 1 required
Shown twice scale

Now we will start with the steam end of the engine, and I suggest that we take care of the **Port Block (12)** first. Take some 20 x 5 brass bar stock, cut to size and mark out all necessary passages. To vertically drill the steam and exhaust passages, you can either use a drill press (**Photo 6**), as I did, or the vertical slide of your lathe (**Photo 7**). DO NOT DRILL THE STEAMPORTS YET. Only drill the hole for the cylinder pivot. We will come to this later. When drilling the cross passages, measure the depth carefully or use a depth stop. Anyway, be sure that these passages do not "meet" each other, short-circuiting the live steam end with the exhaust. Tap the holes to be plugged. Now we have to silver solder the port block to the main frame. Clean the corresponding surfaces thoroughly, apply some solder flux, and clamp them together using a M3 screw through the center hole. To prevent this screw from becoming silver soldered also, grease it well before tightening up.

Lay the assembly down on a fire brick, heat to a bright red and touch

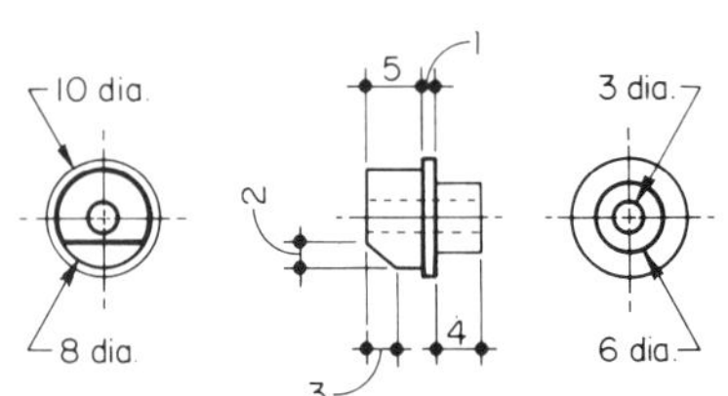

113 LOWER CYLINDER COVER
Brass, 1 required

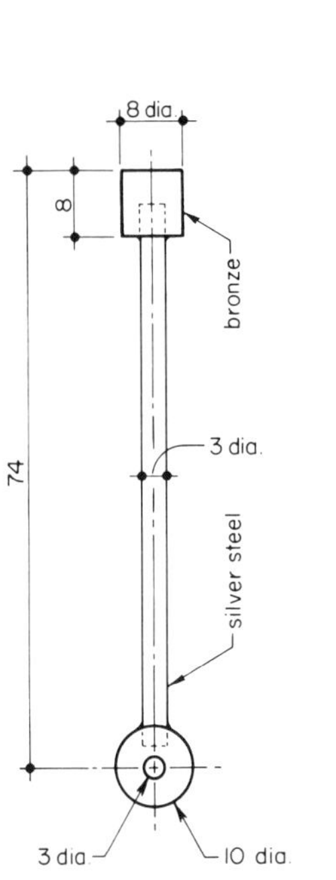

114 PISTON AND ROD
1 required

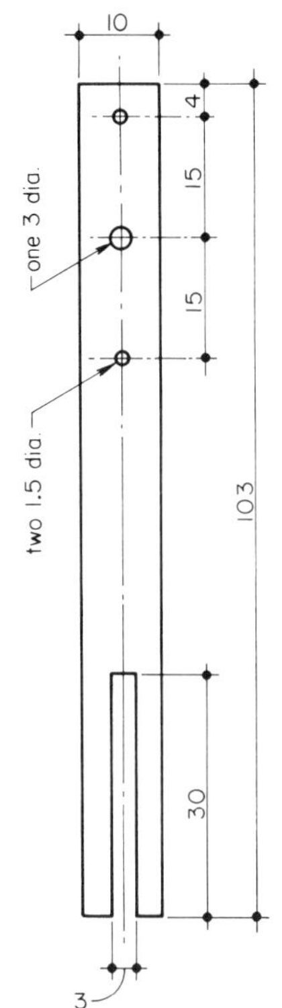

115 DRILLING JIG

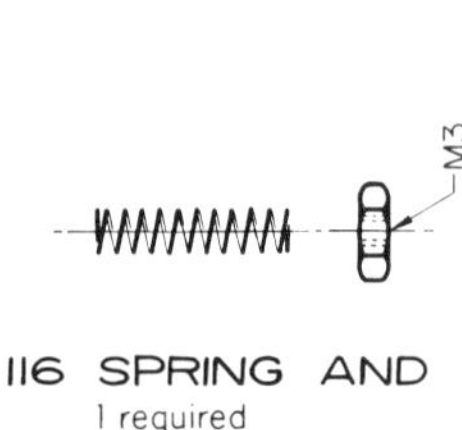

116 SPRING AND NUT
1 required

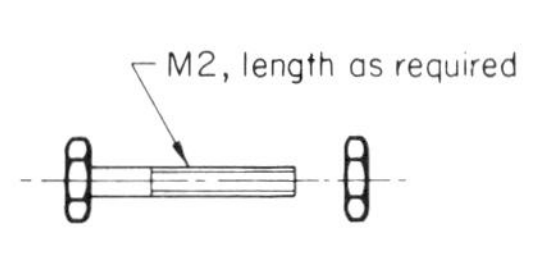

117 BOLT AND NUT
7 required

the joint lightly with silver solder. During this process, the brass material tends to weaken, so take care that the main frame does not bend. Check the bearing bush. It may be possible that it has to be soft soldered again. Remove the clamp screw and pickle.

It may be useful to attach some length (200 mm) of steam pipe now – 1/8" diameter for the steam supply and 5/32" diameter for the exhaust. Leave them straight at first so you can bend them later, to suit your final arrangement.

To find the exact position of the steam ports, use the following method: First make the **Drilling Jig (15)**. Take the main frame with the crank shaft in position. Fit the jig, with a good fitting piece of steel rod, to the port block and with the slotted end on the crank pin. Thus, when turning the crank disk, the jig makes the same movement as the cylinder and the two 1.5 mm diameter holes represent the steam ports in the cylinder block. Put the crank in the top, dead center. Now turn it clockwise to the 90° position. Mark the position of the steam ports on the port block. Repeat this procedure in the 270° position. Remove the jig carefully, centerpunch the four marks and drill the 1.5 mm diameter holes till you reach the cross passages. Clean all parts and passages of any swarf, after which the cross passages can be plugged. The plugs can be sealed with liquid gasket or a touch of soft solder.

Well, you can put together all parts finished so far. The cylinder and piston assembly comes next, and the best we can do is to start with the **Saddle (11)**. Take a 15 mm square piece of brass rod, a little bit longer than required, and chuck in the four-jaw. Center as best as you can, center-drill, drill 8 mm and open out to 10 mm diameter. Cut it in two halves lengthwise, as shown on the sketch, and finish it by filing. Drill a 2.4 mm diameter hole for the pivot and tap M3.

For the **Cylinder (109)**, a piece of tube can be used, but I machined mine from bronze rod. Chuck in the three-jaw and drill a 7.0 mm diameter hole in the usual way. Open out very carefully till the first part of the reamer just enters the opening. *Do not ream*, but part off the tube and square both ends.

Make the **Pivot Pin or Shaft (110)** and screw it home. Clean everything and silver solder the cylinder to the saddle and pickle. Now drill the steam ports using the jig in such a way that it does not face the saddle with the same side as it did the port block. This way, any irregularities in the jig will be properly compensated.

Now ream the cylinder, which concludes this part. I don't think the two **Cylinder Covers (108, 113)** will give you any problems. So, we come to the last parts. Turn the **Piston (114)** from a piece of bronze rod, keeping the diameter at least 1 mm larger than required. Drill a 3 mm hole and part off. Silver solder this part to the piston rod, a 3 mm diameter silver steel rod about 100 mm long.

Chuck the rod in the three-jaw and very carefully turn down the piston to the exact diameter. This method assures you that the piston will be mounted concentric.

Before mounting the "big end," be sure to put the cylinder cover (**113**) on the rod. Mount the big end and secure with a touch of soft solder. We are almost ready now for the final assembly. If you have a fine lapping compound, it may be of advantage to lap the port block and the saddle of the cylinder. If you do this, be sure to clean all ports and passages. The last thing we have to do now is to put the piston in the cylinder, press the cover home and secure with soft solder, doing the same with the top cover in the same "heat." Assemble the engine now, using a lot of light oil. Adjust parts so that everything moves light and true. If you have compressed air available, the first test runs can be made.

If there is leakage on the port faces, it may be that the cylinder will be lifted from the port block due to the pin being not at right angle to the crankdisk or a too tight fit of the big end on the crankpin. After some experiments, it won't take long before the flywheel starts spinning. Oil well and use proper cylinder oil when changing from compressed air to steam.

This concludes our little project and I wonder when the first photographs of your engine will appear in this magazine. I hope that building and steaming your engine will give you as much fun as it has me.

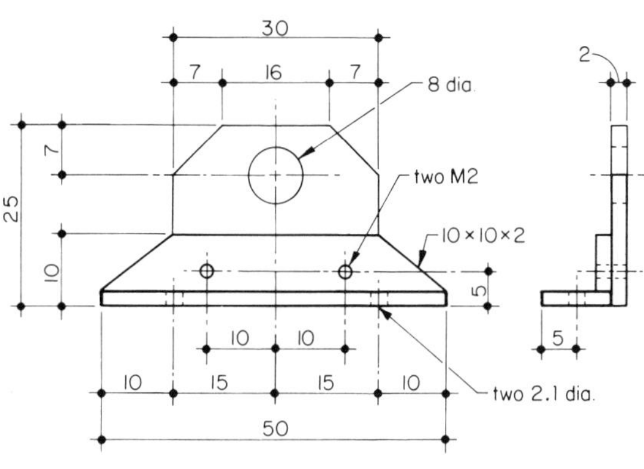

118 SIMPLEX BEARING
Brass, 1 required

A Reversing Duplex

By Jim Lyman

Photos by Image Master Studio

I found great pleasure in building Rob van Dort's *Duplex* (***Live Steam***, September 1983), at 50% larger size and with a reversing feature. I used a system like Jan Gunnarsson's on his "V4 Oscillating Steam Engine" (***Live Steam***, May 1978). It is a simple reversing valve distribution block and piping. The first thing I did was invert the cylinder port blocks, Part 112 (September 1983). Tubing was soldered into the blocks and brought down against the outside of the frames, (Part 101), then out the front, ⅝″ on centers and ⅜″ to the center of the bottom one above the baseplate.

My block is ½″ × 1″ × 3 5/16″ brass. The four passageway holes are drilled in from the ends as in **Figure 1** and tapped for plugs. The rear is drilled for the 4 3/16″ tubes. The rear is then drilled for steam and exhaust to the port blocks, ⅛″ diameter into the passageways, and counterbored to 3/16″ diameter, ⅛″ deep. The four reversing holes are drilled ⅛″ diameter on a ⅝″ hole circle, with care, to match the same locations in the valve block.

The valve block is 1″ diameter × ¼″ thick brass, laid out with four holes on a ⅝″ hole circle, and drilled ⅛″ diameter, ⅛″ deep. Two holes are then milled to meet with a ⅛″ × ⅛″ slot (**Figure 2**). The valve block is then drilled and tapped through the center and on edge for the mounting screw and a reversing lever. The distribution block is drilled for a close bolt clearance and counterbored to clear the size screw head you have used. A small spring is made to fit inside. Use medium pressure to hold the two together; strong pressure is not needed.

To assemble the distribution block, ¼″ steam and exhaust tubes, 3/16″ port tubes, and plugs are all soldered at the same heating. The valve block is then mounted on the distribution block. Apply air or steam to the steam line, move the lever right, then left, and watch it reverse.

I made my flywheel with a pulley on each side – one, 1⅛″ diameter, and the other, 1⅝″ diameter, from a solid piece of aluminum. Care must be used with the steam and exhaust lines. I made the exhaust on the large diameter pulley side from a ¼″ tube 1¼″ long and bent it down into the center slot by the wheel. I do not expect to use steam on this engine, so the exhaust will not be a problem. These tubes could come out the ends of the distribution block; however, passage through the frames makes a much cleaner looking engine.

If you do not have a mill available, the slots may be cut circular in the three-jaw chuck. Make a tool ⅛″ wide, round or square, with clearance to fit into the ⅛″ hole. Then rock the chuck back and forth. The compound needs to be turned parallel to the lathe bed and advanced only a thousandth or two on each forward cut. Now go to the second set of holes, cutting each to a depth of approximately ⅛″.

Reversing may not be necessary, but it is one detail that adds interest and creates conversation, and is probably as much fun to accomplish as building the engine. People cannot believe I can blow in the steam tube and make Duplex go forward, then reverse.

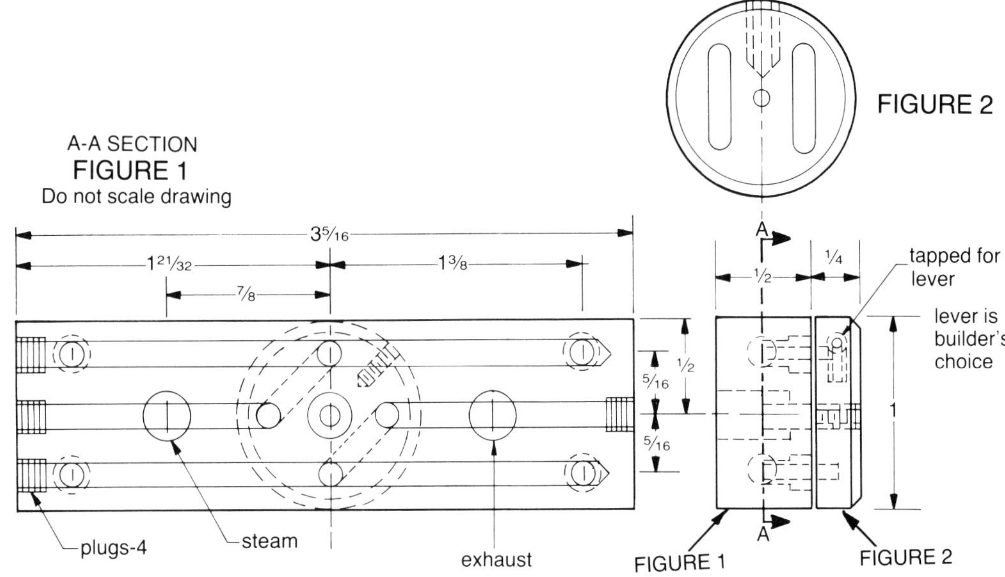

A Toy For Richard

By Richard M. Mitchell

Photos by Harold A. Barry

I've often said, "Life is backwards; as young men growing up we should have an abundance of money and the knowledge of where to travel to enjoy the things that are so dear to us in later life. Then when we are 50 years old, go to work."

When I finished high school in 1937, there were many steamers operating on the lakes, rivers, sounds and oceans of the world, but the Great Depression was on and few publications existed to tell the hobbyist of interesting activities and developments in the Live Steam field. A trip with friends that was supposed to take us to Montreal but ended in Burlington, Vermont, left an indelible mark on my life and has affected many things I've done over the years. The beam engine vessel *Ticonderoga* was weathering the Depression and running during the summer months on Lake Champlain. Although the "Ti" had seen better days, her sidewheels continued to turn day and night. An Army post, Fort Ethan Allen, was located near Burlington, and the soldier boys and the local girls were quick to take advantage of the moonlight nights on the lake. A large, cheap, neon sign reading "Show Boat" was secured to the upper deck for all to see.

The charm of that old steamboat altered our plans and that was as far as we went, but what an adventure. We boarded for a night on the lake, and some of those memories are vivid today. Since that weekend my family and I have ridden on the "Ti" many times, including several rides with members of the Steamship Historical Society. We have steamed to Westport, Port Kent, Plattsburg and St. Albans Bay. Sometimes these cruises lasted as long as 11 hours; once we returned to Burlington at 2:30 a.m.

In 1942 while I was a student at Albany Business College, I went on a school picnic down the Hudson to Kingston Point on the beam engine boat *Robert Fulton*. We returned late in the afternoon on the opposition boat, *Alexander Hamilton*, which had sidewheels also but was powered by an inclined engine. During that summer in Albany, I would frequently go to Recreation Pier after school and watch the *Robert Fulton* come in one day and the *Alexander Hamilton* the next day. What a pleasure to see the men wrap those big steamers around the pier with a spring line and get them in position for the next day's run to New York.

It was sad to me, and many others, that the *Ticonderoga* would cease operations, but she is maintained in the Shelburne Museum.

I am not certain of when I first went to the Mystic Seaport Museum in Connecticut, but I do recall seeing the very beautiful *Mary Powell* beam engine model; something I've seen several times since. In 1948 we drove to Kingston, New York, and back the same day in the pouring rain to see Herman Boyle's beam engine model. This model, now at the Mariners Museum in Newport News, Virginia, does not have the detail or workmanship of the Mystic model, but it is interesting nonetheless. Twice in my life I have stood in front of the glass case and admired the detail of an American

Author Dick Mitchell proudly displays his handiwork.

beam engine model in the Science Museum in England. Other model beam engines near this size have been built over the years and can be seen at the Smithsonian Institution and the San Francisco Marine Museum while three others are now in progress by hobbyists. However, as far as I know, there are less than ten such models in the world.

Many years ago I asked George E. Whitney about the possibility of operating a small launch with a model beam engine, such as the 36-foot *Sweetheart* of 1836 built at the U.S. Navy Yard, New York. Whitney discouraged the idea as impractical but offered no definite reason. The thought of trying to build such a model and put it into a launch of about 18 feet gnawed at me. I even went so far as to go to a junkyard, looked for something I could use as a cylinder and ended up bringing home a massive hydraulic dump truck cylinder, which collected dust under my bench for ten years until I gave it away.

Perhaps what actually got me started to build a model beam engine was Cliff Harris of Gill, Massachusetts, who told me he was going to build a beam engine for a boat. Cliff's shop was a mecca of machines and parts. He had two pistons 2½" in diameter; each piston had two rings with another set of rings under them. These pistons came from a Locomobile steam car; he gave me one piston and kept the other for his beam engine. In some ways his engine, which stood about 5 feet tall, was not an authentic marine beam engine, but those things never bothered Cliff. The cast cylinder measured 2½" × 12" and the sidewheels actually did feather, but there were no steam chests as such. Harris took four cone shutoff valves, bored out the threads in the stem, and made new stems with no threads. These mounted in the steam line and represented the extent of the valve system; they did, however, open with toes and wipers. When the engine was completed, I went down to see it under steam. I don't recall the pressure, but the engine ran extremely well after he got the sensitive little thing slowed down.

Next came the boat, boiler and paddle wheels. A 20-foot hull of steel was built, and Harris constructed a Merryweather-type boiler. He worked feverishly to complete the project, and when the big day finally arrived, Percy Stewart and I went to Gill on the Connecticut River for the christening and maiden voyage. The narrow hull was altogether too top-heavy, but we changed the part in our hair, said our prayers and cast off. The speed perhaps was 3-4 mph, but what a thrill to watch that engine run and listen to the paddles slap the water.

Dick's gleaming model of a Hudson River vertical beam engine pleasantly disputes his claim to "no experience whatsoever with machine tools."

Cliff added stability by sponsoning the sides, adding to the length and moving the engine and wheels closer to the stern. Again we took a cruise up the river. I never rode in *The French King Belle* again. Harris sold the complete boat and a different power plant was installed by the new owner.

This experience was all it took to confirm in my mind that the long smouldering dream would now burst into flame. For me, at 52 years of age, to attempt such a project with my limited knowledge of beam engines, no formal education in engineering, no experience whatsoever with machine tools, and poor health was ridiculous, but I'm a stubborn Vermonter. When I started this project in 1970 I had an old, broken, hand crank blacksmith's drill that I got in the junk yard for $1 and a 1911 combination lathe and milling machine built by

VanNorman in Springfield, Massachusetts. This small but extremely pretty lathe also came from a junk yard for $25.00 and had no power feed.

There were some things I was sure of: Since I had no drawings to speak of and since it was my desire to someday install this in a hull, I knew that most of it would come right off the top of my head. The engine would be one of a kind, not a scale model of any large engine that ever existed. This gave me license to "beef up" many small and delicate parts such as appear in many scale models. I had collected some beautiful pictures which show great detail of beam engines and especially the *Ticonderoga's* engine, which I studied with a passion.

Woodworking came naturally to my brothers and me, as our father worked in an organ factory and framed pictures at home. He possessed many fine woodworking tools and taught us how to use them. Since many early beam engines had wood frames, I decided to build my "A" frame of white oak, and work began in earnest. From old drawings in books, it was fairly easy to see where the tie rods were located; I knew these were important in the final appearance.

I tried to make the frame as near in appearance to the big engines as I possibly could; this meant long threaded rods through laminated small pieces representing many heavy timbers. The horizontal carrying timbers on the bottom are 1½" square and all the rest of the frame is 1" square stock with the exception of the "X" bracing which is ½"×1". Wherever possible, one piece is fastened to the other with a hardwood dowel as well as the tie rods and glue. With a hacksaw, grinding wheel and file, I fashioned from flat steel plate some rather ornate added supports where the "A" frame joints the carrying timbers. These were fastened with brass screws. I made two mistakes that had to be corrected, but in no way do they diminish the strength of the frame. I cannot emphasize enough the importance of taking plenty of time to think things out first, especially when it is a new project and you have no drawings to go by. I should have made the front of the carrying timbers longer to support the engineer's platform; this was rectified later by bolting some longer black walnut stringers alongside the carrying timbers. Often, I've found it is better to make things a little oversize to compensate for my inability to think things through carefully enough in the first place. I also had to add some wedges to the top of the "A" frame to give a longer surface for the beam center bearing. It was necessary to leave out one small brace to later insert the crank. The 30" tall frame is finished with seven coats of spar varnish and looks quite respectable.

So far so good, but from this point I'd be walking in unknown fields. In order for this model to be anywhere near realistic in appearance I felt that castings were mandatory, and this of course meant patterns I knew little about. I will list the castings here, but will detail them more as this story progresses: beam, bronze; two eccentrics, bronze; two air pump crosshead guides, bronze; two steam columns, bronze; two steam chests, bronze; cylinder, cast iron; cylinder head, cast iron; two piston crosshead guides, steel; two beam main bearing blocks, steel; two crank main bearing blocks, steel; and two filler plugs for the spacers in the top and bottom of the cylinder, bronze.

I felt at the time, and I feel now, that a fabricated crank of steel for this type of engine is satisfactory, but I sure wish I knew then what I know now. I made a crank web model from a piece of pine wood and bored the holes with a bit to represent where the crankpin and paddle shaft would go. I then purchased a piece of steel 1" thick and 2" wide from which the crank webs would be cut. I asked my son Gary to cut out the webs with his company's band saw, tack them together with a torch and then mill out the holes exactly as I made the model. What I should have said is, "Make the holes 4½" from center to center for a 9" stroke." I was not careful enough with the holes I bored in the wood and they were not exactly 4½" – a mistake that almost caused serious problems on the cylinder later. I turned the crankpin with shoulders and had a friend thread the ends. This was a press fit into the webs, then secured with thin nuts and pinned. The 1" paddle shaft was cut 15½" long to accommodate some collars inside the bearings (so it would not move sideways), the main bearings, the eccentrics, a short space and eventually the couplings. The shaft was then keyed on both ends. With everything now in place the paddle shaft was welded to the crank webs both inside and outside and the center was cut out, leaving a perfect crank – or so I thought.

At a later time when the shaft bearing blocks were completed and all bolted down and the last piece of wood on the "A" frame was in place, I discovered while rotating the crank by hand that the bearing blocks wobbled; you guessed it, the shaft had become distorted from the welding and was out of alignment. I know now that the proper way would have been to make the paddle shaft out of 1⅛" stock, then when it was completed, put a plug between the webs and turn the shaft down to 1". We all have to live and learn sometime, don't we?

This was very discouraging to me at the time and I did not really know what to do. I had to remove the little piece of wood in the frame and get the crank out and then I started talking to various machinists in this area about the problem. Most told me to start over again, but after talking to about eight men, I found one man who said he would attempt to straighten it for me. He said he had done such a job once before. I did not see him do it but he said he set the crank up in a large lathe and, with several indicators and some large prying bars, he rotated the lathe by hand and bent the shaft cold until the indicators were "right on the money." He never charged me a cent for the job.

There still were questions in my mind that observation and photos could not answer. I had met Connie (Conrad) Milster from Brooklyn, New York (now Chief Engineer at Pratt Institute), and I knew he had worked in the 1950s on the *Robert Fulton* on the Hudson River. I thought he might provide some answers. What I did not know was that during the winter months of 1953-54 Connie had made drawings of the entire Fletcher engine on the *Robert Fulton*. He answered my questions and sent me a photo copy of his drawings of that engine on 193 sheets of paper. Since I had already completed the frame and crank, I only re-copied what I needed for myself and then returned the whole set to Connie. Now I had some drawings that would be valuable to me. Although my engine was not to scale, the design and style of the engine parts were priceless to me and I have studied them extensively.

With the crank straightened out and the precious drawings of Conrad Milster, I now had renewed faith, and was confident that one way or another the beam engine model would, in time, becorne a reality. Now the time had come to think about patterns and castings; a real bugaboo! I redrew Connie's drawing of the beam for a total length of 19" × 8⅜". This pattern took a long time; it was made of sugar pine, and consisted of perhaps 75 pieces. To obtain the proper beading around the edge of the web, I cut pieces of hard twine and glued them to the edge and later filled, using my fingers, all the twists in the twine with an automotive body repair product called *Bondo*. This of course required a lot of sanding and refilling for a smooth job. The little straps and wedges that hold the outside frame of the beam to the web I made in one piece whereas on the big engines, the cast steel and forged steel are indeed secured with straps and driven wedges.

The cylinder pattern was split and involved several pieces, such as "wing pads," on the top outside edge of the flange to provide a stand for the crosshead guides. Directly under these was a wooden dowel to provide support for a brace to the "A" frame. Larger pads were glued to the front top and bottom of the cylinder to eventually accommodate the steam chests. Smaller pads on the lower half of the front of the clyinder are for the middle rockshaft bearing support.

The cylinder head pattern presented no real problem but did contain a vertical plug through the middle that protruded above and below to accommodate the packing gland. The bottom protrusion was split.

The eccentrics were split and were easy to make, but I forgot to glue on a dowel to have lots of thread area for a setscrew, so I had to have a short piece of brass rod silver soldered on later.

The steam chest pattern was split and consisted of a solid block with ample flanges top and bottom to provide room for the lagging. A flat surface was made on the back that would match the pad on the cylinder front.

The crosshead guides for the top of the cylinder and the crosshead guides for the air pump were somewhat alike in appearance. It was necessary to glue on small dowels horizontally, however (some straight and some on an angle), to accommodate the support rods to the "A" frame.

The bearing blocks for the center of the beam and the paddle shaft are in two pieces on the big engines, but in my case the pattern was simply carved in one piece to resemble the real thing.

I did not have to make a pattern for the air pump cylinder as I bought one in bronze at a flea market for $2.

The steam columns were a split pattern. They contained two rings on the outside to which I would later attach several parts of the engine front, and I needed the extra depth of metal for threads.

I know that some of the readers, and especially those in rural areas, have trouble getting castings made; my area is no exception. The old small foundries have pretty much gone the way of the two-bit haircut. I did know that there was a large foundry fifty miles north of here, so I packed up some of the patterns and headed north to have a talk with the foundry manager. He had only to take one quick look at my work to determine I didn't know what I was doing, something I already knew. He sent me back home with all kinds of instructions of what must be done to make them right. He said the beam pattern should have been split but since it was not he would have to cope it down – a slow and expensive process. I made all the changes he instructed me to do and mailed the patterns back to him.

He called me in a couple of weeks and told me the castings were ready. I drove the 50 miles on glare ice roads, I was so anxious to get them. They looked about as I thought they should, but if I had more experience dealing with foundries I would haved asked them not to snag them. I asked him what I owed him and he said, "Mr.

The steam chests and cylinder shown from above. HAROLD A. BARRY

Mitchell, I appreciate what you are trying to do in your shop with your hobby work, but we have castings going out of here every day that are worth over $1,000; your job was too small to even run through the office, so I did it on my noon hour. There is no charge; put them under your arm and don't come back." There were a few swearwords mixed in to flavor his conversation.

Some of the smaller items were later cast in Westminster, Massachusetts, and that foundry man sent the patterns to be cast in steel to a large foundry in Connecticut. I never did get the patterns back for the beam bearing and paddle shaft bearing. This foundry work was not a pleasant experience for me and I was glad when I was back in my shop; ignorance is bliss.

I took the beam casting to my friend Ken Bailey in Cambridgeport, Vermont, who has a large vertical milling machine. He set it up so he could mill out the four holes for the pins without moving the setup. Some parts of the web were very smooth and I did not touch them, but the outside frame was filed and sandpapered until it passed my inspection.

The cylinder, like some of these other castings, was way beyond my limitations in equipment and experience, so when it came time to have it machined I turned to a shop in Brattleboro, Vermont, across the river from my home. I had to sit down with the shop owner before the work was started because he insisted that I know in advance just how much time would be involved and the cost, so there would be no surprises and no argument. The cylinder had to be faced off on both ends and the pads for attachments also had to be faced. Then the cylinder was set up in a lathe and a cut was made near each end to accommodate the steady rest. The lathe was very large and the machinist used a 2″ boring bar to bore the cylinder. I told him that I wanted the ends of the cylinder inside "relieved" so the rings would never leave a shoulder where they stop. I know now that this would be very unlikely, but we went through with it nevertheless.

Rather than monkey around with the real piston that Harris had given to me, the machinist turned a dummy piston with no rings exactly 2½″ in diameter and 1½″ thick – the same as the real piston, and threaded a center hole where he inserted a rod. This was used to check the size of the cylinder as the boring progressed. The

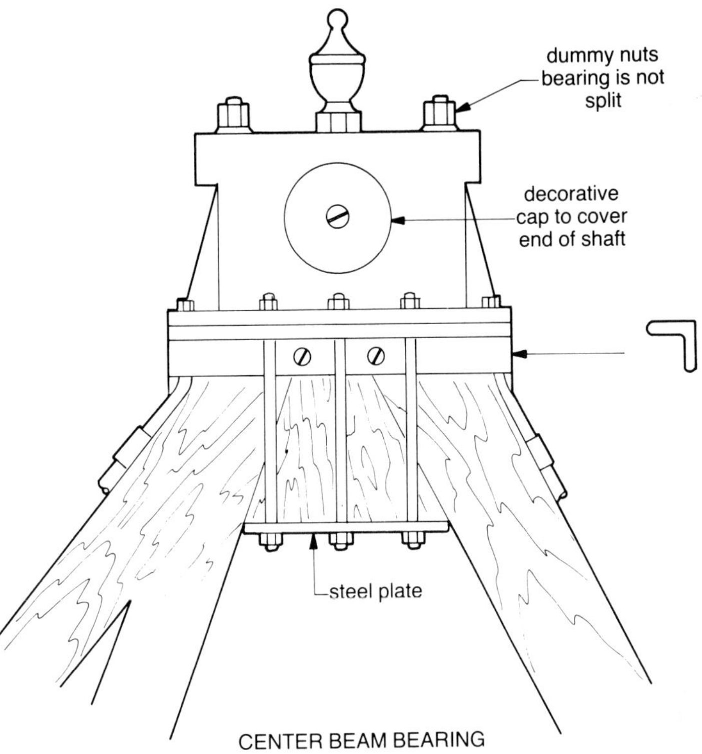

CENTER BEAM BEARING

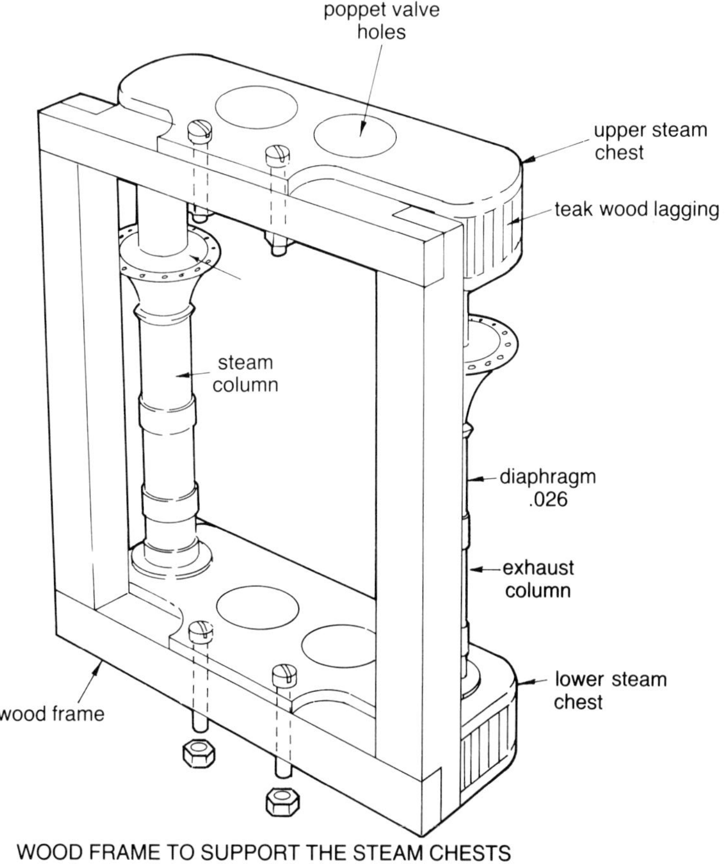

WOOD FRAME TO SUPPORT THE STEAM CHESTS
WHILE THEY ARE BOLTED TO THE CYLINDER

The steam columns and chests. RODERIC M. SCOTT

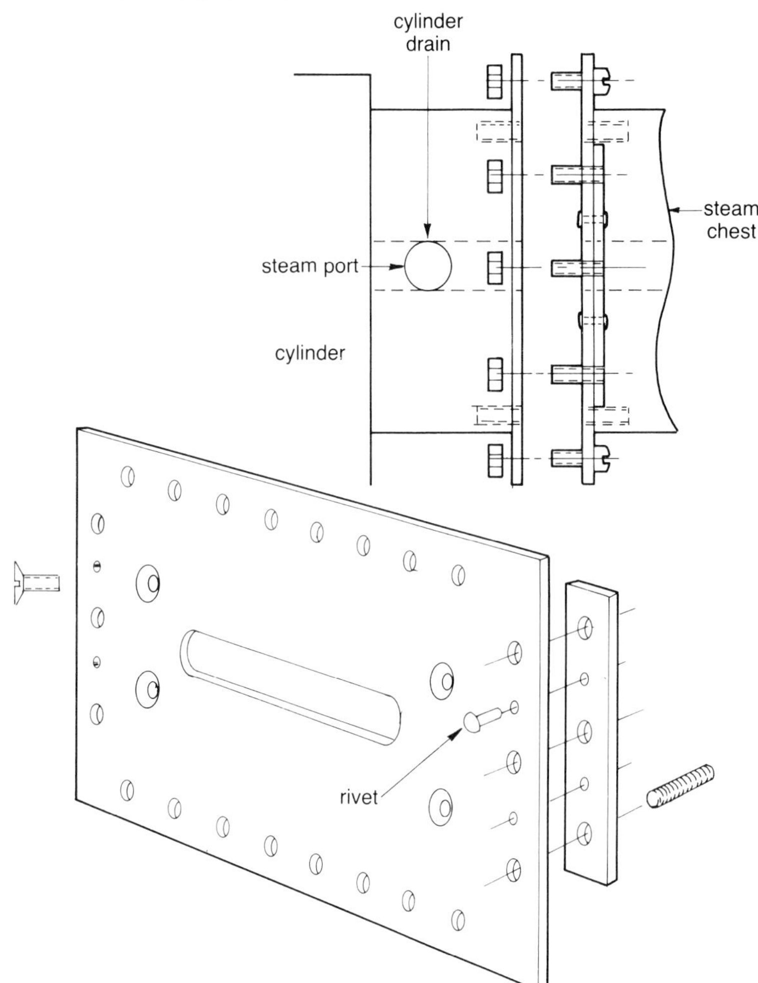

ATTACHMENT PLATES, STEAM CHESTS TO CYLINDER

machinist told me that after the boring was well underway he was going to call me to come in. When I arrived that same afternoon he said, "You sit on this stool and instruct me on every cut on this relief, because if there is going to be a mistake, it will be your mistake, not mine."

I don't recall now, as it was so long ago, whether I forgot about the mistake I had made on the crank webs mentioned earlier or whether I actually discovered this after the cylinder was bored; regardless, the relief was bored for a 9″ stroke when in reality the stroke is actually 8 27/32″. The piston itself does ride past the shoulder but the edge of the ring does not, so all this relief business in my model does not mean a thing. After the cylinder was bored almost to a fit, the machinist and I took it next door to an automotive machine shop where they rebuild truck motors and had it honed to .001″ clearance, constantly using the dummy piston to check it. When it was all finished we set it up on a smooth surface with a newspaper under the bottom. We then put the dummy piston in the cylinder and it coasted down taking about five seconds to reach the bottom.

The steam columns which stand between the chests and in front of the cylinder were quite heavy and over 8″ long, and just about all my little lathe could handle. I drove a long hardwood plug in one end as I had no steady

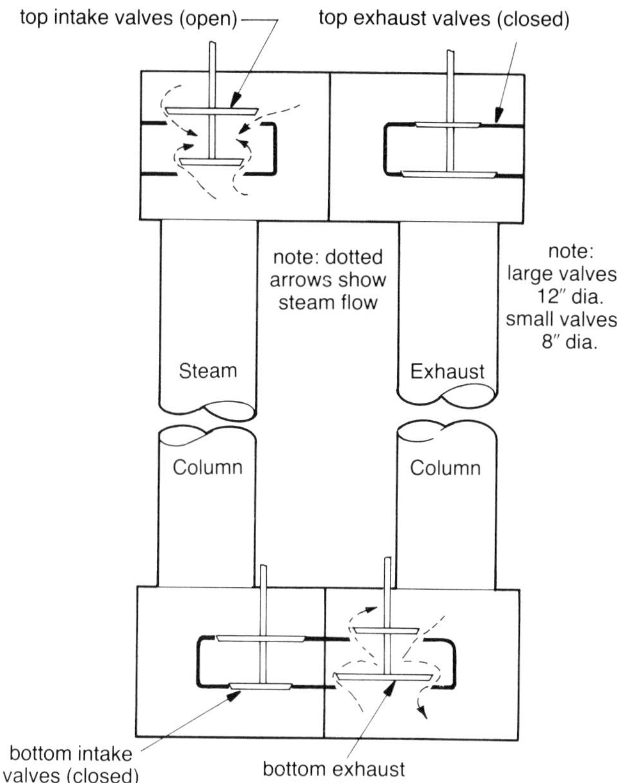

SCHEMATIC DRAWING OF VALVES SHOWING THEM AT BEGINNING OF DOWNWARD STROKE.

RICHARD MITCHELL

A view of the cylinder and steam columns.

rest. I centered the plug as best I could and started to turn. To this day I don't know what made the bronze so hard. I did not have any carbide tip tools so had to sharpen the tool over and over again. It acted as if there was sand in the metal. I did uncover some "rat holes," but they were of no consequence and were later filled.

I have many friends who are very accomplished machinists, but two in particular shared my enthusiasm for this project and were most helpful to me from beginning to end. One is Arthur E. Hughes of East Braintree Massachusetts, and the other is Bernard F. Denny, now retired flight engineer for Pan American, presently living in Virginia Beach, Virginia.

I have been aware for many years that a beam engine has double balanced poppet valves inside the steam chest with the top valve of the pair slightly larger in diameter on the steam column (left) and the bottom valve of the pair being slightly larger in diameter on the exhaust column (right). (This project is now starting to get confusing.) It is true that some of the very earliest marine beam engines had single poppet valves; it is also true that some had only one eccentric, but as better boilers were constructed and the steam pressure rose, the builders used the double balanced valves. The number of letters with drawings, plus the number of phone calls between Art, Bernie and myself to discuss the valves, you would never believe. Although all three of us knew that the best route to take was the double balanced poppet valves, the work seemed to be more than I could handle. We felt that since my single valve was only ⅝″ in diameter it would be best to go ahead on that basis, with the valve opening against the steam pressure (steam on top of the valve). I was elated when Bernie called me and offered to do all the machining on the valve chests. Up to this time I had never done any milling and had no equipment for the work required.

A surprisingly short time passed before the wooden box arrived with the job all done. Bernie had milled out the castings inside, machined the valve seats, and silver soldered the valves to their stems. He had turned beautiful valve covers for the tops of the chests and equally beautiful covers for the bottoms, which contained a lower stem guide with an inside drain hole near the bottom of the guide and a plug in the center of the cover for a drain. He also made the little valve stem arms.

Bernie drilled all the holes to fasten the covers and attach the steam columns, as well as for the ¼″ intake and ½″ exhaust pipes – a total of over 100 holes. I tapped all of these for 3-48 fillister head machine screws and I broke only one tap. It is strange how that little sound of a tap breaking will bring out the worst in a man. Another friend, Frank Fuegeman of Berlin, Maryland, had sent me a new set of taps and dies as a gift, when I started this project.

As work progressed over the years my knowledge and experience grew as did my shop tools. I purchased a new Rockwell/Delta drill press and a used 10″ Logan lathe. I also turned the head stock around on the little Van Norman combination lathe and milling machine and have since used it entirely for milling. It is a joy to watch run with the old original jackshaft and flat belts clicking away. The Van Norman is just not made for anything except very light work, but it does help some.

Bernie and Arthur did come up to see the progress and we got into a

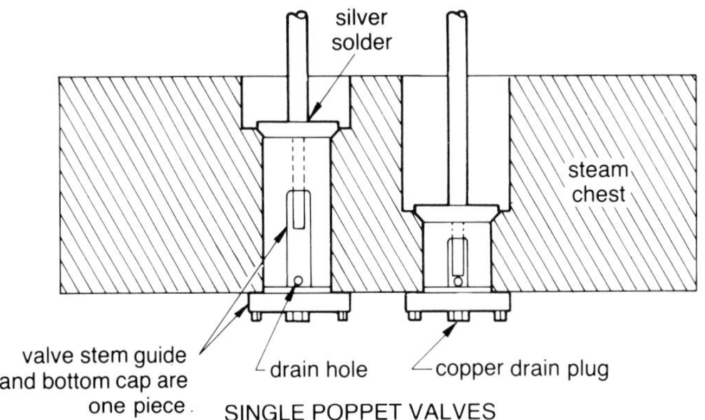

SINGLE POPPET VALVES

discussion regarding the steam columns. I had failed to realize a very important function in setting up the columns. As many times as I had seen the *Ticonderoga* engine and studied the pictures of it, I am embarrassed to tell you I never knew what function the flared joint near the top was for. I had a copy of Connie's drawing but he mentioned nothing about the purpose, so I thought it was for embellishment. As a result of my new lesson I cut off the top of the columns, dished out the flat surface above the "morning glory" and installed a .026" thick brass diaphragm plate. In case any of you, like me, are unaware of the function, the steam columns get hot before all the iron in the cylinder and the diaphragm allows for this expansion, otherwise something might break. On some large engines this plate is ¼" thick steel.

My friends recommended that I make the complete steam chest and column assembly with these units bolted to a steel plate on my bench where I could work on it with ease. Actually, this was mandatory since my .026" thick diaphragm plate would never stand the weight of the top steam chest and certainly not any movement. This procedure worked very well.

The steam columns had to be cut off on the bottom as they were too long. I turned a combination cup and baseplate to fasten to the lower steam chest. The columns were then stood up in the cups and the baseplate was bolted to the chest. With this all in place (including the gaskets), I drilled two holes through the sides of each cup and right through the wall of the steam columns. I threaded the holes and inserted mahine screws. Now I could unbolt the base and top plate from the steam chests to have the cups silver soldered to the bottom of the columns. I knew for sure all the screw holes would again match up.

However, a serious problem developed that I did not realize until later. The column castings were so heavy it took a great deal of heat to get the solder to flow, and one of them warped. When I started to fasten them to the steam chests one stood up like a little soldier and all the holes matched but the warped one tilted away at the top about 3⁄16". If there was ever a time when I thought I would give up on the whole project it was right then. It was days before I could bring myself to even go down in the shop, but the problem was constantly on my mind. I gave this an awful lot of thought and I could not come up with an answer except to take the column off and hand file one side of the base of the cup very carefully until the top tilted back into position. I was thankful that the stock was thick enough to allow that much stock to be removed. This was a case of fitting and filing, fitting and filing, for seven long hours. It finally lined up again and no one would ever notice that one side of the base plate was a little thinner than the other. You are lucky these things do not happen to you!

With my drill press and a file I cut an oblong slot 1 3⁄16" long by ¼" high through the center of the pads on the top and bottom of the cylinder that would hold the steam chests. This was my steam port. I then made four steel plates, 3 3⁄16" long, 2⅝" high, and ⅛" thick. These plates (or flanges) would protrude beyond the pads on the cylinder and steam chests to allow them to be bolted together. (It would have been better had I made them a bit higher for an easier fit.) In each plate I drilled eight holes for 5-40 machine screws across the top and bottom. I also drilled three screw holes on each side of each plate. I then cut my steam port through the plates and drilled and countersunk for four ¼-20 flathead machine screws to be used to fasten the plates to the cylinder pads and the pads on the back of the steam chests.

I then drilled and tapped into the cylinder pad for the ¼-20 machine screws and attached two of the plates to the cylinder pads with a gasket covered with a compound known as *Form-a-Gasket*.

The other two plates to be screwed to the back of each steam chest presented a more serious problem. All the little bolt holes across the top and bottom of the plates would line up as I drilled them together and would stick up and hang down beyond the pads so I could insert the little bolts, but I had three holes on each end of the plate where I could not insert the bolt, although I could get the nuts on. The steam chests were cast with a generous flange on the top and bottom with the exception of the pad on the back which was a flush surface. In time, teak lagging ¼" thick would fill all this area between the flanges. The plate that would be attached to the back of the steam chests was wider than the pad it was to be bolted to. This allowed me room to put 1¼" × ¼" strips of steel on the inside edge of these two plates for more thread surface. I drilled these four little strips and tapped them for 5-40 screws, and I also tapped the three holes on each end of the two plates in the same manner. I then turned the screws through the plate and through the little strips, and cut off the heads. Now I had a total of 12 studs sticking out of the sides of the plates to be bolted to the cylinder plate and these studs were now screwed into a very secure ¼" of thread. I then fastened these plates to the back of the steam chests with a gasket.

At this point I had two of the plates on the cylinder pads. I had the other two plates, with the 12 studs sticking out, on the steam chests. With luck every little bolt hole around the outside would match – are you still with me? Don't give up; I don't.

Now I had the problem of getting the steam chest assembly off the bench and bolted to the cylinder without breaking the diaphragm. I made a wooden frame out of oak much like a picture frame and reinforced it and bolted it to the assembly through the lifting rod holes on the chests. Now I could unfasten the assembly from the bench, stand it up to the cylinder, and nothing could move. I cut the gaskets to go between the plates and was now prepared for the next day's work.

I purchased small nuts from Cole's to fit the 5-40 fillister head machine screws. I had also made myself a little wrench to fit these nuts. I was as ready as I would ever be, but I dreaded the day. I knew the *Form-A-Gasket* would, in time, dry. I also knew I would have to get an early start, would not answer the phone or door, and would not eat until every bolt was in and tight. I started at 7 a.m. and smeared some *Form-A-Gasket* compound on the gasket paper, stood up the assembly by holding the frame and, as luck would have it, all 12 of the little studs fitted into their respective holes. What I did not realize was that the little nuts were so small I could hardly hold them in my fingers and certainly could never get them into the small places where they had to go, so I got my very fine flexible artist's knife, put a little gob of *Form-A-Gasket* on the blade and planted the little nut in the gob; only then could I position the nut where it had to be. Of course this made a dreadful mess on everything, especially my fingers.

Getting the top row bolted was not too difficult, but I knew I must work top and bottom together or they would not be equal and one would "set up" too soon. The part that was extremely difficult was working under each steam chest, a most awkward place. By 2 p.m. I had the 44 bolts and nuts in place and only then did I remove the wood frame. I was tired and hungry. Although the engine was a long way from completion I felt good that this much was secure and I was pleased.

Up to this point I have told you about things that were, in many ways, difficult for me; now I would like to talk about how parts were made and assembled that were lots of fun. In some places I did take short cuts by substitution or omission in relationship to the full-size engines because I still had in mind, at that point, that some day I might put this engine into a boat; the deviations I made were from a practical standpoint rather than museum perfection. However, I did try to have each part resemble the real thing as much as I could. After all, anyone could build such an engine from 2×4s and angle iron and make it work.

The bearing blocks for the center of the beam and paddle shaft were cast in one piece. The base was milled first to allow a true surface to mill the top edges and the bearing hole. The bearings themselves were new electric motor bronze bushings reamed to fit the shaft and then pressed into the holes. A flathead machine screw through the bottom of the block and through the bottom of the bearing holds the bronze from ever moving. I drilled and tapped the tops for a dummy hold-down stud. I actually turned in some cap screws with tall heads and cut the heads off. I put each head in my lathe and drilled and tapped it. I made some brass oil cups that I filled with wicking and painted the blocks a dark green. I drilled and tapped a small hole in the end of the beam

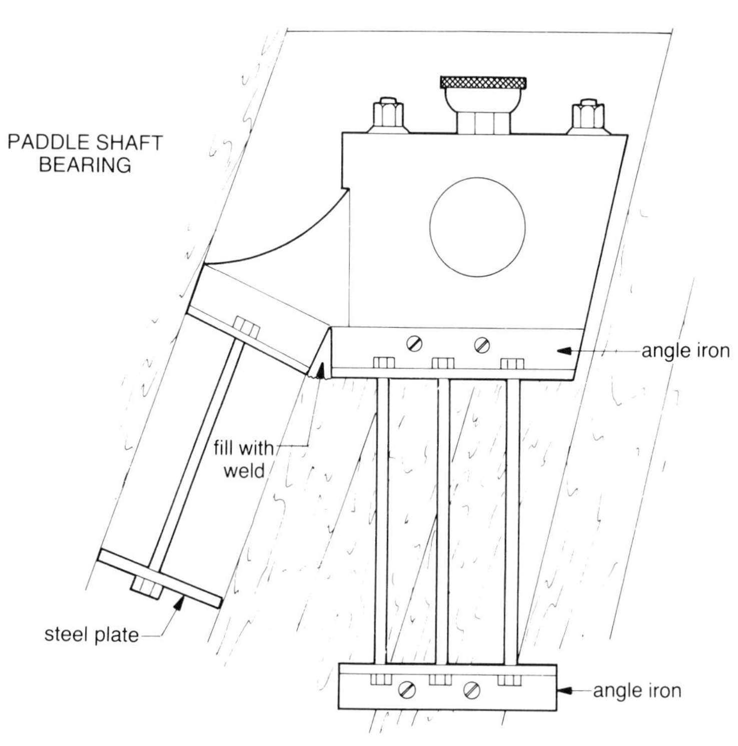

center shaft and turned a nice little brass cap to dress it up. These bearing blocks need a good surface to stand on rather than just the wood itself, so I cut down some small angle iron, rounded the corners, bolted them through the white oak, then carefully filed them to a good fit. The base of the blocks, of course, comes out to the edge of the angle iron and the holes for the hold-down tie rods are drilled through the base and angle iron, so all the holes match.

In the case of the long tie rods that extend to the bottom of the "A" frame, I bought four small turnbuckles, drilled out the threads and retapped them all right-hand, so they are dummies. I fashioned four small pieces of steel by hand to merge the two hold-down rods that extended down from the ends of each bearing block into the one rod that followed the frame. By milling and filing I also made eight small clamps to hold the long rods to the frame of the engine. The tie rod anchor near the bottom of the frame legs could have been just a sawed-off piece of small angle iron, but I found some small "box" iron and cut it away and inserted a small partition in it, and it looks professional. The paddle shaft bearing base is cast and milled on an angle just as I had seen it in the drawing. In this instance I had to cut the little angle irons that would be part of the platform, bend them, have them filled with weld, then file them smooth. The appearance is worth the effort.

The nine gib and key bearings for the crosshead to beam links, air pump rods, and connecting rod are real and good looking but very time consuming. The bronze bearings are square; as a result, I made square straps for the bottom of the rods and curved top straps for the top of the rods so I could have more thread area to accommodate the oil cups, which I made out of brass to resemble a tall grease cup. Most of the slots around the bronze bearings for the straps I did on my limited milling machine, but Frank Fuegeman did make the bearings for the air pump rods for me. Most of the gib and key assemblies were done with drills, hacksaw, grinding wheel and file – a long and tiresome job.

To me the connecting rod presented quite a problem and was slow

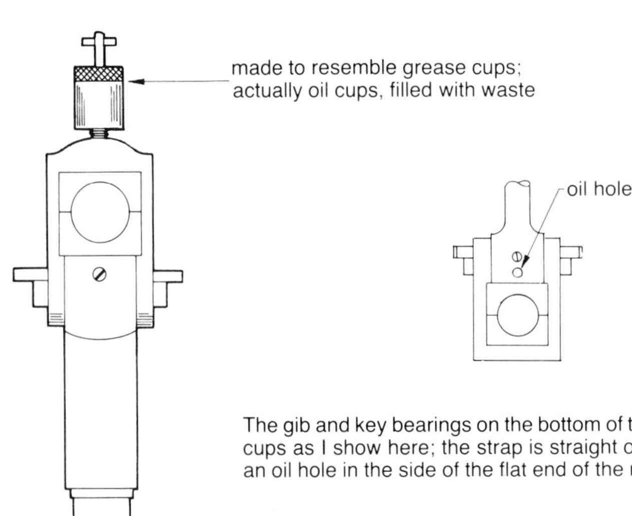

GIB AND KEY BEARING
upper connecting rod

going. That the piston be exactly in the right place in the cylinder when the crank was on dead center, top and bottom, was critical. Because of this very delicate situation, I built a wooden piston, piston rod and a complete connecting rod that would accept the gib and key bearings I had already made. I set up the whole assembly with the wooden rods and then rotated the engine with a crank I had made that fitted the paddle shaft and carefully watched and measured the position of the piston when on top and bottom. This checking was done, with the cylinder head off, through the steam ports. After some slight adjustment on the wooden parts, I again checked and found that 1/16" covered the steam port both top and bottom.

When I bolted the cylinder to the 1/4" steel baseplate I used heavy machine cap screws up through the bottom. Also at that time I bolted the bronze "filler" plug to the base in the same manner. This cast plug fills the space from the end of the cylinder to the edge of the steam port. An exact plug is also bolted to the cylinder head for the same reason, only in this case some of the center of the plug is bored out for the protrusion of the packing gland that sticks below the cylinder head itself. This plug is attached to the cylinder head by four 10-32 recessed head cap screws that go all the way through the cylinder head and extend up a short distance to secure the brass washer that holds the packing gland in place.

I debated for some time just how to build the connecting rod when an idea came to me while traveling near home. I noticed a large turnbuckle on a state highway fence with a forked end. In time, I visited the state highway garage. A very kind man gave me a galvanized rod like the one I had seen that measured 1" in diameter and was long enough so the entire connecting rod could be made in one piece. I cut the holes off the top of the forked end with a hacksaw, then took the rod to a machine shop. With my guidance they heated the forked end and spread it so it would match the bearing surfaces on the beam pin. They also heated the other end and flattened it with a sledge hammer until it was 1/2" thick. I then centered the rod in the crotch of the forked end, set up the other "flattened" end in my four-jaw chuck, turned two slight tapers on the rod and also turned the sides of the fork. It still required a lot of handwork, but I had the wooden model for reference. It came out quite nicely. I eventually attached truss rods on it which protrude out from the center of the rod on turned stanchions.

I found a short piece of thick wall steel pipe the right diameter from which I could make some eccentric straps. I had two round plugs welded on the outside edge, one on each side. I then put it in my lathe, bored it to fit, and faced it off. I drilled holes through the plugs for a 5/32" rod; then, with a hacksaw, split the ring halfway on each plug. These two half sections fitted nicely into the groove I had previously cut in the eccentric.

There are several different designs of eccentric rods in drawings that I had seen, but the one that seemed as pretty as any and would, in my mind, be easy to make had curved webs. I made a drawing on a 1/2" thick pine board of how I wanted it to look, then on my band saw I cut the curve. I then nailed one of these pieces onto a sheet of plywood and nailed the other piece next to it, leaving a crack wide enough to accommodate the thickness of a coat hanger wire. With pliers I bent the wire until it dropped into the slot. I repeated this until I had four curved pieces. I then set up the correct lengths of the 5/32" rod so one end fitted into the holes on the eccentric strap and the other end through a small plate I had fashioned that would be part of the hanger assembly between the eccentric rods and the hooks. With copper wire I wound the outside rods to the curved web wherever they came in contact. I also wound the center of the web where

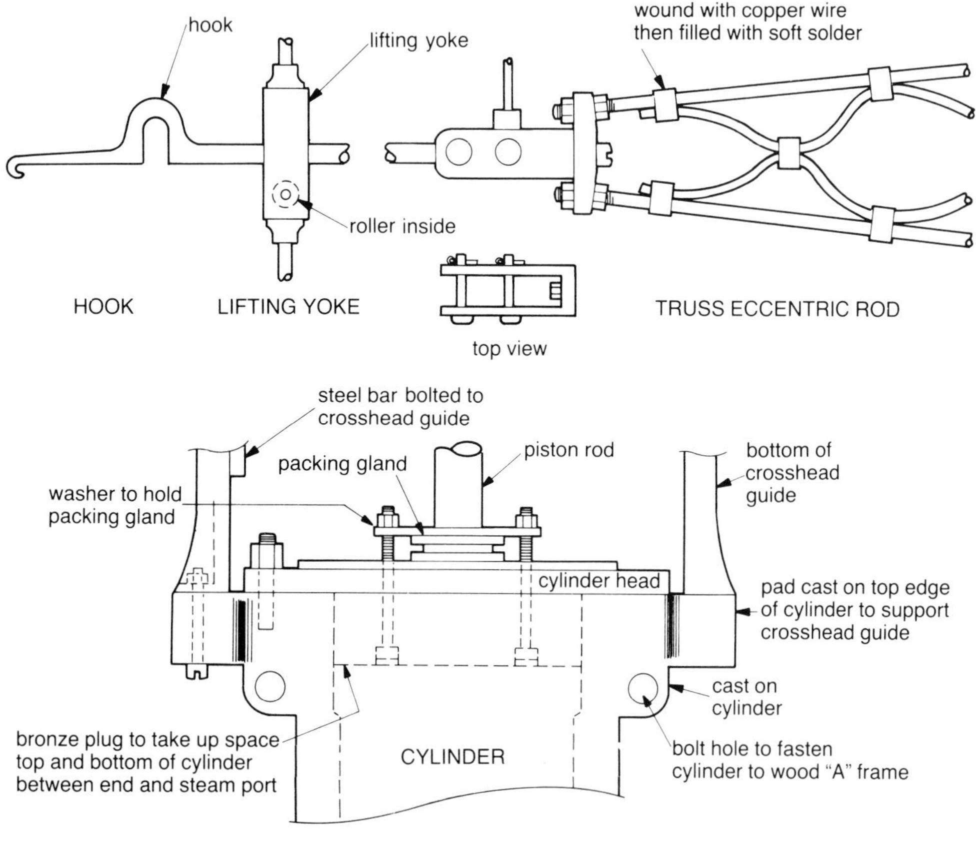

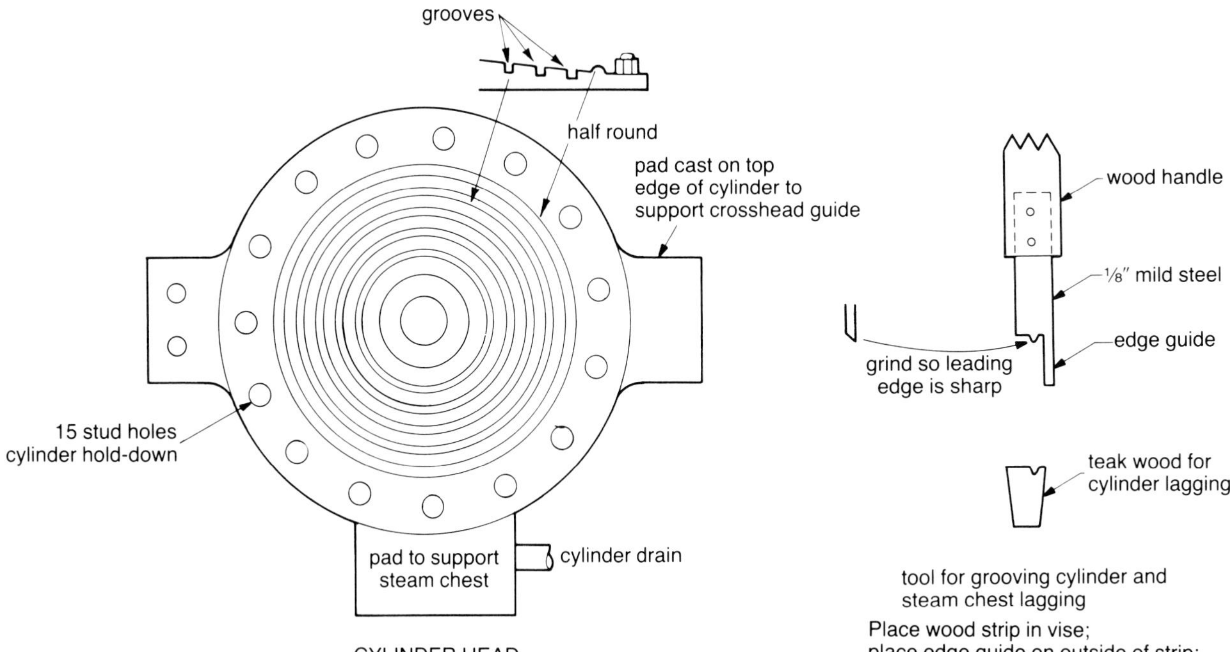

CYLINDER HEAD

tool for grooving cylinder and steam chest lagging

Place wood strip in vise;
place edge guide on outside of strip;
press down and pull tool toward you.

each curve came in contact with the other curve. I pulled the ends of the wire through the web and secured it, then filled the wire with soft solder and cut the loose ends off.

On a full-size engine the eccentric rods and hooks are very heavy, of course, so they are supported by a hanger rod from the frame. Where the small ends of the eccentric rods meet the end of the hook rod, I fashioned a strap that was bolted to the ends of the eccentric rod. With pins, the hooks can be lifted by the engineer without lifting the eccentric rods themselves – a hinge, in effect.

Provision was made on the patterns for the cylinder and steam chests to eventually lag both with narrow vertical strips of teakwood; but to give this wood a professional look I made a hand tool from mild steel that could be drawn along the edge cutting a groove as it traveled the length of each piece. I drew a plan like a piece of pie, except I wanted the strips only ½″ wide to resemble the full-size cylinder. Thirty-eight strips of wood were required to cover the cylinder and each piece was ⅝″ thick to bring it out to the edge of the flange. As each strip was cut, grooved, glued and put into place under large rubber bands, holes were drilled for round hardwood toothpicks to edge-fasten each piece to its neighbor – until the last one, which was simply glued on both edges.

Four narrow copper bands were hemmed to circle the cylinder, but the top and bottom bands had to be cut, due to pads that support the steam chests. The limited space made working in this area difficult, so I fastened the bands to the lagging with round head brass screws. Where the ends met on the back side of the cylinder I made some clamps like those I had seen on one of Frank Fuegeman's 5A engines.

The steam chests were lagged in much the same way, except there are no clamps. A groove was filed on the edge of the wood top and bottom so the band would be flush with the teakwood. All lagging was hand rubbed with linseed oil.

I am sure I spent more time on the engine controls than anything else. It was slow and exacting work to get every piece shaped and fitted properly so it would function as it should. I did not, as previously mentioned, try to make this a model of any real engine and most of the control levers were not included. In fact, the eccentric hooks lever that lifts the yokes is the only one I made. This arrangement of rods, cotter keys and gizmos defies description, at least the way I do things. Due to the shape of the toes and wipers, these were all hand-fashioned, each being a little different than the other. The same detailed handwork applied to the trip shaft and its related small toes and wipers, but I got it done including the starting bar and its little hook and standing socket.

Lining up the 5⁄32″ valve lifting rods through three sets of bearings was very exacting and time-consuming work as each hole must be in alignment with the other. Each contains a

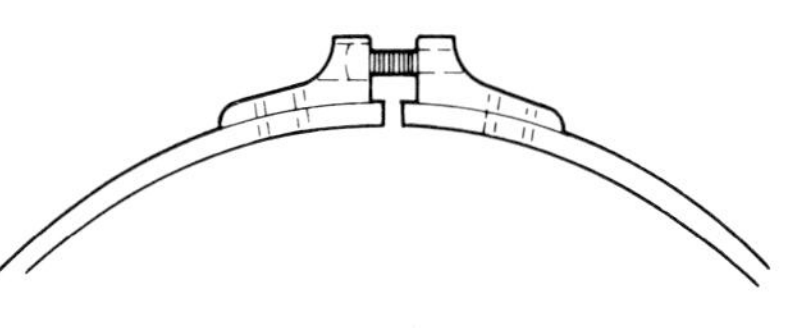

COPPER BAND CLAMP
cylinder lagging

small bronze bearing that is kept in place with a tiny setscrew and each flared top of these little bearings is beveled to keep the oil against the lifting rod.

Actually the beam engine is a simple machine once you have examined each part and perhaps had someone explain some things to you. The thing that bugged me at first was the fact I did not know the rockshaft was in two pieces; while one half is turning in one direction by its eccentric on the paddle shaft, the other is turning the opposite direction by the other eccentric. Hence, as the steam enters the top of the cylinder at the beginning of the down stroke, the exhaust valve is opening in the bottom chest to allow the exhaust steam out and vice versa. Because of the very delicate timing I did not at first cut keyways for all the toes and rockshaft cranks. They were originally set with small Allen screws so they could be changed at will to time the engine. The same applied to the eccentrics on the paddle shaft.

The air pump was one of the last items to be made on my beam engine. In many ways I should have made a true Edwards pump, but time marches on and I wanted to see this model completed, so I used the pump cylinder I had found in the flea market, which has a bore of 1¾". It seemed very functional and had a nice oblong base that was already drilled and tapped so I drilled my baseplate and fastened it from the underside. At the same time I fastened a pipe flange to the bottom of the baseplate with some machine screws serving a double purpose. Since it was my intention to install this engine in a boat with a keel condenser, no inboard condenser was considered.

I made a pattern for the bronze crosshead air pump guides at a much later time and they were cast by Chris Greaves in Connecticut. Since the air pump cylinder already had the machined flange around the middle, it afforded an excellent place to secure the guides. Another machine screw attached the guides to the cylinder top flange. I turned and threaded two ornate steel tie bars to keep the top of the guides in alignment. The brass piston contains the valve. The piston is about ¾" thick and has two water grooves on the outside. The bottom of the piston has a plate with six 3⁄16" holes in it and is soldered in place. On top of these holes lies a brass ring that can flop up and down, covering and uncovering the holes, but cannot come out as there is a "keeper" ring soldered to the top edge of the piston. I have tried this pump by hand with water and it works just fine. I drilled and filed a discharge hole in the upper part of the cylinder wall of the pump and then I found in my junk box (every hobbyist has one) an old motor bearing with a wide flange on one end. I turned another thinner flange for the other end, drilled some holes for a matching flange later and soldered it to the bearing. The thick cast flange would have been best formed with a fly cutter, but my fly cutter is a rattail file. With a small gasket and machine screws I fastened the little discharge pipe to the pump.

The long reach rods operated from a pin on the beam are not tapered and are threaded into the gib and key assembly instead of being all one piece. Small brass collars hide the threads that show on the end and halfway on the rods is another longer, ornate brass collar for decoration.

The crosshead guides that stand on the pump as well as the steam cylinder do contain a steel bar which takes the wear of the crosshead. The cylinder covers for both the air pump and steam cylinder are grooved as in the large engines.

The lower half of the engine showing the air pump.

The engineer's platform was made by gluing strips of mahogany to a piece of plywood, then drilling for round toothpicks which were cut off smooth. The platform was then sanded and varnished.

Frank Fuegeman made some very attractive narrow oil boxes for me that fitted between the steam cylinder cover and the base of the crosshead guide and each has a tiny drain cock. These are to catch the oil that drips from the crosshead guides so it will not run down the lagging. (On some tug compound engines I have seen a brass "comb" on the crosshead that picked up oil from such a box and smeared it on the guide on the upstroke.)

The overall size of my model is 3 feet high, 32" long and 8⅝" wide. (This excludes the black walnut stringers I added to the base and the engineer's platform.)

By now many years have passed and I've had to make some evaluations in my life. I had come to the conclusion some time ago that I had neither the strength nor the ambition to start again to put a steam launch together. This model, even though it has a 2½ × 9" cylinder, develops only ⅕ horsepower at 50 psi and with single unbalanced valves plus a diaphragm so thin it just does not seem practical.

I had thought of having this model in a glass case; someday perhaps I will, but I certainly intend to try running it on steam, so I went to a lot of trouble to remove the old tubes from a Taylor shop boiler, retube it, build a firebox for wood and set it up in my cellar with the smoke pipe out the window.

The big day arrived September 26, 1984, when my friend Cliff Hills came down and we raised steam for a trial run. I had only 25 psi at the most and the engine would not run. I've talked to several steam friends since that day and everyone seems to be in agreement that the pressure was too low, plus the fact that I should not have used 600W steam cylinder oil, but rather *3 in 1* oil with some powdered graphite in it. Some friends also thought I should "break it in" with an electric motor first. I did buy an old motor with a jackshaft, and with the 14" garden cultivator wheels on the paddle shaft I reduced the 1725 rpm on the motor to 35 on the engine. (Some full-size engines ran about 21 rpm, but 35 is a real joy to watch.) The details of

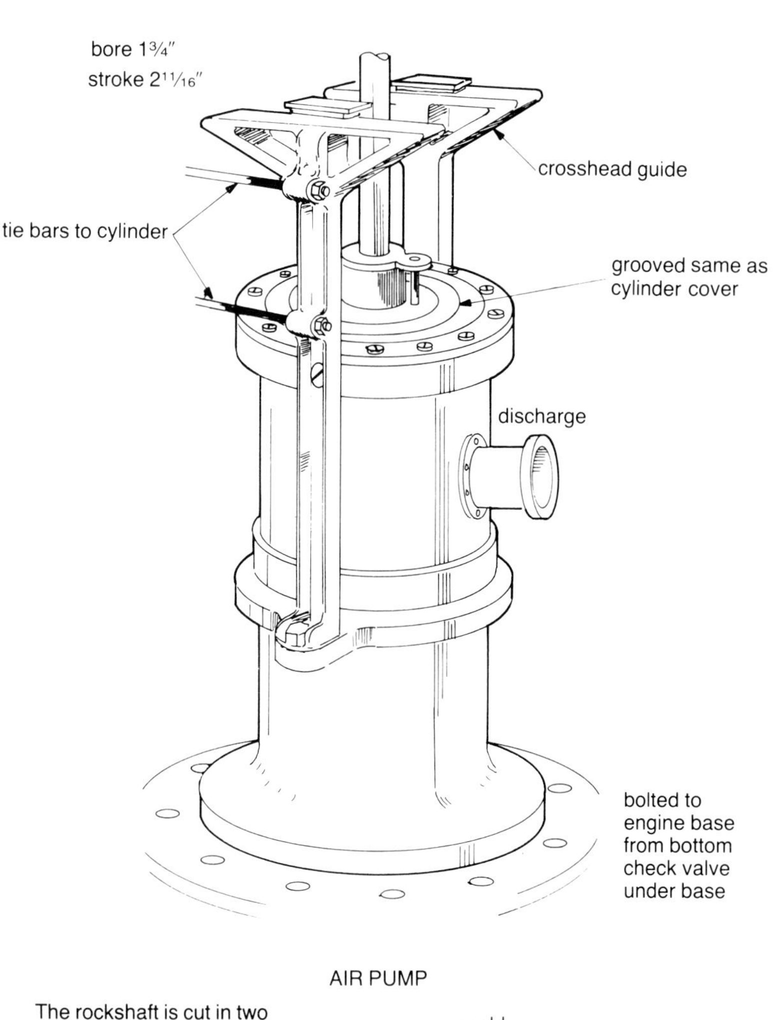

AIR PUMP

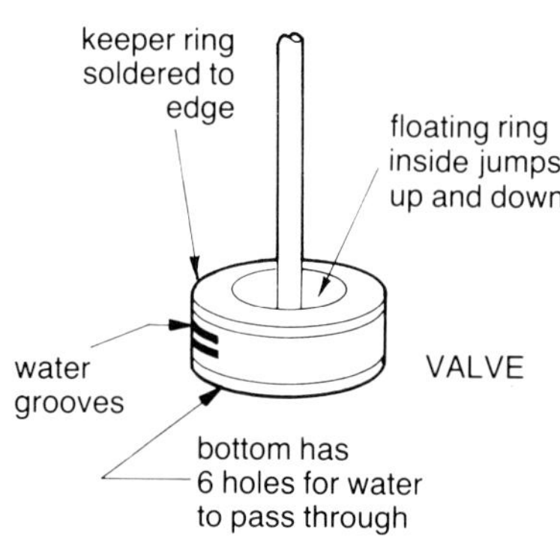

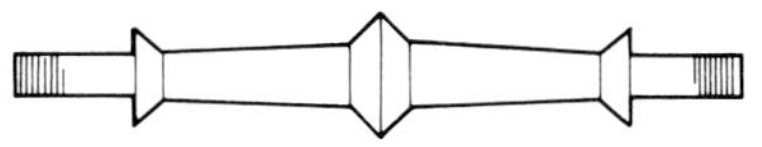

AIR PUMP CROSSHEAD TIE BAR

two on crosshead air pump guides

one larger one on crosshead guide above steam cylinder

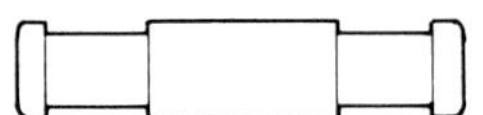

BEAM PIN FOR AIR PUMP

between beam end and beam center

two larger ones for each end of the beam

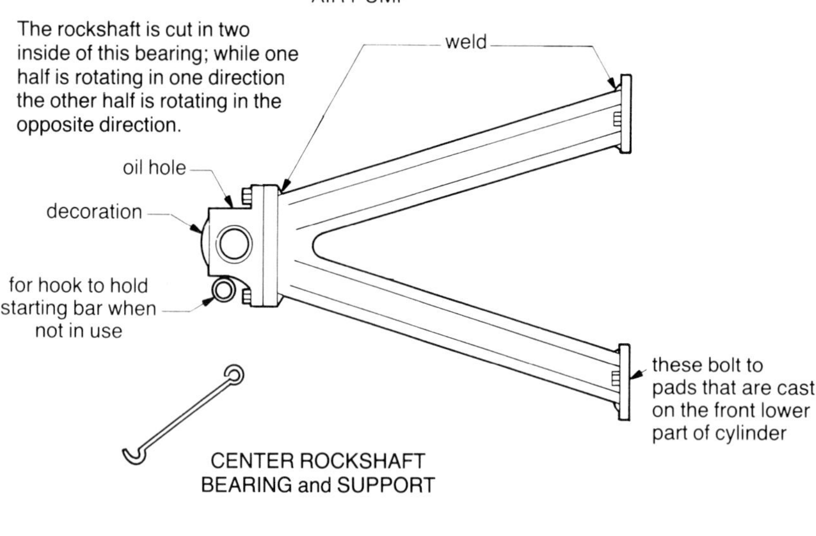

CENTER ROCKSHAFT BEARING and SUPPORT

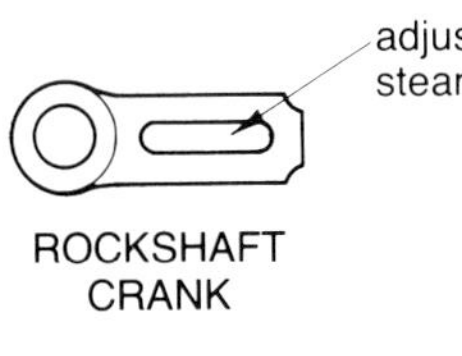

ROCKSHAFT CRANK

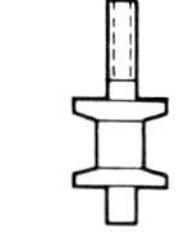

ROCKSHAFT CRANK HOOK PIN

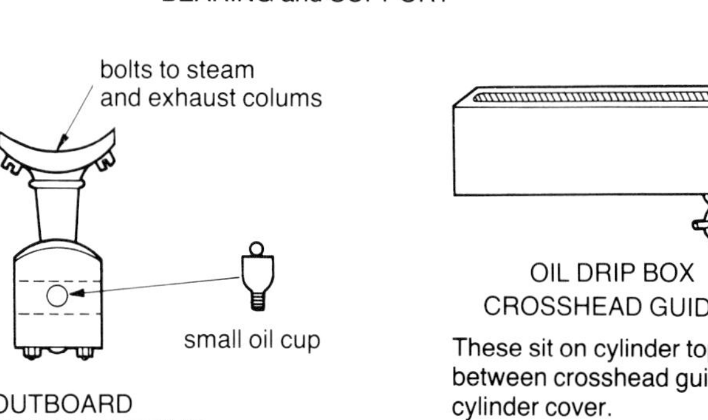

OUTBOARD ROCKSHAFT BEARING

OIL DRIP BOX CROSSHEAD GUIDE

These sit on cylinder top between crosshead guide and cylinder cover.

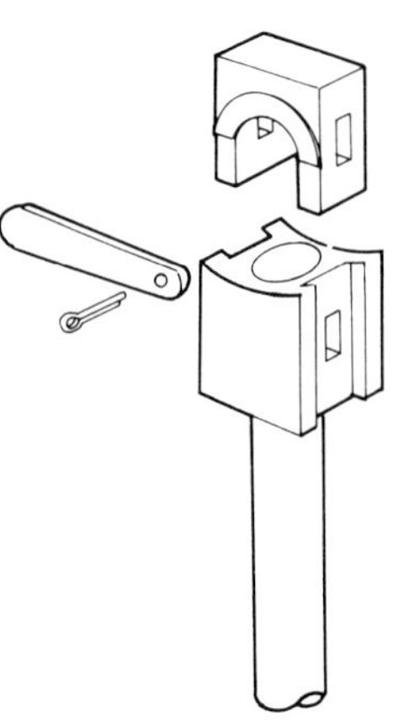

PISTON ROD TO CROSSHEAD GUIDE

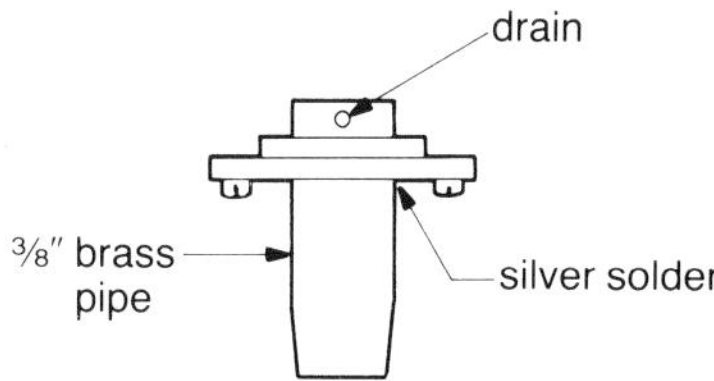

STEAM INTAKE PIPE and FLANGE bolted to bottom of lower steam chest; left side

An assembly like this only with a 1/2" pipe is bolted to bottom of lower steam chest; right side.

Dick Mitchell's model of a Hudson River vertical beam engine (pre-power plant) rises majestically to "full size" at this angle.

the operation of a full-sized marine beam engine is splendidly outlined in the book *Paddle Wheel Steamers and Their Giant Engines* by Bob Whittier, published by Seamaster Boats, Inc., Book Division, P.O. Drawer T, Duxbury, Massachusetts 02331. The price is $7.95.

I am so impressed with the operation, smoothness and quietness of the model I will keep it on the motor, at least for now. The boiler is still piped to the engine and I will try it again on steam with more pressure, of course. At this time [December 1984] it has been run for ten hours for a total of 21,000 turns.

Several friends have come to see the model turn over with the motor, and those who are old enough to remember riding on beam engine boats are fascinated. There is nothing quite like it. Everything works just as it should and, with the cylinder drains open, the air wheezes in and out of the cylinder in its romantic rhythm. The little oil cups on top of the connecting rod rock back and forth with each plunge of the beam end and if you, in your younger life, ever rode on a beam-engined boat, all the memories of those wonderful days return when you see this model operate, even on an electric motor.

Most of my local friends are not steam buffs, but they do come to the house to visit and of course I have to show them my toys. Some have said, "It's very pretty, but what the hell is it?" Others have said, "I know what that thing is; it's a model of an oil rig." I tell them they watch "Dallas" too much. I don't expect them to understand; I don't understand their golf game.

For a hundred years, extending into two centuries, the walking beam steamboat influenced the lives of millions, and although most of the machinery was above deck, few understood the moving parts as they danced in rhythm before their eyes. In spite of the seemingly complicated mechanism, the traveler stood with respect and admiration as these giant boats on both coasts left their pier for a trip to New England, Albany, across San Francisco Bay or around the lake. Gone is the black smoke, the white steam from the whistle and the thrashing paddle wheels that were so much a part of American history.

I am no machinist, but I have learned a great deal and had years of wonderful enjoyment. Every little doodad that I made, whether on the lathe or by hand, I had to rush upstairs to show Lucile. I'm sure she did not understand any of it, anymore than I understand her knitting, but she did think it was pretty, and gave me a smile of approval. Lots of days I ate my lunch with some little shiny component sitting on the table beside me, much the same as when I took my teddy bear to bed with me as a child.

Building this model, I suppose in some ways, was not too unlike the methods used to build the very first big engines of this type in the 1840s. If in my crude way this effort has been an inspiration to some readers, like myself, who have limited knowledge of machine work, then I would like to say, "Go with it," whatever the project. If I can do this as my first endeavor in metal, you certainly can do better.

An Original Mill Engine

"Scrapbox"

By Paul Jacobs

Photos by William Haubert, Jr.

INTRODUCTION

When this engine was conceived, I wanted to build a realistic-looking engine that would run and could be manufactured from scrap materials. The engine is a dual-acting mill-type with uniflow exhaust and a piston valve for admission. The bore is 5/8" and stroke is 3/4". No castings were used. Every part was fabricated or cut from solid material. Even the bolts and functional oil cups were manufactured in my home shop.

If some of my methods seem odd, blame it on my ignorance. I install sash and glass on large construction jobs for my livelihood, and my only exposure to machine practice was in high school and through ***Live Steam***.

I make all my engines from scrap materials, buying as little as possible. This engine cost about $15 in paint and silver solder. For materials – *scrounge*! The base bolt flange was a brass hinge leaf, the cylinder and trunk came from a piece of concrete reinforcing rod. The fly wheel was originally a pulley from an old double-hung window; the piston rod, crank-shaft and several other parts came from stainless steel dowel pins used to hold blocks of stone together. Study the drawings and photos, and if you have a method or design that you prefer, by all means use it.

I used my ancient (1947) 9" South Bend, my homemade mill, a drill press and a Dremel Moto-tool for power equipment. The engine could be made on a Unimat (in fact, I used mine for some parts).

BASE CASTING

Three things are critical on the Base: 1) Ensure that the crank center line will fall in the same plane as the cylinder center; 2) The cylinder can be mounted at right angles to the crankshaft; and 3) Enough offset for the crank disk must be allowed.

Starting with the vertical portions of the base, which are cut from any 1/4" brass available, assemble parts **105**, **106**, **107**, **108** and **110** with screws or pins as shown in **Figure 1**. I use brass escutcheon pins to avoid tapping. Just drill the pin hole to the closest size that you can drive the pin into, and don't drill the full depth of the nail. It will expand and grip when driven in. Remember to clean and flux before pinning parts together.

Silver solder with *Sil-foss* (1310°-1425°) from the inside of the formed box. Run a heavy fillet – no one will ever see it, and it fills any cracks you

may have. Pickle and clean. This portion will be called the Pedestal.

Mount the pedestal in the mill vise. Using a fly cutter, shape the curved sides of the pedestal. On parts 105 and 107, do not cut beyond where **101** and **104** attach. When using the fly cutter with vertical feed, take it easy! Ten or 15 thou and feed down slowly. Alternatively one could file to shape, with a slight change in parts 101 and 104.

Cut out part **109** and drill all the holes shown. Leave the oblong holes slightly undersize and note that you must drill a matching hole in the Pedestal Top (no. 110) to bolt them together.

Fit the remaining base parts. I used a couple of 2-56 screws through the Flange Plate (109) into the Crank Supports and pinned parts **102**, **103**,

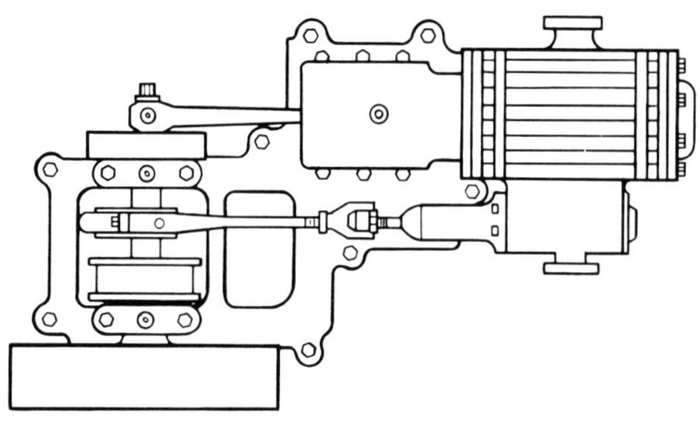

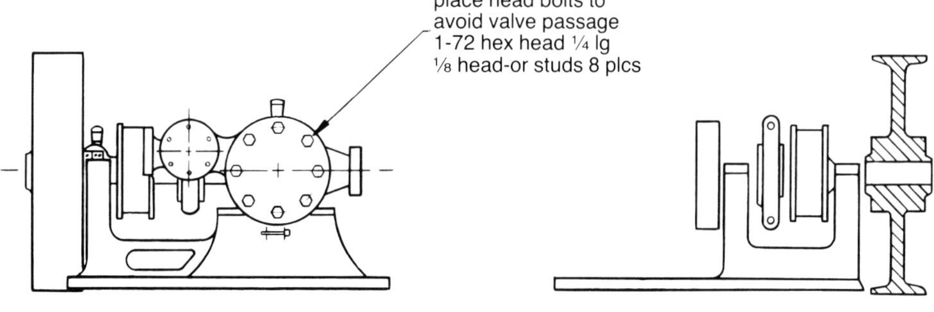

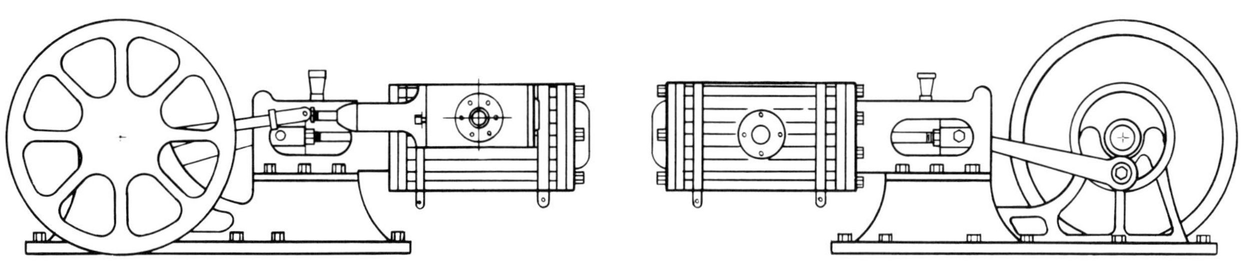

"SCRAPBOX"
GENERAL ELEVATIONS

SECTION A-A

1 13/32
101
110
106
CRANK SIDE
1/8
109

crank
1 13/32
1 5/32
1 1/16
3-48
4 plcs.
9/16
13/16
11/16
3/8
5/16
3/8
9/16
7/8
1
1 3/16
15/16
1/8R
4 plcs.
1/8R
3plcs.
3/16R
1/8 typ.
BASE ASSEMBLY
13/16
1 3/8
31/32
1 5/8
1 13/32
2 11/16
2 13/16
= critical dimension

cylinder
bearing cap no.111
2 required
5/16
3/48 studs
5/16
3/32
crank
1 13/32
7/16
A
A
107
102
105
CRANK END
BASE ASSEMBLY
("casting")
FLYWHEEL SIDE
cylinder
9/16
3/8
15/16
110
108
FRAME CYLINDER END

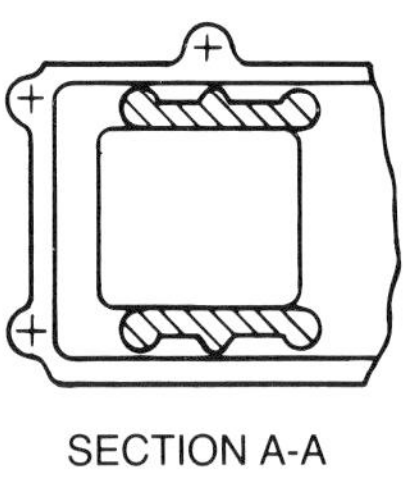

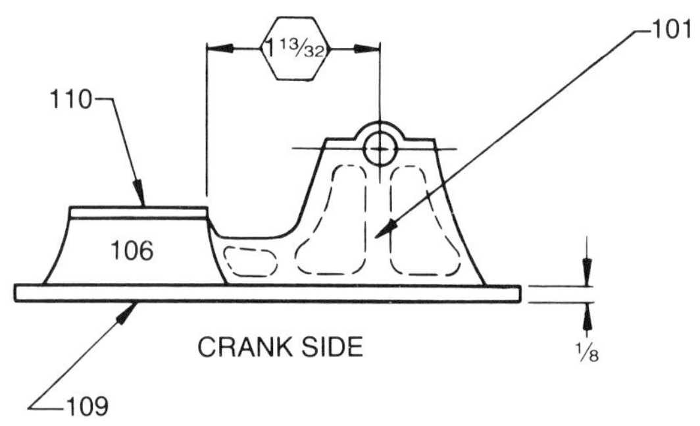

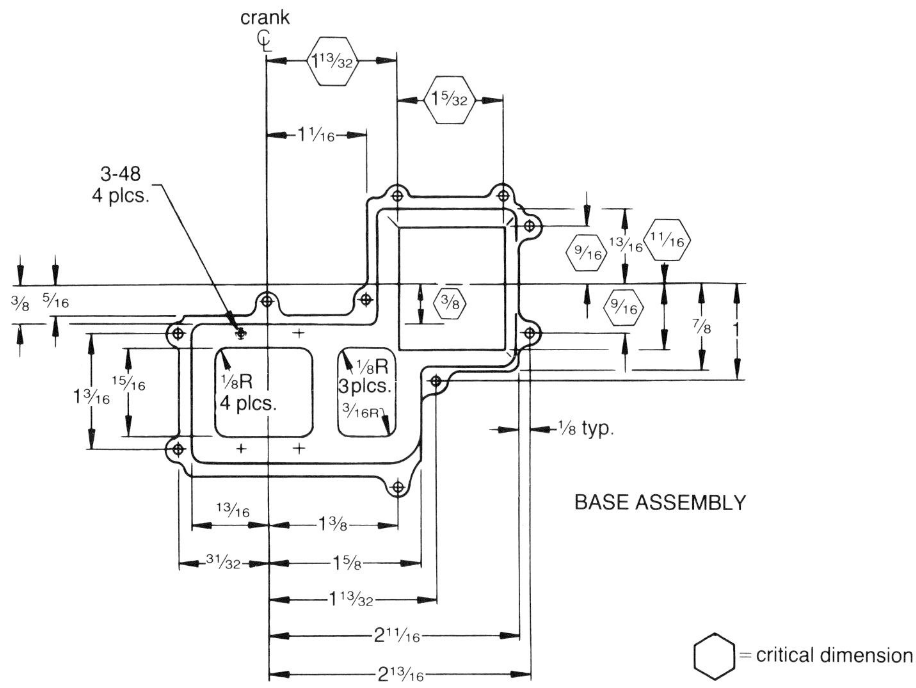

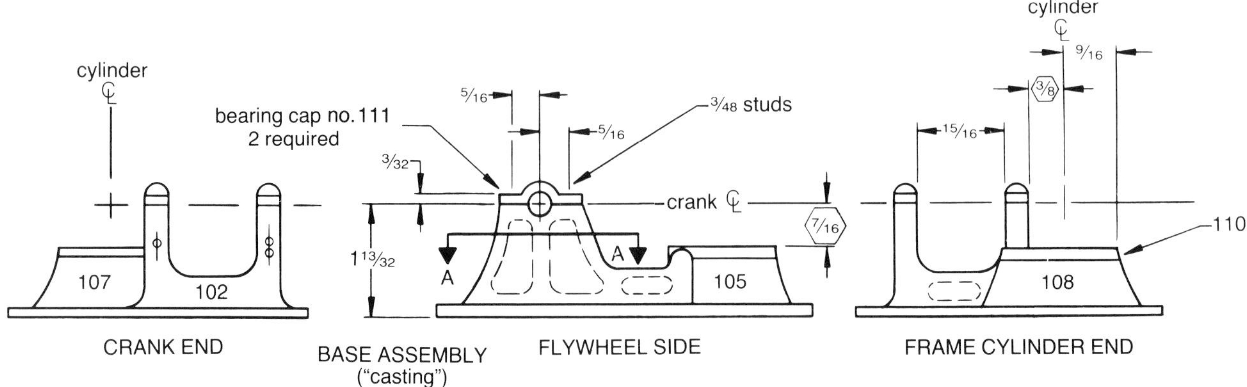

105-106
15/32
107 & 108
1
1 21/32
PEDESTAL SIDES
parts 100 thru 108 are 1/4 brass
7/16
7/16
3/8
1 5/8
1 9/32
100
1/4
3/8
19/32
2 1/2
101
2
CRANK SUPPORTS
3/8
104
19/32
15/16
102,103
3/8
15/16
CROSS MEMBERS
1 13/32
1 5/32
1 1/16
no. 49 drill
10 places
air hole
15/16
9/16
cylinder
9/16
7/8
1
3/16
5/16
5/8
2
1 3/16
15/16
1/8R
3/16R
1/8 typ.
tap 6-32
1 1/16
5/8
31/32
1 3/8
1 5/8
1 13/16
2 11/16
2 13/16
2
1
1 3/16
106
107
108
1 21/32
105
15/16
heavy
fillets
102
103
104
11/16
100
2 15/32
1 1/16
BASE ASSEMBLY
110
1/8 brass
1 1/2
PEDESTAL TOP
109
BOLT FLANGE FOR BASE
1/8 brass. Leave cutouts
undersize & file after assembly

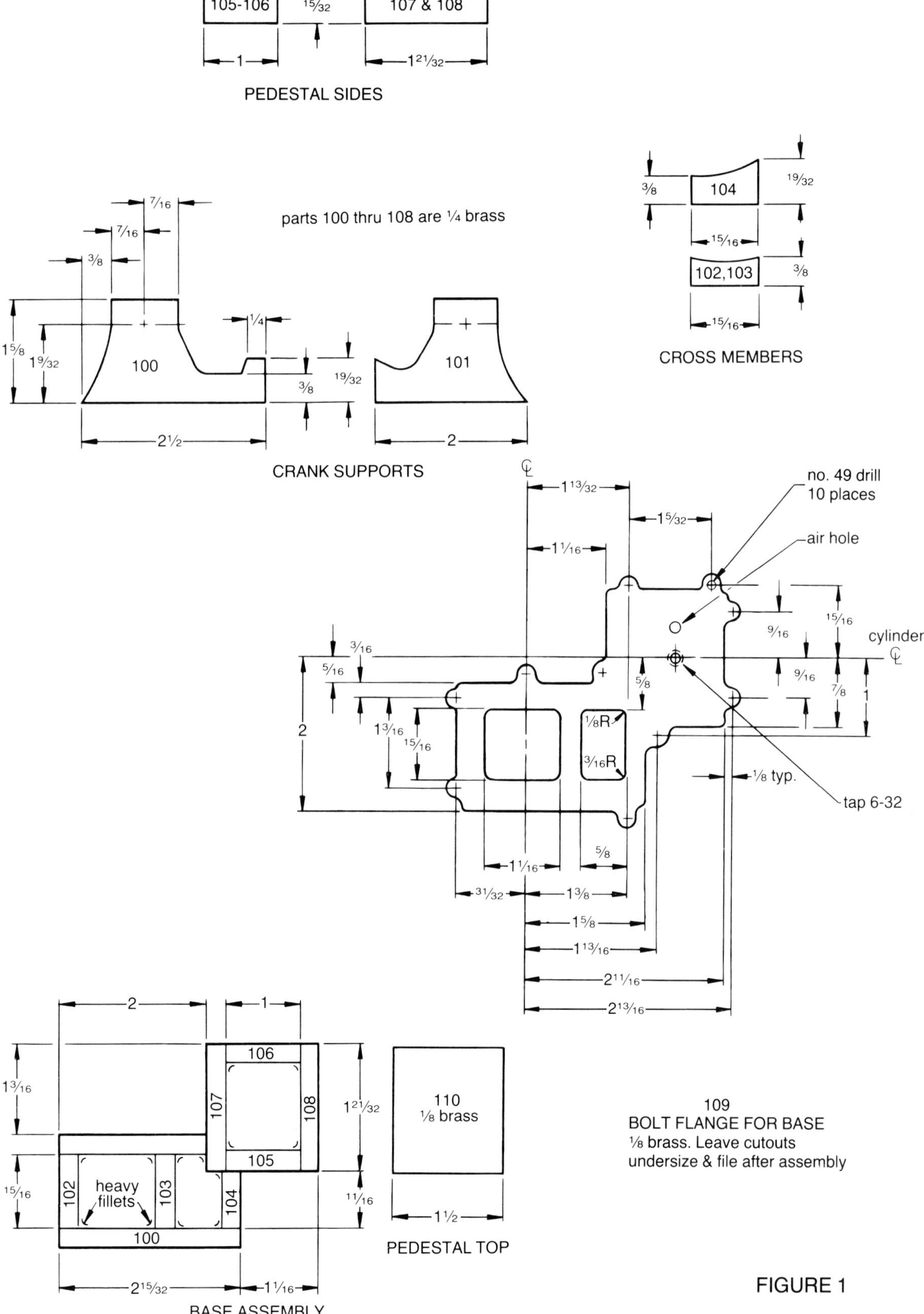

FIGURE 1

perimeter of each area, getting smooth, straight radiused edges. Don't worry about any small cutter marks, we'll take care of those later. Turn the base over and cut the relief areas on the other crank support. You may have to use just a Dremel to do some areas; in fact, you could do all of it with the Dremel, but it's easier to get straight lines this way.

Remove the casting from the mill, get your Dremel and files, and prepare for old manual labor. Don't forget safety glasses when you're using the Dremel on metal! Round and shape all corners except the vertical, and tap the edges of the pedestal. Everything should flare into everything else – no abrupt changes in shape. File oblong holes to be flush with the vertical portions and put a small radius on the bolt flange.

To transform this obviously fabricated and machined object into a casting, we'll use regular household solder. So get your torch, a popsicle stick, a dry cotton rag, and some flux.

Heat the casting slowly, just hot enough to melt the solder. Use a small flame. When the solder starts to flow, move around and coat everything. Use the popsicle stick to push the solder around and wipe the molten solder with the dry rag. You will get nice fillets and smooth surfaces all over. The best way to not solder the bearing caps on is to remove them, so...if the casting gets so hot that the solder doesn't stay where you put it, let it cool off before continuing. Don't worry about solder getting into the flange bolt holes; it's easily removed when you spotface them.

If you don't have a spotface tool about 0.200 in diameter, it's easy to grind a short pilot on a no. 7 drill. Mount your Dremel on the lathe cross-slide, put a no. 7 in the lathe chuck, and put a cutoff disk in the Dremel. Set the carriage stop to allow you to grind a 1/8″ long pilot to 0.073.

Use the Dremel again to touch up the cutting edges. Whatever you use, go around the base and spotface all the flange holes.

Use sandpaper and files to remove any unwanted solder. Tap the oil cup holes, replace the 3-48 screws with studs and nuts, and admire your handiwork!

and 104. Be careful to get the crank supports vertical and parallel. Using *Easiflow* 45, silver solder the lot. Put a heavy fillet on the inside vertical joints. Pickle and clean extra carefully this time.

On a flat surface, mark out the crank center height on both supports. Drop the gauge down and mark the top of the pedestal. Measure back from the top edge of the pedestal 1 13/32″ and scribe a vertical line. Make it long enough that you won't cut it off when you saw off Bearing Caps no. **111**. Mark out the shape of the caps, remembering to allow for the saw cut. Mark out your rib pattern. See section AA in Figure 1.

You will save some work by rough-shaping the bearing caps before you saw them off. Mount the "casting" on the mill table so that the crank center line is parallel to one feed axis. Drill no. 47 for the Cap Bolts. Drill deep enough to get 1/4″ below the crank center. Drill no. 50 for the Oil Cups just to the crank center. Rough-shape the bearing caps with any available end mill. Mount a slitting saw and adjust the quill so that you are cutting just above the crank center. Saw off the caps and put them aside for now. Exchange the saw for a fly cutter, and skim the crank supports right down to the center line. Move over to the pedestal and shove it down the line. It should be pretty close already, so just clean it up to get a nice flat surface.

I used a piece of 4″ angle bolted to the mill table and clamped the casting to the vertical leg to cut the rib patterns and drill the crankshaft holes. Before we can drill for the crank, we must replace the bearing caps. So tap the crank supports no. 3-48, and drill the caps out to a no. 38 drill size. Use screws to attach the caps for the time being.

I always had a hard time tapping small sizes by hand until I mounted a 1/4″ drill chuck on a piece of 3/8″ rod and made a sleeve for the rod. By placing the sleeve in the drill press chuck and the tap in the 1/4″ chuck, I can now tap 00-90's in steel. Just remember to back out the tap and clean it and the hole often.

Back to the mill. Put a straight, 3″ piece of piano wire in the chuck. Clamp the "casting" to the vertical leg of the 4″ angle, high enough to allow you to get at the rib areas with a 1/8″ end mill. Align the oil cup holes with the piece of piano wire, and clamp the "casting" securely to the angle. Remove the wire, insert a small center drill, and drill and ream 1/4″ right through both supports. Again, take it easy!

Change to a 1/8″ end mill and using the "knob-twiddling" method, cut out the relieved areas about 1/8″ deep. Note your quill reading so you can get the same depth in other areas. Stay about 3/32″ inside of your marks. When you get all of one side done this far, change to a ball cutter (I used a Dremel carbide cutter). Run the quill down till the cutter barely touches in the center of one relieved area. Note the quill reading. Gradually move around the

You can do a large portion of the lathe work for the Cylinder and Trunk at one sitting by chucking a steel rod with about 5″ sticking out of the chuck. Turn the rod to 1⅛″ diameter. Shape the Head (**112**) by turning and filing on the extreme end. Set your parting tool to leave a 3⁄32″ flange, and run it in until you have 0.620″ diameter remaining. Withdraw the cutter, move the carriage 1⁄32″ toward the chuck, and part off the head. Put the head aside, and drill or bore what will be the Cylinder (**113**) to 9⁄16″ diameter, 2″ deep. Turn the waist portion to ¾″ OD. Part off to length and put aside.

Turn the Trunk (**118**), working from the crank end. Bore it 9⁄16″ diameter, 1 15⁄32″ deep, flat bottom. Part off to length using the same procedure as used on the head.

Make the Drilling Jig (**148**) from the remaining stub.

Lay the cylinder horizontally on a flat surface, slide a piece of square stock up against the flanges, and scribe each flange. Align one of the holes in the jig with this mark on one end of the cylinder. Clamp it in place, transfer the mark to the jig, and drill all eight holes through the flange no. 53. Move the jig to the other end of the cylinder, align the marks and drill it, also.

Transfer the jig to the trunk, clamp, transfer the mark onto the trunk, and drill the trunk flange. Use the same procedure for the head. Drill the trunk and head bolt holes out to a no. 49 drill size. Tap the cylinder flanges 1-72. Make the Mounting Plate (**119**) and the Flange Blocks (**120**). Use your fly cutter set to 13⁄16″ diameter to cut the mating radii.

On the mounting plate, center the cut 9⁄16″ from one edge, and cut the 1 5⁄32″ length. Use an end mill to cut the flange portions. The Flange Blocks (**120**) are made from two pieces of brass 3⁄16″ × 7⁄16″ × 1″. Run the fly cutter down the 7⁄16″ side, centered. Round the ends and file one end of each to fit the flared end of the trunk.

Starting from the alignment mark on the trunk, scribe three more marks at right angles to each other. These three marks are used to align the flange blocks and the mounting plate. Measure 21⁄32″ from the crank end, and mark, drill and tap all four places 2-56. Attach the flange blocks and the mounting plate in their respective locations with brass screws.

Using *Easyflo*, silver solder the assembly, pickle, and clean, and file the screw head off the mounting plate.

Mount the trunk in the mill vise to cut the slots. To keep the slots in alignment, place a piece of aluminum in the vise as a block and lay one of the flange blocks right on it. Using a ¼″ drill, drill a series of holes along the slot area, through both sides and into the aluminum block. Use an end mill or file the slots to finish size, 5⁄16″ × ⅞″.

Use a couple of screws to attach the cylinder to the trunk and put some layout dye on the exhaust side of the cylinder. Place the base on a flat surface, place the cylinder/trunk assembly on the pedestal. Put your square on the table (blade vertical) and slide it along the cylinder. This establishes one center line for the exhaust port. Disassemble, and make another mark centered end to end. Use a ⅛″ end mill to cut the port.

Now we'll make the Valve Assembly and the Exhaust Fitting. Make parts **114, 115, 116,** and **117.** Part 114, the Passage Block, is made from a piece of ⅜″ square brass. Working from center, lay out the ports and the center screw hole. Drill all three right through the block. Use the fly cutter again to cut the cylinder side radius. Mill the passageways 3⁄32″ deep, almost to each end. Set the fly cutter to cut ⅝″ diameter and cut the radius on the valve side. File or mill the taper. File the cylinder side to a close fit. Drill part **115** rich through (on center) with a no. 42 drill. Enlarge the hole to a no. 21 approximately ⅜″ deep, and tap 10-32. Drop a 2-56 brass screw into the hole and screw the cylinder onto the block. Screw the inlet fitting in and use *Sil Fos* to solder all three parts together. Pickle.

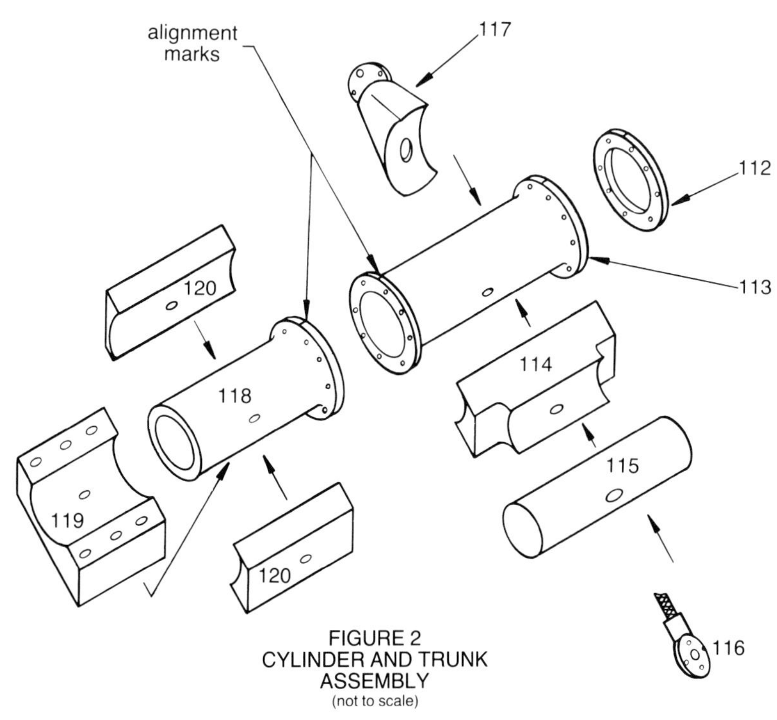

FIGURE 2
CYLINDER AND TRUNK ASSEMBLY
(not to scale)

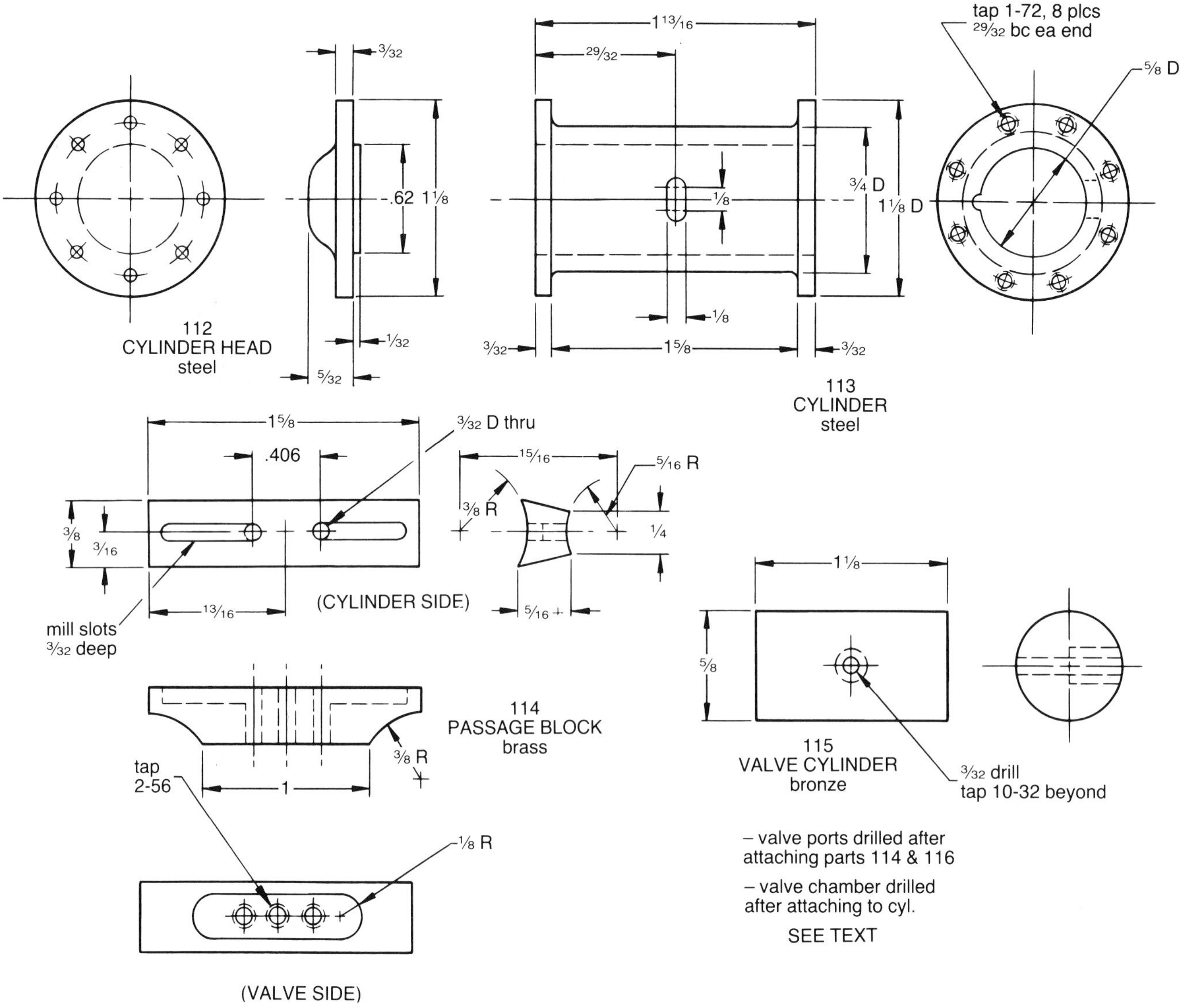

3/32

.62 1 1/8

1/32

5/32

112
CYLINDER HEAD
steel

1 13/16

29/32

1/8

3/4 D

1 1/8 D

1/8

3/32 1 5/8 3/32

113
CYLINDER
steel

tap 1-72, 8 plcs
29/32 bc ea end

5/8 D

1 5/8

.406

3/32 D thru

3/8

3/16

13/16

mill slots
3/32 deep

(CYLINDER SIDE)

15/16

5/16 R

3/8 R

1/4

5/16

114
PASSAGE BLOCK
brass

3/8 R

tap
2-56

1

1/8 R

(VALVE SIDE)

1 1/8

5/8

115
VALVE CYLINDER
bronze

3/32 drill
tap 10-32 beyond

– valve ports drilled after attaching parts 114 & 116

– valve chamber drilled after attaching to cyl.

SEE TEXT

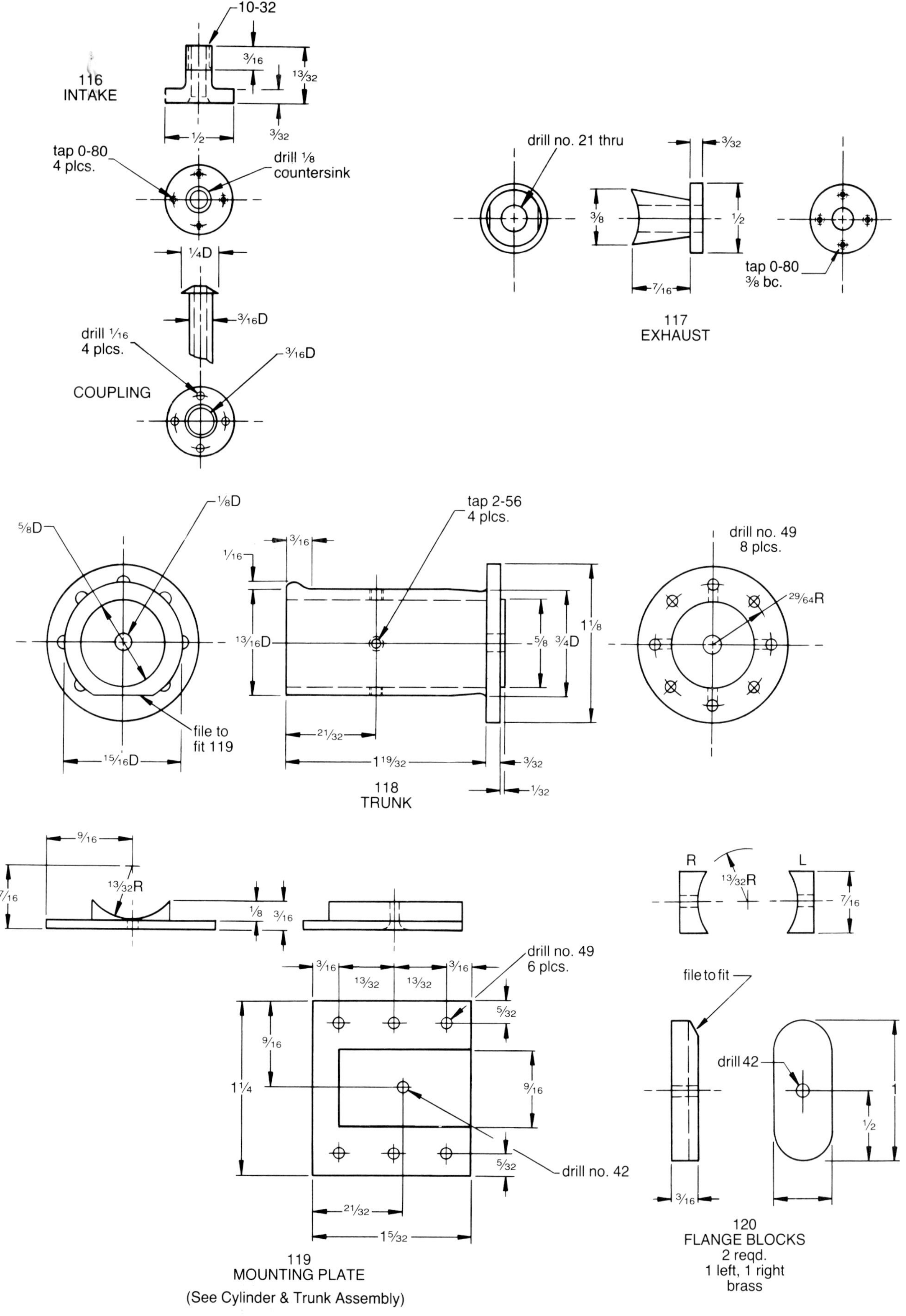

10-32
3/16
13/32
116
INTAKE
3/32
1/2
tap 0-80
4 plcs.
drill 1/8
countersink
1/4D
3/16D
drill 1/16
4 plcs.
3/16D
COUPLING
drill no. 21 thru
3/32
3/8
1/2
7/16
tap 0-80
3/8 bc.
117
EXHAUST
1/8D
5/8D
tap 2-56
4 plcs.
3/16
1/16
drill no. 49
8 plcs.
29/64R
13/16D
5/8
3/4D
1 1/8
file to
fit 119
15/16D
21/32
1 19/32
3/32
1/32
118
TRUNK
9/16
7/16
13/32R
1/8
3/16
R
L
13/32R
7/16
drill no. 49
6 plcs.
3/16
13/32
13/32
3/16
5/32
9/16
1 1/4
9/16
5/32
drill no. 42
21/32
1 5/32
119
MOUNTING PLATE
(See Cylinder & Trunk Assembly)
file to fit
drill 42
1
1/2
3/16
120
FLANGE BLOCKS
2 reqd.
1 left, 1 right
brass

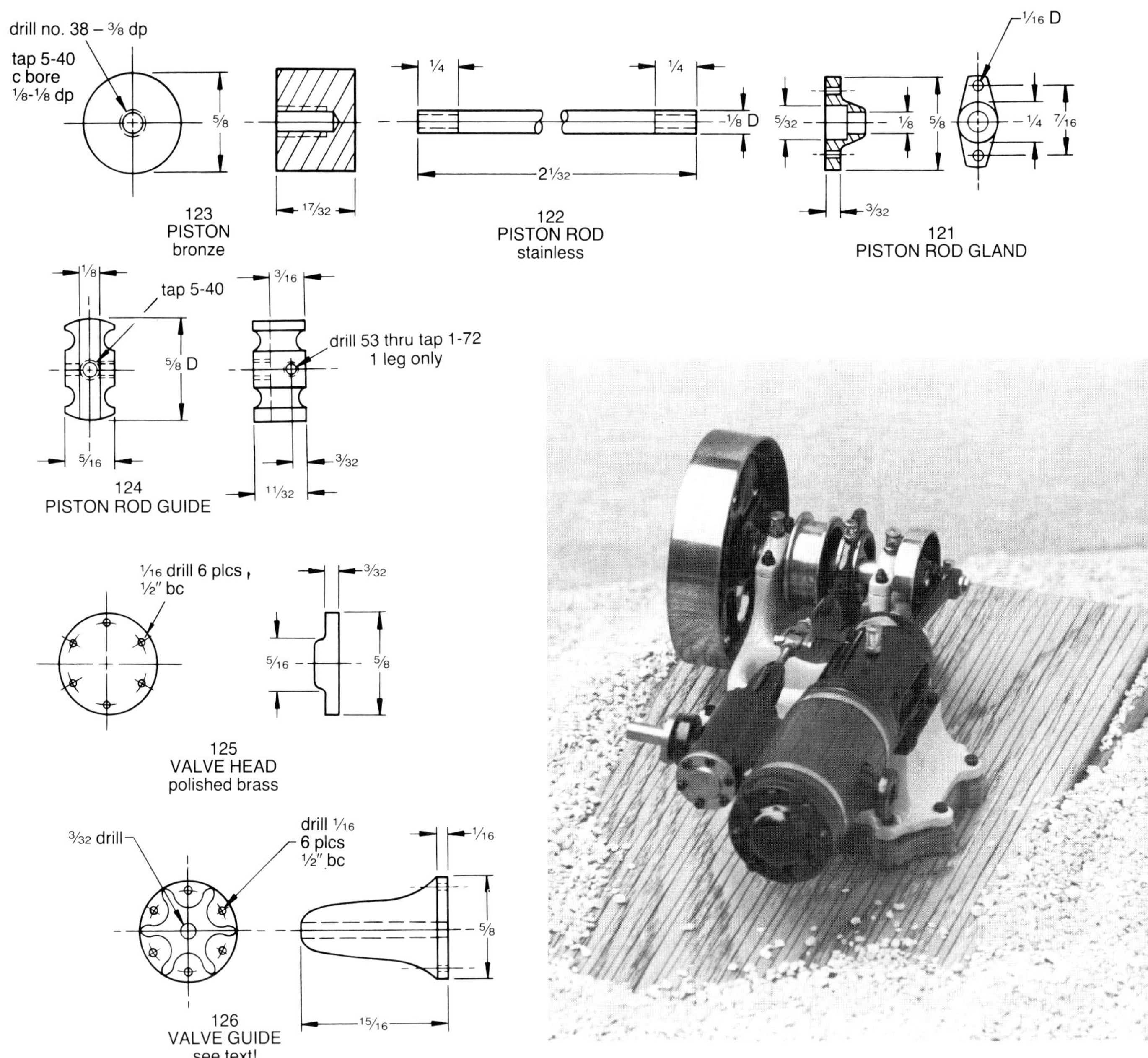

Mount the assembly in the vise with the passage block up. Drill 3/32" diameter through the two ports holes, about halfway into the valve cylinder (115). Use a 4-40 screw and nut to fasten the exhaust fitting in place. Wire or clamp the valve assembly in position to avoid stud holes. I used a wire hose clamp. Use *Easyflo* to silver solder the lot together. Pickle and clean.

Now is a good time to use the soft solder bit (the same method as used on the base) on the valve assembly and the trunk. Clean with soap and water.

Mount the cylinder in the four-jaw as close to center as you can get it, and bore the cylinder out to 5/8" diameter. Use the heaviest boring bar you can get into the hole to get a good finish. *Don't remove the cylinder!*

Attach the trunk to the cylinder, and bore it out to 5/8" diameter, 1 15/32" deep, flat bottom. Center drill and drill 1/8" diameter through the solid end. Lightly countersink the 1/8" hole and put a slight chamfer on the bore of the trunk. Disassemble.

Drill the angled holes 3/32" diameter from each end of the cylinder into the valve passages. Be careful lining it up and mill or file a small flat to aid starting the drill. Make the Valve Cylinder Head (125).

The valve cylinder should be as parallel to the cylinder bore as you can get it. Mount the cylinder in the lathe or use the drill press. Drill and ream the cylinder 5/16" all the way through. While the cylinder is still mounted (I drilled mine), clamp the cylinder head in place – avoid the passageway – and drill 3/64" for the head bolts. Remove the head and tap the holes 0-80. Whenever I have to drill matching holes, I drill the first part tap size and use it to drill the matching holes. Then I drill it out to clearance size.

Mark the Piston Valve, **127**, a close sliding fit in the valve cylinder. A couple of shallow interference grooves could be cut into the outboard ends. Make the Valve Rod, **128**.

Putting the flat bolt seats at the cylinder end of the Valve Rod Guide, **126**, was solved by drilling the bolt holes 1⁄16″ diameter, 7⁄8″ deep, in the end of a 3⁄4″ rod. Then using a 3⁄16″ bit (modified into a counterbore), drill 13⁄16″ deep. The rod was then placed in the lathe and turned to 5⁄8″ diameter. Cutting the flowing shape leaves the flutes exposed. The valve rod hole should be drilled while the guide is still in the lathe. All that remains to be done on the guide is to part off, leaving the 1⁄16″ flange, and sand or file the sharp edges (Dremel sanding disk).

Assemble the piston and rod, insert into the valve cylinder, slide the guide onto the rod to locate and mark the bolt holes. Drill and tap these 0-80 also.

Fabricate the Valve Rod, **130**. Silver solder the 3⁄32″ steel rod into a piece of 3⁄16″ brass, 1½″ × 1¼″ or so. Mark out the center and overall shape. Saw off the cap. Soft solder the cap back in its original position. Check your layout and rough cut and file to shape. Mount the rod on your faceplate and bore the 5⁄8″ ID. The rod was mounted on a stub mandrel to clean up the faces and cut the registers. Tap drill 3⁄64″ for the bolts. Counterbore the cap 3⁄16″ diameter. File and sand to shape. Drill no. 53 for the oil cup, and thread the rod 2-56 if you haven't already done so. Melt off the cap, clean up both parts, and tap for the bolts and the oil cup. Drill the cap out to clearance size and bolt it in place. Make the Cam, **132**, to fit the rod. It's easier to fit the shaft to the hole than vice versa. Make the Coupling, **129**.

The Drive Pulley, **139**, could be made much plainer than shown. You can't see enough of it to justify the fancy web when it's all assembled.

The Crank Disk, **134**, Crankpin, **135**, and Crankpin Bolt, **136**, can now be manufactured. The crank disk was fabricated by turning to shape, disregarding the boss for the pin. The crankpin center was then laid out and drilled ¼″. A ¼″ stub of rod was then silver soldered into the hole. Try to build up nice fillets. The slots were cut by drill-

The pulley I used to make the Fly Wheel, **141**, was drilled for a setscrew and mounted on a short shaft for turning between centers. I turned the flanges off, then shaped the hub and web. The spokes were cut by drilling the corners of the cut out areas, sawing between the holes, and then shaping the spokes by filing and using the Dremel tool.

The crankshaft is simply a length of ¼″ stainless rod. The crank disk key is a 1-72 screw with the head cut off and a screwdriver slot cut in the end. I pressed the disk on the shaft, then drilled and tapped on the joint line. The crankpin bolt, 136, was cut from a hex key and the washer came from the junk box.

The Connecting Rod, **137**, is manufactured by laying out the centers on a 1″ overlong piece of ¼″ × 3⁄8″ brass. Lay out the first pin hole ½″ from one end. Drill both pin holes, center drill each end and mount between centers for turning the taper. Use a sharp cutter and keep it on center, or you may make a pretzel out of it! The ends are turned down somewhat, sawn off, and filed to finish shape.

Make the Guide, **124**, by turning

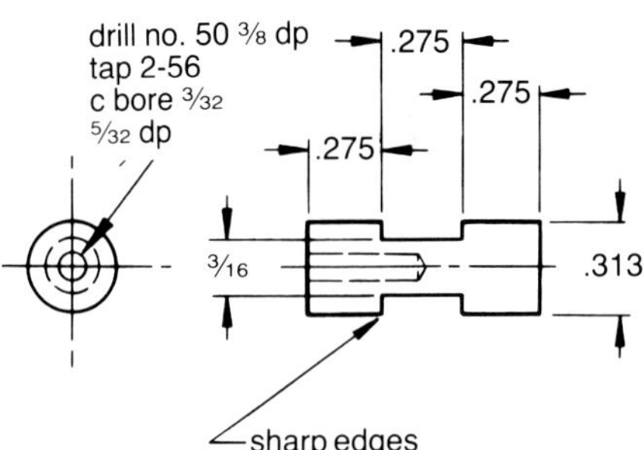

127
PISTON VALVE
close sliding fit in valve chamber
stainless

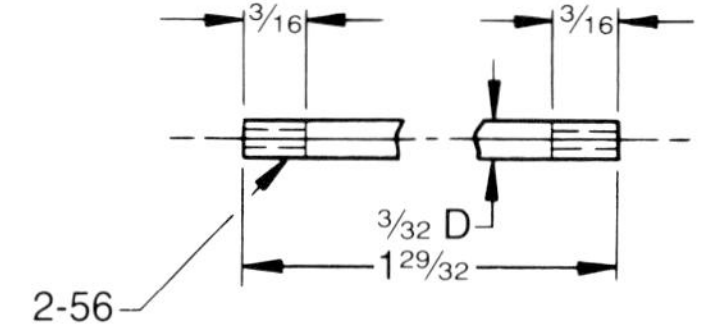

128
PISTON VALVE ROD
stainless

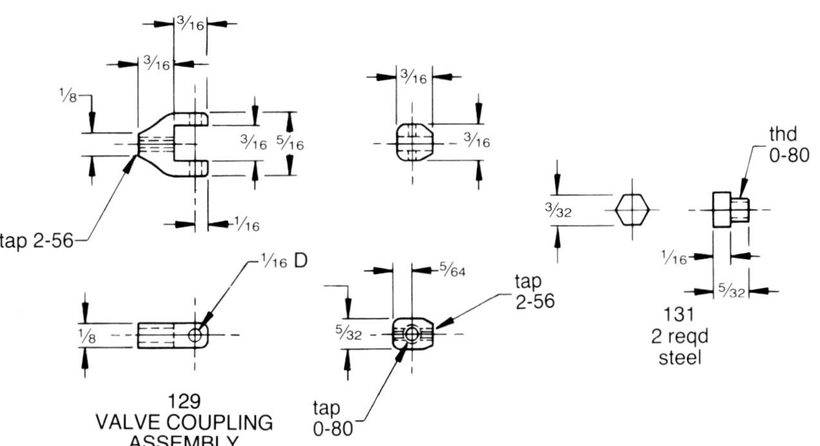

129
VALVE COUPLING
ASSEMBLY

131
2 reqd
steel

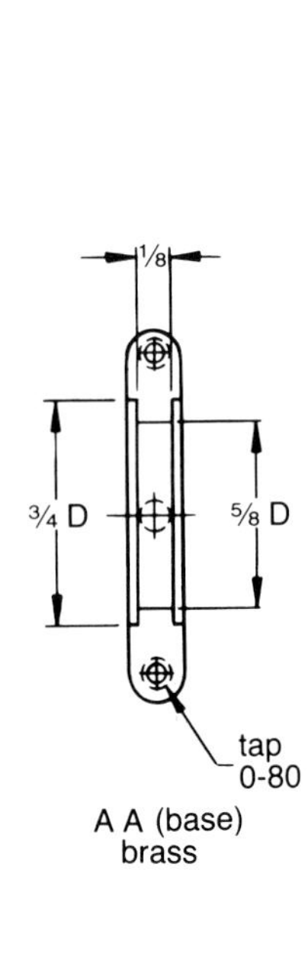

A A (base)
brass

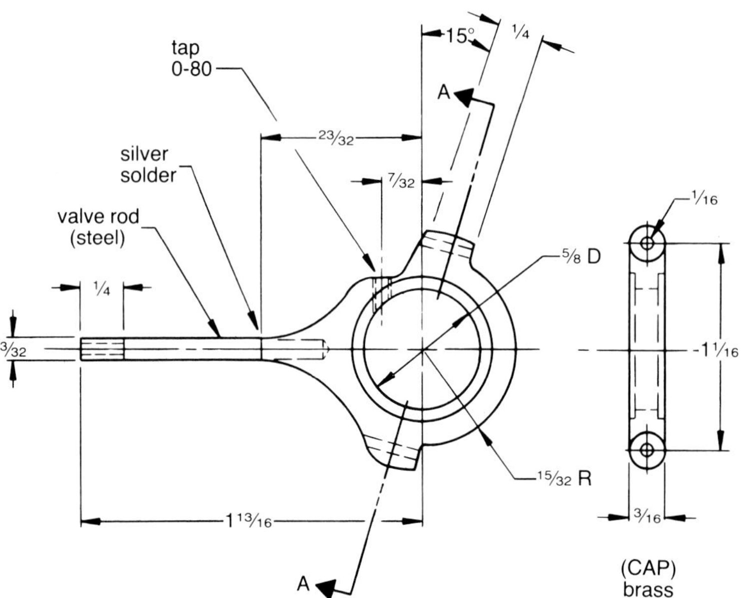

(CAP)
brass

130
COMPLETE VALVE ROD
brass

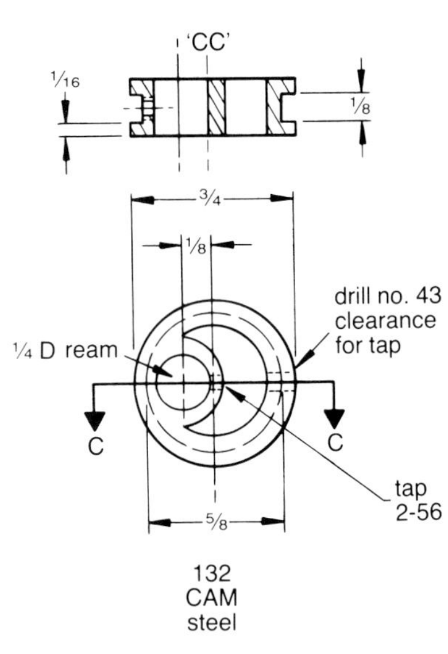

132
CAM
steel

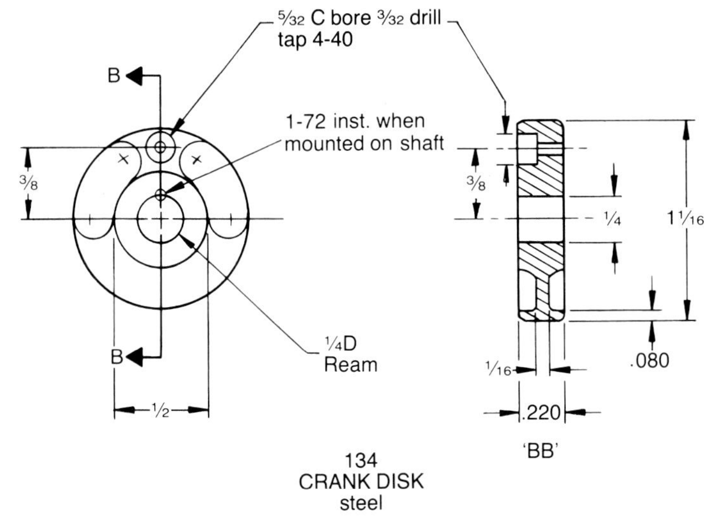

'BB'

134
CRANK DISK
steel

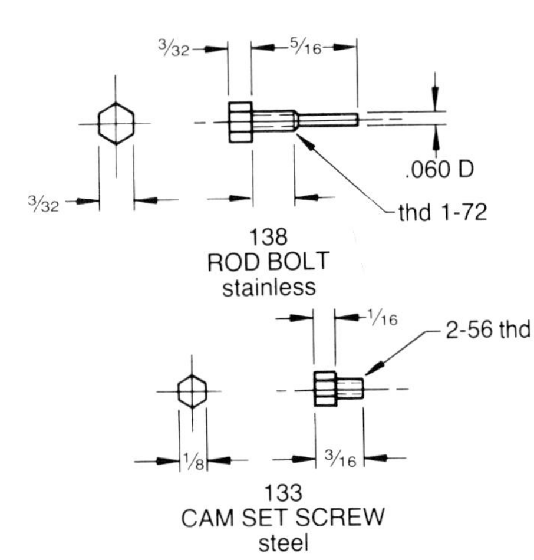

138
ROD BOLT
stainless

133
CAM SET SCREW
steel

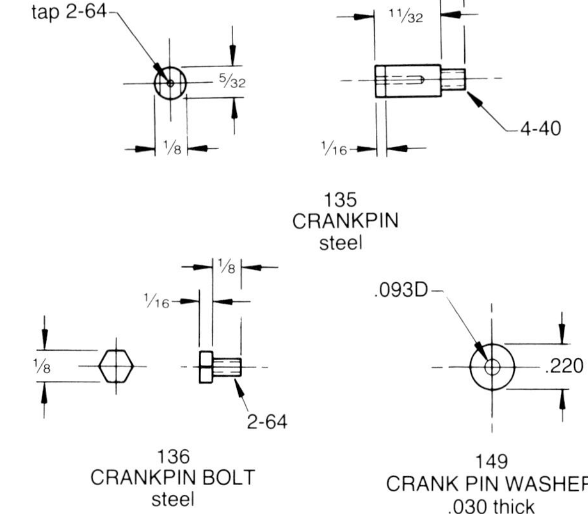

135
CRANKPIN
steel

136
CRANKPIN BOLT
steel

149
CRANK PIN WASHER
.030 thick

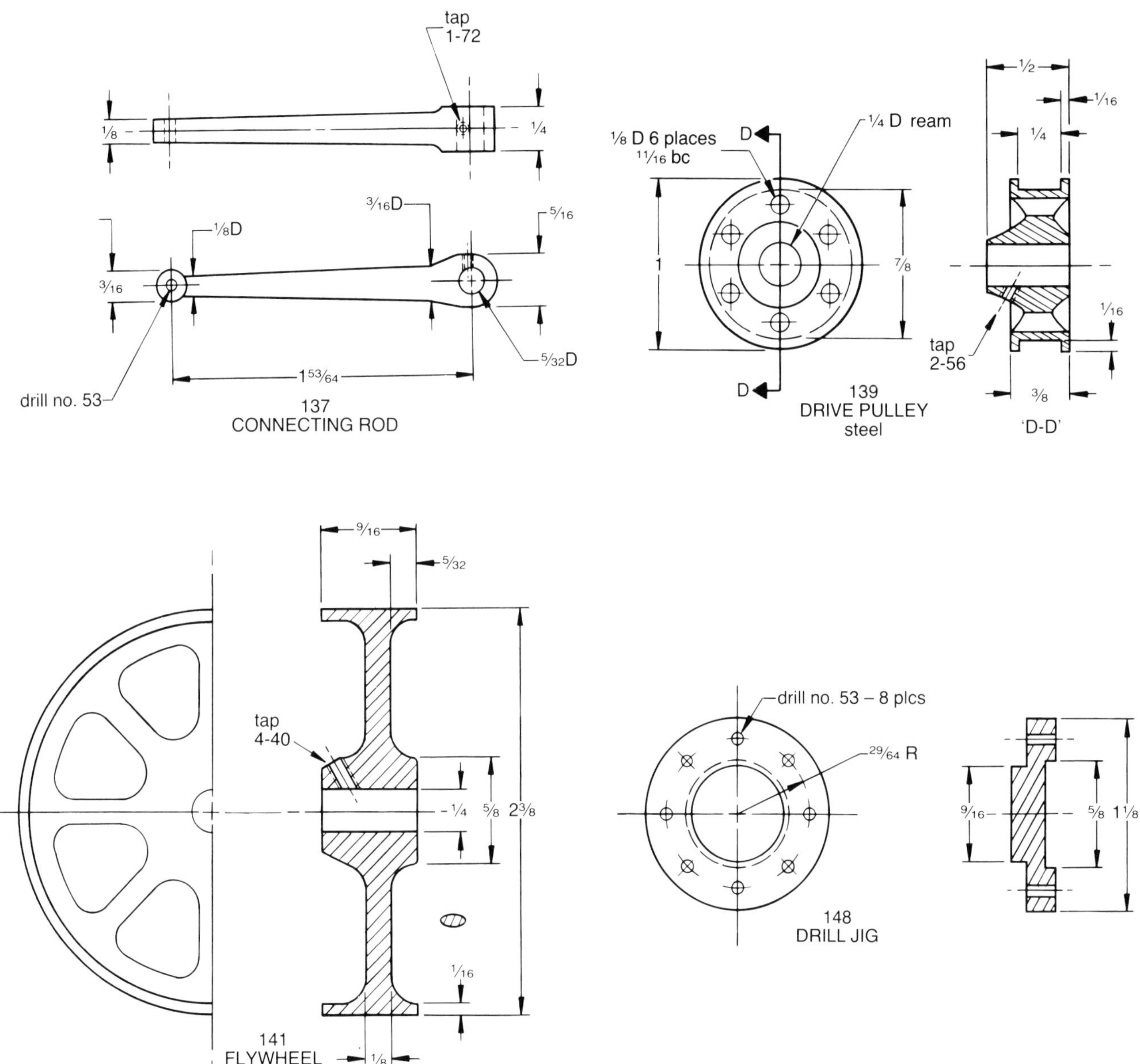

137
CONNECTING ROD

139
DRIVE PULLEY
steel

141
FLYWHEEL

148
DRILL JIG

a piece of brass to 5/8″ diameter, drilling no. 38, and tapping 5-40. To get the rod-receiving slot at right angles to the rod bolt, put the 5/8″ rod in the mill vise (horizontal) with the slot end sticking out the side of the vise. Drill no. 53 right through on center. Don't remove the workpiece. Exchange the drill for a slitting saw. Saw 1/8″ off the top and bottom of the rod. Saw the slot 3/16″ deep on center. Remove the piece from the mill, mark the finish length and saw off close to the line. File to finish shape – use a rattail to cut the grooves. Tap one leg 1-72.

Make the Piston Rod, **122**, the Piston, **123**, and the Piston Rod Gland, **121**. Screw the rod into the guide and insert into the trunk. Slide the gland onto the rod from the cylinder end, and spot the stud holes. Disassemble. Drill and tap 0-80 right through and countersink lightly. Put a drop of *Loctite* near the head of 5/16″ long 0-80 and screw it into the hole (from the cylinder side). This was the easiest way I could think of to put studs in the bottom of a deep recess. The Connecting Rod Bolt, **138**, was also made from a hex key.

Temporarily assemble the engine, lightly clamp the trunk on the pedestal, and adjust its position so everything turns smoothly. When you are satisfied that all is well, mark the mounting bolt holes on the pedestal. Disassemble, drill the pedestal No. 53 and tap 1-72.

There are two sizes of oil cups (**Figure 3**) to be fabricated; three cups have a 2-56 base and are slightly larger overall than the other two with 1-72 bases. The drawings show the smaller one. Construction is the same for both sizes.

We'll need something to hold the bases for machining and polishing, so make a threaded bushing by putting a 1" long piece of 1/2" brass rod in the collet. Center drill, drill no. 53 and tap 1-72. Reverse the piece in the collet and drill no. 50 to connect with the 1-72 end. Tap 2-56.

It's best to make the bases (**142**) first, then the glass tube (**143**), and finally the cap (**144**). Turn a 1/4" brass rod down to 1/8" diameter for approximately 1/2". Turn the end down to 0.073 for 1/4". Use a tailstock die holder and thread 1-72. By reversing the die, you can get a thread or more closer to the shoulder.

Be careful – you don't want to break the stem off in the die! If you do happen to break one off, use an Exacto knife to cut a slot in the stub, and back it out with a small screwdriver.

Use the Dremel with a cutoff disk to cut the stem to 3/32" long, and put a small chamfer on the end. Center drill and drill no. 69, 3/16" deep. Place a rag across the ways and cut off the base 1/16" beyond the shoulder. Machine all the bases to this stage.

Obtain a length of 1/4" or 3/16" glass lab tubing. Place your propane torch so the flame is horizontal. Hold the tubing vertically and move it into the flame so that about 1" is below the flame. Rotate the tube slowly; as it begins to glow and stretch, move it away from the flame a little. Keep rotating the tube and keep it vertical. When it has stretched out to a shape something like the one in Figure 3, move it out of the flame and let it cool. Keep it vertical! It will harden in less than a minute, although it will still be hot.

FIGURE 3
OIL CUPS
see text

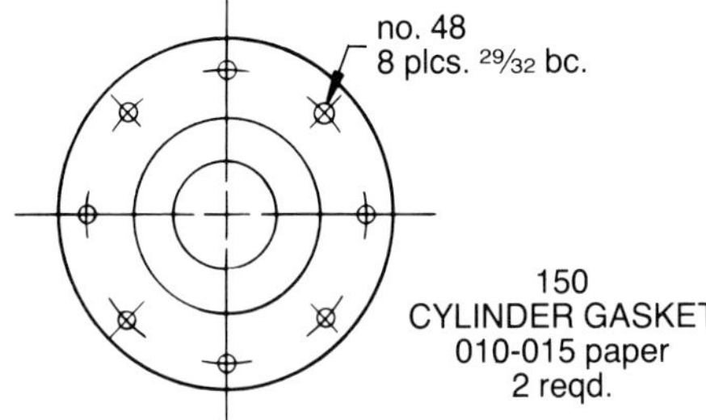

150
CYLINDER GASKET
010-015 paper
2 reqd.

Measure the diameter along the stretched portion. Use a grease pencil or marking pen to mark the small end (about a 3/32" diameter is needed to fit into the base). Nick the tubing with a triangular file – a couple of strokes just hard enough to cut into the surface will do. Snap it off between thumb and forefinger. Cut it long because it probably won't break square. Use a file, grinding wheel or carborundum paper to square the end. Cut the larger end in the same manner. Measure the diameter of the small end.

Put a base in the threaded bushing we made earlier and drill into the end with the next larger size drill – just until it cuts its full diameter. I reground an old bit to cut the flat bottom, leaving

a recess for the tube to fit into. If your recess is too tight, enlarge it; if it's too loose, shorten the tube.

Since stretching the tubing is not a very precise operation, the sizes required may vary somewhat from the drawing. Just make any necessary adjustments and keep the matching parts together.

To make the caps, turn a rod about 30 thou larger than the larger end of the tube. Put a 1/32″ deep recess for the tube in the end, and drill no. 50 about 1/8″ deep.

Now it gets a little tricky. I tried using a regular cutoff tool with no success – it either collapsed the cap, or left it too ragged to use. Anyhow, I ended up using the trusty Dremel and a cutoff disk to cut the cap off 1/16″ long. Don't forget the rag across the ways!

To assemble the oil cups, use a small amount of silicone sealant (bathtub caulk) on the end of the tube and push it into the base. Wipe off any excess and try not to get any sealer inside the tube. The cap is attached in the same manner.

All of this tedious work becomes worthwhile when you can admire such a tiny, yet functional, oil cup. So persevere! The lagging was made by turning a piece of hardwood to 1 5/32″ diameter, 1 5/8″ long, and boring out to 3/4″ ID. To simulate individual boards, turn a threading bit 90° counterclockwise to normal. By feeding the cutter into the wood and moving the carriage back and forth, cut small horizontal grooves about 3/16″ apart, all around the cylinder. Cut the cylinder in half lengthwise, and carve, file and sand to fit closely around the cylinder. The bands are 3/32″ wide strips of 0.015″ brass sheet, triple folded on one end and soft soldered to get enough thread depth for the 0-80 hex head screws.

Most of the fasteners (packaged by Wm. K. Walthers, Inc.) can be purchased at a model train shop. I am stubborn, so I made mine. Appliance enamel was used to paint the engine. It gives a smooth, tough, high-gloss finish, but it's tricky to use on such small stuff.

Polish everything that isn't going to be painted, and finish assembling the engine. Don't forget the gaskets (**150**), and pack the piston rod gland with graphited asbestos yarn. To adjust the valve, set the high point of the cam even with the crankpin, and adjust in small increments to get the best running position.

I hope you enjoy "Scrapbox" as much as I have.

A Three-cylinder Oscillating Steam Engine

By Samuel K. Hodgson

Photos by Author

I have always been fascinated with small oscillating cylinder steam engines. In my collection, I have several single cylinder engines, so this time, I thought I would enjoy making one with three cylinders from some of the scrap material around my shop.

This simple little steam engine is fun to make, and not very complicated. Perhaps the most difficult part is drilling the steam passages in the main plate.

I'd suggest you start with the Base (Part 3), which can be wood or metal – I made mine from one piece of steel, but you could use a press-fitted pin, if desired. The Flywheel (Part 4) can be either brass or steel. If you have the brass material, that would be my choice – highly polished.

I made my cylinders from aluminum, but you could use steel or brass. They must be made of a different material than the Part 6 and 7 Pistons. I'd suggest you make the cylinders of aluminum and the pistons from brass. You will note the pistons are two types, in order to fit on the crankpin.

The three springs can be purchased, and reworked to fit. The Caps (Part 9) look good made from brass, and then polished. All of the aluminum parts should be highly polished, starting with various grades of emery paper, and then using *Scotch-Brite* and *Simichrome*. You can easily attain a mirror finish. The combination of the aluminum and brass parts makes a beautiful model.

Of course, it will run in either direction, depending on where you apply the air or steam pressure.

whichever you may have around. Next, fabricate the Main Plate (Part 1). I used .625" aluminum plate. The steam passages must be carefully laid out as shown, and drilled 5/32" diameter. Next, drill and ream the ten holes in the face of the plate, as required. I suggest using air pressure to check if the passages are clear and connect where necessary.

If this checks out, then it is time to plug the ten places as shown with drive fit plugs. Add the two inlet and exhaust holes in the sides of the plate. These are tapped 5/16-24. Then make the brass bushing (Part 2), and press into place. Re-ream the .375" hole after the press fit. You will notice the hole coordinates for all holes in the face are given in case you drill these on your milling machine.

Then start on the Crankshaft (Part 8).

Bill of Materials

PART	NO. REQ'D	NAME	MATERIAL
1	1	Main plate	aluminum
2	1	Bushing	brass
3	1	Base	wood or metal
4	1	Flywheel	brass or steel
5	3	Cylinder	aluminum
6	1	Piston	brass
7	2	Piston	brass
8	1	Crankshaft	steel
9	1	Cap	brass
10	1	Spring	steel
11	3	Bolt	6-32 × 3/4" Allen head
12	4	Bolt	8-32 × 3/4" Allen head
13	1	Setscrew	10-24 × .25" Allen head

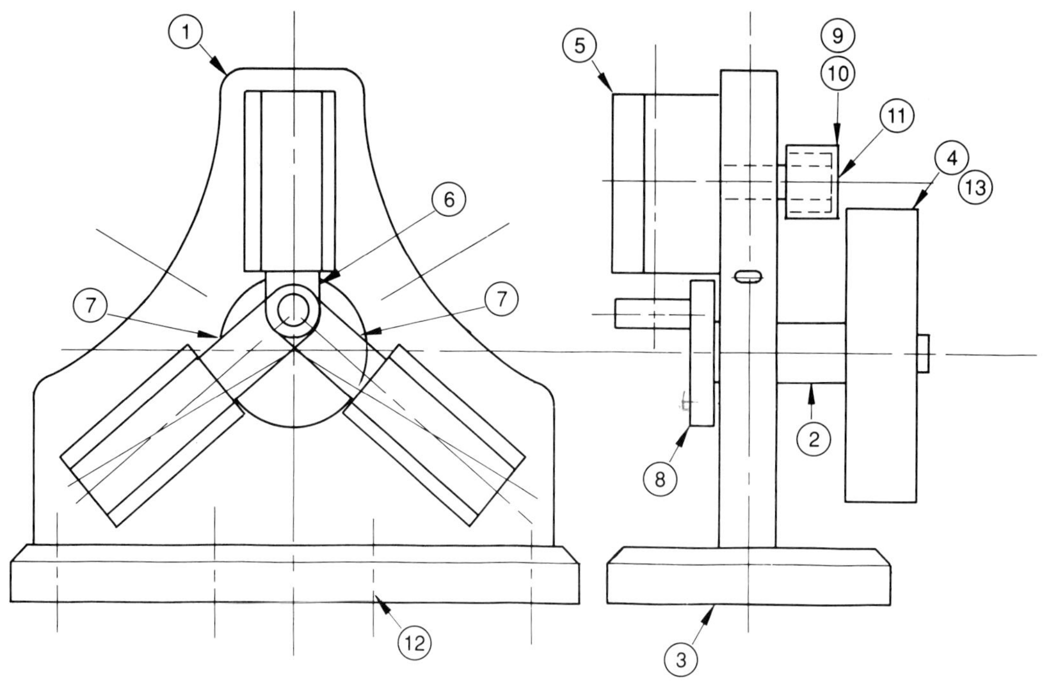

1
2
3
4
5
6
7
7
8
9
10
11
12
13

.180
.180
.080
.080
1.50
12°
.625" R
56°
60°
drill "I" (.272")
tap 5⁄16-24
drill No. 50 (.070")
oil holes
3.25" R
1.750
15°
ream .500"
4.875
30°
.250" R
2.00
1.50
drive fit plugs
10 places
1.892
2.178
ream
.375"
drill No. 30 (.128") × .50"
tap 8-32
drill 5⁄32"
all steam passages
.625
.251
1.666
1.666
1.666
.251
.156
.156
5.50
1.531
.656
drill No. 50
(.070") oil
ream .375"
.750" dia.
.180
.180
MAIN PLATE 1 aluminum
BUSHING 2 brass

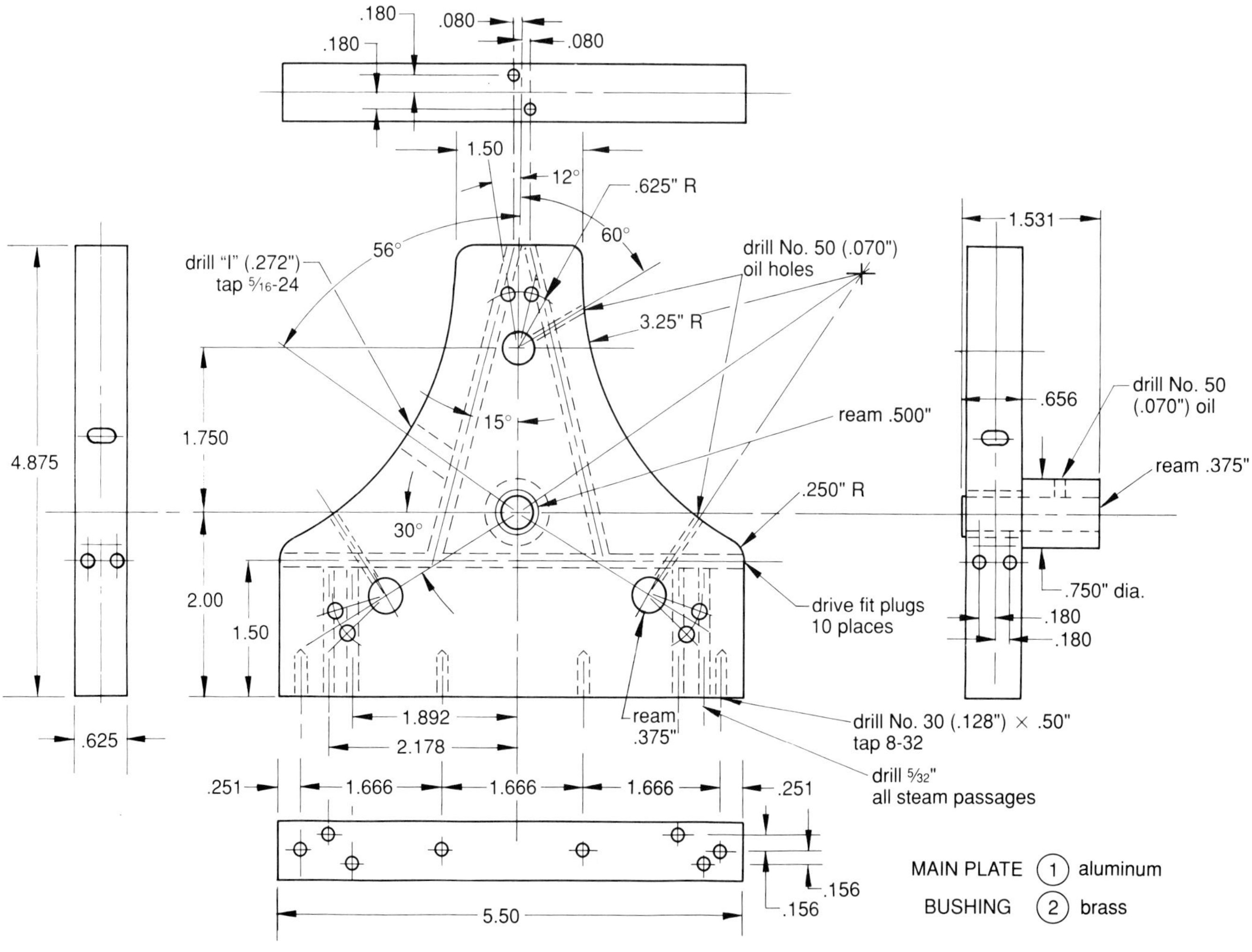

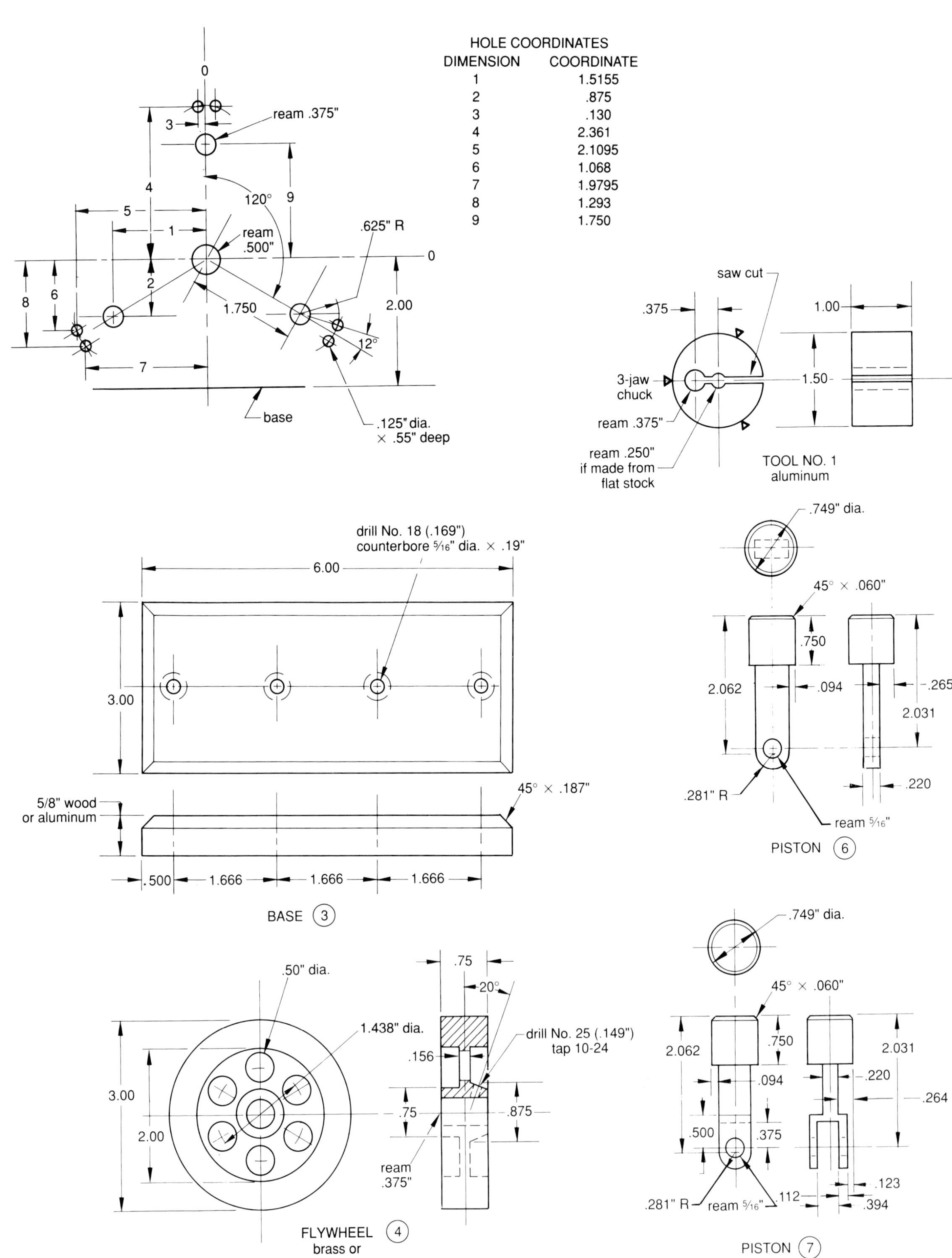
HOLE COORDINATES
DIMENSION COORDINATE
1 1.5155
2 .875
3 .130
4 2.361
5 2.1095
6 1.068
7 1.9795
8 1.293
9 1.750
0
ream .375"
3
4
120°
9
5
1
ream .500"
.625" R
0
8
6
2
1.750
2.00
12°
7
base
.125" dia. × .55" deep
saw cut
.375
1.00
3-jaw chuck
1.50
ream .375"
ream .250" if made from flat stock
TOOL NO. 1
aluminum
.749" dia.
drill No. 18 (.169")
counterbore 5/16" dia. × .19"
6.00
45° × .060"
.750
3.00
2.062
.094
.265
2.031
45° × .187"
.281" R
.220
5/8" wood or aluminum
ream 5/16"
.500
1.666
1.666
1.666
PISTON 6
BASE 3
.749" dia.
.75
.50" dia.
20°
45° × .060"
1.438" dia.
drill No. 25 (.149")
tap 10-24
.156
2.062
.750
2.031
3.00
.75
.875
.094
.220
.264
2.00
.500
.375
ream .375"
.123
.281" R
ream 5/16"
.112
.394
FLYWHEEL 4
brass or steel
PISTON 7

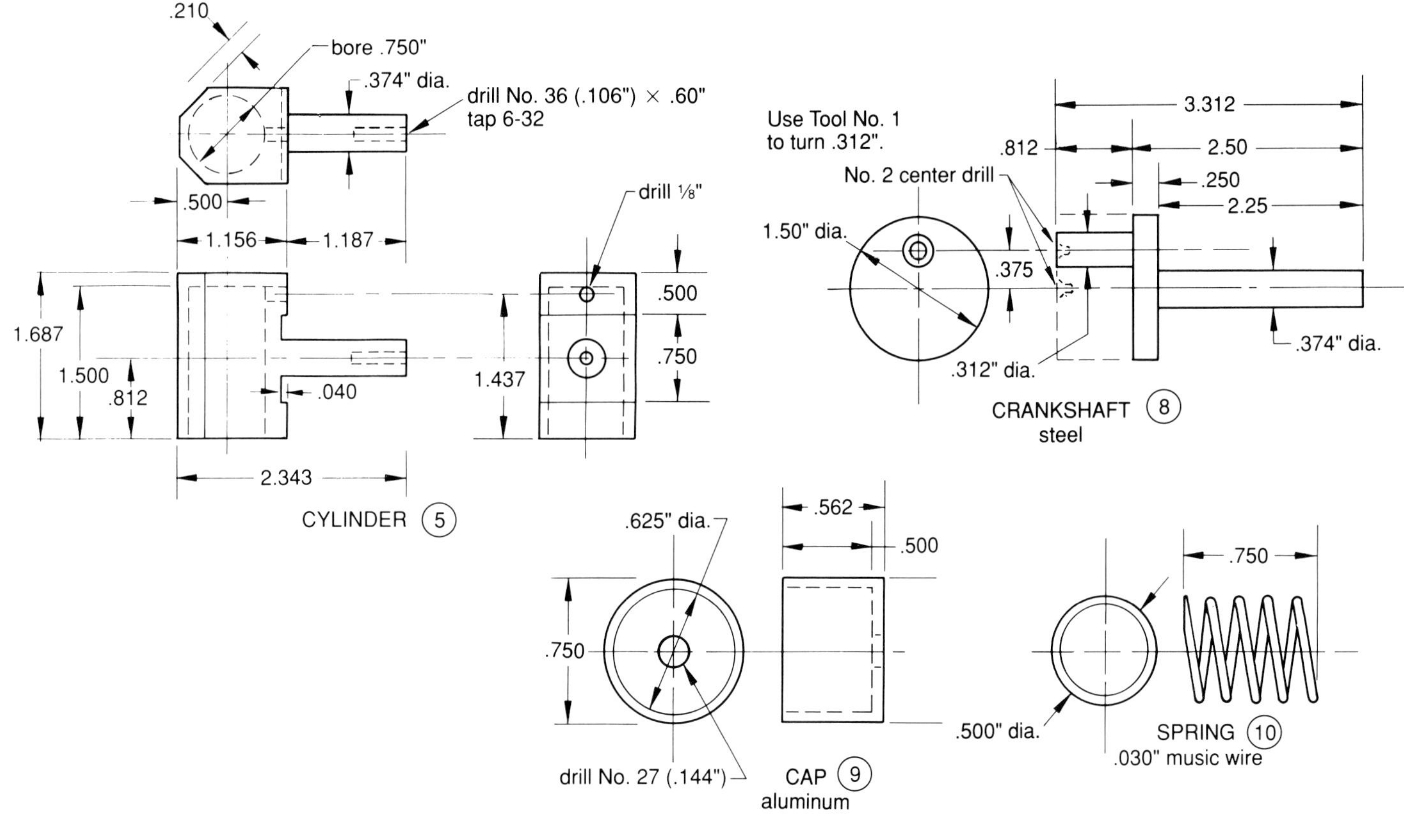
.210
bore .750"
.374" dia.
drill No. 36 (.106") × .60"
tap 6-32
.500
1.156
1.187
drill ⅛"
.500
.750
1.437
1.687
1.500
.812
.040
2.343
CYLINDER 5
Use Tool No. 1
to turn .312".
3.312
.812
2.50
No. 2 center drill
.250
2.25
1.50" dia.
.375
.374" dia.
.312" dia.
CRANKSHAFT 8
steel
.562
.625" dia.
.500
.750
.750
drill No. 27 (.144")
CAP 9
aluminum
.500" dia.
SPRING 10
.030" music wire

Brasso

A Small Beam Engine

By W. Marshall Black

Photos and drawing by the Author

Brasso is a decorative, working replica of a beam engine. There were no preliminary drawings. It was made up as I went along, following recollections of an old model once seen in a London shop. The size was dictated by odds and ends of brass from my scrap box. The sketch included here was made after completion. Working without drawings is a recreation for me – I can do what I please. But to do this, parts *must* be built in a logical sequence.

Brasso is about a 30-hour project. If you would like to go at it, but have no scrap box, I've included a bill of materials. Many advertisers in ***Live Steam*** will sell you short lengths of stock. I've tried to indicate the minimum lengths needed, but why not get a foot of every size? Then you, too, will have a scrap box. The power tools used were a 6" Atlas lathe with milling attachment, drill press, belt sander, and polishing wheel.

Brasso has been run so far only on air. Slowest smooth speed is about 100 rpm at 15 psi. This is a bit fast. A slower speed could be achieved with a larger flywheel, and this would be more faithful.

This little engine has instantly appealed to all who have seen it on my desk. Why is this? First, I think, is the use of polished brass – this says it is a decorative replica, not an authentic scale duplicate. In short, the model is a sort of unpretentious cartoon. Second, the free architectural turnings seem to speak of an earlier time; aside from a few clues, the thing could be passed off as being 200 years old. Third, the overall proportions seem right. The yoke-tenons are a bit grotesque, but even this adds to the appeal. If too perfect, a model becomes like a watch – beyond the ken of most viewers. Finally, a comment on designing and building out of your mind's eye rather than drawings: This is not exactly a beginner's sport, but if you have been a good observer over the years, it is a most enjoyable and challenging thing to do.

The flywheel disk has been faced, drilled and reamed, and a recess cut to form the rim and hub. A scant 1/32" of stock still connects rim and hub.

The spoke holes have been drilled through the rim and into the hub, spokes inserted, and soft soldered in.

You might begin with the Flywheel (**1**). I began this without any idea that I was going to make a beam engine – a disk of 2¾" diameter × ½" brass in the scrap box just seemed to want to be turned into a spoked wheel. Chuck the stock and face off both sides. Then cut out the annular recess between rim and hub as shown in **Photo 1**. The recess must be deeper than the finished wheel thickness. Drill and ream 3/16". Divide the rim into eight equal divisions and scribe lightly. Remove from the chuck and center punch the rim at these eight divisions and on the finished center line. Drill 3/32" for the spokes right through the rim and just into the hub. Insert the spokes and soft solder (**Photo 2**). Note that the hub and rim are still part of the original stock. Next rechuck with the flat face of the stock outward, and skim off the excess

The wheel has been chucked with the flush face out; the excess thickness has been faced off, exposing the spokes and hub. The hub should project a bit on both sides.

The finished flywheel. It has been dressed by chucking on the shaft. Loctite 271 was used to secure wheel to shaft.

The column base is being tapped ¼-32. Note the "free" turning to produce a contoured architectural form.

thickness, exposing the spokes as seen in **Photo 3**. Then chuck a length of 3⁄16″ diameter steel shaft, cut long, slip on the wheel and secure with *Loctite* 271. Let the lathe run at speed to assure a concentric set. Finally, finish up the rim with light cuts which also remove the spoke nubbins; form the hub OD and the inside of the rim and you are done (**Photo 4**). A beam engine should have a very large flywheel; one 3¾″ diameter would not be excessive on this model, if you have the stock. But you may need an aircraft drill to penetrate the hub.

Somehow my finished flywheel recalled to mind a very old brass beam engine I had once admired. Subconscious at work? In a flash I inventoried my brass scraps and saw that everything was there for a beam engine.

The Cylinder Barrel (**2**) came next out of ¾″ diameter stock. Drill the piston rod hole 3⁄32″, then drill and ream ⅜″ about 1½″ deep. The stroke is going to be 1″. The extra depth allows for piston thickness and threads for the Base or Head (**3**). The entire exterior shape had to be finished before cutoff because of the varying OD's. This is a pitfall of working without plans, but if you get cornered there is usually a way out.

The bore was lightly lapped using an underside bar of ⅜″ diameter mounted in the tailstock chuck. Beware of seizing here. Finally a 7⁄16-20 tap was run in about ¼″ making just enough threads. The base or head (3) was turned up free-form out of 1″ diameter stock. Become an artist here – imagine you're forming the base for an architectural column. This nicety will set your model apart from the crowd. The maximum OD of the base should be about ⅞″.

On to the Main Column. The Base (**4**) is a larger version of the cylinder base (3). The maximum OD is 1″. Follow the same style closely. **Photo 5** shows this piece being tapped ¼-32. Note the outer (upper) OD has been left cylindrical so it can be reverse-chucked to face off the bottom and tap 4-40. The contouring of this cylindrical portion can be done when mounted on the mating Column Shaft (**5**). The column shaft should have a pleasing contour. Form this by turning sections to increasingly smaller OD, then smooth out the ledges with a flat file. Again, form the capital as a rough miniature of the base. Leave a little peg for registering when soldering to the top bearing.

The Column-top Bearing (**6**) was milled from ½″ square stock using my new milling attachment; this was so

Cylinder, Column, Flywheel, and Baseplate. The column top bearing has been roughed out by milling.

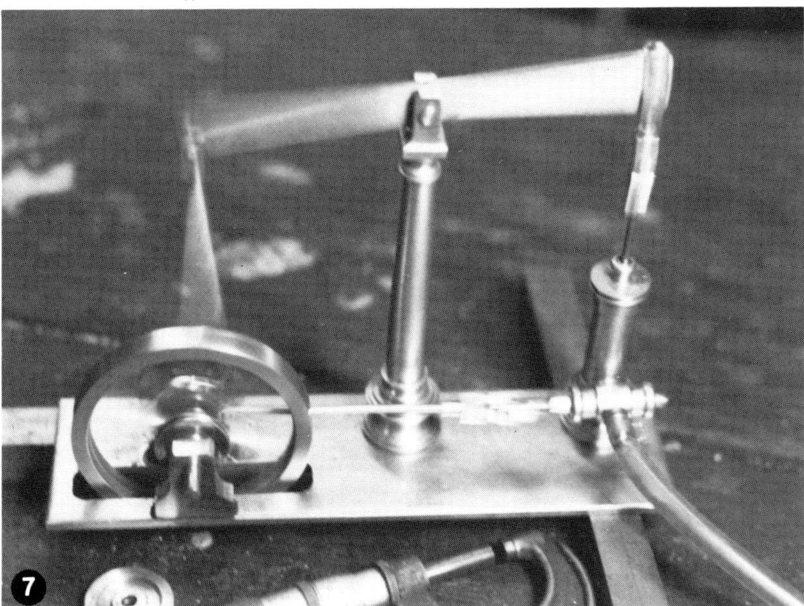

A most happy moment – first test. Photo at 1/15 sec, f-2, with 100w light bulb. (I'm not a camera bug.)

easy I had to stop and reminisce how things like this had been formed for over 25 years with hacksaw and file. (I've never been blessed with elaborate tooling.)

Photo 6 was taken about this point, nine hours into the project. A suitable Base Plate (7) had been found of 1/8 × 2 × 7⅜" plate. A little narrower than desirable, but a bird in hand... Besides, 2" is the maximum vertical width in the clamping space of the milling attachment, a coincidence that would make easy the cutting of the slot for the flywheel. It was at this time that the entire finished engine look shaped in my mind.

A Beam (**8**) length of 5½" was dictated by the baseplate length – real engineering. The beam was sawed from 1/8 × ½" bar and is shaped like an elongated diamond. I went too fast here; it should be more like an elongated ellipse. Soft, hand-generated lines are always preferable, and would have been more authentic, also.

With the beam in hand, the approximate center distances between crankshaft, column and cylinder were marked out, and attention shifted to mounting the flywheel. A bar of ¼ × 1" brass looked likely for the Main Bearing Pedestals (**9**). By happy coincidence, if the shaft center were ¾" up from the baseplate this would correspond nicely to the height of the steam "chest" center line and permit it to be soft soldered to the cylinder without interference with the cylinder base (3). In other words, the eccentric rod would be level at the extreme valve stroke as shown in the sketch. So the bar went into the milling attachment and three deep U-shaped notches were cut with a ½" end mill. These formed the profile of the main bearing pedestals in side view. The two Pedestals (**9**) apeared when the bottoms of the U notches were sawed through. They were clamped together for drilling and reaming 3/16".

The Steam Chest (**10**) was turned up from ½" diameter stock, cut off 1" long, then rechucked for drilling and reaming 3/16" diameter. A length of 3/16" steel rod was lapped through, later to become the Valve Spindle (**20**). The steam chest (10) was held to the cylinder (2) with a spring clamp for generous soft soldering. The steam port was drilled through, about No. 55. On the off-cylinder side this hole was opened out for a 5-40 thread for the Inlet Nozzle (**11**).

Next came a bit of layout on the baseplate – to locate the pedestals, flywheel slot, and center line of the beam on the width. This was done working from right to left in the end view. The center line, marked A on the drawing at upper left, is of course also the center line of the column and cylinder marked A at lower right in the partial plan view. A fat 1/8" was allowed for the Eccentric (**13**) and, for no good reason, a fat 1/8" for a matching Inside Sheave (**12**). (Later this became the drive sheave for a Dummy Governor, **23**). Finally, 1/16" was thrown in for potential washers. All this, plus the flywheel hub width, set the distance between the main bearing pedestals. By good luck all would fit in on the 2" wide baseplate, and the eccentric rod could be nearly straight when viewed from the top. Who needs plans when he has faith?

The eccentric (13) was made from a nubbin of ¾" D steel – a flat, scant 1/8" thick. A scant 1/16" wide groove was cut on the periphery. The disk was offset 1/8" in the four-jaw, then drilled and reamed 3/16" to yield a ¼" valve stroke. The Eccentric Strap (**14**) was formed like a wedding ring from 1" D and is 1/8" wide. At opposite ends of a diameter, one hole was tapped 2-56 for a socket head Retaining Screw (**15**); the other was tapped 4-40 for the eccentric rod. Utter simplicity. The eccentric and the governor sheave were promptly fastened with *Loctite* to the

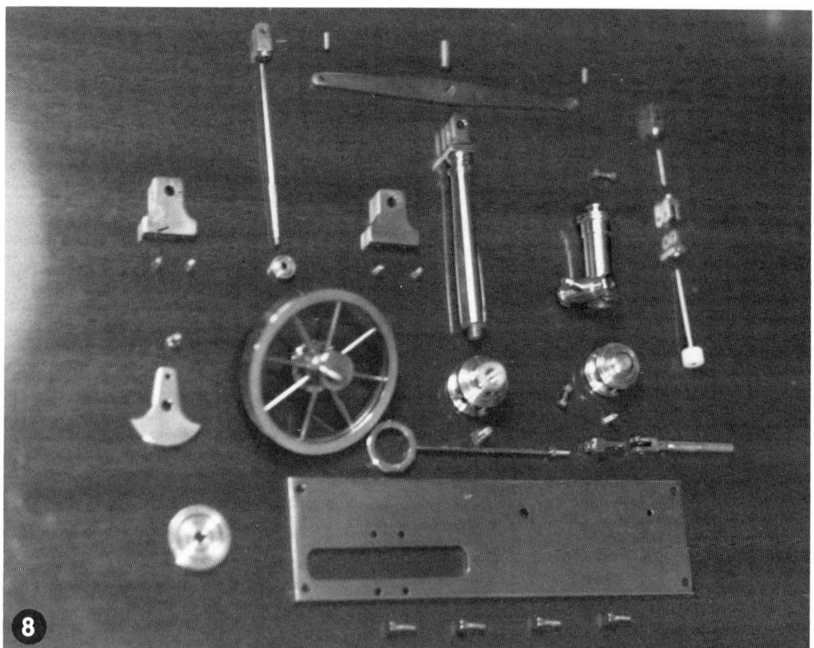

The basic kit ready to assemble – just bolt 'em together.

crankshaft. But there was an oversight here; see if you can see what it is before I tell you.

Time now to do some mounting (the groove in the baseplate for the flywheel had been milled). To save precise layout work, the mainbearing pedestals were strung on a temporary shaft and clamped to the baseplate in correct position. This lash-up was outlandish but the tap drill size for four 4-40 screws were drilled through the baseplate and into the pedestals with no doubt about future alignment. The beam was then drilled for its 3⁄16" main pin and two 1⁄8" pins, and served for final location of the baseplate holes for the column and cylinder.

The Crank Disk (**15**) was made from a disk of 1⅜" D, faced to about 1⁄8" thick, then drilled and reamed 3⁄16". It was then profiled as shown with saw, rotary file, and scraper, largely to add interest but also a little bit of counter weight. The crankpin was tapped 5-40, 1⁄2" off center for the 1" stroke. Then it dawned. I would have to set the timing by using setscrews on this crank, not the eccentric, because the latter was now permanently fixed. Oh well, a couple of 2-56 setscrews would fix that, even absent any bosses. (Who needs plans when he has faith?) We are now about 18 hours into the project.

I used to hate making yoke-tenon joints – all that sawing and filing. But these were fun with my new milling attachment. Two sets are required, one for the Eccentric Rod marked **16**, and one for the Piston Rod, marked **17**. The pins are 4-40 bolts having an unthreaded portion near the head. Similar Yokes (**18**) are made for the beam. The pins for these are 1⁄8" D and secured with 2-56 socket head setscrews in the beam. By the way, a nice and cheap assortment of small end mills and reamers is available from Kitts, a ***Live Steam*** advertiser.

The Connecting or Crank Rod (**19**) is formed from 3⁄16" D rod and tapped 4-40, male, each end. The length is determined from a measurement with the beam level and crank in mid stroke position. The Angular Link (**20**) is a bit of 3⁄32" D rod. This is threaded 4-40 on each end long enough to allow adjustment. A 4-40 thread is too large for 3⁄32" D (3-48 is too small) but it will work with *Loctite* help. Note that the tenon at the end of the piston rod is secured thereto with another 2-56 setscrew. The rod is 3⁄32" D steel, left long for now. The piston was turned from a bit of *Teflon*, but a string-packed version of steel would do fine. With the connecting rod mounted, crank disk setscrews tightened, piston and rod installed, the piston rod length is determined by visually observing where it should be cut so that the piston does not "bottom" or "top" out, while rotating the flywheel through 360°.

We now drill a secret port in the cylinder. It is shown at B on the drawing – use a No. 60. The engine works without this port, but it frees things up. Its purpose is to release pressure in the cylinder after the cutoff event when the bottom of the piston is at top dead center. A similar port is located at the top of the bore to avoid compression. The cylinder is now screwed to its base with a bit of *Permatex* to seal things up.

It remains to make the Valve Spindle (**20**) and Eccentric Rod (**21**). Make a trial valve spindle from the 3⁄16" D lapped stock mentioned earlier. It's about 1¾" long. Neck 1⁄2" of length down to take a 3-48 male thread. Screw this in the yoke of 16 and loosely lock with a jam nut. Now, with the main crank in the mid down stroke position shown on the drawing (180° ahead of the eccentric), the eccentric has reached maximum right-hand travel. Measure and cut the eccentric rod, 21; a slight offset bend may be required. The eccentric end is threaded 4-40 and fastened with *Loctite* into the eccentric strap. The

Crankside view of the basic kit assembled and on display.

A governor, pump rod, and guard fence have been added. The spoked power takeoff sheave was made as illustrated for the flywheel, except the spoke holes were drilled clear through, spokes inserted clear through, soldered, then drilled out again and reamed in the three-jaw.

other end is threaded 3-48 with a little extra length of thread to permit adjustment. This is screwed into the tenon.

Now adjust the valve spindle so that the point of its full 3⁄16" D is just flush with the left end of the steam chest – but at this time the spindle is not *in* the chest, but lying *on* top of it. A mark on the steam chest has been made at the port location. We must make two pencil marks on the valve spindle between which a groove will be cut to admit steam. Since the valve spindle is now at its right-hand-most travel, the left edge of the groove should be about centered on the port. Make a mark on the spindle. Observe the admission period by moving the flywheel, i.e., crank, through the 180° of the power side (left side) of one revolution. Admission should occur with the crank about 15° past its highest point, and cutoff about the same amount before the lowermost crank position. The latter spindle position relative to the admission port mark position determines the right boundary of the steam groove. The groove will be a scant 3⁄32" wide. The exhaust lip on the spindle is the end of a flat filed on the cylinder side of the spindle. The bridge should be about two port diameters wide. When events look okay, cut the groove, file the flat, and assemble. Be sure the crank is locked tightly to the shaft with the two 2-56 setscrews. Oil around. Hold the flywheel against the vee belt drive of some tool to exercise the new engine for a minute or two. All should move quite freely.

It's typically now 11:30 p.m. and you must rise at 5:30 a.m. to go to work, but who can resist a first trial on air. I love to watch a little engine make its first revolutions. After a minor adjustment or two she soon will be spinning merrily (**Photo 7**). You will probably watch it till 1 a.m. I'd never seen a beam engine work. The combination of movements up and down, side to side, wiggle and waggle is fascinating. Success at 25 hours into the project.

A walnut Wood Base (**22**) was shaped up using the drill press to rout out the flywheel groove with a ½" end mill. Some hex head 6-32 bolts were used for the tie-down – better looking than slotted wood screws. Now tear everything down, get out the *Brasso* and polishing disk and shine everything up. **Photo 8** shows the "kit" ready to assemble. **Photo 9** shows the engine on display. You can stop here or go ahead with a few more details.

Since I had made a governor sheave, I decided to make a Dummy

Governor (**23**). It really does nothing, but I'd seen one on the old antique – a really outsized one. The flyballs are .36 calibre lead pistol balls, but 3/8" D bronze balls would have been great (available from Saturated Steam, a ***Live Steam*** advertiser). The balls are secured with light music wire, about .015", and *Loctite*. A belt Fair-lead (**24**) will have to be made. The top is a loop of brass wire – tiny sheaves could be used now that I see just what angles the belt makes. The governor belt is presently a rubber band. Mickey Mouse, but I haven't found anything better.

Another touch was to add a Dummy Pump (**25**). Similar takeoffs appear on big engines and in this model, the pump rod adds to counter weight and makes for smoother operation. The final item was a little fence or guard for the crank – this, too, recalled from the antique. We are now 30 hours into the project.

Photos 10, 11 and **12** show the finished engine. A spoked power takeoff pulley was made, following the technique described for the flywheel. This is shown as item **26**. The polished brass was sprayed with a Brookstone lacquer to maintain the shine for a few years. I think the 1/8" globe valve (Cole's) is out of place here; it looks store-bought. But it is handy for a throttle.

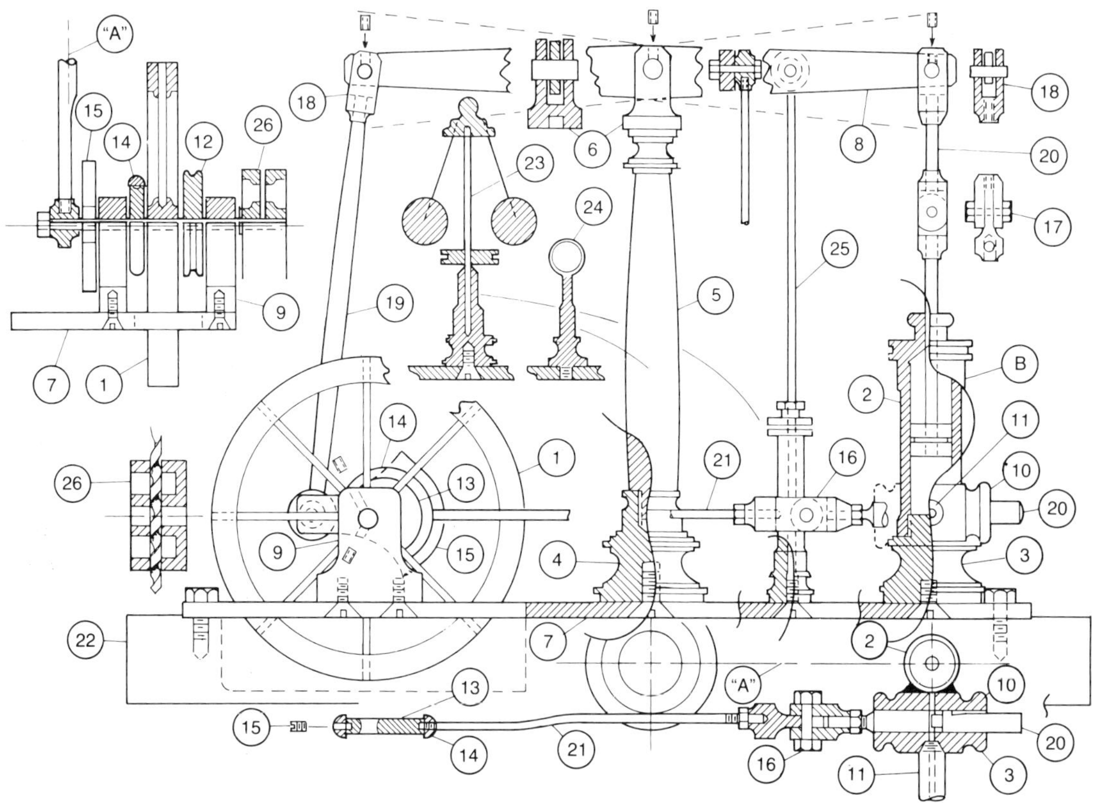

BILL OF MATERIALS
(Includes Excess for Chucking and Cutoff)

Size-Inches	Material	Length–Inches	For
1-D	brass	6	Column Base 4; Cylinder Base 3; Eccentric Strap 14; Governor Sheave 12; Belt Wheel 26
3/4-D	brass	4	Cylinder 2
1/2-D	brass	6	Column 5; Steam Chest 10; Crank Bearing; Pump-rod Bearing; Governor Sheave 23
3/8-D	brass	4	Pump Body 25; Governor Stand 23, Piston (optional = *Teflon* or steel)
1/4-D	brass	2	Governor Belt Fair-lead 24
3/16-D	brass	5	Connecting Rod 19
3/32-D	brass	24	Eccentric Rod 21; Angular Link 20; Flywheel Spokes
1/2-Sq	brass	2	Column Top Bearing 6
1/4-Sq	brass	8	All Yoke and Yoke-Tenon Joints 16, 17, 18
1/4 × 1	brass	6	Main Bearing Pedestals 9
1/8 × 1/2	brass	6	Beam 8
1/8 × 2	brass	7 1/2	Baseplate 7 (could be up to 2 1/2″ wide)
2 3/4-D	brass	1/2	Flywheel 1 (could be up to 3 3/4″ D)
1 3/8-D	brass	*	Crank 15; *Finished thickness = 1/8″ (could be cut from plate)
3/4-D	steel	*	Eccentric 13; *Finished thickness 7/64″
3/16-D	steel	5	Mainshaft; Beam Pin; Valve Spindle 20
1/8-D	steel	2	Beam Pins; (2 required, 3/8″ long)
3/32-D	steel	6	Pump Rod 25; Piston Rod
3/8-D	bronze	balls	Governor Weights (Or .36 calibre lead balls, painted)
3/4 × 8 1/2	wood	8	Hardwood Mounting – To suit, 22
			Fastenings
2-56	steel	1/8	Socket Head Setscrew – 6 required
2-56	steel	3/8	Hex Head Bolt and Nut – 1 required
4-40	steel	3/8	Hex Head Bolt and Nut – 2 required
3-48	steel		Nut – 2 required
4-40	brass	1/4	Flathead Screw – 7 required
6-32	brass	3/8	Hex Head Bolts – 4 required

Loctite No. 271

Andy's model

An Easy-to-build

Speeder

from Mamod and Wilesco Parts

By Andy Sprague

Photos by Frank Medina except where noted

Quick and Dottie Carlson aboard their speeder on the Hobo Railroad in Lincoln, New Hampshire.

HOWARD PIERPONT

Introduction

It wasn't until some months ago that I learned of the existence of the speeder hobby, but I'm sure you young Live Steam enthusiasts, and future machinists and engineers to whom I'm addressing this article, are far more knowledgeable on this subject than I. As far as I can find out, no one seems to know where the name "speeder" originated. It certainly doesn't fit a machine that travels this slow, nor should it be expected to.

All this started for me when my friend Dick called and said he had purchased a used gasoline-powered railroad handcar, and was in the process of jazzing it up with a roof, windshield, lights,

JIM WALCZAK

Old mail bags carry the wood fuel on the back porch of the Carlson railcar.

JIM WALCZAK

The Carlsons take a moment for maintenance during a fall color outing with other speeders on the Maryland & Pennsylvania Railroad in Muddy Creek Forks, Pennsylvania.

and a new paint job. When he's finished, he'll join other speeder friends on excursions through the countryside, riding on abandoned rail or authorized track with permission of the railroads.

Subsequently, I received photos of a group of Live Steamers who mounted steam engines on their railcars. Now I'm excited. I want to learn more about this steam car business.

Luckily, I was able to contact Quick Carlson, a steam railcar owner, to discover how he operates his speeder (for technical information, see "Landlubber" in the Mail Stop column, ***Live Steam***, August 1990). Quick told me he rides the rails from Tennessee to New Hampshire, along with other devotees, at motorcar meets arranged by the two clubs he belongs to.

Although in its infancy, the steam-powered railcar movement is expanding, and I'm sure we'll be hearing more of this interesting hobby in the not-too-distant future.

JIM WALCZAK

Quick Carlson's speeder.

All things considered, I doubt I'll ever be the proud owner of a standard track steam speeder. However, why not a model that can operate on 4-3/4" gauge club tracks (or on a floor or outside on a flat surface minus the wheel flanges)? Here's one you can build using only a power drill, soldering torch, and the usual hand tools.

The trick is to build the machine without having to construct the engine, boiler, wheels, or gears. These items, which are Mamod and Wilesco parts, can be obtained commercially from Frank Van Meeuwen at Diamond Enterprises. Their ads can be seen frequently in ***Live Steam***. Frank told me he has all components in stock, or can order them for you, and will give Live Steam readers a 20% discount by mentioning where they saw the ad.

Other than this, everything you need can be scrounged up or obtained in your local hobby shop and/or hardware store. All the nuts and bolts are the same size (6-32 × 1/2"), and the model can be assembled or disassembled in ten or fifteen minutes.

Once you have all the components, it shouldn't take more than three or four weekends to complete your engine. Here is a list of parts to order.

From Diamond Enterprises and Book Publishers, Box 537, Alexandria Bay, New York 13607, Attn: Frank Van Meeuwen:

Sp-5 Mamod two-cylinder engine with tubing connected

D-305 Wilesco 3 × 6" vertical boiler

Wilesco Whistle (if desired)

Wilesco pressure gauge (if desired)

Two Wilesco boiler filler pop valves

One Wilesco 2" diameter large tooth gear

One Wilesco 3/4" diameter large

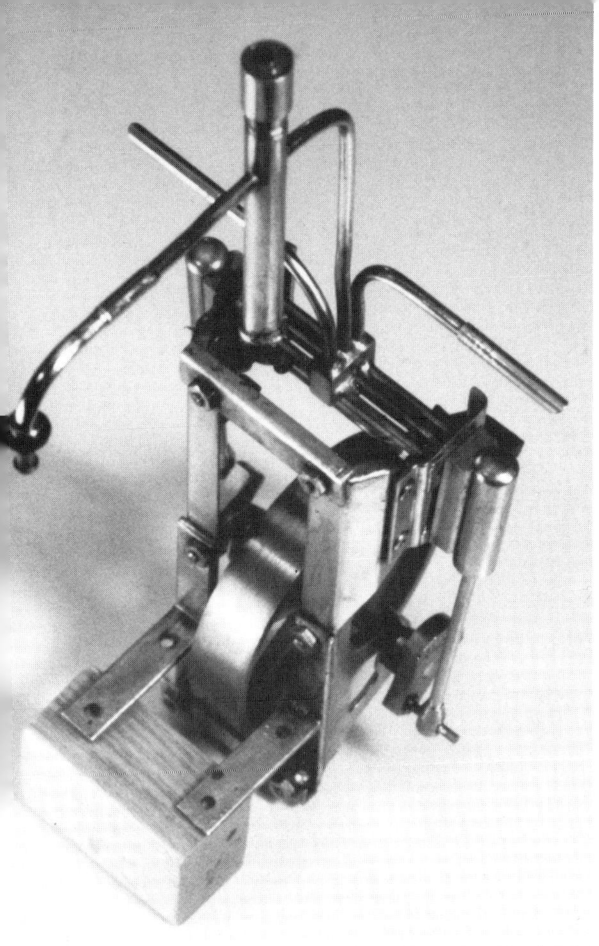

Andy's engine.

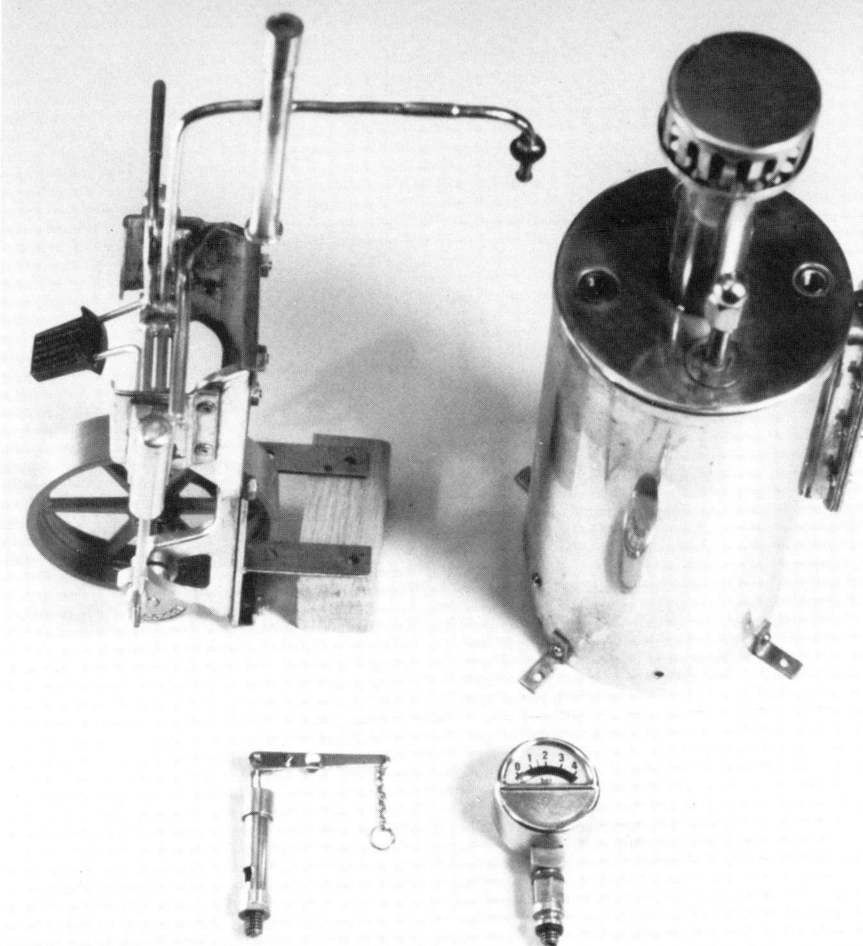

The boiler.

The chassis top.

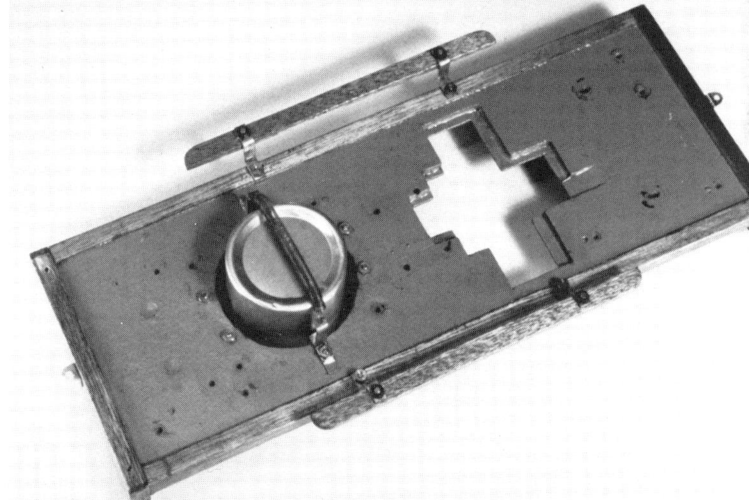

The chassis underside.

tooth gear with setscrew

One Wilesco 1-1/4" diameter small tooth gear with setscrew

One Wilesco ladder chain

One bag of fiber washers

Four Mamod 1-3/4 × 1/2" pulley wheels with setscrews

Well, that's it, and with the help of the following photos and text, you're on your way. When you've completed your model, why not send a snapshot of it to Joe Rice at ***Live Steam***? I'm sure he'd want to publish a picture of it.

Good luck, and happy steaming.

Engine

The Engine is a two-cylinder single-acting unit from a SP5 Mamod stationary model. The original support was the base of the model, so you will want to add two top and bottom cross braces plus the right angle supports to attach the engine to the chassis at the flywheel axle level.

The engine will arrive with tubing attached, but you will have to re-bend it to form the exhaust lines and the steam pressure line. If you don't have a screw connection for the boiler, you can solder it in, and use a short length of plastic tubing for a disconnect.

The lubricator is made from a bicycle tire valve and a short piece of 1/4" brass tubing.

The engine is equipped with a lever for two speeds forward and reverse operation, but the engine seems to work best in fast forward. Part of the engine frame and tubing were brass plated for me by a friend.

Boiler

The Boiler is from a Wilesco D-305 fire engine, and is fastened to the chassis by four right angles made from a 1/4" brass strip from the hobby store. The boiler has a large water gauge, but comes without fittings.

I added a whistle and pressure gauge, but these items are not really necessary. The pressure gauge, should you want one, will have to be soldered onto a stripped pop valve, as the gauge threads don't fit the boiler. In any case, a couple of pop valves will work fine.

I added a bicycle valve filler pipe for convenience so I wouldn't have to remove the whistle or pressure gauge when filling the boiler.

Chassis

The platform, or Chassis, is made from a piece of 1/8" fiberboard, decked and edged with 3/8" wide mahogany strips scrounged from an old window blind. I just happen to like a mahogany and brass combination, but 1/4 × 15-1/2 × 5-1/2" plywood will work as well.

Note the placement of the fuel can in the photos. Running boards, of course, are optional.

Burner

As with Bill Harris' beautiful steam roller, I too fooled around with a not-too-reliable alcohol burner, but eventually opted for the easy-to-use Sterno fuel in the small size can.

The photos show how the 1/4" brass strips secure the can in the 2-3/4" circular opening, and the spring holds the can in place.

The gel fuel fires up easily, and will raise steam in about 10-20 minutes, depending on how much water is in the boiler.

Also, if you're as cheap as I am, and would like to save a few bucks on the cost of Sterno, you can stuff an empty can with cotton, fix a piece of window screening on top, fill the can with alcohol, and you'll get a nice flame for all the times you'll be testing the engine.

Wheels

The four Wheels, two of which are powered, are Mamod 1-3/4 × 1/2" pulley wheels with setscrews. These are not the same wheels you see in the photo. This substitution makes for better track operation. The change was made at the last minute, so there was no time for a new photo. This is also the same for the can covers that make up the wheel rims. Substitute the milk cans for two 6 oz. tomato paste cans.

Slice off the tops and bottoms, and epoxy to the inside of the pulley wheels. Make sure the outer can rims face the inside of the track.

The axles are pegboard hooks, and can be purchased at a lumberyard that sells pegboard – or if you're lucky, your friendly local merchant will give you a couple, as happened in my case.

The Sterno *can held in place on top with 1/4" brass strips.*

The Sterno *can is held in place underneath with a spring.*

The wheels.

The drive mechanism with the ladder chain and gearing shown.

The wheel supports to the chassis can be seen in the photo showing the gearing. They are 7/16" scrap metal strips bent to 4-1/8 × 1-1/2". Note that the bolt holes on the gear axle support are slotted to facilitate easy ladder chain tension.

Gears

The Gears required are listed with other needed parts at the beginning of the article. Note that the reason for the 1-1/4" gear is only to have a setscrew collar for the 2" large tooth gear which has none. It can be soldered or bolted to the large tooth gear. If you have a setscrew collar, you won't need the extra gear.

The 3/4" gear goes on the engine axle next to the flywheel, and has its own setscrew.

The ladder chain is the correct length, and does not have to be altered.

Look at the photo showing the underside assembly. Note the can cover rims facing inside the track, and the large gear wheel assembly.

Decorative Parts

What might be called decorative parts are the log and toolboxes, bench seat and end railings.

The bench seat is of wood with legs formed from coat hanger wire, as are the end railings. They are divided by soldered-on tin squares.

The log and toolboxes are made from the mahogany strips. The toolbox holds two screwdrivers and a wrench.

The fake headlights are large brass tacks soldered to the top railing.

Running

The final photo shows my speeder steamed up and going through a test run at speed while sitting on a couple of bricks. Below the engine are two wood strips that make up a 2-foot work track. This arrangement makes a good base to work on the machine, once you've attached the wheels to the chassis.

The underside assembly.

A test run up on blocks.

Speaking of track, the rail you see in the cover photo is discarded indoor lighting track I found out in the street, minus the wiring. Bolted together, it made a nice 4-3/4" gauge, 10-foot test track I could lay out in my apartment.

(Editor's note: Quick Carlson belongs to two clubs that may be of interest. The clubs are: Motor Car Collectors of America (MCCA), c/o Mark Mayfield, 5 Bay View Hills, Wever, Iowa 52658; and North American Railcar Operators Association (NARCOA), c/o Joel Williams, Box 82, Greendell, New Jersey 07839. According to Mr. Carlson, both clubs have a quarterly magazine, but they are devoted primarily to gas-powered motorcars. However, there is definitely a steam power movement emerging. He knows of four steam cars for standard gauge in various stages of operation, and two in the planning stages.)

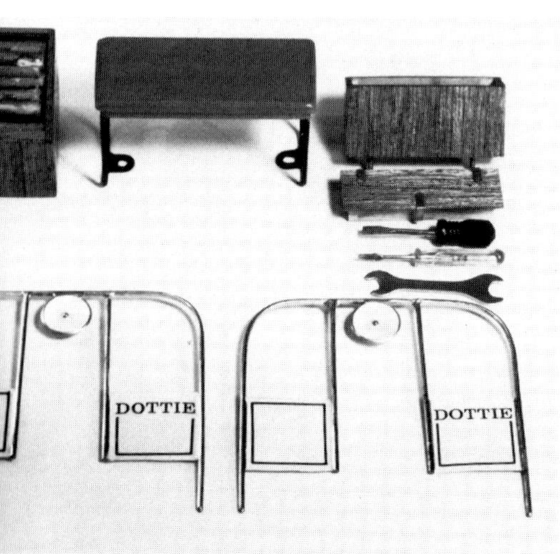

The decorative parts for the speeder.

A Speeder Update – An Alternative Engine

By Andy Sprague

Photos by Author

To those young Live Steamers who are building or contemplating building the speeder described in the January 1991 issue of ***Live Steam***, I've been informed by Frank Van Meeuwen at Diamond Enterprises that the SP5 Mamod engine suggested for the model is no longer available, as it has been discontinued by the manufacturer.

An alternative engine supplied by Diamond Enterprises is the Wilesco D48, a much more powerful unit, and a real beauty. It has double-acting slide valve cylinders, and is self-starting with a fully reversible steam regulator and an infinitely variable R/C connection that can be joined to the reversing lever. This is a great engine for marine application with its additional geared axle which, as seen in the photos, has been removed; it is not needed for the speeder.

This engine is actually easier to install than the original one; there is no frame support to strengthen. Just a couple of angle supports, and she's in place. The flywheel axle gear, ladder chain, and other accessories remain as before.

Here's an operating tip: I've discovered when operating the speeder that because the boiler is quite large, it is not necessary to fill the boiler to the usual water level. Filling the boiler to 1/2 or even 1/3 with water will give the ol' girl plenty of running time. You don't need the extra water weight. Good luck with your speeder, and have fun!

The Tesla Turbine

By R. S. Hedin

Photos by Author

Around the year 1900 Nikola Tesla, the inventor of the alternating current motor, developed a different kind of steam turbine. It had no blades or buckets but only smooth disks closely spaced on the rotor shaft. The steam entered tangentially via a nozzle and spiraled around between the disks, exiting through holes near the rotor shaft. Friction between the steam and the sides of the disks turned the rotor. It is said that Tesla's first turbine, the size of a "hat box," put out 30 hp with 125 psi steam.

My model (**Photos 1 and 2**) was made from a written description of the turbine and does not pretend to be a copy of the original Tesla unit. However, it works well on compressed air and probably would produce more torque on steam.

The construction of this model includes a number of options. The full-blown unit can be made as shown, or with only one nozzle, or without the valves and piping. Made as shown, the turbine will run in either direction, depending on which valve is open.

Starting construction with the case, make parts 1, 2 and 3 shown on the drawings. The tubing (2) is silver soldered to the plate (1). Then after chucking on the inside and centering the tube, the plate is bored and faced to fit the .800" diameter of the bearing housing (3). The housing is then silver soldered into the plate. Again chuck the assembly on the large tube as before, and bore the bearing housing to fit the ball bearings. Also, take a cleanup cut on the outside diameter at the same setup. This diameter will be used later for boring the inside of the rotor case. At this point the decision is made to install one or two nozzles and mill the pockets in the case as shown. The end mill will leave a radius in the corner; file this to a sharp corner so the nozzle will fit up tight against the plate (part 1).

To finish the case, make parts 4, 5 and 6. Soft solder these parts in place.

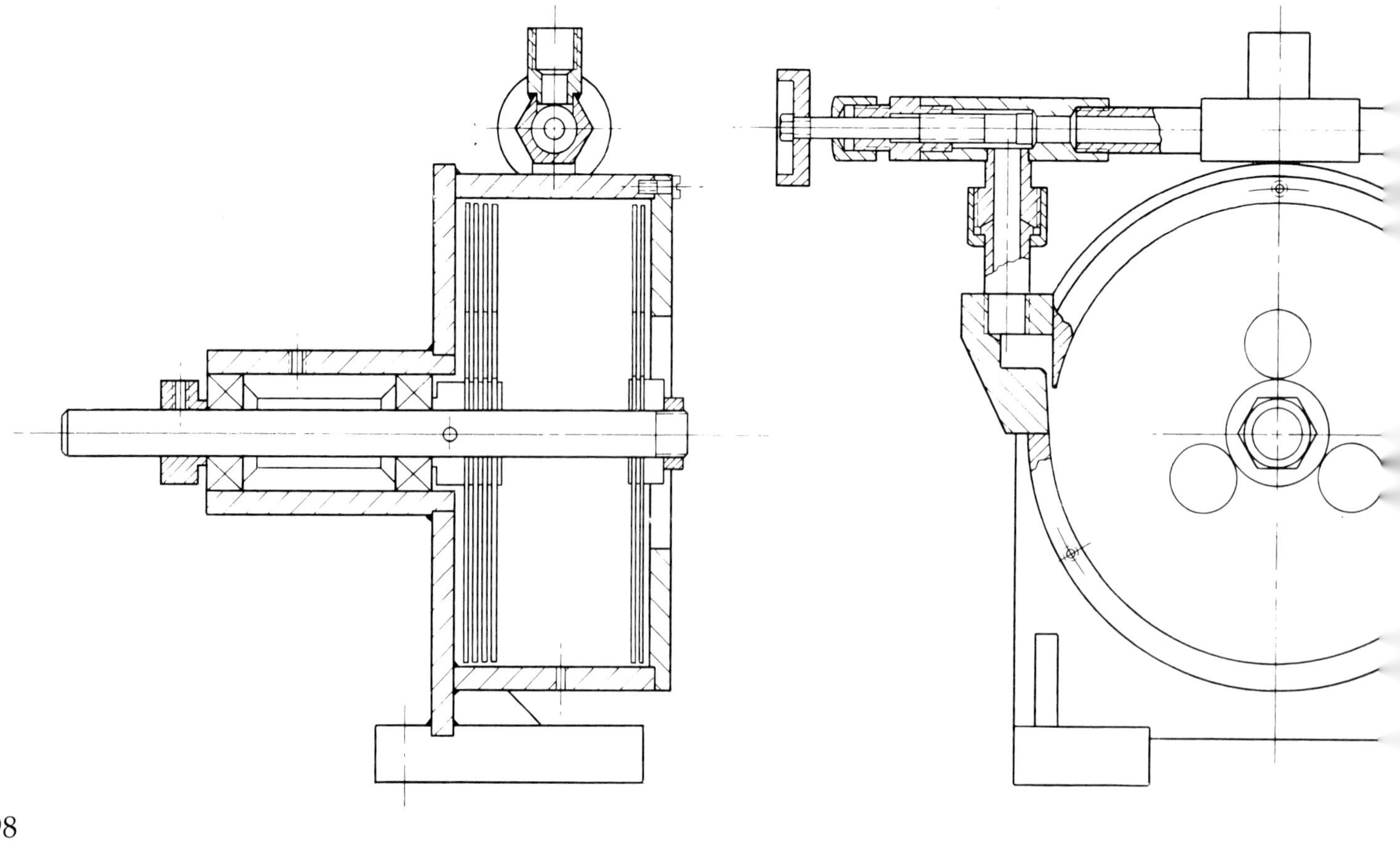

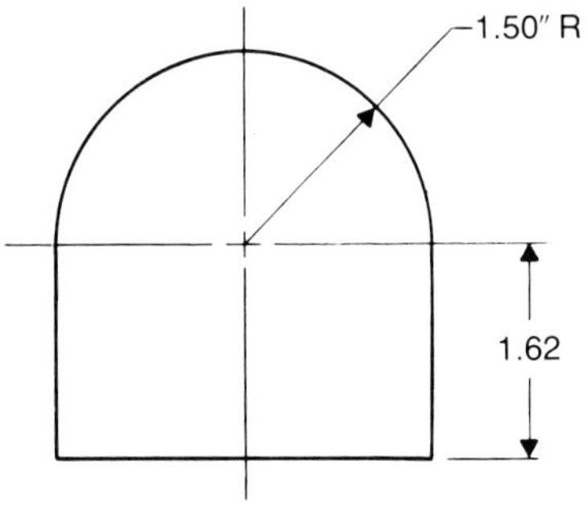

1.50″ R

1.62

① .125″ PLATE
brass, 1 required

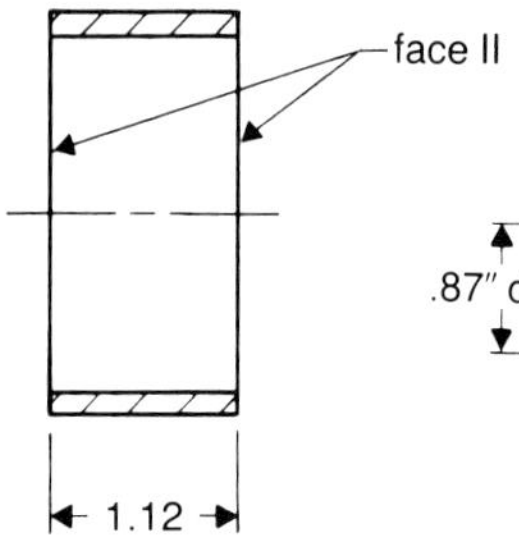

face II

1.12

② TUBING
2.75″ OD × 2.50″ ID, brass

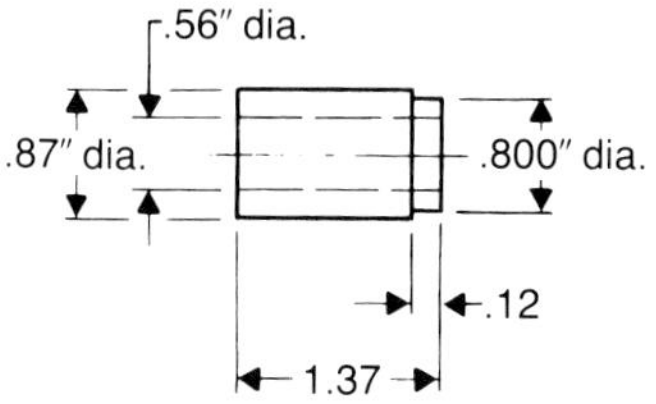

.56″ dia.

.87″ dia.

.800″ dia.

.12

1.37

③ BEARINGS HOUSING
brass

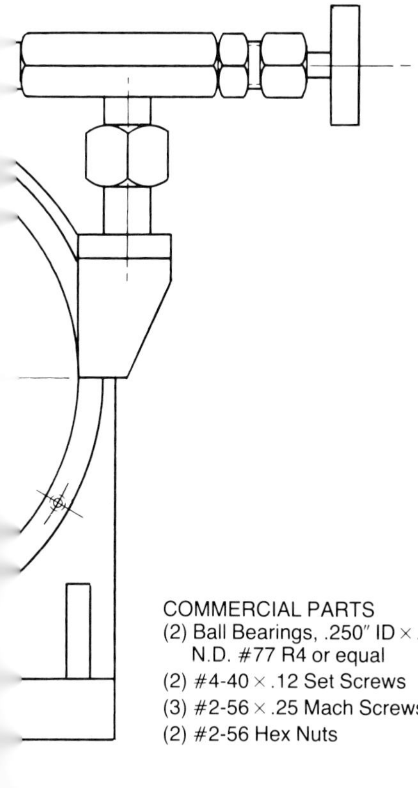

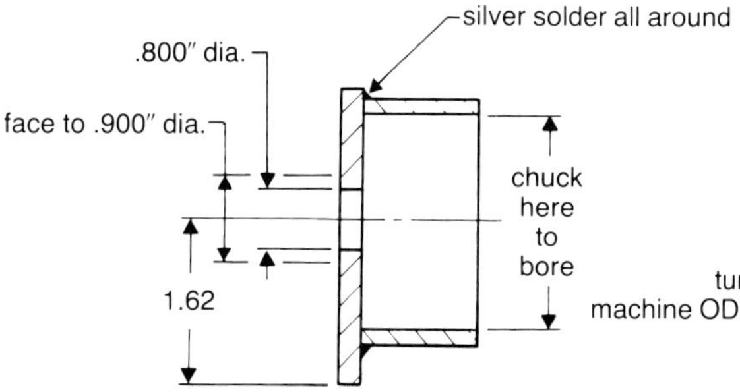

.800″ dia.

face to .900″ dia.

silver solder all around

chuck here to bore

1.62

ASSEMBLY ① & ②
Step 1

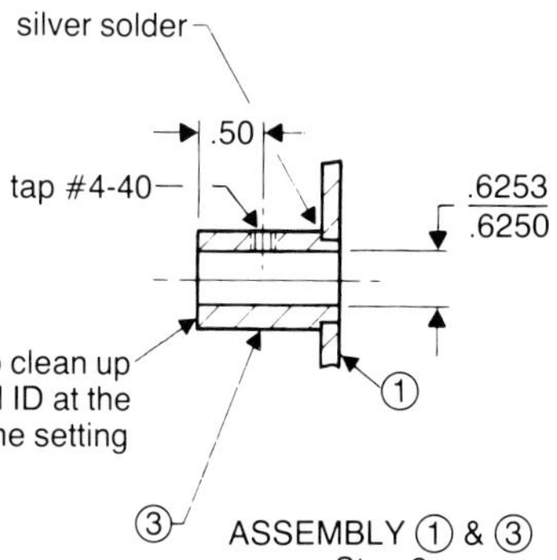

silver solder

.50

tap #4-40

.6253
.6250

turn to clean up
machine OD and ID at the same setting

①

③

ASSEMBLY ① & ③
Step 2

.010 .010

file out radius flush with plate, 2 places

mill from this direction

remove sharp edge, 2 places

②

①

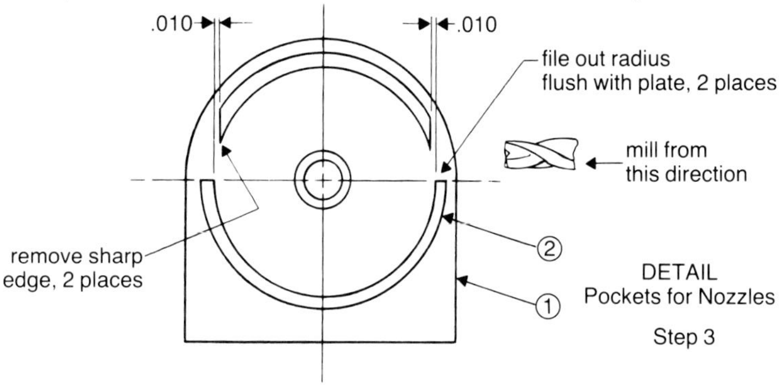

DETAIL
Pockets for Nozzles
Step 3

COMMERCIAL PARTS
(2) Ball Bearings, .250″ ID × .625″ OD × .196″ wide
N.D. #77 R4 or equal
(2) #4-40 × .12 Set Screws
(3) #2-56 × .25 Mach Screws
(2) #2-56 Hex Nuts

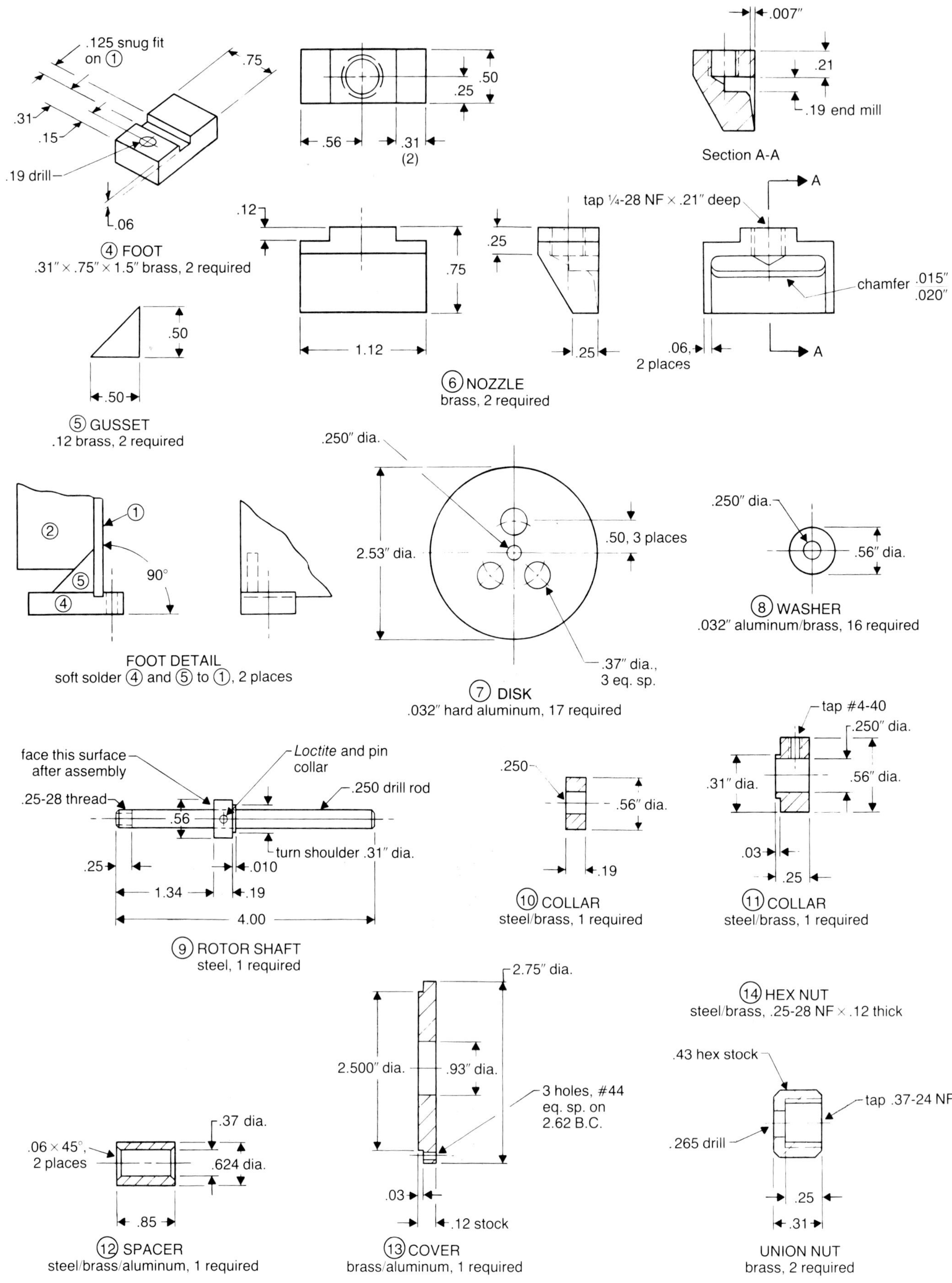

.125 snug fit on ①
.75
.31
.15
.19 drill
.06
④ FOOT
.31″ × .75″ × 1.5″ brass, 2 required
.50
.25
.56
.31 (2)
.007″
.21
.19 end mill
Section A-A
.12
.75
1.12
.25
.25
tap ¼-28 NF × .21″ deep
A
chamfer .015″ .020″
.06, 2 places
⑥ NOZZLE
brass, 2 required
.50
.50
⑤ GUSSET
.12 brass, 2 required
.250″ dia.
2.53″ dia.
.50, 3 places
.37″ dia., 3 eq. sp.
⑦ DISK
.032″ hard aluminum, 17 required
.250″ dia.
.56″ dia.
⑧ WASHER
.032″ aluminum/brass, 16 required
90°
FOOT DETAIL
soft solder ④ and ⑤ to ①, 2 places
face this surface after assembly
Loctite and pin collar
.25-28 thread
.250 drill rod
.56
turn shoulder .31″ dia.
.25
.010
1.34
.19
4.00
⑨ ROTOR SHAFT
steel, 1 required
.250
.56″ dia.
.19
⑩ COLLAR
steel/brass, 1 required
tap #4-40
.250″ dia.
.31″ dia.
.56″ dia.
.03
.25
⑪ COLLAR
steel/brass, 1 required
2.75″ dia.
2.500″ dia.
.93″ dia.
3 holes, #44 eq. sp. on 2.62 B.C.
.03
.12 stock
⑬ COVER
brass/aluminum, 1 required
.37 dia.
.06 × 45°, 2 places
.624 dia.
.85
⑫ SPACER
steel/brass/aluminum, 1 required
⑭ HEX NUT
steel/brass, .25-28 NF × .12 thick
.43 hex stock
tap .37-24 NF
.265 drill
.25
.31
UNION NUT
brass, 2 required

For strength use a solder that has a small amount of silver with the remainder tin. If the turbine is to be used with steam, drill a small hole at the lowest point in the case to drain the condensate. The inside of the case, the 2.50″ diameter, is bored to a cleanup, because a small amount of the nozzle projects into this diameter. Chuck on the OD of the bearing housing. Also, face to clean up the end of the case, including the nozzle blocks. Complete the cover, item 13, and spot the holes in the case. Drill and tap for no. 2-56 screws.

The rotor disks are made from flat aluminum sheet. They can best be cut using a flycutter in a drill press. The center hole is reamed .250″. The spacing washers can be made in the lathe by parting off slices of stock with a .250″ hole. With items 7, 8, 9, 10 and 14 completed, assemble the rotor and turn the OD of the disks to about .005″ smaller than the inside diameter of the case. Round the edges of the disks with a smooth file.

With items 11 and 12 completed, the turbine can be assembled for testing. The setscrew in the bearing housing keeps the spacer (12) in place, and the collar (11) keeps the rotor assembly from shifting. The .31″ diameter of the collar is placed against the ball bearing inner race. The entire rotor assembly with the ball bearings is adjusted endways by loosening the setscrew in the housing. Test the turbine on compressed air at about 40 to 50 psi.

The parts for the valves and piping are, in the main, self-explanatory. The female union is silver soldered in the valve body in the same manner as the tee. The valve stem is packed with graphited string or something similar. The completed valves and pipes are assembled on the turbine with the pipes loose in the tee. The pipes are then soft soldered in the tee.

All that remains is to disassemble to clean and paint the case.

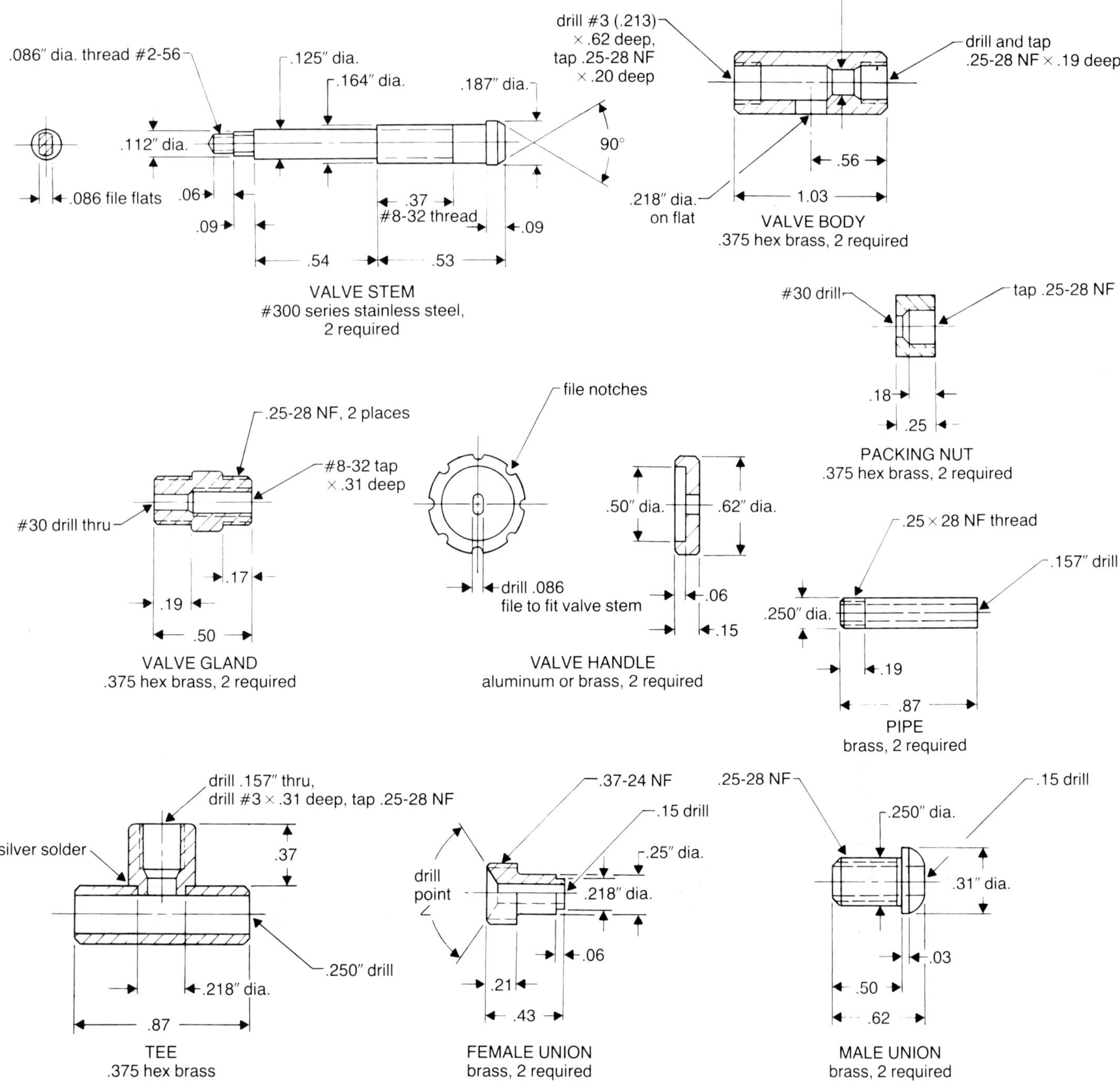

VALVE STEM
#300 series stainless steel, 2 required

VALVE BODY
.375 hex brass, 2 required

PACKING NUT
.375 hex brass, 2 required

VALVE GLAND
.375 hex brass, 2 required

VALVE HANDLE
aluminum or brass, 2 required

PIPE
brass, 2 required

TEE
.375 hex brass

FEMALE UNION
brass, 2 required

MALE UNION
brass, 2 required

NDC-1

A twin-column, twin-cylinder, self-starting mill engine

By Paul Jacobs

Photos by Anthony Molnar

My "NDC-1" was inspired by an engine I saw in the Science Museum in London, England, in January of '92. The museum model was quite large (approximately two feet tall), and was attributed to John Musgrave, 1843. The staff at the museum was very helpful but could not locate any drawings of the engine. Their photo library was, however, able to provide an 8-1/2 x 11" glossy print of the engine. Since I was leaving for home the next day, I settled for the photo intending to "maybe later" scale it.

Sometime later, a friend gave me a copy of an article on Non-Dead-Center engines written by Sam Clogston. After a phone call to Mr. Clogston, the "maybe later" idea quickly moved to the drawing board to become the *NDC-1.* Why NDC-1? Well, it has no dead centers (self-start-

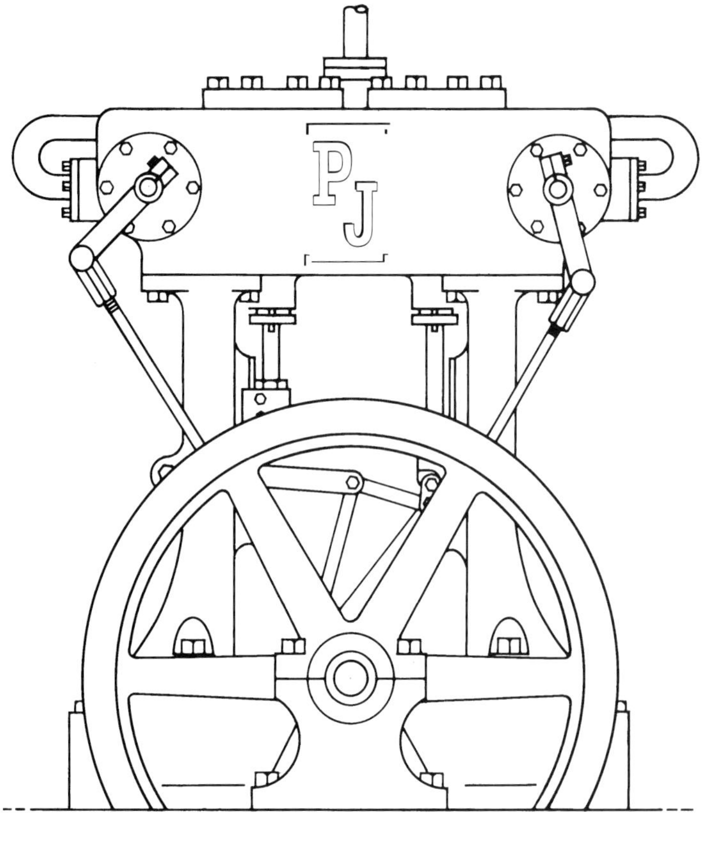

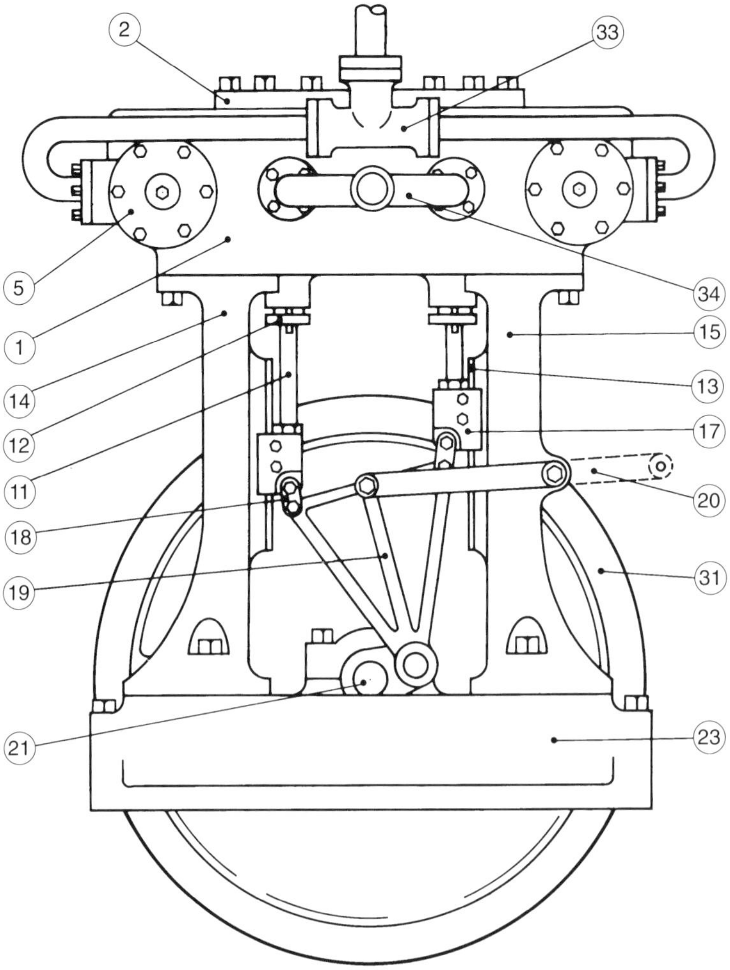

1

2

ing). Why "1"? It seems, with some alterations, the overall height of the engine can be drastically reduced, thus allowing for marine use...maybe later. This particular design was used primarily in the textile industry and was manufactured in various sizes from 10 to 200 hp.

I made patterns and cast parts as the design evolved, ending up with 22 castings—mostly aluminum. The flywheel is cast iron, and the eccentric strap and piston rod glands are brass (**Photo 1**).

Construction is pretty straightforward and does not require any special tricks or procedures. There are many parts that are machined and fitted to a previous part. Access to a milling machine greatly simplifies things, and I

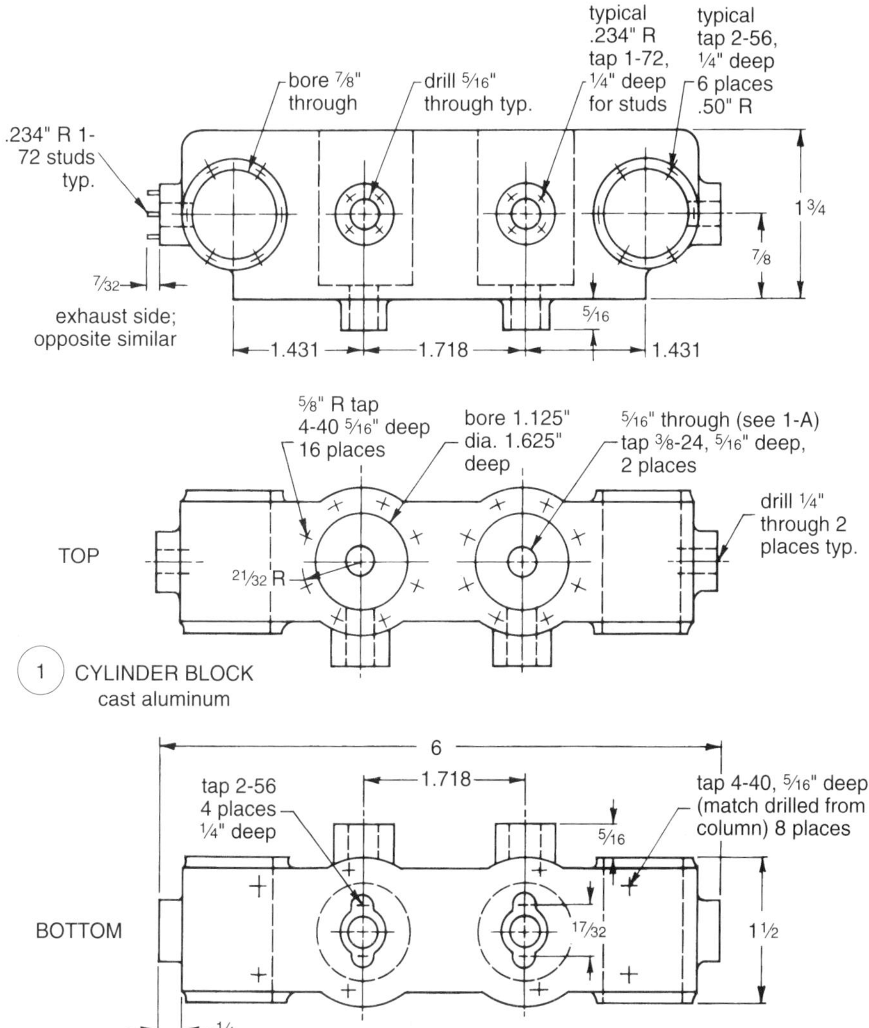

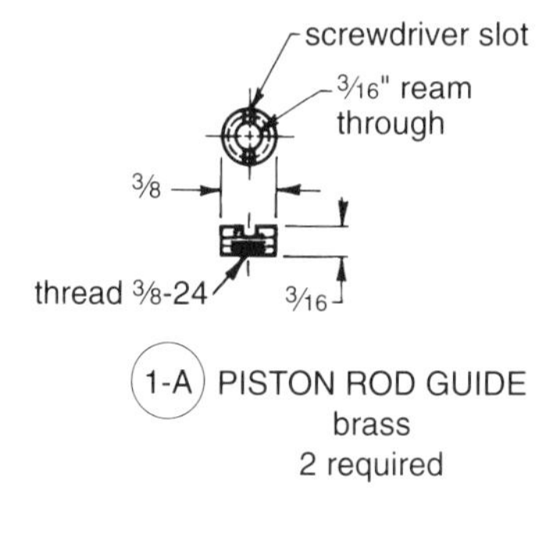

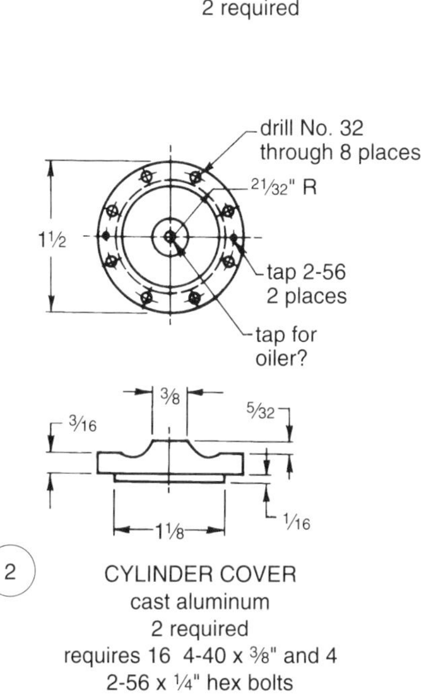

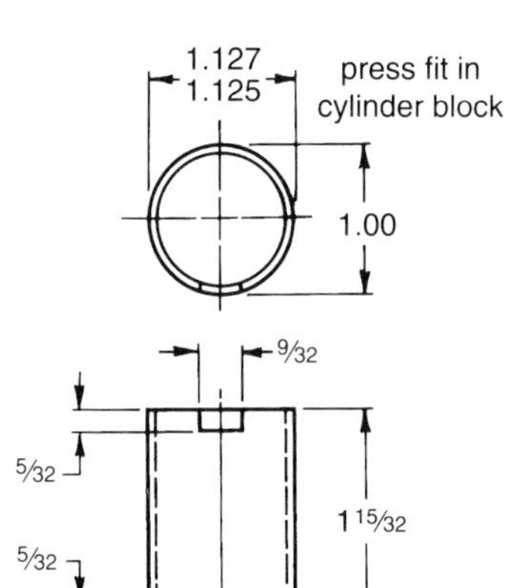

3 CYLINDER SLEEVES
steel
2 required

Note!
Check the port alignment before pressing the sleeve in. Press the sleeve 0.140" below the top of the block.

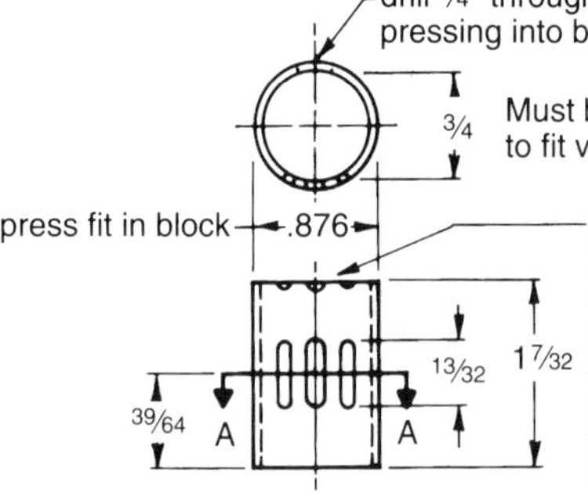

Note!
Put a small notch on this edge of the sleeve at the same time you cut the ports. Put the notches on the exhaust side of the block; they will be invaluable when timing the valve.

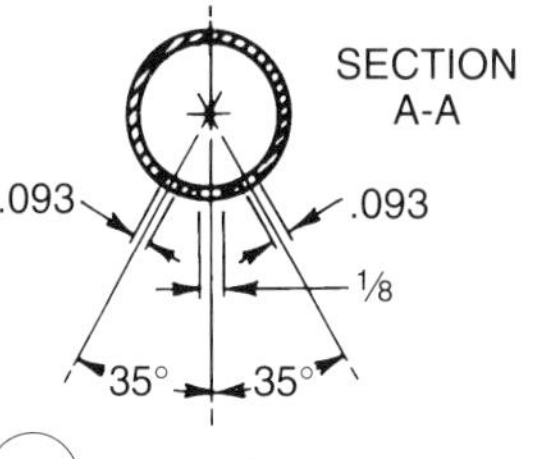

Note!
The sleeves were made from schedule 80 pipe.

Again – check the port alignment *before* pressing into the block.

4 VALVE SLEEVE
steel
2 required

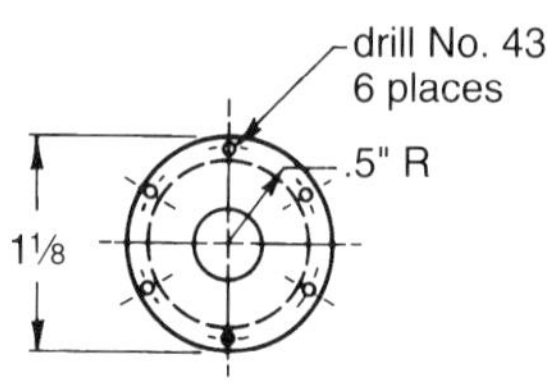

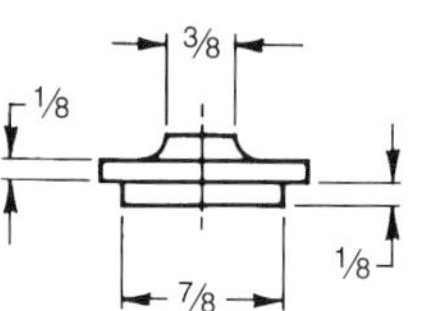

5 VALVE COVER, EXHAUST SIDE
cast aluminum
2 required
requires 12 2-56 x 1/4" hex bolts

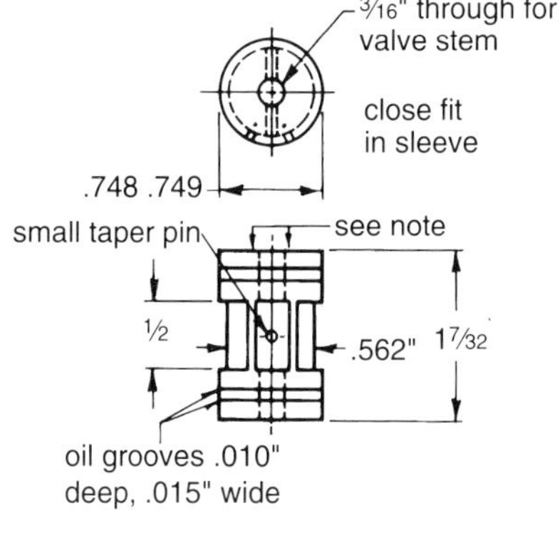

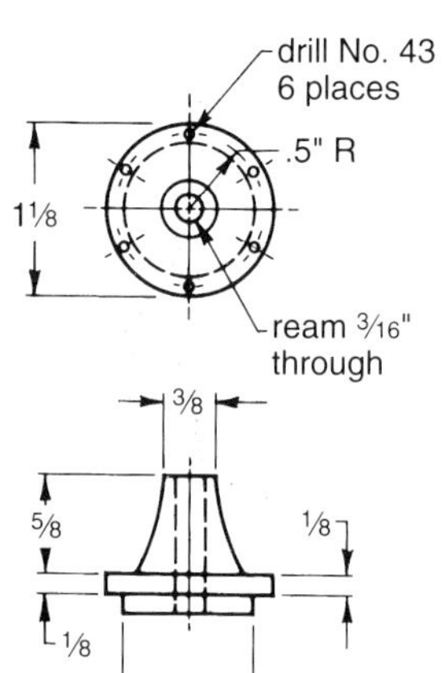

6 VALVE COVER, FLYWHEEL SIDE
cast aluminum
2 required
requires 12 2-56 x 1/4" hex bolts

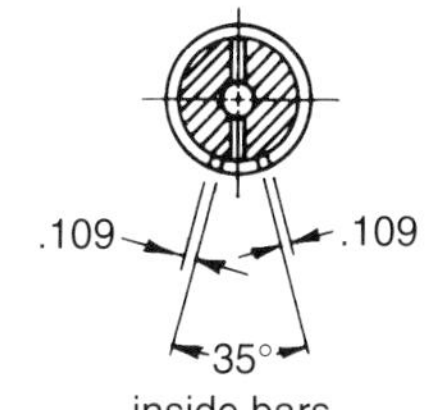

inside bars

Note!
Mark where the bars are located on the end of the valve. Align with notches on the valve sleeve to time.

7 VALVE
brass
2 required

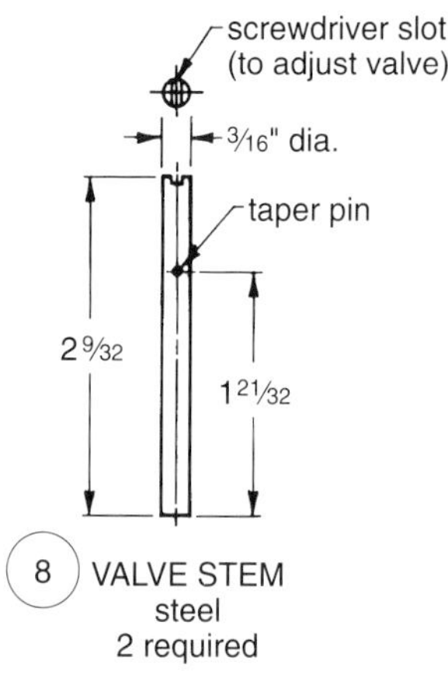

8 VALVE STEM
steel
2 required

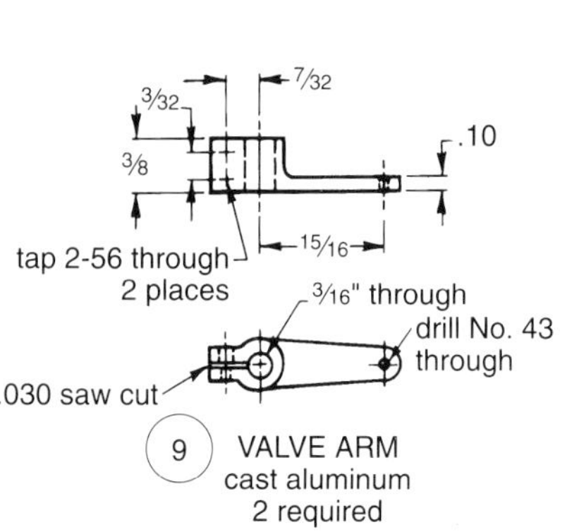

9 VALVE ARM
cast aluminum
2 required

3

4

5

6

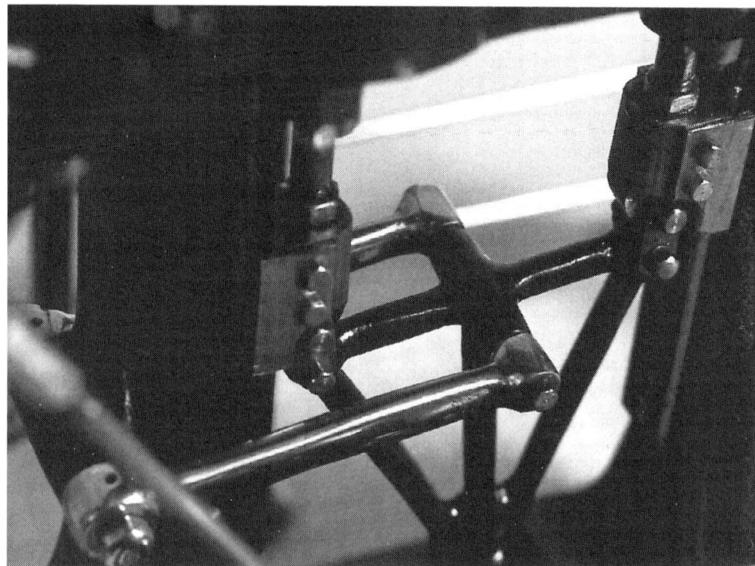

7

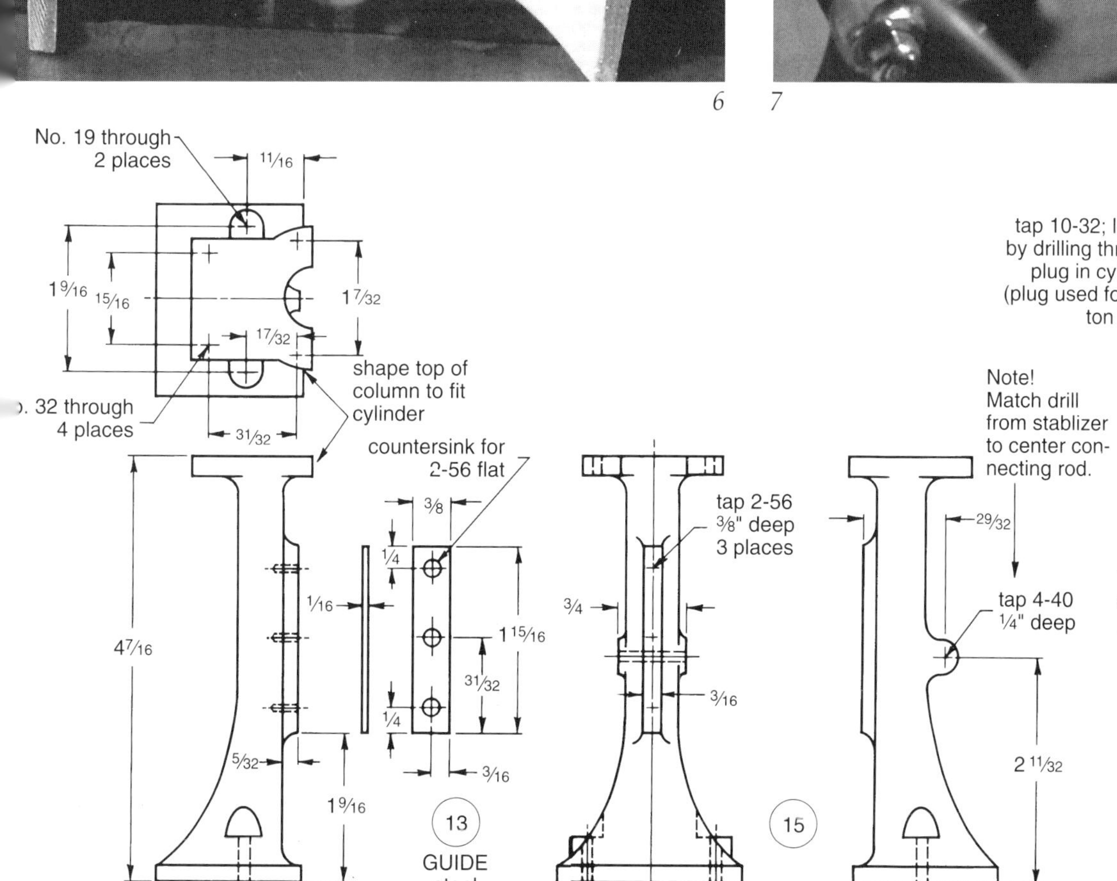

No. 19 through 2 places
11/16
1 9/16
15/16
1 7/32
17/32
shape top of column to fit cylinder
... 32 through 4 places
31/32
countersink for 2-56 flat
3/8
1/4
1/16
1 15/16
31/32
1/4
3/16
4 7/16
5/32
1 9/16
1 9/16
14
13
GUIDE
steel
2 required
tap 2-56
3/8" deep
3 places
3/4
3/16
15
Note!
Match drill from stablizer to center connecting rod.
29/32
tap 4-40
1/4" deep
2 11/32

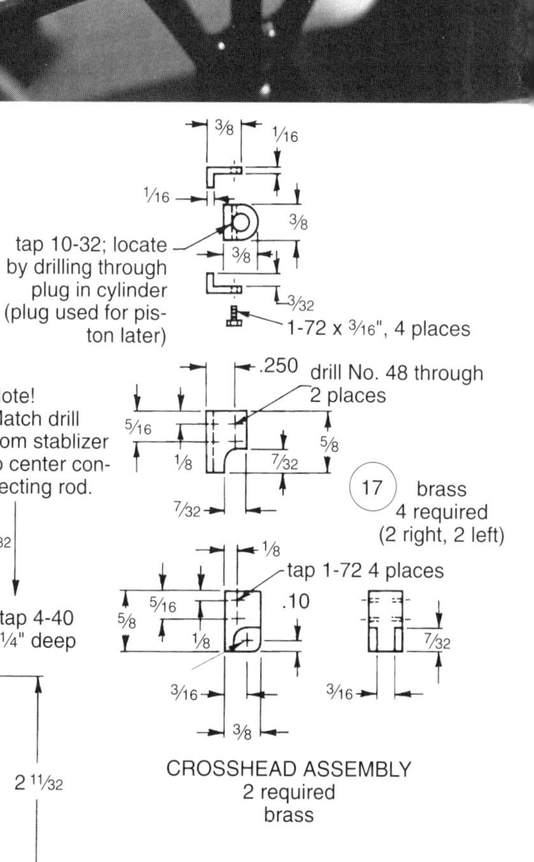

3/8
1/16
1/16
3/8
tap 10-32; locate by drilling through plug in cylinder (plug used for piston later)
3/8
3/32
1-72 x 3/16", 4 places
.250
drill No. 48 through 2 places
5/16
1/8
5/8
7/32
7/32
17
brass
4 required
(2 right, 2 left)
1/8
tap 1-72 4 places
5/16
.10
5/8
1/8
7/32
3/16
3/16
3/8
CROSSHEAD ASSEMBLY
2 required
brass

used my mill for most of the machining.

I will assume the builder has some experience in modeling and machining. As such, some parts may be glossed over. I will attempt to cover the areas that could create problems, and offer you some of my solutions.

The cylinder block (1) is all important since it determines the location and sizes of many of the parts. When boring the cylinders and the valve cavities, be sure to center on the bosses. The porting is cast in (cored) and will appear during machining. All of the tapped holes in the block, except for the piston rod guides (1-A), should be match-drilled from the part to be attached (columns, covers, and manifolds). All the machine work on the block was done on the mill, using 1-2-3 blocks and an angle plate. By mounting the block right side up, with the exhaust bosses facing out, you can skim the top, bore the cylinders, tap for the rod guides, and trim the valve bosses and the steam and exhaust bosses (**Photos 2** and **3**).

That done, rotate the block 90°, the top against the angle plate, exhaust ports up. Now you can drill the exhaust bosses and bore the valve cavities. Remember to locate centers from the bosses; there is not a lot of excess metal here, and the center distances are not critical. Rotate again to clean up the rod gland faces, and drill them to accept the glands. While the block is mounted in this position, go around and clean up the column mounting areas.

After all this mill work, move over to the lathe for a while. Turn the two cylinder sleeves (3) from schedule 80 pipe. Note that they are to be pressed into the block, so make them one or two thousandths over whatever the cylinder bore in the block measures. Turn the two valve sleeves (4) from schedule 80 pipe. Note that these are also a press fit in the block. Turn two pieces of brass for the valves (7). Leave them about 1/2" longer than the designated dimension for now. Put several small oil grooves on each end, and drill and ream 3/16" through. Since the valve must be a close fit, it would probably be a good idea to bore the sleeves a little undersize and hone them after pressing into the block.

My procedure for cutting the ports in the sleeves and the passages on the valves was as follows: Mount the rotary table on the mill with the axis of the table chuck parallel with the X-axis of the mill table. Chuck a sleeve snugly in place. Center the sleeve under the spindle and lock the Y-axis (**Photo 4**). Now taking light cuts, cut the ports as accurately as possible. Don't forget to put a little dimple on the outer end of the sleeve before you rotate to the next port. After all three ports are cut, remove and deburr the sleeve. Be careful not to round the port edges over. It may help to visualize the semi-rotary valve as a D-valve setup that has been wrapped around a cylinder.

8

BILL OF MATERIALS – PARTS

Part	Qty.	Description	Material	Source
1	1	Cylinder block	aluminum casting	furnished w/kit
1-A	2	Piston rod guides	3/8" brass rod	stock
2	2	Cylinder covers	aluminum casting	furnished w/kit
3	2	Cylinder sleeves	schedule 80 pipe, 1"	stock
4	2	Valve sleeves	3/4" schedule 80 pipe	stock
5	2	Valve covers	aluminum casting	furnished w/kit
6	2	Valve covers	aluminum casting	furnished w/kit
7	2	Valve	3/4" brass rod	stock
8	2	Valve stems	3/16" steel rod	stock
9	2	Valve arms	aluminum casting	furnished w/kit
10	2	Piston assembly	1" aluminum rod	stock
11	2	Piston rods	3/16" steel rod	stock
12	2	Piston rod glands	brass casting	furnished w/kit
13	2	Crosshead guides	1/16 x 3/8 x 2-1/2" steel	stock
14	1	Column	aluminum casting	furnished w/kit
15	1	Column	aluminum casting	furnished w/kit
16	2	Piston rings	1", purchase or make to print	stock
17	2	Crosshead assembly	3/8" brass bar	stock
18	4	Shackles	1/16 x 3/16 x 5/8" steel	stock
19	1	Connecting rod	aluminum casting	furnished w/kit
20	2	Stabilizer arms	aluminum casting	furnished w/kit
21	1	Crankshaft fabrication	3/8 x 4" steel rod, 3/8 x 5/8" steel bar	stock
22	1	Crankshaft bearing	5/8" brass rod	stock
23	1	Base	aluminum casting	furnished w/kit
23-A	1	Bearing cap for base	aluminum casting	furnished w/kit
24	1	Outboard bearing stand	aluminum casting	furnished w/kit
25	1	Outboard bearing	5/8" brass rod	stock
26	1	Eccentric	1-1/16" steel rod	stock
27	1	Eccentric strap	brass casting	furnished w/kit
28	2	Valve rods	1/8 x 4-1/2" steel rod	stock
29	1	Valve rod end	steel fabrication	stock
30	2	Valve rod ends	steel fabrications	stock
31	1	Flywheel	cast iron	furnished w/kit
32	1	Drive pulley/sheave	aluminum casting	furnished w/kit
33	2	Steam manifold assemblies	1/4" x 20-gauge brass tube	stock
34	1	Exhaust manifold fabrication:		
	2		1/4" copper ells	furnished w/kit
	1		3/8" copper ell	furnished w/kit
	1		tee, 3/8" brass rod fabrication	stock
	1		3/8" copper tubing, 8"	stock

The valves (7) were cut using this same setup. Machine the cavities as shown on the drawings. Note! The ports in the sleeves are centered 35° apart, but the bars on the valve have a 35° separation between them. Make the bars the same width as the bars in the sleeve. Again, don't forget to mark the end of the valve to show where the bars are located. When the valve is assembled you cannot see either the bars or the ports. Not having these marks on the valve and sleeve will definitely make timing the engine very difficult.

I used a taper pin to fasten the valve on the spindle (8). Any type of fastening would work as long as the valve won't move on the spindle. Remove the valve from the mill and trim it to length. Insert and fasten the spindle with the slotted end toward the end of the valve with the marks for the bars. Set the valves and sleeves aside for now.

You will need a means to locate the columns (14 and 15), so turn an aluminum bar about 1-1/2" long to a close fit in the cylinder bore. Tap drill No. 21 clear through. We will use this piece as a drill guide for now. Eventually it will be used to make the pistons.

Machine the columns (14 and 15) making sure to keep the top and bottom surfaces parallel, and the crosshead guide surface at right angles, centrally located on the columns (**Photos 5** and **6**). The top flange was cast oversize to ease setup, and will have to be shaped to fit the cylinder block. Leave it a little oversize and file it to fit after mounting to the block.

Make up the crosshead guides (13) and fasten them in place. Make up the crosshead assemblies (17), but don't drill and tap for the piston rod yet (**Photo 7**). Slide a crosshead into place on either column. Insert the drill guide into the appropriate cylinder, and set the block on the top of the two columns. Drop the tap drill (or a suitable rod) through the hole in the guide and align the crosshead centrally under the point of the rod or drill. Clamp the column in place and remove the drill guide to spot the column mounting holes on the block. Remove the column and drill and tap the four 4-40 holes. Bolt this column in place and repeat the process for the other column.

With both columns mounted to the block, clamp a crosshead in place on the guide and spot the piston rod location using the drill guide again, thus insuring a minimum of misalignment. Do the same for the other crosshead. You will have to remove the crossheads to drill and tap them 10-32.

Now is a good time to press the sleeves in place, so remove the columns. Using a small square, slide the blade into the valve cavity and align the blade edge with the edge of one of the cast-in ports. Transfer a small mark to the face of the valve boss on the flywheel side of the block. Do this for all six edges (three ports). Align the port marks on the sleeve so they are centrally located with the marks on the valve boss, and press into the block 0.130" to 0.140" below the surface of the boss. Repeat the process for the other valve. Now is the time to drill the steam passage into the valve cavity. Just drill through the steam boss and through the sleeve. Deburr and hone the sleeve to a close sliding fit with the valve. It might be a good idea to mark each valve so it can be returned to its proper sleeve.

Check the cylinder bore to be sure the exhaust passage connects to the exhaust port. It should be about 1/4" wide and 3/32" deep. If not, use a Dremel or equivalent to carve out the passageway. Align the ports on the sleeve with the cast-in ports, and press the sleeve into place. If you haven't done so already, install the piston rod guides (1-A). Screw them in tight.

You can make up the piston assemblies (10), and the piston rods (11), using the drill guide for stock. Make the rods first. Tap both ends of the drill guide 10-32 and saw off a piece long enough to make the piston body. Screw it onto the rod for turning to size and shape. Cylinder sleeve bore minus 5 to 10 thousandths. The rings I used were as shown; if yours are different, make the appropriate changes but don't make the piston any longer than shown.

Assemble the piston body, ring, and piston top. Screw this assembly onto the rod. Use *Loctite!* Insert the piston and rod assembly into the cylinder and wrap a few strands of packing around the rod. I used *Teflon*, but graphited yarn will work fine. The *Teflon* was an experiment that seems to be working well. Loosely install the rod gland (12). Attach the crosshead to the rod using a thin locknut, and remount the column to the block.

BILL OF MATERIALS – FASTENERS

Part	Qty.	Description	Use	Source
1	16	4-40 x 3/8" hex bolts	cylinder covers	stock
	4	2-56 x 1/2" hex bolts	cylinder covers	stock
	16	1-72 x 1/2" studs	steam/exhaust manifold	stock
	8	4-40 x 3/8" hex bolts	fasten columns to cylinder	stock
	4	2-56 x 1/2" studs	hold rod glands	stock
	24	2-56 x 3/8" hex bolts	fasten valve covers	stock
9	4	2-56 x 3/8" hex bolts	valve arm clamps	stock
	4	2-56 nuts	valve arm clamps	stock
	2	2-56 x 3/8" hex bolts	connect valve rods to arms	stock
10	6	1-72 x 3/8" flathead screws	ring retainer	stock
11	2	10-32 nuts (thin)	lock rod to crosshead	fabricate
12	4	2-56 nuts	adjust piston rod gland	stock
13	6	2-56 flathead screws	fasten guide to column	stock
14-15	4	8-32 x 3/4" hex bolts	fasten columns to base	stock
17	8	1-72 x 3/16" hex bolts	fasten clamps to crosshead	stock
18	4	2-56 x 1/2" hex bolts	shackle bolts	fabricate
20	2	1-56 x 1/2" hex bolts	fasten stabilizer arm to rod	stock
	2	4-40 x 1/2" hex bolts	stabilizer arm pivots	fabricate
23	4	8-32 x 1-3/8" studs	fasten base to sub-base	stock
24	4	6-32 x 3/4" studs	fasten bearing caps	stock
	4	6-32 nuts	fasten bearing caps	stock
	2	8-32 x 1/2" hex bolts	fasten bearing stand to base	stock
26	1	6-32 x 1/4 Allen setscrew	lock eccentric	stock
27	1	2-56 x 3/8" hex bolt, brass	guide screw	stock
	1	2-56 nut	guide screw	stock
	1	2-56 x 1/2" hex bolt	valve rod pivot	fabricate
28	4	5-40 nuts (thin)	lock valve rod ends	fabricate
31	1	8-32 Allen setscrew	lock flywheel	stock
32	4	4-40 x 3/8" hex bolts	fasten pulley to flywheel	stock
33	16	1-72 nuts	fasten manifold to block and tee	stock
33	18	1-72 x 1/4" hex bolts	fasten "tee" flanges	stock
34	8	1-72 nuts	fasten manifold to block	stock

NOTES: All of the fasteners shown above are steel unless otherwise marked.

All bolts and nuts are "scale" sizes, and can be purchased from any of several regular advertisers in ***Live Steam***.

All exposed bolt heads and nuts should be polished.

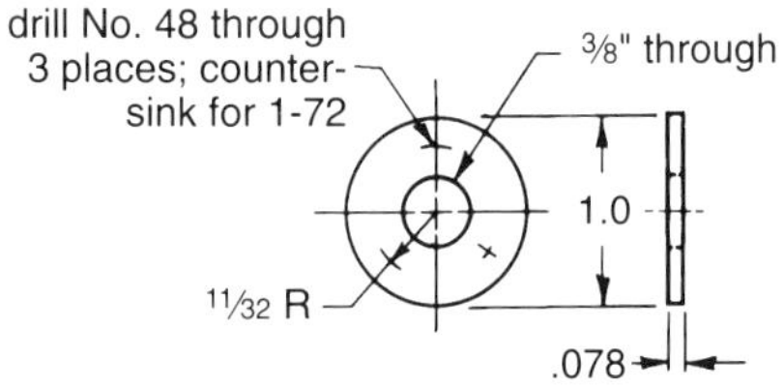

drill No. 48 through 3 places; countersink for 1-72

3⁄8" through

1.0

11⁄32 R

.078

(10A) aluminum 2 required

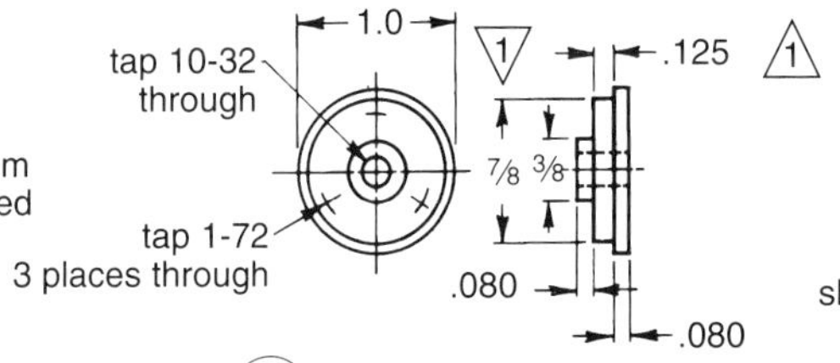

tap 10-32 through

1.0

tap 1-72 3 places through

(1) .125 (1)

7⁄8 3⁄8

.080

.080

(10B) PISTON ASSEMBLY aluminum 2 required

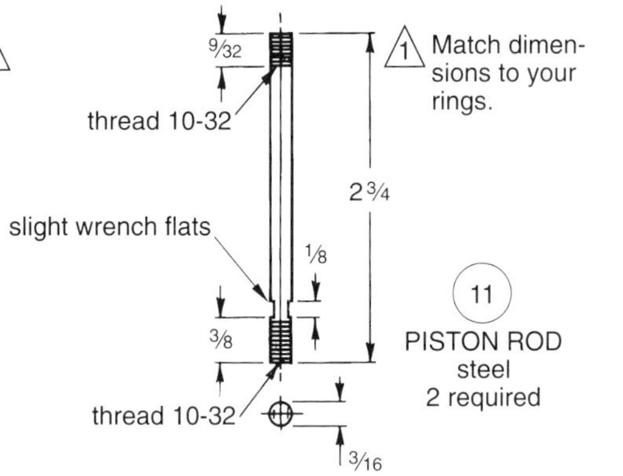

9⁄32

thread 10-32

(1) Match dimensions to your rings.

2 3⁄4

slight wrench flats

1⁄8

3⁄8

thread 10-32

3⁄16

(11) PISTON ROD steel 2 required

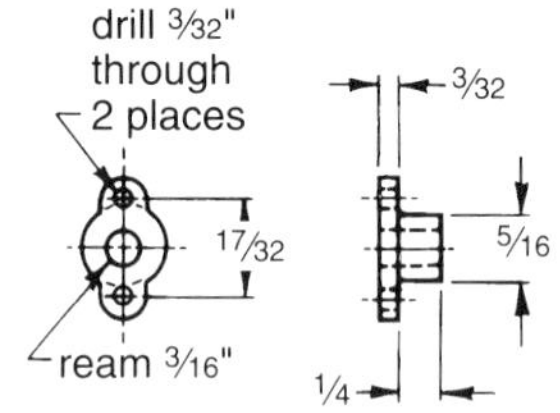

drill 3⁄32" through 2 places

17⁄32

ream 3⁄16"

3⁄32

5⁄16

1⁄4

(12) PISTON ROD GLAND brass casting 2 required

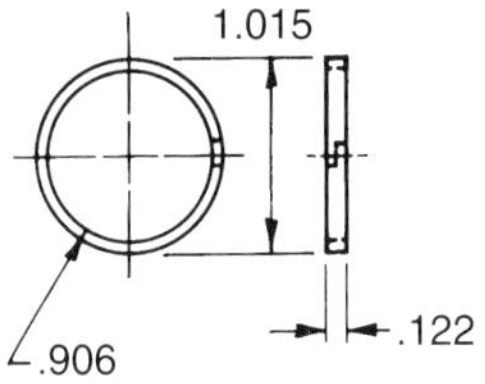

TOP VIEW

3⁄16

1.718

.859

tap 2-56 1⁄4" deep 2 places

3⁄4

3⁄32" through 2 places

1.937

3⁄16

oil

ream 1⁄4"

9⁄16

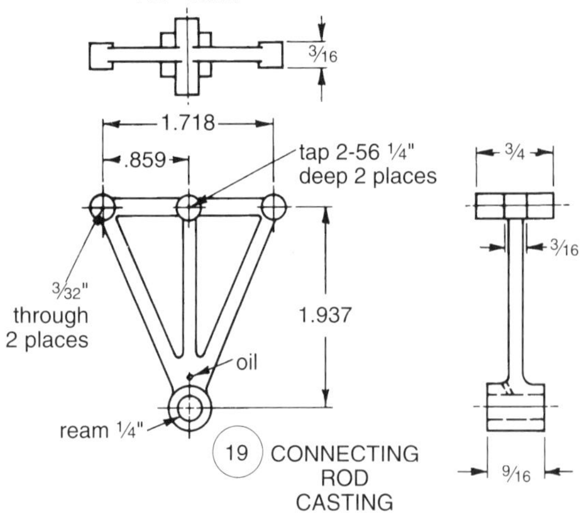

(19) CONNECTING ROD CASTING

1.015

.906

.122

(16) 2 required

1" commercial rings or make to above drawing

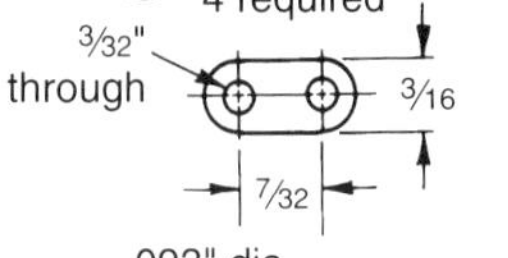

(18) 1⁄16" steel 4 required

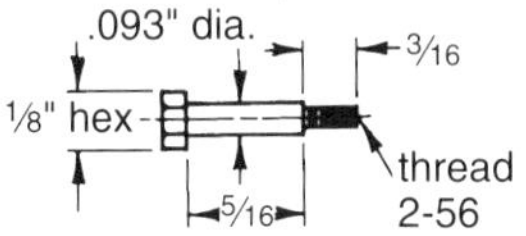

3⁄32" through

3⁄16

7⁄32

.093" dia.

3⁄16

1⁄8" hex

5⁄16

thread 2-56

SHACKLE BOLTS steel 4 required with nuts

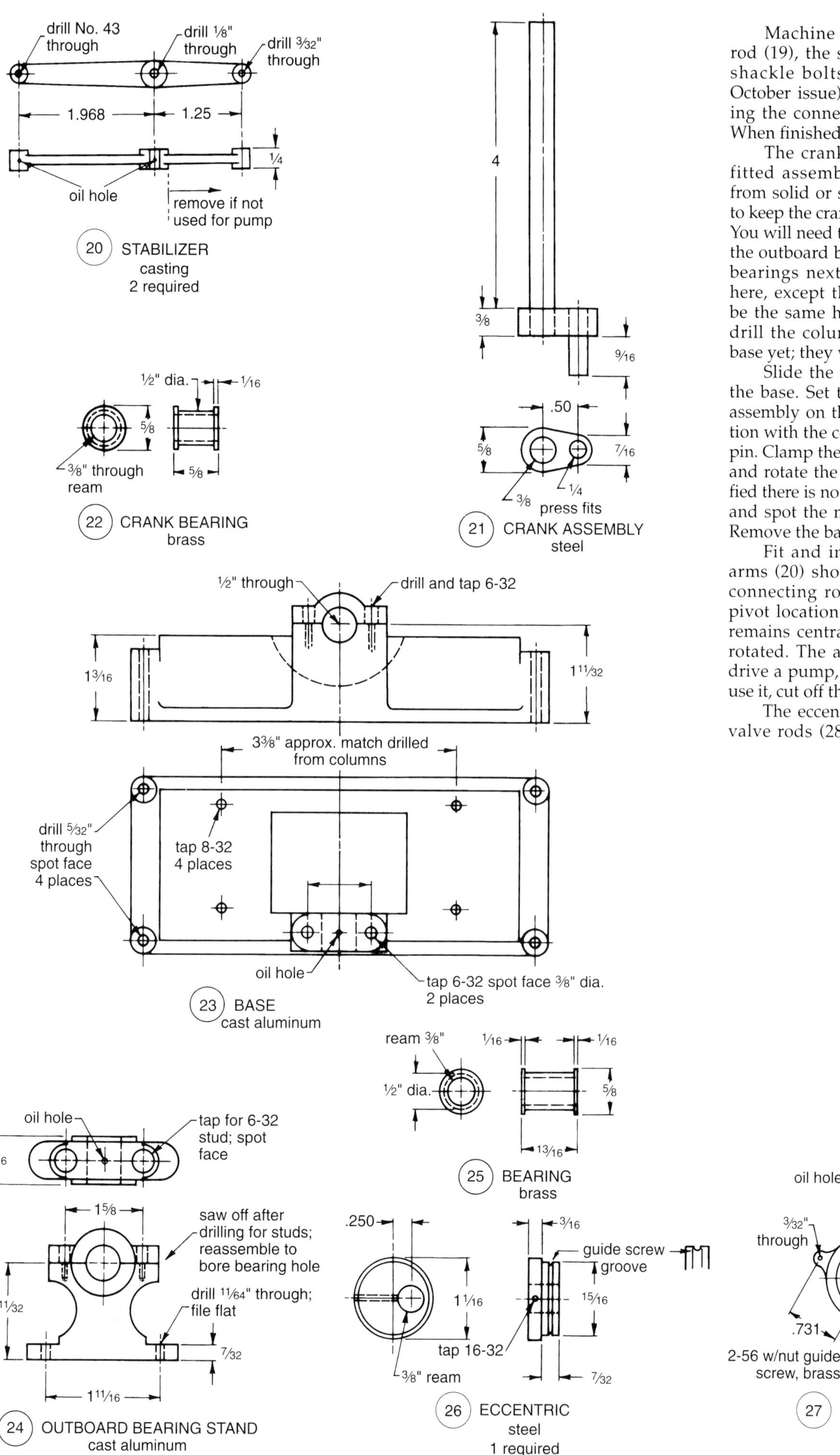

Machine the triangular connecting rod (19), the shackles (18), and the four shackle bolts (Photo 7 – September/ October issue). Be careful to avoid bending the connecting rod while drilling it. When finished, install it.

The crankshaft is shown as a press fitted assembly; it could be machined from solid or silver soldered. Just be sure to keep the crankpin parallel with the shaft. You will need the base (23), the cap, (23-A), the outboard bearing stand (24), and their bearings next. There is nothing critical here, except that the crank centers must be the same height on each piece. Don't drill the column mounting holes in the base yet; they will be match drilled later.

Slide the crankshaft into position in the base. Set the cylinder block/column assembly on the base and slide into position with the connecting rod on the crankpin. Clamp the columns loosely to the base and rotate the crank. When you are satisfied there is no binding, tighten the clamps, and spot the mounting holes in the base. Remove the base to drill and tap.

Fit and install the stabilizer/pump arms (20) shown in Photo 7. Fasten the connecting rod end first, then spot the pivot location on the column so the rod remains centrally located as the crank is rotated. The arm is cast long enough to drive a pump, etc. If you are not going to use it, cut off the excess and round the end.

The eccentric (26), the strap (27), the valve rods (28), and the valve rod ends

(29 and 30) can be made up and installed. The rod ends could be brass, but in real life, they would be steel. In either case polish them.

The flywheel is shown having a 5″ diameter, but this is not critical, so turn it to suit yourself. Put a slight crown on the periphery. The four 4-40 holes in the hub are used to attach the drive pulley/sheave (32), so this surface must be at right angles to the crank bore. I show a setscrew being used to lock the flywheel in position. I gave some thought to using a key, but decided it wasn't necessary. I would advise you to face and bore the pulley and mount it on the flywheel for finish turning. There is enough metal available in the pulley to cut rope grooves if so desired. If you use a flat belt, put a slight crown on the pulley (1-1/2° each side).

Make up the manifolds (33 and 34), shown in Photo 8 (September/October issue). Olives are shown as seals on the manifolds. They could be brass, copper, or O-rings, or as the prototype uses, *Teflon*. Your choice. Bending the steam lines can be very aggravating. I made several sets before I was satisfied. The appearance of the graceful curves is worth the effort. These are pretty tight bends, so anneal the tube often and persevere. Don't try to put a bend right at the end of the tube. Leave it long, and trim to proper length after all bending is complete.

The sub base is a matter of personal preference. The prototype engine is

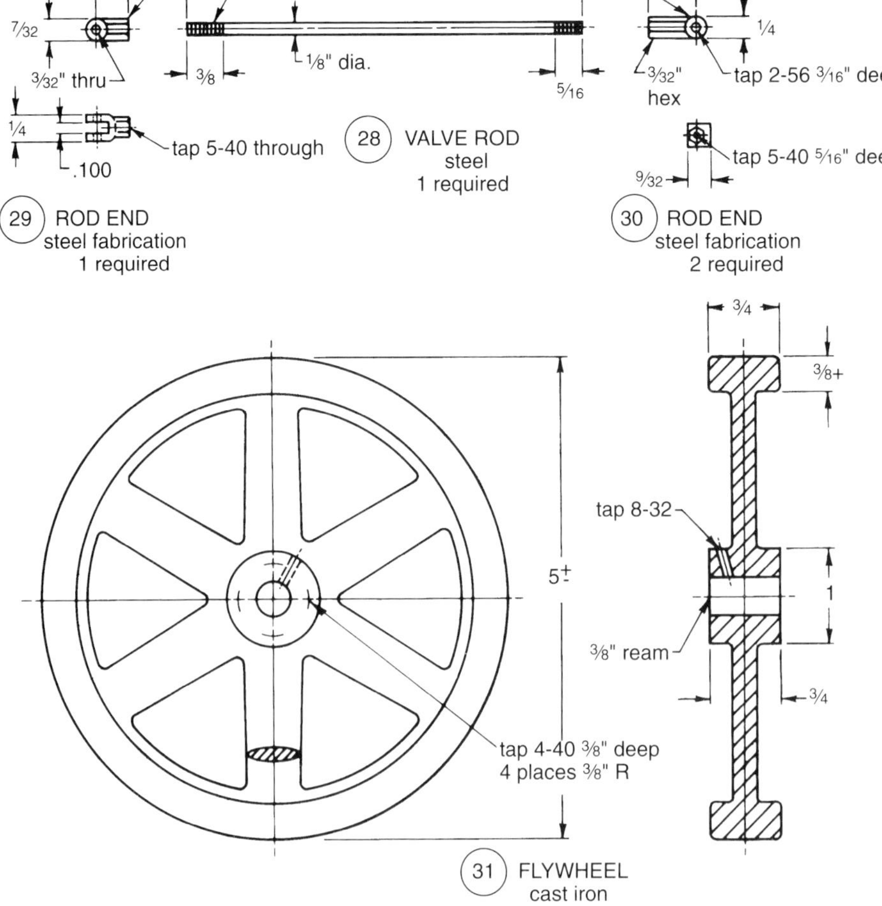

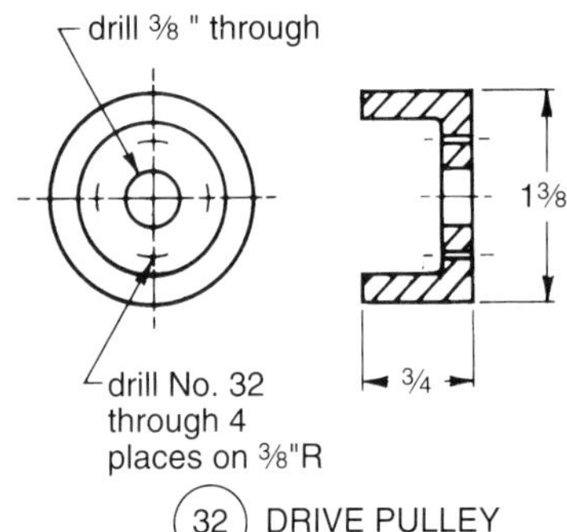

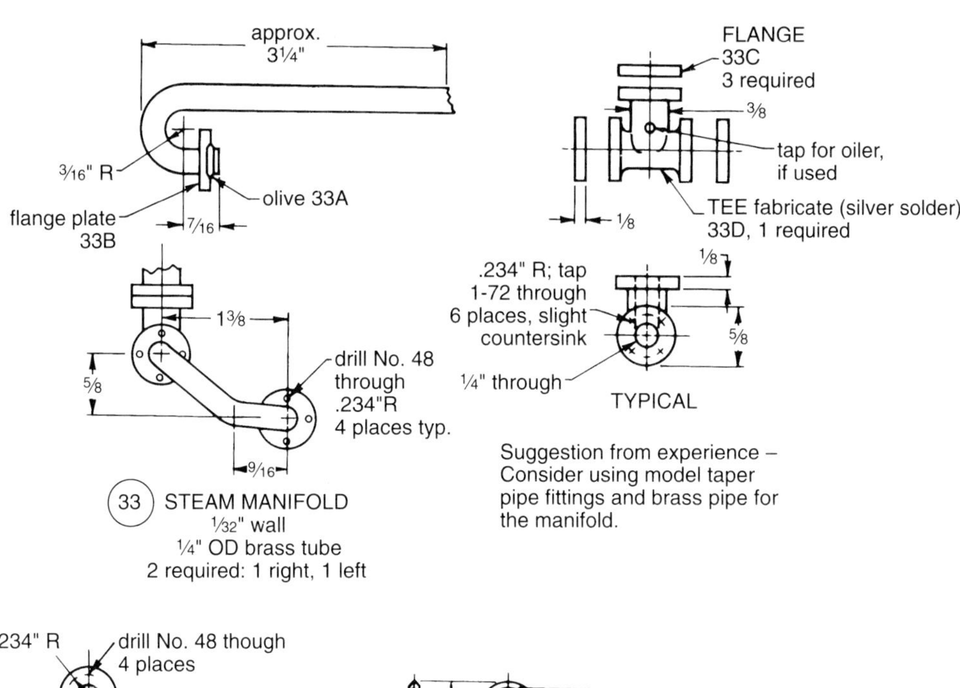

33 STEAM MANIFOLD
1/32" wall
¼" OD brass tube
2 required: 1 right, 1 left

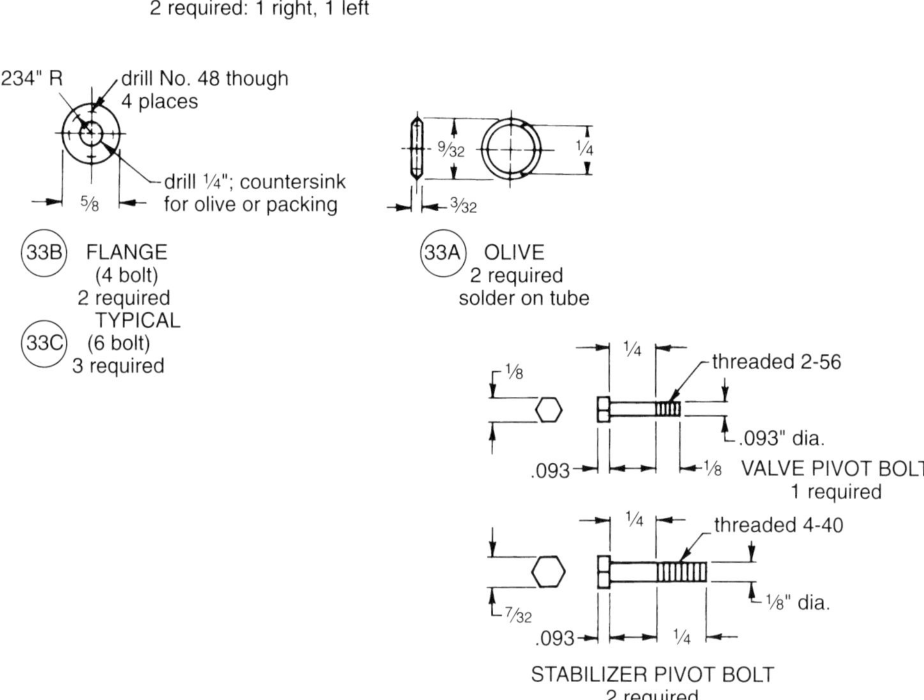

33B FLANGE
(4 bolt)
2 required
TYPICAL
33C (6 bolt)
3 required

mounted on a piece of *Corian* (counter top material) with an ash edging. Miniature bricks such as used on doll houses would look nice. Whatever you use, be careful to keep the outboard bearing in the same plane as the base.

To time the engine, start by setting the eccentric high point 90° in advance of the crankpin. Slide the valve arms (9) onto the spindles; leave the clamp screws loose for now. Remove the cylinder covers and the rear valve covers (exhaust side). Turn the crank to raise one piston to the extreme top position. Using a small screwdriver, adjust the valve for this cylinder to align the bars to the "just opening" position.

Tighten the clamp screws on the valve arm. Now move the piston to its extreme bottom position and compare the bar alignment. The bars should be in the same relative position as they were at the first setting. If not, split the difference and recheck both settings. Get it as even as possible. Follow the same procedure to set the valve for the other cylinder.

Remember to always turn the crank in the same direction when setting the valves. Replace the cylinder covers and supply some air. The prototype started on 15-20 psi. After some fiddling around with the valve and eccentric and installing head gaskets, it starts on 7-10 psi and runs on 3-5. After you are satisfied with the timing, reinstall the valve covers and put locknuts on the clamp screws.

This engine is not reversing, as most mill engines ran only one direction. It could be made reversible by several methods, the simplest probably being a slip eccentric.

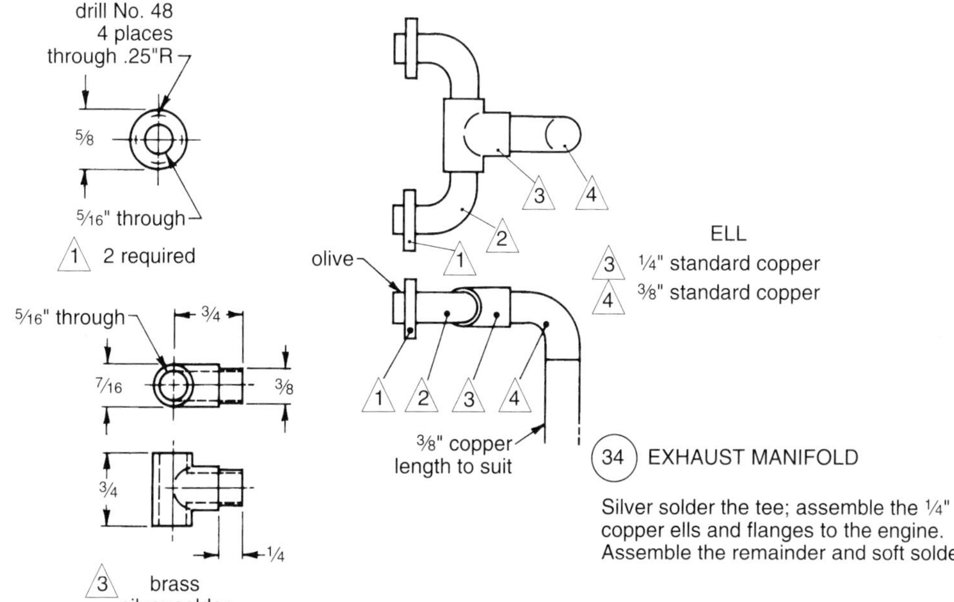

34 EXHAUST MANIFOLD

Silver solder the tee; assemble the ¼" copper ells and flanges to the engine. Assemble the remainder and soft solder.

Castings for this engine are available from the author: Paul E. Jacobs, 1745 Glastonberry Road, East, Toledo, Ohio 43613.

The Mystery Machine

By Arnold Teague

Photos by Author

We began the engine, dubbed "Aaron's Mystery," by drilling through both sides of the tube (4). After the necessary de-burring, I was looking around for stock for the valve core (2) and found a length of 6 gauge copper wire in the salvage pile. It slipped nicely into the tube, so I filed it to form the port passages. It was installed by soldering in the hole opposite the intake (steam?) port. The wheel rim (3) was formed from the same copper wire, as were the plugs (13, 16 and 17) – building up as required with tube to suit the situation.

The piston was capped at the top to avoid distortion that might cause problems with "free fit" in the cylinder. (This is very wasteful of expansion area, but efficiency was not a consideration.)

Using my chain saw file, I notched out the manifold tubes as a matched pair. Every modelmaker should have chain saw files in his collection. Generally of good quality, they are finetoothed, have no taper, and come in fractional sizes. Matching spacing of these notches (pipe saddles) is the only really critical dimension, because they determine the alignment of the main and pivot bearings. We filed one end of each, placed a tube in the saddles across the pair, and filed the second saddle in both tubes at the same time.

When work was completed on tubes (4) and (15), they were placed on a flat surface, ports up, and tubes (18) were placed over the ports. (Port spacing, maybe a little wide, was designed to allow room for the less skilled to operate and to make a more stable structure.) They were held in place with a weight, and then soldering was completed. All joints were pre-trimmed and, if the fit was good, needed no additional solder. Since OD and ID dimensions are stock, only lengths need to be considered, and they aren't very critical.

With a little care and good cleanup, the engine can be run by lung power. It may not be a typical steam or air engine, and no one said it was efficient. The engine runs better vertically, as shown, to take advantage of gravity during the exhaust stroke. The machine was fun to make and provided an opportunity to better know a grandson. Aaron's Mystery Machine was made for kids and is to be made by kids – young and old!

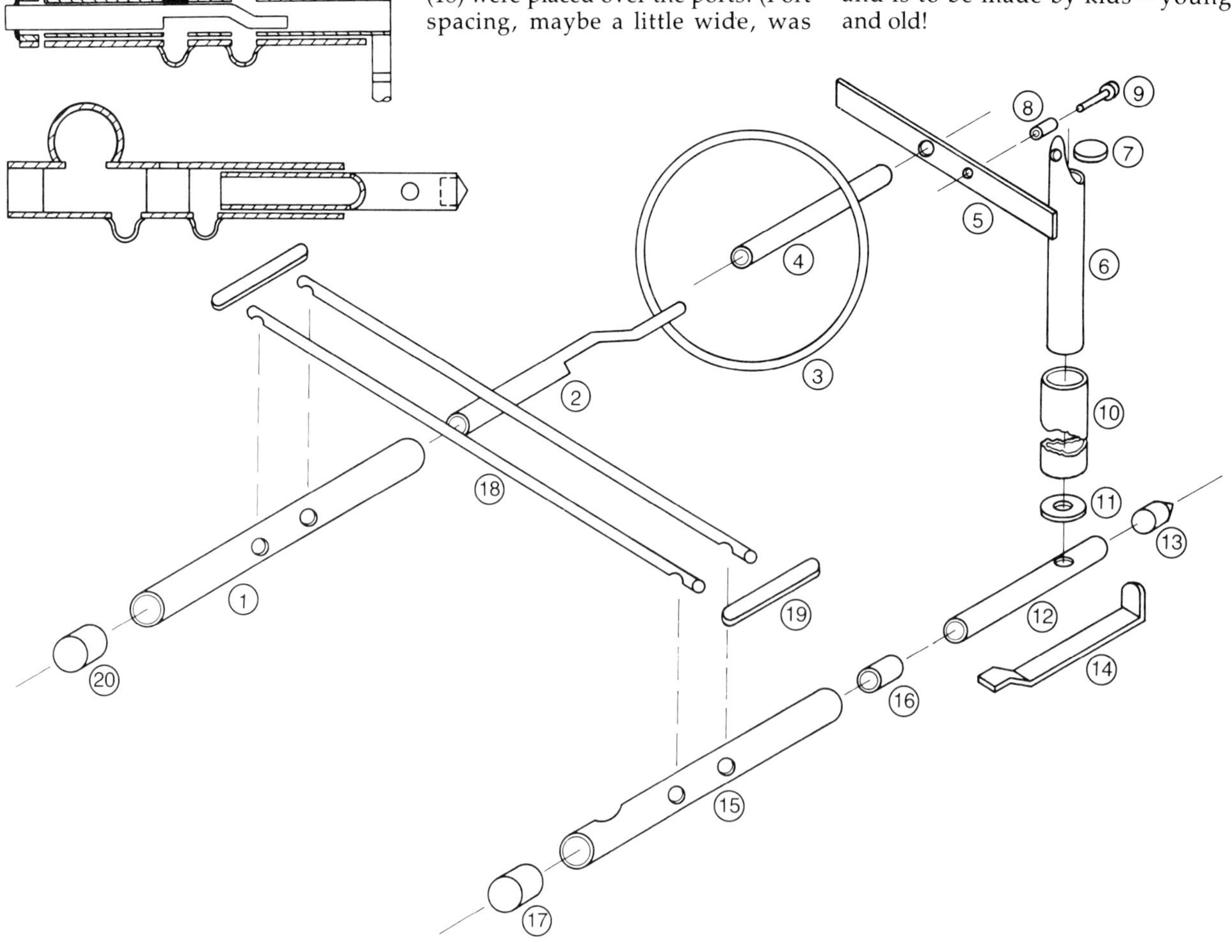

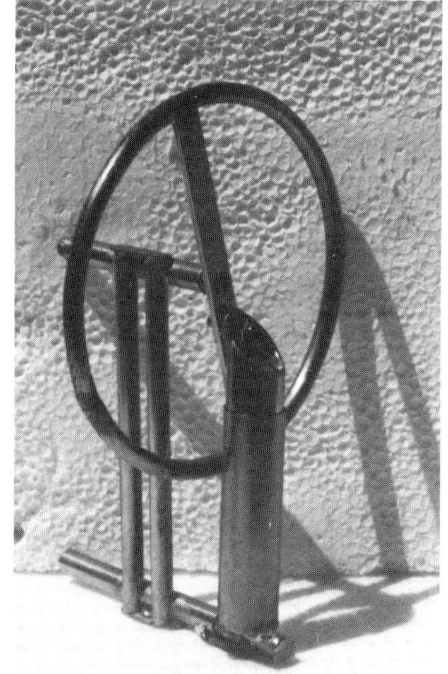

The photo series shows a display of the machine parts, the assembled machine, and the finished product ready for operation.

(1) Main bearing and valve housing	7/32 × 1 1/2
(2) Valve core – (copper wire, 6 ga.)	17/64 × 1 1/2
(3) Wheel rim (6 ga. cu.)	17/64 × 9 1/4
(4) Main shaft & valve ports	3/16 × 1 1/2
(5) Wheel spokes (brass flat)	1/16 × 1/4 × 2 15/16
(6) "Piston" (capped tube)	15/32 × 1 7/8
(7) "Piston" cap (from tube wall)	1/64 × 15/32∅
(8) Crank pin sleeve	1/8 × 5/32
(9) Crank pin	piece of 4d nail
(10) Cylinder tube	1/2 × 1 7/8
(11) Cylinder head (see (7))	1/64 × 1/2∅
(12) Cylinder support pivot tube	3/16 × 1 1/16
(13) Pivot tube plug (6 ga. cu.)	17/64 × 3/16
(14) Pivot tube retainer	1/32 × 3/16 × 1 1/8
(15) Pivot bearing and feed tube	7/32 × 2
(16) Center plug (port separation)	7/32 × 1/4
(17) End cap	7/32 × 1/4
(18) Manifold tubes	3/16 × 3 1/2
(19) Manifold tube caps (see (7))	
(20) Main shaft retainer	7/32 + 3/16 × 3/16

Note: This "as built" materials list is not intended to be restrictive but to simply give some idea of scale. They are post-construction dimensions!

"Woody"

By John W. Reichart

Photos by Author

This little engine was never intended to run on steam, but it does run nicely on compressed air. It is simply a nice heirloom to leave a grandchild, and a trophy to display your craftsmanship. By making a simple adapter out of wood, your shop vacuum sweeper can run the engine. The vac simply sucks the piston up and down while compressed air would push the piston.

Before starting to cut wood, study the drawing and understand the underlying principle by which it works. The cylinder oscillates on the frame as the engine runs. This motion creates the valve action that allows the pressure to push the piston down while at the same time allows air below the piston to exhaust. As the cylinder oscillates across, the reverse is true. As the ports align and the piston is pushed up, the air above the piston exhausts. This is technically called a 1½" bore × 2" stroke, double-action, oscillating cylinder, stationary steam engine.

If you are a good craftsman and accustomed to making precision wood parts, then fabricate them using your own methods. If you need guidance, then follow the steps that I outline

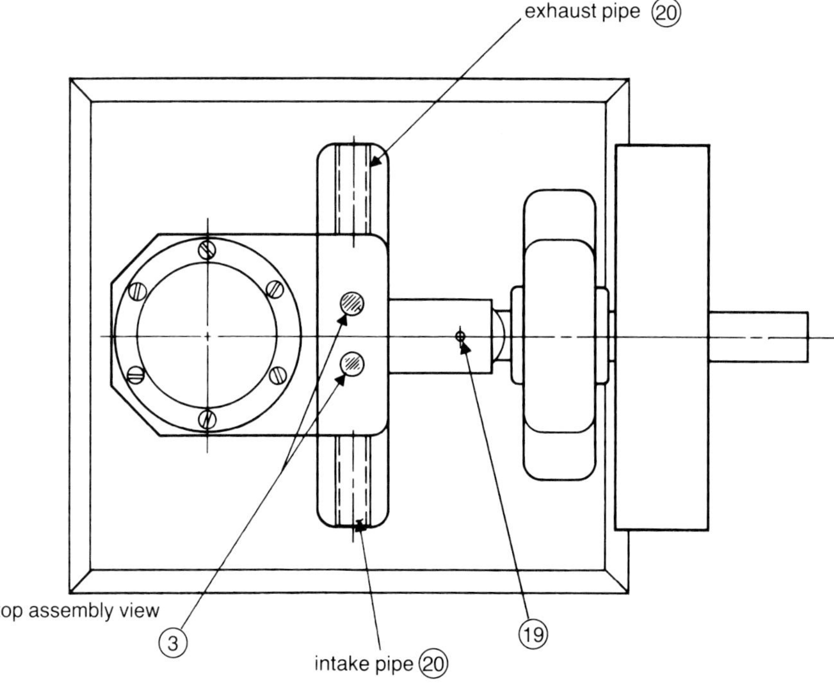

PT. NO.	NAME
1	Base
2	Main Frame
3	Plugs (2 req'd.)
4	Outer Bearing Support
5	Cylinder
6	Cylinder Pivot Rod
7	Cylinder Head Cover
8	Cylinder Lower Cover
9	Piston & Rod
10	Piston Rod End
11	Assembly Pin
12	Flywheel
13	Crankshaft
14	Crank Arm
15	Crankpin
16	Spacer
17	Bearings (4 req'd.)
18	Spring Housing
19	Assembly Pin
20	Intake/Exhaust Pipe (2 req'd.)

QUAN.	HARDWARE
13	No. 4 × ½" pan hd. SS sheet metal screws
4	No. 12 × 2" pan hd. sheet metal screws
1	Spring: Ajax Wire Specialties no. 67-x
1	Brass name plate
2	Escutcheon pins – for name plate
	Elmers Carpenter Glue
	Tung oil for finishing

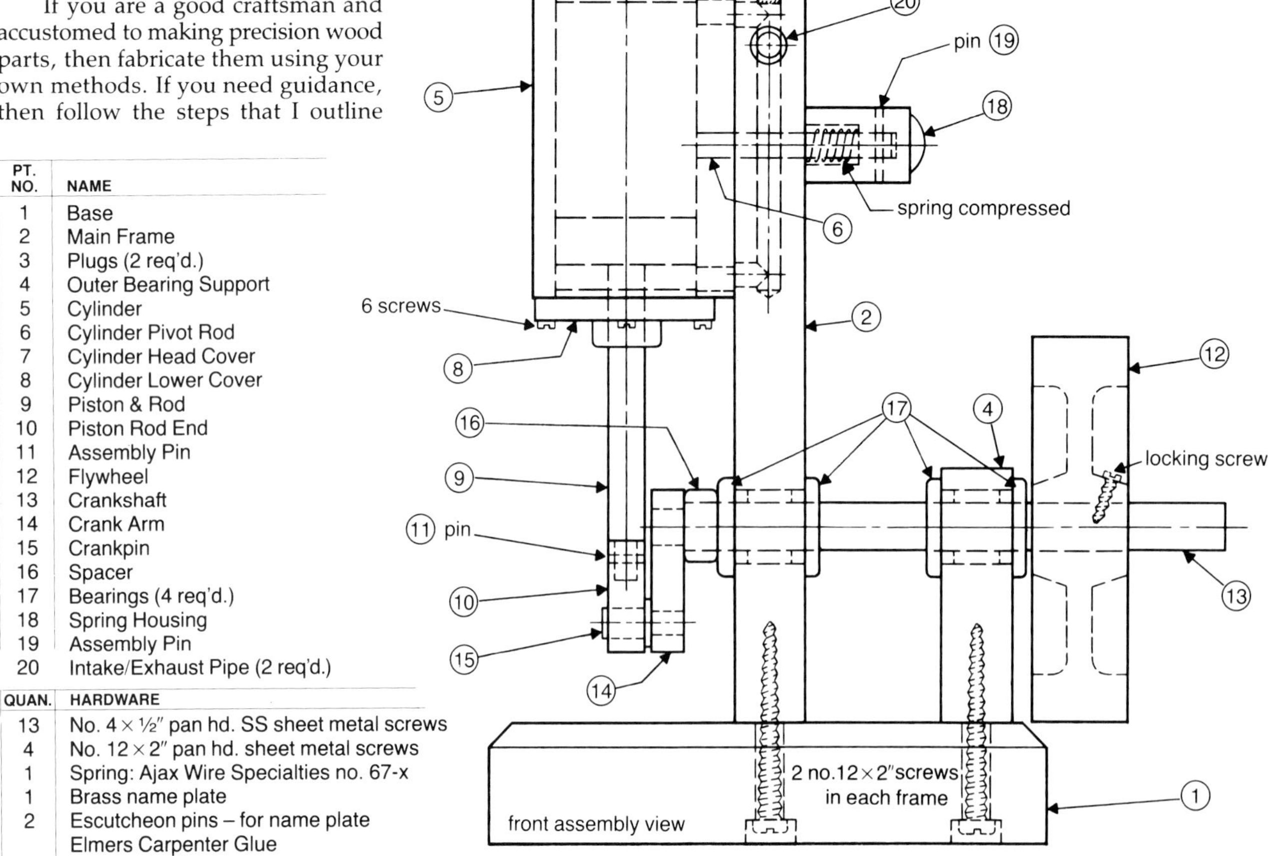

here. All wood parts must be good hardwood. Use all the same wood, or mix them up as you desire.

To drill precision holes, use wood bits with a *spur point* and a drill press. To eliminate splitting or breaking the small parts, plus keeping warping to a minimum, I recommend that these parts be laminated. This simply means sawing thin wood pieces, then criss-crossing the grain and gluing them together. That will give you a very strong

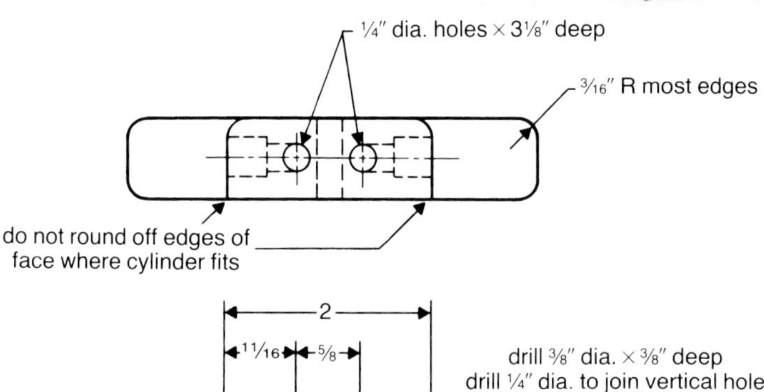

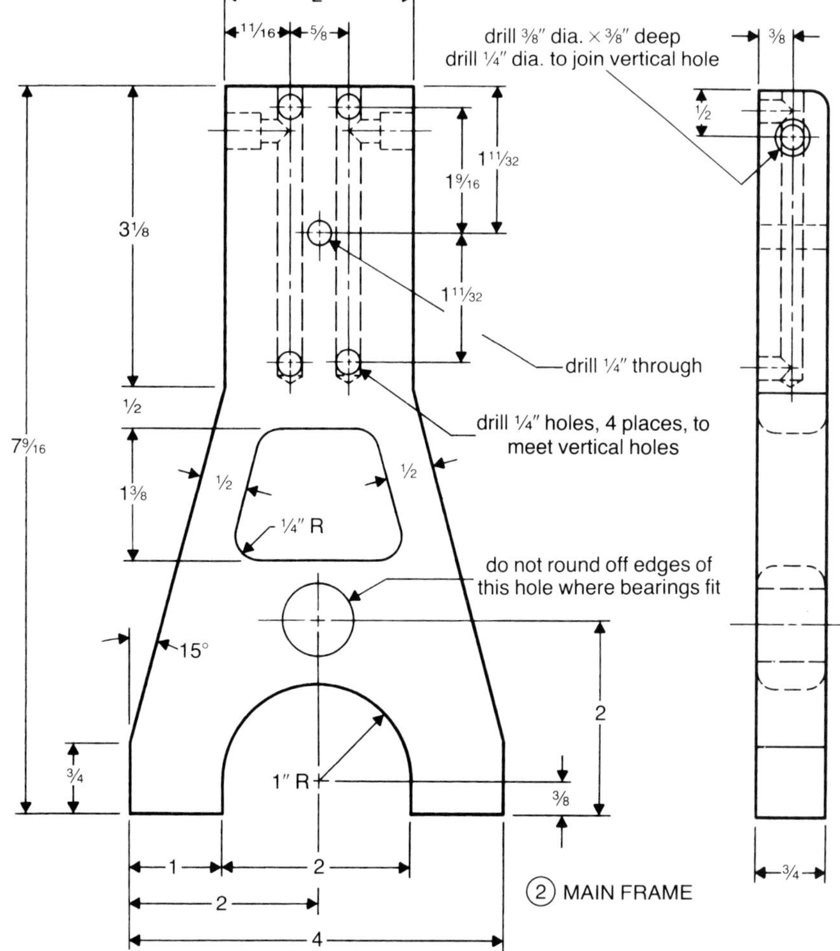

hardwood piece from which to make the particular part.

While this is essentially an all-wood steam engine, I strongly suggest that you use the screws indicated. The engine can be glued or doweled together, but then it can never be disassembled. Make the parts in the order that is shown here.

Main Frame (2)

Cut accurately and square the piece ¾″ × 4″ × 7⁹⁄₁₆″. It is okay to have it slightly thicker. Draw on this piece the complete shape, and lay out all the holes. Using a 90° angle block and drill press, drill the two long vertical ¼″ holes, 3⅛″ deep. Then drill the four ¼″ holes half through to meet the vertical holes. These are valve ports. Next, drill the ¼″ hole through where the cylinder mounts.

Drill four ½″ diameter holes at the corners of the trapezoidal cutout. These form the radii. Then drill the ¾″ hole for the main bearing. Complete the shape with a jigsaw and then sand smooth. Round off the edges using a router and ³⁄₁₆″ radius cutter. Do not round off the ¾″ bearing hole or the bottom of the legs that attach to the base. Also, do not round off the sides and top that fit against the cylinder. Drill two side holes ⅜″ diameter × ⅜″ deep where intake and exhaust pipes fit. Then, in these same holes, drill ¼″ holes into the vertical ports. Then give the piece a final finish sanding all over. Be sure all sawdust and chips are out of all ports.

Plugs (3)

Make two short 1/4" diameter plugs. Glue them into the holes in the top of Part 2 and sand them off.

Outer Bearing (4)

Make the Outer Bearing in a similar fashion to Part 2. Again rout off all edges except the 3/4" hole and the bottom edges of the feet.

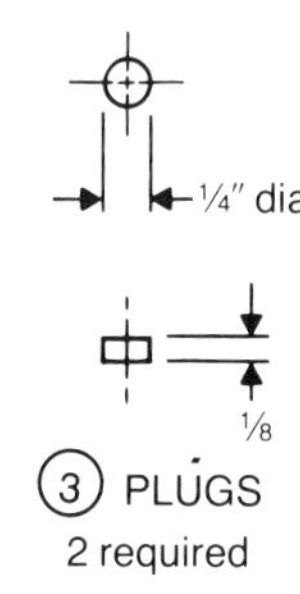

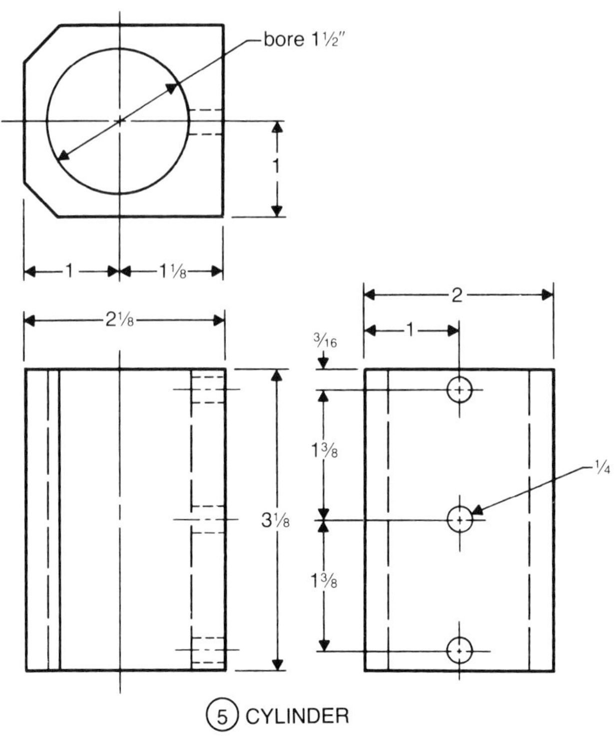

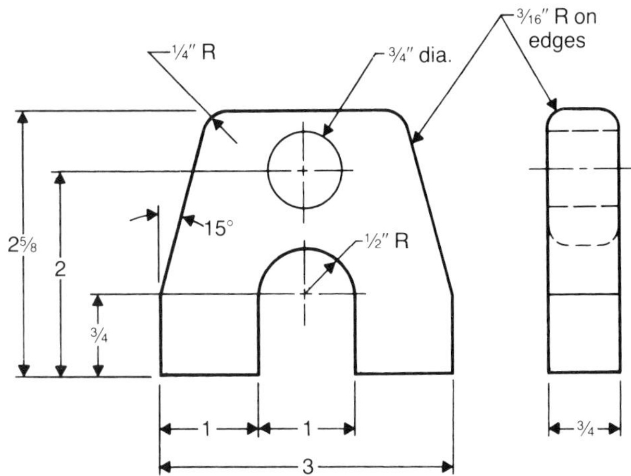

Cylinder (5)

The Cylinder is the most difficult piece to make for "Woody." Fabricate it any way you desire, but the steps I describe here are the methods I used. Because this is turned between centers, you can remove it from the lathe and test if for a nice sliding fit in the Cylinder (5) and Bottom Cover (8). Do not make it too close a fit. When the fit is complete, cut off the extending ends of the rod.

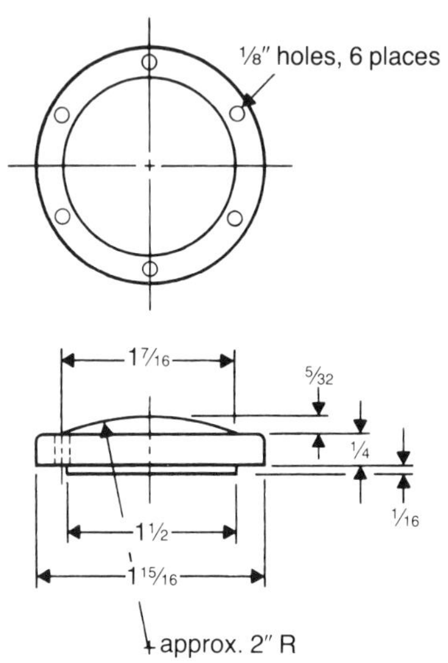

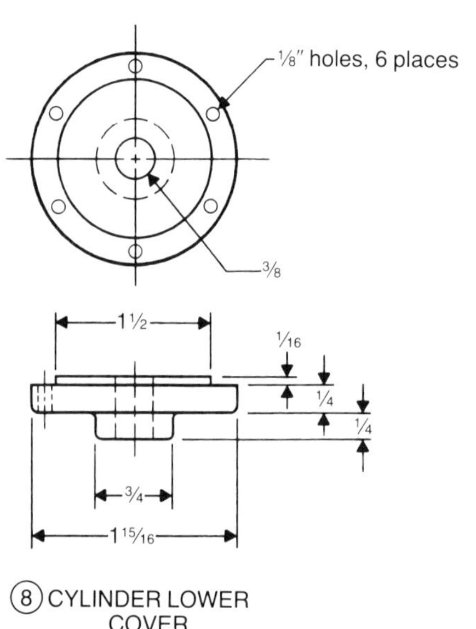

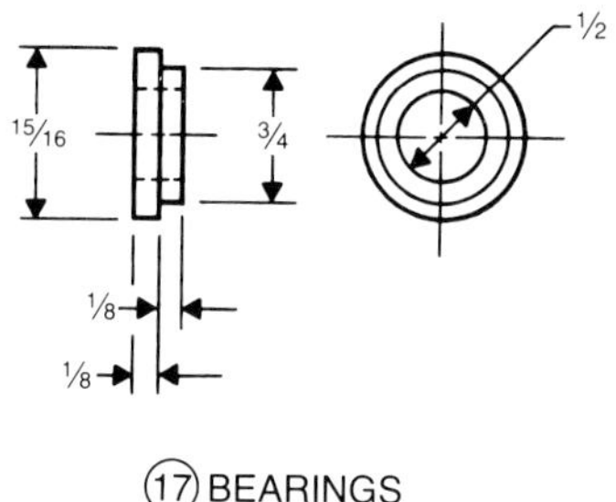

⑰ BEARINGS
4 required

Bearings (17)

The Bearings must be laminated. Saw several strips 3/32″ × 1⅛″ × 8″ to 10″ long, and sand the sides flat. Then cut them into 16 pieces 3/32″ × 1⅛″ × 1⅛″. Glue four pieces together crossing the grain. (Make four such pieces.) When they are dry, rough-saw each to 1⅛″ diameter. Then chuck each in the lathe and turn the ¾″ to fit the frame. Accurately drill the ½″ hole through the center. Do all four parts.

Next, make a jig. In the lathe, chuck a piece of ¾″ dowel about 1½″ long. Turn the end about ¼″ long and a diameter that will allow the bearings to push on firmly. By hand, press the bearings on and finish the other end to the dimensions shown and sand smooth. Glue these four bearings into the frame members.

Base (1)

The size and shape of the Base can be to your own taste. The dimensions shown were used on the model engine.

6
drill 15/64″ holes, 4 places
5⅜ 3
2
1 11/16
1 3/16
3
¾
¼″ bevel
1¼
5/16
counterbore 7/16″ dia.

① BASE

Sub Assembly

Assemble the Frame (2) and the Outer Bearing Support (4) to the Base (1). By now, both frame members should have the bearings glued in place. Make a ½″ diameter steel or wood shaft about 5″ long that will slide into the bearings of both parts 2 and 4. With this alignment shaft in place, clamp both 2 and 4 to the base in the proper location. Using a ¼″ electric drill, drill the screw starter holes into the four feet of Parts 2 and 4. Then put in the four mounting screws, and remove the clamps and alignment rod.

Crankshaft (13)

I doubt that a commercial dowel rod is accurate enough for this part. You would be wise to turn this piece in the lathe to the dimensions shown. When the Crankshaft is turned complete, fit it into the assembled bearings. Do not polish the shaft for a fit, but rather sand out the bearings until the shaft rotates freely.

Crank Arm (14)

The Crank Arm must be laminated. Make two pieces approximately 1″ × 2″ × 3/16″ thick. One of these must have grain lengthwise and the other must have grain crosswise. Glue them together with grain crossed. Lay out and dirll and cut to the proper shape. Then smooth the edges and sand.

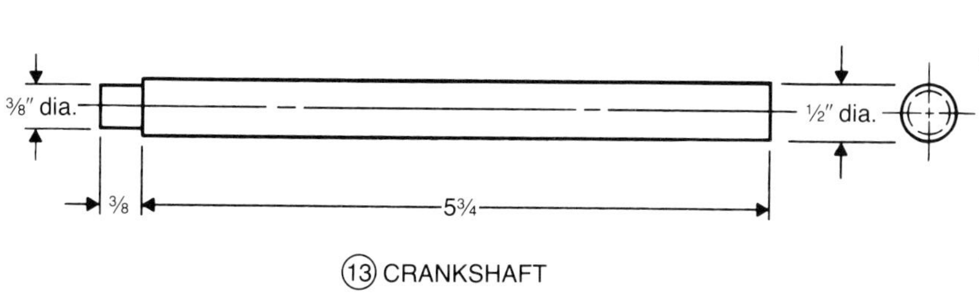

⑬ CRANKSHAFT

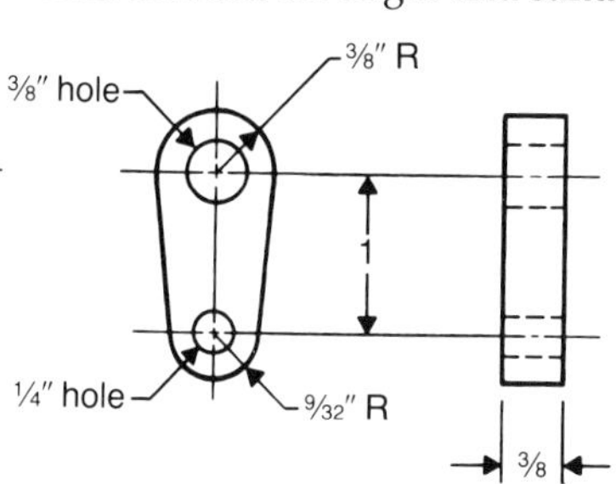

⑭ CRANK ARM

Crankpin (15)

The Crankpin is simply turned to the dimensions shown.

Piston Rod End (10)

The Piston Rod End must be laminated. It is made in a similar fashion to Part 14.

Crankshaft Assembly

When all of Parts 13, 14, 15, and 10 are finished, and all fit properly, then glue the crank together (Parts 13, 14 and 15). Do not glue on Part 10.

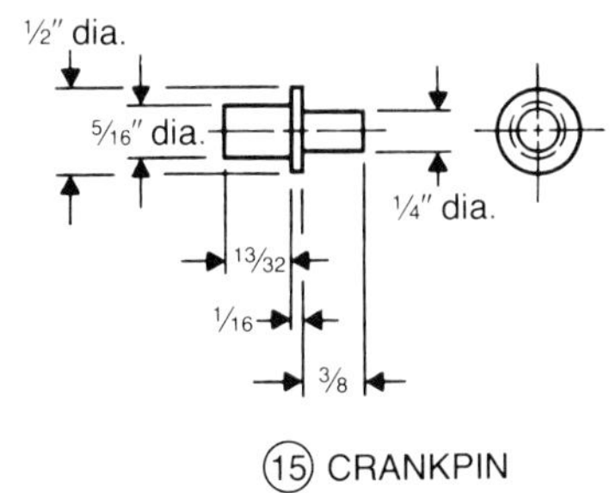

⑮ CRANKPIN

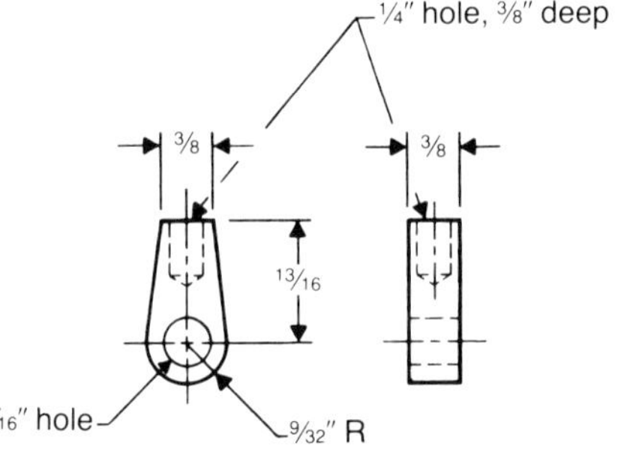

⑩ PISTON ROD END

Flywheel (12)

Select a very heavy piece of wood for this. It is possible that this can be made from one good solid piece. However, I made mine as follows: Saw a piece to 1⅛" × 2⅛" × 14". Set your miter gauge at 30° and saw six triangular pieces.

Glue them together as a hexagon. Then rough-saw the hex to a round shape. Finally, turn the piece to final dimension and bore the center hole in the lathe.

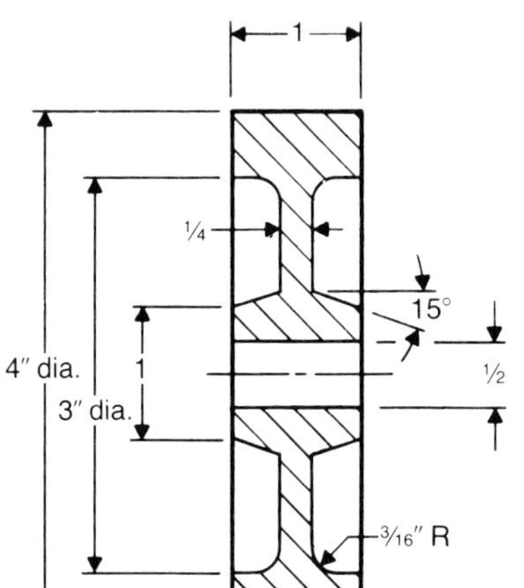
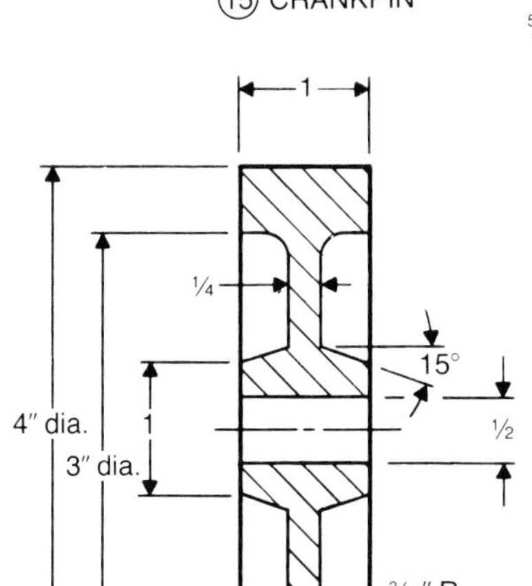

⑫ FLYWHEEL

Cylinder Pivot Rod (6)

Before making the Cylinder Pivot Rod, find the appropriate spring. At a local hardware store, I found a large assortment by Ajax Wire Specialties Company. For the model, spring no. 67-X was used. If you can find this exact spring, then proceed with the dimensions shown. Otherwise, make or find a light compression spring about as shown. If your spring is different, you may have to alter the dimensions of Part 6 and Part 18. When all is assembled, the spring must hold the cylinder firmly against the Frame, Part 2. Cut a ¼" dowel to the dimension shown. Be sure this turns freely in Part 2. Glue the dowel into the cylinder. To insure that this rod is perpendicular to the cylinder face, simply insert it into the proper hole in Part 2 for the glue to dry.

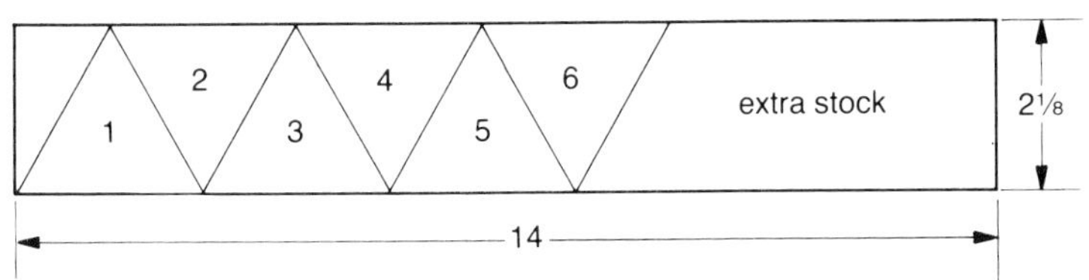

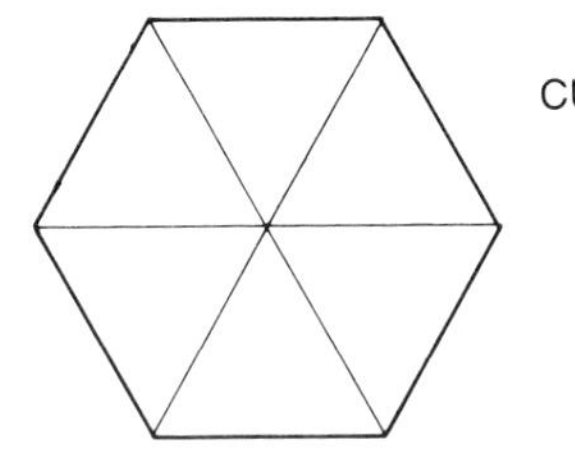

FLYWHEEL CUTTING PLAN

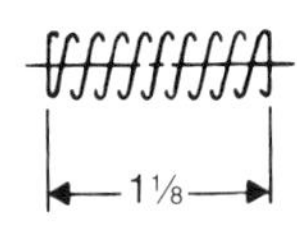

SPRING

5⁄16" OD – slips ¼" .030" .030" wire
Ajax Wire Specialities Co. no. 67-X
or similar

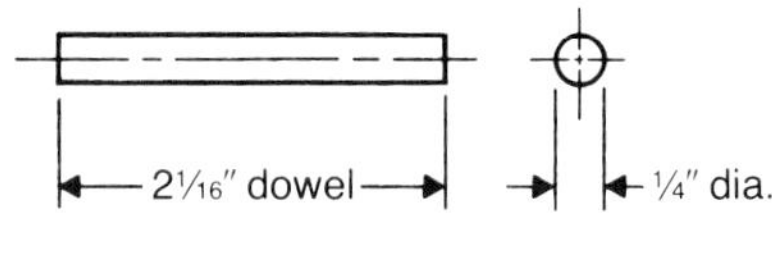

⑥ CYLINDER PIVOT ROD

Spring Housing (18)

Turn the Spring Housing from solid stock. Simply turn to the dimensions shown if you have the proper spring. If not, make this part so it will slip over the spring and compress it, and at the same time hide the spring from view. The grooves are for appearance only.

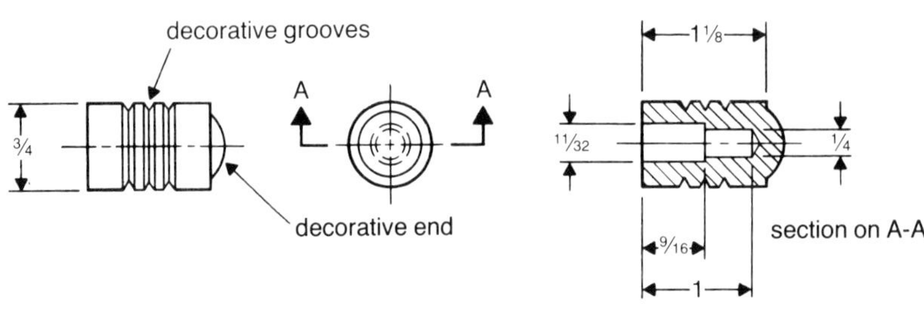

⑱ SPRING HOUSING

Assembly Pins (11) and (19)

These two wood pins are 1/16″ to 3/32″ in diameter. They can be found on cotton swabs in drugstores. Or perhaps the druggist can furnish wood "applicator" sticks that are used by doctors as sticks for cotton swabs. Another possibility is making these wooden pins from a section of a round toothpick. Whenever you have a suitable stick, simply drill an appropriately sized hole and lightly tap in these two pins. Use a small finishing nail backward to tap them out for disassembly.

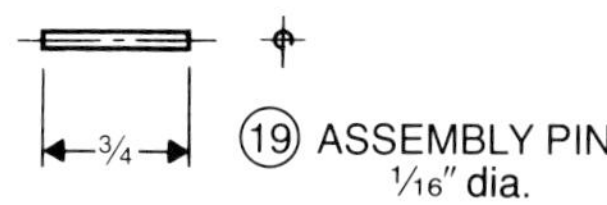

(19) ASSEMBLY PIN
1/16″ dia.

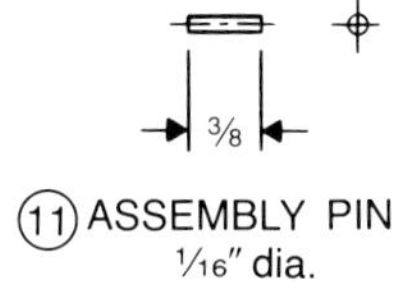

(11) ASSEMBLY PIN
1/16″ dia.

Spacer (16)

When the engine is fully assembled, make a wooden spacer to fit on the crankshaft. The width of this spacer must fit loosely in the space available for it. This spacer and the flywheel control the end play in the crankshaft.

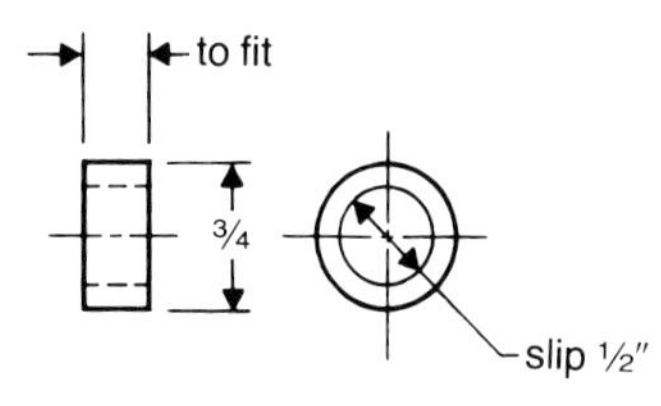

(16) SPACER

Intake and Exhaust Pipes (20)

These pipes are made of solid wood. Turn the two wooden tubes per the dimensions shown and glue them in place.

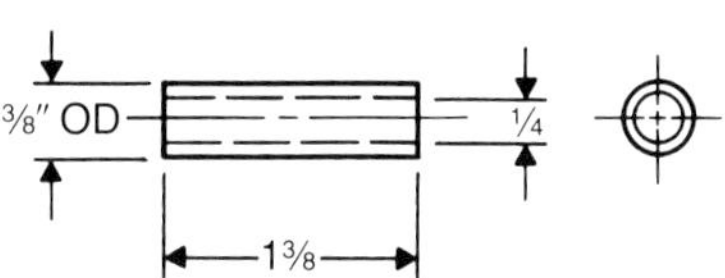

(20) INTAKE/EXHAUST PIPE
2 required

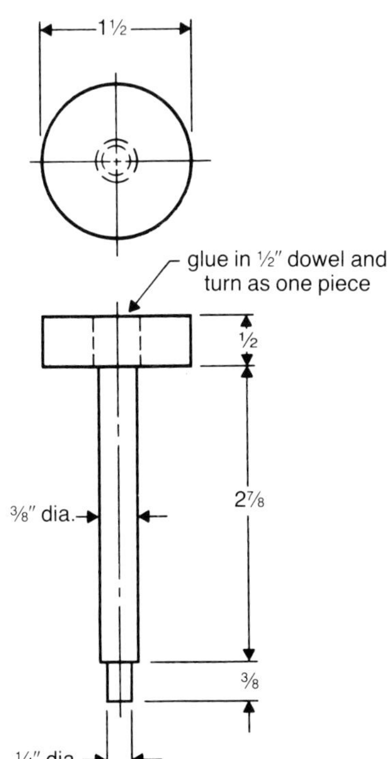

(9) PISTON & ROD

Final Assembly

Slip the piston into the cylinder. Then slip Part 8 over the piston rod and against the cylinder. When the piston and rod slide freely, drill the six starter holes and put in the screws. Attach the cylinder head cover (7) with six screws. Put on Part 10 (Piston Rod End) and put in pin 11. Then put in the crankshaft. Slide the cylinder in place and complete the spring assembly and insert pin 19. Then mount the flywheel. Now as the crankshaft is turned, your engine moves. Slide the flywheel up close to the bearing. After spacer 16 is made and in place, the flywheel can be fastened to the shaft with a screw.

Check It Out

Now your engine is ready to run. Simply blow hard into the intake pipe and spin the crank. Your engine should run. If not, work out the tight spots until it does. For prolonged running, use your shop vac. Make an adapter (a wood turning) to adapt your vacuum hose to the intake pipe. An air compressor and light pressure will really spin your engine.

Finishing

Completely disassemble and sand all parts clean and smooth. Using a small rag, wipe tung oil over all parts according to directions on the can. Your engine deserves a brass nameplate. Either make one or buy one at your local trophy store. A suggested size is about 3/4″ × 2″. On the nameplate use a name of your choice or call it "Woody." Include your name and the completion date. Now set "Woody" on the mantle for all to enjoy.

Duplex Pump

By Jeffrey C. Maier

Photos by Author

My duplex steam pump is not a scale model of any particular pump. I saw a working pump at an antique engine show, and was fascinated by the elegant motion of the mechanism, particularly the fact that no rotating parts were involved. With the memory of this pump, along with a few minutes of close-up video tape, I decided to design my own. The result has 1" steam cylinders, .75" water cylinders, and up to a 1.5" stroke. It is able to run smoothly down to about 20 psi on compressed air.

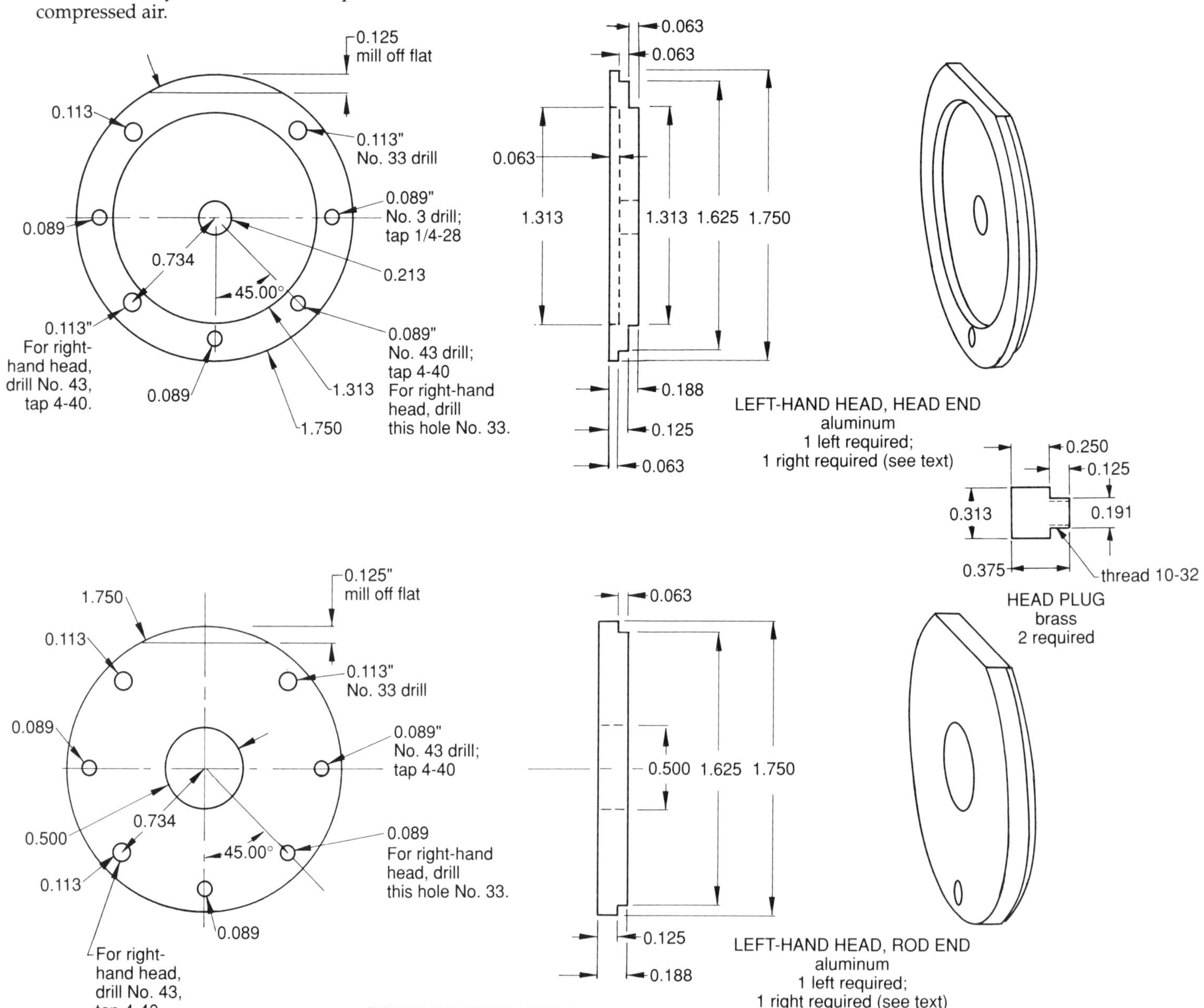

0.125
mill off flat
0.113
0.113"
No. 33 drill
0.089
0.089"
No. 3 drill;
tap 1/4-28
0.734
0.213
45.00°
0.113"
For right-hand head, drill No. 43, tap 4-40.
0.089
1.313
1.750
0.089"
No. 43 drill;
tap 4-40
For right-hand head, drill this hole No. 33.

0.063
0.063
0.063
1.313
1.313 1.625 1.750
0.188
0.125
0.063

LEFT-HAND HEAD, HEAD END
aluminum
1 left required;
1 right required (see text)

0.250
0.125
0.313
0.191
0.375
thread 10-32

HEAD PLUG
brass
2 required

0.125"
mill off flat
1.750
0.113
0.113"
No. 33 drill
0.089
0.089"
No. 43 drill;
tap 4-40
0.500
0.734
0.113
45.00°
0.089
For right-hand head, drill this hole No. 33.
0.089
For right-hand head, drill No. 43, tap 4-40.

0.063
0.500 1.625 1.750
0.125
0.188

LEFT-HAND HEAD, ROD END
aluminum
1 left required;
1 right required (see text)

STEAM CYLINDER HEADS

1

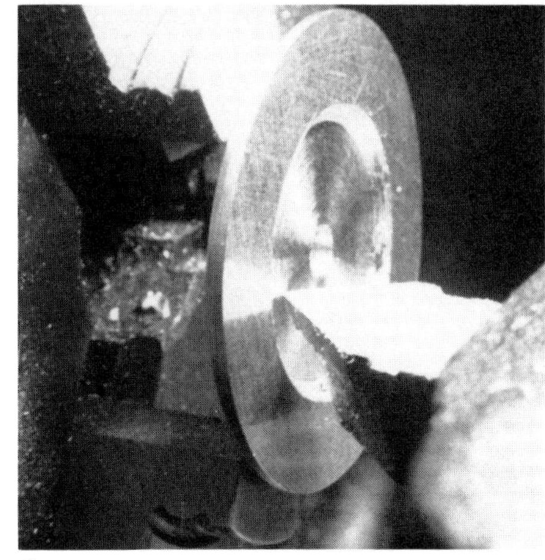

3

4

2

5

Many of the choices I made regarding materials, setups, and sizes were done with my own tools and available materials in mind. There is nothing sacred about the way I did anything, and I would encourage anyone wishing to build this project to experiment with and improve upon my design.

The instructions for building the pump fall naturally into two sections: the steam cylinders and the water cylinders. Let's begin with the steam cylinders. My usual practice is to make the cylinder block first, and then make all the pieces that attach to it. This time, I decided I wanted to be able to assemble the steam cylinders as much as possible when I had the block finished. So, the first pieces to make are the cylinder heads. Rough cut a circle larger than 1.750" out of some .188" thick aluminum. Drill a No. 11 hole through the approximate center and screw it into a mandrel on the lathe which has been previously drilled and tapped for 10-24. Turn the outside to 1.710". Turn a step .063" deep to 1.313". This step will fit into the cylinder block. Turn another .063" deep step to a diameter of 1.625" (**Photo 1**).

A similar process is used to make the cylinder head that goes at the rod end of the cylinder block. However, this piece has only one step – .063" turned to a diameter of 1.625". This head does not seal off the rod end of the cylinder. Its purpose is mainly cosmetic in that it holds the thin sheet brass shroud to the steam cylinders. **Photo 2** shows this head being turned. Next, turn the head end head over and grip it in the three-jaw chuck by one of the steps. Turn the central depression 1.000" in diameter and .063" deep, as shown in **Photo 3**. Drill out the central hole with a No. 3 drill and tap 1/4-28, as in **Photo 4**. Place the rod end head in the three-jaw chuck, gripping it by the step previously turned on it. **Photo 5** shows the head being drilled through with a .500" drill.

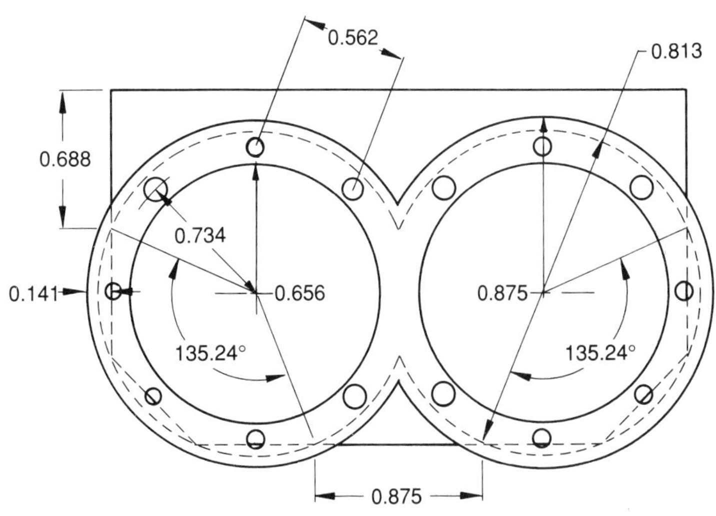

CYLINDER HEAD ASSEMBLY DETAILS

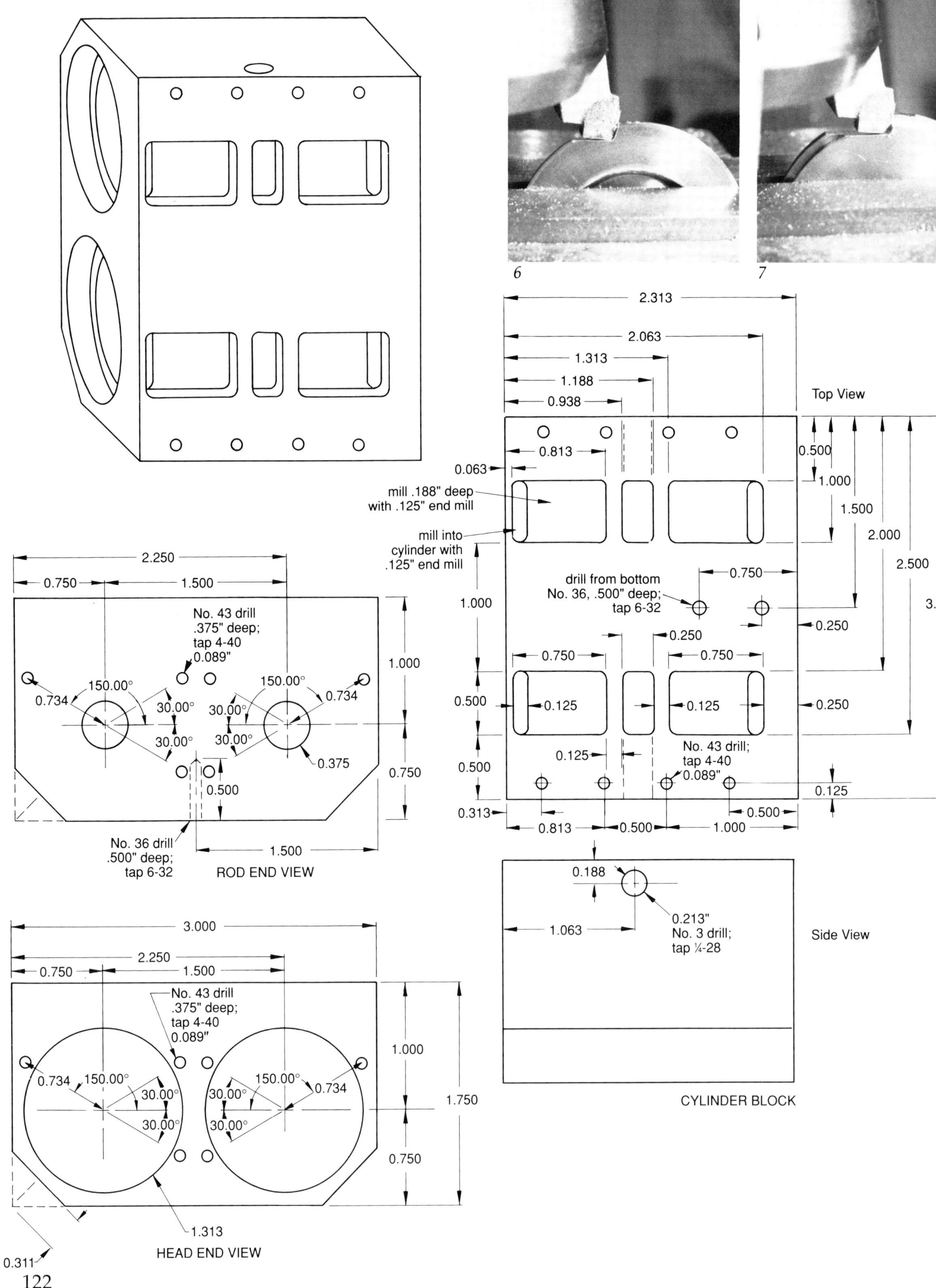
6
7
2.313
2.063
1.313
1.188
0.938
Top View
0.813
0.063
0.500
1.000
1.500
2.000
2.500
mill .188" deep with .125" end mill
mill into cylinder with .125" end mill
drill from bottom No. 36, .500" deep; tap 6-32
0.750
1.000
0.250
0.750
0.750
0.500
0.125
0.125
0.250
0.125
No. 43 drill; tap 4-40 0.089"
0.500
0.125
0.313
0.813
0.500
0.500
1.000
0.188
1.063
0.213" No. 3 drill; tap ¼-28
Side View
CYLINDER BLOCK
2.250
0.750
1.500
No. 43 drill .375" deep; tap 4-40 0.089"
1.000
150.00°
0.734
30.00°
0.375
0.750
0.500
No. 36 drill .500" deep; tap 6-32
1.500
ROD END VIEW
3.000
2.250
0.750
1.500
No. 43 drill .375" deep; tap 4-40 0.089"
1.000
0.734
150.00°
30.00°
1.750
0.750
1.313
0.311
HEAD END VIEW

8

9

10

11

In order for the heads to fit next to each other, both at the head and rod ends of the cylinders, a cut of .125" will have to be made on each head. Clamp the head end heads in the milling machine vise as seen in **Photo 6**. Position the cutter so it just grazes the highest point on the head. Move the table in the longitudinal direction so the cutter is clear, and lower the spindle by .125". Feed the table slowly and cut off the desired .125". Clamp the other head end head in the mill and repeat this operation. **Photo 7** illustrates removing .125" from the rod end heads. Note that the heads may be clamped in the mill vise without regard to angular position, as the holes that attach the heads to the cylinder block are not yet drilled.

Let's make the cylinder block next. Mill a block of aluminum to a size of 3.000 × 2.313 × 1.750". Clamp this block in the milling machine vise so the 3.000" dimension is parallel to the cross slide travel. Use a .125" end mill to cut the steam ways into the block as **Photo 8** illustrates. When the steam ways are finished, turn the block in the vise so the 2.313" dimension is parallel to the cross slide travel, as seen in **Photo 9**. Using the same .125" end mill, cut slots at the far ends of the four outer steam ways. Cut as deep as the mill will go. These slots will eventually connect with the outer ends of each steam cylinder. Remove the block from the milling machine and set it aside.

Mill a piece of .094" thick brass to 3.000 × 2.313". This will be the valve plate. Clamp this piece in the milling machine vise as illustrated in **Photo 10**. The 2.313" dimension will be parallel to the mill cross slide travel. Using a .125" end mill, cut slots as shown in the drawings. Set stops on the mill table in the longitudinal direction so the slots may be milled gradually, .03" to .04" in depth per cut. Do not run the cutter all the way to the stop on each pass. Stop just short, and after the plate has been cut all the way through, then run the table all the way to each stop, ensuring a nice, smooth cut.

Leaving the stops at the same settings, move the cross slide to cut the next slot. This will be the exhaust port, which is .25" wide. Cut a single .125" wide slot as before, then move the cross slide .125" to cut the second slot. After both slots are all the way through, run the table to each stop and then move the cross slide to clean up the other edges. Advance the cross slide .125" to mill the last slot, in the same manner as the first .125" wide slot. Now, set new stops on the table to cut the other set of slots. Remove the valve plate from the vise and set it aside.

Locate and center punch the positions of the center of each steam cylinder. Return the cylinder block to the milling machine, as illustrated in **Photo 11**. Shim the block up off the bottom of the vise by 3/8" or so to allow space for drill bits to come through. Center one of the cylinder locations under the mill spindle and lock it tightly in place. Several cutting operations will take place here, so the table must not move. Drill all the way through the block with a .375" drill. After backing the drill out, install a .500" drill and drill down to a depth of 2.063". Back out this drill and remove it and the drill chuck. Install the boring head in the mill. Begin boring to a depth of 2.063" each time, taking about .04" to .05" in diameter with each cut, until a diameter of 1.188" is reached. Continue cutting .04" to .05" in diameter, except now bore to a depth of 1.938". Continue boring until a diameter of 1.313" has been reached. You will have cut a step located right at the edge of the rod end steam way. This step will serve as a stop for the cylinder sleeve, so it gets inserted to the exact depth. Unlock the tightly clamped (and immobile) mill table, and locate the center of the other cylinder under the spindle.

Repeat all of the above drilling and boring operations for the second cylinder.

12

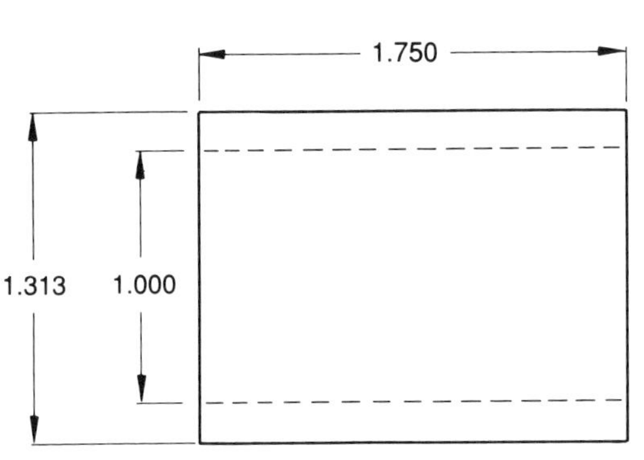

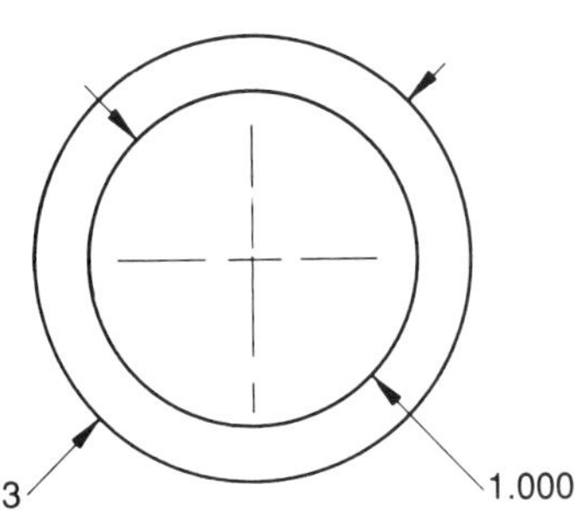

Size for a tight press fit in the cylinder block.

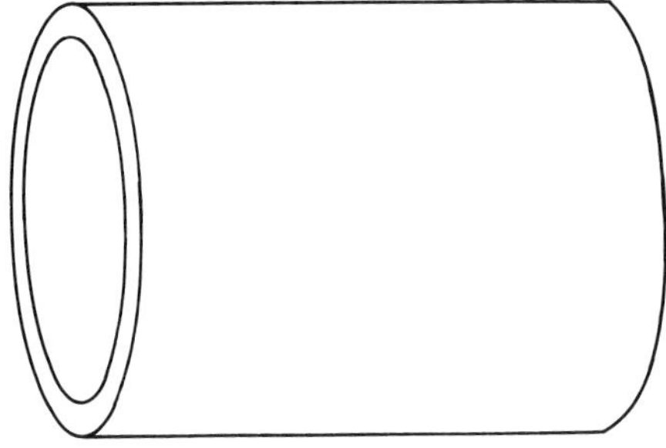

CYLINDER SLEEVE
brass
2 required

Turn and bore the cylinder sleeves on the lathe. Measure the exact diameter of the holes in the cylinder block and turn the sleeves .0005" larger for a tight press fit. Bore the inside of the sleeve to 1.000" while it is still in the lathe. You may press in both sleeves after both cylinders are bored, or you may do as I did (Photo 11) and press the first one in before boring the second cylinder.

Photo 12 illustrates the manner in which the block is cut down at the corners. The reason for this is to allow the sheet brass cylinder shroud to be able to clear the block, and wrap around it with no obstructions. Clamp the block in the mill vise at a 45° angle. Using a .500" end mill, lower the spindle until the mill just begins to cut the edge of the block. Set the spindle travel indicator to 0. Begin lowering the spindle, and cutting away at the block until it has been lowered by .311". This odd value will give a flat edge at 45° which, if continued around, would inscribe an octagon that would fit evenly around the cylinder bore. This flat edge could be milled down to any depth that cleared the shroud but didn't cut into the cylinder sleeve. Making an octagon to fit seemed to be an elegant compromise.

Locate and center punch the locations on the block for the exhaust port holes. Clamp the block in the milling machine vise as shown in **Photo 13**. Center the exhaust hole location under the spindle. Using a No. 3 drill, bore a hole through the block into the exhaust port until the tip of the drill just clears the outer edge of the hole. The drill bit is in this position in Photo 13. Back out and remove the drill and clamp a 1/4-28 tap in the drill chuck. Lower the chuck and start the tap by hand. When it is in as far as it can easily be turned by hand, loosen the drill chuck, raise it out of the way, and

13

14

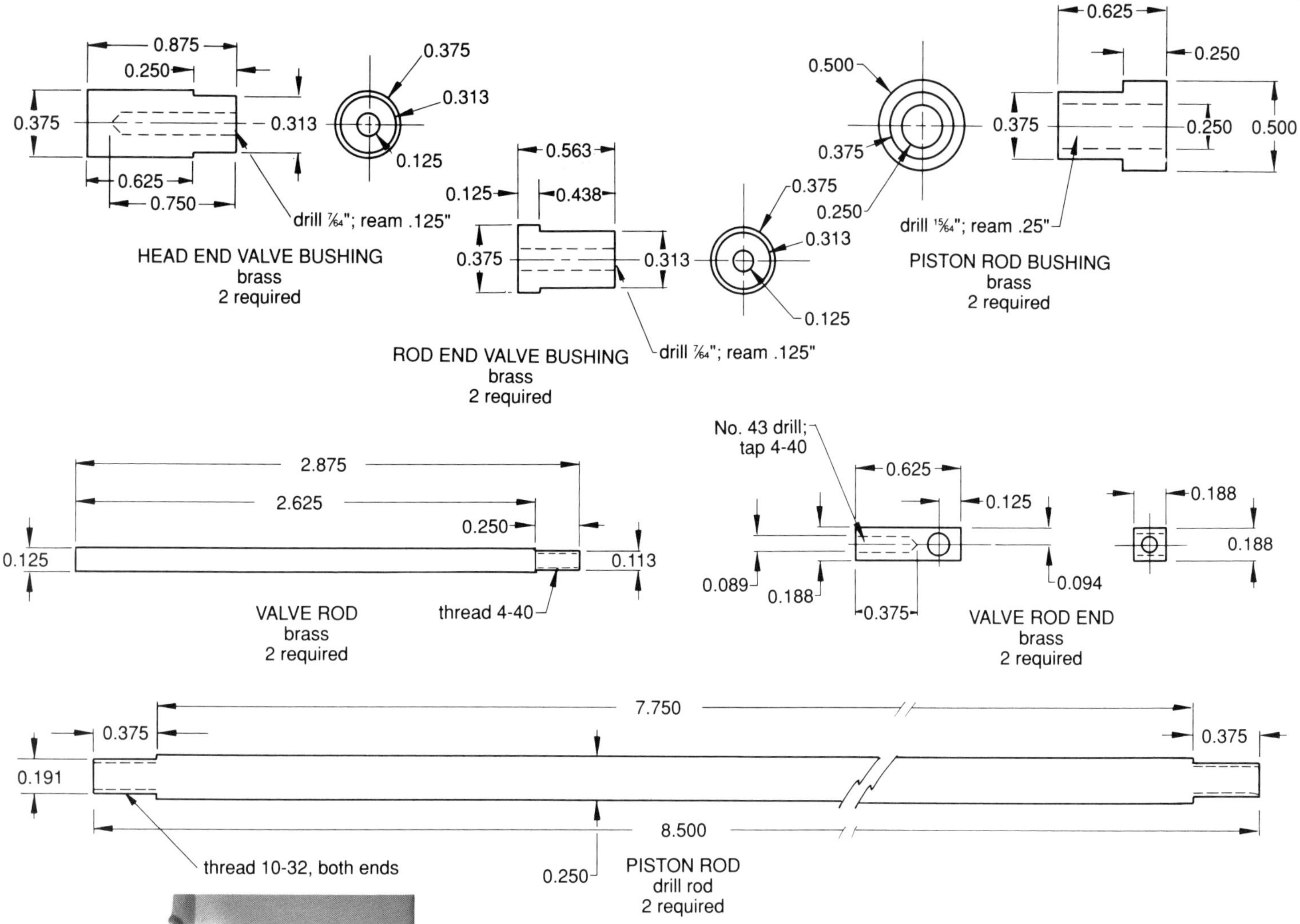

0.875
0.250
0.375
0.313
0.625
0.750
0.375
0.313
0.125
drill 7/64"; ream .125"

HEAD END VALVE BUSHING
brass
2 required

0.563
0.125
0.438
0.375
0.313
0.375
0.313
0.125
drill 7/64"; ream .125"

ROD END VALVE BUSHING
brass
2 required

0.625
0.250
0.500
0.375
0.250
0.375
0.250
0.500
drill 15/64"; ream .25"

PISTON ROD BUSHING
brass
2 required

2.875
2.625
0.250
0.125
0.113
thread 4-40

VALVE ROD
brass
2 required

No. 43 drill;
tap 4-40
0.625
0.125
0.188
0.188
0.089
0.188
0.375
0.094

VALVE ROD END
brass
2 required

7.750
0.375
0.375
0.191
8.500
thread 10-32, both ends
0.250

PISTON ROD
drill rod
2 required

15

finish the tapping job with a tapping handle. Unclamp the block from the vise, turn it over, and drill and tap the hole for the other exhaust port.

Make the piston rod bushings next. These are a press fit in the block, so turn them about .0005" oversize. Turn down .250" of a piece of .625" diameter brass rod to a diameter of .3755". Center drill and drill through with a 15/64" bit, followed by a .250" reamer (**Photo 15**). Remove the bushing, turn it around, and face off the other end. Press both bushings into the .375" holes in the rod end of the cylinder block. Make the valve rod bushings next. Again, make the turned down ends about .0005" oversize for a press fit into the steam chest. On the head end bushings,

16

17

18

19

20

7.625
4.156
3.469
Top
0.250
.188
.188
0.059"
No. 36 drill
tap 6-32
0.750
0.500
0.500
0.250
0.375
1.875
0.688
0.106"
No. 36 drill
tap 6-32, 4 places
1.875
4.156
3.469
BASE BAR
aluminum
1 required
0.750
0.250
0.125
0.500
0.141"
2 places
Top View
1.875
0.688
0.125
1.875
7.625

BASE BRACKET

21

22

drill in to a depth of .750" with a 7/64" drill. Finish the hole with a .125" reamer. Run it into the blind hole as far as it will easily go. For the rod end bushings, drill through with a 7/64" drill and finish with a .125" reamer.

Make the cylinder head plugs from lengths of .313" diameter brass rod, as shown in the drawings. After threading the plugs, install them in the head end cylinder heads with a drop of *Loctite*. Lay out and center punch the locations of the head bolts on both the head end and rod end cylinder heads. Clamp the block in the milling machine vise as seen in **Photo 16**. Place the two cylinder heads on as shown, and clamp down on each head plug. Drill with a No. 43 drill .500" deep. Note that only three holes are drilled into the block through each cylinder head. These holes are the only ones that have been drilled in Photo 16.

Photo 17 shows the setup for drilling the holes in the rod end heads. Again, the only holes drilled in Photo 17 are the ones that actually go down into the block. Unclamp and remove the cylinder heads.

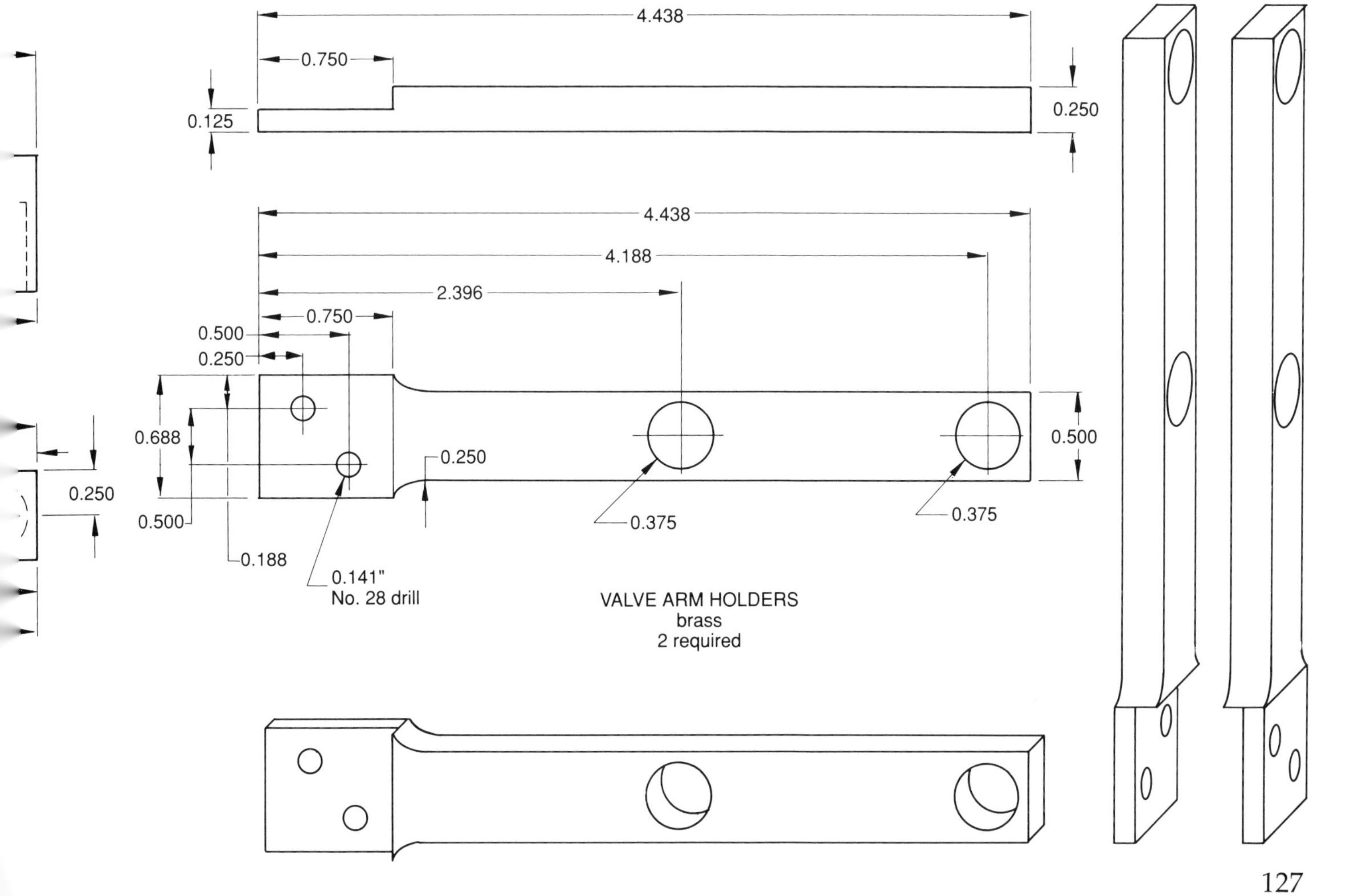

4.438
0.750
0.125
0.250
4.438
4.188
2.396
0.750
0.500
0.250
0.688
0.500
0.250
0.188
0.141"
No. 28 drill
0.250
0.375
0.375
0.500

VALVE ARM HOLDERS
brass
2 required

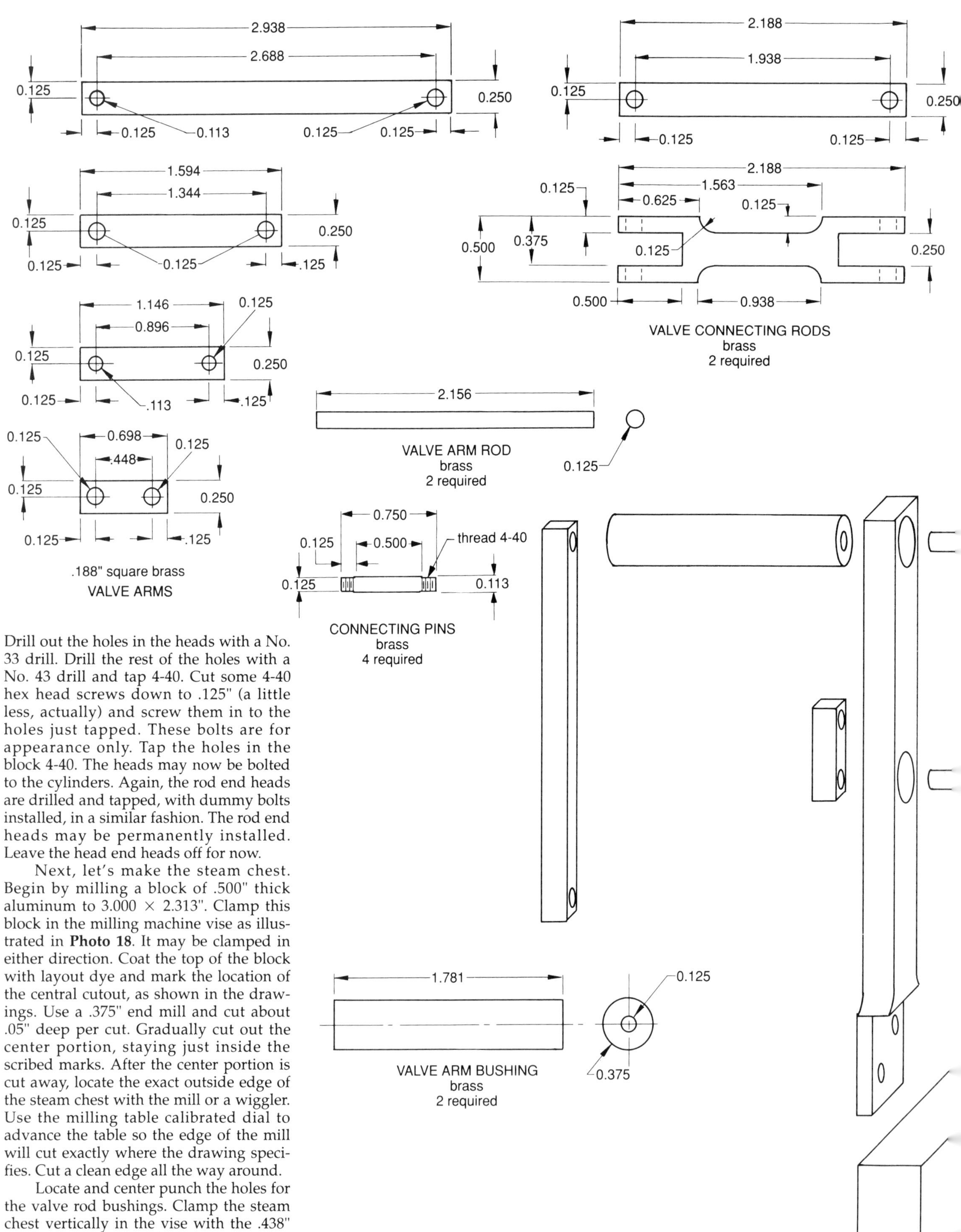

Drill out the holes in the heads with a No. 33 drill. Drill the rest of the holes with a No. 43 drill and tap 4-40. Cut some 4-40 hex head screws down to .125" (a little less, actually) and screw them in to the holes just tapped. These bolts are for appearance only. Tap the holes in the block 4-40. The heads may now be bolted to the cylinders. Again, the rod end heads are drilled and tapped, with dummy bolts installed, in a similar fashion. The rod end heads may be permanently installed. Leave the head end heads off for now.

Next, let's make the steam chest. Begin by milling a block of .500" thick aluminum to 3.000 × 2.313". Clamp this block in the milling machine vise as illustrated in **Photo 18**. It may be clamped in either direction. Coat the top of the block with layout dye and mark the location of the central cutout, as shown in the drawings. Use a .375" end mill and cut about .05" deep per cut. Gradually cut out the center portion, staying just inside the scribed marks. After the center portion is cut away, locate the exact outside edge of the steam chest with the mill or a wiggler. Use the milling table calibrated dial to advance the table so the edge of the mill will cut exactly where the drawing specifies. Cut a clean edge all the way around.

Locate and center punch the holes for the valve rod bushings. Clamp the steam chest vertically in the vise with the .438" thick edge down and projecting out as seen in **Photo 19**. Locate the spindle over the center punch mark, which is projecting over the edge of the vise. Drill through both ends of the steam chest with a .313" drill. Back out the drill, unclamp the steam chest, and turn it around in the vise. Drill the second .313" hole in the same manner. Remove the steam chest from the vise and press in all four bushings. Actually, I should say beat them in with a rubber mallet. At least I know they will not come out on their own. Locate and center punch the steam inlet hole. Drill with a No. 3 drill and tap 1/4-28.

Cut a 3.000 × 2.313" piece of .063" thick aluminum. Locate and center punch the locations for all the holes. This will become the steam chest cover as well as a drilling template for all of the bolt holes. Clamp the cylinder block in the milling machine vise as shown in **Photo 20**. Place the valve plate, steam chest, and steam chest cover on the block. Make sure the valve plate and other pieces are oriented correctly. Place clamps as seen in Photo 20. Tighten them down a little bit.

Use a straightedge to align all four sides of the valve plate, chest, and chest

23

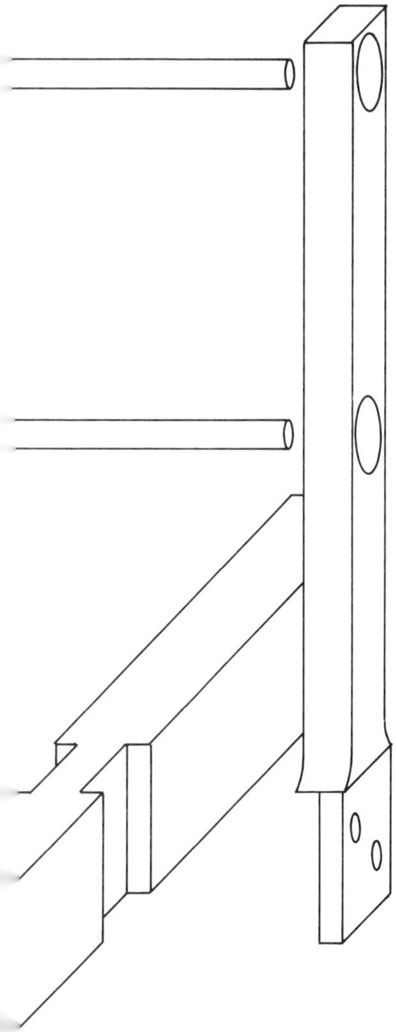

VALVE ARM ASSEMBLY

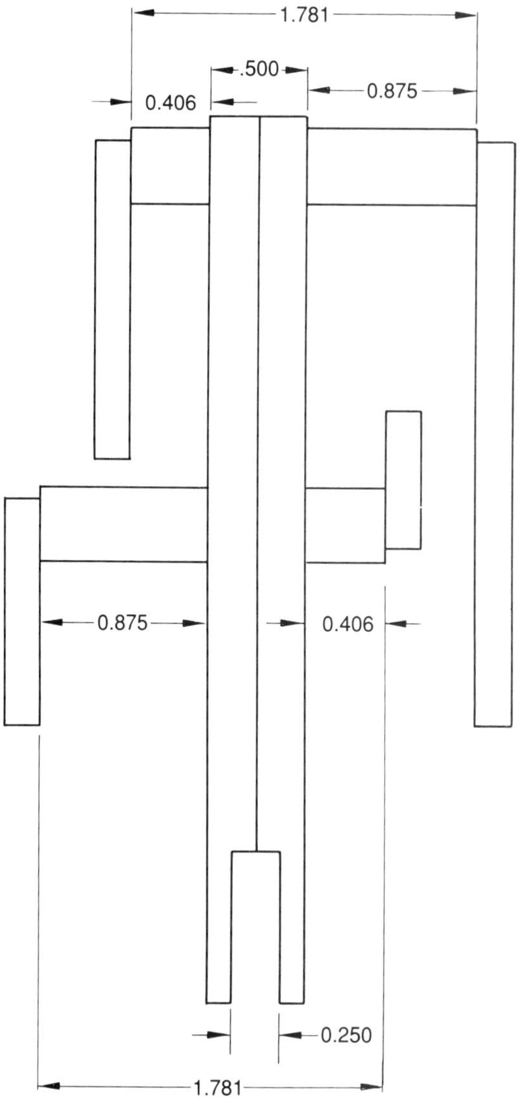

VALVE ARM HOLDERS

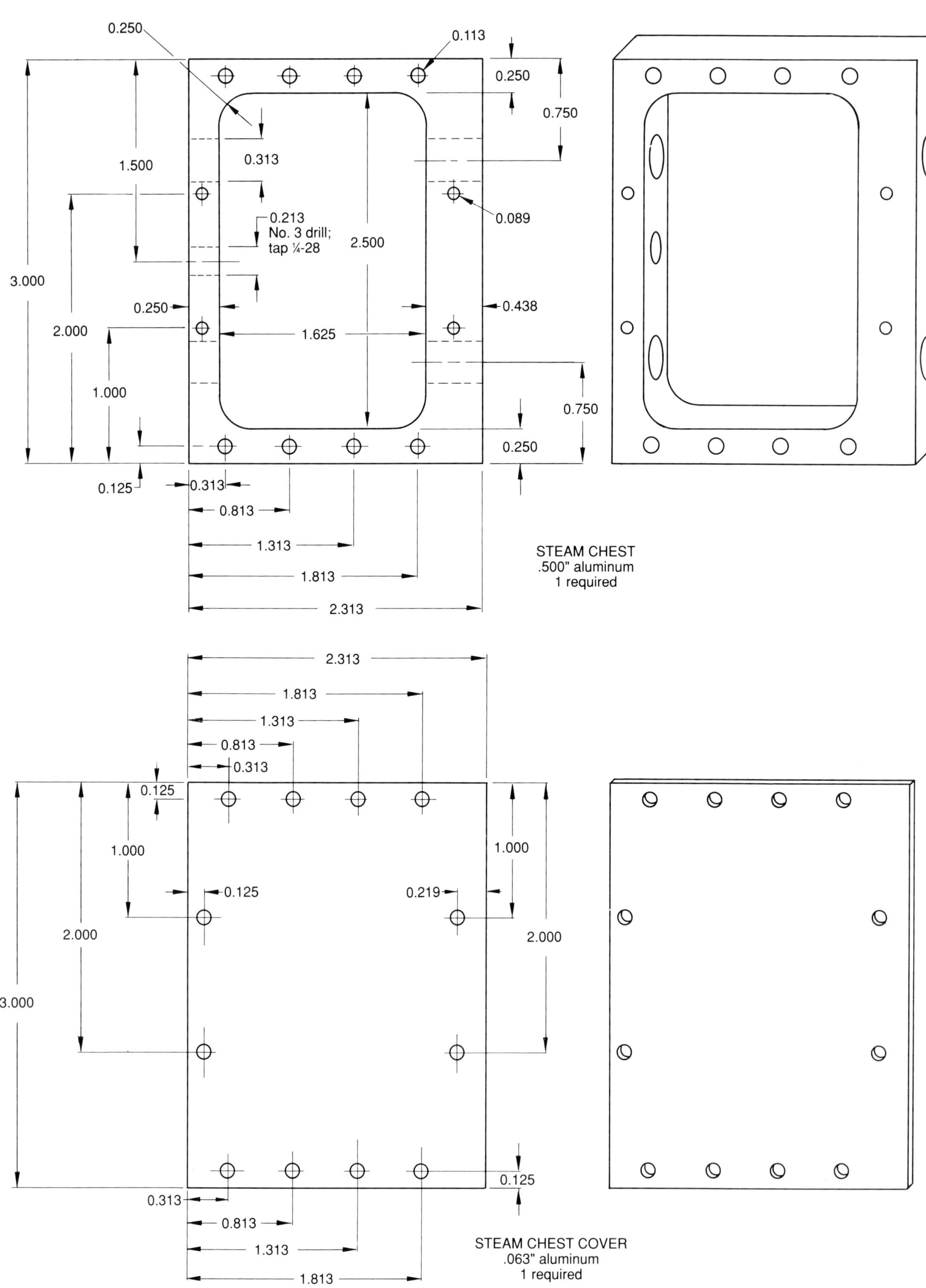

STEAM CHEST
.500" aluminum
1 required

STEAM CHEST COVER
.063" aluminum
1 required

24

25

26

cover to the block. Tighten down the clamps. Chuck up a No. 43 drill and drill the eight holes on the outer edges (exhaust port edges) so the depth into the cylinder block is .500". This means the depth of the hole as measured from the top of the steam chest cover is 1.156". Each hole is a slow process. After about the first .5", the drill clogs every .063" or less, and must be backed out and cleared. Use plenty of cutting fluid and go slowly. It takes a while, but it can be done. I still have the same drill bit I started with. Alternatively, drill deep enough to just drill into the cylinder block.

After all pieces are removed, the holes in the block may be drilled to their .500" depth. Drill the four holes adjacent to the head and rod ends only deep enough to just go through the steam chest. This makes a total depth from the cover of .563". After all the holes are drilled, use a center punch and make a light mark on the block, and the edges of the valve plate, steam chest, and cover. These will allow the parts to be easily assembled later. Unclamp the parts and drill out all holes in the steam chest cover with a No. 33 drill. Drill out the eight holes on the exhaust port sides in the steam chest. Tap the other four holes 4-40. Tap all holes in the cylinder block 4-40.

This finishes all the non-moving parts for the steam cylinders.

We'll turn our attention and cutting bits to the baseplate bracket next. Rough cut a length of .500" thick aluminum and mill it to .750 × 7.625". Clamp this piece in the vise as shown in **Photo 21**. Use a .500" end mill to cut the .125" deep groove centered in the bracket. Turn the bar over and cut the other groove. Be careful to mill these grooves exactly adjacent to each other. Pick one of the .500" wide edges to be the bottom. Drill the No. 28 holes located .250" and .750" in from each end, then counterbore all four holes with a .375" end mill to a depth of .375". These holes will attach the steam and water cylinders to the bracket, and allow the screw heads to remain hidden. Bore the blind No. 36 holes and tap 6-32. These holes will be used to attach the bracket to the baseplate.

Next, we'll make the valve arm holders. Begin with two pieces of .25" thick brass. Mill them to .688 × 4.438". Clamp them to the milling table and mill with the side of a .500" end mill until only .750" of the .688" width is left. Do this on both sides of the holder so the width of the upper portion is .688", with the radius of the end mill blending the narrow portion into the wider portion, as shown in the drawing. Do not drill the .375" holes for the valve arm bushings yet. Mill out a piece from the .688" wide end that is .125" deep and .75" wide. Do this to both pieces. Next, clamp the two arm holders to the base bracket as shown in **Photo 22**. Locate and center punch the locations for the two diagonal holes. Drill through the holder

27

and into the bracket with a No. 36 drill. Turn the assembly over, re-clamp it, and drill the two diagonal holes in the other valve arm holder. Make sure the diagonal holes in each holder are opposite the holes in the other one. Remove the holders and drill out the two holes in each with a No. 28 drill. Drill the four holes in the bracket through with the No. 36 drill and tap all four 6-32. Place the holders back on the bracket and fasten with No. 6 screws.

After the valve arm holders have been installed on the base bracket, locate, center punch, and drill the .375" holes for the valve arm bushings. Make these bushings next. They are a simple length of .375" brass rod, turned to a length of 1.781" and drilled and reamed .125". Install these bushings in the holders as shown in **Photo 23**. Solder them in place. Each bushing projects .875" from the edge of the valve arm holder. The .875" projections are opposite each other, as may be seen in Photo 23. Make the valve arm rods from .125" brass rod or drill rod. Make the valve arms from .188" square brass rod. Drill and ream the .125" holes in the ends of each valve arm. Install the valve arms as seen in Photo 23 and the exploded view in the drawings. After aligning the arms, solder them in place. Be careful not to allow any solder to flow into the bushings, unless you want a static model.

Mill two pieces of .25" thick brass to a size of 2.188 × .500" for the valve connecting rods. Clamp one of the blanks upright in the milling machine vise (**Photo 24**). Using a .250" end mill, cut a slot down to a depth of .500", cutting about .05" per cut. Turn the blank over in the vise and cut a similar slot on the other end. Now, clamp the connecting rod sideways in the vise as illustrated in **Photo 25**. Using the same .250" end mill, cut down the center portion as shown. Raise the cutter and move the table in the longitudinal direction so the other side may be cut down in the same manner. Locate and center punch the locations for the two holes. Drill through with a 7/64" drill followed with a .125" reamer (**Photo 26**).

Make the valve rod ends, and pins for attaching the valve connecting rods next. These are all simple parts and the drawings should provide sufficient information. Assemble all of the parts made thus far and check the valve gear for fit and smooth operation. **Photo 27** illustrates this assembly. Now the project is beginning to take shape. Since I'm eager to get it done and operating, I'll take any excuse to assemble what parts I've finished.

Now, it is time to make the remainder of the pieces for the steam cylinders. Starting from the top down, we'll make the valves, valve nuts, pistons, rings, and rods. Begin by milling two blocks of steel to .75 × .75 × .438" thick. Notice from the drawing that a .250" wide slot and a .125" wide slot cross each other on the topside of the valve. Mill the .250" side slot first. Clamp the valve in the milling machine vise and center the cutter with the cross slide Lock the cross slide in place. Lower the spindle until the mill just grazes the surface of the valve.

Set the calibrated collar for the spindle to 0. Move the table longitudinally so the mill clears the end of the valve. Lower the spindle by .03" or so and make a pass through the valve. Continue cutting until a depth of .344" is reached. Please note that the valve face is milled up by .063" from the bottom, leaving only .031" of material between the bottom of the valve face and the bottom of the slots on the back. Take several cuts of shallow depth, or take a few cuts as much as .100" deep. I tried this method, and it worked well as long as I fed the table very slowly, and used lots of cutting fluid.

Take the first valve face out of the vise and install the second one. Everything should still be set up properly to mill the .250" wide slot in the second valve. Should be, but check it all anyway. Remove the valve and turn it 90°. Install a .125" end mill. Again, since the valve body is square, the .125" end mill should be centered. If it is, cut the .125" slot, again to a depth of .344". **Photo 28** shows the cutter just emerging from the slot as it reaches the proper depth.

Clamp the valve face up in the vise. Using the cross slide and longitudinal feeds, position the .125" end mill such that it is located in one corner of the valve cutout. Since the mill I used was center cutting, I was able to feed it straight down to the required depth of .063". At this point, set the calibrated collars on both the cross slide and longitudinal feed to 0. Slowly move the cross slide a distance of .375". This is the .500" width of the valve cutout minus the .125" width of the mill.

Lock the cross slide and feed the table by .375". Now lock the table, unlock the cross slide, and feed it back in the other direction by another .375". Last, lock the cross slide again, unlock the table, and feed it .375" back to the starting position. You now have a .125" wide groove that accurately defines the perimeter of the valve face cutout. Unlock both the cross slide and table and, leaving the mill at the same depth, cut out the remaining metal in the center. **Photo 29** shows this after all the chips have been made (and vacuumed up just before the shutter clicked).

The valve nuts are made from small blocks of brass. Mill two blocks to a size of .750 × .375 × .313". Drill and ream a .125" diameter hole in the .313" side centered in the .750" dimension and .125" from the edge. This is the hole the valve rod will pass through. Turn the block 90° and drill a No. 43 hole into the .125" hole. The No. 3 hole is centered in both directions. Tap this hole 4-40. It may be necessary to drill the No. 43 hole all the way through so the 4-40 tap will go sufficiently deep. The use of a bottom tap would make this unnecessary. After tapping, run the reamer through the .125" hole to clean it up.

28

29

30

31

Make the piston rods next. These are simply lengths of .250" diameter drill rod 7.750" in length with additional .375" lengths of 10-32 threads on each end. Rough cut a circle of .375" thick aluminum. Drill and tap the approximate center 10-32. Screw it on one end of the piston rod and chuck the whole affair in the lathe, leaving the piston close to the chuck. Turn the piston to the proper

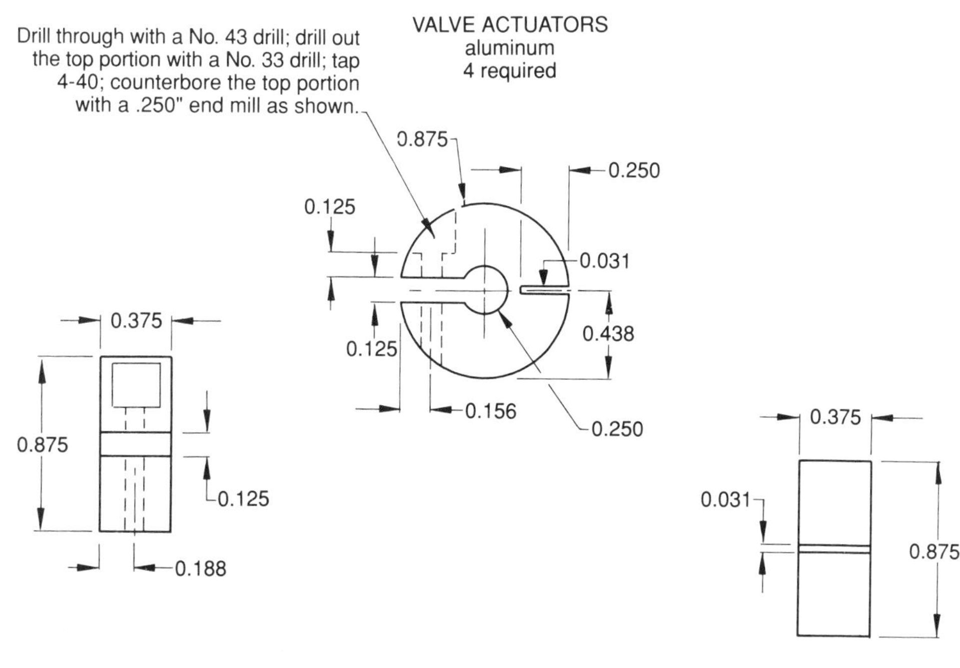

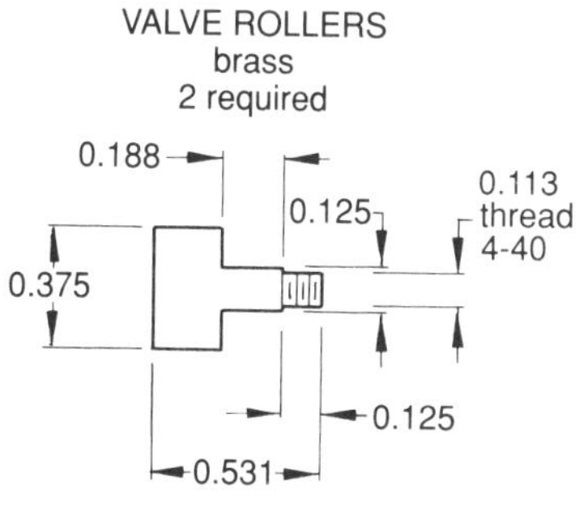

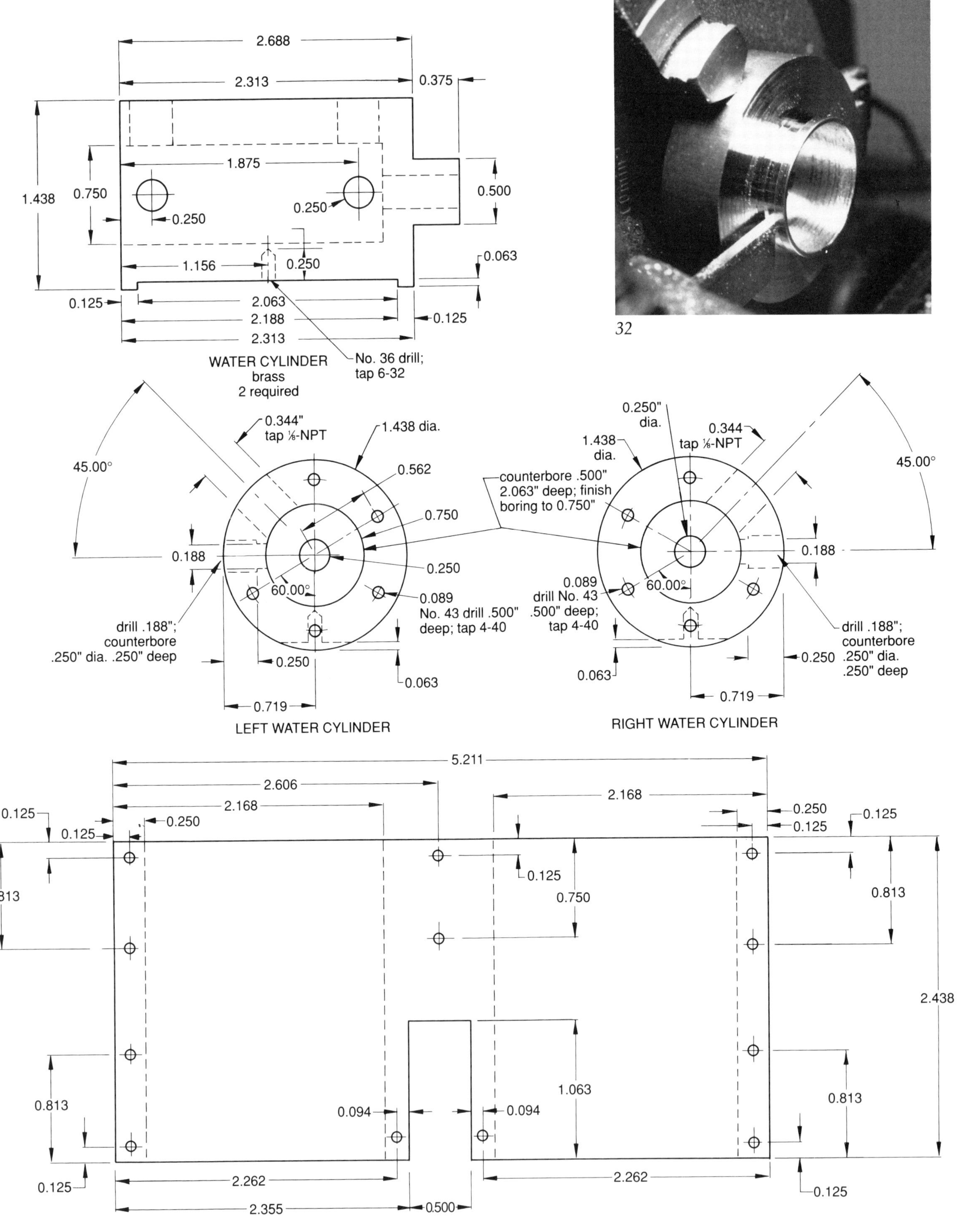

32

When installing the shroud, wrap it around the steam cylinders and mark the location of all the holes as they line up on the cylinder block. From these locations, drill No. 50 holes .250" deep and tap 2-56. Install the shroud with 2-56 screws.

33

34

diameter of 1.000", less .002" to .005" for a sliding fit in the cylinder. Use a 3/32" wide cutoff tool to cut the slot for the ring. Position the tool in the middle of the piston. Slowly feed it in until the diameter of the groove is .910" (**Photo 30**).

Now it's time to make the rings. I have always wondered how to make piston rings, and quaked in my boots at the prospect. Then along came Village Press's excellent book, *The Shop Wisdom of Philip Duclos*. There is a nice chapter on making model piston rings. After reading it, I decided to give it a try and found it very easy. I had some rod ends of aluminum nickel bronze handy, so, somewhat arbitrarily, I decided this would be the material for the rings.

Chuck a piece of the ring material in the lathe. Measure the exact diameter of the steam cylinder. Let's suppose that it comes to 1.000". Now, find the circumference of the cylinder, which will be 3.142". Add the size of the ring gap, which I chose to be .063". This gives a total circumference of 3.204". Now, divide by pi to get back to the diameter, which will be 1.020". Turn the outside of the bronze ring blank to this diameter.

Using the rule of thumb in Philip's book, the ratio of ring diameter to thickness is 25:1. This means the rings should be 1.020/25" or .041" thick. I used .040", which would give an internal diameter of .940". Bore the ring blank to this diameter. **Photo 31** illustrates turning the final outside diameter.

Next, position the cutoff tool so the ring will be .094" wide to fit in the piston groove. Cut off the ring (**Photo 32**). Clamp the ring in the milling machine vise and locate the middle. As shown in **Photo 33**, use a .063" end mill to cut the gap. Clean up the gap with a file, and clean up the edges of the ring with emery cloth. Compress the ring and attempt to fit it into its cylinder (**Photo 34**). If it doesn't fit, file the gap slightly larger until it will just fit in the cylinder. Slip the ring over the piston (**Photo 35**). It should be able to slide around in the groove without binding.

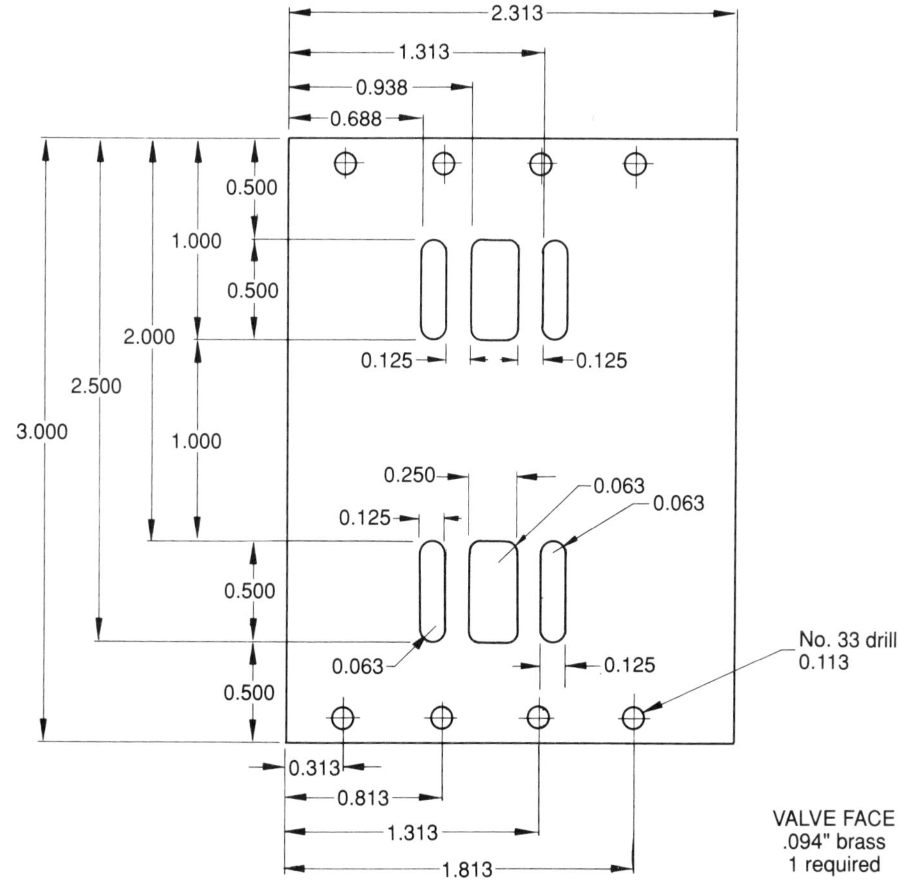

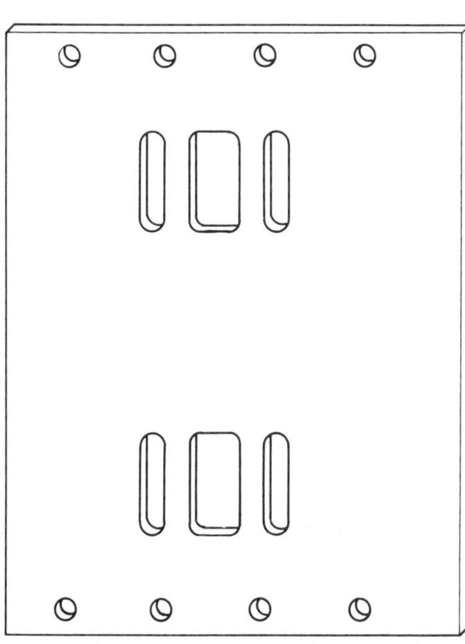

VALVE FACE
.094" brass
1 required

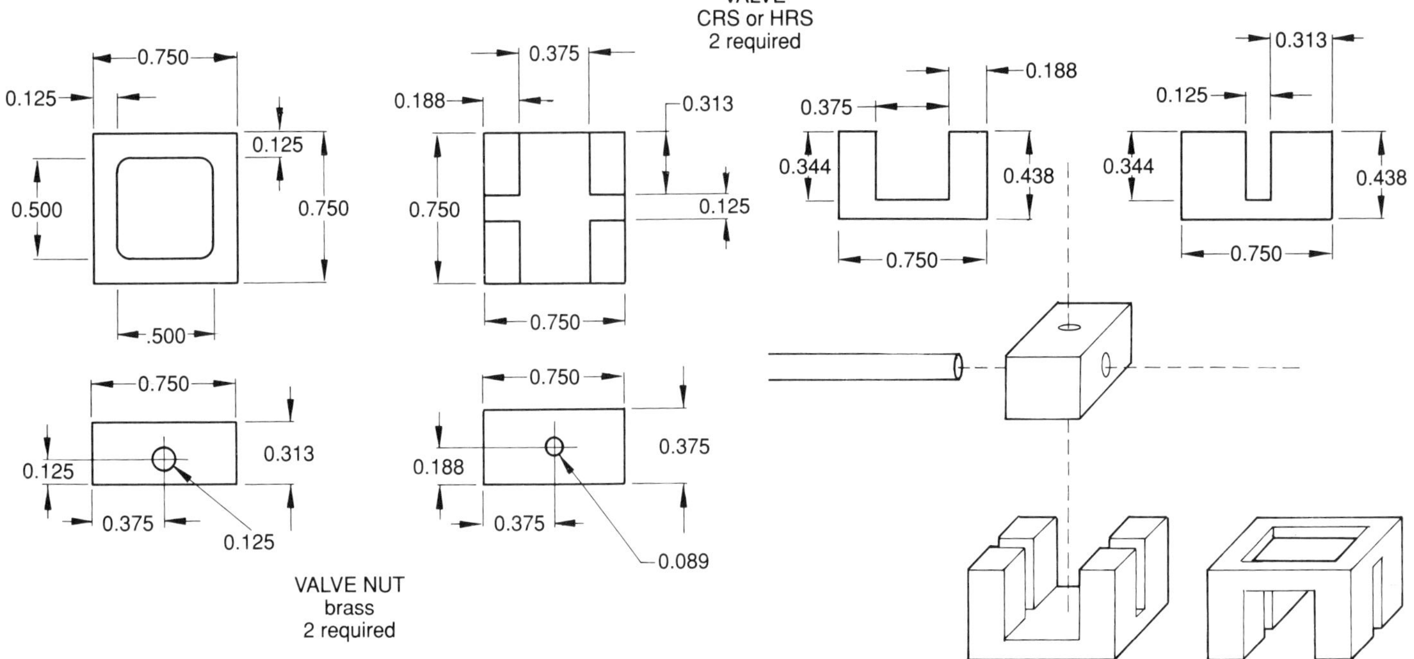

Make the valve actuators next. Begin with an aluminum rod .875" in diameter. Cut off four pieces .375" thick. Drill and ream a .250" diameter hole through the center of each one. Clamp the actuator in the milling machine vise and cut a .125" slot from the outer edge into the center .250" hole. Now, turn the blank 90° and use a .031" slitting saw to cut a groove in to a depth of .250". This makes it easier to squeeze the actuator so it will clamp tightly to the piston rod.

Locate the edge of the actuator and move the table longitudinally .156" so the spindle is positioned halfway between the edge of the actuator and the edge of the central .250" hole. Center drill this location, followed with a No. 43 drill all the way through. Back out the drill and chuck up a No. 33 drill. Drill through only the top section, until the hole extends into the previously cut .125" slot. Back out the drill and install a .250" end mill. Counterbore the No. 33 hole until there is .125" between the top of the .125" slot and the bottom of the counterbored hole. This allows the screw head a place to sit.

Tap the No. 43 hole 4-40. After the valve actuators have been made, make the valve rollers. These are a simple turning job, as detailed in the drawings. Finally, the steam cylinder end can be completely assembled. Insert the pistons into the cylinders.

Compressing the rings can be a touchy business, but it can usually be done with the aid of tweezers, needle nose pliers, or long fingernails. Slide on one valve actuator as the rod is pushed out through the cylinder bushing. When the end of the rod clears the valve arm (and roller) slide the second actuator on.

Bolt on the heads. Install the valves and valve nuts. Leave the valve nuts loose. Position the valves directly in the center of their travel. Position the valve arms so there is .250" of space between the outer edge of the rod end valve bushing and the square valve rod end. Clamp the valve nuts in place. Position each piston half-

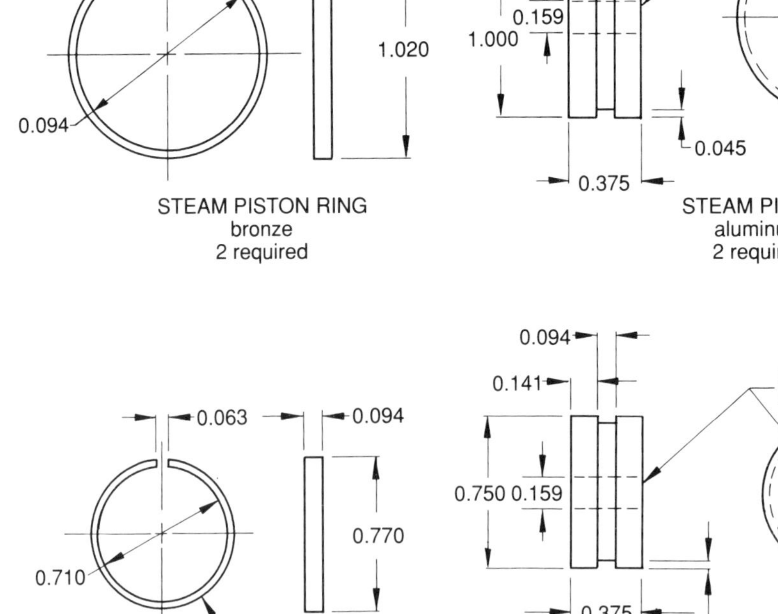

35

36 37

way down in the cylinder. With the valves still positioned as before, clamp tight the actuators on either side of the roller. Install the steam chest cover. The result should appear as in **Photos 36** and **37**.

At this point, I couldn't resist the temptation to try and run it. It will run, on about 20 to 40 psi of compressed air. However, there are no water cylinders to provide any damping, so it runs quite fast and tends to get stuck. In order to make it run at all, I had to provide some damping. I placed the palm of one hand in front of the threaded rod ends meant for the water cylinders, and stuck my thumb behind the valve actuators to catch the rods in the other direction. The result was that it ran, fast, and pummeled my hand. However, it was worth a little discomfort to enjoy the fruits of my labors before the project was completely done. You may also use this opportunity to make sure everything works well together, without any binding.

Now we can begin on the water cylinders. These cylinders are made from pieces of 1.500" diameter brass rod. Cut lengths of the rod and face off each end so the overall length is 2.688". With the cylinder clamped in the three-jaw chuck, center drill and drill through with a 15/64" drill. Follow this with a .250" reamer (**Photo 38**).

Next, use a .500 drill to counterbore the existing hole to a depth of 2.063". This is illustrated with **Photo 39**. This hole will allow the boring bar to fit and continue widening the hole. Use a boring bar to bore the cylinder out to a diameter of .750" to a depth of 2.063", as shown in **Photo 40**. Without removing the cylinder, turn the outside diameter to 1.438" (**Photo 41**). Now, remove the cylinder, turn it around, and turn the remainder of the outside to 1.438". At this time, turn down .375" of the end (with the .250" hole) to a diameter of .500". Remove the cylinder from the lathe and clamp it in the milling machine as shown in **Photo 42**.

Since no other holes have been drilled through the side of the cylinder, the angular position of the cylinder is not important. Install a .500" end mill and lower the spindle until the mill just kisses

38 39

40 41

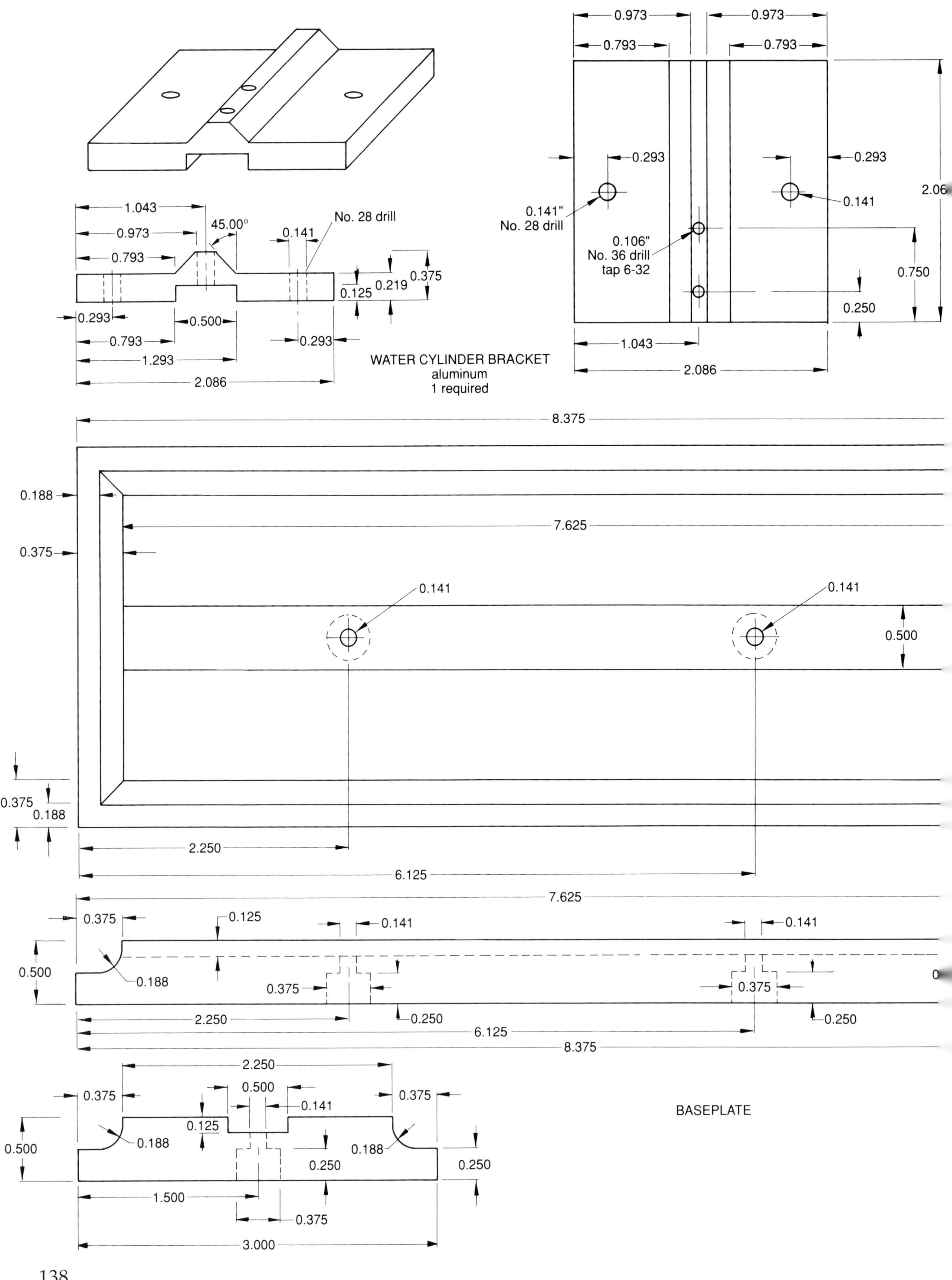

1.043
0.973
0.793
45.00°
No. 28 drill
0.141
0.125
0.219
0.375
0.293
0.500
0.793
1.293
2.086
0.293
0.973
0.973
0.793
0.793
0.293
0.293
0.141" No. 28 drill
0.141
0.106" No. 36 drill tap 6-32
0.750
0.250
1.043
2.086
WATER CYLINDER BRACKET
aluminum
1 required
8.375
0.188
7.625
0.375
0.141
0.141
0.500
0.375
0.188
2.250
6.125
7.625
0.375
0.125
0.141
0.141
0.500
0.188
0.375
0.375
2.250
0.250
0.250
6.125
8.375
2.250
0.375
0.500
0.375
0.141
0.125
0.188
0.188
0.500
0.250
0.250
1.500
0.375
3.000
BASEPLATE

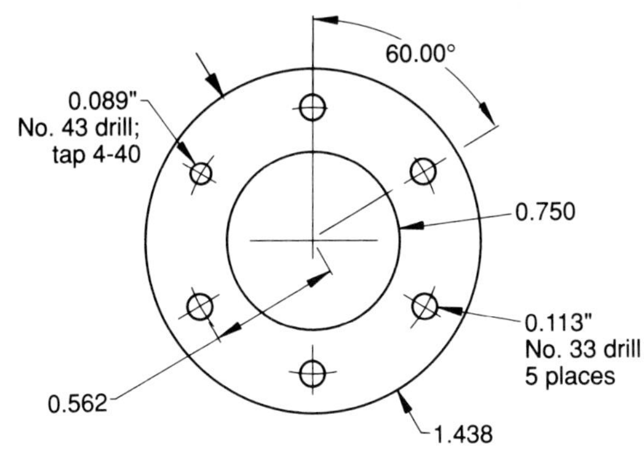

LEFT WATER CYLINDER HEAD
aluminum
1 required

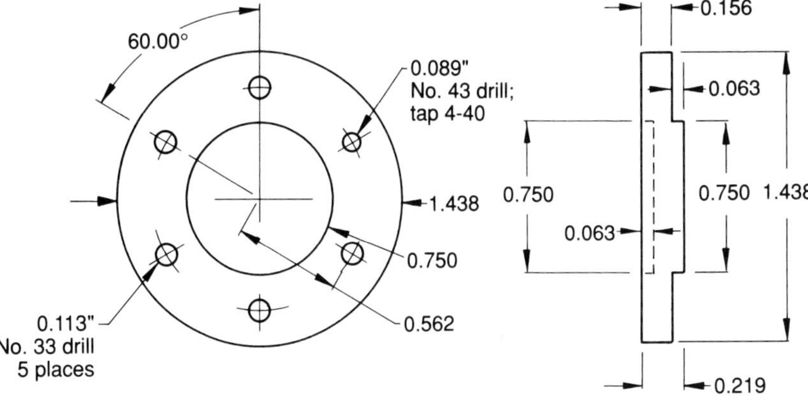

RIGHT WATER CYLINDER HEAD
aluminum
1 required

the top of the cylinder. Move the longitudinal feed so the mill clears the cylinder and lower the spindle by .063". Using the cross slide, locate the outer edge of the mill .125" in from one end of the cylinder. Feed the table and cut a .500" wide slot at one end of the cylinder. Now, locate the outer edge of the mill .125" in from the other end of the cylinder. Again, mill out a .500" wide slot. Mill out the remaining material in the center of the cylinder, to achieve a flat spot as seen in Photo 42.

Drill the holes for the check valves next. The flat surface previously milled on the cylinder will be used to locate the angles for these holes. Clamp the cylinder with the rod end facing you in the milling machine vise. Use a 45° angle block (I used a drafting triangle) to tilt the flat surface on the cylinder up 45°. Locate the spindle directly over the mid line of the cylinder and lock the table. Using the cross slide, locate and center drill a hole 1.875" from the head end (the end with the .750" hole). Drill through with a .344" drill. Clamp a 1/8-NPT tap in the drill chuck and start it by hand. Remove the tap. The hole will be finished later.

Locate and center drill a hole .250" from the head end. Again, drill through with a .344" drill and start the threads with a 1/8-NPT tap. Loosen the cylinder and use a square to place the flat surface at right angles to the milling machine table. As before, locate and center drill a hole 1.875" from the head end. Drill through with a .188" drill, and counterbore with a .250" drill to a depth of .250" (**Photo 43**). Drill and counterbore another hole located .250" from the head end. Now, drill the other cylinder in a similar manner.

Please Note: the holes in the other cylinder must be a mirror image of the first cylinder, as illustrated in the drawings. The check valves will project to the outside from both cylinders. Finish tapping all four 1/8-NPT holes in both cylinders. Deburr the holes where they break through into the cylinder bore. I found that running the tap in until about three threads were visible was about right to screw in the check valves and have them tighten well (remember that the 1/8-NPT is a tapered thread).

Cut out two rough circles of .250" thick aluminum for the water cylinder heads. Clamp the rough blank in the three-jaw chuck as straight as possible. Face off the end, and turn to a diameter of .750" to a depth of .063". Remove the blank, turn it around, and clamp it back in the chuck using the .063" step just turned. Turn the outer diameter to 1.438", to match the diameter of the cylinder. Next, bore a recess .063" deep and .750" in diameter. Remove the cylinder head, and finish the other head in a similar fashion.

Making the water cylinder bracket next. Begin with a .375" thick piece of aluminum milled to 2.063 × 2.086". The 2.086" dimension was calculated so the edge of the bracket will match up with the edge of the flat cutout on the cylinder when the two cylinder centers are spaced the proper (1.500") distance apart. Using a .500" end mill, cut a slot .125" deep down the center of the bracket, parallel to the 2.063" dimension. Take the bracket out, and turn it over. Mill from the outside edge in .793" and down .156". Do this on both sides of the

42

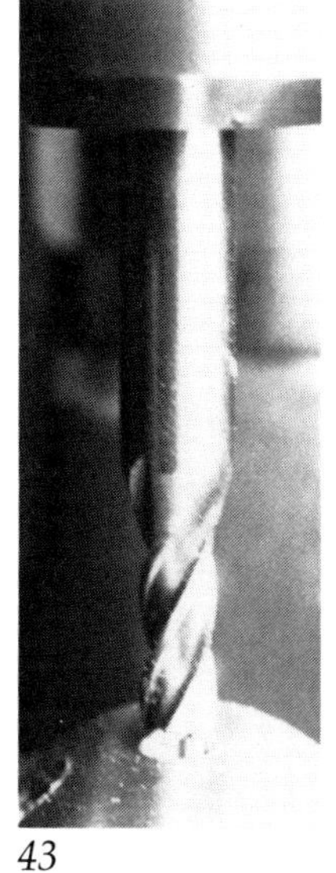
43

44

45

46

bracket, such that there is a central ridge in parallel with the .125" deep groove now located on the bottom side of the bracket.

Next, as shown in the drawing, mill a side of the central ridge at a 45° angle. This provides clearance for the edges of the water cylinders. Locate, center punch, and drill with a No. 36 drill the two holes .250" and .750" from one end of the bracket, and in the center of the .125" deep channel. Tap these holes 6-32. Also, locate and drill the two No. 28 holes in the milled down surface of the bracket. Bolt the bracket to the base-plate bracket. Place the water cylinders on the bracket, inserting the piston rods in each. Determine the exact position where the rods slide in and out of the cylinders with the least amount of binding. Using the holes in the bracket, mark the location of the hole on the flat portion of each water cylinder. Remove the water cylinders, and drill a No. 36 hole .250" deep and tap 6-32. Fasten the cylinders to the bracket.

This assembly is now clamped upright in the milling machine vise as shown in **Photo 44**. Lay out and center punch the six holes in each water cylinder head. Place the heads on the cylinders, and clamp as shown in Photo 44. Using a No. 43 drill, drill five holes to a depth of .500" into the cylinder (total depth of .656" including the head). Note that I just said to drill five holes. Like the steam cylinder heads, one of the head bolts is a dummy. Do not drill the hole which would, if drilled, go through the 1/8-NPT hole in the cylinder. After all holes have been drilled, remove the head and drill out the five holes with a No. 33 drill. Drill the sixth hole with a No. 43 drill and tap 4-40. Cut down a hex head 4-40 screw to a length of .125" and install it in this hole. Turn the cylinder assembly around in the vise and clamp the second head in place. Drill it in a similar fashion.

Now the check valves may be installed. I thought long and hard about how to design this portion of the pump. The overriding factor was that I did not really want to make my own miniature check valves. Fortunately, the local hardware store had some neat little ball check valves with a 1/8-NPT connection on the inlet end and a 1/4" compression fitting on the other. **Photo 45** shows one of these valves taken apart.

The ball sits in the little cup in the

47

48

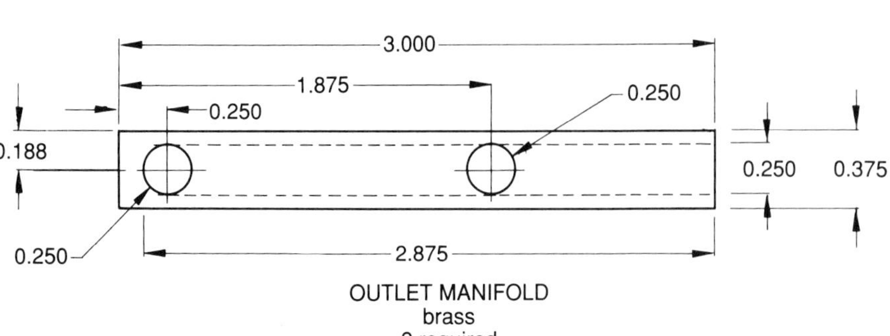

OUTLET MANIFOLD
brass
2 required

49

50

51

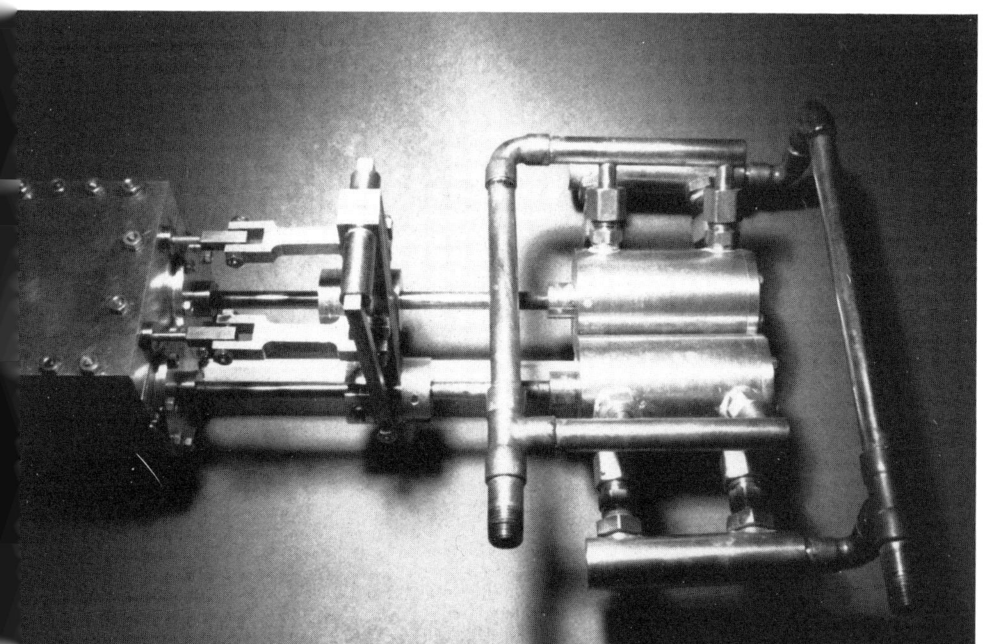

52

foreground, and then presses on the spring inside the body of the valve. The cup that the ball sits in may be screwed in and out to adjust the spring tension. I found out, the hard way, that this adjustment screw must be held in place with a little *Loctite*. I assembled the pump, and ran it. It worked fine, for a short time. It seems the pumping action caused the adjustment screw to back out on several of the valves, depositing the screw, ball, and spring in various internal nooks and crannies of the pump. So, while it is still easy, adjust the spring tension, and place a drop or two of *Loctite* on each one.

Wrap the threads of each valve with *Teflon* tape. Install four of them in the 1/8-NPT holes in the two cylinders. These will be the outlet valves. Cut four pieces of .25" OD copper or brass tubing .875" long, and solder them into the four .25" diameter holes in the two water cylinders. Place the compression nut, and then the compression ring, over each piece of tubing. Assemble the other four valves, as seen in **Photos 46** and **47**.

Make the inlet manifolds next. Begin with a piece of .625" diameter brass rod. Face off both ends so the overall length is 3.000". Turn down one end to a diameter of .375" to a depth of .375". Center drill and drill with a .313" drill (**Photo 48**) to a depth of .875". This places the bottom of the blind hole .125" in from the other end of the manifold. Clamp the manifold in the milling machine vise. Block it up as shown in **Photo 49**. Center drill and drill through into the .313" hole (not all the way through the manifold) with a .438" drill. This first hole is located .438" from the blank end of the manifold. Move the table longitudinally 1.625", and center drill and drill a second hole.

Photo 50 illustrates how the bushings for the check valves are installed. Begin with a brass 1/4-NPT to 1/8-NPT bushing from the local hardware store. Clamp the hex head in the three-jaw chuck, and turn down the 1/4-NPT thread until a smooth outer diameter of .438" is obtained. Next, cut off the bushing until .250" remains beyond the hex head. This will appear as the bushing in the lower left foreground of Photo 50. Smear with flux, and solder the modified bushings into the manifold. Screw all four inlet valves into the two manifolds, and then clamp down the compression nuts to fit the valves to the water cylinders.

The outlet manifolds are similar to the inlet ones. These must accommodate a .25" OD piece of tubing as opposed to a 1/8-NPT thread. Begin with a piece of .375" diameter brass rod. Face off both ends so its length is 3.000". Center drill and drill with a .250" drill to a depth of 2.875". As with the inlet manifold, clamp this in the milling machine vise. Drill a .250" hole into the central bore .250" from the blank end, and another 1.625" from the first hole. Solder two pieces of .25" OD tubing .875" long into the holes in each

53

manifold. Fit the .25" OD tubing with compression nuts and rings, and tighten these on to the four outlet check valves. **Photo 51** shows a close-up of the inlet and outlet manifolds.

The four inlet and outlet check valves must now be connected together. In doing this, I pretended I was plumbing my bathroom. I used thin wall, .375" OD brass tube and 3/8" copper sweat fittings. **Photo 52** illustrates the way I did it. There is no right way to do this, and it should be done at the convenience of the individual builder.

There is still the baseplate and steam cylinder shroud to make. However, my eagerness got the best of me at this point, and I just had to see it run. So, I connected it as you see in **Photo 53**, where it sucked water out of the bucket and pumped it

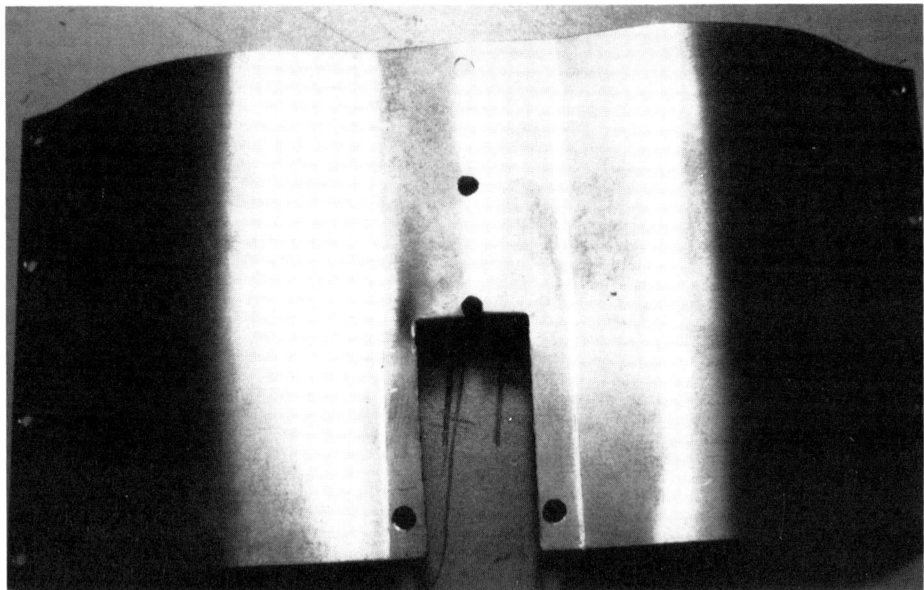

54

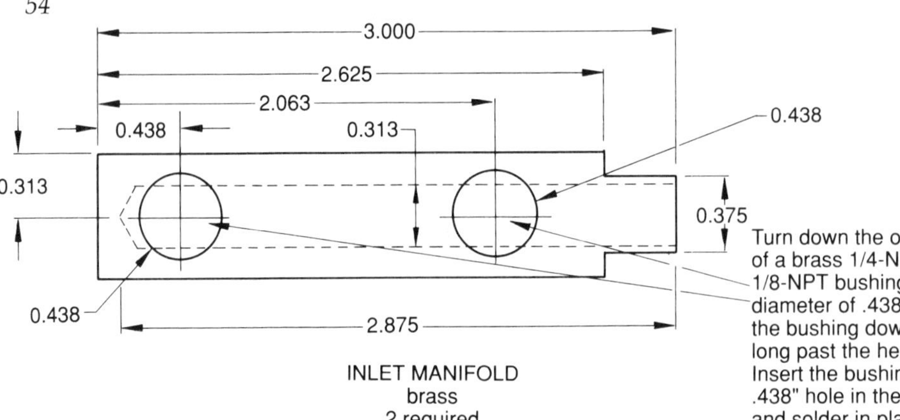

55

56

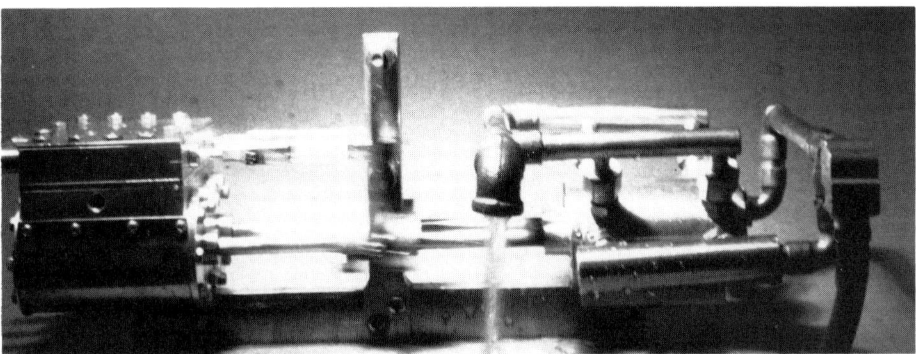

57

58

straight back in again. It ran quite well between the pressures of 20 and 50 psi. Below 20, it stopped. Above 50, at least pumping into no back pressure, the water cylinders would cavitate. Anyway, the water squirted from the outlet pipe quite vigorously, splashing everywhere. Since there was always at least one chamber pumping, the water came out in a continuous stream, as I had hoped it would.

Back to work, now. The baseplate is made from .500" thick aluminum milled to an initial size of 8.375 × 3.000". Use a .500" end mill and cut a .125" deep slot down the center of the base, in parallel with the long dimension. The base bracket of the pump will sit in this. I found it necessary to widen the groove by .125" at the center in order to clear the screw heads which hold the valve arm holders to the base bracket. Turn the bracket over. Locate, center punch, and drill with a No. 28 drill the two mounting holes. Counterbore with a .375" end mill to a depth of .250".

Turn the base over and clamp it in the milling vise with some sacrificial shims between the jaws of the vise and the bracket. Install a .375" end mill. Lower the spindle until the mill just touches the surface of the plate. Move the table in the longitudinal direction so the mill clears the baseplate, and lower the spindle .250". Now, move the cross slide such that the edge of the mill is .188" in from the edge of the baseplate. In a manner similar to making the steam valve face, cut a .188" wide × .250" deep step all the way around the baseplate. When this is finished, install a .375" ball end mill, and cut another step .188" in from the edge of the first step and also .250" deep. This leaves a nice decorative base with a radius edged step. The pump may be bolted to the baseplate. Slide the base bracket into the slot on the baseplate and screw it down with two 6-32 screws.

Photo 54 illustrates the steam cylinder shroud. Cut out a piece of .031" thick sheet brass as shown in the drawings. Drill .094" holes as shown. Wrap the shroud around the steam cylinders, and use the holes as a drilling template. After marking the locations of all 12 holes, drill into the block with a No. 50 drill to a depth of .250". Tap 2-56 and install the shroud. **Photos 55** and **56** show the finished shroud.

Well, now your pump is complete. Use some *Permatex* blue to make gaskets for the steam cylinder heads, valve plate, steam chest, and chest cover. An oiler for your compressed air line, or displacement lubricator for steam, are all that is needed for lubrication. **Photos 57** and **58** provide a parting shot of the pump in operation and the shop it was made in. Happy pumping!

A Junkbox Steamroller

By Andy Sprague

Photos by Neelon Crawford

Introduction

Thinking back to my early youth, I can recall the two summer months I spent each year with my family in the Green Mountain State. Starting from Long Island, New York, my dad would pack us up in the ol' Studebaker, strap suitcases to the running boards, and head for our cottage on Lake Eden in Vermont. The first thing Dad did on arrival was to shave my head right down to the skin. A few days of getting my bare feet toughened up and I was ready to attack summer.

Next to catching lake perch and cooking them on the beach, the best time I can remember was watching the big black steamroller puffing its way along the road behind our cottage. Sometimes it was preceded by a tank wagon watering down the road.

Eventually, Bert, the engineer, would give me rides and try to explain to me how the big brute worked. (I often wondered if the old boy was as bald as I was.) Enter Live Steam into the life of a small boy.

This was all great fun for me until one summer, after arriving at the cottage, I discovered a beautiful little redheaded girl had moved in next door. Her name was Jane, and she came from Texas. For the rest of that summer, catching perch, smoking cornsilk and riding the steamroller were of low priority.

I don't know what happened to Jane or the old steamroller, but I hope they are both making someone else happy up there in the Green Mountains of Vermont.

Steamroller

For any of you younger readers (or the "kids at heart") who might like to build a model of the old roller, let me tell you how I constructed mine.

As far as materials are concerned, they all came from the junk box. And the only power tool I used was a hand drill with a broken trigger. Give it a try!

The Body/Chassis

The Body is constructed of wood and aluminum – mostly wood – with a band of light iron around the bottom to hold everything together. The curved part in the front is carved from wood with the exception of the rectangular box attached to it. If you can get your hands on a band saw, you could zip this part out in no time. My box is hollow, and contains clock gears for steering. I think this was a mistake. If I were doing it over again, I'd make the "box" of solid wood. Drill a hole for the roller shaft and

secure it with a spring for tension, topped by a pin or nut.

So, to recap – the light iron band was from the junk box, the aluminum from a window frame, and the wood from a tree.

The Boiler

The Boiler you see in the photos is just an outer shell. The "working" boiler is inside. The shell is made from an insect spray can. The real boiler is a section of 2" brass tube from the junk box. The ends were sealed with scrap sheet brass with a ⅜" brass flue tube in the center.

All soldering was done on the kitchen stove. The stack is just a bit of brass pipe from an old lamp. It was slipped over the boiler flue tube. The decorative brass ring on top was left on from the same piece of pipe. I just thought it added a nice touch.

Water for the boiler enters through an automobile tire valve, with the cap jazzed up by using a little brass tubing. I made a little working door at the bottom of the boiler to light the burner, but a hole there would work just as well.

The steam line is ⅛" copper tubing, and runs from the top of the boiler down inside the shell and up through the floor next to the engine.

The Burner

A short cut was taken here; I should have installed an alcohol tank in the rear and run tubing to the boiler, but I was in a hurry to see the ol' girl rolling. The burner is just the cap from the bug juice spray can bolted to a hinge and screwed to the undercarriage. About fifteen minutes work was all it required. The hinge is necessary so the cap can swing down to be filled with *Sterno* jelly. The *Sterno* works well, and will keep the machine running for almost half an hour. I suspect the long run is partly due to the low gearing which puts very little strain on the engine.

The Gears

The Gears are from two sources: an old wind-up alarm clock and a busted electric can opener. I extended the crankshaft and engine base about 3" so the gearing would be on the other side of the roller, gearing down as I go. The last gear is the small one from the can opener, and is so small it has only five teeth on it. The large gear for the rear roller is also from the can opener, and was a wee bit smaller than the diameter of the soup can. This gear is connected to the small one by a ladder chain which operated the can opener in the first place. I realize that not all gearing in electric can openers operate with a ladder chain arrangement, but they all have some kind of high/low gears which could be adapted for the roller.

The Engine

Sorry, I have to plead guilty to not having built the Engine – it's store-bought. Here follows my excuse.

Many years ago, in Tokyo, Japan, I was exploring one of their beautiful department stores. While walking through the toy department, I saw a glass case containing three little stationary steam plants. I inquired as to their price, and they came to about $3.60 each (American). I purchased all three engines, each packaged beautifully in its own little box. After thinking for a moment, I decided to buy a fourth engine and learned there was only one box left in the whole store. The saleslady returned from the stock room carrying a big carton, explaining that it was the last "box." You guessed it – the carton contained eighteen engines, and not being of sound mind and body, I walked out of the store with 21 steam plants!

Examining the engines more closely at home, I discovered the boilers to be less than great, but they did make nice alcohol tanks. The engines were fine, with flywheels and double-acting cylinders made of brass and chrome plate.

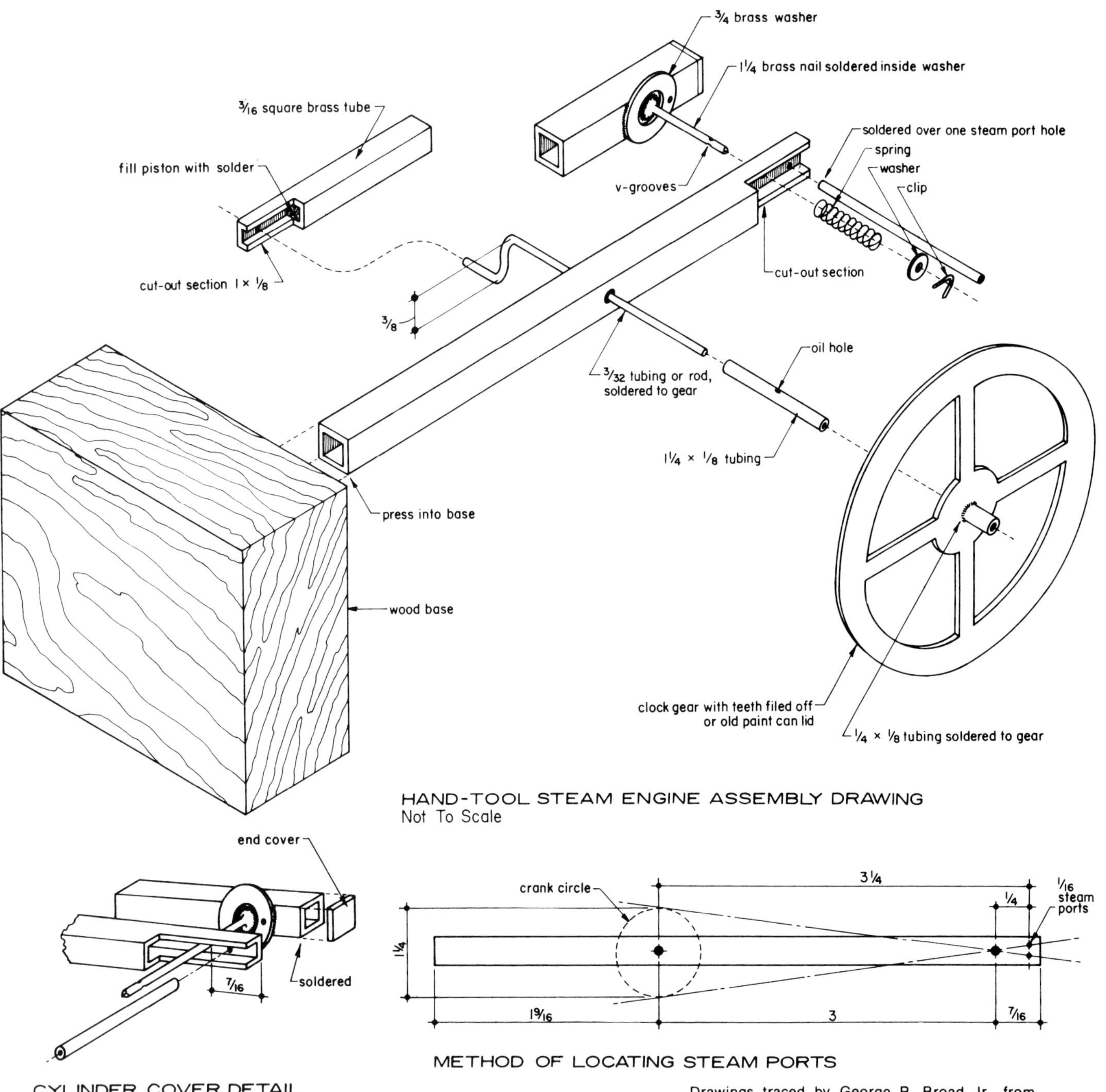

HAND-TOOL STEAM ENGINE ASSEMBLY DRAWING
Not To Scale

CYLINDER COVER DETAIL

METHOD OF LOCATING STEAM PORTS

Drawings traced by George R. Broad Jr., from originals by Andrew Sprague.

Over the years, the engines have all disappeared into various projects, with the exception of the last one which powers this steamroller.

There is a workable alternative engine I can recommend. If you can gain access to a copy of ***Live Steam*** from December 1977, or the book *Steam and Stirling Engines You Can Build*, you'll find an article by me called "Hand-Tool Steam Engine." That simple little engine can be re-proportioned to power the roller. By substituting 1/4″ square tubing for 3/8″ or 1/2″ tubing, and reducing the engine height by about half, you will have a nice little engine to do the job. The drawings are reproduced here for your convenience and interest.

The Rollers

There is little to explain about the Rollers; they are simply soup cans. Remove the tops, empty the contents, and resolder the tops back on. You could use an epoxy glue here, too. The axles are cut from a coat hanger (why waste good brass?).

That's about all there is to it. Look at it this way – you won't go hungry building this model; you can always eat the soup. I like the cream of mushroom myself, but you might prefer the chicken or vegetable. Good luck!

STIRLING HOT AIR ENGINES

1

Fire Eater Engine

By Philip Duclos

Photos by Author

One of the amazing features of this very intriguing engine is that its energy source is merely a clean burning denatured alcohol flame positioned near the cylinder porthole. This is not a Stirling cycle motor; it's usually referred to as a "flame sucker." An even more accurate title would be "atmospheric" or "vacuum" engine. This little mechanism is not powerful, yet when properly adjusted it will attain speeds up to 1,100 rpm (**Photo 1**).

Even though it emits a smart, crackling "pop" like a gasoline motor, the similarity ends there. For instance, the power stroke of this engine occurs when the ringless piston moves toward the cylinder head. As the piston approaches the end of this stroke, a fast-acting slide valve opens the cylinder porthole. When the piston begins its outward stroke, the flame is sucked into the cylinder. Near the end of this stroke, the slide valve quickly closes the porthole. In a small fraction of a second, hot gases trapped in the cylinder begin to cool, thus creating a vacuum within the cylinder. Outside atmospheric pressure now pushes the piston inwards with enough force to keep the engine in motion until the entire cycle is repeated in the next revolution. The motor speed is controlled by the proximity and size of the flame near the porthole. Although this is a very simple engine with a minimum amount of parts, you'll find it to be a fascinating and challenging project, well worth the effort.

Our little motor has a 1" bore by a 1-3/4" stroke and is about as modern as an ancient design can get. It boasts an adjustable cam for fine tuning and a semi-balanced crank arm for optimum performance (**Photo 2**).

2

One inherent problem with this type engine is proper lubrication for the cylinder and piston. Oil, of course, would be the answer for an internal combustion motor, but our little contrivance is weak. Believe it or not, oil on the piston causes excessive drag; heat in the cylinder soon gums the oil and the engine will grind to a halt. I find that the lubricating problem can be overcome by occasionally coating the cylinder walls with fine graphite powder. Because of its free machining ability, stock aluminum was chosen for all the major parts, including the flywheel. If you prefer a steel flywheel, its weight would have to be reduced by narrowing the rim width and thickness approximately fifty percent. The cylinder could also be of steel or bronze. If the cylinder is made from aluminum, it's not advisable to have an aluminum piston. A bronze, cast iron, or steel piston is preferable – less chance of scoring.

The partially completed cylinder, the cylinder pedestal, and the crankshaft bearing bracket are displayed in **Photo 3**.

Begin work on the cylinder pedestal. Machine the blank piece to the proper length, width and thickness, being careful to render the base end of the piece as square as possible. Proceed by accurately laying out center lines on the base end of the pedestal for the two threaded blind holes; use the mill to precisely drill and tap them. Follow by step-cutting each side of the plate down to form the beginning of what will be the foot of the unit (**Photo 4**). Now scribe center lines for the cylinder hole and the 1/8" push rod hole, but drill or ream only the 1/8" hole at this time (**Photo 5**).

The next operation is to form the contour of the pedestal (**Photo 6**). First, adjust the center line of your mill spindle to the true center of your rotary table. Lock the longitudinal table travel. Position the work on a sacrifice piece

3

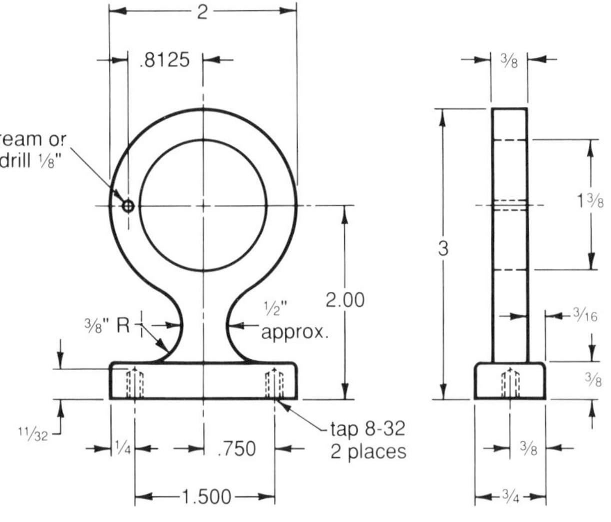

CYLINDER PEDESTAL
aluminum or steel
1 required

4

5

6

7

8

9

10

of flat scrap metal. Adjust the position of the blank by hand until its center lines are true to the mill spindle. Then clamp the piece tight. Note that both hold-down clamps are placed on one side of the work, thus allowing free space to contour one-half of the unit (**Photo 7**). Use a 3/4" end mill; position it not only in front of the work but also about 1/32" below the work so the cutter will actually mill into the sacrifice piece of metal supporting the whole unit. Use the cross slide to gradually advance the cutter into the work. Stop machining when all flat spots around the side and top end of the blank have barely disappeared. Write down the reading on the calibrated collar of the cross slide; you'll need it later on.

The next step is to transfer the two hold-down clamps to the opposite side of the work without disturbing its position (**Photo 8**). Remove one clamp and secure it tightly to the opposite side; then place the second clamp in its new location. Now mill the remaining section of the contour.

Transfer the work to the mill vise and carefully smooth out both little ridges that remain on the foot section (**Photo 9**).

The cylinder hole in the pedestal can be bored either in the mill or lathe. Just make certain the face of the pedestal is running true and is centered properly. Do not overtighten the chuck jaws if you use the lathe. After boring the hole to size, remove the work and smooth all sharp edges on the pedestal; follow by polishing it.

The cylinder is next (**Photo 10**). Machine down the outer end of the piece as shown, but leave the outer step diameter about .010" oversize for now (this is the section that will be pressed into the cylinder pedestal).

A 3/32" wide cutoff tool is used to form the fin slots, so set the compound slide parallel to the work and use its calibrated collar to accurately space the fins. Proceed by drilling and boring the blind cylinder hole. When nearing the correct

11

12

13

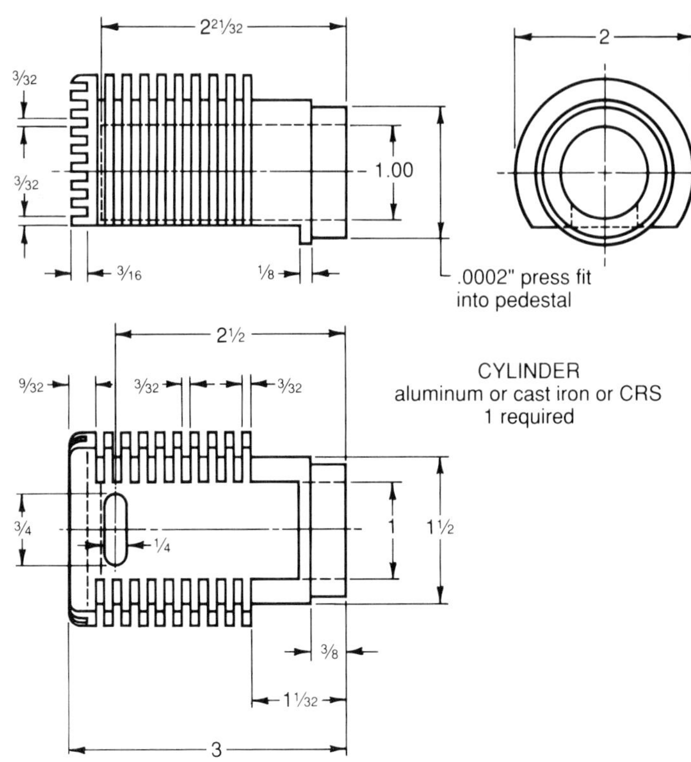

diameter, check for taper. The finished bore should be as smooth as possible. Now prepare to finish machine the outer end step section for a .0002" press fit into the pedestal. Use a rather narrow and pointed tool bit. Hone a small radius on its cutting tip. Employ a fine carriage travel and apply aluminum cutting fluid during this operation (charcoal lighter fluid or sulfur base cutting oil will do in a pinch). When approximately .001" over the correct diameter, run the tool back and forth at the same setting to ensure that it has stopped cutting. Then very slightly advance the tool to machine off a few tenths of a thousand at a time until the desired size is reached.

Suppose (heaven forbid!) that we've goofed and this section is now undersize. That means either make a new cylinder or a new pedestal. The easiest choice would be a new pedestal. But wait! There's also another option, one that's often considered sneaky and improper. Simply semi-knurl the offending diameter enough to slightly increase its size.

Continue by parting the cylinder from the stock, leaving excess metal to face off the head end.

Before pressing the cylinder into its pedestal, please examine **Photo 11**. It shows the cylinder after the pedestal is attached. Be

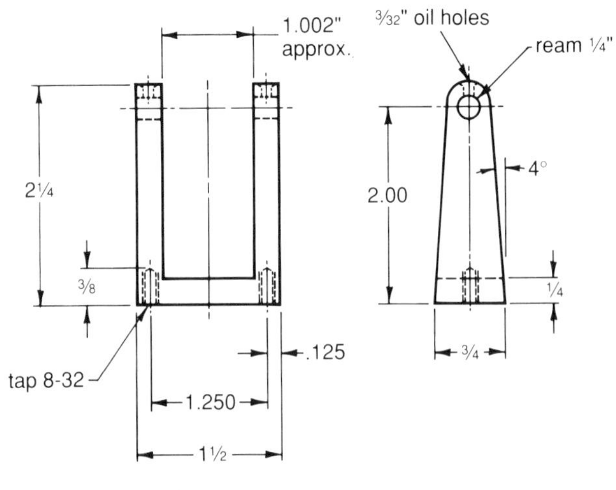

CRANKSHAFT BEARING BRACKET
aluminum
1 required

14

15

16

17

18

certain the valve push rod hole in the pedestal is on the correct side of the cylinder before pressing the parts together. Then clamp the unit in a vise for machining the large flat on the cylinder side. Extend the head end of the cylinder to clear the side of the vise. Wedge an adjustable parallel in the vise to equalize vise pressure on the cylinder and pedestal foot. After milling the flat area, scribe center lines for the porthole. This can be done right in the vise without disturbing the setup (**Photo 12**). Bring the mill spindle over the slot center line. A 1/4" end mill is used to form the 3/4" long opening. Continue by milling the fins on the cylinder head with a 3/32" slitting saw (**Photo 13**). Start from the top and work down. This completes the cylinder, except for smoothing it up.

Next on the agenda is the crankshaft bearing bracket. There are several methods for removing the excess metal in the middle of the aluminum block. If a 1" end mill is available, the flywheel slot could be gradually milled downwards (**Photo 14**). In this

19

20

case, the blank stock piece would have to be at least 1/4" longer than needed to give the vise sufficient gripping surface to hold the work securely – very dangerous otherwise!

A smoother job can be accomplished by positioning the blank on parallels as shown in **Photo 15.** Allow the piece to extend outward from the side of the vise a reasonable distance. Thus, later on, the thickness of each bracket arm can easily be measured with a micrometer. Now position a 5/16" end mill – or one no larger than 3/8" – about 1/64" away from the scribed layout line. The purpose is to gradually rough out a slot along the guide line to the intersecting line near the base end. After this slot is cut through the piece, move the end mill over to the other parallel line, staying away from it about 1/64". Mill the second slot through. Then mill through what's left of the surplus metal close to the intersecting line near the base.

The space between the two bracket arms must now be widened to 1.002" (approximately). First, mike the outside width of the bracket. Subtract 1.002" from that reading. The result is divided by 2. The answer will be the final thickness for each arm of the bracket. **Photo 16** shows the completed milling for this section of the bracket. Continue by accurately squaring off the base end of the bracket (**Photo 17**). Prepare to scribe accurate center lines for the two blind threaded bolt holes in the base (**Photo 18**). Make some type of identifying mark on one side of the bracket. Scribe the cross line for the first bolt hole exactly .125" from that side. On assembly, that side of the bracket should be positioned facing towards the connecting rod crank arm.

The center line for the crankshaft bearing holes must be placed precisely 2.00" from the base. If your scribed lines are accurate, use a wiggler to locate them; otherwise, use an edge finder (**Photo 19**). Next, machine the 4" taper on the bracket arms with the aid of an angle vise (**Photo 20**).

BILL OF MATERIALS

QTY.	PART	MATERIAL	FINISHED SIZE
1	Baseplate	aluminum or steel	4¾ × 7½ × ¼" or thicker
1	Cylinder pedestal	aluminum	¾ × 2 × 3"
1	Cylinder	aluminum, cast iron or CRS	2" OD × 3"
1	Crankshaft bracket	aluminum	¾ × 1½ × 2"
1	Flywheel	aluminum	3⅜" OD × 1"
1	Crankshaft	CRS	¼" OD × 2¾"
1	Piston	bronze, cast iron or CRS	1" OD × ¾"
1	Connecting rod	aluminum	3/16 × 5/16 × 3 11/32"
1	Crankpin retainer washer	CRS	5/16" OD × 1/32"
1	Crankpin	CRS	3/16" OD × 3/16" plus
1	Wrist pin	CRS or dri11 rod	⅛" OD × 29/32"
1	Wrist pin yoke	aluminum	5/16" OD × 11/16"
1	Crank arm	aluminum	¼ × ½ × 2"
1	Cam roller fork	aluminum	11/32 × ½ × 1⅛"
1	Cam roller	CRS	½" OD × 3/16"
1	Cam roller shaft	CRS	¼" OD × 11/32"
1	Cam	aluminum	15/16" OD × ¼"
1	Valve	CRS, cast iron, or bronze	5/32 × ½ × 15/16"
1	Valve spring	.015" spring wire	11/64" OD × 1 9/16", 32 turns
1	Valve flat spring	steel shim stock	.007 × ⅝ × 1 29/32"
1	Valve push rod	CRS or drill rod	⅛" OD × 2⅝"
1	Fuel tank	brass door knob	Weslock, stock No. SV600, *Sunray*
1	Fuel tank spout	brass tubing	7/16" OD × 1⅛"
1	Fuel tank lid	aluminum	1" OD × ⅜"
2	Tank clamps	aluminum	⅜ × 7/16 × 1"
2	Clamp springs	.025" spring wire	3/16" OD × ⅜"
4	Socket cap screws		8-32 × 9/32"
4	Socket cap screws		4-40 × ½"
1	Socket cap screws		4-40 × ⅜"
2	Hex nuts		5-40
1	Hex nuts		4-40
1	Hex nuts		6-32
2	Socket setscrews		8-32 × 3/16"
1	Socket setscrews		6-32 × ⅛"
1	Socket setscrews		4-40 × ⅛"

Although the flywheel is easily machined from aluminum (**Photo 21**), care must be taken to drill and ream a true running shaft hole. Be gentle with the center drill when spotting location for the hole and never allow the drill to bang into the work. After machining the first side of the flywheel, reverse it in a four-jaw chuck, allowing enough of the finished perimeter of the flywheel to be exposed for trueing up with a dial indicator. After completion of the lathe work, the optional spoke holes can be drilled through the flywheel. An easy method is to center the work on the mill rotary table. Elevate the flywheel on parallels to avoid drilling surplus holes in the rotary.

The location for the setscrew holes in the flywheel hub are spot drilled with a long center drill. The work is tilted about 10° (**Photo 22**). It's prudent to complete all of the engine parts before mounting anything to the baseplate. Please examine **Photo 23**; it illustrates how the crankshaft parts will appear after assembly.

Begin work on the piston and connecting rod units (**Photo 24**). Visible are the bronze piston, aluminum connecting rod, tubular wrist pin, and the wrist pin yoke. The nut secures the piston to the wrist pin yoke.

The piston needs very little explanation except to mention that it's advisable to rough out the OD of the piston first, leaving it about .010" oversize. Then drill and bore the ID to size. Now return to the OD and carefully finish it, rendering it as smooth as possible. The piston should be from .0015" to .002" smaller than the cylinder bore; any larger than that seems to add to the problem of scoring in the cylinder. More than .002" clearance means excessive piston leakage, resulting in a hard starting, pepless motor.

The piston is now cut from the stock piece, allowing enough length to face off the head end. The piston should be gripped very gently in a three-jaw chuck for this operation. If a 1" collet is available, use that instead, but don't overtighten it on the work.

Machine the connecting rod blank to the proper overall length, width, and thickness. Lay out center lines for the wrist pin and crankpin holes, then drill and ream them to size (**Photo 25**). Continue by step-cutting each side of the arm (**Photo 27**). Remove the work, and by hand, round off any sharp edges on the con-rod.

Photo 28 shows how the wrist pin yoke was slotted, and in **Photo 29** is a view of the assembled unit.

Visible from the left in **Photo 30** are the steel crankpin bushing with its retaining screw and washer, then the semi-balanced crank arm (note the circular brass weight plugged into one end). Finally, at the right, is the fast-acting aluminum cam.

Photo 31 illustrates the beginning of the crank arm. Near the right-hand end of the blank is the threaded hole for the crankpin bushing. Next to that is the reamed crankshaft hole. Then follows the countersunk bolt hole that will secure the cam to the crank arm. Last is the 3/8" reamed hole for the press fitted brass (or steel) counterbalance weight.

In **Photo 32**, a portion of the crankpin end of the arm is being rounded with the aid of the rotary table. A circular headed bolt was inserted in the arm as a means of centering the work. Run the indicator around the bolt head. Follow by rounding the opposite end of the arm (**Photo 33**). Then continue by rounding the step shoulder adjacent to the crankshaft hole (**Photo 34**). Finally, mill the taper on the crank arm (**Photo 35**).

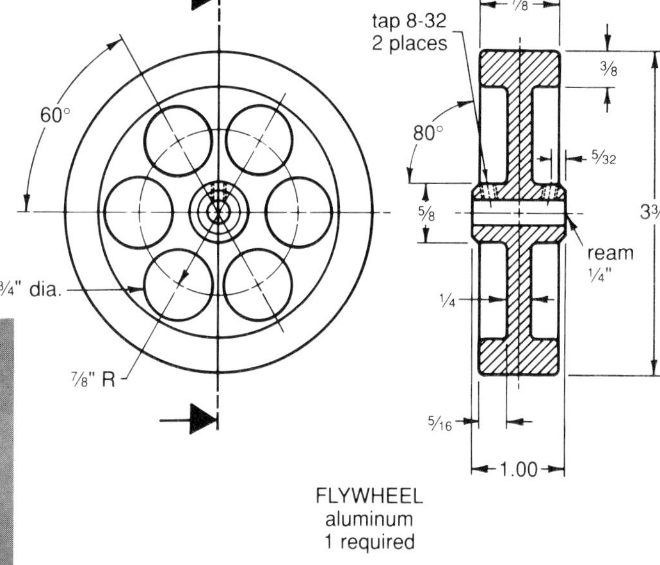

FLYWHEEL
aluminum
1 required

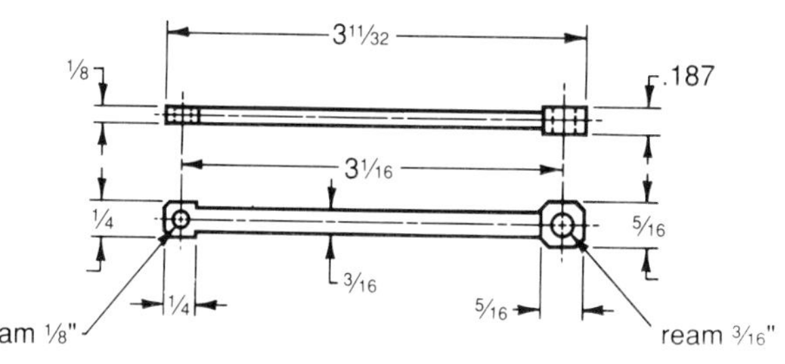

CONNECTING ROD
aluminum
1 required

21

22

23

24

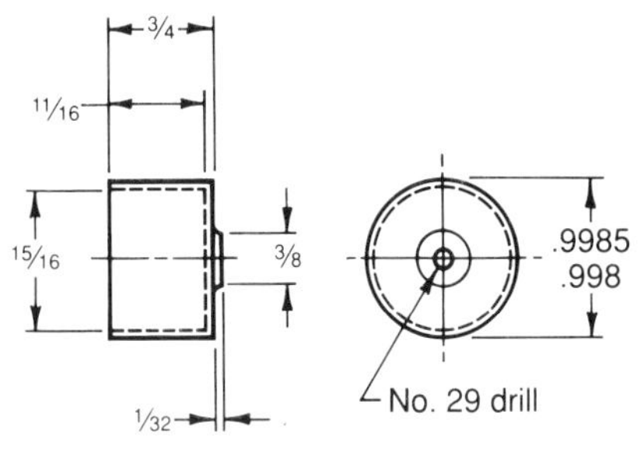

PISTON
bronze, cast iron or CRS
1 required

25

26

27

28

29

ream ⅜"
press in a brass
or CRS plug
2
5/16
.250
1/8
3/4
drill and counterbore
for a 4-40 bolt
tap 6-32
tap 4-40
1/2
7°
1/4
.282
.875
5/32
CRANK ARM
aluminum
1 required

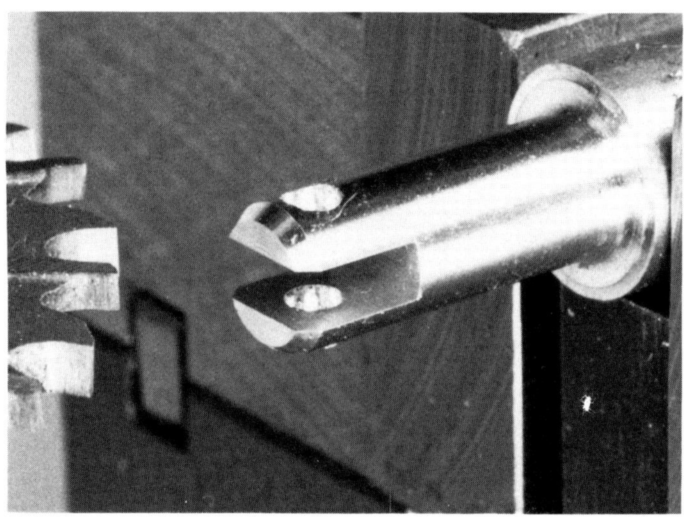

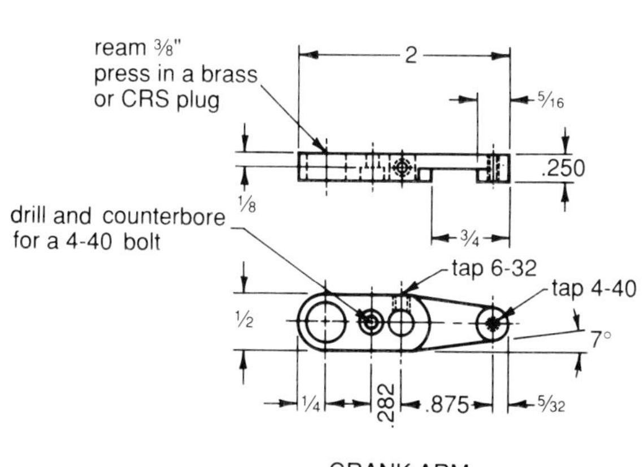

30

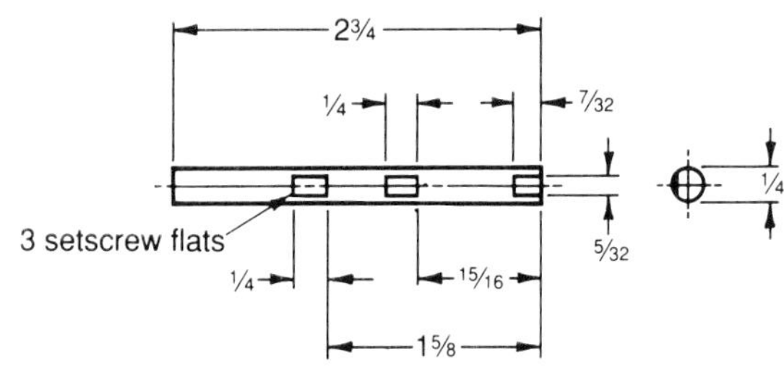

CRANKSHAFT
CRS
1 required

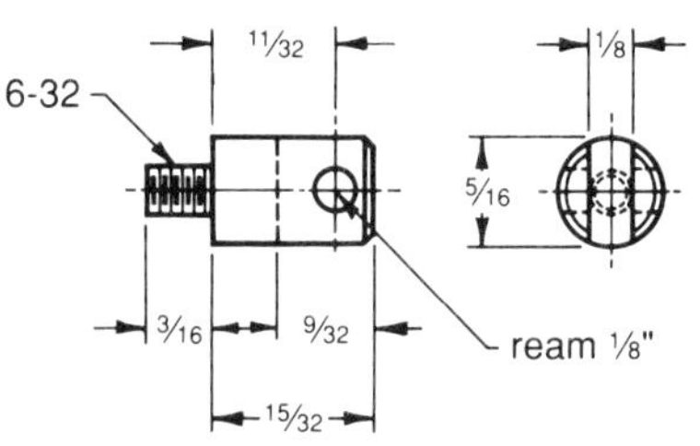

WRIST PIN YOKE
aluminum
1 required

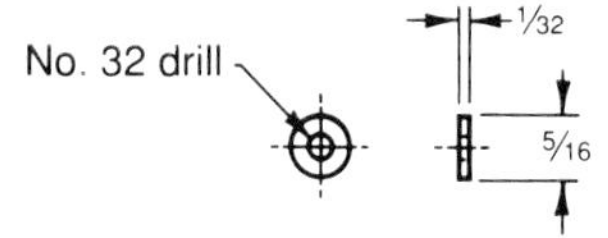

CRANKPIN RETAINER WASHER
CRS
1 required

31

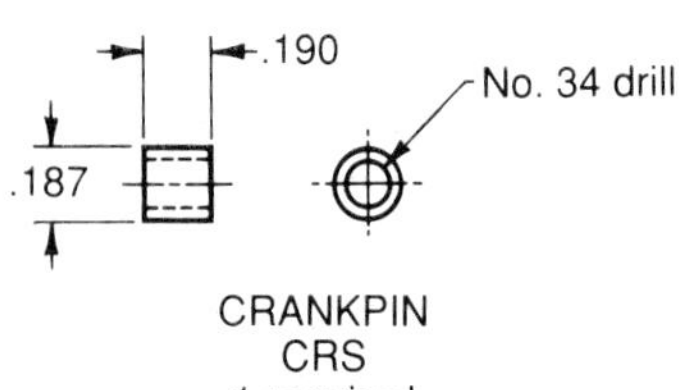

CRANKPIN
CRS
1 required

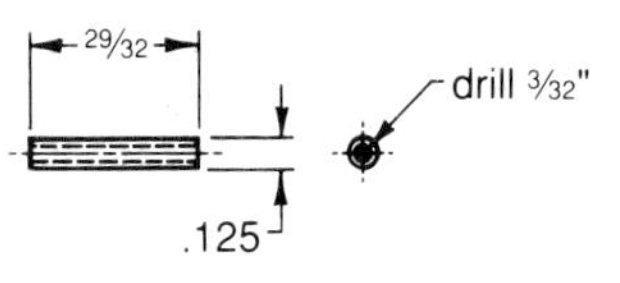

WRIST PIN
drill rod or CRS
1 required

32

33

34

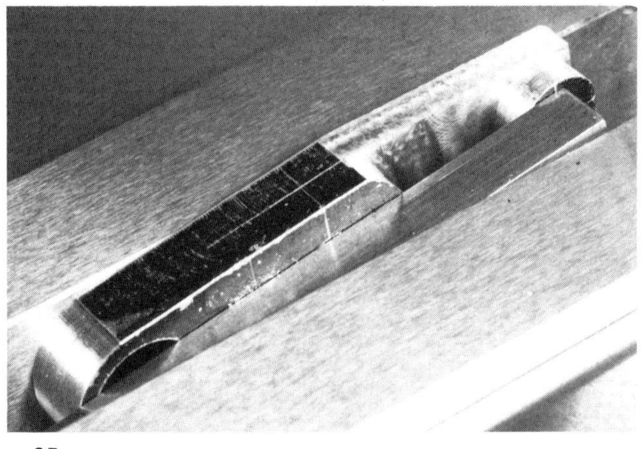

35

Cam

Begin work on the Cam by turning the stock piece to the proper diameter. Drill and ream the shaft hole about 3/8" deep. Mount a cutoff tool in the lathe as if to part the disk at its proper thickness (.250"). However, merely run the cutter into the work about 1/4" deep, leaving the disk still attached to the stock. Now transfer the work to the mill and rotary table.

First, center the rotary true to the mill spindle. Then set the mill longitudinal table calibrated collar to zero for a table movement later on, to the right. Now lock the table. Set the calibrated collar on the cross slide to zero, for a table movement away from you...of course, note the location of the cross slide, thus enabling you to bring it back to this exact position at will. Proceed to mount the work stock piece vertically in a small vise. Now move the cross slide from its zero setting exactly 9/16" away from you and lock it. Place the vise on the rotary table and, using a dial indicator in the spindle, shift the vise by hand until the work is centered true to the mill spindle. Then clamp the vise securely to the rotary.

For better visibility, it's best to position the end mill in front of the work, so move the cross slide farther away from you, and install either a 1/2" or 3/8" end mill. Lower it enough to mill the 1/4" wide rim of the cam (**Photo 36**). With the cutter in motion, advance the cross slide towards you until the cutter makes contact with the work. Then gradually feed inwards, using the rotary crank to mill an arc on the cam. When the high point of the arc reaches about 1/16" from the rim of the cam center hole, begin measuring across the middle of the arc to the opposite rim of the cam. Stop milling when this reading reaches .625" (**Photo 37**).

The next step is to mill the cam adjusting bolt slot in the face of the cam; that means the work will have to be relocated true to the center of the rotary table. Return the mill cross slide back to its original zero setting and lock it. That should center the mill spindle with the center of the rotary. Install an indicator in the spindle. Loosen the clamps holding the vise and shift the vise by hand until the hole in the cam runs true to the spindle. Clamp down the vise, and install a 1/4" end mill. Unlock the longitudinal table travel, and move the table to the right .281" from its zero setting, then lock the table.

With the aid of the rotary crank, gradually mill out the curved slot to

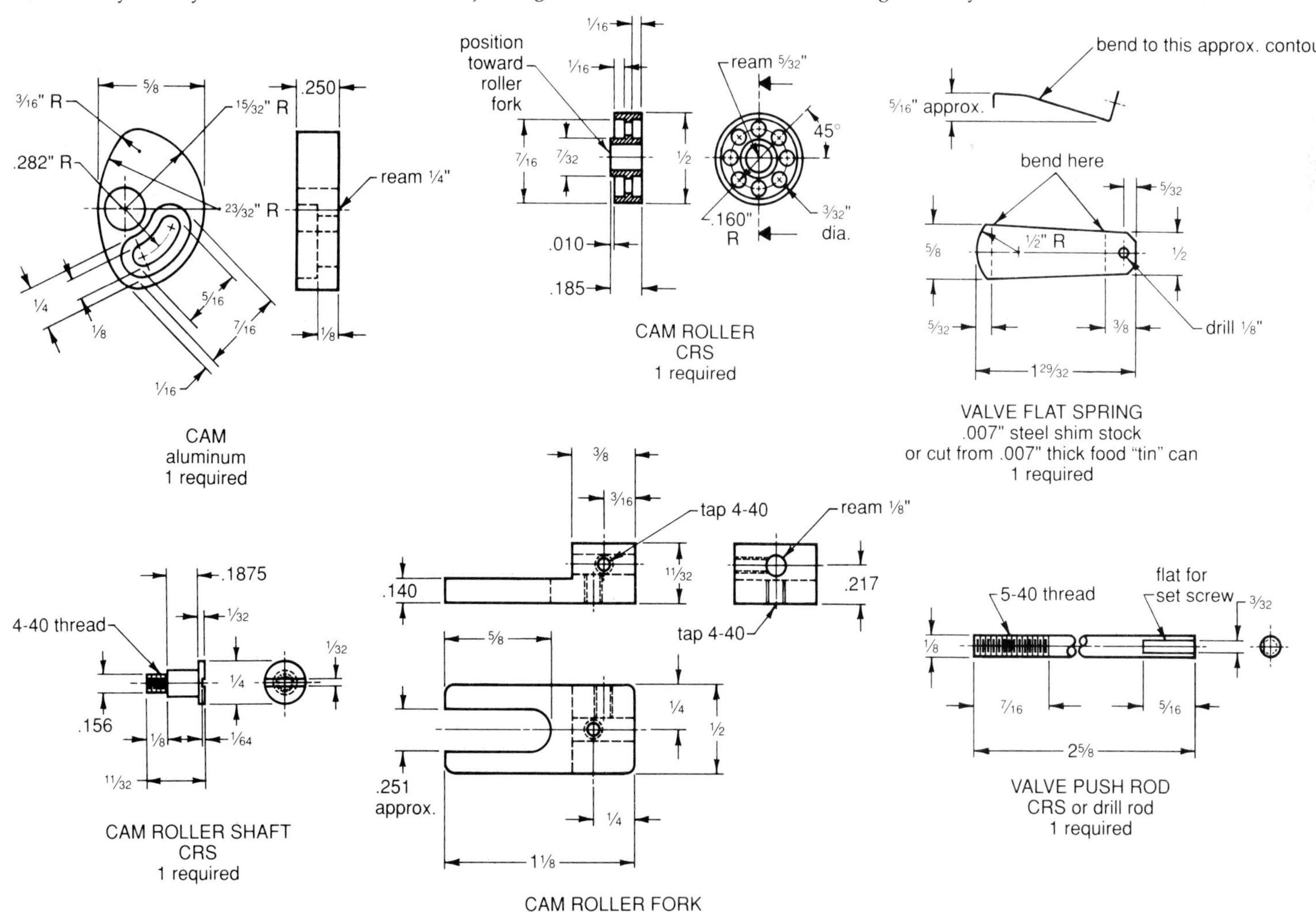

CAM
aluminum
1 required

CAM ROLLER
CRS
1 required

VALVE FLAT SPRING
.007" steel shim stock
or cut from .007" thick food "tin" can
1 required

CAM ROLLER SHAFT
CRS
1 required

CAM ROLLER FORK
aluminum
1 required

VALVE PUSH ROD
CRS or drill rod
1 required

36

37

38

39

40

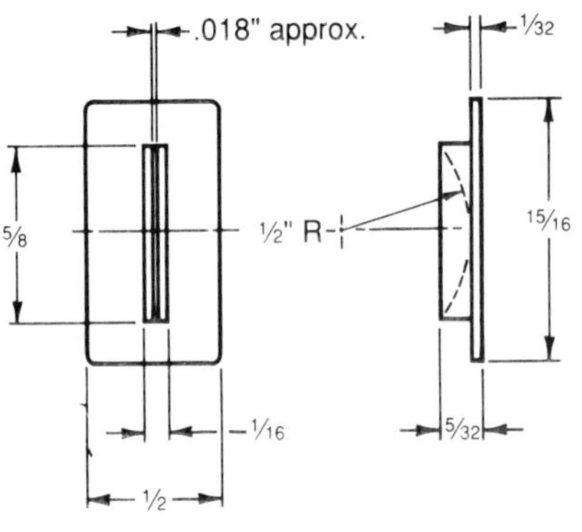

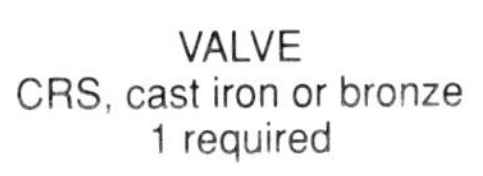

VALVE
CRS, cast iron or bronze
1 required

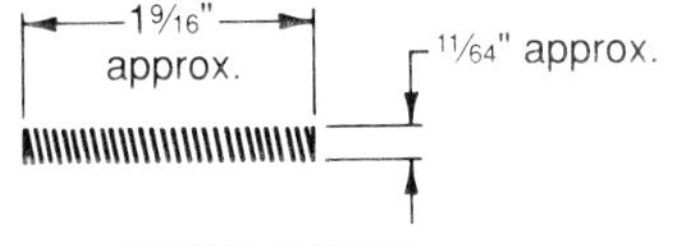

VALVE SPRING
32 turns of .015" dia. spring wire
1 required

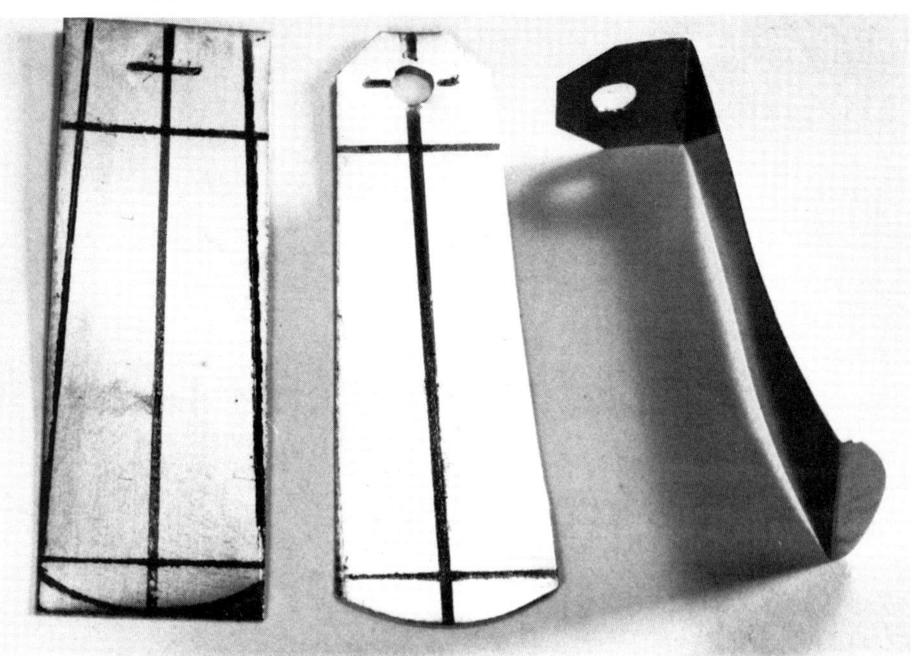

41

42 43

44

45

the proper depth (**Photo 38**). Then install a 1/8" end mill, and gradually cut a narrow slot all the way through the cam. Return to the lathe, and part the cam from its stock piece. The sharp tips on the cam lobes are rounded by hand or with a disk sander.

The elemental yet effective slide valve and flat spring are illustrated in **Photo 39**. Parts for the valve push rod assembly (minus one setscrew) are displayed in **Photo 40**. The flat spring on the left has its curved tip resting in a loose fitting shallow slot in the valve plate. Next are the compression spring and the push rod, followed by the cam roller fork and the roller wheel. Above the fork is the roller shaft.

The flat spring is cut from .007" steel shim stock or from the side of an ordinary food can that is also .007" thick – either will work. The three simple steps of forming the spring are shown in **Photo 41**.

The slide valve can be machined from steel, cast iron, or bronze. The blank piece of metal to be used should be made 1/8" thicker than the finished product specifies. The extra thickness is for gripping in the vise during the machining process. Scribe layout lines on the block and mount it in the mill vise (**Photo 42**). Set the mill spindle to the center line of the work. Install a 1" diameter by .018" jeweler's slotting saw to form the slot (**Photo 43**). Run the cutter straight into the work. (The saws are readily available from ENCO, 5000 West Bloomingdale Avenue, Chicago, Illinois 60639).

Proceed by positioning the work as shown in **Photo 44**. Step cut each end first, then gradually mill the sides to form the thin wall that runs parallel to the slit (**Photo 45**). Now turn the piece upside down in the vise, gripping it on the narrow wall section just machined. Gradually mill off the surplus metal (**Photo 46**). It's important that this surface is rendered as smooth as possible, so sand it on a flat surface. Begin sanding with medium fine grit emery paper, placed face up on the flat surface, until the tool marks disappear. Then use a finer grit paper and finally polish it on 600 grit paper. Be certain to smooth any sharp edges around the valve plate – otherwise they may dig into the aluminum surface of the cylinder when the engine is in motion.

46

The aluminum baseplate should be machined so its edges are square and parallel to each other. My piece of metal also had to be lightly machined on both sides to flatten it. The optional bevel around the edges was formed with a ball end mill.

It would be possible to eliminate the metal base entirely and mount the engine components directly to a hardwood base, providing it is perfectly flat.

A suitable fuel tank is the next item to tackle (**Photo 47**). A small old-fashioned oil can makes an ideal tank – that is, providing you can find one! Well, I couldn't locate one in any of the stores, so ended up buying an ordinary keyless-type door knob that was easily converted into a tank. The one in the photo is from a Wedlock closet/hall door knob set, stock No. SV600, design – *Sunray*.

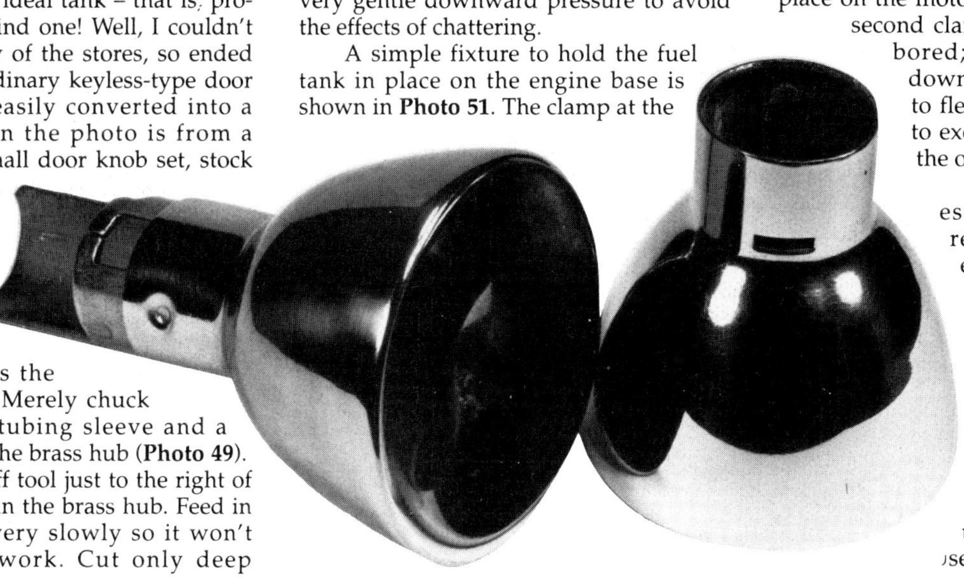

The two knobs from the set are shown in **Photo 48**. The one at the left is the easiest to work. Merely chuck in on the steel tubing sleeve and a small portion of the brass hub (**Photo 49**). Position the cutoff tool just to the right of the indentations in the brass hub. Feed in the cutoff tool very slowly so it won't grab onto the work. Cut only deep enough to part the brass from the steel inner sleeve.

Use an angle vise in the milling machine to drill the hole in the tank for the wick tube. The diameter of this tube is not critical; from 3/8" to 1/2" is suitable. Whatever size is chosen, check to see if you have an end mill the same diameter (within a few thousandths): it will be utilized to drill the hole in the tank. First, center drill the location for the spout hole (**Photo 50**). Then follow with the end mill, using a low spindle speed and a very gentle downward pressure to avoid the effects of chattering.

A simple fixture to hold the fuel tank in place on the engine base is shown in **Photo 51**. The clamp at the left has oversize bolt holes, thus allowing for some adjustment of the clamp when in place on the motor base. The holes of the second clamp are deeply counterbored; springs on the hold-down bolts allow the clamp to flex up and down slightly to exert a springy tension on the out-of-round tank.

No explanation is necessary for making the remaining parts of the engine; there is nothing tricky at all in their construction.

Upon completion of all the engine parts, accurately scribe center lines for the countersunk bolt holes that will secure the cylinder unit to the baseplate. Use the milling machine to

47

49

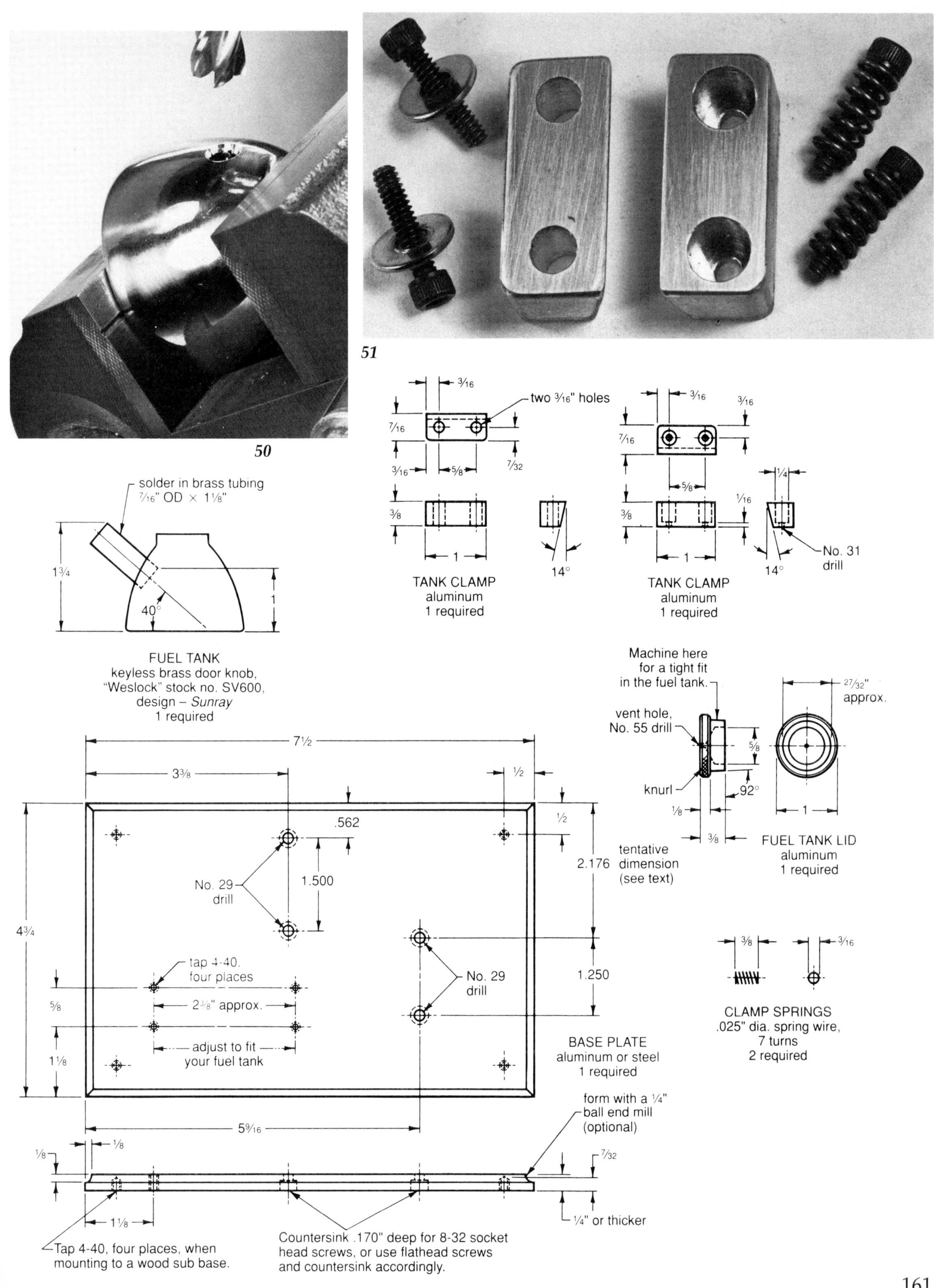

50
51
3/16
two 3/16" holes
7/16
3/16
5/8
7/32
3/8
1
14°
TANK CLAMP
aluminum
1 required
3/16
3/16
7/16
5/8
1/4
1/16
3/8
1
14°
No. 31
drill
TANK CLAMP
aluminum
1 required
solder in brass tubing
7/16" OD × 1 1/8"
1 3/4
1
40°
FUEL TANK
keyless brass door knob,
"Weslock" stock no. SV600,
design – Sunray
1 required
Machine here
for a tight fit
in the fuel tank.
27/32"
approx.
vent hole,
No. 55 drill
5/8
knurl
92°
1/8
3/8
1
FUEL TANK LID
aluminum
1 required
7 1/2
3 3/8
1/2
1/2
.562
4 3/4
No. 29
drill
1.500
2.176
tentative
dimension
(see text)
tap 4-40,
four places
No. 29
drill
1.250
5/8
2 3/8" approx.
adjust to fit
your fuel tank
1 1/8
BASE PLATE
aluminum or steel
1 required
3/8
3/16
CLAMP SPRINGS
.025" dia. spring wire,
7 turns
2 required
5 9/16
form with a 1/4"
ball end mill
(optional)
1/8
1/8
7/32
1 1/8
1/4" or thicker
Tap 4-40, four places, when
mounting to a wood sub base.
Countersink .170" deep for 8-32 socket
head screws, or use flathead screws
and countersink accordingly.

precisely drill the holes, since they must line up perfectly with the threaded blind holes in the cylinder pedestal. Upon completion, bolt the cylinder unit to the base. Now apply layout bluing to the baseplate in the area where the crankshaft bearing bracket will be situated (**Photo 52**).

Please examine **Photo 53.** When attempting to locate the lateral position for the bracket, it's essential to allow about .003" clearance between the cam roller fork and bracket. This will permit the roller fork to slide freely back and forth.

Referring to **Photo 54,** clamp the baseplate to an angle plate. Insert the piston into the cylinder as shown. Allow the height gauge scribe to lightly contact the perimeter of the piston. Write down the height gauge reading. As an example, let's assume the cylinder bore is 1.00", and the piston diameter is .998". Therefore, to find the center line of the cylinder, lower the gauge one-half the diameter of the piston – minus .001". Make a note of this reading. Now, let's assume the connecting rod crankpin bushing is .190" in length. One-half of that length should be positioned on one side of the center line of the cylinder and the other half on the other side. So now lower the height gauge .095".

This new reading should place the scribe point on the gauge even with where the outer face of the crank arm will be. Now add up the thickness of the crank arm, plus the thickness of the cam, and also the fork section of the cam roller fork. To this total, add .003" for clearance. Then lower the height gauge that total amount. Scribe the horizontal line as in **Photo 55.** In theory, the side edge of the bracket should be placed in line with the scribe. Because nothing is perfect, double check by temporarily clamping the bracket on the line. Use the setup shown in **Photo 56.**

52

Install only the valve push rod and roller fork. Both the push rod and fork should slide back and forth without binding. It could bind up and down as well as sideways. If binding occurs, determine what's causing it. The bracket may have to be shifted laterally a few thousandths either direction. After everything checks out satisfactorily, scribe the center line for the first bolt hole exactly .125" below the proper guide line, then the second one below that. Again, accuracy in drilling the holes is essential for matching with the blind threaded holes in the bracket.

When assembling the entire motor, bear in mind all moving parts must function freely! First, wipe off any oil that may be in the cylinder. Coat your finger generously with fine graphite powder and thoroughly rub it all over the inside of the cylinder. Then install the piston.

The flat spring that clips to the slide valve should be bent enough to exert a little pressure against the slide valve. Rub graphite powder to the area where the slide valve moves back and forth.

The push rod compression spring should be only strong enough to keep the cam roller in contact with the cam at all times. Observe the cam roller when operating at top speed; that will tell you if the spring is strong enough.

This engine is designed to run in a clockwise direction when viewed from the fuel tank side. When the slide valve is in the closed position, the outer edge of

53

54

the slide valve should only extend approximately 1/32" beyond the porthole.

For the first trial run, adjust the position of the cam so the bolt that secures it to the crank arm is approximately in the center of the curved recessed slot in the cam.

Lightly oil all of the moving parts, except the cylinder and slider valve. Don't forget the wrist pin, but wipe out any excessive oil around it, thus avoiding cylinder contamination.

The wick for the fuel tank is composed of cotton yarn, or a piece of cloth rolled up and inserted into the tube. The wick should extend inside to the base of the tank. Also, the wick in the tube should be just tight enough so the exposed end can easily be adjusted in or out.

Use only completely denatured alcohol for fuel. Not every drug store will have it in stock, so keep hunting, or ask them to order it for you. A pint will last a long time. Be certain to drill a small vent hole in the tank cover, otherwise excessive pressure in the tank will force fuel out of the spout and you'll have more fire than you bargained for!

When the engine is cold, the heat from the wick flame will usually create moisture condensation around the porthole area. This causes the slide valve to stick rather strongly to the cylinder. Prewarm the cylinder slightly with a small hand torch. Finally, position the wick flame about 3/8" away from the porthole and give the flywheel a fast turn. The motor should come to life with a definite pop! pop! Then adjust the position of the flame this way or that to control the speed.

55

Remember, the faster your Fire Eater goes, the hotter it gets. It's best not to run the engine at top speed longer than two or three minutes at a time. A safe speed would be around 500 or 600 rpm. Enjoy!

56

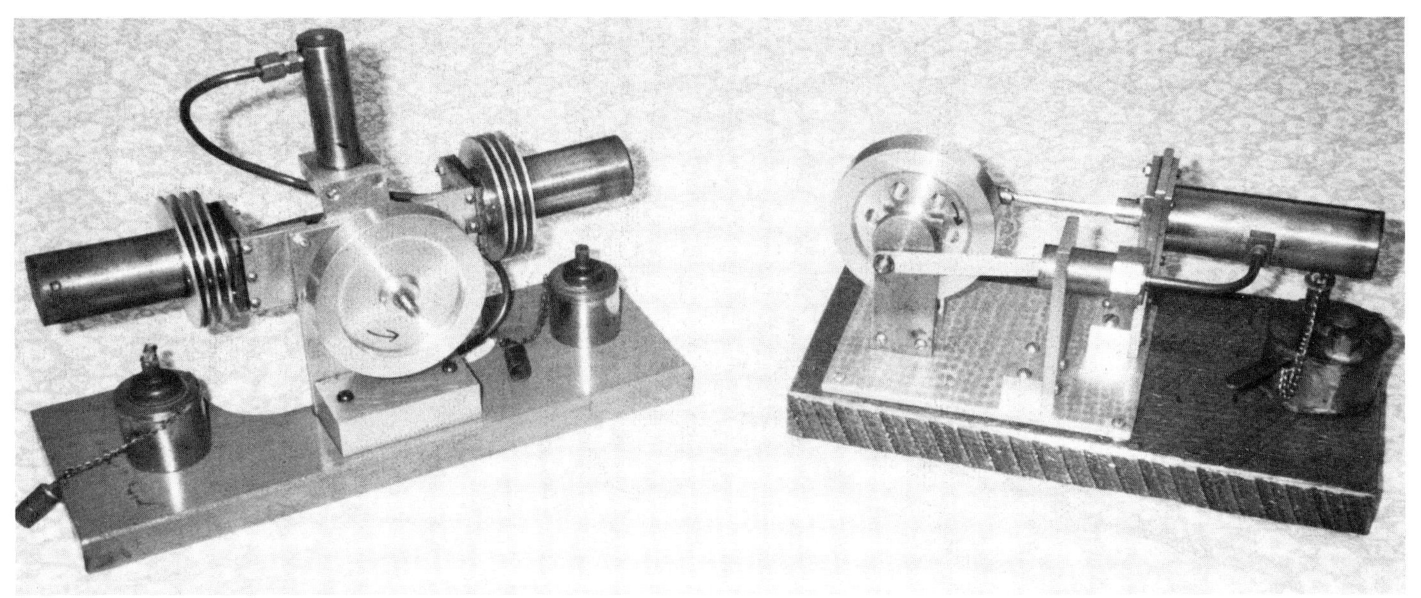

Stirling Hot Air Engine

By Ray J. Colin

Photos by Author

Here's a nice little Stirling-type hot air engine of my own design that you may find an enjoyable project. It runs with an alcohol burner, and starts easily after a short warmup period.

I use Marvel *Mystery Oil* for lubrication. *Loctite* 290 is the best adhesive I've found, which is good up to 400° F for joining parts like the power cylinder to the standard, the end cap on the power cylinder and copper tubing between the displacer and the power cylinders. I have found that vacuum cleaner tubing is good material for the displacer cylinder – thin-walled steel tubing. The choice of materials is up to the builder, and small changes in dimensions are not generally critical.

The two crank disks are set at 90° to each other, and the exact location determines the rotation. Good workmanship is needed, with no binding of parts. The fit of the displacer cylinder rod and power piston are of primary importance, with .001" clearance.

Enjoy your little hot air engine.

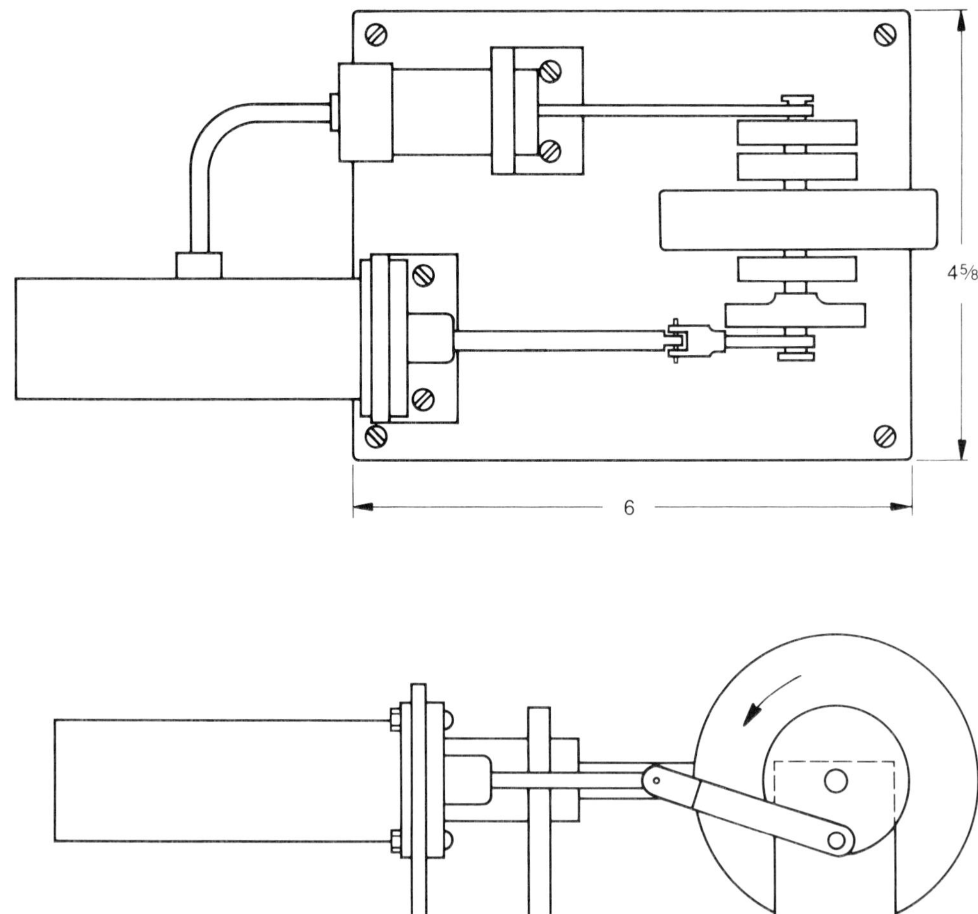

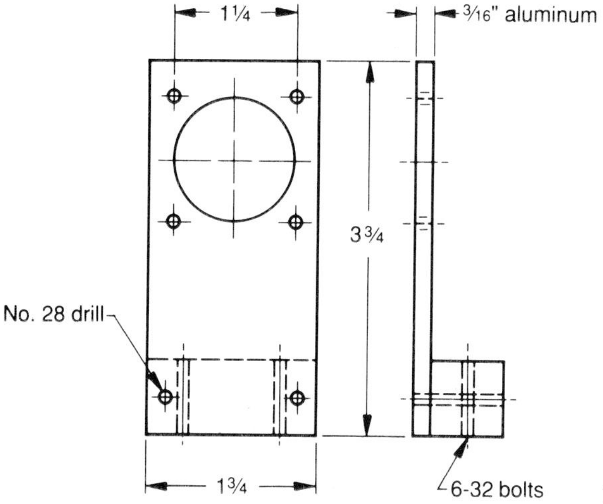

1¼
3⁄16" aluminum
3¾
No. 28 drill
1¾
6-32 bolts

DISPLACER CYLINDER
STANDARD
assembled with 4-40 bolts

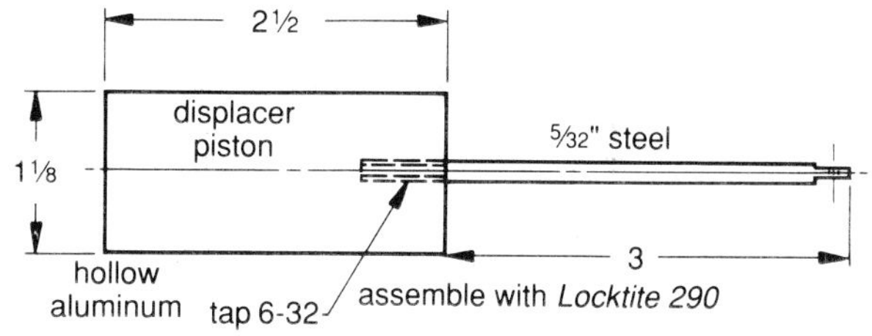

2½
displacer
piston
1⅛
5⁄32" steel
3
hollow
aluminum
tap 6-32
assemble with *Locktite 290*

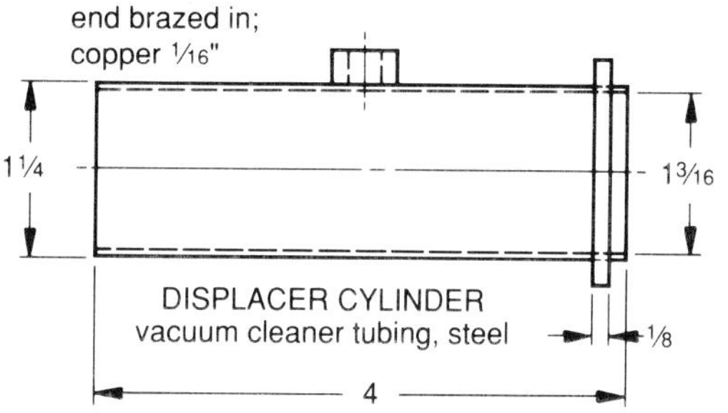

end brazed in;
copper 1⁄16"
1¼
1 3⁄16
⅛
4

DISPLACER CYLINDER
vacuum cleaner tubing, steel

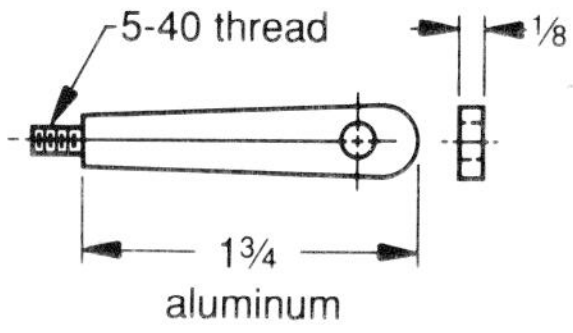

5-40 thread
⅛
1¾
aluminum

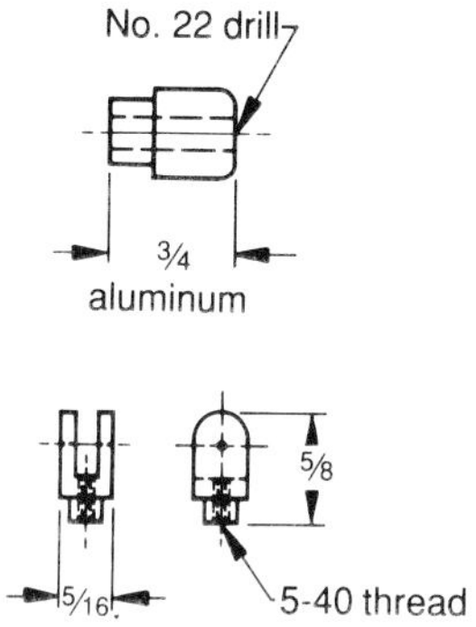

No. 22 drill
¾
aluminum
⅝
5⁄16
5-40 thread

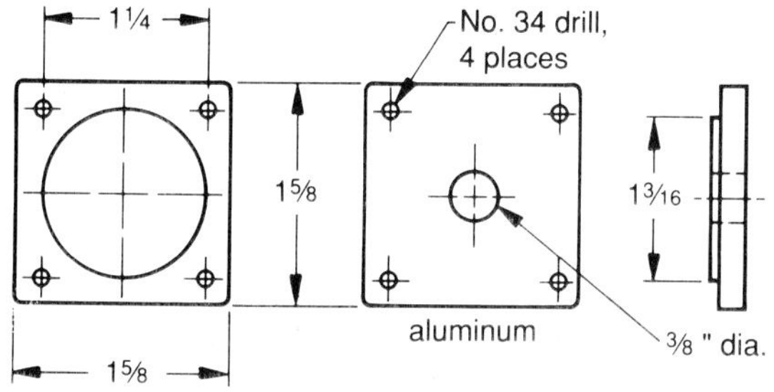

1¼
No. 34 drill,
4 places
1⅝
1 3⁄16
aluminum
⅜ " dia.
1⅝

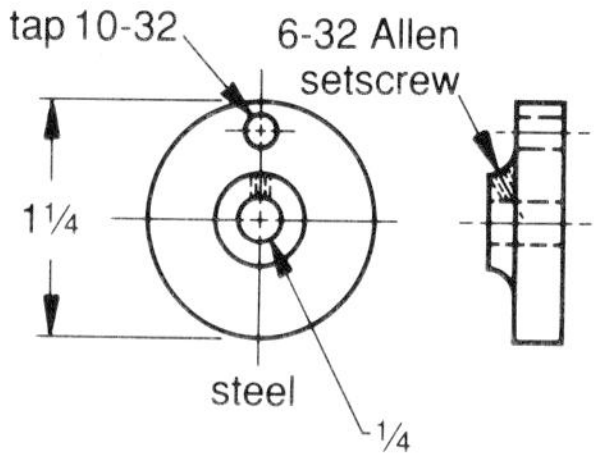

tap 10-32
6-32 Allen
setscrew
1¼
steel
¼

DISPLACER CYLINDER PARTS

oil hole
3
⅞
No. 28 drill
6-32
1¼
5⁄16
¾

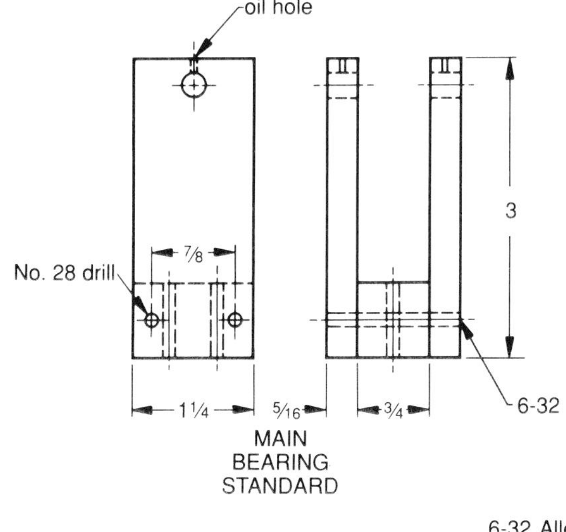

MAIN
BEARING
STANDARD

6-32 Allen setscrew
3

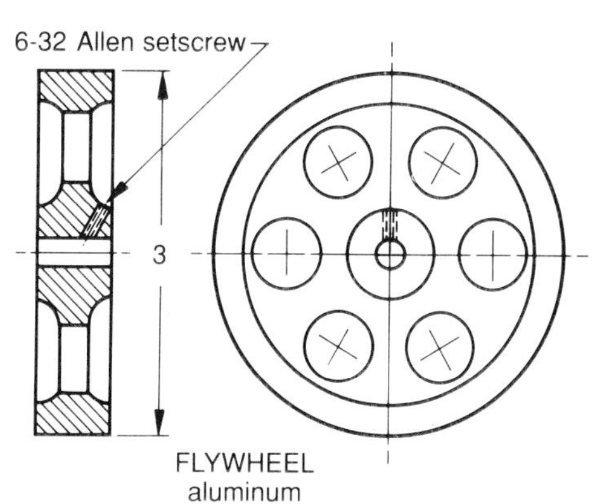

FLYWHEEL
aluminum

The power cylinder and cap are cemented with *Loctite 290*, as is the power cylinder to the standard.

⅞
¼
3½

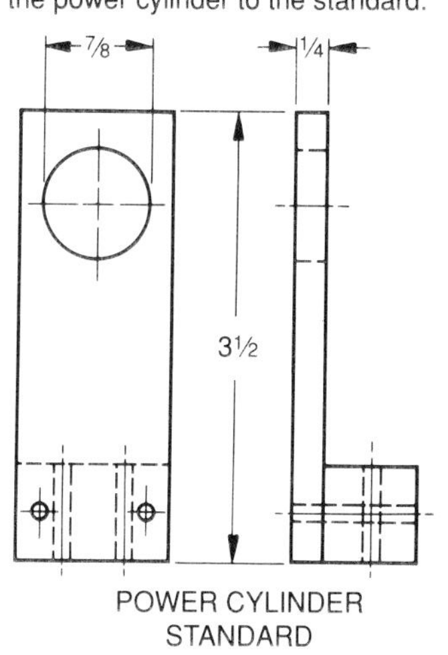

POWER CYLINDER
STANDARD

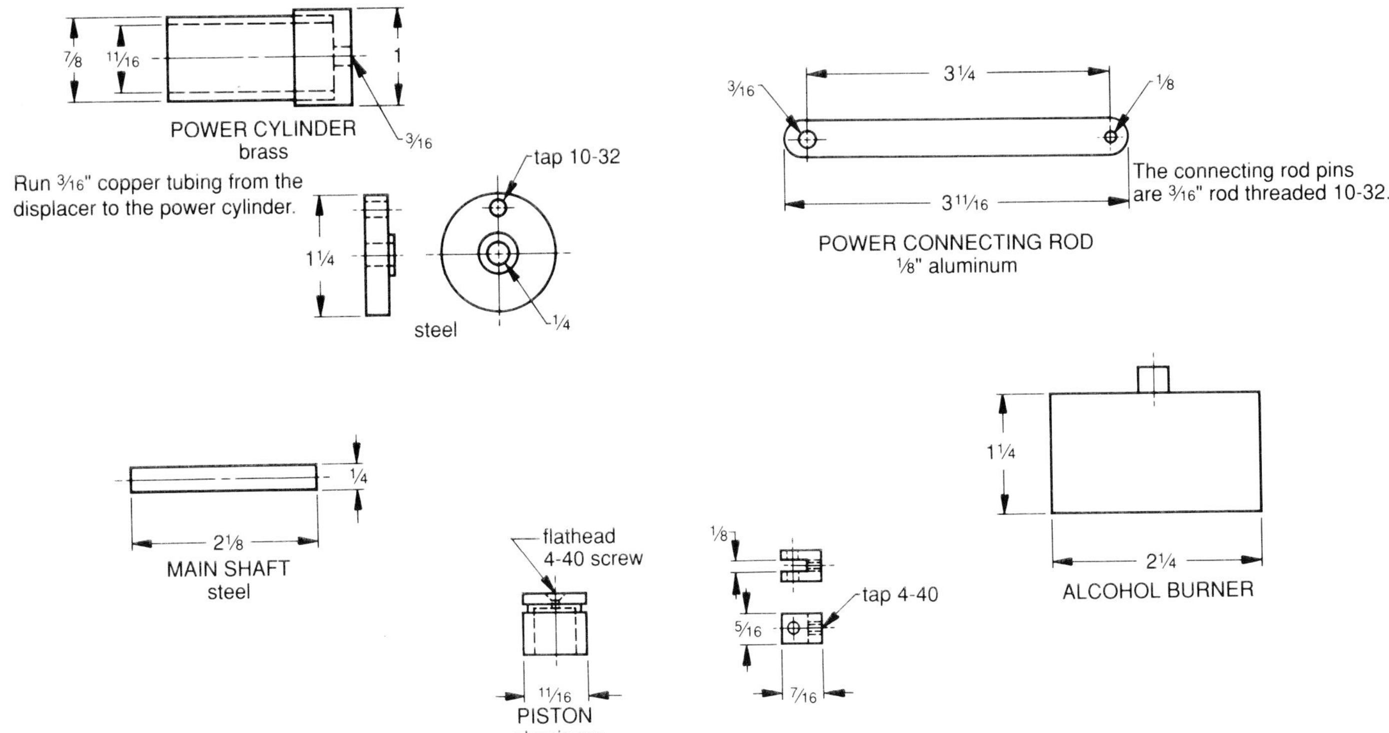
7⁄8
11⁄16
1
3⁄16
POWER CYLINDER
brass
Run 3⁄16" copper tubing from the displacer to the power cylinder.
tap 10-32
1 1⁄4
1⁄4
steel
3⁄16
3 1⁄4
1⁄8
3 11⁄16
The connecting rod pins are 3⁄16" rod threaded 10-32.
POWER CONNECTING ROD
1⁄8" aluminum
1⁄4
2 1⁄8
MAIN SHAFT
steel
flathead
4-40 screw
11⁄16
PISTON
aluminum
1⁄8
tap 4-40
5⁄16
7⁄16
1 1⁄4
2 1⁄4
ALCOHOL BURNER

A Simple, Low-cost Stirling Cycle Engine

By Tim Kraemer

Photos by Author

1

Here is a Stirling cycle engine that can appeal to the beginner and advanced home machinist alike. As a classroom display, it is what scientists call an "elegant" exhibit of the principles behind all heat engines. This is also a gratifying project in that it is fun to make, the parts are cheap (mostly tin and aluminum cans), it doesn't take long to build, and it works very well. A beginner with a lathe should have no difficulty with it and an experienced home shop machinist could put it together in no time at all.

This walking beam Stirling engine was designed by Don Olson, a farmer in Parshall, North Dakota, in 1983. The original intent of the engine was to amuse the grandkids. After the grandkids got some mileage out of the engine, he took it around with him when visiting relatives elsewhere in the country. Since then, I have begun to see this design of engine appear in shows and most recently in the letters to the editor section of *Gas Engine*.

Photos 1 and **2** and **Figure 3** give the overall design. The basic structural materials are wood and cans. I don't know if it could be made entirely out of metal, but I would recommend that you first make one this way, since this design of engine is not terribly powerful. Except for the displacer and piston, the dimensions and materials are not critical. Nevertheless, there are a few details to follow that will possibly save you some trouble.

The order of construction is to first build the basic engine and mount it on the base; then the walking beam and flywheel are mounted in relationship to the basic engine. Almost all of the parts are held together with a high quality epoxy such as *J.B. Weld*. If you feel so motivated, you could soft solder it together, but this is a relatively low temperature engine operating at low pressures.

Piston and Cylinder

The cylinder for the piston is a 3-1/4" length of steel tubing with an ID of 1". The one pictured in **Photo 4** is a piece of scrap just before being cleaned up and made smooth on the inside with a bit of steel wool.

A cup-shaped piston is machined from aluminum to the dimensions given in **Figure 5**. You will note I have not included any tolerances. Make the piston to just fit the cylinder and still slide easily. Before taking the piston out of the lathe, drill a hole through the center and tap it for a convenient size slotted screw you have on hand. I drilled 13/64" and tapped for 1/4-20. Then soft solder a 1/4" length of 1/8"

ID brass tubing onto the slot. This will be the bearing for the crank to the flywheel.

Cut the bolt to a length that will put the top of the tubing on the screw head slightly below the edge of the piston cup shape when turned into the threaded hole of the piston. (The screw must not protrude beyond the face of the piston.) Fix the screw in place with either a high quality epoxy or one of the aluminum solders on the market. The piston rod is a 1/8" brazing rod bent as shown in Photo 4. The Displacement Chamber in **Photo 6** shows the piston and its rod along with the displacement chamber and the displacer. (We'll get to the displacer shortly.)

The displacement chamber was made from an old oil can for two-cycle engines. It is slightly more than 6-1/4" long and slightly more than 2-1/2" wide. Only one end is cut off, so there is a closed end. A 1/2" to 3/4" hole is placed halfway up the side of the can and the 3" piston cylinder is joined so the hole on the displacement chamber is surrounded by the piston cylinder. Again, the means of joining the cylinder to the can is up to you, but epoxy would be the easiest.

The Displacer

This is the trickiest part of the engine and even this isn't too difficult. The displacer is an empty "light" beer can. It must fit inside the displacement chamber with somewhere between 1/32" and 1/16" clearance all around. You might have to search around the trash bin behind a bar in order to get a couple of cans the right size. All of the engines built

2

walking beam 13" long
hole directly above center of flywheel
hole directly above center of displacement chamber
rod is 10" long
cooling can filled with water
cylinder clamp
18
flywheel 5½" dia.
1¼
displacement chamber
holes for exhaust
walking beam support
flywheel stand
base
No. 10 can for firebox
cylinder
¾
2
4½

FIGURE 3

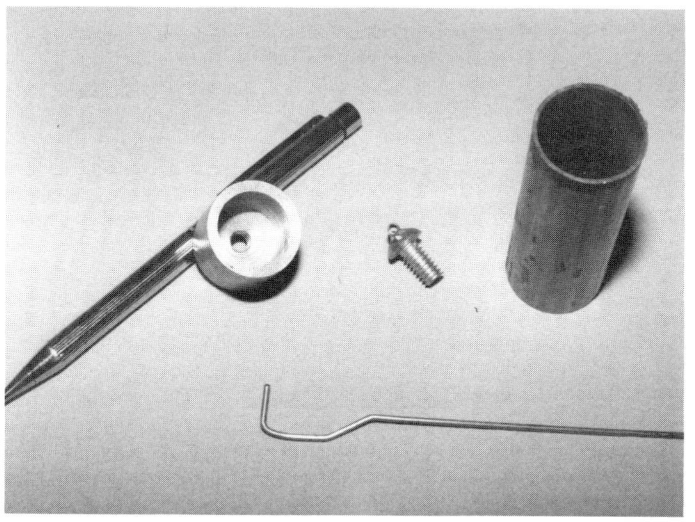

4

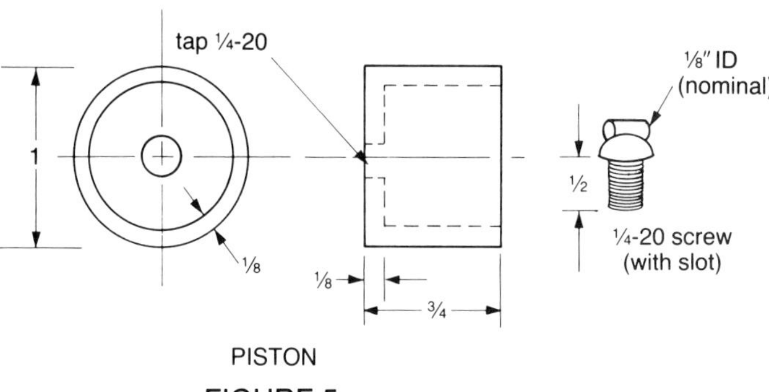

FIGURE 5

around Parshall used a Stihl snowmobile engine oil can as a displacement chamber and a displacer made from "Coors Light" cans. I am sure other cans would work, but this is what I have used. Now, refer to **Figure 7** and **Photo 8** in the following discussion.

It takes two beer cans. Cut off 3/8" of the bottom of one can and 4-1/4" of the other can. (Once a hole is started, a sharp knife or razor does a good job here.) Put a hole in the center of both bottoms. Thread about a 1/2" of a 10" length of 1/8" brazing rod, and run this rod through the shorter can bottom, threaded end first. Place a nut on the threads, and run the threaded portion through the longer can. Place another nut on the rod, and tighten both to hold the larger beer can. Now slide the shorter beer can bottom into the top of the larger beer can bottom so their edges are fairly flush. (Remember, none of these dimensions are critical.) Next, with a small piece of wood on the inside edge, and a nail on the outside, put some dimples around the cans so they are crimped together.

6

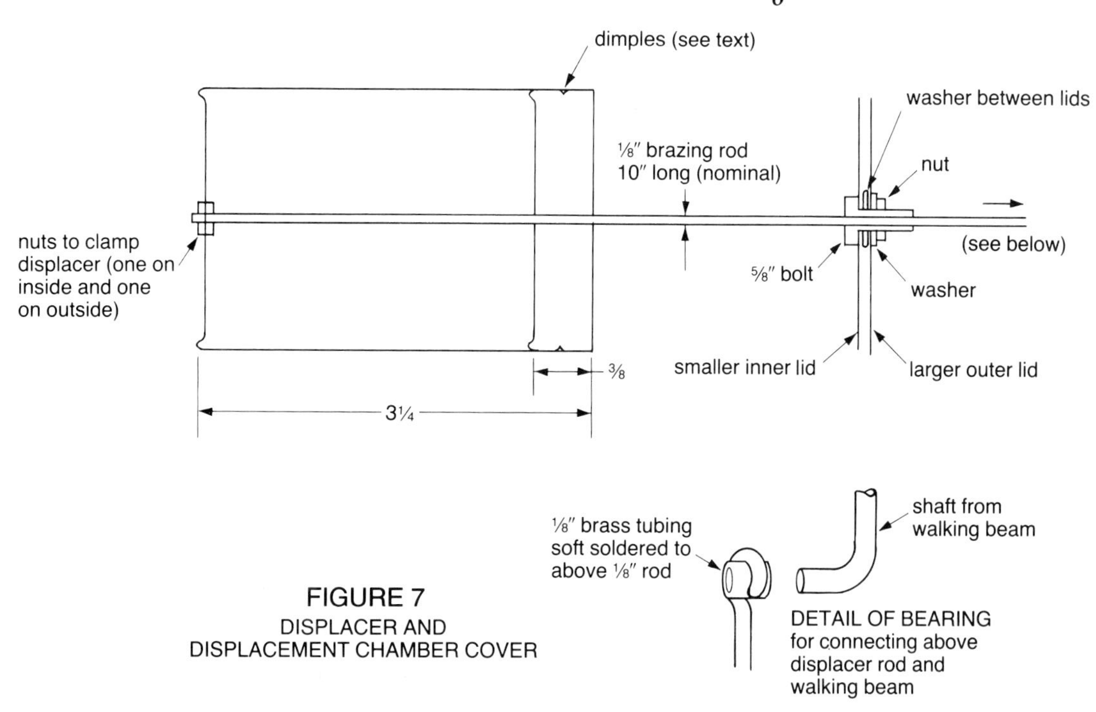

FIGURE 7
DISPLACER AND
DISPLACEMENT CHAMBER COVER

The next task is to put a cover on the displacement chamber. Face off the head of a 5/8" bolt that is threaded all its length, and drill a hole through the center that is 1/8" in diameter. If you have a good eye you could use a drill press, but it would be more technically correct to drill this hole with a lathe after the bolt has been faced. Run this bolt through two tin can lids with a washer between them, and another washer and nut on the outside lid. The can lids are two different diameters. The larger one will cover the top of the displacement chamber and the lid under it, which is slightly smaller than the ID of the can, is there for centering everything in the displacement chamber.

The end of the 10" rod that extends out of the displacer is soft soldered to a short stub of brass tubing which will be engaged by a hook that descends from the walking beam.

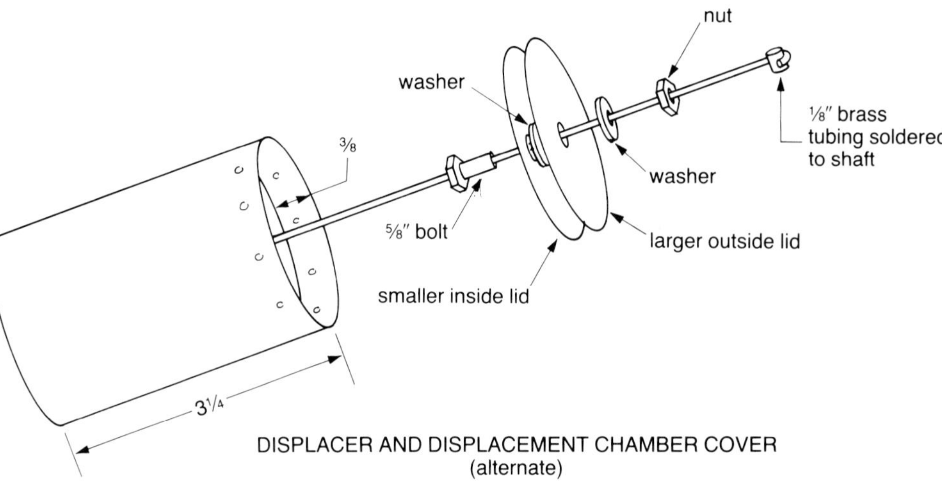

DISPLACER AND DISPLACEMENT CHAMBER COVER
(alternate)

FIGURE 7A

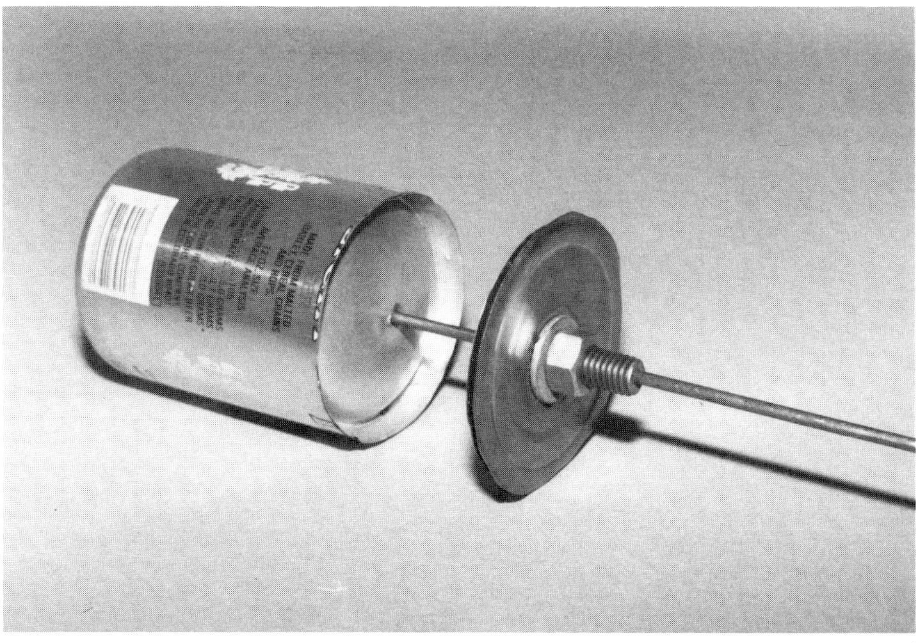

8

Finishing the Engine

Get two discarded number 10 tin cans (the size peas, beans, and such come in). If they have been used one end is already open, so you still need to make a hole in the center of each of the closed ends that will fit the displacement chamber. One can goes around the top portion of the chamber above the piston cylinder, and the other goes around the bottom below the cylinder. Cut a door in the bottom can for the burner, and drill or punch a ring of holes around the top portion of the can so exhaust can escape. The displacement chamber is placed in the bottom can; seal the top can to the chamber with epoxy so it will not leak water. This will be the radiator.

Place the displacer inside its chamber, and see that it moves up and down with no resistance; if it doesn't, add a drop or two of light oil. Seal the lid to the chamber.

The Cylinder Clamp

As illustrated in **Figure 9**, the cylinder clamp has a hole the size of the cylinder OD and a slot cut with a saw. When the threaded rod is tightened, the wood clamps the cylinder very effectively. The height of the hole from the base is the same as the height of the cylinder from the base. The height was 4-3/4" for the machine illustrated. All of the wooden fixtures are mounted with countersunk wood screws through the bottom of the base.

The Flywheel

The flywheel is a 5-1/2" disk cut from 3/4" thick wood. A hole slightly smaller than 1/4" is drilled through the center of the disk, and a 3" length of 1/4" welding rod, threaded for 1", is press fit into the hole. Place one nut on each side of the disk tight enough to hold the disk on the rod, and true up the flywheel on the lathe if necessary.

Next, locate a wood screw 1-1/4" away from the center of the flywheel for later connection to the piston rod and the walking beam shaft. The location of this screw determines the throw for this engine. The mount for the flywheel has a hole at the center height of the cylinder (5-1/4" in the model pictured). A piece of 1/4" ID brass tubing is placed into a 1/4" hole in the mount with a saw slot and threaded rod for tightening, just as in the cylinder clamp. When the shaft is slid into the mount, the flywheel should turn freely. The flywheel and walking beam are shown in **Photo 10**.

The Walking Beam

The mount for the walking beam is 2" at the base and 18" high. (The taper from base to top is "just for pretty.") Don't fasten this to the base until everything else is lined up. The walking beam itself is 13" long. When the beam is horizontal to the base, the holes for the connecting rods must be exactly over the center of the flywheel center, and exactly over the hole on the displacer nut-bearing. A 1/4" bolt with no threads on the shank keeps the walking beam in place. The hole on the beam for this bolt must be a little larger so the beam can move on the bolt with no friction. Place a couple of washers between the stand and the beam, as detailed in **Figure 11**.

Alignment

Turn the flywheel so the off-center wood screw is at its closest position to the piston cylinder. Place a short stub of brass tubing over the threads of the wood screw; this will be the pivot. With the piston rod, move the piston almost all of the way into its cylinder. Then bend it around the pivot, and cut off the remaining rod. Next move the flywheel so the pivot is at its highest point. Hook a length of 1/8" brazing rod through the hole on the walking beam, and bend the other end around the pivot.

Soft solder both rods to the tubing on the pivot. In the original model, the distance between pivot and beam was

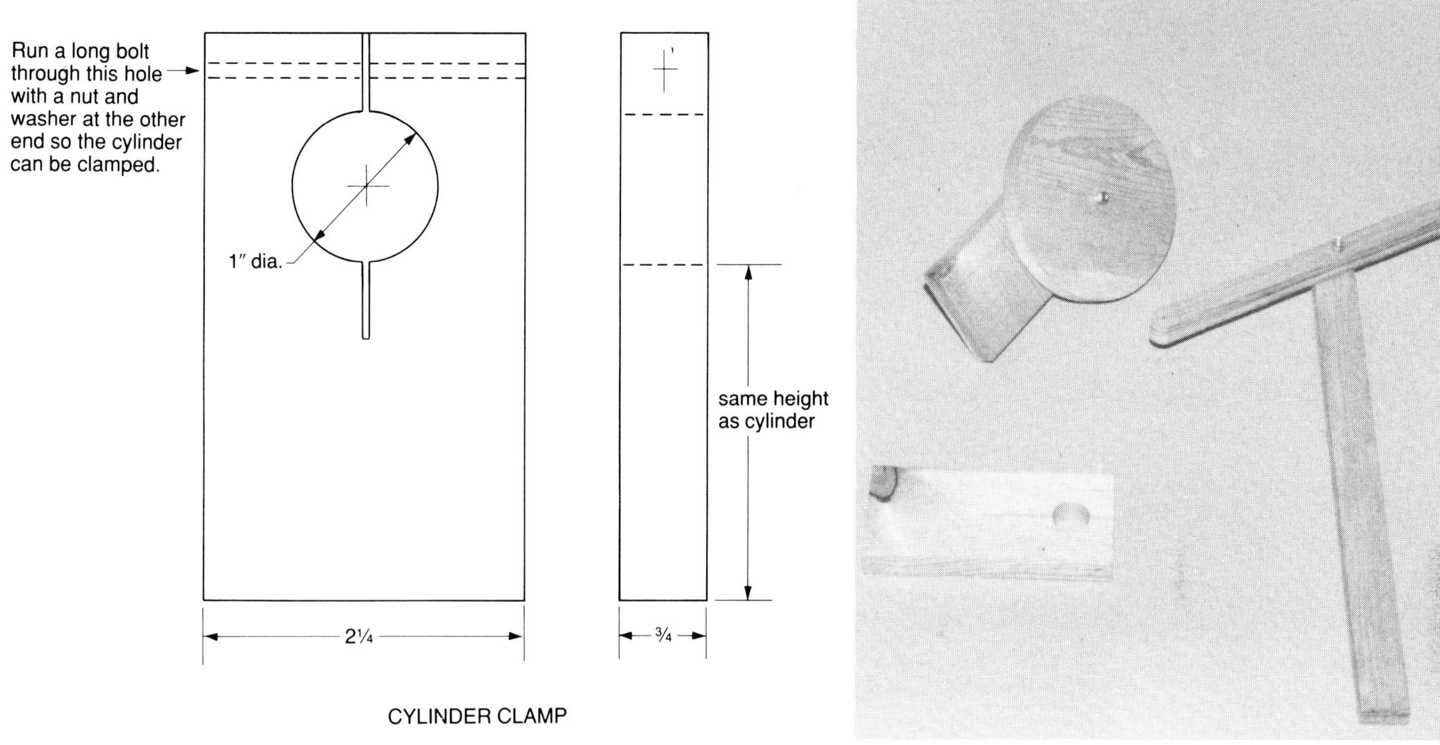

CYLINDER CLAMP

FIGURE 9

10

10". Keep the pivot at its highest position, and hook another brazing rod on the other end of the walking beam. This rod has a second hook bent to engage the stub of tubing soldered to the displacer rod. If everything is set up correctly, moving the flywheel should make the piston move in and out. When the pivot is at its lowest point, the displacer should be at its highest. The hook connecting the displacer rod to the beam can be adjusted by rebending the rod, and thereby make the final "fine tuning."

Burner

All heat engines need a source of heat. There are any number of possibilities, but the heater shown in **Figure 12** is easy to make. Simply squeeze shut one end of a short piece of 3/4" copper pipe, and drill a 1/4" hole close to the bottom. Insert 10" of 1/4" OD copper tubing, and solder both the tubing and the bottom of the pipe. (Use whatever dimensions you happen to have available.) Stuff some cotton into the pipe, and solder the other end of the copper tubing to the bottom of a fuel tank cut from the bottom of a tin can. Use gas line anti-freeze or any other source of methanol as a fuel.

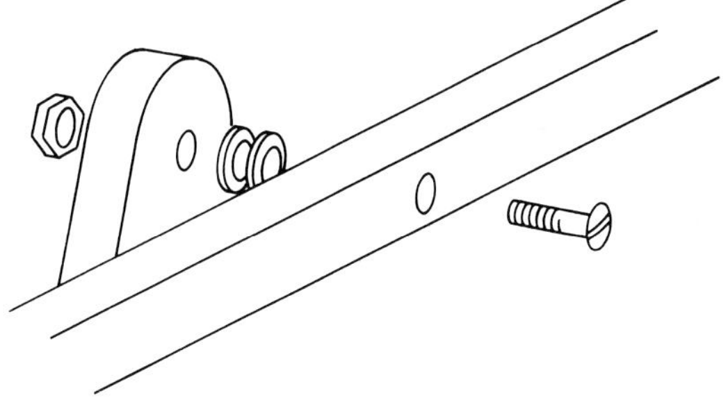

DETAIL OF WALKING BEAM AND MOUNT

FIGURE 11

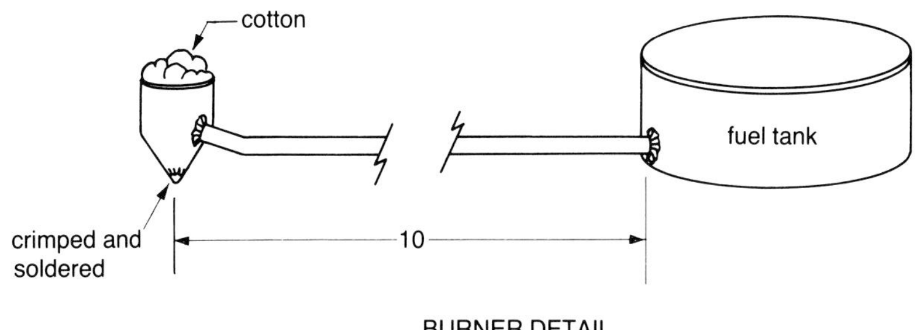

BURNER DETAIL

FIGURE 12

Running

Fill the top can surrounding the displacement chamber with water. Put some fuel in the burner, light it, and put the flame under the displacement chamber. The engine should start right up at about 150 rpm. Give the flywheel a little help if it doesn't. This engine really goes if it's set up in a cold garage in January, just as you would expect with any heat engine. Now that you have built this simple engine, you will probably think of improvements and new designs, so get to it.

BOILER WORKS

An Automatic Electric Model Boiler

By D. E. Johnson

Photos by Author

Weather conditions frequently prevent steaming model boilers outdoors with any degree of comfort. I've tried solid and liquid fueled firing in the basement shop; this resulted in serious stack gas complaints from the upstairs management! Also, it's difficult to tend the fire, handle the engine, and instruct a couple of active grandsons all at the same time. My next problem, a small alcohol fire on the workbench resulted from a crack in an antique burner and required a couple of squirts from the shop fire extinguisher. At this point, I decided to consider alternative methods for cleanly generating model engine quantities of live steam in the shop or even on the kitchen table.

As a heat source, an electric immersion heater seemed practical. This could perhaps be controlled automatically by a steam pressure switch or a thermoswitch (thermostat) immersed in the boiler water. Investigation showed pressure switches to be bulky, expensive and perhaps difficult to fine-tune.

As revealed by the steam tables found in engineering handbooks, for every different absolute pressure (PSIA), there is a unique corresponding temperature. Therefore, if the laws of thermodynamics are still in effect, a reasonably sensitive thermoswitch should, in theory, switch the immersion heater on and off with varying demands for steam at a given pressure.

Theory is, of course, wonderful; the big question remains would it actually work, or might the system go into "open-loop," chasing its tail with wild excursions above and below the desired pressure?

Well, the design shown herein turned out to work perfectly! On the first test, with temporary wiring, a hose exhausted steam into a bucket. It was gratifying to rapidly open and close the stop valve and, via the pilot light, watch the thermoswitch cycle the immersion heater to maintain whatever steam pressure you've dialed into the system.

Photo 1 shows the general arrangement of the boiler and accessories. A Stuart 10V engine is connected to the steam line and stop valve with a Stuart type 1851 displacement lubricator teed in at the steam chest. A Stuart No. 145-3 hand pump feeds makeup water from the feedwater tank seen at the upper right of the photo. The knob at the left end of the boiler adjusts the thermoswitch setting and thus the steam pressure. The immersion heater at the right end of the boiler extends into the electrical junction box, where all electrical connections are made and concealed. The on-off switch and the

1

"heater-on" pilot light are visible on the side of the junction box.

Some modelers may wish to add things like a dummy stack and revise the junction box to look more like the firing end of a stationary boiler.

Note that for steaming engines the size of the Stuart 10V, the hand pump and water tank are not really needed since the boiler capacity is sufficient to steam these smaller engines perhaps 45 minutes without makeup water. The pump is handy for steaming larger model engines which have higher water rates. I used the pump shown to hydro-test the boiler. It can be removed in a couple of minutes to test other boilers as required.

Let's briefly discuss the basic numbers involved in the design so, using a few guidelines, a builder can upsize or downsize the system to suit different requirements. We will also begin construction of the basic boiler. In Part 2 we will make the boiler heads and steam dome, assemble, hydro-test, do the electrical wiring, and get steaming.

The boiler and heating element were sized to steam model engines like the Stuart 10V (3/4" bore × 3/4" stroke) under load, as well as larger engines lightly loaded.

To find the required wattage of the immersion heater, we need to first make some reasonable assumptions. Although a properly broken-in Stuart 10V will, under no load, idle merrily along on less than 5 psig, let's assume under full load the steam chest pressure required is 30 psig (45 psia) at 750 rpm.

Looking in the steam tables on the line for 45 psia, the total heat (hg) for 1 lb. of dry steam is 1171.5 Btu, and the specific volume (vg) a this condition is 9.4 cu. ft./lb. Now we need to find the hourly volume of steam required, and its weight, which will lead us to the wattage required for the heater.

For the 10V engine, bored 3/4", we can calculate or look up in a table the area of the piston; .442 sq. in. Then the volume of steam the engine will need is:

$$\frac{\text{(.442 piston area) (.75 stroke) (750 rpm) (2 double acting)}}{\text{(1728 cu. in. in a cu. ft.)}} = .288 \text{ cu. ft./min.}$$

This ignores the steam savings from early valve cutoff, but the error introduced will be on the conservative side, and will be partially offset by boiler radiation losses, also ignored in the interest of simplicity.

The steam requirement in lb./hr. is:

$$\frac{\text{(.288 cu. ft./min.) (60 min.)}}{\text{(9.4 cu. ft./lb.)}} = 1.84 \text{ lb./hr.}$$

The Btu/hr. requirement is:

(1.84 lb./hr.) (1171.5 Btu/lb.) = 2155.6 Btu/hr.

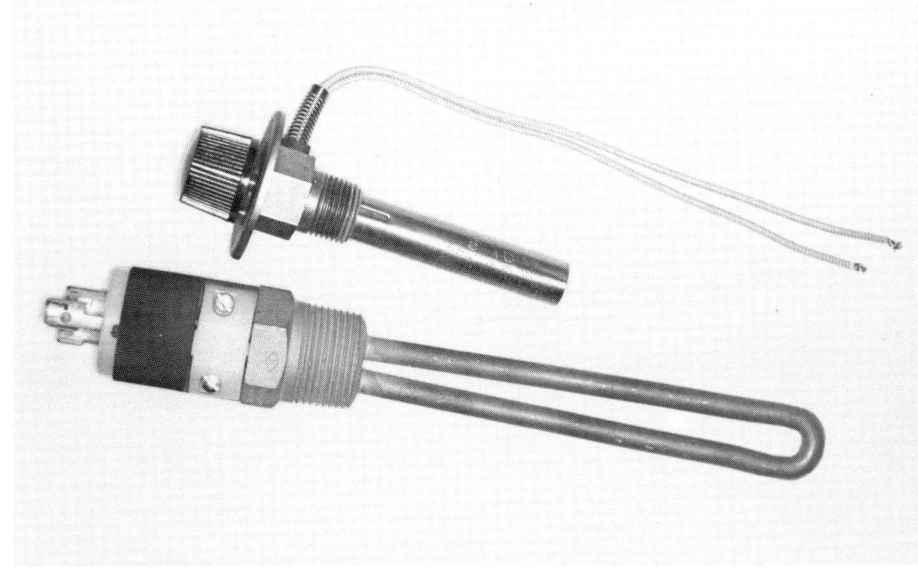

2

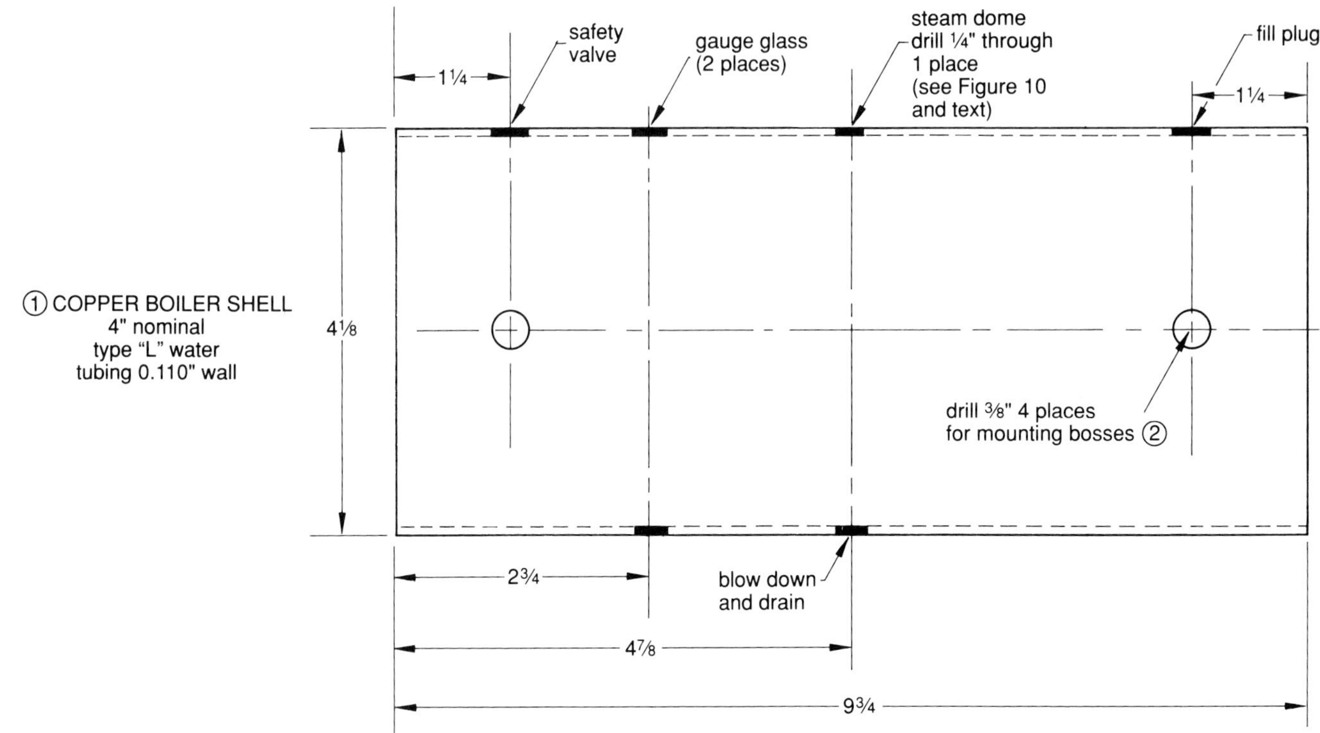

BOILER SHELL AND MOUNTING

FIGURE 3

4

5

And the indicated heater wattage is:

$$\frac{\frac{(2155.6 \text{ Btu/hr.})}{(1000 \text{ watts/kw})}}{(3413 \text{ Btu in 1 kw-hr.})} = \text{632 watts min. required for heater}$$

This means a 750-watt immersion heater would steam the Stuart 10V at full load with some capacity to spare. I chose to use a 1000-watt unit since it is dimensionally equivalent to the 750W unit and 1 kw is nearly the maximum load the thermoswitch (10 amp capacity) can control directly; ie., without an intermediate relay. The 1 kw heater provides the ability to steam, at light loads, engines substantially larger than the 10V.

Photo 2 shows the *Chromalox* heater and thermoswitch. These are high quality industrial process components, and should last a very long time in this application. The thermoswitch, having fast temperature response and extreme sensitivity, is the key to close control of the heater.

Anyone planning a larger boiler would probably choose a higher capacity 220V heater controlled by the thermoswitch via a relay. Solid-state power relays handling heavy AC loads are manufactured by National Controls Corporation.[(1)]

I chose the length of the boiler shell to accommodate the combined length of the heater and thermoswitch when each is installed at the lowest possible location in opposite heads.

Using the previously determined water

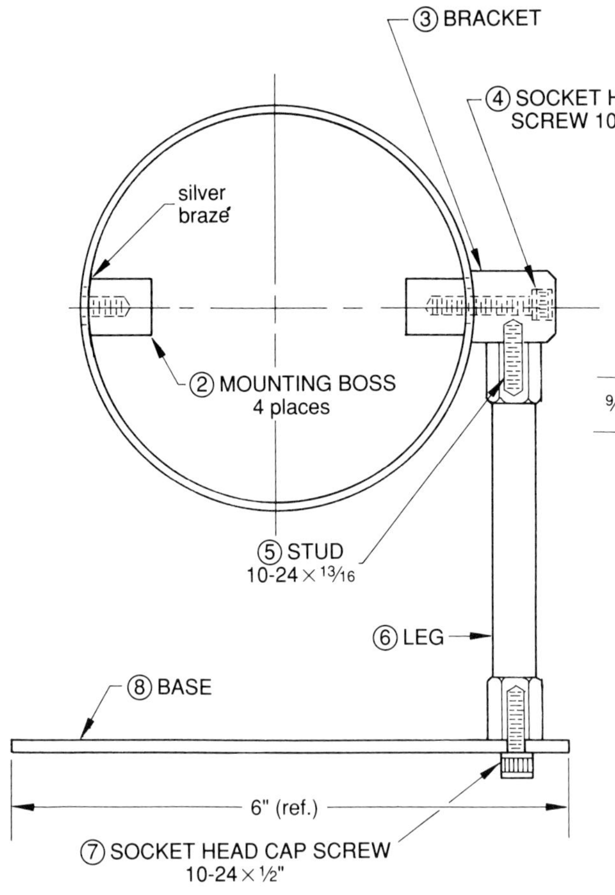

③ BRACKET

④ SOCKET HEAD CAP SCREW 10-24 × 1"

silver braze

② MOUNTING BOSS 4 places

⑤ STUD 10-24 × 13/16

⑥ LEG

⑧ BASE

6" (ref.)

⑦ SOCKET HEAD CAP SCREW 10-24 × ½"

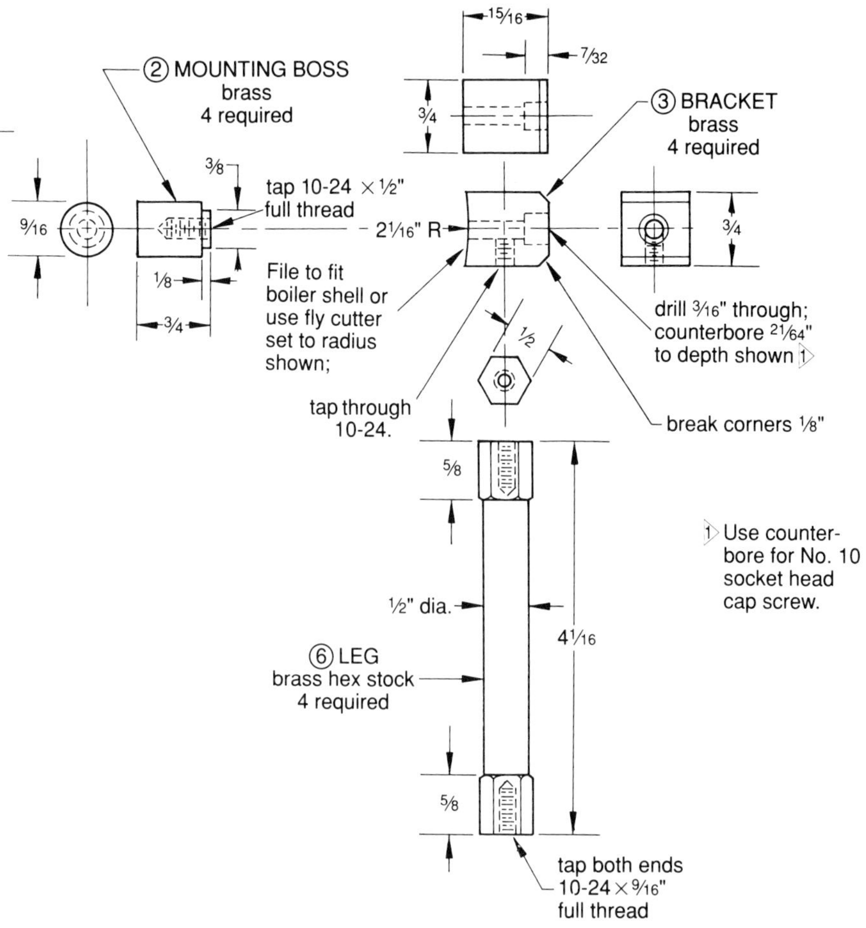

② MOUNTING BOSS brass 4 required

9/16

3/8

tap 10-24 × ½" full thread

1/8

3/4

15/16

7/32

3/4

③ BRACKET brass 4 required

2 1/16" R

3/4

File to fit boiler shell or use fly cutter set to radius shown;

tap through 10-24.

½

drill 3/16" through; counterbore 21/64" to depth shown ①

break corners 1/8"

5/8

① Use counterbore for No. 10 socket head cap screw.

½" dia.

4 1/16

⑥ LEG brass hex stock 4 required

5/8

tap both ends 10-24 × 9/16" full thread

MOUNTING DETAILS

FIGURE 6

rate of 1.84 lb./hr., the boiler shell diameter was calculated to provide water capacity for 45 minutes steaming (without a feed pump) and with the heater element well submerged at the end of the period. A nominal 4" diameter shell meets these requirements.

Figure 3 shows the hole locations in the shell and the method of assembly for the mounting legs.

Whenever a threaded connection or accessory penetrates the shell or heads, a pre-threaded ferrule must be silver-brazed in place, since the material is too thin to provide sufficient thread area by itself.

All of the shelf-stock Stuart model steam components shown were mail ordered from ***Live Steam*** advertisers. Builders will have individual preferences of manufacturers and suppliers; there are many similar components on the market. For this reason, purchased ferrules aren't listed in the Bill of Materials. These ferrules should be ordered with the steam fittings, and the required hole sizes determined by the builder.

The only ferrules shown in the drawings and Bill of Materials are those to be made by the builder. While making the two water gauge ferrules (35), make a third one for the blowdown and drain valve (46) (found in **Figure 9**).

Before drilling ferrule holes in the boiler shell and heads, I prefer to collect all of the fittings with their respective prethreaded ferrules, then measure each ferrule and drill accordingly. I drilled slightly

7

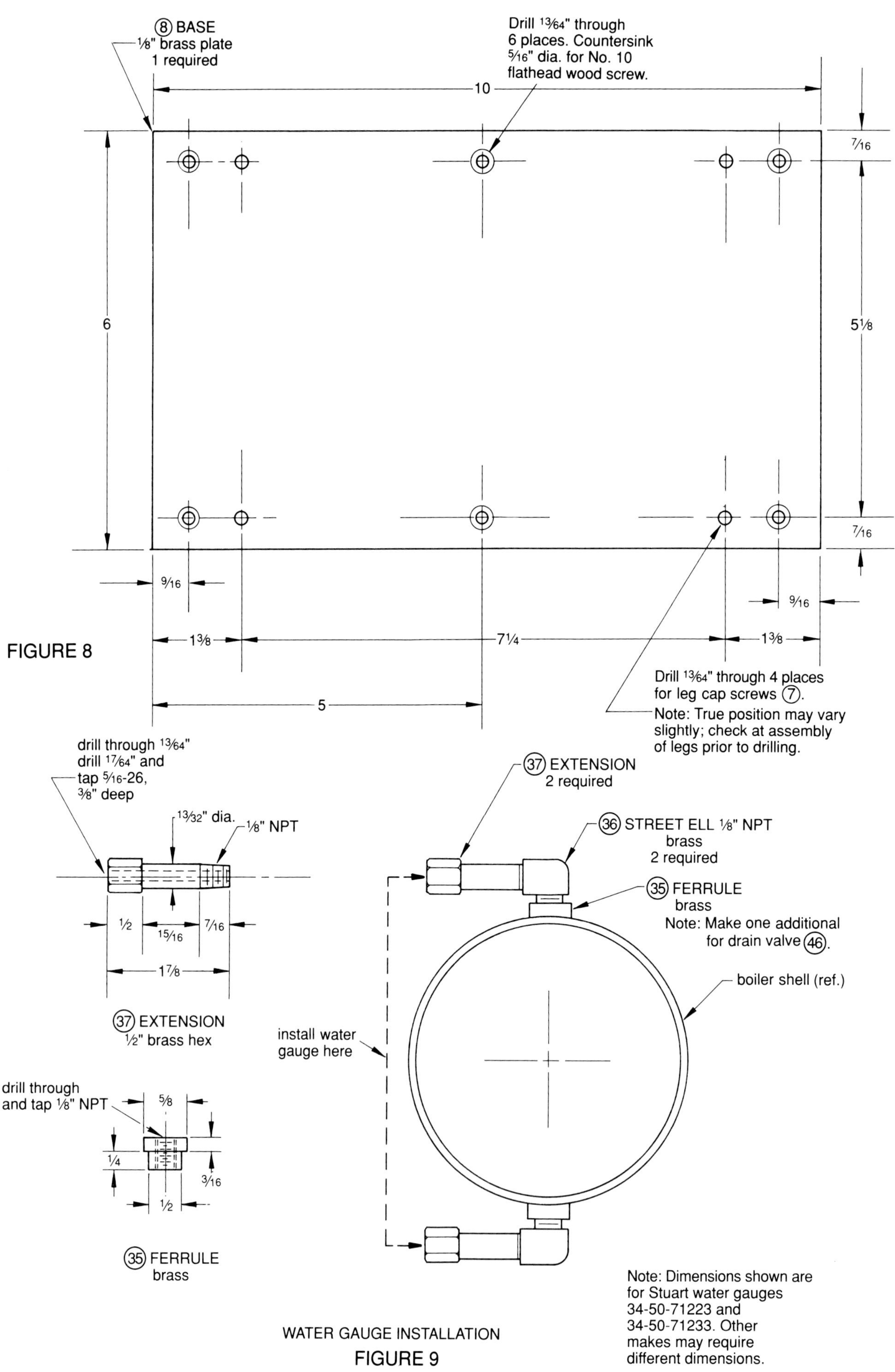

WATER GAUGE INSTALLATION

FIGURE 9

BILL OF MATERIALS					
PART	NAME	NO. REQ'D.	MATERIAL	SIZE	P/N – SOURCE – REMARKS
1	Boiler Shell	1	copper	4" dia. × 9¾"	4" nominal dia. type "L" water tubing (0.110" wall)
2	Mounting Boss	4	brass	9⁄16" dia. × ¾"	—
3	Bracket	4	brass	¾" sq. bar × 5"	—
4	Cap Screw	4	steel	10-24 × 1"	socket head
5	Stud	4	steel	10-24 × 13⁄16"	make from 1" screws
6	Leg	4	brass	½" hex bar × 17"	—
7	Cap Screw	4	steel	10-24 × ½"	socket head
8	Base	1	brass	⅛" plate 6 × 10"	—
9	Head – Thermostat End	1	copper	16 gage (.0647")	approx. 4½ × 4½" hot rolled sheet
10	Head – Heater End	1	copper	16 gage (.0647")	approx. 4½ × 4½" hot rolled sheet
11	Ferrule – Thermostat	1	bronze	½" NPT	make from plumbing fitting (see text)
12	Ferrule – Heater	1	bronze	1" NPT	make from plumbing fitting (see text)
13	Stay	4	copper	¼" dia. × 44"	hard temper rod
14	Stay Bushing	8	brass	9⁄16" rod × 2½"	—
15	Plug – Head Center	2	brass	⅜" dia. × 1"	—
16	Steam Dome	1	brass	1¼" dia. × 2"	—
17	Dome Stay	1	copper	¼ × 2"	hard temper rod
18	Hex Nut	1	brass	¼-20	—
19	Frame – J Box	1	aluminum	2½ × 2 × 4¾"	use hard alloy for easier machining
20	Cover – J Box	1	aluminum	⅛ × 2¼ × 4¾"	Note 20 and 21 are identical except for 1.60" hole in 20 and grommet hole in 21.
21	Cover – J Box	1	aluminum	⅛ × 2¼ × 4¾"	—
22	Screw – R-H	12	brass	4-36 × ⅜"	cover fasteners
23	Pilot Light	1	—	⅝" panel mount 120 volt	Radio Shack or similar supplier
24	Switch – Push Button	1	—	panel mount 120V 10A min.	Radio Shack or similar supplier (toggle switch is alternative)
25	Grommet	1	rubber	as required	protects cord 26 at J-box Radio Shack or similar supplier
26	Appliance Cord – 3 conductor	6-8 feet	—	No. 16 AWG minimum	hardware store
27	Plug – 3 Pin	1	—	120V wall outlet size	Use heavy duty plug. Hardware store.
28	Immersion Heater	1	—	120 volt, 1000 watt	Chromalox Co. P/N TM – 1101G [1]
29	Thermostat (Thermoswitch)	1	—	120 volt 10 amp capacity	Chromalox Co. P/N 17100 [1]
30	Cover – Feedwater Tank	1	brass	2¼" bar × 2	—
31	Shell – Feedwater tank	1	brass	2" OD tube × 3"	—
32	Lower Head – Feedwater Tank	1	brass	2" dia. x ¾"	—
33	Standpipe – Feedwater Tank	1	copper	⅝" OD HD tube	—
34	Base – Feedwater Tank	1	brass	2" OD × ⅞"	—
35	Ferrule – Water Gauge	3	brass	⅝" dia. × 1½"	2 required for water gauge, 1 required for drain valve 46
36	Street Ell	2	brass	⅛" NPT	hardware store
37	Extension – Water Gauge	2	brass	½" hex bar 4"	—
38	Pressure Gauge	1	—	1⅝" dial 100 psi	Stuart P/N 34-50-71141
39	Syphon – Pressure Gauge	1	copper brass	fits (38) threaded 7⁄16-26	Stuart P/N 34-50-71134
40	Water Gauge	1	brass	¼" glass	Stuart P/N 34-50-71223 (1 cock) or P/N 34-50-71233 (no cock)
41	Safety Valve	1	brass	60 psi	Stuart P/N 34-50-71323
42	Steam Stop Valve	1	brass	5⁄32" dia. tube	Stuart P/N 34-50-71542
43	Check Valve – Boiler Feed	1	brass	for ¼" dia. tube	Stuart P/N 34-50-71664 (optional - see text)
44	Filling Plug	1	brass	threaded ½"	Stuart P/N 34-50-72101 (see text)
45	Feedwater Pump	1	bronze	½" bore × 1" stroke	Stuart P/N 34-50-71453 (optional - see text)
46	Valve – Blowdown and Drain	1	brass	⅛" NPT ¼" tube right angle pattern	Lasco Mfg. Co. P/N 17-1109 or equivalent hardware store

[1] Find local Chromalox distributor in Yellow Pages under *Electric Heating Elements* or phone Pittsburgh, PA, sales headquarters, (412) 323-3900.

undersize and carefully opened the holes with a long-taper reamer.

The boiler shell is difficult to hold on the drill press table. Even if you have a large machine vise, resist any temptation to use it as it is very easy to squeeze the shell out of round.

Photos 4 and **5** show a plywood jig that can be made in a few minutes. This jig holds the shell very firmly for drilling and fitting operations. Tightening two nuts on the threaded rod shown bends the jig ends slightly inward, gripping the ends of the shell. The 1/4" threaded rod will be used in another tooling setup in Part 2.

Figure 6 shows the boiler mounting parts required. The concave ends of the mounting brackets (3) were machined by holding them in the lathe milling attachment, and running across with a fly cutter or boring head set at 2-1/16" radius. This could also be done by careful filing.

The mounting bosses (2) can now be silver-brazed inside the shell, as shown in **Photo 7**. A piece of scrap is tapped to accept a short length of threaded rod, forming a jacking screw to hold two bosses for brazing.

Small diameter wire silver-brazing alloy is easy to apply in small quantities exactly where needed, whereas larger diameter material tends to run all over, giving the joint a poor appearance.

But handling fine silver-brazing wire is difficult because it curls badly. This problem can be overcome by using an ordinary draftsman's lead holder as a handle. Feed the wire right through the handle as shown.

The brass base is shown in **Figure 8**. This part locates the lower ends of the legs and also serves as a heat shield to protect the wooden mounting board.

Figure 9 shows the parts needed for the water gauge installation. With the extensions in place, a water gauge will fit in the position shown by the dashed line.

The Bill of Materials is complete as shown except for the mounting board, a few brass wood screws, and the previously noted ferrules. Many fittings in the Stuart line require a soft aluminum washer for sealing. These come in packets of a given size and different thicknesses, as well as one packet of assorted sizes. Different thickness washers allow the fitting to be properly aligned (if required) when fully tightened. When obtaining fittings, be sure to get these little crush washers, if needed.

[1] National Controls Corporation, 1725 Western Drive, West Chicago, Illinois 60185 • 1-800-323-2593

Before getting started on the final assembly silver brazing, we need to form the heads and machine the steam dome, the stays, and the stay bushings.

Figure 10 shows the steam dome (16) machined from brass bar stock. The 2-1/16" radius to match the boiler shell curvature can easily be formed using the lathe milling attachment and a fly cutter, just like forming the brackets (3), Figure 6, Part 1. The silver brazed joint between the dome and the boiler shell turns out to be in tension rather than shear. In silver brazing, shear joints are always preferable from a loading and safety standpoint. Since the design doesn't easily accommodate a shear joint, the dome stay (17) is installed to eliminate any doubt about the tension joint.

Lay out and drill a circle of 11 holes and a circle of 12 holes, 1/16" diameter and roughly equally spaced at the radii shown. Be careful not to fill any of these holes when silver brazing the stay (17) and nut (18) inside the boiler shell.

The steam dome is drilled for two or more ferrules to accept outlet fittings of the builder's choice. I drilled one side to fit the ferrule for a small engine stop valve, and the other side for a ferrule threaded 1/8" npt. This ferrule is essentially the same as Part 35, Figure 9, and is plugged with a 1/8" npt pipe plug until needed.

The boiler heads (9 and 10) shown in **Figure 11** were formed by rolling in the lathe. This technique and the tooling required for these specific heads is described in a previous article: "Roll Forming Copper Boiler Heads and Similar Parts," ***Live Steam,*** March 1991. Roll forming is fun and particularly indicated when more than a couple of heads are to be made. For those who elect the more traditional hammer-forming method, **Figure 12** shows the tooling required and the dimensions of the blanks. The 1/4" diameter centering pin hole aids in centering the blank, and is also used to position the finished heads during silver brazing. Regardless of the forming method used, the heads will probably have to be annealed at least twice during the process. This consists of heating the part to a dull red, and allowing it to air cool. Water cooling is faster but may cause some distortion.

The large ferrules (11 and 12) are silver brazed in the heads prior to assembling the heads and shell for brazing. Anyone having large pipe taps can make these ferrules from scratch. It was much easier for me to find a bronze 1" npt tee and a 1/2" npt union at a salvage yard. Practically any brass or bronze fitting with the correct threads will do. Screw each fitting onto a short pipe nipple and saw off the part of the fitting not needed. Then chuck the pipe nipple in the lathe to finish the ferrule. I found the fitting to make Part 11 with a hex body, but Part 12 turned out to be round. Be sure to form two wrench flats on either 11 or 12, if they are round. This allows a wrench to be applied directly to the ferrule during installation of the heater and switch, eliminating any possible strain on the head itself.

If the feed pump is omitted, I'd suggest at least installing a suitable ferrule for an inlet check valve at the position shown on Part 10 (Figure 11). This ferrule can then be plugged. This minor effort will eliminate a messy problem later if a feed pump were to be retrofitted.

Make the stays, bushings, and the small plugs shown in Figure 11. The stays are dimensioned a bit long and filed or belt-ground flush with the bushings after silver brazing.

It's fairly difficult to cut clean threads on copper rod. I made a search through a collection of antique machinist's handbooks, looking for a lost secret recipe for copper threading lubricant. I mixed up some of the oddball and obscure materials recommended, and the resulting concoctions were universally worthless! These formulas appear to be a combination of folklore and superstition.

I tested some mixtures of my own, based on more modern technical information. The best copper threading lubricant developed is a mixture of SAE 80W-90 Hypoid Gear Oil EP (extreme pressure) and moly-filled auto chassis grease. These items are available at any auto

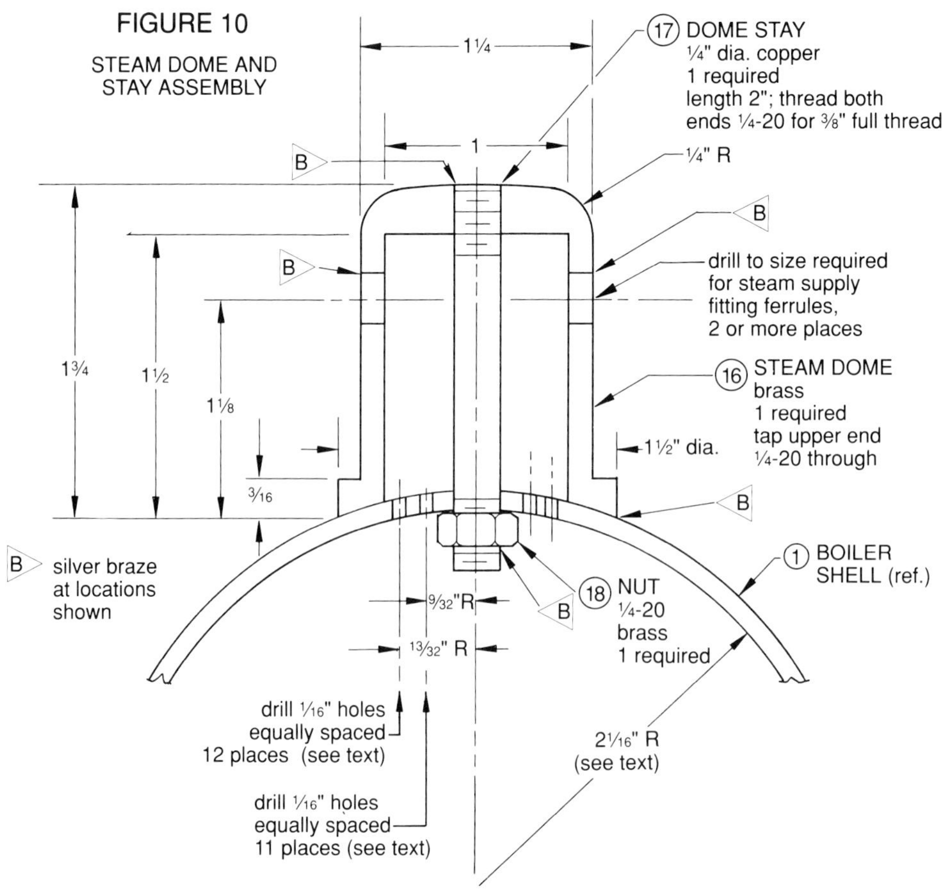

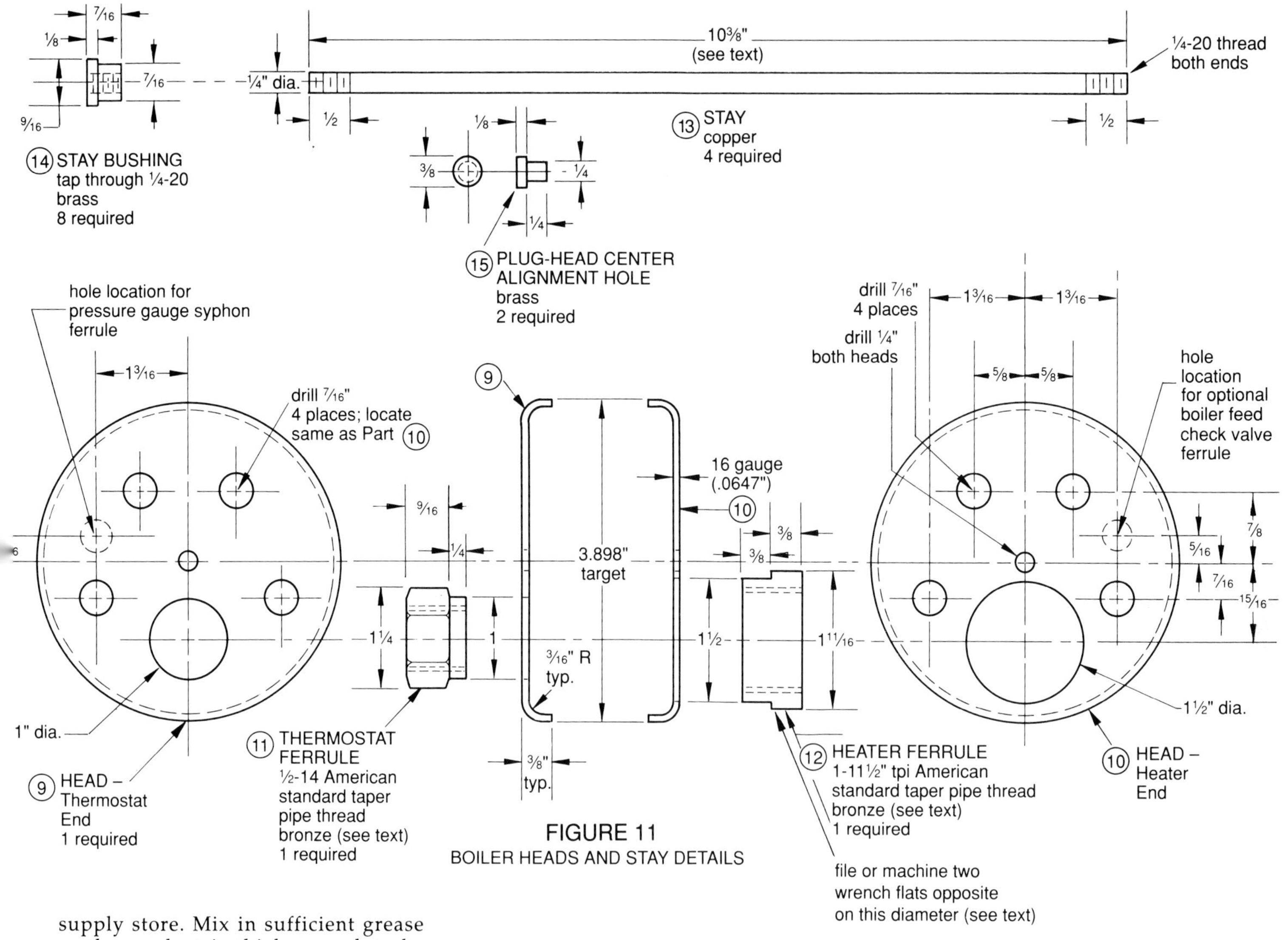

7/16
1/8
9/16
7/16
1/4" dia.
10 3/8"
(see text)
1/4-20 thread
both ends
1/2
1/2
13 STAY
copper
4 required
14 STAY BUSHING
tap through 1/4-20
brass
8 required
1/8
3/8
1/4
1/4
15 PLUG-HEAD CENTER
ALIGNMENT HOLE
brass
2 required
hole location for
pressure gauge syphon
ferrule
1 3/16
drill 7/16"
4 places; locate
same as Part 10
1" dia.
9 HEAD –
Thermostat
End
1 required
9/16
1/4
1 1/4
1
11 THERMOSTAT
FERRULE
1/2-14 American
standard taper
pipe thread
bronze (see text)
1 required
9
16 gauge
(.0647")
10
3.898"
target
3/16" R
typ.
3/8"
typ.
3/8
3/8
1 1/2
1 11/16
12 HEATER FERRULE
1-11 1/2" tpi American
standard taper pipe thread
bronze (see text)
1 required
file or machine two
wrench flats opposite
on this diameter (see text)
drill 7/16"
4 places
drill 1/4"
both heads
1 3/16
1 3/16
5/8
5/8
hole
location
for optional
boiler feed
check valve
ferrule
7/8
5/16
7/16
15/16
1 1/2" dia.
10 HEAD –
Heater
End

FIGURE 11
BOILER HEADS AND STAY DETAILS

supply store. Mix in sufficient grease so the product is thick enough to be "buttered" on the work and not drip away. (Hypoid oil by itself also works well as a bedway and slide lubricant).

For easier threading, reduce the diameter of the rod in the threaded area about .006"; i.e., a .250" rod is carefully reduced to .244"-.245" at the ends.

The throats of most small dies are bellmouthed on one end, making for easier starting on most materials. Many are marked "Start From This Side." For cleaner threads on copper rod, reverse the die in the holder, and start from the non-bell-mouthed side. If your die is split and adjustable, run the thread in two passes.

Never try to start the die free-handed. Use the lathe, pulled through by hand. If you don't have a die holder for the lathe, start the hand-held die stock and die by applying pressure to the die with the tailstock ram.

The boiler shell is ready for final assembly after the steam dome as well as all ferrules and mounting bosses are silver brazed in place (**Photo 13**). Silver braze the stays and stay bushings to the heater-end head (10), working on the inside of the head as shown in the photo. Braze the heater ferrule (12) at the same time.

1/2
3/16" R
3.761" dia.
FORM BLOCK
(tooling) hardwood
or metal
16 gauge
.0647" thick
drill 1/4"
through all
3 parts
4 3/16" dia.
COPPER BLANK FOR
BOILER HEADS
Part 9 and Part 10
1/2
3" dia.
CLAMP BLOCK
(tooling)
hardwood or metal
1
1/4" dia.
CENTERING
PIN (tooling)
steel

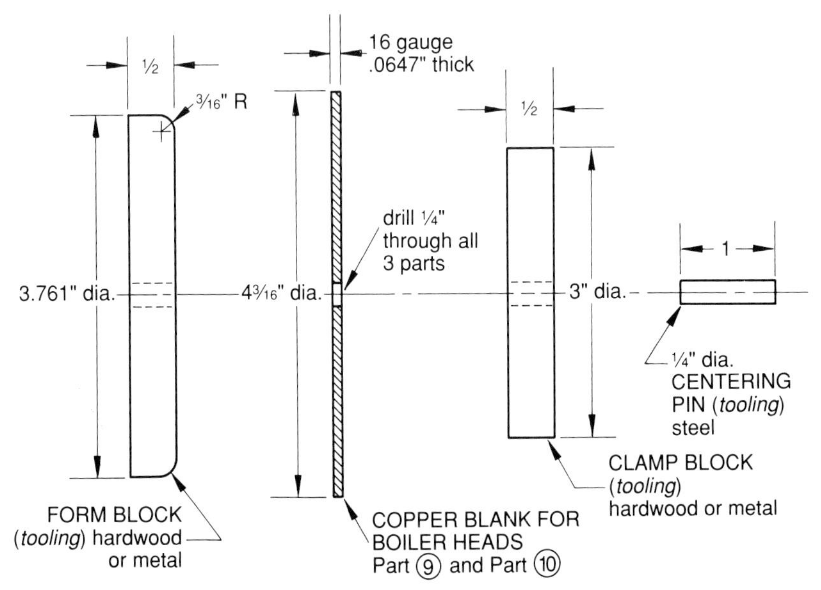

FIGURE 12
TOOLING FOR HAMMER – FORMING BOILER HEADS
(see text)

Now slip both heads into the shell, spacing them with the piece of threaded rod from the jig shown in Photo 4, Part 1. Use a nut on each side of each head. These nuts and the rod are fairly easy to remove after both heads are brazed.

It's no doubt possible to silver braze both heads at the same heating, saving time and torch fuel. To ease handling and fluxing, I brazed one head at a time, thus two "heats" were required. **Photo 14** shows the thermoswitch-end head (9) 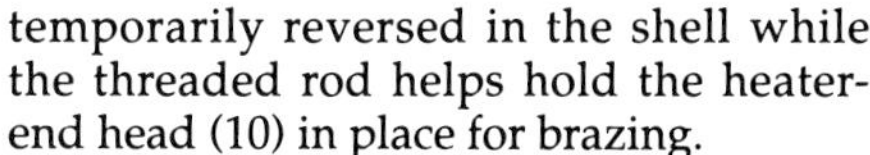
temporarily reversed in the shell while the threaded rod helps hold the heater-end head (10) in place for brazing.

Time and torch fuel can be saved by fluxing the joints heavily, and preheating the assembly in the kitchen oven to about 450°F. This dries and shrinks the flux, and is a good check to see if enough flux was applied. Add some more if the joint isn't heavily covered. The flux acts like a sponge, soaking up oxides during silver brazing, and it's practically impossible to use too much, particularly when using an acetylene torch, which seems to generate more oxides than other types of torches.

Copper conducts heat away from a joint to be silver brazed very efficiently, and the shell with the two heads amounts to a fairly large chunk of copper. The temperature required is moderate (1200-1300°F), but the quantity of heat required is substantial! One or two small hardware store type propane torches will not accomplish the silver brazing. It's necessary to gain access to a larger heating torch or take the parts to a small welding shop willing to do odd jobs.

I used my light duty Victor J-100 oxy-acetylene torch with a Victor No. 5-113 tip throttled back to a fairly soft neutral flame. *Handy Flux* made by Handy & Harman was used for all joints.

All small fittings were silver brazed using *Easy-Flo 45*. The heads and the two large ferrules were brazed with *Sil-fos*, a less expensive material that fills relatively large joint clearances very nicely. For tighter joints, *Sil-fos 5* is recommended. *Sil-fos* fillers are advertised as self-fluxing on copper and copper alloys. Maybe so, but I found a heavy application of flux made the brazing easier and improved the joint appearance. I suspect this apparent flux requirement is related to the use of an oxy-acetylene torch.

These *Sil-fos* alloys should not be used where there is a possible exposure to sulphur, as in firing a boiler with fossil fuels. Since we are "firing" with electrici-

13

14

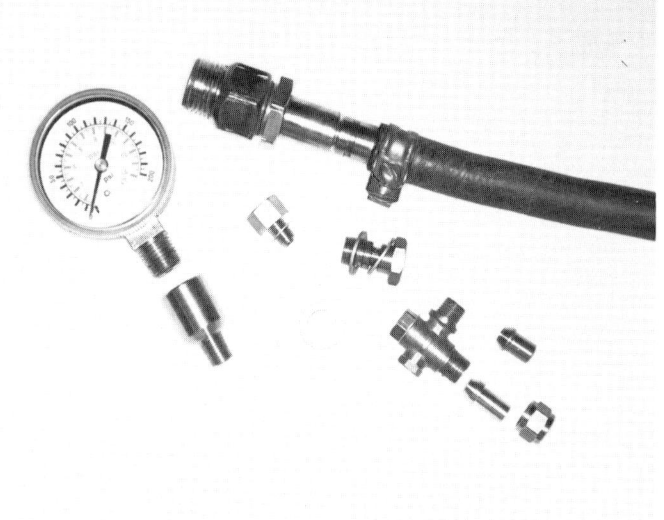

15

16

17

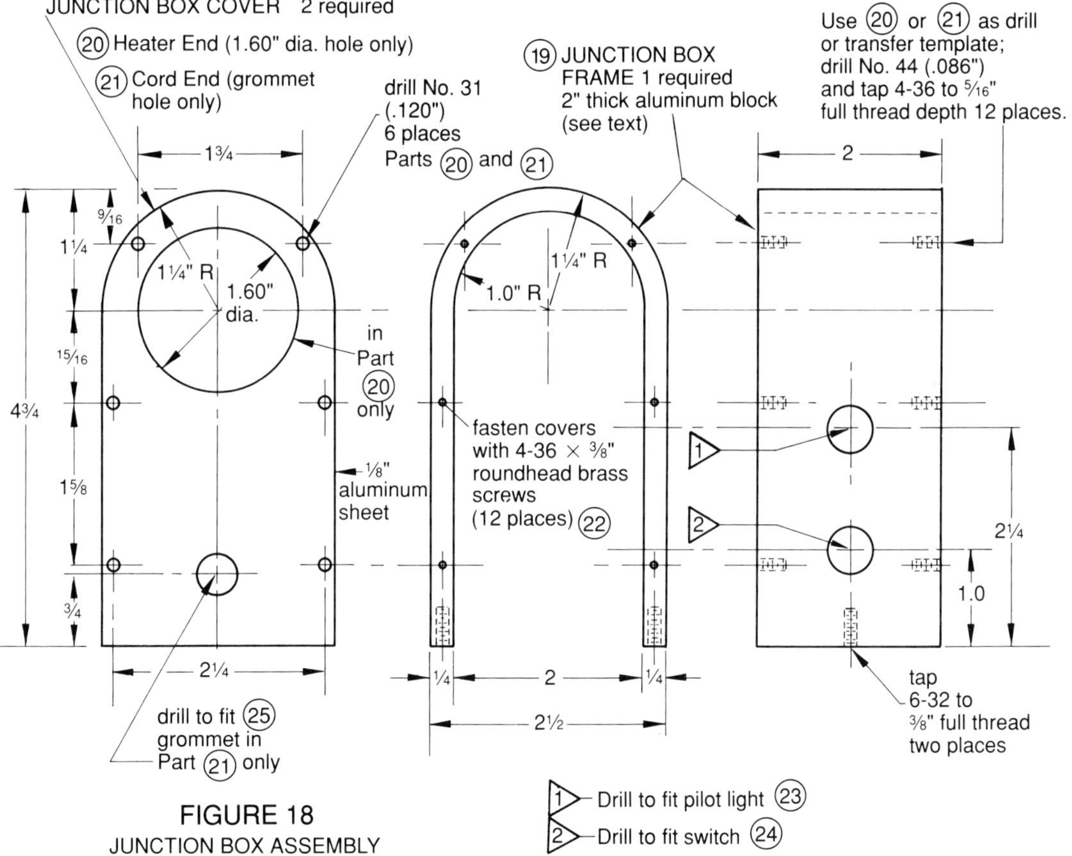

FIGURE 18
JUNCTION BOX ASSEMBLY

ty, there should be no problem. All of the above silver brazing alloys are Handy & Harman products.

Remove the threaded rod from the head alignment holes, and install the two small plugs (15). These are soft-soldered in place using a small propane torch. This avoids reheating the heads to brazing temperature.

After brazing, the boiler will be an awful mess – covered with hardened flux and multi-colored oxides. It's time for a pickle bath. Many people use a dilute solution of sulfuric acid and water. I obtained a 2-1/2 lb. can of *Sparex* No. 2, as offered by several ***Live Steam*** advertisers. This makes one gallon of pickle solution. Using a plastic dishpan, immerse the finished boiler for 15 minutes or so, and with just minor scrubbing, the boiler comes out amazingly clean and bright! The solution can be stored in a plastic jug.

Now we're ready for the hydro-test. A preliminary test can be made by connecting the boiler to the domestic water supply using a garden hose of the fabric-reinforced type that can be fully shut off without bursting. Note that this does not constitute a complete hydro-test unless the boiler is to be operated at a very low pressure, and is fitted with a safety valve that relieves at less than half the domestic water pressure!

A few simple pieces of test hardware are needed as shown in **Photo 15**. At the top of the photo, a collection of fittings from the scrap box and a short piece of hose connect the garden hose to the thermo-switch ferrule. The right-hand end of the short hose ends in a hose coupling. The hose coupling could just as well be sweat-soldered to the adapter fitting.

Below the test gauge is an adapter made from scrap brass that connects the gauge to the upper water gauge ferrule. The lower one is plugged with a 1/8" pipe plug, not shown. The little hex plug to the right of the gauge is installed in place of the safety valve. Next is the hollow threaded fitting that retains the operator's pressure gauge syphon banjo. (This comes with the syphon.) Just below this fitting, and what looks like a washer in the photo, is a brass sleeve made to the same dimensions as the syphon banjo. This sleeve and the hollow fitting blank off the operator's pressure gauge ferrule. The inlet check valve is shown with its standard tubing cone and a machined solid cone used with the cone nut to blank off the valve.

Photo 16 shows the boiler connected to the garden hose and under pressure. I used *Loctite Teflon* pipe thread sealant on all tapered pipe threads including the heater seen installed at the extreme right of the photo. This material serves as a lubricant as well as a sealant, reducing the torque required to seal pipe threads. Be sure to use a wrench on the heater ferrule when installing the heater; don't attempt to hold the ferrule by gripping the boiler.

The operator's pressure gauge was left connected for this test to check its accuracy against the test gauge since the domestic water pressure wasn't expected to exceed this gauge's limit of 100 psi. It turned out to be 80 psi as seen on the test gauge.

Remove the fill plug and open the stop valve; then turn on the water until it floods out both places. The boiler is now full and ready to be pressurized. A couple of leaks showed up right away. The Stuart union cock installed as a blowdown and drain valve leaked badly in spite of multiple efforts to lap it in. It finally had to be replaced by the Lasco valve (46) seen in **Photo 17.**

The fill plug came with an aluminum crush washer, and required excessive wrench force to hold pressure. This wasn't acceptable to me. Chuck the hex plug in the three-jaw, and machine a shallow elliptical groove under the head just behind the threads. Then roll an appropriately sized O-ring over the threads, bearing against this groove. Now the plug will hold 150 psi when tightened with two fingers.

A drip from a pinhole leak at the steam dome base is seen in Photo 16. I'm told these can be caulked using a dull center punch. Another repair method I used was to drill the pinhole with a 1/16" drill about 1/32" deep, and fill with soft solder, heating with the small propane torch. This works well.

In Photo 17, we're going for the real hydro-test. I decided to try for 150 psi and a 30-minute hold without pressure decay. The operator's pressure gauge was removed, and the previously described blank banjo sleeve installed in place of the syphon. I installed the thermoswitch, and connected the pump to the inlet check valve. Then I filled the boiler. At around 120 psi another pin-hole leak appeared at one mounting boss as seen in the photo. This was repaired with soft solder as previously described. Then 150 psi was easily sustained. This test pressure is, in my view, adequate for use of a 60 psi safety valve, and actual operation in the 40-50 psi range.

Details of the electrical junction box are shown in **Figure 18** and **Photo 19**. The J-box frame was band-sawn from a 2" thick block of aluminum scrap, and finished on the narrow belt grinder. Holes for the pilot light (23) and the on-off switch (24) are drilled in the frame. I used a red pilot light which is on whenever the thermoswitch feeds power to the heater.

1

20

The push-button on-off switch has a light in the button which is on whenever the switch is in the on position – i.e., power is available to the thermoswitch.

The frame is fastened to the mounting board with two countersunk screws passing through the board. One J-box cover has a large hole that slides over the heater shank; the other has a small hole to fit the cord grommet. Remove the plug furnished with the heater, and solder all wiring directly to the heater terminals.

My 13-1/8 × 17-1/2" oak mounting board shown is made up of ten pieces 1-5/16" square, edge glued and dowelled. Four small rubber feet raise the base slightly to provide an easy finger hold when moving the assembly. Be sure to make the board large enough to mount your engine(s) and driven equipment.

Wires running from the thermoswitch to the J-box are concealed in the following manner. While laying out pieces for edge-gluing, arrange it so one glue line joint will intersect both the thermoswitch wire outlet and the J-box. Before gluing, plow a centralized blind slot about 5/8" square in one of the pieces on the edge to be glued. (Don't run the dado saw or router bit through the ends of the piece.) Mark the slot location carefully and proceed with the gluing. When the clamps come off, drill about 5/8" diameter into the slot, from the top of the board, in the area covered by the J-box, and also below the thermoswitch wire outlet. Make a short wire race by soft-soldering a piece of 1/2" rigid copper tubing to a 1-1/2" diameter brass mounting flange, as shown in **Photo 20**, below the thermoswitch dial. Push the thermoswitch wires through the tube and through the concealed slot in the mounting board, fishing them out through the hole at the base of the J-box. It takes most visitors quite a while to figure out if anything is really hooked up, and where the wiring is!

The wiring diagram (**Figure 21**) is self-explanatory. Be sure to use an on-off

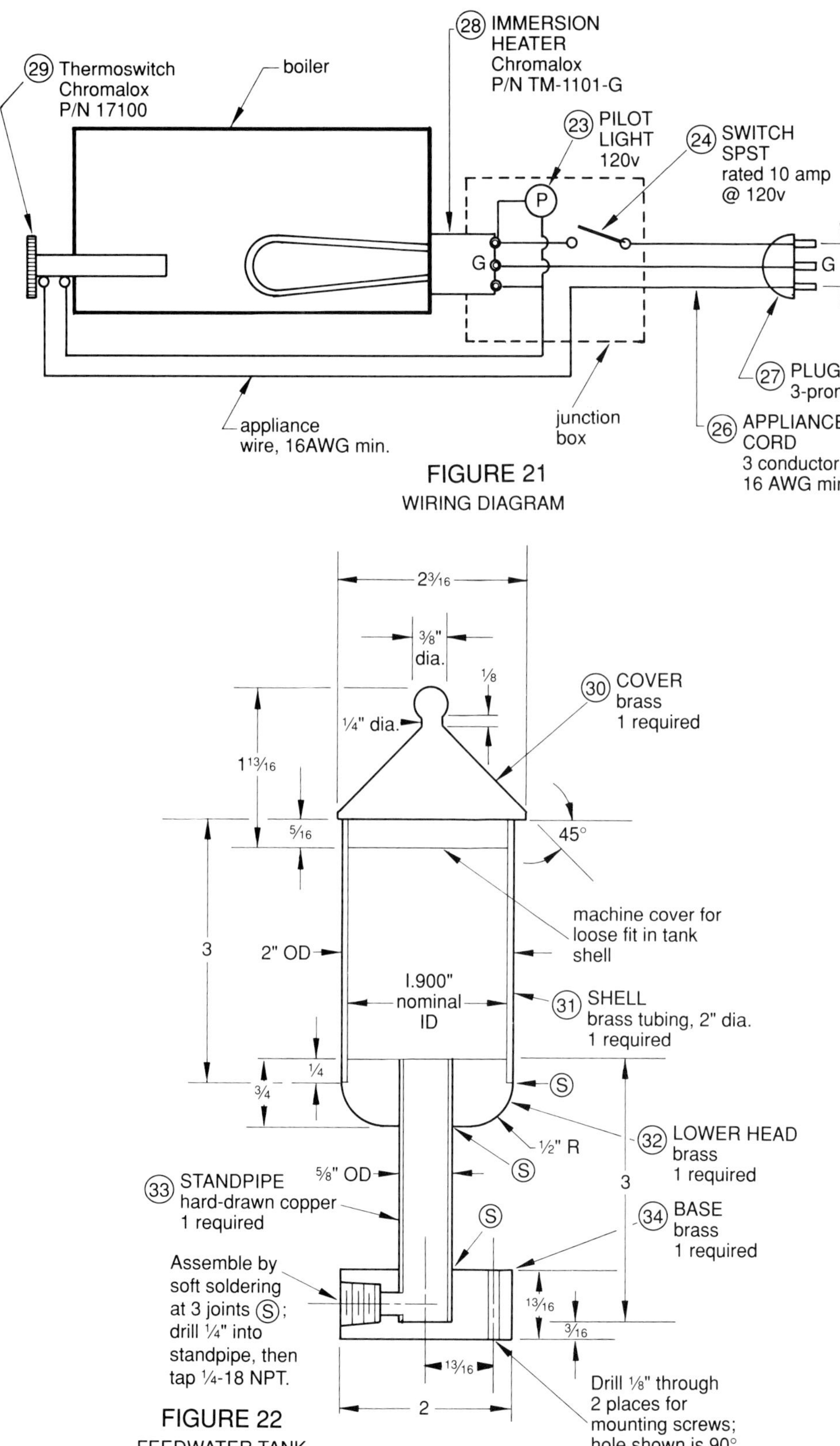

FIGURE 21
WIRING DIAGRAM

FIGURE 22
FEEDWATER TANK

switch having a minimum rating of 10 amps at 120V.

If a feedwater pump is used, a water tank will be required to supply the pump. Any configuration that suits the builder will work. **Figure 22** and Photo 19 show the tank I built, using material from the scrap box. The Stuart No. 145-3 pump shown was machined per print except the bore was machined 9/16" instead of 1/2", and a "quad-seal" was used on the plunger in place of the O-ring specified. Quad-seals are similar to O-rings, but are shaped with four lobes. In cross section, they look like a four-leaf clover. They are much more resistant to spiral failure in high pressure reciprocating service.

During the first heating trial, test the safety valve for its set pressure and flow capacity. Fill the boiler about 2/3 full of water. Temporarily jumper-wire across the thermoswitch wires in the J-box so the thermoswitch is out of the circuit – i.e., the heater is on whenever the on-off switch is on. Carefully approach the anticipated relief pressure of the safety valve until it pops. My valve actuated at exactly the advertised pressure of 60 psi. Continue with the heater full on and the safety relieving until it is certain the valve has sufficient flow capacity to vent all the steam the heater can produce. The pressure should not creep up.

Next, return the thermoswitch to the circuit and remove the fine adjustment dial. (This dial is restricted to one turn for fine adjustment.) Turn the adjuster screw in or out the required number of turns to approach the desired working pressure; then install the fine adjustment dial.

The pilot light will go on and off as the thermoswitch cycles the heater to hold pressure at a given steam demand. If the pilot light stays on continuously, the steam demand is equal to or exceeds the heater capacity.

The boiler is now ready for service. The lagging on the steam supply line in Photos 19 and 20 is coarse cotton tying cord wrapped tightly and saturated with several coats of clear model airplane dope. Trials show this lagging to be effective in reducing condensation in the supply line, particularly when running at low steam flow.

Always maintain the boiler water level comfortably above the heater element. The heater has a high watt-density, and its life will be reduced if not completely submerged.

A builder's plate showing the builder's name, date, and the basics of the hydro-test is a nice addition to the mounting board. There are a number of ways to produce an inexpensive plate. (See the Yellow Pages under Engravers-Metal, or build your own engraving pantograph from Rudy Kouhoupt's plans in the November/December 1990 *The Home Shop Machinist*, $5.00 postpaid.)

For long term storage, the boiler can be vented and dried out with a heat lamp, or filled completely full of distilled water. Distilled water is inexpensive enough to use for steaming in any area where tap water may produce boiler scale.

Building and operating this boiler has given me a great deal of pleasure. I hope this article will encourage and assist others having a need for a similar boiler.

Roll Forming Copper Boiler Heads

By D. E. Johnson

Photos by Author

Running small model engines on compressed air lacks a certain realism, and for some time I had a small stationary steam boiler on my list of projects.

Having zero experience in boiler construction, I read all the literature I had, up to the part about hammering the heads over a hardwood form. At that point, I always postponed the project since my past performance in hand-forming sheet metal has been disappointing, to say the least!

One day I was in a factory machine shop dedicated to mock-up and prototype work and noticed a machinist at a large lathe roll-forming an aluminum tank head. Upon inquiry, I was advised they roll-form parts like this fairly often if only a couple of pieces are required. If production quantities were later needed, a set of press dies would be built to reduce costs.

After seeing this, I decided I could probably do at home, on a very reduced scale, what the big boys over at the factory were doing with fairly heavy plate.

I should state here that building the tooling and accomplishing the roll-forming operations on small boiler heads is well within the range of the beginning machinist/boilermaker.

2

1

Small boiler heads and similar parts produced in this manner are amazingly accurate and attractive. This project turned out to be pure fun from start to finish!

I certainly can't claim this roll-forming technique to be an original idea. A considerable amount of handbook-type literature exists on the old art of metal spinning and its close relative, roll-forming.

Roll-forming in the lathe amounts to clamping a round blank of the material to be formed between two plates which are then rotated slowly in the lathe. Pressure is applied to the blank with a roller, gradually coaxing the blank to conform to the shape of the form plate. The roller tool is mounted on the compound, whose effective angle is increased in increments to gently wrap the blank around the form plate.

Photo 1 shows the tooling and two finished boiler heads. At the top is the form plate, pressed and brazed onto a shank for chuck mounting. To the right are four cap screws and the clamp plate. Further right is the roller tool holder and the alignment pin. Two finished boiler heads are in the foreground. Note that the one on the left has some threaded stay bushings dropped into place for checking.

At first glance, this sure seems like a lot of tooling to roll a few boiler heads! Actually, the tooling is easy to make from generally available scrap box supplies and turns out to have several secondary applications which greatly speed the whole boiler project.

Most stationary vertical or horizontal model steam boilers are going to have lots of holes in the heads – for stay bushings, fire tubes, gauge glass and inlet check bosses, etc. Clean round holes are very difficult to drill in copper sheet stock with standard point drills unless the sheet is firmly clamped between a drill guide plate and a backing plate. Therefore, what better way than to make the entire layout of head holes directly on the rolling form clamp plate and use the clamp plate as a drilling guide? This will provide assurance that stay rods or fire tubes will be lined up. Some of the holes thus generated will be used to bolt the clamp plate and head blank to the form plate.

This application is shown in **Photo 2**. A copper blank located with a centering pin is being drilled with drill stabilization furnished by the clamp plate. The holes shown are for the stay bushings, and are repeated in tapped holes in the form plate to accept the clamping cap screws. The drill shown is size 7/16", turning at low speed. Automotive hypoid rear axle oil (the heavy stuff with the EP additive) works as well as anything for a drilling lubricant and is inexpensive. The relatively large holes in the copper sheet are very clean and acceptable as drilled.

Another advantage of the roll-forming tool is that the copper blanks can be machined to the correct diameter in the lathe in just a couple of minutes, versus the tedious process of band sawing and filing or belt grinding to a scribed line. This alone was to me worth building the tooling. Note in Photo 2 the rough blank is a lumpy shape quickly roughed out on the band saw and drilled/reamed for the locating pin.

Then in **Photo 3** and **Photo 4** the blank is quickly rounded up to the desired diameter. Before grinding a tool bit specifically to handbook angles for copper, try a dead-sharp bit known to cut aluminum well. I did, and it cut fine.

One more advantage with this tooling: after the rolling operation is complete, should tolerance accumulations cause the finished head to be perhaps a few thousandths too large in diameter (mine came out perfectly), it is very easy to take an adjusting skim-cut on the head flange just rolled, or do a bit of filing with the lathe running. Caution: don't overdo this built-in convenience! Excessive material removal will reduce the flange strength. If anything more than a light skim cut is required to fit the boiler shell, the diameter of the form plate itself should be reduced, then re-roll the oversized head.

After you have made all the boiler heads you need, the form plate and shank assembly constitute a nice little auxiliary faceplate to which hard-to-hold work shapes can be bolted, clamped, or even tack-welded.

3

Photo 5 shows the start of a rolling operation. If possible, obtain hot rolled copper sheet for the head blanks; this will eliminate the need for annealing before the first rolling pass, since the hot rolled sheet will be soft. During the rolling, each head will have to be removed from the tool twice for annealing, thus the convenience of tapping threads in the form plate versus using nuts on the cap screws. Take your choice here.

For rolling, the lathe is run at lowest back gear speed and the compound is set about 10° off parallel with the lathe axis for the first pass. Feed the roller in with the compound against the copper sheet, and the sheet will magically "flop over" to run parallel with the roller face. You'll be amazed at how little pressure is required. Back off the roller pressure immediately; when the copper blank is

4

5

running parallel to the roller face, any further pressure only serves to work harden the copper. The working surfaces of the roller and form plate must be as smooth and free from imperfections as you wish the copper work to be. Any scratch or nick in the surfaces forming the copper will immediately show up in reverse image on the work, much as striking a penny with dies at the mint.

The angle of the compound is increased in 10° to 15° increments, gradually rolling the copper blank around the form. Always work with the flat of the roller contacting the blank. Never let the outside diameter corner of the roller contact the blank. Doing so will result in a beautiful unwanted groove in the nicely radiused flange. A shallow groove formed in this manner can be blended out with a file while the lathe is running; a deep groove means starting over with a new blank.

As the rolling proceeds, you will feel the required pressure increase due to work hardening of the copper. About one-third and two-thirds through the flanging process, it will be necessary to remove the blank from the tool for annealing.

6

The heads for a nominal 4" boiler shell represent a fair volume of copper. It is unlikely that one or even two hardware store type propane torches will be adequate to anneal these heads.

The quantity of heat required is substantial. Also, it will take more heat than two of these little torches can provide to successfully silver braze these heads into a boiler shell, even if the proverbial three-handed machinist is available. It will be necessary to use some higher capacity heating system.

Notwithstanding a lot of popular press to the contrary, I found my oxy-acetylene welding torch ideal for annealing these heads and, later, silver brazing them into the boiler shell. It's true that the oxy-acetylene flame is a bit hot for copper and for silver brazing filler material. A fairly large tip should be used, with a "soft" flame running at less than maximum output.

I used a Victor 8-T29 multi-flame heating tip in my Victor J-100 light duty welding torch for annealing the heads. Place the pieces to be annealed on a *new, clean* firebrick or piece of *clean* steel plate. Caution: don't throw the piece to be annealed on the dirty firebrick brazing bench as I did the first time. The hot copper will pick up spent flux and brazing spelter from the old bricks like a sponge, creating a severe cleanup problem.

Play the torch in a circular motion around the partially formed flange part of the head until the area becomes dull red under average shop lighting – not in direct sunlight. The blank is now annealed and ready for the next rolling operation. Whether you cool the parts in a bucket of water or just let them air-cool while you sweep the floor for ten minutes has no bearing on their resultant softness. Because rapid chilling of hot parts can sometimes lead to warpage, I prefer to let the parts air-cool.

There is no need to pickle the heads until rolling is complete. A little warm water and fine steel wool will remove the minor scale which forms during annealing.

Photo 6 shows a finished head ready for a boiler shell fit test. In this view, the clamp plate has been removed, and three cap screws hold the head in place. Note that the roller is in the 90° position, having just completed the final rolling cycle.

Figure 7 shows how the copper blank is sandwiched between the form and clamp plates. Head holes for various boiler designs will differ in size and location, therefore the clamping cap screw layout is not detailed.

The form plate was reamed for a press and also brazed to the shank. If a heavy press fit is obtained, brazing or welding is probably not necessary. This would allow the use of an aluminum form plate instead of steel material. A lot

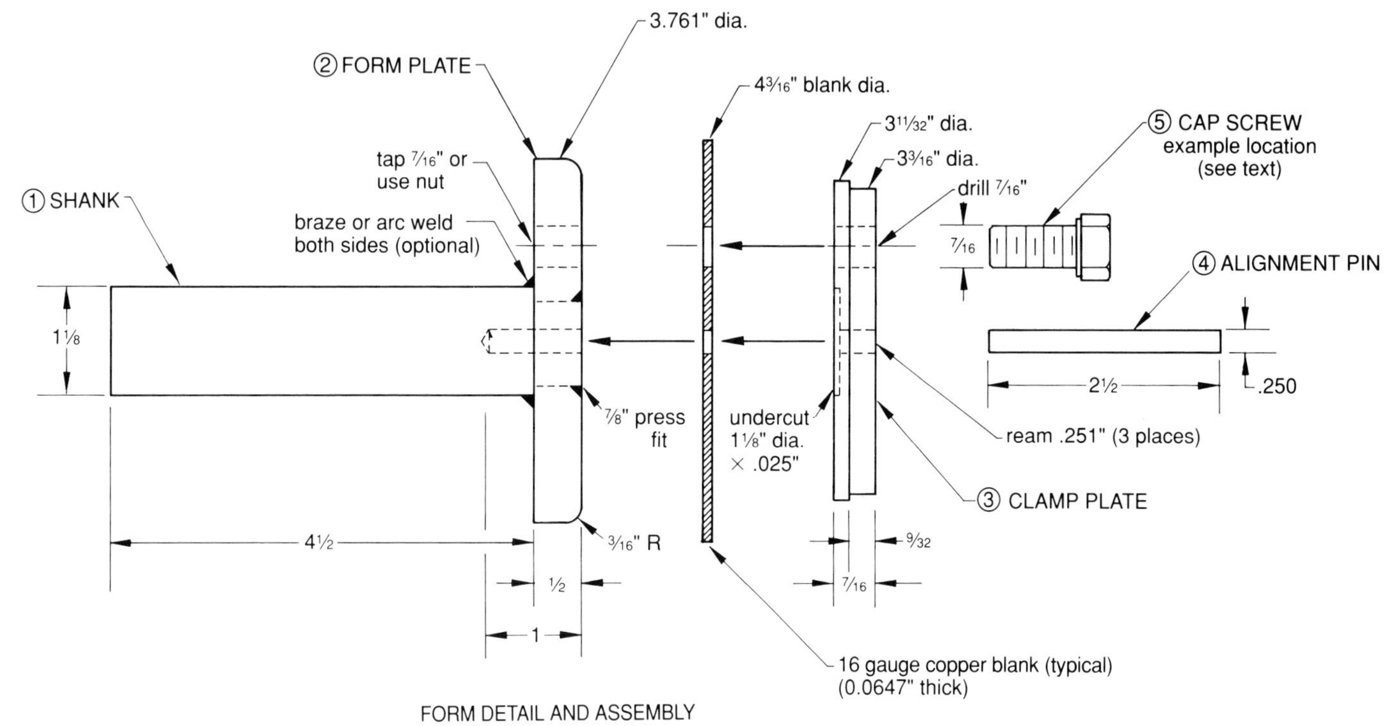

FORM DETAIL AND ASSEMBLY

FIGURE 7

DIMENSIONS OF COPPER WATER TUBING (INCHES)

NOM. SIZE	OUTSIDE DIA.	INSIDE DIAMETER			WALL THICKNESS		
	TYPE K-L-M	TYPE K	TYPE L	TYPE M	TYPE K	TYPE L	TYPE M
1	1.125	0.995	1.025	1.055	0.065	0.050	0.035
1¼	1.375	1.245	1.265	1.291	0.065	0.055	0.042
1½	1.625	1.481	1.505	1.527	0.072	0.060	0.049
2	2.125	1.959	1.985	2.009	0.083	0.070	0.058
2½	2.625	2.435	2.465	2.495	0.095	0.080	0.065
3	3.125	2.907	2.945	2.981	0.109	0.090	0.072
3½	3.625	3.385	3.425	3.459	0.120	0.100	0.083
4	4.125	3.857	3.905	3.935	0.134	0.110	0.095
5	5.125	4.805	4.875	4.907	0.160	0.125	0.109
6	6.125	5.741	5.845	5.881	0.192	0.140	0.122

Table 8

HOT ROLLED COPPER SHEET & PLATE

GAUGE	THICKNESS (INCHES)	WEIGHT PER SQ. FT.	
		OZ.	LB.
21	0.0323	24	1.50
19	0.0430	32	2.00
18	0.0485	36	2.25
16	0.0647	48	3.00
15	0.0750	56	3.50
13	0.0950	72	4.50
10	0.1290	96	6.00
9	0.1560	115	7.19
7	³⁄₁₆	139	8.69
3	¼	185	11.60

Table 9

of variations are possible here depending upon the contents of your scrap box. The simplest possible method might be to true up a piece of water pipe and braze or arc-weld it to the form plate. The form plate is, of course, trued up and turned to size after assembly to the shank.

The next thing to determine is the outside diameter of the form plate. For small boilers like this, most people will probably use copper water tubing for the shell. **Table 8** lists the important dimensions of water tubing in the sizes of most interest to boiler builders. This information was hard to find, and is reproduced here for form plate sizing calculations and particularly to assist scratch builders in making strength calculations.

Note in Table 8 that no dimension of any schedule pipe is equal to the nominal size. If our head is to go inside the shell, we need the shell inside diameter as shown in the table. If you measure your shell material, record several diameters, and calculate an average figure. This product is manufactured as water pipe, not mechanical tubing; a few thousandths out-of-round is to be expected. It is perhaps best to read the inside diameter from the table directly.

Table 9 shows the thickness of various gauges of hot rolled copper sheet and

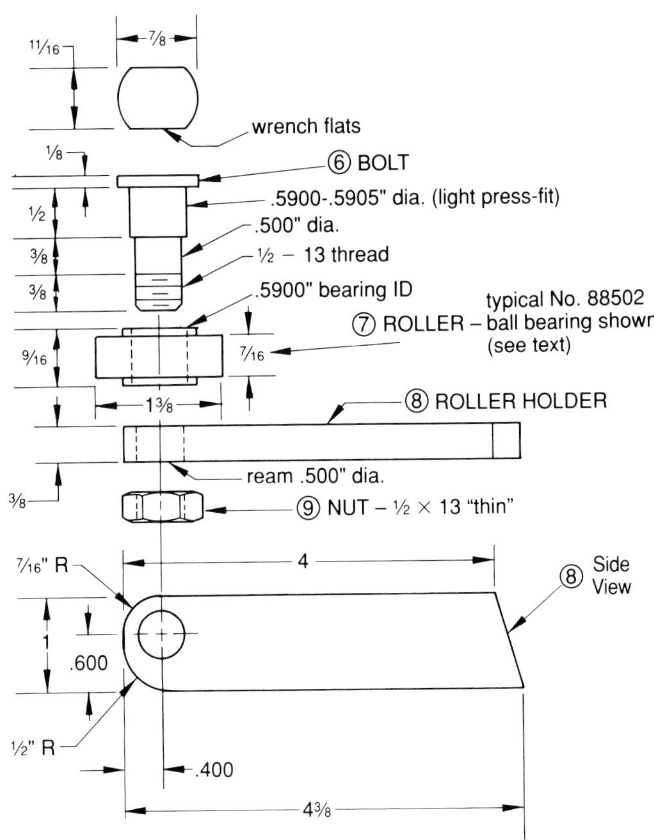

ROLLER TOOL DETAIL AND ASSEMBLY

FIGURE 10

plate. My boiler was constructed from a nominal 4" type L shell and 16-gauge (0.0647") hot rolled copper sheet for the heads.

With the above data, the form plate diameter is calculated as shown in the following example:

3.905	ID of 4" Type L shell (Table 8)
−.065	head flange thickness (Table 9)
−.065	same
−.007	silver brazing capillary clearance[1]
−.007	same
3.761	form plate diameter

[1]A rather large clearance was selected because *Sil-Fos* was to be used as the brazing filler. *Sil-Fos* likes large capillary clearance. Less clearance should be used for *Easy-Flo 45*.

Referring again to Figure 7, the clamp plate can be made of aluminum or steel. A portion of the outside diameter is relieved to roughly 3-3/16" diameter to provide extra clearance for the thin bolt head of the roller tool. A slight undercut was made at the center to concentrate clamping pressure nearer the outer diameter.

A convenient way to machine this piece is to bolt it directly to the form plate using the alignment pin and clamping cap screws, with some flat washers used as spacers.

The final dimension to be determined is the OD of the copper blank itself. Unless one is skilled in sheet metal bend allowance calculations, this is somewhat a cut and try situation. I found that, as a rule of thumb, adding 7/16" to 1/2" to the form plate diameter results in a blank diameter which will roll easily and produce an adequate flange. Much deeper flanges are easily rolled if desired.

Figure 10 shows the roller tool holder with appropriate dimensions to fit the lantern-style tool post of the South Bend 10K lathe. According to my South Bend handbook, these dimensions will be identical for 9" series lathes.

Whatever lathe and tool holder system is used, the objective is to mount a small steel roller on the compound in the simplest manner. The center line of the roller should, of course, be approximately the same height as the lathe axis.

As a convenience, I used a scrap box ball bearing having the inner race thicker than the outer race. This simplifies matters, since the bearing can be bolted directly against the tool holder and still be free to rotate. If a bearing with equally thick inner and outer races is used, a spacer washer will be needed to shim the inner race.

If you don't have a scrap box ball bearing candidate, there is no need to buy one. A plain machined steel roller and a few drops of oil will work just as well. The actual rolling operation is so short, no wear can take place.

I hope this rather lengthy dissertation will serve as encouragement to those contemplating construction of a boiler.

In a subsequent article, I will continue a description of techniques "discovered" and problems overcome in building my small stationary boiler.

BILL OF MATERIALS

PART NO.	NO. REQ'D	NAME	MATERIAL	SIZE
	1	Shank	steel	1 1/8" dia. × 4 1/2"
	1	Form Plate	steel	4 x 4 × 1/2"
	1	Clamp Plate	aluminum or steel	4 x 4 × 7/16"
	1	Alignment Pin	drill rod	.250 × 2 1/2"
	as req'd	Cap Screw	steel	as req'd
	1	Special Bolt	steel	7/8" dia. × 1 3/8"
	1	Roller	ball bearing[1] No. 88502	1 3/8" dia. × 9/16"
	1	Roller Holder	steel	1 × 4 3/8 x 3/8"
	1	Nut – "thin"	steel	1/2 × 13"

[1]Plain steel roller may be substituted (see text).

RELATED TOPICS

The Use and Storage of Propane

By Christopher Leggo

Photos by Author

TANKS AND TORCHES

Propane is widely used and could be better understood. Propane is the third in a series of hydrocarbons which starts with methane, proceeds to ethane, then to propane and butane. Following is pentane and a whole series. The series is put in order of the number of carbon atoms and are all of the same type of molecular structure.

Butane and propane have become popular as fuels because they are liquids at elevated pressures which makes getting a large quantity of fuel in a small space easy. Used in the gaseous form, the fuel is allowed to expand into a lower pressure and propane does so at a ratio of 278 to one. The vapor pressures in the tank are not so high that a heavy tank is needed, and when pressure is released to facilitate pumping, the losses to atmosphere are not great. Butane has a tank pressure of about 25 psi at room temperature and can be stored in "tin cans." It is safely used in cigarette lighters made of plastic. Look into a *Bic*-type lighter and you can see the liquid.

Propane has a tank pressure of about 125 psi at room temperature and a stronger tank is needed; but even then, it is nothing like the oxygen or CO^2 bottles.

If a tank contains all gas, its contents may be measured by its pressure. If a tank contains liquid and gas and the liquid evaporates as the gas is withdrawn, the pressure in the tank is constant until all the gas is evaporated.

In the case of propane, while there is still liquid in the tank, the pressure is a function of the temperature only and in no way indicates the weight of propane left in the tank. Only when all the liquid is gone does pressure fall with usage. Therefore, weighing is the only way to tell how full the tank is, even if you had a pressure gauge on the tank, which you don't.

Propane has a heating value of about 20,000 Btu/lb. which is about as high as any common fuel gets. It is cheaper than gasoline and almost as easy to buy. It is used for camp stoves, lanterns, barbeques, lift trucks in factories, and general heating in remote areas because of its mild exhaust. Tanks seldom blow up, but there are severe dangers under certain conditions if the tank or its plumbing leak. Propane gas is heavier than air and can collect on floors or pits or in the bilges of a boat where it can be ignited if not detected and dispersed.

Construction and Operation of Bottles

There are three widely used types of bottles and several types of not so common bottles, one of which can be modified for use in models (**Photo 1**). The trailer (or barbeque) bottle comes in several sizes from about 5 lbs. and up. It is made of heavy steel, has a built-in safety valve, filling vent, a *left*-handed thread for connection, and is refillable at trailer suppliers and many gas stations in areas where campers go. If you have one of these bottles, it can be used for your barbeque, for your brazing torch, and for refilling smaller bottles.

Probably the most common bottle is the 14.1 oz. size sold in hardware stores, auto supplies, and even grocery stores. The 16 oz. size is almost as common and differs only in its size and shape. Both are considered disposable and are not made for refilling, although we will talk about that later. The outlet of the bottle is fitted with a 1″-20 thread, a "tire" valve, and an O-ring seal (**Figure 2**). The tire valve is pushed open when the appliance is screwed on and gas is allowed to flow. It is the O-ring that makes the seal. The cork gasket is secondary.

The 10% safety valve is recessed on the top of the tank and serves two purposes. It is made like a tire valve but works the other way. It is spring loaded closed; pressure above that at which it is set will open it. The "inlet into the outlet" is at about 90% full

1 — *Left to right, the "trailer"-type bottle, a 14.1 oz. bottle, the 16 oz. bottle, and a modified "minnie" torch bottle.*

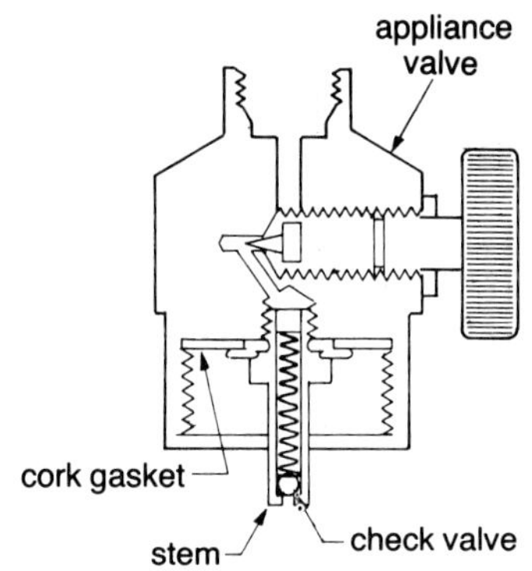

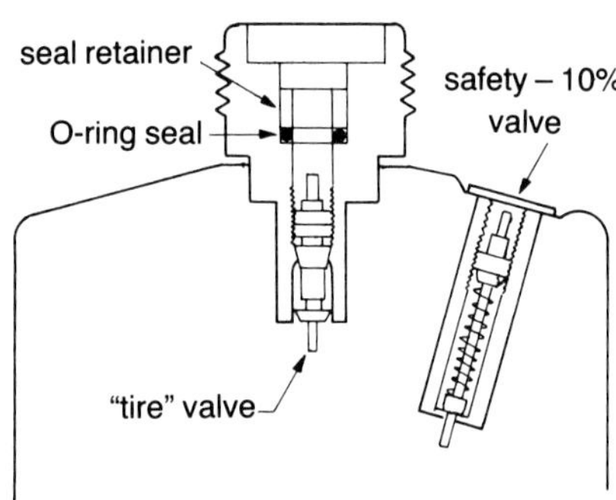

Cross section of 14.1 and 16 oz. bottles. Details may differ in various makes.

FIGURE 2

level and is used when the tank is filled to insure that there is about 10% of tank unfilled. This 10% will be occupied by gas and below it there will be liquid. This space is necessary to accommodate temperature changes where the bottle is stored. If it were not for this "steam space," expansion of the liquid would certainly rupture the tank.

The appliance valve has some features which are worth noting. The stem is positioned so that when the valve is screwed onto the tank, it depresses the tire valve in the bottle and gas can flow. The stem contains a check valve so that gas (or liquid, if the bottle is upside down) cannot go back into the bottle. The needle valve can regulate flow but in most cases is used wide open.

A fourth type of bottle is the 7 oz. or "mini" torch bottle. It is of the same diameter as the 14.1 oz. tank but only half its length. The thread on the outlet is 9/16-24 and is not compatible with the common appliances. Fittings for this smaller size are available but a little hard to find. Because the "regular" sizes are so easy to come by, it is probably the best plan to sleeve the thread up to 1-20. More on this later.

All the common torches have a maximum flow rate of about 3 oz. per hour. If any more than that is removed from the common bottle, the heat of evaporation of the liquid into gas takes heat out of the liquid and the bottle becomes progressively colder with time until the pressure drops exceedingly. The pressure in a propane tank is very temperature sensitive. A normal pressure of 125 psi at 70° F will raise to 200 on a hot day and go to 50 on a cold day. Excessive draining will lower the temperature of the bottle on any day if heat is not supplied somewhere. At moderate use, enough heat gets through the walls of the bottle so that pressure is kept up, but at great flow rates, pressure, and therefore heat output, will drop.

One of the ways to overcome this difficulty is to design the torch for use of the gas at a reduced pressure. In this way, the pressure in the bottle can be reduced considerably before the flame is affected and more heat can be utilized for a longer time. The Turner "Tornado" (shown on the 14.1 oz. bottle in Photo 1) and the "swirl"-type torches all use a pressure regulator in the on-off valve and the burner is designed for this reduced pressure. The regulators are made so small you may not be aware they are there.

Even at reduced pressure usage, the tank may become exceedingly cold. Operators of large locomotives who sink the bottle in a water tank will find ice in the water after a couple of hours on a not-so-warm day.

The Refillable Bottle

BernzOmatic makes a 14.1 oz. bottle that has special provisions for refilling it from a trailer bottle (**Photo 3**). A vent is built into the housing of the safety valve and can be used without disturbing the safety valve setting. The use of this bottle reduces the cost of propane from 2-3 dollars to about 10 cents. It works just like refilling your trailer bottle at the trailer supply.

The refillable is connected to the source at a point below the liquid level. The vent on the refillable is opened so that air and gas will escape, allowing the bottle to be filled with liquid. The source is then turned on and liquid flows into the bottle. The gas that escapes to atmosphere comes from the evaporation of the liquid as the bottle is being filled. Vaporization during the filling will reduce the temperature so that frost will form on the outside of the bottle. When the level of the liquid reaches the 10% valve, liquid then issues from the vent and the liquid supply can be closed (**Photo 4**). The vent is then closed and the refillable can be removed from the source.

The BernzOmatic *refillable bottle reduces the cost of propane to about 10¢ per filling.*

When the bottle is full, a heavy mixture of gas and liquid issues from the vent.

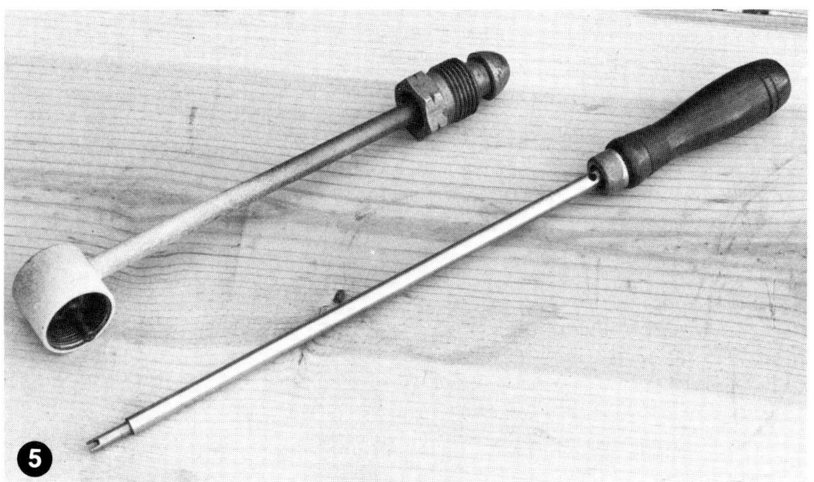

The refilling adapter sole with the Bernz refillable bottle and the long reach valve stem tool necessary to refill other bottles.

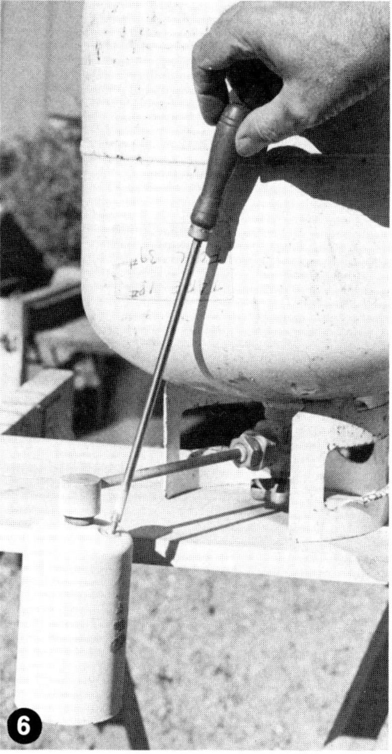

Refilling the 7 oz. bottle. The valve tool is ready to close the safety valve when full and the supply valve is closed.

Having gas escape from the vent assures you that the bottle is not overfilled. For a 14.1 oz. bottle, it takes about two minutes.

Very little liquid can be transferred if the bottle is not vented and even less fuel value can be transferred as gas is taken from the source. Liquid must be taken from the source and the bottle must be vented if its maximum capacity is to be utilized. If the bottle is not empty at refilling, there will be a great loss of gas before it starts accepting liquid. It is always more economical to refill an empty bottle, to say nothing of the safety.

A notice on all disposable bottles says that transporting a refilled bottle is subject to a $25,000 fine. It doesn't say that you can't do it, but you ought to be aware of the hazzards involved. To fill a disposable bottle, you must release the safety valve so that the bottle will vent, but there is no clear-cut way of knowing where to reset it. I have seen refilled bottles with the safety valve screwed down tight because the owner did not know how it worked, let alone where to set it. He was walking around with a bomb, and quite a bomb at that. There are 750,000 ft. lbs. of energy in a 14.1 oz. bottle. That's enough to lift two loaded 747's a foot off the ground.

A bottle from the supplier has the safety valve set at 285 psi but that information doesn't help you much. However, if you take a new bottle at a known temperature and unscrew the safety valve until gas escapes, you can count the turns. Now, on the refilled bottle, after it warms up to the same temperature, you can bring it to release, and screw it down the same number of turns. It may not be exact, but at least you will be in the right ball park. I have found that 2½ turns release pressure on a new bottle on a moderate day.

The disposable bottle is refilled exactly like the refillable ones except that the safety valve is used for a vent. It will be necessary for you to make yourself a long reach tool, at least a foot long, to operate the tire valve (**Photo 5**). Liquid (LP) gas, like dry ice, can cause severe burns if exposed to the skin for any length of time.

It is best not to remove the safety valve when refilling but merely to release it. There are several threads left before it comes out. Reinserting it in the stream of supercold propane might well be impossible. It is probably best to leave the tool in the valve while the bottle is filling so that you are ready to close down the valve when the bottle is full (**Photo 6**).

The easiest way to determine how much propane is in the bottle is to weigh it (**Photo 7**). Weigh the bottle empty and when it is full, and mark the bottle. This is a good idea for all your bottles, even the trailer bottle. Don't be surprised if the weight of gas in the bottle differs by an ounce or two from the nominal value. Any sort of a scale or balance will do. We don't have to work to the nearest ounce.

Weighing the bottle is the best way to determine the contents. This bottle shows 8 oz. left.

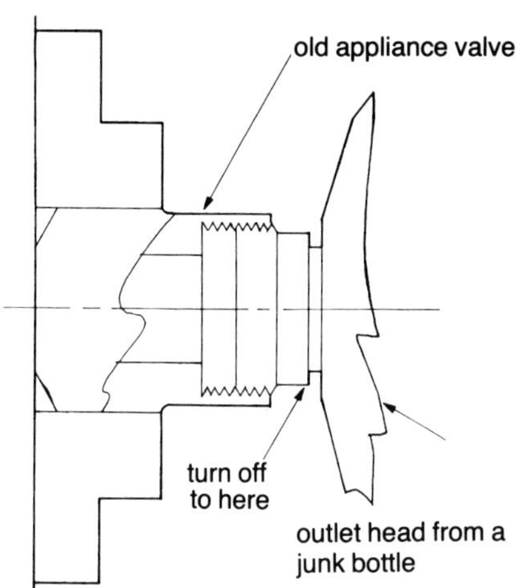

An old appliance valve is used for chucking the bottle head for turning.

FIGURE 8

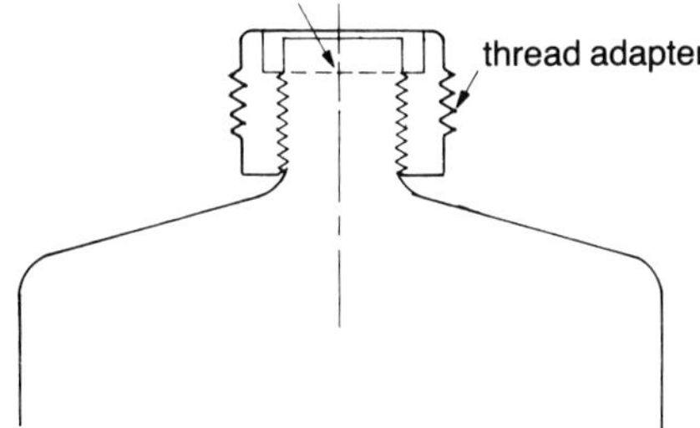

The adapter lip must stand proud of the smaller so that sealing is not disrupted.

FIGURE 9

10

An attempt to make up a very small bottle. It leaked from my bad welding.

11

Hook tool used to remove the plastic O-ring retainer from the neck of the bottle.

Modification of the 7 oz. Bottle

To modify the smaller bottle for use with the common connectors on torches, a disposable tank must be destroyed to get some parts. It is also helpful if you have a junk torch valve that you can sacrifice. Cut the threaded head off the old tank and screw it into the junk valve head which is chucked in the lathe (**Figure 8**). Turn off the remaining sheet metal and drill it through at the tapping size for 9/16-24. It will not be necessary to remove the valve, O-ring, and plastic seal retainer unless you want to save them. The drill will do that for you. Tap 9/16-24, and using a husky pair of pliers, unscrew the head from the valve body. Save the valve body for the next time and screw the thread adapter onto the 7 oz. bottle, making sure that its upper surface is just above that of the smaller thread (**Figure 9**). Stake it together or use *Loctite* so that when you unscrew the appliance, it will stay with the bottle. The threads need not be tight. It is the O-ring that makes the seal.

The stem of gas appliances is screwed into its valve body and the hex on the base of the stem may be 5/16 or 3/8. If it is 5/16, you are home free. If larger, it will interfere with the remainder of the thread head of the smaller bottle. In this case, chuck up the whole bottle, and *carefully* turn off the top of the smaller thread. Stuff the hole with a scrap of rag so as not to get chips in the tire valve.

Photo 10 shows a failure in trying to make up a miniature bottle for use in a very small boat. The bottom was cut off a 14.1 oz. bottle and fitted to the sawed off top. My welding was not gas tight and the bottle leaked. If a good welder had done it, it may have worked. If you weld on one of these tanks, you will have to remove the valves, the O-ring, and the plastic O-ring retainer. A tool is shown in **Photo 11** for removing the plastic retainer. It must be large enough just to slip into the retainer and hook on its lower edge. These plastic retainers are easy to ruin and a tool like this must be used if you want to reuse it. There is no reason you can't make up your own container of any configuration for propane, but make sure it has a 10% valve and a safety valve. If you hydrostatic test the tank, go to 500 psi or so.

BOTTLES AND BURNERS

Let's look at some of the properties of propane:

PROPERTIES OF PROPANE

Specific volume of gas (14.7 psi and 70°F)	8.6 cubic feet per lb.
Specific volume of liquid	.03 cubic feet per lb.
Expansion ratio, liquid to gas	270:1
Specific gravity of gas (air equals 1.00)	1.52
Density of liquid at room temperature	31 lbs. per cubic foot
or	4.2 lbs. per gallon
Density of gas	.116 lbs. per cubic foot
Boiling point	-43°F
Latent heat of vaporization	183 Btu/lb.
Specific heat of gas	.34 Btu/lb./degree F
Heat of combustion (gas)	2316 Btu/cubic foot
Heat of combustion (liquid)	20,000 Btu/lb.
Air to fuel ratio	14.5:1 by weight
Air to fuel ratio range to burn	Narrow
Temperature of combustion	3400°F
Temperature-pressure relationship	(see **Figure 12**)

BURNING RATES

Common torch	2-3 oz./hr.
"Tornado"-type torch	4-5 oz./hr.
"blowtorch"-type burner	8-10 oz./hr.
Cast iron stove-type burner with reduced pressure	10-12 oz./hr.
Grosse-Holtfort locomotive	
two "blowtorch"-type burners	16 oz./hr.
Downey steamboat (***Live Steam***, August 1976)	3.5 lb./hr.
GGLS club locomotive (1½" Pacific)	4 lb./hr.

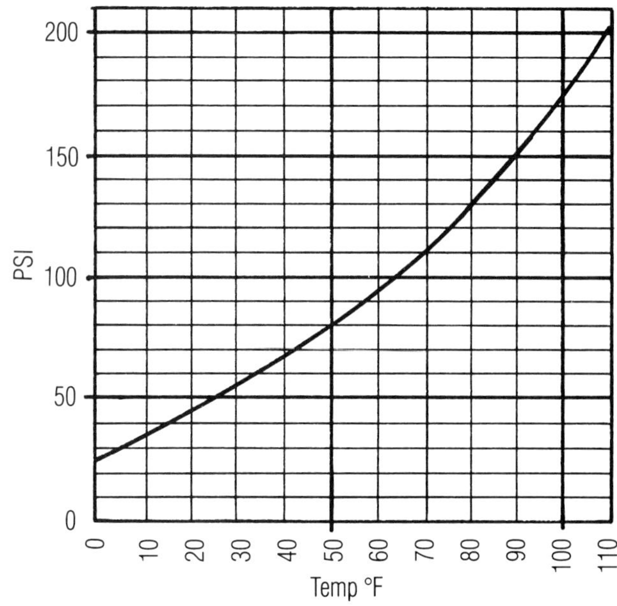

Temperature-pressure relationship of propane in a closed container containing both liquid and gas.

FIGURE 12

The contents of the bottle can be weighed before and after the burning test or constantly weighed while the test is taking place. The following rates will give you an idea of various burning rates and are approximate only because they do not take into account the cooling of the bottle as gas is extracted. Some figures are from actual measurements, others are from literature and verbal reports.

Burner Testing

All of the following tests were made on a moderate day (65-75°F) with the bottle and burner in open air and the bottle and burner on the scale while the test was being run (**Photo 13**).

The bottle being used is a modification of the 16 oz. standard propane bottle. It is fitted with a thermometer well and a 200 psi pressure gauge. Additional outputs are fitted so that gas or liquid can be withdrawn with the bottle lying on its side. The standard outlet is not disturbed and may be used as well (**Photo 14**).

The first test (**Figure 15**) was the "common" torch, the one you get with the propane kit you buy at the hardware store. The test was run for 30 minutes, at which time both temperature and pressure seemed to want to level out. Consumption started out high as a result of the high initial pressure in the bottle and reduced as the pressure leveled out to 64 psi. This was the point where heat passing through the walls of the bottle just matched the heat of evaporation of the gas being generated in the bottle. The temperature does not match theoretical because of lag in the system. Contents of the bottle measured 2 oz. at the start of the test and 1 oz. at the end, enough to insure that there was still liquid.

Theoretical steam output at this burning rate would be 2.2 lbs./hr. or .56 oz./min.

Figure 16 shows the same test with the Turner "Tornado" burner. This burner has a built-in regulator in the valve and reduces pressure to about 15 psi; the burner is designed to use gas at this reduced pressure. Here the consumption was a steady 5.4 oz./hr. After 12 minutes I could see that this could take all afternoon, so I stopped the test and bled the bottle by 2½ oz. to reduce the pressure and temperature. The test was restarted at 16 minutes, the temperature and pressure being reduced considerably. Because the "use" pressure was still below the pressure of the bottle, the consumption stayed at the steady 5.4 oz./hr. Temperature and pressure actually rose for the remainder of the test,

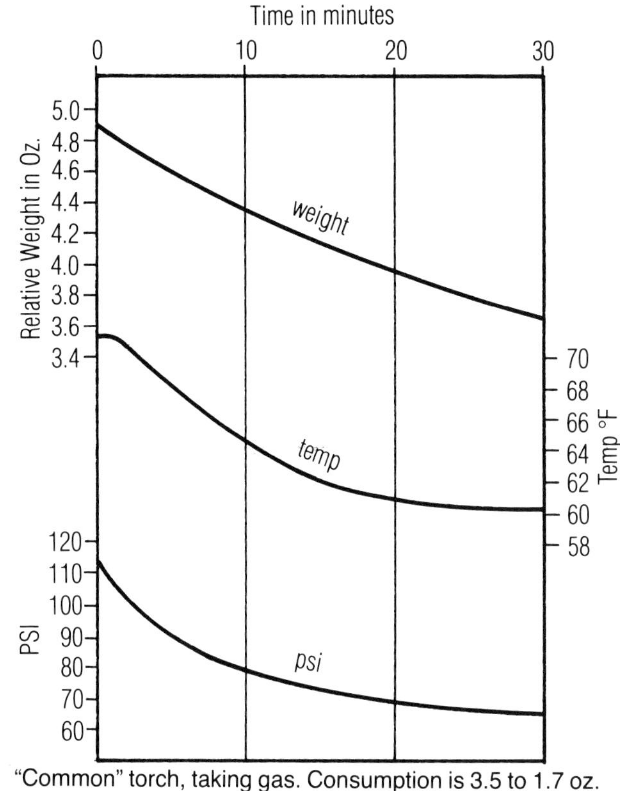

"Common" torch, taking gas. Consumption is 3.5 to 1.7 oz. per hour as pressure is decreased.

FIGURE 15

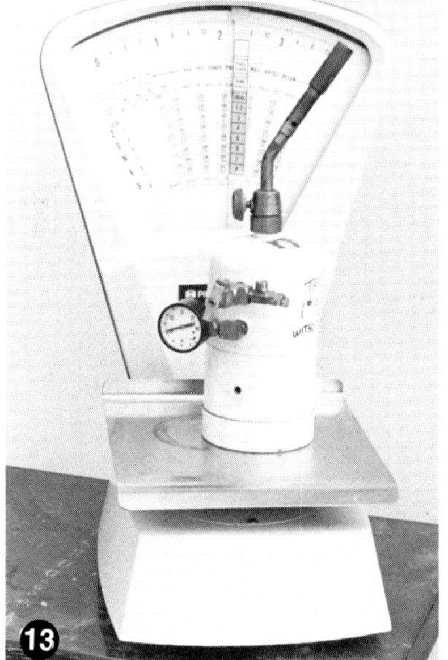

Testing burning rates of propane appliances by measuring their weights over a period of time.

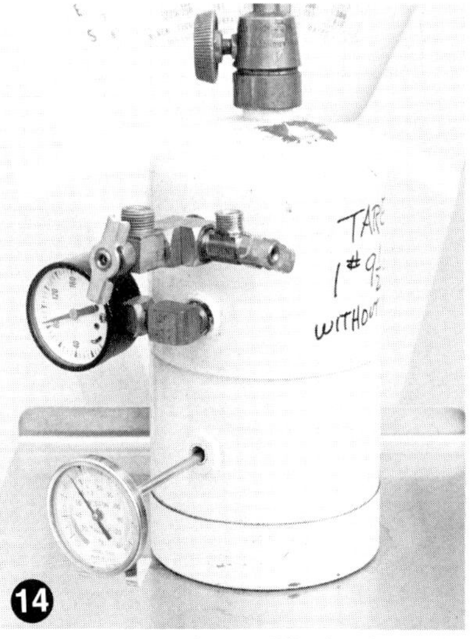

The 16 oz. bottle modified to include a pressure gauge, a thermometer well, and both gas and liquid outlets.

showing that the steady state conditions were somewhere below the first half of the test and somewhere above the second half of the test. If the test had been continued, temperature and pressure would have stabilized at the point where heat transferring through the walls of the bottle would have been just that needed to vaporize the gas being used. Theoretical steam production here would be 7 lbs./hr.

The Turner "Industrial" burner is a replacement head for the standard torch. Its heat output is high and so is the consumption rate (**Figure 17**). While output was 21.6 oz./hr. at the start, it fell to 6.6 oz./hr. after 13 minutes. During this time, temperature fell to a stabilization point of 37°F and pressure to 32 psi. Any propane burning system which takes gas out of the bottle will suffer a reduction of pressure as gas is withrawn. Pressure will continue to drop if heat is not supplied somewhere. If the gas is being burned at the bottle pressure, consumption will fall until stabilization is reached. Steam generation would have been 28 lb./hr. if the 21.6 oz./hr. rate could have been maintained.

To test recovery, measurements of temperature and pressure were continued with the burner shut off. After a further 17 minutes, pressure recovered to 95 psi and temperature to 63°. Again, there will be a temperature lag and it will not be exactly as theoretical.

Model boat burners are usually run directly off the bottle and will suffer the effects of reduced pressure. Those who run propane in locomotives use the gas at a reduced pressure and seldom see any ill effects.

The steel water heater burner of about 2½" diameter (**Photo 18**) is in common use in locomotives at Golden Gate Live Steamers . It will burn with pressures up to 30 psi without blowing out and 5 psi will keep the flame at the holes. Consumption rates for this burner are charted in **Figure 19**. The burner was run for 14 minutes at 10 psi where the consumption was 5.3 oz./hr. and steady with drop in temperature and pressure as shown. I then played with the pressure and stopped at 30 psi where the flame was somewhat in danger of blowing out but still stable. Consumption at this rate was 8.4 oz./hr. and bottle pressure fell to 30 psi where it affected the use pressure. Pressures of 2-10 psi are used for these burners at the track and two or three of them are used in the

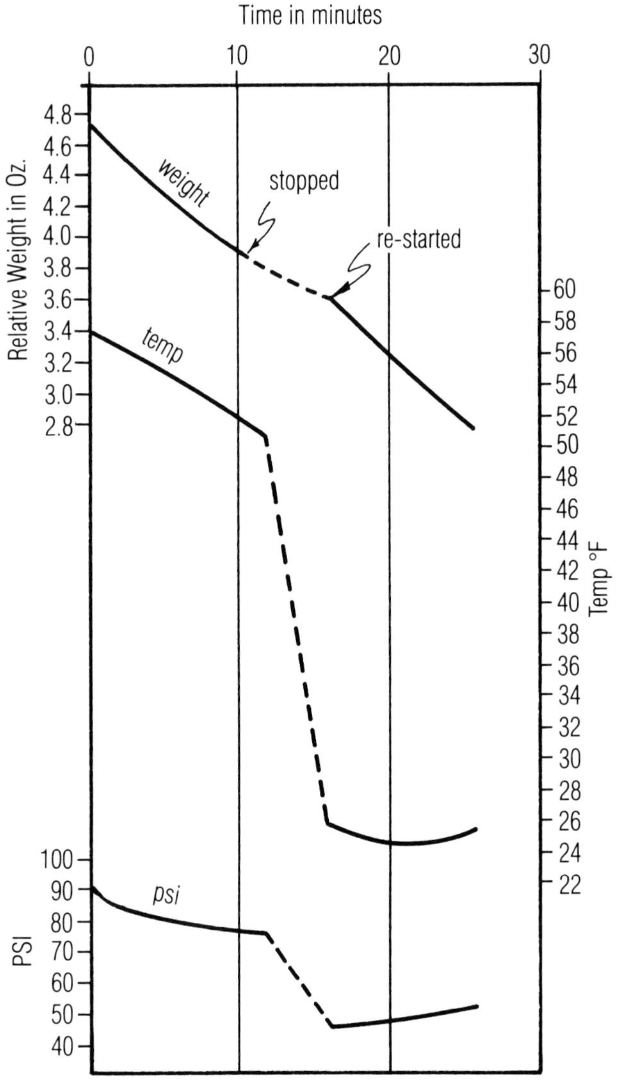

Turner "Tornado" taking gas. Consumption is a steady 5.4 oz. per hr. and reduction in pressure does not affect output.

FIGURE 16

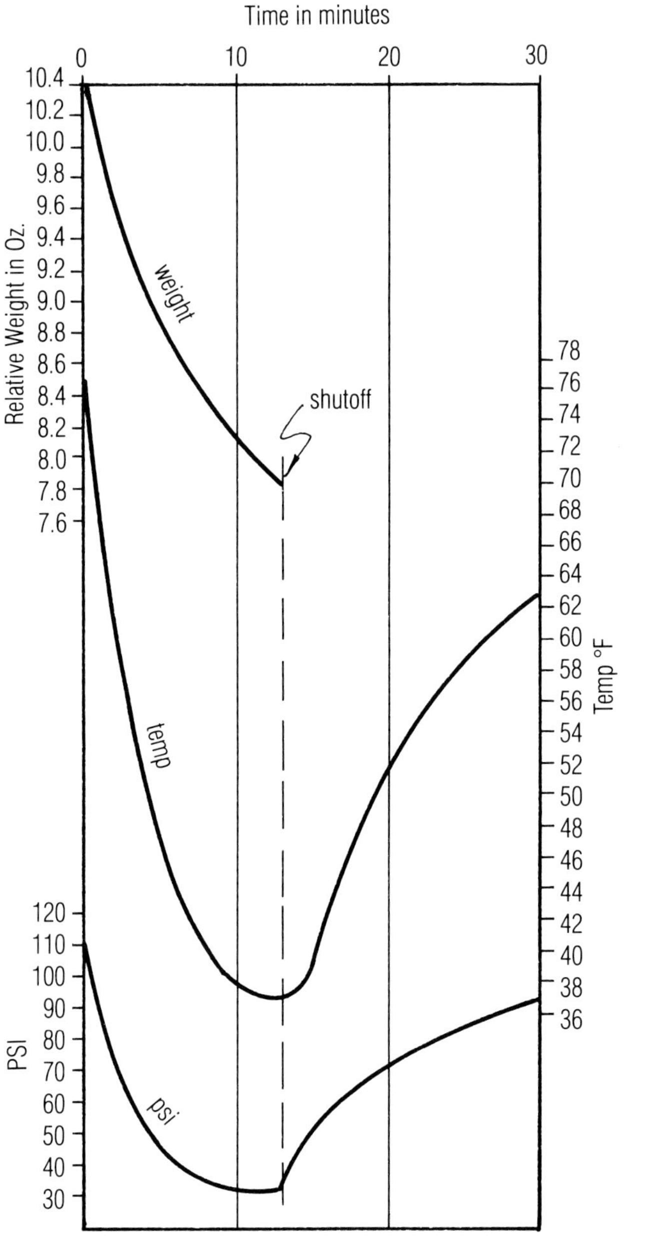

Turner "Industrial" burner taking gas. Output will fall until heat balance is established.

FIGURE 17

18 *The versatile and "almost indestructible" sheet metal water heater burner as used on many locomotives.*

firebox. These burners are considered "almost indestructible" and are a good solution to the burner dilemma. They are small enough to fit into a ¾" scale firebox and the fire can be regulated with the pressure regulator. Theoretical generation is about 6.5 lb./hr. per burner.

The cast iron kitchen range or oven burner is designed to use about ½ psi. The regulator for this pressure is common enough at propane suppliers and the adjustable jet allows fine tuning of the flame. Consumption is a steady 10 oz./hr., and although temperature and pressure drop off dramatically (**Figure 20**), it would take severe conditions for the bottle pressure to drop off below the use pressure of ½ psi. Generation would be 13 lb./hr.

Using gas at a reduced pressure goes a long way to obtaining a high and steady output from a propane burner. Taking liquid from the bottle would insure that the bottle will not freeze up and reduce pressure. But it is still necessary to supply the heat of vaporization somewhere. To supply the heat of vaporization of the gas, I tried a warming trick. Liquid is taken from the bottle and expanded in an orifice which is submerged in water

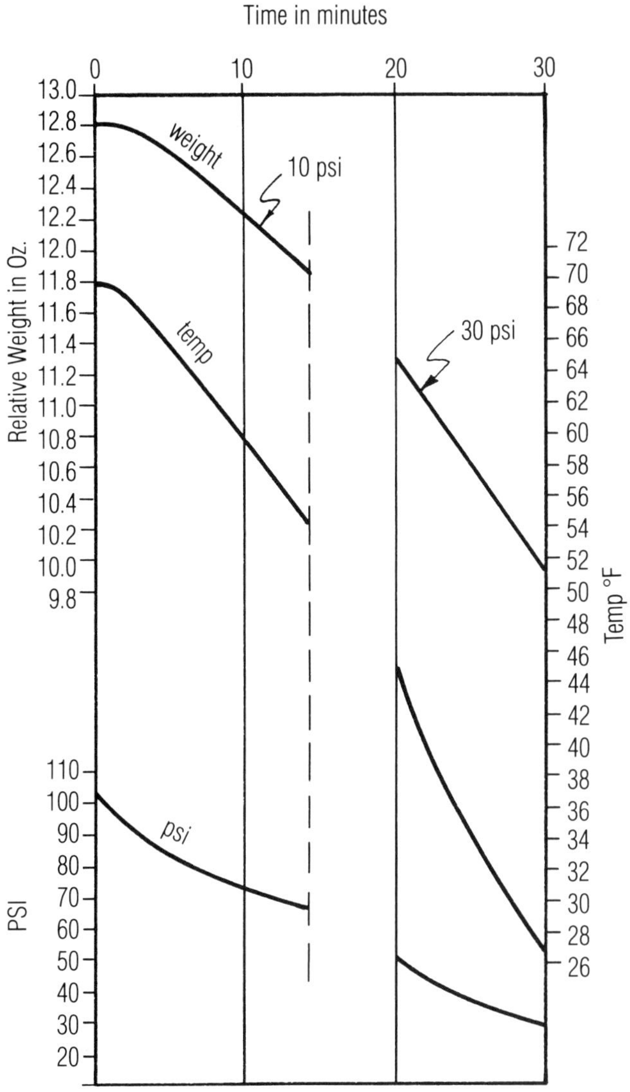

The sheet metal "water heater" burner will burn at a great range of reduced pressure and is a step in the right direction.

FIGURE 19

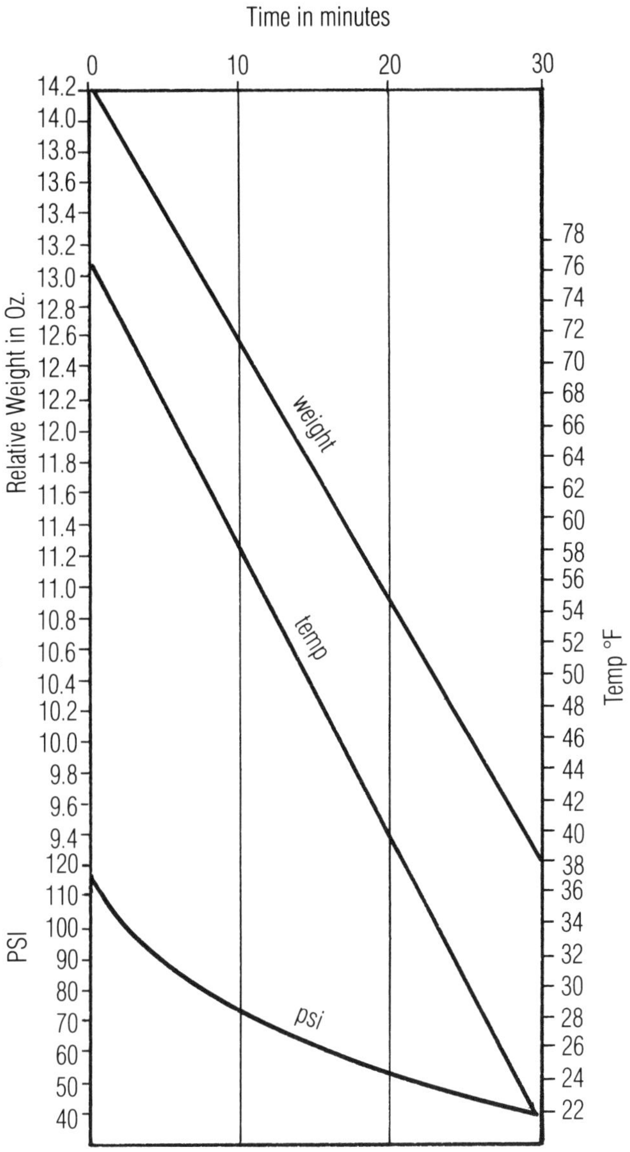

Cast iron burner as used on your kitchen stove. "Use" pressure is 12″ of water or about ½ psi.

FIGURE 20

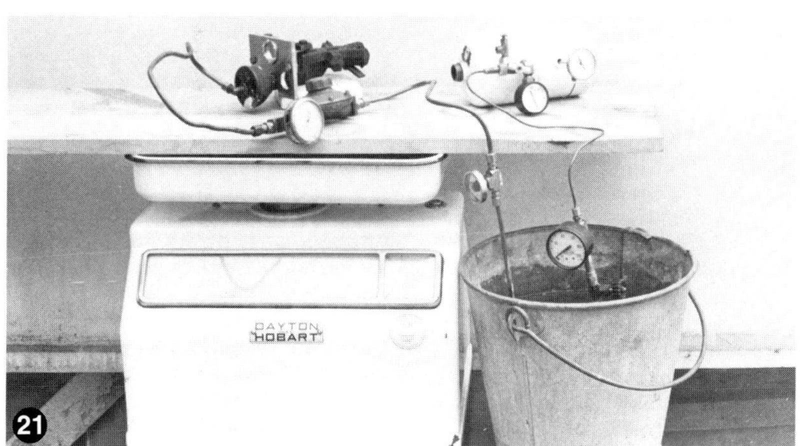

Bottle, coil, regulator and burner are supported on the scale. Liquid is expanded, warmed, regulated, and burned.

(**Photo 21**). The gas then flows through about two feet of ¼" tubing in the water and then to the ½ psi regulator. The orifice was adjusted so that bottle pressure was reduced to about half as it passed through the orifice. This would insure that expansion was taking place there and that would be the place to supply the heat of vaporization.

Pressure just before the orifice was the same as the bottle pressure and was assumed to be still liquid because the line was still at room temperature. A freshly filled bottle was used for the test and had an initial pressure of 65 psi and a temperature of 38° (**Figure 22**). Contents of the bottle at the start was about 6 oz. Con-

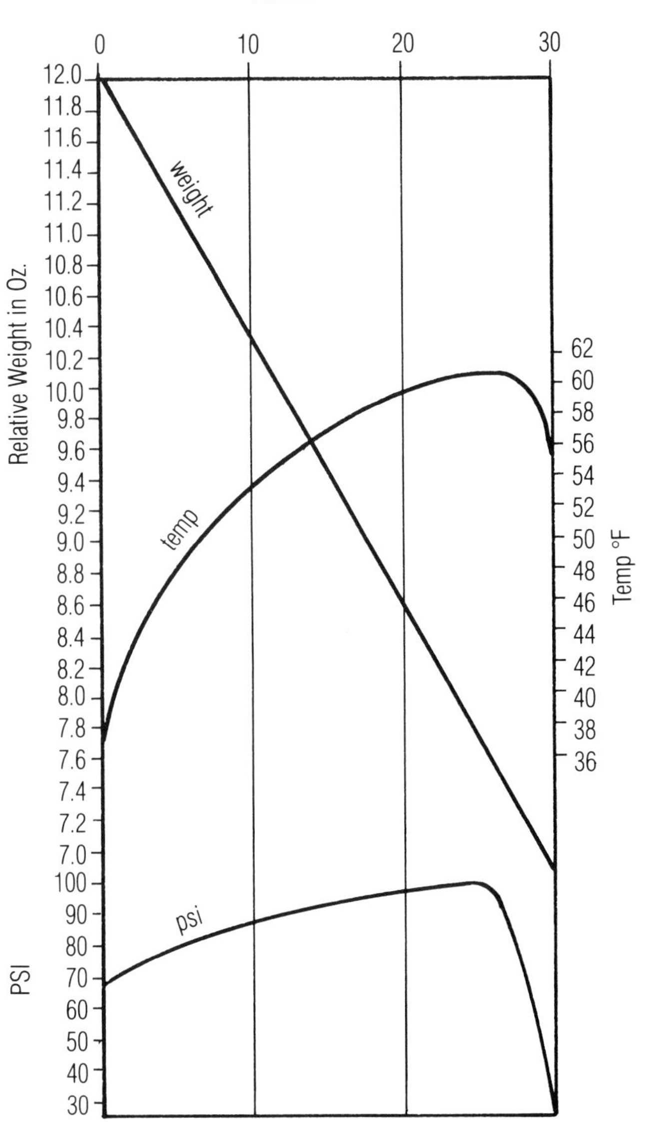

The cast iron burner with liquid taken from the bottle and warmed after expanding to a gas.

FIGURE 22

sumption was a steady 10.2 oz./hr. and temperature and pressure did not drop but actually rose, with every indication that they were heading for room temperature and pressure.

At 25 minutes, both temperature and pressure started to drop. This was a dramatic development and my first thought was that something was wrong; actually, the bottle had run out of liquid and the reaction was that of a bottle with only gas in it. Sure enough, on removing the bottle and weighing it, it read zero contents.

Temperature drop in the bucket of water was not detectable, although I could be forced to admit to a 1° drop. If all the heat of vaporization was going into the water, and it had to go there or through the walls of the piping, theoretical temperature drop would be about 2° in this time period.

In a model boat, this orifice could be placed outside the hull. The pond would be an infinite heat sink and the bottle would always maintain ambient temperature. Although this may be awkward in a model boat, the system could be used to advantage in a full size launch. The biggest complaint in launches seems to be the freezing of the propane bottle. In models, a better way might be to run the liquid through an orifice located on the surface of the boiler, but we'll talk about that next time.

All these burning tests were made in open air and may not apply to a closed furnace space. Any burner gets air from two sources. Primary air is that which is mixed in the venturi of the burner. Any gas flame needs secondary air which must be supplied to the combustion space. No burner will survive if shoved into a hole where there is no secondary air, but if you've ever tried to braze inside a firebox, you know this. Too much secondary air will just cool the fire and waste heat.

So what do we know so far? 1) Heat output will drop if pressure falls below that which the burner was designed; 2) if pressure is to be maintained, heat must be supplied where liquid propane turns into gas; and 3) the right amount of primary and seconary air must be supplied for complete combustion.

We are now in a position to design a burner and propane system which will give us high output at a sustained rate. Some control will be needed to make it automatic and we will take that up next.

Automatic Fire Control for Propane

To this point we have discussed handling and storage of propane, properties of the liquid and the gas, and characteristics of bottles and burners.

We can now put this information to use. Propane offers one great advantage over coal or gasoline burners. It is a *gas* system and the gas can be stored in the form of a liquid, therefore enabling us to store large quantities of fuel in a small space. The liquifaction of the gas also allows us to draw it at a constant pressure from the container. The greatest advantage, however, is the possibility of using a fire control device, regulated by the pressure in the boiler itself, allowing hands-off operation of the boiler. This is not such a great advantage in locomotives where the operator is in constant attention, but is very useful in a model boat which is limited in water supply and away from the operator for long periods of time. A fire control system will turn down the fire at a given pressure and thus keep the boiler from blowing off. When the pressure reduces, the fire will turn on full again.

In my 33″ steamboat, the safety

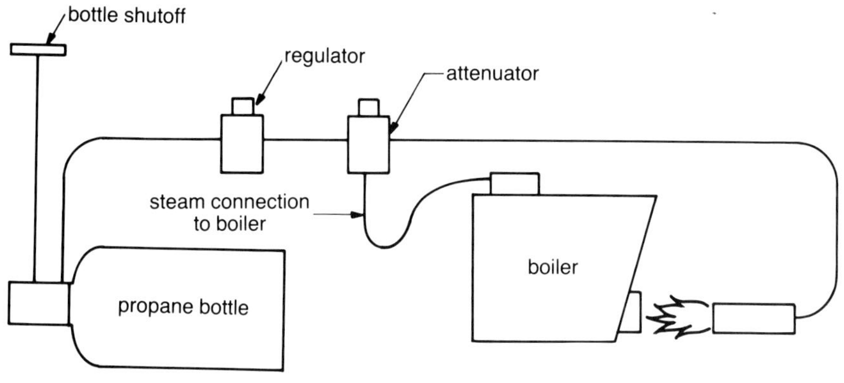

FIGURE 23

Diagram of a pressure regulated propane burner for a 33" model boat. Be sure to put a loop or syphon in the line to the attenuator.

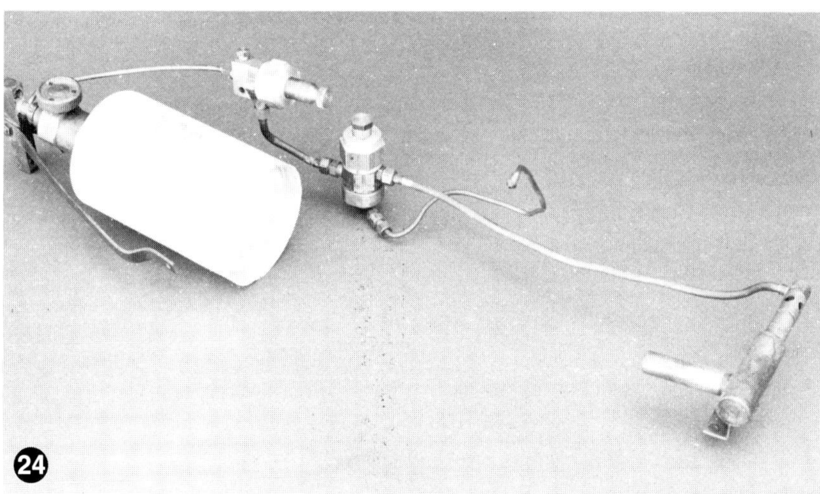

The hardware of the system. All components must be homemade, although an appliance valve can easily be modified for the bottle connection.

The hardware installed in the boat. The main gas valve is the capstan on the foredeck. Radio gear is under hatch covers.

valve is set for 50 psi and the fire control is set for 40 psi. The safety never blows and the fire can idle indefinitely at 40 psi. When the throttle is opened, the fire immediately comes up to full blast. Capacity of this boiler is 3.6 lb./hr. at 40 psi.

The basic diagram of the system is shown in **Figure 23**. It consists of a regulator to reduce bottle pressure to about 30 psi, the attenuator which shuts down gas flow at about 40 psi, and a homemade burner. Because the boat runs only for a short time and heat loss in the bottle is of no consideration, the bottle is placed without regard to whether gas or liquid is fed.

Configuration of the equipment is as shown in **Photo 24** and is installed in the model as in **Photos 25** and **26**. The regulator is patterned after the one built into the Turner Tornado torch. It uses a tire valve and can be built into a very small space (**Figure 27**). The body of the valve can be 1" hex, although 1⅜" takes the bind off a little. More later on construction. The attenuator is very similar to the regulator except that it has another diaphragm on the bottom to push the valve closed, and a connection to steam pressure (**Photo 28** and **Photo 29**).

The burner was modeled after the Turner again. Configuration of the boat demanded that a special one be built. I got it to work by seemingly endless experimentation with orifice sizes, tube lengths, and "turbo" devices. I'd like to describe how to make a successful burner, but I have to admit to not understanding exactly what the parameters are.

To set the valves, the attenuator is screwed down all the way so that it will be open, and the fire lit off. The regulator can then be adjusted to any rate up to the point where the fire blows out. When boiler pressure builds up to a desired amount, the attenuator is screwed back so the flame almost

The regulator and attenuator must be easily removable but need not be available for ordinary running.

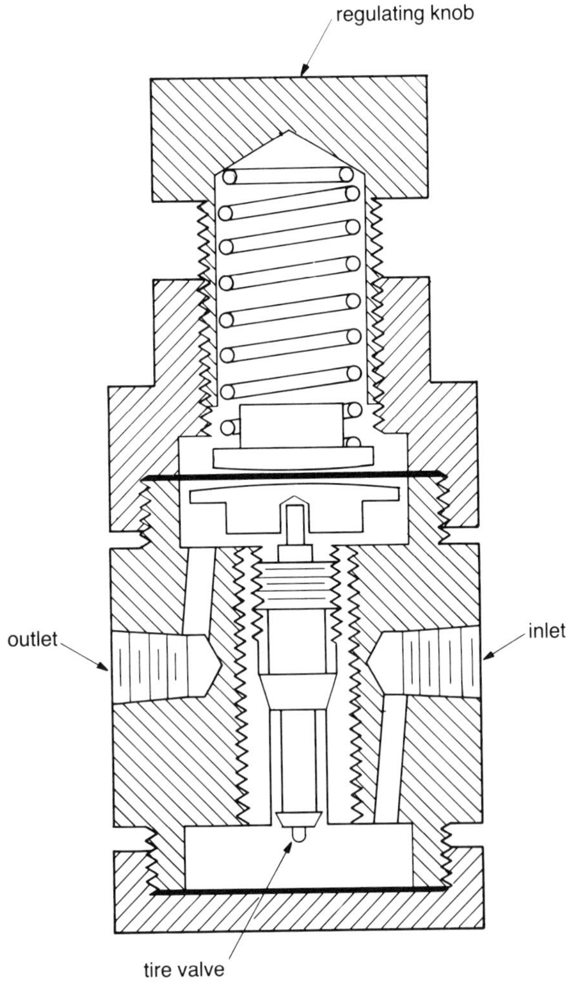

regulating knob

outlet

inlet

tire valve

FIGURE 27

The gas regulator uses a "tire" valve and rubber diaphragms. Pads must be crowned so as not to cut into the rubber. Material may be brass or aluminum.

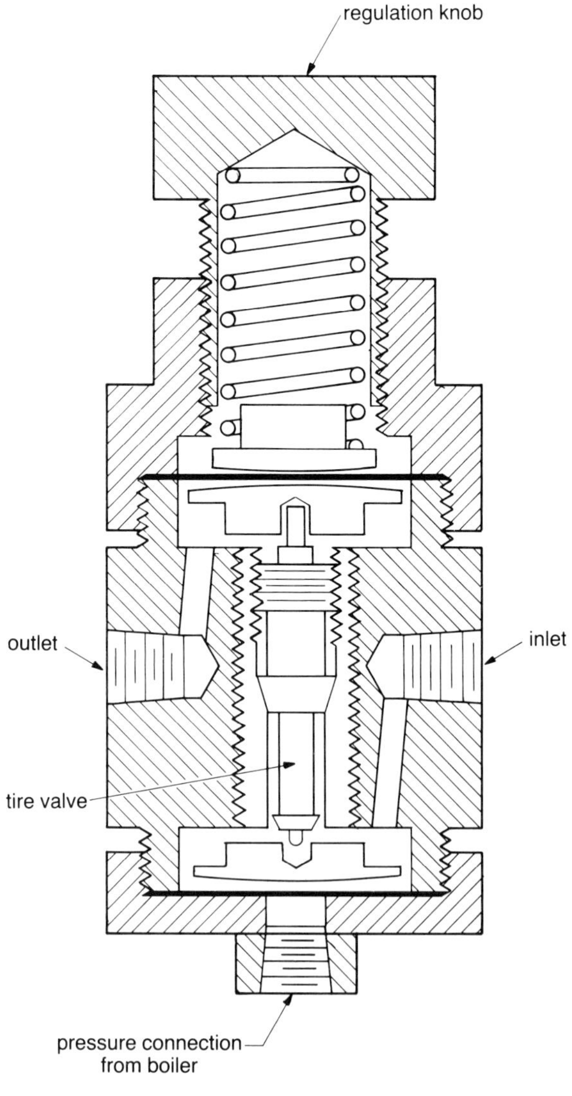

regulation knob

outlet

inlet

tire valve

pressure connection from boiler

FIGURE 28

The attenuator is similar to the regulator except for the lower diaphragm. Only about .015" motion is necessary on the valve.

Both regulator and attenuator may be made very small. The steam pressure pipe may be brought in on the side of the lower cap just as well.

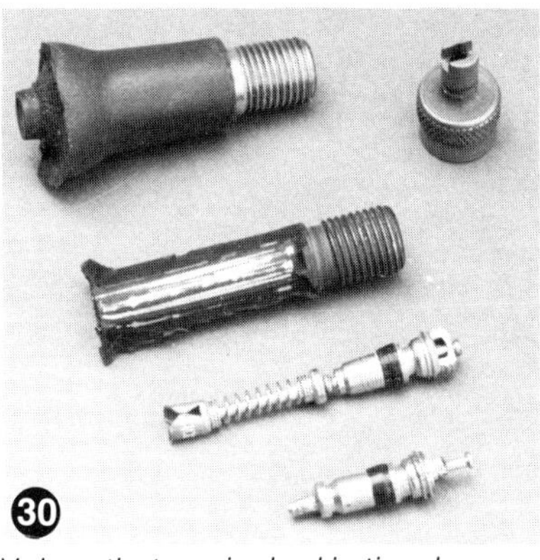

Valves that are junked in tire shops and are quite satisfactory for our use. The shorter valve core must be used.

Boiler, propane tank, and plumbing are on one base plate for easy removal. A mica window allows viewing the fire.

shuts off. After that, the operation is automatic and the burner may be lit by using the bottle shutoff valve.

I don't want to get into specifics of construction of the regulator and attenuator, but there are a few tips I can give and some pitfalls to warn about. The valve is a common tire valve complete with its sleeve as it comes off the floor of a tire shop (**Photo 30**). The outside of the sleeve is threaded 5⁄16-32, which is a common model engineering size. The body of the valve is threaded this size and then the sleeve is silver soldered or loctited into the body. The top end of the sleeve should stand proud of the body by about 1⁄8". Solder and then cut off. Care must be taken so that end caps do not cut into the diaphragms if they are made of rubber. The diaphragms may be made of almost any material. The motion is small enough that even brass diaphragms may be used. Sealing the diaphragms could be something of a problem. If they are rubber, you will need a ring of some sort so you don't squeeze it out of its seating. Diaphragms are used throughout the attenuator to eliminate any glands that are sure to leak.

The attenuator is made just like the regulator except that a diaphragm is applied at the bottom to close the valve when boiler pressure is enough to overcome the regulator spring. In the original articles of 1987, flow was described as going in the reverse direction from the regulator, which was in error. The device works that way but the valve will snap shut and not open again until the boiler pressure reduces by about 10 psi. It will also be necessary to provide a pilot flame. Running in the same direction as the regulator, gas

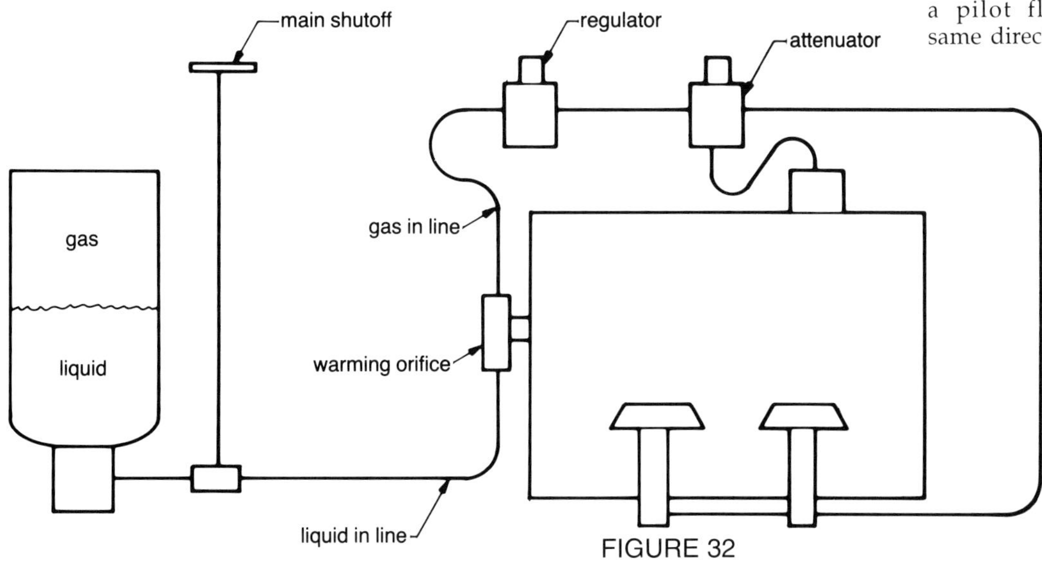

FIGURE 32

Diagram of boiler and gas system for a six-foot boat. Liquid is taken from the bottle and expanded at an orifice on the side of the boiler.

A commercial regulator and homemade attenuator. The pressure gauge on the gas line will be removed when confidence in the system is sufficient.

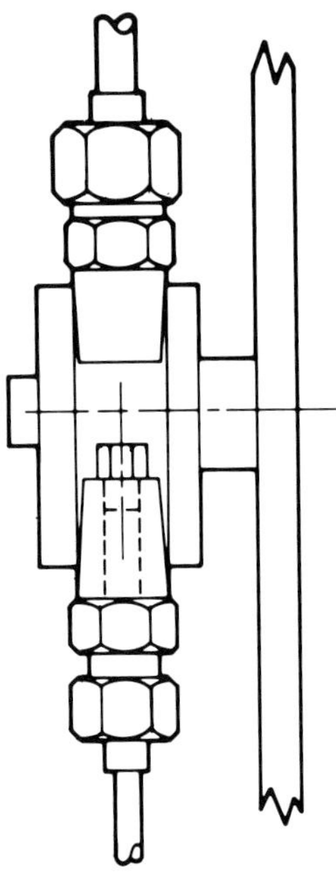

FIGURE 34

The orifice is bolted to the side of the boiler so that heat is supplied the expanding gas. Heat supplied can be regulated by the size of the mounting stud.

The front end of the experimental boiler. Feedwater temperature reads about 200° F at a steady state. The blowdown valve is at the lowest point of boiler.

flow attenuates slowly and never shuts down completely. In this model, flow starts to slow down at about 38 psi and is at a minimum at 40 psi. It must be pointed out that this attenuator will not work at full bottle pressure because bottle pressure is greater than boiler pressure and the lower diaphragm will not be able to overcome pressure on the other side of the diaphragm. It should also be pointed out that, although the attenuator has all the features of a regulator, it does not act as such and both regulator and attenuator must be used.

Photo 31 depicts a boiler of larger capacity for a 71" model boat. **Figure 32** is the flow diagram. In this case, a commercial regulator was used (**Photo 33**). Because of the larger expected output of gas, the bottle is arranged to feed from the bottom so that liquid is taken from the bottle and it will not freeze up. the expansion orifice (**Figure 34**) is about .015" diameter and is fastened to the side of the boiler to supply the heat of vaporization, the propane being in liquid form up to that point. There is some frosting of the regulator when starting up, but when steam is up, heat balance seems to be all right. Heat supplied to the sink may be regulated by the size of the stub that connects it to the boiler and the place on the boiler to which it is fastened.

The output of this boiler is 8 lbs/hr at 80 psi with two miniature water heater burners at about 7 psi gas pressure; with forced draft, it has been run at 35 psi on the gas with an output of 22 lbs/hr at 80 psi. Attenuation is set so that reduced flame is at a minimum at 93 psi. Upon opening the throttle, the flame is full again at about 80 psi.

Photo 35 shows the business end of this boiler. It is equipped with a feedwater heater, a five tube superheater, two reheat superheaters, and thermometer wells for feedwater and boiler temperature. This boiler was made for experimental work but was put together so I can use it in the six-foot boat.

There is no reason this system could not be used for locomotives or stationary plants. It requires very little more apparatus than ordinarily required for gas burning. I have found it quite comforting to know that I am not wasting water and heat through a blowing safety valve. To take full advantage of the system, however, you must have a boiler that puts out more steam than your engine can use. That could be a larger problem for many model boats.

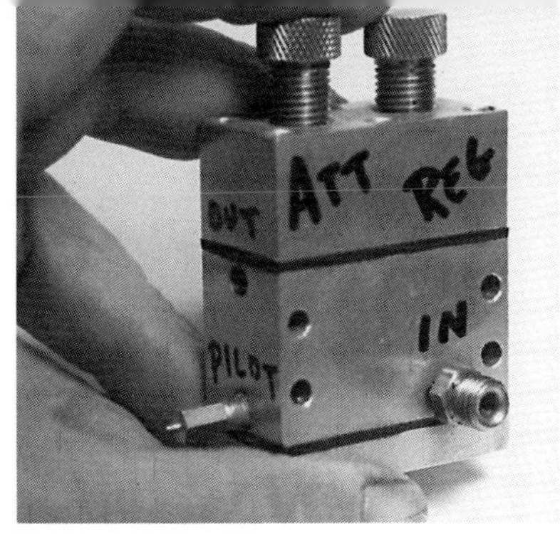

Combination unit is bolted together with 6-32 Allen screws. Pilot outlet, if desired, is regulated but un-attenuated. The unit can be mounted away from the boiler if gas is taken from the bottle.

ADDENDUM

When Joe Rice asked me to reprint this for *Steam and Stirling, Book 2*, I asked to make a few corrections and to add some material. Since the publication of this series in 1986, there have been some significant developments along the lines of fire control.

It started about 1990 at the Model Engineer Exhibition when Malcolm Beak of St. Albans approached me and started the conversation by telling me he has "pinched" my idea for the attenuator. Not only had he reduced it in size but had combined the regulator and attenuator in one compact unit (**Photo 36** and **Figure 37**). In return he gave me his design for automatic water control which works very nicely, but that is another story.

Malcolm's design has several advantages. It is made of aluminum which is just as suitable and easier to work, it saves space and a lot of plumbing, and the clamping of the diaphragms is such that no danger exists of squeezing them out of their seatings.

It also leads to mounting the unit directly on the firebox of the boiler and feeding heat directly from the fire to the regulator. Remember, we said that heat must be provided at the point where liquid propane becomes gas, and it may just as well be done at the regulator if you are taking liquid from the bottle.

The first try at this was to mount the regulator-attenuator on copper plates and extend these plates right into the flame (**Photo 38**). This worked all right, but the second design was better (**Photo 39**). With all out gas flow, the regulator is just warm to the touch. The heat sinks were made large to begin with and trimmed until the regulator operated at the proper temperature.

All in all, this makes for a neat and tidy installation, and the boiler may be run and cycled for long periods of time feeding liquid to the system and with no subsequent freezing of the bottle.

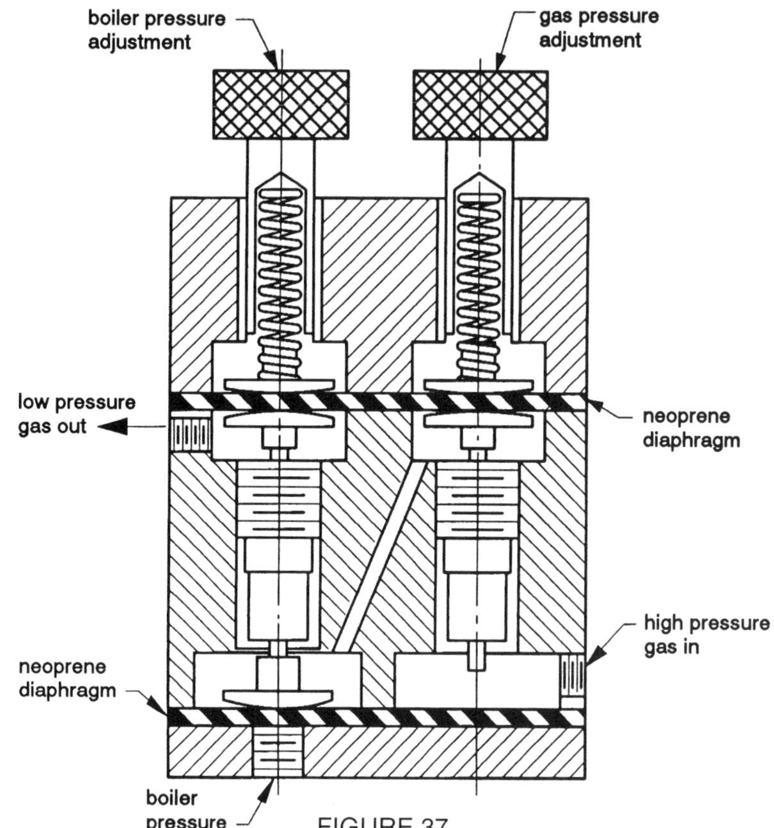

FIGURE 37

Combination regulator-attenuator. Unit is small, light, easily made from common materials. Note flow is from bottom to top in both cases.

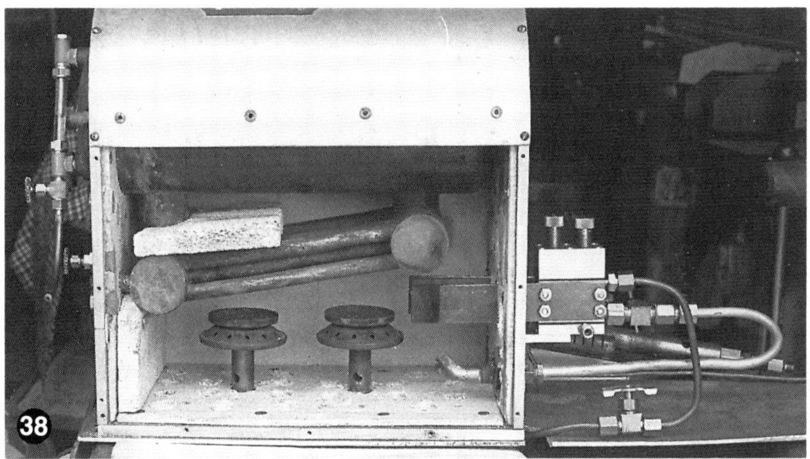

Combination regulator and attenuator mounted on copper plates sticking into the fire to furnish the heat necessary to turn liquid propane into gas.

Unit and heat sink sandwiches removable mounting plate. Sink extends into fire and is cut away until heat flow is right. Slotted burner is steel, and uses a .015" orifice.

Stirling Engine Work

By Andrew Ross

Photos by Author

Imagine a little engine for your bicycle, canoe, or campside generator set that is as quiet as a sewing machine. It runs on kerosene, and its nonpoisonous flue gases are practically odorless. It starts easily, and, with only seven moving parts, it should run without repair for many hundreds of hours, burning less than one-half liter of kerosene per hour.

Such an engine was developed 30 years ago and incorporated into a 200 watt generator set (**Photo 1**) by the Philips Company of Holland; it is the modern stirling "hot air" engine.

Unfortunately, only about 100 of these units were made, and stirling engine research soon passed them by in the pursuit of more efficient, but less practical, helium and hydrogen engines.

Eleven years ago, I first read the Philips hot air engine literature (including references 1 and 2, noted at the end of this article); I found it extremely exciting, but also puzzling. Why, after 30 years, were such simple, reliable, and quiet engines totally unavailable? This puzzle so intrigued me that I decided to build my own stirling hot air engine.

Initially, my aim was to build an engine of a few horsepower, mount it on a bicycle, and have some fun with it. I expected the whole project to take about a year. How incredibly naive these early expectations seem today!

My first engine was overly complex. It featured two cranks, scotch yokes with rollers, two cylinders, and a newly patented speed control system. After nine months of work, I wisely decided to completely rebuild it as a "simpler" rhombic drive engine (**Photo 2**). After many more months of effort, it was ready for the initial run. To my great surprise and frustration, it would not run.

Mistakenly thinking the problems were involved in the rhombic geometry, I designed a V-2 stirling to be "quickly" made from a freon compressor. Five months later, this engine (**Photo 3**) was ready to test. My frustration and despair were complete when it, too, refused to run. It was becoming apparent that the stirling literature, which I had by now studied rather carefully, did not tell all that one needed to know to build stirling engines.

Correspondence with Dr. Ted Finkelstein, one of the leading authorities on stirling engines, set me on the right track. He suggested I simplify my designs and minimize thermal conduction losses.

Pursuant to Ted's advice, I redesigned the top portion of the 65 cc rhombic (**Photo 4**) and, at last, it ran. On its first run it turned only 200 rpm, but it was quiet, and I was elated.

I immediately set about to build a brake to test power. I then made, over a long period of time, a series of improved propane burners. This burner work paid off; from an initial

4

5

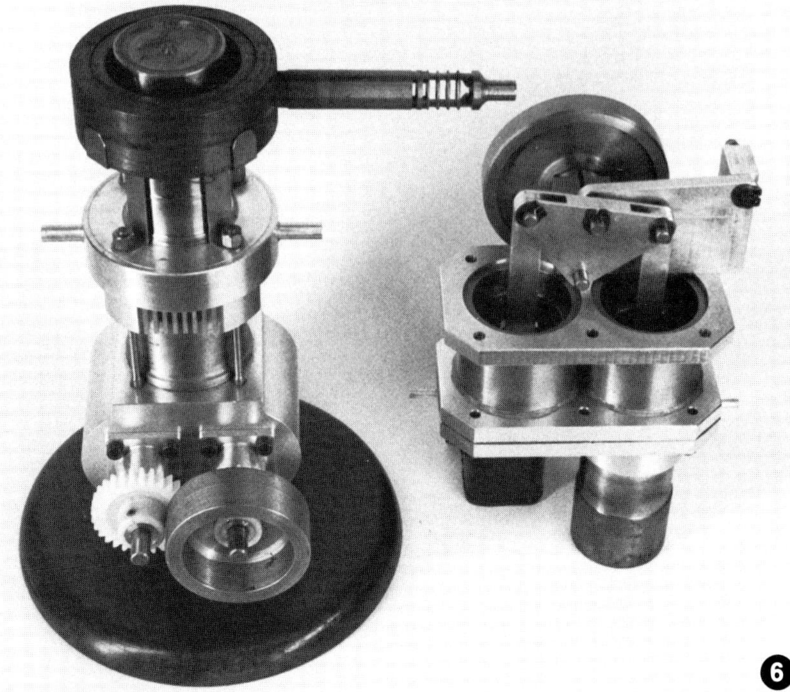
6

7

output of only 1.5 watts at 750 rpm, power went up, step by step, to its present 81 watts at 1600 rpm (**Photo 5**). The engine beneath the burner has remained essentially the same.

With a running engine to work on, I soon realized that my initial aims were unreasonable. Obtaining several hundred watts was going to be challenge enough, let alone several horsepower. But, along with the limitations, there appeared unsuspected opportunities as well. It became apparent, for example, that the low pressure air engine had considerably more potential in terms of both speed and power than the literature suggested.[1] It also became apparent that, despite the extensive literature, the stirling was still relatively unexplored, and that there was immense opportunity here for creative imagination and investigation. Indeed, what had started out as a simple shop project with an anticipated "easy victory," had turned into a demanding mental challenge in an exciting new technology.

The 65 cc rhombic became one of my best engines. It has been the basis of many tests on alternate coolers, heaters, and regenerators; and

1. The Philips 200 w engine was a medium pressure machine, with 140 psi crankcase pressure.

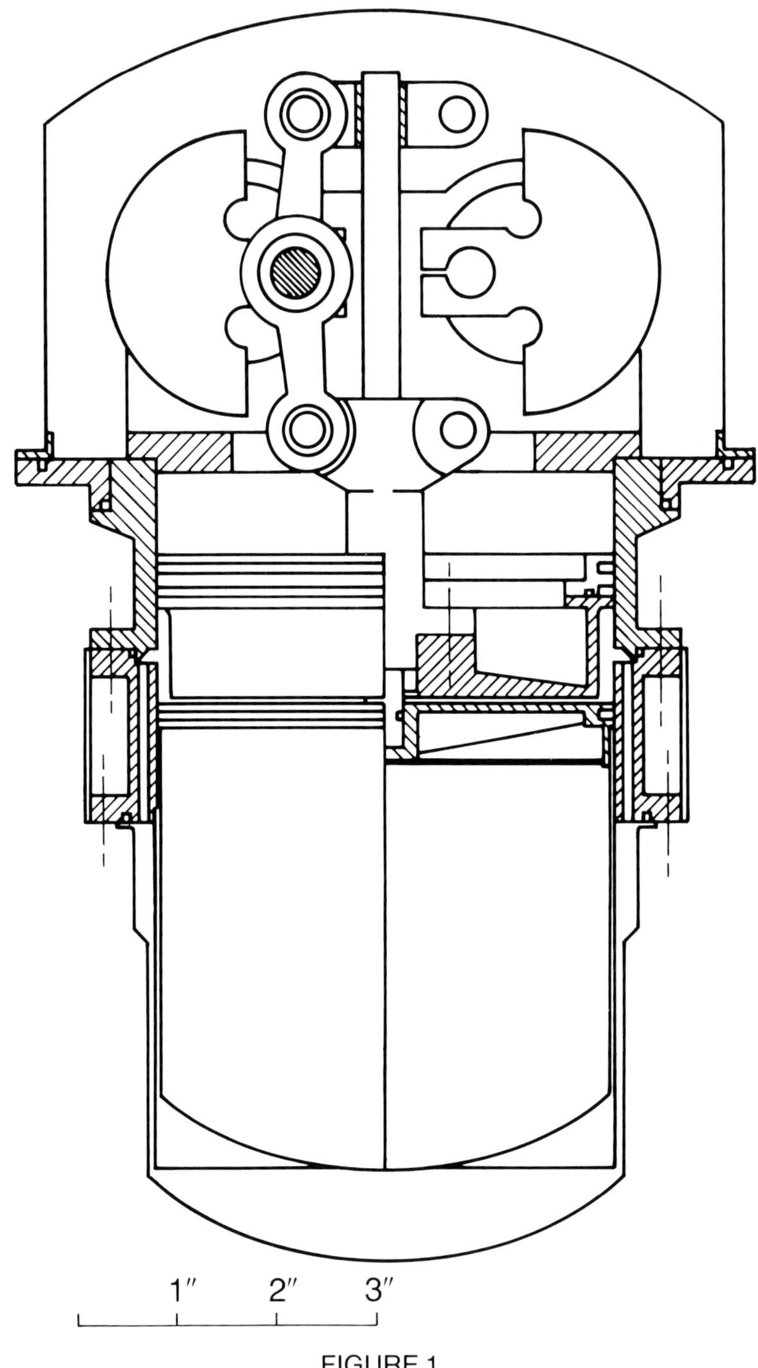

FIGURE 1

through it all it has run many hours on minimal lubrication without giving any trouble.

The success of this machine inspired a series of other rhombic designs, some actually built, others not. Among engines actually built were an 11 cc demonstrator engine (**Photo 6**, left side), a 100 cc test engine with which very little was ever done (**Photo 7**), and a 300 cc test engine built under a D.O.E. grant (**Photos 8** and **9**, and **Figure 1**). Both the 11 cc and 300 cc engine have been described at length in other articles.

Perhaps more interesting were the designs not built. During the D.O.E. work, it occurred to me that the rhombic drive lent itself to use in a low pressure pancake engine. If one greatly increased the bore relative to the stroke (6:1 or 8:1 ratios), and used the cylinder head instead of the cylinder sides for the heater, then a very compact engine with ample heater surface area was possible. Several new versions of the 65 cc engine were designed along these lines, and engine dimensions were incredibly reduced (**Figure 2**). A 110 cc version of

The engine to the left represents the 65 cc rhombic, with 1" crankthrows and 2.125" bore. The engine to the right is also 65 cc, but with .5" crankthrows and 3" bore. The dotted line shows further height reduction possible if the top, instead of the sides, of the cylinder head, are made to be the "heater." Both drawings are to a common scale.

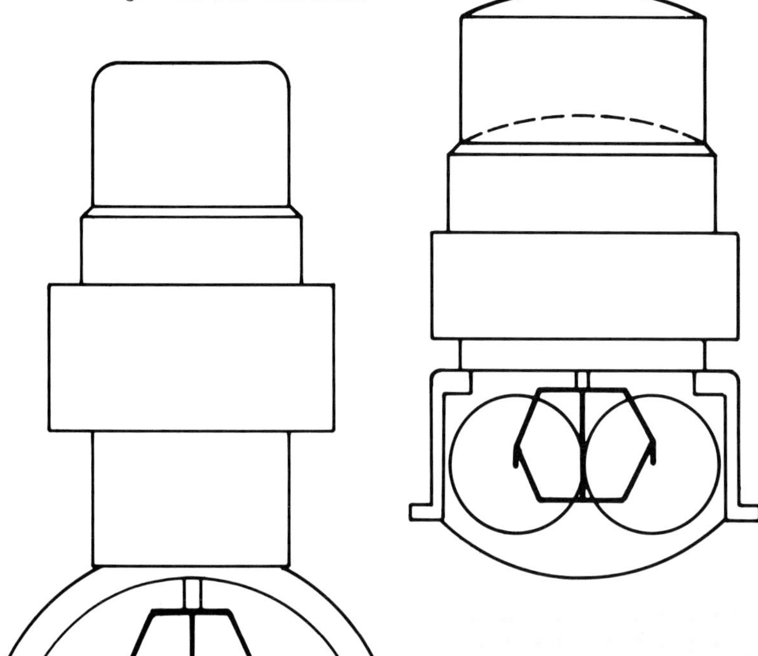

FIGURE 2

the 11 cc engine was not only designed, but also begun (**Photo 10**). It features needle bearings throughout, a 4" bore and ½" crankthrow. Its overall height is 5", actually less (because of the cylinder head heater) than the 11 cc, and its diameter is 5". This engine has ample surface area to produce 100 watts on air at atmospheric pressure. I believe it represents a promising approach for a compact, high speed, low pressure, stove-top air engine (with diaphragms it could also be a simple helium engine).

After the initial successes with the rhombic, I began looking for simpler approaches. The two cylinder piston/displacer machine seemed one possible answer, so a 38 cc V-2 version of this arrangement was built (**Photos 11** A and B), incorporating the burner, heater and regenerator of the 65 cc rhombic. It was indeed simple, and its power and speed were promising, but its efficiency was considerably poorer than the rhombic,

10

11A

11B

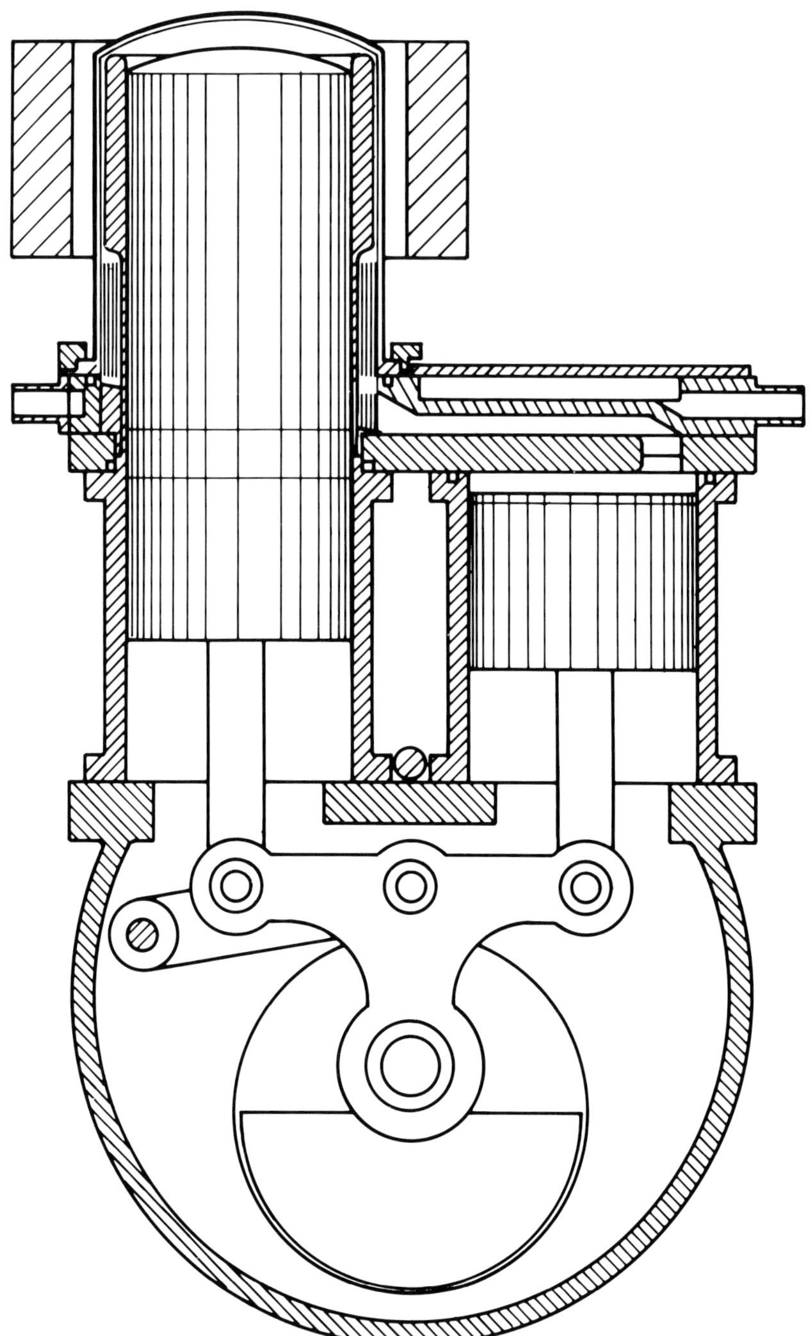

FIGURE 3

and no further engines of this type have been built.

Still in quest of simplification, an 11 cc two-piston (Rider type) engine (**Photo 12**), similar to the 11 cc rhombic, was built. This engine turned out to be very fast (3600 rpm) and very easy to make. The only crucial point was that the piston fits had to be superb. This engine became a "test-bed" for a number of modifications, including the tubular heat exchanger shown in the photo.

Shortly after finishing this engine, I invented a balanced crankshaft mechanism ("yoke drive" or "Ross linkage," **Figure 3**) for the two-piston engine that had the advantage of relieving the pistons of almost all side loads. This design makes possible a simple, long-life low friction engine with dry lubricated pistons. It has long been considered desirable to avoid using oil lubrication in air

2. The Philips 200 watt engine did use an oil filled crankcase.

stirlings for safety and other reasons.[2] The yoke drive seems to be a significant advance in small engine design.

The 11 cc Rider was modified successfully to the yoke drive (Photo 6, right). A 50 cc yoke drive engine was then designed and built, based on the heater, regenerator, and burner of the 65 cc rhombic (**Photo 13**). This engine was initially a great disappointment; I ran it for only a few minutes before foolishly deciding it had no future. Several years later, while demonstrating the 11 cc Rider for a visitor, I noticed that the Rider always seemed to take longer to come up to speed than the rhombic. In an instant, I decided I'd better re-test the 50 cc. Sure enough, with a little longer run it showed very good promise indeed. I quickly built the balance shaft, to see if my now-patented balance scheme really worked; it did. All this was a year and a half ago, and I've concentrated on yoke drive Riders ever since.

The 50 cc was obsolete in various ways, so I designed a small 35 cc yoke engine that would incorporate most of what I'd learned over the years about building stirlings. The idea was to offer it as a kit to serious stirling researchers, some of whom desperately needed hardware upon which to test ideas. The resulting engine (**Photo 14**) was the best natural runner I'd ever built. Its friction was very low, its speed high. It's been the subject of a separate article, so I won't go into great detail here. Its peak power with air working fluid at atmospheric pressure is 44 watts at 2750 rpm. Free speed is 4500-4700 rpm, when things are right.

My first stirling field test was conducted in March, 1981, when this engine was incorporated into a miniature outboard rig, and mounted on a 17-foot canoe. Performance was mild, but encouraging. The test was also great fun; at last, one of my engines was doing something more or less useful.

Putting this engine in kit form took much longer than I expected. Sales were satisfactory, but it became clear that a simpler engine was necessary for those who had never built a stirling before. The V-15 (**Photo 15**) was designed around the old 11 cc Rider, but in V form, to fill this niche. It has been well received, and makes a very quiet and impressive little demonstrator engine.

Meanwhile, the late John Mazur of New York suggested simplifying the 35 cc design by using a unit block construction. He kindly sent me eight blocks to my design carved from barstock by his sophisticated tape-controlled machines. Other internal simplifications were also incorporated and the phase angle was in-

18

19

creased from 90° to 100°. This 30 cc engine (**Photo 16**, right, and **17**) is now in the very competent hands of Dr. Jim Senft, who plans to do various tests with it.

This engine was slated to replace the 35 cc kit, but, after John's untimely death, I decided to up-size the engine to 60 cc. This decision was partly rational (a 60 cc engine could produce a useful 100 watts of power with a simple unfinned heater), and partly emotional (I was ready to settle on one engine for extensive development, and it appealed to me to make it the same displacement as the inspiring Philips machine).

The 60 cc (**Photo 18**) has only three hours running time so far, but it shows considerable promise. It, too, is a "natural runner," with a present free speed of over 3500 rpm. My initial plans are to make it truly quiet, which means a lot of thought is going into bearings and bearing substitutes (flexible members, etc.). Next, operating life will be tested, and, if necessary, improved. Only then will any attempt be made to test or improve power. I have already done some work on investment cast stainless heaters (**Photo 19**), and this will be one element of "hop-up" that will, at last, be explored. There are numerous other exciting approaches to investigate, and various new field tests to conduct; truly, the adventure is just beginning.

During these many years of effort I've enjoyed the advice, encouragement, and friendship of many internationally-known stirling engineers, but I would particularly like to acknowledge my gratitude to Bill Martini, Joe (Graham) Walker, and (especially) William Beale.

My aim for the 60 cc is to develop it into a fine little stirling air engine for the hobbyist or experimenter, and to make it available as a pre-machined kit. At such time as that occurs, the puzzle of the stirling hot air engine that has so intrigued me these last 11 years will finally be resolved to my satisfaction.

References

1. deBREY, H., et. al. "Fundamentals for the Development of the Philips Air Engines." Philips Technical Review, IX, No. 5 (1947), 97-104.
2. van WEENEN, F.L. "The Construction of the Philips Air Engine." Philips Technical Review, IX, No. 4 (1947), 125-134.

The use of sealants in place of solder

Make a See-through Displacement Lubricator

By William T. Roubal

Photos by Author

Steam engines require internal lubrication in order to operate properly and give long years of service. One type of lubricator for model steam engines is the displacement lubricator. It has no moving parts and is easy to make; delivery of oil to the engine occurs as water from the steam line condenses in the lubricator. In so doing, a small amount of oil is displaced from the lubricator and swept into the engine.

The usual displacement lubricator for model stationary steam engines is of all-metal construction. However, by using glass for the main body of the reservoir, the operator has a visual "dip stick" for monitoring the oil level. When the reservoir fills with water, the drain plug is removed, the water is drained off and the lubricator is refilled with oil.

The see-through lubricator described here is assembled without the use of solder, using two special sealants instead. Both sealants withstand continuous exposure to water, steam, oil and many solvents. Anaerobic sealant No. 4177, made by 3M, is used for assembling brass parts; *anaerobic* because cure proceeds only in the *absence* of oxygen, such as at the glue line between parts out of contact with air (anaerobic means in the absence of oxygen, as contrasted to aerobic, in the presence of oxygen). This sealant is exceptionally strong and a good solder substitute. The second sealant is more conventional (two-part epoxy resin) and exhibits considerable resiliency in the cured state. It is ideal for bonding together materials with differing expansion and contraction rates (glass-to-metal).

The first step in making the lubricator is making the glass reservoir. I use 1" lengths of heavy wall borosilicate glass tubing (Corning Pyrex Brand laboratory tubing, 9.5 mm nominal OD, catalog No. 237650, obtainable through scientific supply houses). Cut the tubing as I described in my article on making see-through oil cups (***Live Steam*** Magazine, June 1978). Grind both ends square as follows: insert the glass piece into a 25⁄64" diameter hole drilled through a small block of wood. Then, applying finger

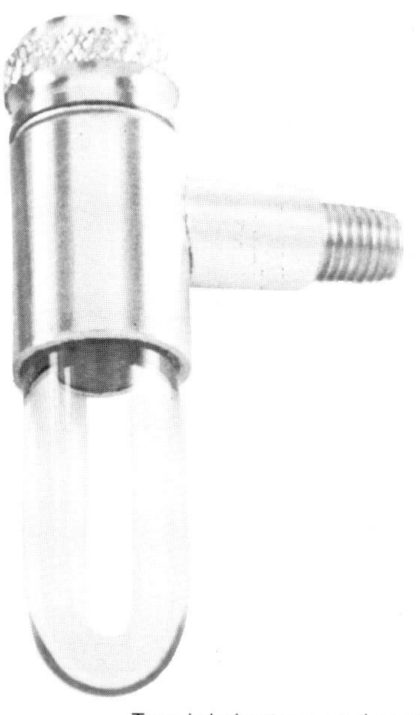

Two lubricators and component parts are displayed in approximately 2X actual size. From left to right, top row: top cap, bottom cap, and steam delivery pipe. Bottom row: the assembled lubricator, the bottom cap drain plug, the top cap filler plug, and a simplified lubricator (no drain, see text). Note the Teflon flat washers on the drain and the filler plugs.

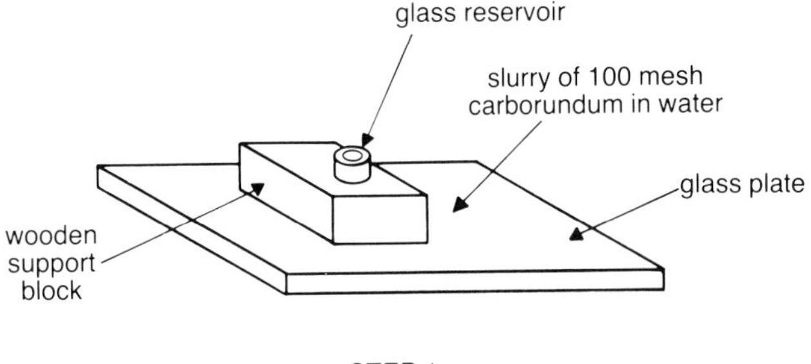

STEP 1

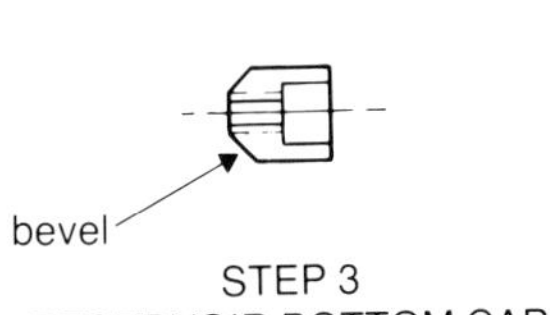

STEP 3
RESERVOIR BOTTOM CAP

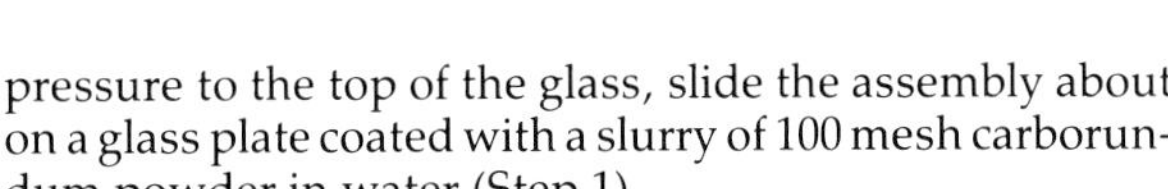

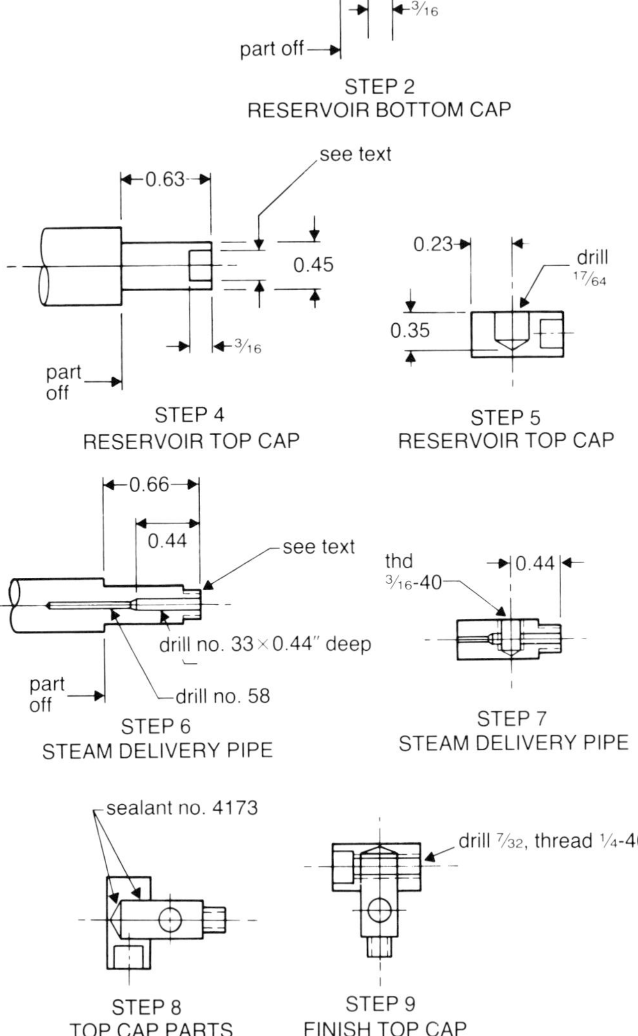

STEP 2
RESERVOIR BOTTOM CAP

STEP 4
RESERVOIR TOP CAP

STEP 5
RESERVOIR TOP CAP

STEP 6
STEAM DELIVERY PIPE

STEP 7
STEAM DELIVERY PIPE

STEP 8
TOP CAP PARTS ASSEMBLY

STEP 9
FINISH TOP CAP

pressure to the top of the glass, slide the assembly about on a glass plate coated with a slurry of 100 mesh carborundum powder in water (Step 1).

The bottom cap of the reservoir is fabricated from brass. Chuck a short length of 1/2″ round brass rod in a three-jaw chuck, and drill a shallow pilot hole and bore it out to an ″ID which is 0.004″ larger than the OD of the glass by 3/16″ deep. Drill a No. 38 diameter hole 1/2″ deep and tap this 6-40 to a depth of 0.4″. Reduce the OD of the rod to 0.45″ and part off to the left of the line shown in Step 2. Reverse the piece in the chuck, take a light facing cut, and bevel the end as shown in Step 3.

For the top cap, chuck another length of 1/2″ round brass rod in the chuck, bore a recess for the glass (0.004″ oversize by 3/16″ deep as above), and reduce the diameter to 0.45″ for a distance of about 0.7″. Part off to the left of the line in Step 4. Do *not* drill the hole for the filler plug at this time.

Center the top cap on its side in the drill press vise (***LS***, September 1978), and drill a 17/64″ diameter hole to a depth of 0.35″ (Step 5).

For the steam delivery pipe, chuck a length of 5/16″ round brass rod in the three-jaw chuck and turn a 3/16″ to 1/4″-long stub with the correct diameter and thread size to fit the threaded hole on the inlet side of the steam chest on your engine (3/16-40 is a popular thread size for small engines and is used on several of the Stuart models). Reduce the diameter of the rod for a slip fit into the 17/64″ diameter hole of Step 5. Drill a No. 33 hole 0.44″ deep, followed by a No. 58 hole for a total hole depth of 0.8″, and part off to the left of the line in Step 6.

Center the delivery pipe on its side in the drill press vise and drill a 5/32″ diameter hole to a depth of 0.2″, spacing the center of the hole 0.4″ from the threaded end (Step 7). Thread the hole 3/16-40 for a steam delivery line using a bottom tap. Tap the hole while the piece is still in the vise, turning the drill press chuck by hand.

Remove all oil and grease from the top cap and steam delivery pipe with chloroform or lacquer thinner (caution! *use good ventilation*), and then scrub the external surfaces with soap and hot water, followed by a thorough rinse in clean water. Place the parts on a small tray folded up from aluminum foil and dry the parts in a warm oven.

Treat the parts by spraying them all over thoroughly with 3M Scotch Bond Primer-Activator, No. 4181, obtainable in a pressurized can. Allow the parts to dry five

STEP 10
RESERVOIR FILLER PLUG

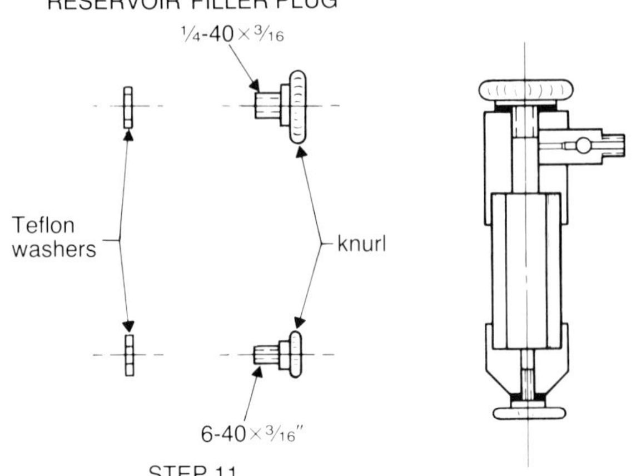

STEP 11
RESERVOIR DRAIN PLUG

A much better sealant than that listed in the original article for sealing glass to metals is Armstrong's A34 Epoxy resin, available from J.S. Switzer Associates, 15116 Downey Ave., Paramount, CA 90723. Phone No., 213-774-0740.

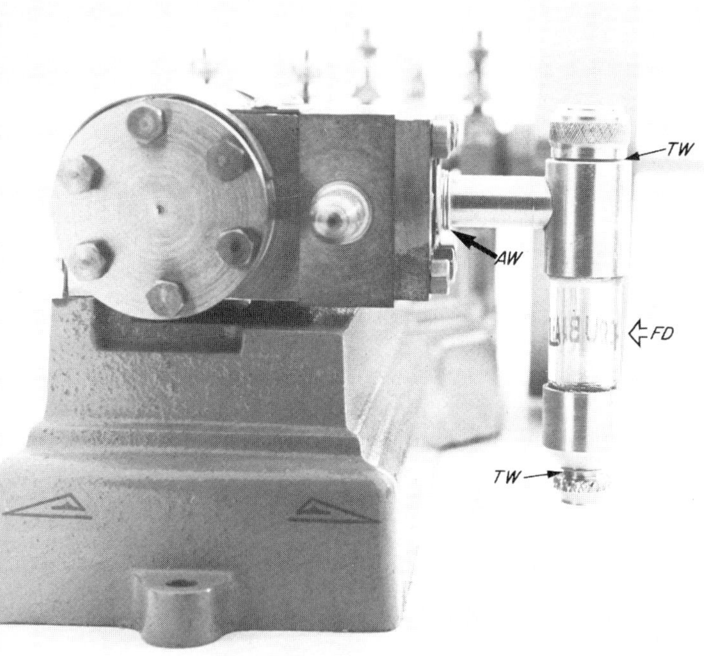

The lubricator in the right foreground is in place on a steam engine. ***AW*** *identifies soft aluminum washers, which provide a steam-tight fit plus alignment of the lubricator.* ***TW*** *identifies Teflon flat washers, and* ***FD*** *is a fire-on decal used for permanent marking of glass (***Live Steam***, November 1978).*

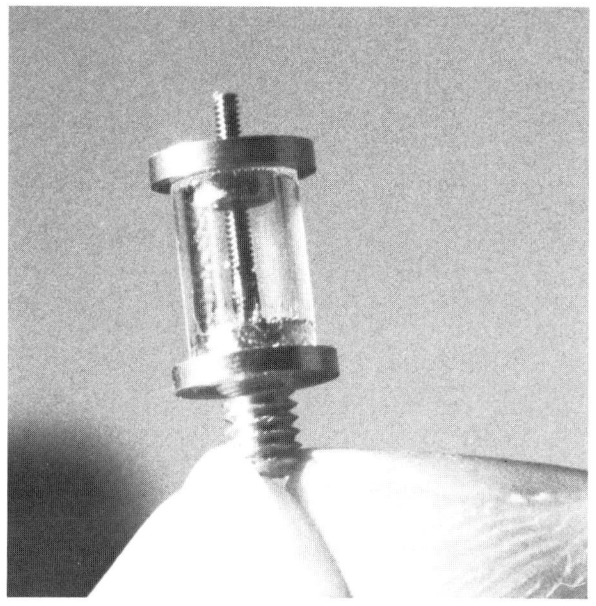

Shown above is another example of the author's tiny lubricators.

minutes. Coat the 17/64" diameter hole in the lubricator top cap with 3M's Scotch Bond anaerobic bushing assembly sealant No. 4173. Align the delivery pipe so that the threaded hole is perpendicular to the long axis of the top cap, and insert the delivery pipe into the coated hole. Do not hesitate when inserting the pipe into the hole and pushing it home; the sealant sets quickly! Allow the sealant to cure two hours at room temperature (Step 8). If the oil delivery hole gets plugged with sealant, drill it out later.

Now chuck the assembly in a three-jaw chuck, drill a 7/32" diameter hole, and thread it 1/4-40 as shown in Step 9. Make a threaded top cap filler plug as shown in Step 10. Also make a threaded bottom cap drain plug as shown in Step 11. Cut gaskets from thin Teflon sheeting for use as flat washers on the filler and drain plugs in order to insure pressure-tight assemblies. A set of laboratory cork borers is ideal for cutting gaskets.

Clean the glass reservoir and bottom cap with solvent, soap and water. Rinse, and then heat to dryness in a warm oven. Assemble the remaining parts as follows: Chuck the bottom cap in the drill press drill chuck, beveled end down, with a portion of the unbeveled end protruding from the chuck. Lower the quill and lock it. Grasp the protruding end in the drill press vise and clamp the vise to the table. Loosen the jaws of the drill chuck and raise the quill, but do not disturb the bottom cap. Chuck the top cap either by the use of the threaded extension screwed into the filler hole or by the portion of the top cap above the steam delivery pipe, if possible.

Insert the glass reservoir into the bottom cap, center it, and lower the quill until the glass seats in the recess in the top cap. Lock the quill. Fill the space between the glass and metal of the bottom cap with A271 epoxy resin (J.S. Switzer Associates, 15116 Downey Avenue, Paramount, California 90723) and allow the resin to harden overnight. Remove the bottom cap with attached reservoir from the vise, reverse the top cap in the chuck, lower the quill and grasp the top cap in the vise. Loosen the chuck, rechuck the bottom cap and lower it until the glass seats in the recess of the top cap. Add resin and allow it to harden. Although the assembly sequence sounds quite complicated, it really isn't, and it insures near perfect concentricity of the parts in the final assembly.

Photo 1 shows the assembled see-through lubricator (2" long overall) together with its component parts. A simpler version is also shown; the bottom drain assembly has been deleted in this lubricator. Condensed water is aspirated from the unit by inserting a hypodermic syringe or drawn-out eye dropper through the filling hole. The overall length of the shorter version is 1½".

Undoubtedly, other sealants and resins will make good metal-to-metal and heat cycleable glass-to-brass seals. Two combinations that *won't* are: No. 4173 for sealing brass to glass, and *Scotch-Grip* 1099 for sealing glass to brass. For joints that aren't exposed to steam or other hot environments, however, No. 4173 is quite satisfactory for sealing glass to many metals. This is especially true if the glass is first metalized (coated with a mirror of metal such as that obtainable by firing a coating of Englehard Industries' Liquid Organic Silver No. A2282 (Englehard Inc., Electro Metallics Division, East Newark, New Jersey 07029) onto glass.

If the glass reservoir should ever get broken, you can break out the remnants with a screw extractor along with a pick made from a piece of hardened drill rod. Be careful not to mar the external metal surfaces in the process. Use a good cylinder oil in the lubricator.

Flywheel Tapered Bushing

By Robert C. Johnson

Photos by Author

Every engine we build has at least one flywheel; it can be as modest as a simple metal disk or as elaborate as a finely detailed casting. In either case, it is the most visible part of the project and, therefore, a real disappointment if it doesn't run true. With a little extra time and effort, you can mount your flywheel with a simple tapered bushing, and it will run "true." And it can be installed and removed as many times as you like without damaging the crankshaft.

Since the flywheel is not required to transmit high torque, a keyway is not necessary, and using an appropriate taper will provide a good tight fit for model engine applications.

The flywheel described here is for the hot air engine *Poppin,* found in the November 1980 issue of ***Live Steam***. *Poppin* was designed by Dr. J. R. Senft. The flywheel is made in three parts: the outer ring, which has three internal diameters; the web which will sport the internal taper; and the tapered bushing, which has the outer taper and the crankshaft bore. I like to mix different materials, mostly for aesthetic purposes. However, on this project, it got me into a little trouble. I used aluminum and brass which turned out to be too soft. I intend to use steel on all future projects.

First, construct the outer ring. This is a simple turning operation, so little will be said. Since concentricity is one of our primary goals, face one edge and all internal bores in the same setup. Face the opposite edge to within a few thousandths, and don't bother with the OD at this time.

The inner web is next. Turn the hub that will be the small end of the taper first, and leave a few thousandths for clean-up later. Flip the web and turn the shorter hub, face square, and drill a 7/16" clearance hole. Next, bore the taper.

Tapers are generally thought of in terms of inches of taper per foot of length. The self-holding variety, such as Morse, has a taper of around 5/8" per foot and an angle from the center line of about 1-1/2°. For use with a flywheel, this taper would be near the smallest limit. A small angle will hold very well. However, it will also be more difficult to remove. For flywheels, I've been working with tapers from 3/4" per foot to 1-3/4" per foot, or between approximately 2° and 4° from the center line. There is a wealth of information about tapers in the *Machinery's Handbook*.

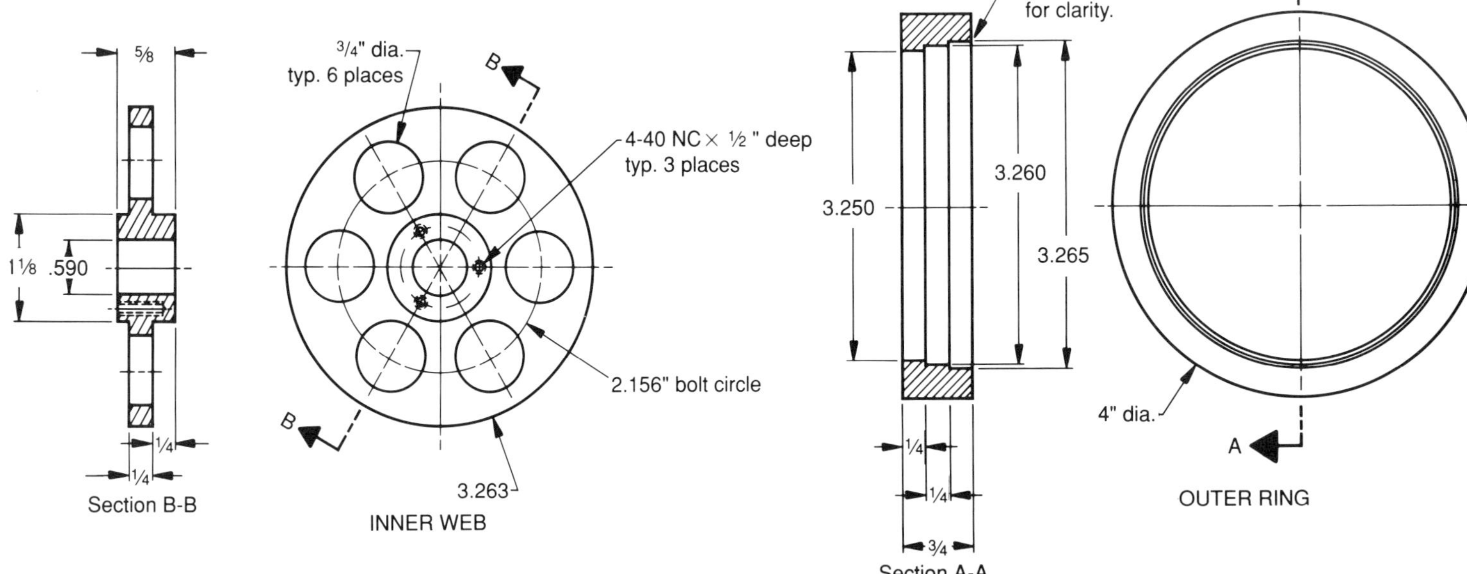

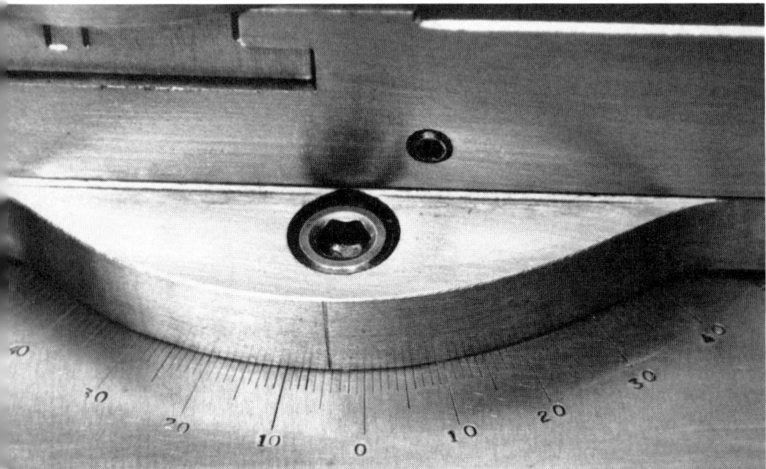

Set the lathe compound at 4°, more or less. Don't disturb this setting until the tapers are complete.

Bore the taper in the web first.

Turn the taper on the bushing, being very careful not to unscrew the chuck on a lathe with a threaded spindle.

Bore the bushing in the same setup as the taper to maintain concentricity.

Cut off the bushing after you're satisfied with the fit in the web.

Locate and drill holes with the web and bushing assembled.

Tap one of the mounting holes in the web before drilling and tapping the others. This hole will be used to clamp the bushing to the web.

Finish locating and drilling holes for mounting and removal.

Use a slitting saw to cut the slot in the bushing.

Assemble the bushing and web. Finish turn + .003" for 3 thou pressed fit into the outer ring.

Pushing the cold inner web into the hot outer ring.

The finished flywheel on the incomplete hot air engine Poppin.

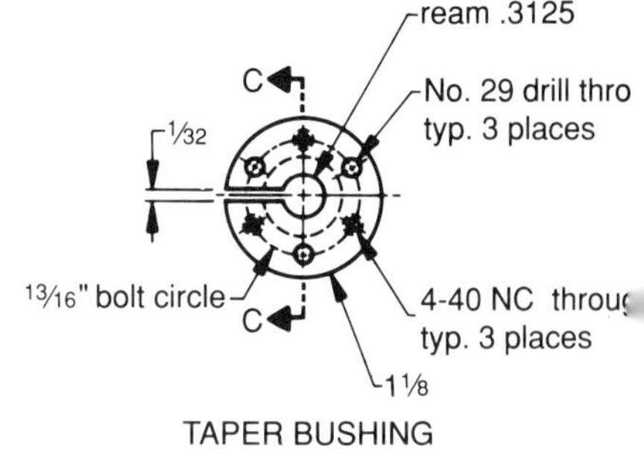

TAPER BUSHING

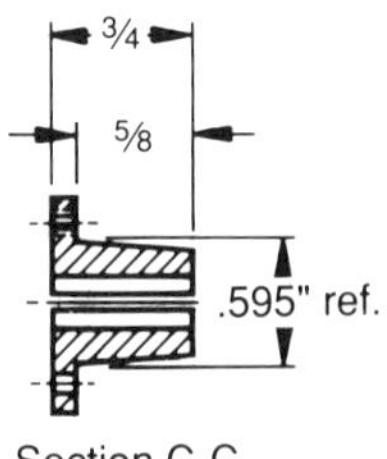

Section C-C

Wood Flywheels

By D. A. Drayson
Photos by Author

When making some of the older models, the modelmaker has to come up with a wood flywheel, and there seems to be a number of ways to do it. The way I make up one usually gives me a pretty true running flywheel, and some control over the rim weight.

To start, use wood screws to secure a disk of 2 × 6" or 2 × 8" wood to a faceplate. Use screws only long enough to hold the disk securely. Turn the disk diameter so it is an inch or two larger than the finished diameter of the flywheel. Then take a light cut across the face to true it up.

Next, glue a cardboard disk to the one on the faceplate (same diameter). The cardboard from a shoebox is about the correct thickness. With a compass, draw a circle on the cardboard the diameter of the finished flywheel and another, the OD of the hub.

Now you can make up the pieces that form the flywheel. They consist of 12 segments for the rim, six for the fillers between the spokes, six spokes, a couple of pieces of brass or whatever pieces of metal you have in your scrap box, and last but not least, a length of soft solder wire.

You can now remove the faceplate from the lathe, and glue up six of the 12 segments to the cardboard disk, making sure they will finish up to the OD circle drawn on the cardboard. Be sure to get glue on the ends of the segments. Also add a wood disk at the center to support the spokes.

When the glue is dry, put the faceplate back on the lathe, and turn the ring to its finished ID and OD. Then take a face cut to true up the ring and center hub disk.

The next step is to assemble the six spacers and the spokes onto the wood ring that you now have on the faceplate.

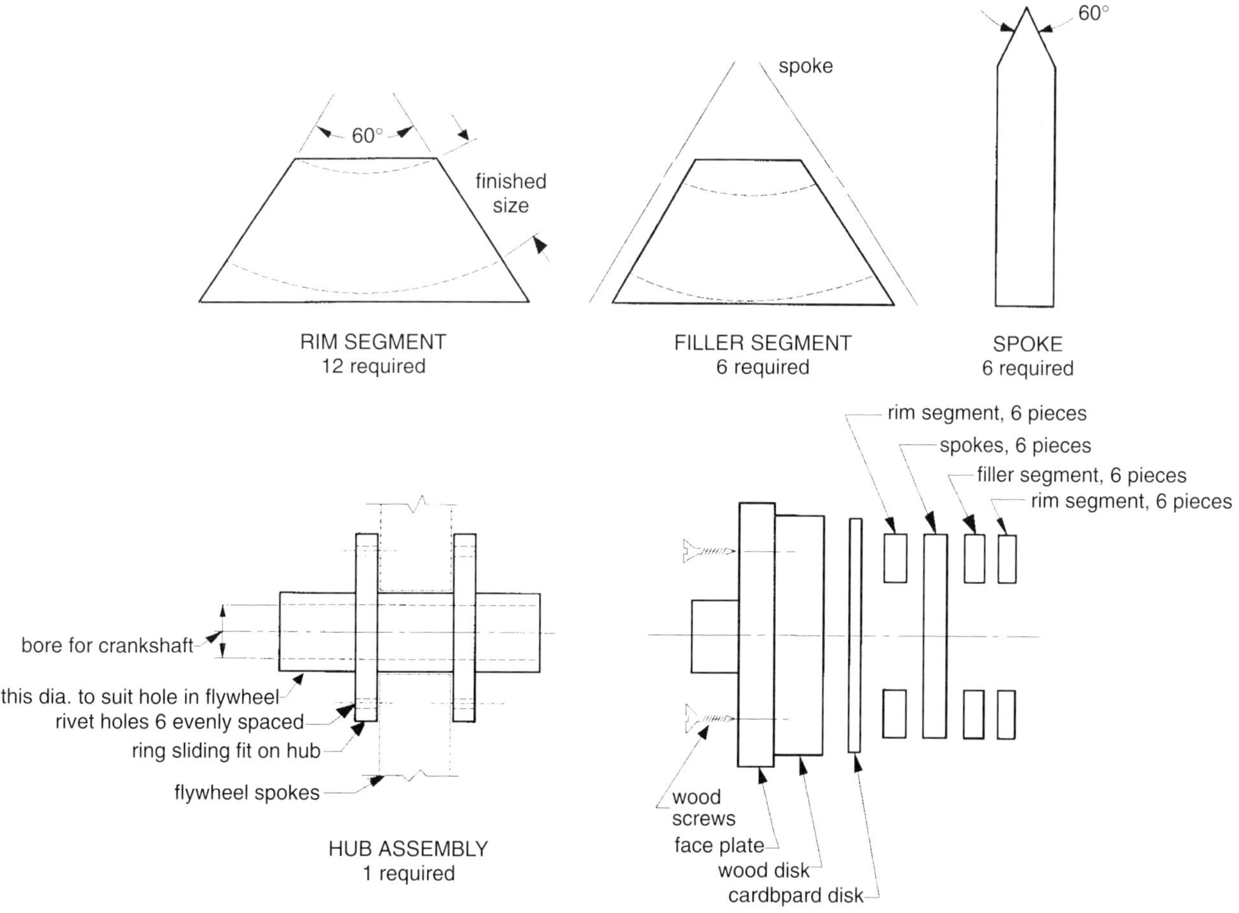

A wood flywheel installed.

The pattern and casting.

The split pattern.

Once you have these fitted, tack them in place with small brads, but only enough so you can lift them off and put them back in the same location. Be sure to number each piece and its location.

Now remove all the spokes. Remove one spacer at a time and apply glue to the back, then press it back into position, making sure no glue oozes out into the space for the spokes.

When this has dried, put the faceplate back on the lathe and turn the ID and OD to match the ring. Before gluing in the spokes, you should cut your radii on the edges; it's a lot easier than trying to do it after everything is glued up.

Because this flywheel has a metal hub, the disk in the center is only a support for the spokes, so before gluing in the spokes, put a piece of wax paper over the center disk. Make certain the spokes are in their right location, and glue them in. Don't forget the tips.

When this has dried, take a light cut across the face of the rim and at the center to form a seat for the metal hub. Then drill and bore a hole for the hub assembly. At this time, you can cut a groove in the rim just wide enough to fit in the solder wire and deep enough to be below the surface.

You will find it easier to put in the wire if you first grab one end in the vise, and give it a yank with a pair of pliers on the other end. This gets the kinks out.

Now glue the last six segments in place, and when the glue dries, turn their OD and ID to match those already finished. Also take a light cut across the face. Make sure that when you glue up these pieces, you stagger the joints. Using a thin knife, and rotating the faceplate by hand, you can separate the flywheel from the disk.

Turn a recess in the disk so the finished side of the flywheel is an easy press fit into the recess, and the side of the flywheel is up snug against the bottom of the recess. A wood screw and washer through the center holds the whole thing secure, and a light cut across the face to clean off any cardboard finishes the turning. The flywheel is then removed and the hub installed. A light sanding and a stain finish the job.

Wood patterns solid or split can also be made in a similar manner, but don't forget added material for machining and draft angles so the pattern can be pulled.

I hope this helps to keep the wigglewobbles out of your flywheels.

A Simple Alcohol Burner

By Andy Sprague

Photos and drawing by the Author

To the young readers of ***Live Steam***, I thought I would pass along the following. Some time ago, I came into possession of a Wilesco 5" horizontal boiler equipped with a butane gas burner (**Photo 1**). For some reason, I could never get the burner to work properly. Either the least little whisp of air would extinguish the flame, or when it did work, it would function for only five or six minutes. Besides that, I was going broke feeding it the Ronson butane fuel at $3.65 a can.

I decided to build my own alcohol burner made from junk parts, and the results were very satisfying. Take a look for yourself (**Photo 2**).

The fuel tank is a 3 oz. *3-in-One* oil can with a 1/2 x 5" brass tube soldered to one end and capped at the other end. Three 1/4" holes were spaced and drilled on top of the tube and 1/4 x 1/2" brass tubing soldered into each hole, leaving about 3/8" extending on top.

The three burner cups are the brass ends of expended 20-gauge Winchester shotgun shell casings picked up on the deck of a cruise ship. The centers were popped out, and soldered over the tubing to a depth of 1/8".

1

2

Two inches of rope wick were pushed into the tubes, leaving about 1/8" above the tubes. A coil of 1/8" string wick was then wound around the bottom of the cups.

The cup tops are the brass and copper screens taken from old faucet aerators (I save everything), and soldered on top of the cups.

Note: It is best to keep the burner tops above the level of the alcohol tank. Otherwise, they tend to overflow. **Figure 3** should explain everything reasonably well.

When in operation, this little unit vaporizes beautifully with a blue flame that would make any self-respecting kitchen gas range proud, and will steam the boiler for about 25 minutes.

The photo shows the burner as applied to a Diamond Enterprises D-48 boiler, and hooked up to a V-4 Saito engine given me by my steam pals Frank and Marion Bielens. Good luck and happy steaming!

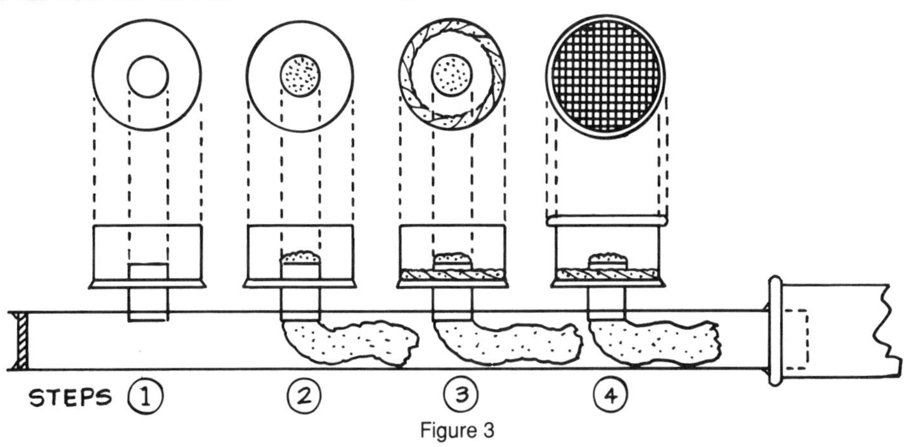

Figure 3